Project Management Techniques and Innovations in Information Technology

John Wang
Montclair State University, USA

Information Science
REFERENCE

Managing Director:	Lindsay Johnston
Senior Editorial Director:	Heather A. Probst
Book Production Manager:	Sean Woznicki
Development Manager:	Joel Gamon
Development Editor:	Development Editor
Acquisitions Editor:	Erika Gallagher
Typesetter:	Jen McHugh
Cover Design:	Nick Newcomer, Lisandro Gonzalez

Published in the United States of America by
   Information Science Reference (an imprint of IGI Global)
   701 E. Chocolate Avenue
   Hershey PA 17033
   Tel: 717-533-8845
   Fax: 717-533-8661
   E-mail: cust@igi-global.com
   Web site: http://www.igi-global.com

Library of Congress Cataloging-in-Publication Data

Project management techniques and innovations in information technology / John
Wang, editor.
     p. cm.
  Includes bibliographical references and index.
  Summary: "This book presents the latest research, case studies, best
 practices, and methodologies within the field of IT project management,offering research from top experts around the world in a variety of IT project management applications and job sectors"--Provided by publisher.
  ISBN 978-1-4666-0930-3 (hardcover) -- ISBN 978-1-4666-0931-0 (ebook) – ISBN 978-1-4666-0932-7 (print & perpetual access) 1. Information technology--Management. 2. Project management. 3. Management information systems. I. Wang, John, 1955-
  HD30.2.P758 2012
  658.4'038--dc23
                           2012000024

British Cataloguing in Publication Data
A Cataloguing in Publication record for this book is available from the British Library.

All work contributed to this book is new, previously-unpublished material. The views expressed in this book are those of the authors, but not necessarily of the publisher.

Table of Contents

Section 5
Project Outcomes and Conception of Success

Section 6
Implementation of IT Projects for Commercial Environment, Agencies, and Governments

Detailed Table of Contents

Section 1
Resource Allocation and Scheduling

Chapter 1

Mihalis M. Golias, University of Memphis, USA
Maria Boilé, Rutgers University, USA
Sotirios Theofanis, Rutgers University, USA
Heidi A. Taboada, The University of Texas at El Paso, USA

Berth scheduling can be described as the resource allocation problem of berth space to vessels in a container terminal. When defining the allocation of berths to vessels container terminal operators set several objectives which ideally need to be optimized simultaneously. These multiple objectives are often non-commensurable and gaining an improvement on one objective often causes degrading performance on the other objectives. In this paper, the authors present the application of a multi-objective decision and analysis approach to the berth scheduling problem, a resource allocation problem at container terminals. The proposed approach allows the port operator to efficiently select a subset of solutions over the entire solution space of berth schedules when multiple and conflicting objectives are involved. Results from extensive computational examples using real-world data show that the proposed approach is able to construct and select efficient berth schedules, is consistent, and can be used with confidence.

Chapter 2

Dan Trietsch, American University of Armenia, Armenia

Crashing stochastic activities implies changing their distributions to reduce the mean. This can involve changing the variance too. Therefore, crashing can change not only the expected duration of a project but also the necessary size of its safety buffer. We consider optimal crashing of serial projects where the objective is to minimize total costs including crashing cost and expected delay penalty. As part of the solution we determine optimal safety buffers. They allow for activities that are statistically dependent because they share an error element (e.g., when all durations have been estimated by one person, when weather or general economic conditions influence many activities, etc). We show that under plausible conditions the problem is convex and thus it can be solved by standard numerical search procedures. The purpose of the paper is to encourage software development that will include valid stochastic analysis for scheduling and crashing using current estimates and historical performance records.

A critical success dimension in projects is the ability to complete a project within an estimated duration. In that regard, effective project scheduling techniques in an uncertain environment is of interest in many organizations. In this paper, the authors use an analytic approach to analyze the behavior of time duration distributions of projects in stochastic activity networks, and propose a simple computation scheme for approximating their distribution. The findings offer an understanding of the large gap between PERT and simulation results, and the deviation of projects from their intended schedules. In addition to providing theoretical framework, the proposed approach also recommends a simple practical pragmatic technique that computes the time distribution of project duration. This is a simple and handy tool for the project manager that may replace simulation. As a byproduct, the earliest start time.

Section 2
Requirements Uncertainty and Technological Risks

The Waterfall approach has been the dominant approach for enterprise systems (ES) implementation since the 1970s. It offers ES project managers a simple, step-by-step way to make ES projects manageable and minimize drawbacks. The main criticism of this approach centres on its inflexibility regarding requirement uncertainty. In this article, the authors challenge this criticism. By means of an in-depth case study of a Waterfall approach-based ES implementation project within the maintenance department of one of the world's biggest airline companies, this article will illustrate how it deals with requirements uncertainty and required flexibility in practice.

Chapter 5

A risk evaluation model for IT projects using fuzzy inference is proposed. The knowledge base for fuzzy processes is built using a causal and cognitive map of risks. This map was specially developed for IT projects and takes into account the typical lifecycle and the risk taxonomy created by the Software Engineering Institute. The model was used to compute the technological risk of an e-testing project. This project was positioned on the middle level of the risk map, implying that the probability of encountering technological difficulties depends on the number of technologies used and their market maturity. A software system for validating the model was also developed.

Section 3
Knowledge Management and Placement of Project Teams

Knowledge is now becoming the most valuable asset of the construction organisations to gain competitive advantages by improving quality while reducing cost and time of work completion in projects. Knowledge Management (KM) is the most effective way to deal with the intellectual capital of the organisations through facilitating the capturing and sharing of existing knowledge and creating new innovative knowledge. The most useful knowledge in construction projects is tacit knowledge since it includes the people ideas, perceptions and experiences that can be shared and re-used to improve experiences and enhance abilities of employees for problem-solving and decision-making. Many of methods have been adopted to deal with knowledge in the construction organisations, but they are still far from enough, particularly in dealing with tacit knowledge gained from construction projects. This paper presents a methodology for dealing with tacit knowledge efficiently and effectively in construction projects. A case study has been conducted to evaluate the proposed KM method and to test its importance and usefulness in the construction industry.

Despite the clear relevance of the Information and Communications Technologies (ICT) market in world economics and the evident lack of success of software projects, organizations devote little effort to the development and maturity of the software project manager profession. This work analyzes the figure of project manager from the perspective of the Team Software Process (TSP), and it considers the required skills, attitudes and knowledge for a software development project. The basis for the study is the analysis of relevant references from the literature for their subsequent categorization into different competency concepts. The results of the analysis are compared with the contributions which the Guide to the SWEBOK® and the PMBOK® Guide models provide of the profiles of the project manager. The results indicate that the literature relating to the Team Software Process is focused on the definitions of skills and attitudes, and to a lesser extent on knowledge components. The lack of the definition of the components which comprise competency constitutes a challenge for software development organizations.

This paper, through the voices of two professors and a student, describes an educational experience that exposed students to virtual teams constructed between Information Technology Project Management classes of two branch campuses of the Pennsylvania State University. This experience focused on overcoming the communication problems of virtual teams in order to strengthen team building dynamics. Since working on virtual teams was the first experience for the students, attempts were made to control some aspects of the virtual team environment by eliminating cultural and time differences. The variable to be in focus was the building of trust in a virtual environment. By eliminating all other variables such as time zones, cultural and disciplinary backgrounds, etc., students could experience the efforts required to build trust in a virtual environment. Students were given pre and post experience surveys. The results indicate that initially many students were very apprehensive about virtual teams; however, after completing the course, most students expressed positive attitudes and a general understanding of techniques to work effectively in virtual teams. In addition, almost all teams commented on how important they felt virtual teams would become in the future as digital technology continues to improve.

Section 4
Acquiring Managerial Experience

Chapter 9

Learning curves are used extensively in business, science, technology, engineering, and industry to predict system performance over time. Although most of the early development and applications were in the area of production engineering, contemporary applications can be found in all areas of applications. Information technology project management, in particular, offers a fertile area for the application of learning curves. This paper applies the concept of half-life of learning curves to information technology project management. This is useful for predictive measures of information technology system performance. Half-life is the amount of time it takes for a quantity to diminish to half of its original size through natural processes. The approach of half-life computation provides an additional decision tool for researchers and practitioners in information technology management. Derivation of the half-life equations of learning curves can reveal more about the properties of the various curves with respect to the unique life-cycle property of information technology.

Chapter 10

What behavioral competencies do experienced IT project managers apply when facing critical situations in their projects, and how have they developed those competencies? In this paper, the authors answer these questions. The authors interviewed 23 experienced IT project managers from 11 organizations, focusing on critical situations that they now managed differently from their earlier, novice, practices, and on how they had learned to develop these different approaches. The authors discuss a variety of management development and training interventions. They use a thematic analysis to identify the key competencies being applied and learning methods experienced by this set of managers. Results suggest that IT project managers are drawing on a different set of competencies from those required for project management in other industries. Additionally, this paper reveals the importance of informal learning channels, often involving project experiences, for the development of IT project management competencies.

The iterative and incremental development (IID) approach is widely adopted in information systems development (ISD) projects. While the IID approach has played an important role the management of many ISD projects, some of the key techniques have not received critical appraisal from the academic community. This paper aims to fill the gap and examines three such techniques through a case study. First of all, the gap between the theory of user participation and the reality of user's lack of real influence on design and development is explored. The author proposes the concept of "participatory capture" to explain the side effect of user participation. Secondly, the assumption that evolutionary prototyping converges to a successful design is questioned. Thirdly, the side effect of the timeboxing technique is considered. The paper suggests that the IID approach represents the learning approach as categorized in Pich et al. (2002) and it might be ineffective in dealing with the significant uncertainties in ISD projects.

This paper examines the process leading to a formalised co-operation. A comparative case study of Research and Development (R&D) collaborations illustrates how, during the process of formalising, the creation of shared understanding of the co-operation is supported or hindered. When participants are involved in setting goals, writing work plans, and creating the rules for the co-operation, each participant will have a better understanding of their relationship with others, their own role and responsibility and those of the others. In this study, the authors identify five possible factors that encourage or discourage the partners to use the process of formalising for the purpose of sensemaking.

Section 5
Project Outcomes and Conception of Success

The effect of user participation on system success is one of the most studied topics in information systems, yet still yields inconclusive results. Contingency-based concepts attempt to resolve this issue by providing a plausible explanation which indicates that users can only generate expected results when there is a need for users to participate in the development process. As a different approach, this study adopts a mediating perspective and asserts that influence due to the effectiveness of participation determines the final outcomes. Based on control theory, and viewing user participation in reviews as one kind of control, we propose that the influence users can generate through participation determines project outcomes. Data collected from 151 information systems personnel confirms the relationships and that an ability to achieve quality interactions among developers and users heightens the achievement of user influence.

Chapter 14

In researching IS phenomena, many different theoretical lenses have been advanced. This paper proposes the use of Margaret Archer's Morphogenetic Approach to Analytical Dualism (MAAD) as a social theoretic approach to explain why social phenomena may occur in a case study. This paper provides a brief overview to MAAD, providing a description of its tenets and methodology for use in an empirical study. As an example, the author applies MAAD to the implementation of Lotus Notes in the Alpha consulting organization as reported by Orlikowski (2000). This approach shows that the differential success of the implementation efforts in the different organizations was due to the diverse cultures and possible experiences with technology found in those organizations. This example shows that the use of this social theory can provide explanatory purchase where social phenomena are involved. For practitioners, it suggests that structural analysis at the beginning of a project may provide direction as to how to make the project more successful.

Chapter 15

This paper presents an in-depth insider's case study of a "runaway" information systems (IS) project in a U.S. State government agency. Because such projects are politically sensitive matters and often obscured from public view, details of how such projects operate are not well understood. This case study adds new details to the body of knowledge surrounding IS project escalation and de-escalation. The authors' resulting project narrative details how this project went out of control for so long, raising important questions for future research in theory development for both IS project escalation and de-escalation. The paper argues that a punctuated equilibrium approach to analyzing "runaway" IS projects are a more fruitful area to explore than are "stage models."

Section 6
Implementation of IT Projects for Commercial Environment, Agencies, and Governments

Service-oriented architecture (SOA) have been adopted by organizations in a wide variety of industries, however, best practices have still yet to mature. This article, which is part of a larger study on SOA, develops a normative decision model introducing key factors that influence the timing and approach of adopting a SOA. The decision model is based on the results of multiple case studies of organizations that had either employed or were considering implementing a service-oriented architecture project. The results indicate that there are four main areas an information technology (IT) manager needs to assess to determine when and how to move towards a SOA: the maturity of relevant standards, the technology gap, the organizational gap, and the nature of the benefits expected from a SOA. Analyzing these results suggest that differences in the business environment need to be considered in the decision of when and how an IT manager should pursue the move to a service-oriented architecture.

Implementing an e-procurement system is a challenge for local government; however, lessons learned through the identification of these challenging issues allow local government ICT project managers to checklist these issues and ensure a successful e-procurement system rollout in their respective organization. For this study, qualitative research design and analyses were used to identify and rank the emergent issues. Through pattern-coding analyses of the interview transcriptions, twelve key issues emerged to be found as the common barriers of successful e-procurement rollout. In this regard, the author's research is significant given that the return of investment is crucial to a local government's administrative functions as well as for effective and efficient service delivery.

Chapter 18

Inter-organizational cooperations between public and private partners, called public private partnerships (PPP), are increasingly gaining more importance concerning renewal, standardization, and optimization of the information technology (IT) infrastructure of public sector organizations. Reasons for this trend include the search for partners with necessary technological and innovative knowledge of sourcing IT and the identification of cost-saving potentials. Unfortunately, IT-PPP-cooperations are particularly susceptible to failure due to the clash of different cultures. Divergent understandings, expectations, and pressure from the relevant stakeholders hinder a working partnership. Therefore, in this exploratory, qualitative single-case study from the German TollCollect IT megaproject, the authors draw on findings from boundary spanning literature to explain how establishing preconditions for boundary spanning and actively bridging the gap between the partners, moderated by external stakeholder support, affects the formation of mutual trust and success of an IT-PPP-megaproject.

Chapter 19

This paper is a qualitative study regarding m-government in a developing country in Eastern Europe with a poor infrastructure and a democratic history—Albania. To understand why m-government is unavoidable and necessary for Albania, the authors provide an overall picture of the country's current telecommunication infrastructure, which explains some of the current e-government initiatives, and their level of implementation success and barriers to progress. In addition, this paper presents possible benefits of m-government for Albanians, along with possible future applications, challenges, and issues in their implementation.

Preface

PROJECT MANAGEMENT TECHNIQUES AND INNOVATIONS IN INFORMATION TECHNOLOGY

"Project Management Techniques and Innovations in Information Technology" belongs to *Advances in Information Technology Project Management series* book project. There are six sections and 19 chapters in this book.

RESOURCE ALLOCATION AND SCHEDULING

Section one consists of three chapters. Mihalis M. Golias, Maria Boilé, Sotirios Theofan, and Heidi A. Taboada propose "A Multi-Objective Decision and Analysis Approach for the Berth Scheduling Problem" in chapter 1. The berth scheduling problem deals with the allocation of berth space and service time slots to vessels at marine container terminals. Ocean carriers compete over the available berths, and service time slots and several factors affect the decision of the terminal operator to assign the available quay side resources. As with most real-world scheduling problems, the berth scheduling problem is explicitly multi-objective as the terminal operator is faced with pressure by liner shipping operators for increased effectiveness and punctuality of services (berthing and vessel loading/unloading operations). These objectives include reduction of vessel turnaround time, increase in port throughput, keeping the customers' satisfaction at a desired level, and minimizing the emissions of the vessels on-route and at the port. Addressing these objectives simultaneously and selecting the *best* berth schedule can present a challenge to terminal operators. In this chapter, the multi-objective berth scheduling problem is studied, and a methodology for selecting a subset of schedules over the entire feasible space is proposed. The methodology allows the port operator to efficiently evaluate the majority of the feasible berth schedules, and select the ones with a dominant performance over a number of different objectives. The approach presented herein ranks the objectives non-numerically in order of relative importance, without having to specify weight values and allows for the selection of a small number of competing schedules to be selected even in the case where the relative importance of the different objectives cannot be determined. The proposed methodology is repeatable and reliable, and a significant decrease in the solution space can be obtained without any sacrifice in the objectives' performance. The proposed method can further be applied as is to other scheduling/assignment problems for which computing the competitiveness of a solution over a number of alternatives is not feasible.

In chapter 2, Dan Trietsch explores "Optimal Crashing and Buffering of Stochastic Serial Projects." His first paper on optimal safety time in a project context (with Boaz Ronen) was written in 1986. This chapter is on the problem of optimal crashing of stochastic activities. Whereas it is possible to solve the problem by sample based optimization, the task is greatly facilitated if serial subprojects can be combined to single tasks. This chapter shows how to do that, and thus constitutes an important link in the development of a better comprehensive approach to project scheduling. The crucial point is that it is not correct to just focus on the mean, because crashing a stochastic activity also changes its variance. Often, as an activity is crashed, its variance is reduced too. As a result, crashing may be more beneficial than suggested by analyzing only the mean. Results are provided not only for independent activities but also for positively correlated ones. Since completing this chapter Dr. Trietsch has been involved in further research on project scheduling, published in *EJOR* (with Lilit Mazmanyan, Lilit Gevorgyan, and Ken Baker; doi:10.1016/j.ejor.2011.07.054). This research shows the particular relevance of the lognormal distribution both for single project activities and for serial subprojects. The lognormal distribution is shown to provide statistically valid fit for project activities. It also provides an excellent approximation for sums of lognormal distributions even if they are positively correlated. Finally, chapter 2 shows how to account for the Parkinson effect (hidden earliness). Nonetheless, the results of this chapter can be easily applied in combination with the new insights. Thus, this chapter remains an important building block in the new project scheduling framework Trietsch is working on, designed to replace both traditional PERT and Critical Chain. For more on the new framework, see his forthcoming *IJPM* paper (with Ken Baker), "PERT 21: Fitting PERT/CPM for Use in the 21st Century" (doi:10.1016/j.ijproman.2011.08.001).

In Chapter 3, Yuval Cohen and Ofer Zwikael provide "A New Technique for Estimating the Distribution of a Stochastic Project Makespan." Timely completion of large and mega projects remains a challenge and a critical stumbling block despite the introduction of various project scheduling techniques. While the gap between PERT and reality, and even between PERT and simulations, has been addressed by many papers, only general explanations were given to this gap, and only scant insight was offered for better estimation of project's duration. This chapter suggests an approach that will help mitigate/eliminate the shortcomings of the aforementioned approaches; its complexity is low, it gives an accurate estimate of the project's makespan probability in chosen points, and its precision could be adjusted as desired by adding or subtracting estimation points (complexity is linearly proportional to the number of points). In addition, the chapter gives an important insight based on an analytical approach connecting the network structure to this estimation gap, and suggests a technique for better estimating a project's duration. The chapter analyzes the behavior of time duration distributions of projects in stochastic activity networks and proposes a simple computation scheme for approximating their distribution. The effect of parallelism is illustrated and gives a strong support for conservative estimations of project duration. A simple algorithm for estimating the makespan cumulative distribution is presented. The algorithm is based on forward recursive computational approximations and was validated by comparison to simulation results. The technique calculates for each AOA node a piecewise linear approximation of its distribution function. Thus, the accuracy of the proposed technique depends on the number of linear segments in the approximation. While this may be a limitation, the computational complexity of adding a new linear segment to the project distribution function is proportional to the number of nodes. The findings offer understanding of the large gap between PERT and simulation results, and the deviation of projects from their intended schedules. In addition to providing theoretical framework, the proposed approach also proposes a simple practical pragmatic technique that computes the time distribution of project duration. This is a simple and handy tool for the project manager that may replace simulation. As a byproduct, the earliest start time distribution for each activity is also estimated. This chapter gives project scheduling practitioners a practical tool for estimating the project duration distribution in the presence of task time variability. The proposed technique may be applied in many organizations, and assist in estimating realistic project durations.

REQUIREMENTS UNCERTAINTY AND TECHNOLOGICAL RISKS

Section two involves two chapters. In Chapter 4, Huub J.M. Ruël, Tanya Bondarouk, and Stefan Smink present "The Waterfall Approach and Requirement Uncertainty: An In-Depth Case Study of an Enterprise Systems Implementation at a Major Airline Company." The authors address the issue of the high failure rates of Enterprise Systems (ES) implementation projects. Many project management methodologies and tools have been developed throughout the years that claim to contribute to ES project success, and the importance of project management is fully acknowledged in the literature. In software project development studies, the Waterfall approach is the one referred to predominantly. However, in response to growing environmental uncertainty and flexibility, the Waterfall approach is being criticized for its rigid character. The authors of this chapter contribute to this debate by starting from the assumption that the Waterfall approach in practice is not as ill-suited to the dynamics of ES projects as its critics claim, since it is still the most widely used approach for ES implementation projects. The leading research question therefore is: How does a Waterfall approach-based ES project cope with requirements uncertainty?

As an alternative to the Waterfall approach, a new form of ES project management has emerged since the late 1990s, called the Agile approach. It took until 2001 before the concept of the Agile approach was formally born. In that year a group of prominent practitioners agreed upon the basic values of the Agile approach as laid down in the Manifesto for Agile Software Development. The Agile approach accommodates the volatility of requirements and focuses on collaboration between developer and end-users.

By means of an in-depth case study, the authors collected data about an ES project at a major airline company during eight months of full-time access to project meetings, project documentation, and direct observations and by conducting semi-structured interviews with project managers and team members. Through data triangulation and interviewing different stakeholders, the authors were able to reconstruct the 'story' of the ES project. The in-depth case study makes clear that a Waterfall approach-based ES project deviates in practice to certain, but crucial extent from its features as presented in the literature. In practice a Waterfall approach-based ES project includes a joint (developers plus end-users) design and coding stage, and involves a number of iterations. In this way, adjustments to the requirements can be made and changes included before a final design is approved.

Furthermore, the case study shows that requirements are subject to change in an ES project. However, a Waterfall approach-based ES project does not turn out in practice to be as simplistic and inflexible as opponents of the approach claim. It does include features typical of an Agile approach, such as iterations, early releases, and frequent end-user feedback, though in a more moderate way. By doing so, a Waterfall approach-based ES project keeps its original focus on planning, but is more flexible in responding to requirements uncertainty and changes. In the in-depth case study at the major airline, this turned out to be sufficient and resulted in successful user acceptance of a new ES. Interestingly, the impact of requirements uncertainty and changes in practice was less than the literature suggests. The authors' main conclusion is that the demise of the Waterfall approach for ES implementation projects is not imminent. In practice, this approach seemed to be an appropriate one to successfully implement an ES.

In Chapter 5, Constanta-Nicoleta Bodea and Maria-Iuliana Dascalu demonstrate "IT Risk Evaluation Model Using Risk Maps and Fuzzy Inference." The chapter presents an interesting risk evaluation model, based on fuzzy reasoning. The core part of the proposed model is a causal cognitive map of the project risks, which is defined starting from the Software Engineering Institute risk taxonomy. The fuzzy model considers risks according to their source (management, cost, technology, production, environment, and schedule) and the project lifecycle (initiation, planning and resource procurement, design and implementation, bug fixing and installation, and maintenance). The model quantifies the risks based on the crisp values of the risk sources, but due to the fuzzy logic mechanisms, the results are more than single-point estimates. The following two phases are defined by the authors in order to work with the model: the risk identification, using a database designed by experts and the development of the risk map and fuzzy inference components. The causal cognitive map is used to describe the propagation of risk throughout the project, according to the transitivity principle of the risk propagation chains.

The fuzzy rules applied by the fuzzy inference components are built on two parameters: the probability of risk occurence, and the impact on project development. Each phase of the model is thoroughly documented using numerical values. In order to validate the model, the authors have developed a software tool implementing the basic fuzzy sets operators, the main defuzzification methods, and the required inference rules. The chapter presents a case study for computing the technological risks of an e-testing project. The input values, the classification of the input values into suitable fuzzy sets, the calculation of the membership level of each input value, and finally, the fuzzy reasoning steps, are all provided. Two defuzzification methods were applied: the Centre of Gravity (COG) and the Middle of Maximum (MOM). These two defuzzification methods reveal similar results, meaning that the model is valid. The conclusion is that the technological risk has a low probability of occurence, because the technological maturity is somewhere between high and very high and the number of applied technologies are medium-high. The authors conclude that the risks for this particularly IT project type are strongly related to the number of applied technologies and the market maturity.

KNOWLEDGE MANAGEMENT AND PLACEMENT OF PROJECT TEAMS

Section three has three chapters. In Chapter 6, Min An and Hesham S. Ahmad focus on "Knowledge Management in Construction Projects: A Way Forward in Dealing with Tacit Knowledge." Knowledge is now becoming the most valuable asset of the construction organizations to gain competitive advantages by reducing cost and time while improving the quality of projects. Construction projects are in knowledge-intensive environments where many interrelated components work together in a complex manner. Knowledge Management (KM) is the most effective way to deal with the intellectual capital of the organizations through facilitating the capturing and sharing of existing knowledge and creating new innovative knowledge. The most useful knowledge in construction projects is tacit knowledge. Tacit knowledge is personal and exists in individuals' heads and memories in the form of experiences and know-how. However, in many circumstances, tacit knowledge is not easy to be shared and re-used to improve experiences and enhance abilities of employees for problem-solving and decision-making. These situations call for a method of managing such knowledge to solve construction problems and achieve a high quality of construction projects. Many of methods have been adopted to deal with knowledge in the construction organizations, but in any case, they are still far from enough since most KM models only provide a communication platform and much creative knowledge work still depends entirely on human activities.

This chapter provides an overview of the classification of data, information, explicit and tacit knowledge. This classification will help organisations identify the types of knowledge with different nature that may need different procedures, tools and methods to process and manage. Subsequently, by exploring the main challenges of KM implementation in construction organisations the chapter reviews and discusses problems of current approaches of managing tacit knowledge. In order to distinguish the differences in nature and processing procedures for the different types of knowledge, a novel KM methodology to facilitate understanding, implementing, and applying a KM system in the organisations is presented in this chapter with a particular emphasis on dealing with tacit knowledge in construction projects, which covers identifying knowledge resources, knowledge processing, identifying processing resultants, IT and non-IT tools in order to enhance the implementation and application and effectively assess the overall performance of the KM system. Then a case study is used to demonstrate its importance and usefulness of this KM methodology in the construction industry. The chapter concludes with a consolidated overview of a method and procedure for better understanding, dealing with, and benefiting from the dynamic nature of knowledge, which helps the organisations capture, share, and manage knowledge effectively and efficiently.

Marcos Ruano-Mayoral, Ricardo Colomo-Palacios, Ángel García-Crespo, and Juan Miguel Gómez-Berbís deal with "Software Project Managers under the Team Software Process: A Study of Competences Based on Literature" in Chapter 7. The authors present an interesting approach to identify the competencies for software project managers. Given that competency is the ability of an individual to perform a job properly, this work is interesting for both practitioners and researchers alike. Instead of identifying competences through job analysis or task analysis, the authors did a remarkable work in which they review the Team Software Process (TSP) literature to highlight skills, attitudes and knowledge components. This componential profile of the team leader role in TSP can be considered pioneer in the software engineering management scenario. This study identified "Work quality as a challenge" as the most cited skill followed by "Combine forces," "Maintain team communication;" and "Identify key issues"; "Job facilitator" as the most important attitude followed by "Collaborative leadership," "Respect," and "Commitment"; and finally, "Build and maintain an effective team," as the most cited knowledge component followed by "Lead risk evaluation and tracking," "Participate in the configuration control board," and "Handle funding issues."

In this work, this group of researchers from Universidad Carlos III de Madrid, Spain, compares obtained results with the Guide to the Software Engineering Body of Knowledge and the Project Management Body of Knowledge Guide models in order to provide a comparative with the most important initiatives present in the literature. The work discovers that TSP literature is more focused on the definition of skills and attitudes than in dealing with knowledge components. The importance of this work lays on the intrinsic relevance of the TSP, a set of practices that lead software engineering teams that are developing software-intensive products to reach a disciplined engineering practice. The lack of the definition of the components that comprise competency constitutes a challenge for software development organizations that use TSP, whose project managers should confront the task with full capacities, and without the help of established and recognized competencies. The main conclusion of the work is that the style of management enabled by TSP permits the team leader to concentrate on aspects such as the management of human resources, delegating some others, such as the management of quality, to team members.

In Chapter 8, Sadan Kulturel-Konak, Clifford R. Maurer, and Daniel L. Lohin show "Teaching Students How to Effectively Work in Virtual Teams." A virtual team (also known as a geographically dispersed team) is a group of individuals who work across time, culture, space, and organizational boundaries using webs of computer-mediated communication (CMC) systems. Geographic distance typically precludes face-to-face (FtF) interaction and has impacts on a team's task processes as well as its socio-emotional processes. Meanwhile, virtual teams in the workplace are becoming increasingly popular. Educators understand the need to prepare students for working in virtual teams. However, although knowledge about the challenges of virtual communication and virtual team work is increasing, there is still need for more work focusing on the teaching strategies in order to enhance students' virtual team literacy.

This chapter first reviews related prior work emphasizing the importance of virtual teams as skills to be addressed by undergraduate education. Then, through the voices of two professors and a student, the chapter describes an educational experience that exposed students to virtual teams constructed between Information Technology Project Management classes of two branch campuses of the Pennsylvania State University. At both campuses, students had the opportunity to form nucleus teams (i.e., subteams) with people of their choice. Subteams were then matched to form the geographically dispersed teams. This experience focused on overcoming the communication problems of virtual teams in order to strengthen team building dynamics. Students experienced that they should not have expected the dynamics to be the same as if everyone were in the same room. Professors designed assignments so that students interacted with team members in the other location since it could be tempting to focus only on those in the same location (i.e., their own campus) with them. Another variable to be in focus was the building of trust in virtual teams. The problem to be solved by the virtual teams concerned a growing company that had experienced growth but also recognized that it had problems due to a lack of consistent adaptation of technology within the organization.

Students were given surveys before and after this virtual team project experience. The results indicate that initially many students were very apprehensive about virtual teams; however, after completing the course, most students expressed positive attitudes and a general understanding of techniques to work effectively in virtual teams. In addition, almost all teams commented on how important they felt virtual teams would become in the future as digital technology continues to improve.

ACQUIRING MANAGERIAL EXPERIENCE

Section four contains four chapters. In Chapter 9, Adedeji B. Badiru stresses "Half-Life of Learning Curves for Information Technology Project Management." It is a natural process for people to learn, unlearn, and relearn. Capturing this process in a quantitative framework is essential for making effective decisions in any operation, particularly in an information technology environment, where human-machine interfaces are common. Because the degradation of learning does not follow a linear path, it is essential to monitor the various stages of the learning, unlearning, and relearning processes. This is exactly what the chapter on half-life of learning curves presents. The methodology presented in the chapter is new and innovative. The chapter presents an excellent analytical modeling of the stage when a learning profile has degraded to half of its initial value. This is useful for predicting the magnitude and behavior of learning over time. The author did an excellent job of pointing out that the half-way point is of most interest in tracking the degradation path of learning. That half-life point can be used for project planning and control purposes.

With the techniques in this chapter, something similar to a breakeven analysis of learning can be done because the upswing of learning and the downswing of learning conceptually intercept at some point. It is of decision interest whether that interception point occurs before or after the half-life point. For the purpose of training in information technology operations, an organization can use the half-life computational technique to estimate what fraction of training retention remains after some point in time and what level of retraining might be needed. Practitioners often speak of "twice as much" and "half as much" as benchmarks for process analysis. In economic and financial principles, the "rule of 72" refers to the length of time required for an investment to double in value. These common "double" or "half" concepts provide the motivation for using the half-life properties of learning curves as presented in this chapter. The longer the half-life of a learning curve, the more stable it is. This innovative chapter provides a good analogy for modeling learning curves with the recognition of increasing performance or decreasing cost with respect to the passage of time. Useful definitions from the chapter are: "Half-life of a learning curve is the incremental production level required to reduce cumulative average cost per unit to half of its initial level." "Half-life of a forgetting curve is the amount of time it takes for performance to decline to half of its initial level."

In Chapter 10, Hazel Taylor and Jill Palzkill Woelfer analyze "Critical Behavioral Competencies for IT Project Managers: What Are They? How Are They Learned?" The authors acknowledge the need to improve the performance of IT projects and the role of behavioral competencies of IT project managers in project outcomes. The chapter begins with a review of research related to project management skills and an in-depth discussion of the competencies described in general management and project management literatures, to provide a starting point for examining skills required specifically for IT project management. Potential avenues for learning these skills are discussed. From this background in the literature, the authors ask, "What behavioral competencies do experienced IT project managers apply when facing critical situations in their projects, and how have they developed those competencies?"

Through the analysis of data gathered in interviews with 23 experienced IT project managers, the authors identify the most important behavioral competencies of IT project managers and the ways that these managers have learned these skills. From this analysis, the authors make two primary contributions. The first contribution takes the form of an empirically derived set of specific behavioral competencies that are important for managers of IT projects with team leadership, concern for order, quality and accuracy, relationship building, impact and influence, and organizational awareness being most important. The second contribution relates to the learning methods used by IT project managers and formal development interventions that IT project managers have experienced. The most frequently employed learning methods are reflection on experience, observation of other project managers, formal training, and working with a coach or mentor. IT project managers also encountered a number of development interventions such as formal project management training, other management training, performance appraisals, participating in communities of practice, coaching and mentoring, and 360-degree feedback.

The authors present two key findings related to these learning methods and development interventions. First, although formal project management training provides a foundation for the development of IT project management skills, many of the IT project managers interviewed did not receive formal training until later in their careers. Second, IT project managers often employ self-reflection as a learning method and persist in seeking out new learning opportunities throughout their careers. Thus, the opportunity exists for organizations to foster life-long learning among IT project managers by providing a situated learning environment wherein junior project managers take part in formal training early in their careers and then receive feedback while being encouraged to reflect on their practice. Building on the work presented in this chapter, the authors are currently pursuing a follow-up study to develop a validated model of behavioral competencies for IT project managers.

Chapter 11, entitled "Questioning the Key Techniques Underlying the Iterative and Incremental Approach to Information Systems Development," was written by Angus G. Yu. The iterative and incremental development (IID) approach is widely promoted and adopted in information systems development (ISD) projects. While the IID approach has played an important role in the management of many ISD projects, its key techniques have not received critical appraisal from the academic community. Through a case study, this chapter fills the gap and examines three techniques of user participation, to evolutionary prototyping and timeboxing that are common to many IID methodologies.

First of all, the gap between the theory of user participation and the reality of user's lack of real influence on design and development is explored. While acknowledging behaviour-based explanations for difficulties caused by user participation, the chapter introduces an alternative structural explanation based on the concept of participatory capture within the agency-theoretic framework. This is significant since the new explanation not only explains the side effect of user participation, it points to a structural solution to issues that seem to be inherent in the user participation process. Secondly, with regard to evolutionary prototyping, the chapter suggests that its underlying assumption of converging and converging to success is problematic. As a result of the assumption, the IID approach in general does not provide a strategy to deal with the risk of the converged solution not meeting client requirements. Thirdly, the technique of timeboxing is considered. The chapter highlights its bias toward the supplier without adequately considering the needs of the client. The use of the timeboxing technique is likely to result in the supplier providing a system with less functionality and lower quality without proportionally reducing the client's cost.

The study is relevant to the on-going evaluation of agile methodologies incorporating similar techniques. It is also relevant to the broad question of how to deal with the significant uncertainties in ISD projects. The chapter finishes by referencing an existing framework of categorising product development strategies into instructional, learning, and selectionist approaches. It is suggested that IID represents the learning approach, which is a step forward from the instructional approach. However, the chapter postulates that to overcome the significant client-supplier and developer-user information asymmetry and development uncertainties, there is a need to incorporate the "selectionist" approach in ISD project methodologies.

Sanne Bor and Kees Boersma study the "Processes in R&D Collaboration" in Chapter 12. The chapter examines the process leading to a formalized co-operation of innovation in two cases: TechStar, and SciNet. Both cases were Research and Development (R&D) collaborations selected for funding by the European Commission (EC) under Framework Programme Six (FP6). In order to be eligible for the funding, the two cases needed to formalise their collaboration, whereby both the organisation of the collaboration as well as the activities were put into contracts, the consortium agreement and the contract with the EC.

The participants interviewed in TechStar reflected rather negatively on the formalisation process demanded by the EC. They reported that the formalisation process was unnecessary in that their research would have been done in the same way without the consortium agreement and contract, and that the demands of the EC were burdensome and bureaucratic. The participants of the other case, SciNet, on the other hand reflected positively on the formalisation process demanded by the EC. They reported that it was demanding, but that the contract and agreement help in understanding what is expected from them and how decisions should be made, and that the process helped in better understanding how they can work together with the other partners.

In order to understand this difference, Bor and Boersma illustrate how during the process of formalising, these two cases differ in the way that they use the formalisation process for simultaneously creating a better understanding of the collaboration, the expectations and the partners. The concept of sensemaking is used to grasp this possible sequential process of increasing of understanding by participants of their relationship with the other participants, their own role and responsibility and those of the others as well as the possibilities of collaborating due to better understanding what each participant is doing, interested in doing and capable of doing. The authors argue that using the formalisation process for simultaneous sensemaking adds value to the collaboration as well as can help in creating success of the collaboration due to the participants having a better understanding of the whole, the partners, and process.

The authors identify five factors that encourage or discourage the partners to use the process of formalising for the purpose of sensemaking: 1) the network configuration, 2) the extent to which partners already know one another, 3) the similarity of the partners, 4) the dependence of the partners on one another, and 5) the attitude towards formalisation. The authors urge practitioners to see formalisation not as an end in itself, but as a means for sensemaking. The authors believe this will lead to a situation in which the innovation process is supported by the different participants, problems will be able to be solved more easily, and this will lead to a more efficient innovation process.

PROJECT OUTCOMES AND CONCEPTION OF SUCCESS

Section five covers three chapters. In Chapter 13, Jack Shih-Chieh Hsu, Houn-Gee Chen, James Jiang and Gary Klein highlight "The Role of User Review on Information System Project Outcomes: A Control Theory Perspective." For quite a few years now it has been assumed that having users participate in the development of an information system will improve the outcomes of a development project. However, past research shows that participation by users has at best minimal impact. The authors take the challenge of determining why the wisdom of practice does not garner much research support. The authors contend that the contingency perspective taken by researchers does not consider the type of influence required for users to have an impact on final project outcomes.

Basing a model on contingency theory essentially forces actions to be taken based on task needs. This is obviously a valid consideration, but the actions taken could be done by any party without broad influence. Thus, should a user conduct an activity for the sake of participation, there is no structure to influence the outcome of the system as a whole, being limited to the scope of a particular task.

The authors of this study contend that this approach does not allow the necessary influence over the project at large. Instead, the authors alter the traditional view of user participation by drawing on control theory. This change in perspective allows for those in control to wield influence over a broader project scope. Under this assumption, the users become controllers as participants rather than as performers of a limited number of tasks. This assumption is a unique contribution to the field of information technology project management.

To refine the proposition, the authors consider the function of system reviews by users. The greater the intensity and frequency of reviews, the greater the opportunity the users have to influence the outcome of the project. The caveat in this situation is that the users and developers be effective in communicating their ideas and concerns to one another. Thus, the role of the user is elevated from one of conducting tasks within the project to one of potentially altering the path the project will follow. This increases the influence a user has to a greater extent than task completion.

Based on this logic, the authors then test the proposition. A sample validates the model indicating that participation as a controller explains a substantial portion of the success achieved by an IT project. This significant work by the authors of this study indicates researchers should consider control aspects in future models, but more importantly indicates how managers of technology projects should work to position users to have an ability to influence outcomes rather than perform a limited number of tasks.

Michael J. Cuellar prefers "Using Realist Social Theory to Explain Project Outcomes" in Chapter 14. The author takes on a significant issue in project management: Why did the project turn out the way it did? To address critical issue, Dr. Cuellar's contribution is to provide a methodology to apply Archer's Morphogenetic Social Theory, a general sociological theory whose key concern is to identify the reasons for change or non-change in social structures, to the problem. This is particularly appropriate for IT project management as IT projects are inherently social activities whose goal is the creation and/or implementation of IT artifacts.

In Archer's theory, social structures are held to be relationships between roles, which are positioned sets of practices such as a business process or organization. In any change effort such as an IT project, the different groups associated with the project (agencies) have different perspectives (situational logics) toward the existing social structures and the change effort. Additionally, resources such as money, expertise, and sanction are variously distributed amongst the agencies. When an agency begins an effort to make change, the agencies interact and in the process, they are defined and realigned, and resources are redistributed. On the basis of the realigned resources, the social structure is either transformed or not on the basis of mutual agreement, negotiation, or power imposition depending on the negotiating strength of the parties.

To use this theory for explaining project outcomes, first the author identified the social structure for which he wished to explain how it changed or did not change. Then data must be collected on the existing social structures and agencies, a history of interaction and negotiations around the resulting form of the social structure. Finally, the author analyzes the contractions within the structure, the resources available to the agencies and their situational logic. From the history, the chapter examines the strategies and tactics that they used to accomplish their goals. Finally, there is a power analysis of the negotiation. This drives out the causal factors explaining the results of the change activity.

This methodology provides the macro- and micro-level concepts that become the explanatory engine for identifying why the project achieved the results that it did. In so doing, the author balances structures and agencies not giving priority to either but allowing for identifying the dynamics between them. For practitioners, this approach allows them to understand the strengths and weakness of their social position prior to beginning a development or implementation effort and take steps to improve the chances of success. An example case study is provided to illustrate this methodology.

In Chapter 15, M. Keith Wright and Charles J. Capps offer "Runaway Information Technology Projects: A Punctuated Equilibrium Analysis." This wonderfully detailed case study presents a rarely seen inside view of a runaway Information Systems (IS) project in a(n) (unidentified) U.S. State government agency. Such out of control projects have been repeatedly shown to be one of the most egregious sunk costs in the global economy. This agency was targeted because it was well known as one of the most inefficient healthcare related agencies in the U.S. The principal investigator (PI) had a unique perspective; being both an academic and a certified IS auditor, he got permission from the agency's Director of Internal Audit (IA) to perform the project monitoring function for a long-troubled IS project in return for collecting research data.

The resulting ethnographic project narrative contained herein precisely chronicles how that project went out of control for so long, and because of this unique hybrid practitioner-academic perspective, the accompanying case study adds many new details to the IS project escalation literature. The chapter clearly explains the over-simplification in existing popular models of IS project escalation and de-escalation, and illustrates how a punctuated equilibrium analysis can be a more fruitful predictive tool than are "stage models," which are based on temporal processes.

Many important insights emerge from this case study. It suggests that project escalation should be expected to occur in most large IS projects and that when it does, it will do so in a manner consistent with that of an organization in "equilibrium." This indicates that future models of the escalation/de-escalation process should focus less on "projects" and more on the life cycle of the underlying business problem. The study raises the following specific research questions: What are the most important organizational choices forming the "deep structure" of information systems (IS) project organization? Are U.S. State government IS projects more prone to escalation than projects elsewhere? How can large organizations be structured to prevent project escalation? What are the factors governing when IS project redefinitions are used mainly for political purposes rather than to address real business problems? What are the factors governing when an IS project can be de-escalated without "revolutionary" organizational change? How do IS projects function during revolutionary periods? How do IS project revolutionary periods conclude? How is an organization's perception of its self-efficacy related to IS project escalation? The chapter cleverly illustrates benefits that can result when academia partners with the professional IS audit community.

IMPLEMENTATION OF IT PROJECTS FOR COMMERCIAL ENVIRONMENT, AGENCIES AND GOVERNMENTS

With four chapters, section six concentrates on "Implementation of IT Projects for Commercial Environment, Agencies and Governments." In Chapter 16, Andrew P. Ciganek and Marc N. Haines introduce "Service-Oriented Architecture Adoption: A Normative Decision Model for Timing and Approach." Successful project managers seek best practices and process improvements. This chapter introduces a normative decision model that reveals the most salient factors helping project manager to determine the appropriate timing and approach for adopting or expanding a Service Oriented Architecture (SOA) based on Web services. As SOA is becoming more entrenched as an architectural paradigm for information systems, organizations are expanding the scope and sophistication of SOA deployments. Questions of how and when to move ahead with SOA initiatives are as pertinent today as in the earlier days of SOA.

IT practitioners should pay particular attention to the decision flow representing the key questions and possible actions necessary for moving forward with SOA. The normative decision model offers direct guidance leveraging multiple best practices identified by adopters of SOA. There are four main areas an IT manager needs to assess to determine when and how to go ahead with a SOA project: the maturity of relevant standards, the technology gap, the organizational gap, and the nature of the benefits expected from a SOA. The authors provide specific instructions for practitioners based on the decisions that IT managers make in these four areas for the timing, scale, and usage of services.

The authors' seminal work examining SOA should help guiding both practitioners and researchers as the literature on the topic of SOA matures. The multiple case study approach used in this chapter proved to be appropriate for shedding greater insight into the complex nature of adopting SOA. A semi-structured interview script with eight open-ended questions was used during the interview process. This approach ensured consistency among all interviews and addressed the firm's organizational and IT background, the perspective and involvement of the interviewee, current SOA initiatives, expected benefits, the key challenges, long-term solutions and temporary workarounds, as well as key lessons learned in dealing with a SOA.

Scientific theory examining SOA is still maturing, and the authors offer an important contribution to this growing field in the literature. The authors interviewed multiple individuals from eight organizations in this study. These organizations represented varying levels of SOA adoption in multiple industries which gave a more balanced and comprehensive representation of the challenges organizations faced, attesting to the study's rigor. Researchers are encouraged to expand upon this work by either validating the findings through an independent study, examine SOA adoption for latter adopters, or refine the authors' normative decision making model using a similar, rigorous methodological approach.

In Chapter 17, Rugayah Hashim checks the "Issues in Electronic Procurement Project Implementation in Local Government." Electronic procurement was one of the first pilot projects implemented under the Malaysian e-government flagship in 1997. Till today, the e-procurement project has not been fully and successfully implemented because of several glitches and issues. Within the scope of local governments in Malaysia, eighteen pertinent issues were identified; namely, inter-departmental coordination, organizational directives, existing system or legacy system, organizational support, written procedures, planning model, organizational ICT expertise, organizational culture, individual support, leadership, strategic planning, individual ICT expertise, financial and budgeting issues, internal and external politics, standardization, timeframe and scheduling issues, human resources, and finally, adequate staffing. By converting these issues into a checklist, local government administrators would be able to ameliorate problems synonymous with project management resources such as extended timeframe and budget.

In addition, addressing these common barriers to successful e-procurement rollout would result in a significant return of investments for the federal, state and local governments. Furthermore, the Malaysian government is insistent that all public service delivery systems maintain a high standard of efficiency, effectiveness, integrity and accountability. With e-procurement, the transparency involved with government tenders and biddings would eliminate bribery among the vendors or suppliers and the civil servants working in the procurement department. Reforms in local authorities' administrative functions are crucial to the government's machinery, particularly the third tier of government as they are the ones that work closely with the grassroots, a.k.a., the citizens. Moreover, local authorities have limited resources, especially skilled manpower and money; thus, these constraints further inhibit the implementation of a sophisticated system project. Within these two realms, if the local authority leadership is weak and lacks the ICT expertise or know-how on e-procurement, the failure of the project is doomed from the start.

Nevertheless, inter-departmental coordination issues need to be eliminated as information sharing should not be provincial in nature. As such, organizational directives have to be similar or parallel, and the tasks of ensuring the integration of entity goals lie heavily on a strong and competent leader. Since e-procurement is rather contemporary, local authorities with legacy systems would need to update their computer peripherals for proper system integration. This would require organization support by letting the immediate department authorized to implement the e-procurement system have access to new equipment, and a skilled and adequate number of staff. Once the internal and external politics are taken care of, the success of e-procurement implementation and usage are ensured.

Chapter 18, entitled "Establishing Preconditions for Spanning the Boundaries in Public Private IT Megaprojects," was written by Roman Beck, Oliver Marschollek, and Robert Wayne Gregory. In recent decades, public-private partnerships (PPP) gained increasing attention for realizing public infrastructure projects. Due to different interests and corporate cultures of public sector and private sector organizations, the realization of infrastructure projects in the context of a PPP often causes collaboration difficulties, which lead to cost and time overruns. Therefore, this chapter focuses on exploring how the failing course of action of a public-private IT megaproject can be stopped and how the project can be turned around successfully. Based on the theoretical insights of boundary spanning literature, this chapter examines how public sector and private sector differences can be overcome to bridge the cultural divide in IT PPP projects. In particular, the analysis sheds light on the organizational preconditions for and activities of boundary spanning to reestablish a previously violated public-private relationship.

The analysis shows that the organizational preconditions of boundary spanning consist of establishing an unbiased relationship with the stakeholders, expertise in both fields of practice for developing mutual understanding, and the power to enforce changes in collaboration practices. Establishing these preconditions could only be realized by installing IT PPP managers with an unbiased relationship to the partnership project, which need to be familiar with the different cultural environments and possess the formal power to enforce changes in governance structures. In addition, it became evident in the analysis that specific activities are necessary to actively span the boundaries for reestablishing a sustainable partnership and turn around the project's course of action. In order to reestablish the partnership relation and mutual trust between the parties, partnership employees need to be shielded from external influences, such as media cover stories. Thereby, an open communicative culture can be maintained, which enables understanding mutual expectations and negotiating compromises on project realization.

Closer collaboration within the partnership and with all stakeholders as well as an increasing belief in project success was also supported by continuous external stakeholder support, such as positive announcements of politicians and transport associations in public media. Summing up, turning around troubled IT PPP projects necessitates establishing an unbiased relation between public and private parties and continuously nurturing the partnership relation as well as all stakeholder relations. Using boundary spanning theory, this chapter adds to the extant literature by identifying the antecedent conditions for and the activities of boundary spanning on an organizational level to bridge the cultural divide in interorganizational cooperation's.

Silvana Trimi and Kozeta Sevrani summarize "Development of M-Government Projects in a Developing Country: The Case of Albania" in Chapter 19. Albania is a Balkan former communist country, which has been striving to overcome obstacles toward its goal of joining EU and improving its citizens' life. However, recently the nation seems to have stagnated. Allegations of corruption have tainted every election since 1992 and politics seems to roll from one crisis to next because of the constant battle between the two major political parties. Every election's results have been disputed, parliament has been boycotted, fingers pointed both ways, and neither is showing any willingness to put the country before their political and self-interests. Institutions are weak, and laws are very often ignored. Bribes and corruption have penetrated in all levels of the government. The government is not transparent even for the impact of the global financial crisis on the country. Citizens are unhappy with the levels of corruption, lack of transparency, and the speed of progress toward an advanced country. The political turmoil is damaging Albania's EU accession process as EU requires applicants to be well-functioning democracies.

Today, information and communication technologies (ICTs) are used innovatively by governments worldwide to conveniently and economically deliver services, engage citizens, and increase transparency. The Albanian government also has successfully initiated and developed several e-government services. Many e-government projects, even when designed successfully, are canceled or not fully utilized because of the lack of awareness and/or lack of technologies (network infrastructure and access devices) to access these services, a problem quite prevalent in most poor countries. In Albania, fixed-line infrastructure is still very poor, particularly in rural areas. The majority of population has no desktop access to the Internet. However, they do have wireless access, with a penetration of around 90%. Thus, the best and perhaps the only way to serve citizens and businesses with timely and locality-based information, perform transactions, participate in decision making, and increase transparency is through m-government applications.

In this chapter, the authors develop the point of importance in introducing m-government applications in Albania, the types and the benefits to the users (individuals, businesses, and government) and to the country's progress toward democracy. The Albanian government not only should start designing m-government applications, but it should also make them a priority because: (1) e-government is still at early stages, and synergy between the two (e- and m- services) can be explored and duplications avoided; and (2) m-government can be the only, the quickest, the easiest, and most efficient way to provide government services, increase transparency, and citizen-participation, thus helping the country to get out of its stagnation and progress toward democracy and EU integration.

John Wang
Montclair State University, USA

Richard Peterson
Montclair State University, USA

Section 1
Resource Allocation and Scheduling

Chapter 1
A Multi–Objective Decision and Analysis Approach for the Berth Scheduling Problem

Mihalis M. Golias
University of Memphis, USA

Maria Boilé
Rutgers University, USA

Sotirios Theofanis
Rutgers University, USA

Heidi A. Taboada
The University of Texas at El Paso, USA

ABSTRACT

Berth scheduling can be described as the resource allocation problem of berth space to vessels in a container terminal. When defining the allocation of berths to vessels container terminal operators set several objectives which ideally need to be optimized simultaneously. These multiple objectives are often non-commensurable and gaining an improvement on one objective often causes degrading performance on the other objectives. In this paper, the authors present the application of a multi-objective decision and analysis approach to the berth scheduling problem, a resource allocation problem at container terminals. The proposed approach allows the port operator to efficiently select a subset of solutions over the entire solution space of berth schedules when multiple and conflicting objectives are involved. Results from extensive computational examples using real-world data show that the proposed approach is able to construct and select efficient berth schedules, is consistent, and can be used with confidence.

DOI: 10.4018/978-1-4666-0930-3.ch001

INTRODUCTION

Berth scheduling can be described as the problem of allocating berth space to incoming container vessels; a valuable resource of container terminals. Shipping lines, and therefore vessels, arrive at a container terminal over a period of time and compete for service at the available berths. Different factors affect the decision of a container terminal operator when deciding on the position and time slot assignment of each vessel along the terminal's quay. Fierce terminal competition and the need to maximize resource utilization have led marine terminal operators to the development and application of a rich variety of berth scheduling policies (Steenken et al., 2004). Some of the factors affecting the berth scheduling policy to be applied include, the type and function of the port (dedicated or private terminal, transshipment hub, etc), the size of the port, the location, nearby competition, type of contractual agreement with the vessel carriers, among others (Theofanis et al., 2009).

Most real-world scheduling problems, like the berth scheduling problem, are implicitly or explicitly multi-objective. In the case of the problem addressed in this paper, several objectives (minimization of vessel turnaround time, maximization of port throughput, maximization of revenues, etc) can be considered by container terminal operators when defining berth schedules. Usually, these multiple objectives are non-commensurable and gaining an improvement on one objective often causes degradation performance in at least one other objective (i.e. minimization of the makespan of the berth schedule and minimization of the number of total quay cranes (QCs) employed). The majority of the berth scheduling policies found in the literature have not captured current port operators practices (Steenken et al., 2004; Theofanis et al., 2009), and until recently (Boile et al., 2007; Imai et al., 2007; Hansen et al., 2008; Golias et al., 2009;) researchers had not recognized the importance of simultaneously optimizing for the different objectives that a port operator needs to consider when scheduling for the berthing of vessels.

The later research presented a set of non-dominated berth schedules as the final solution of the problem, known as the Pareto-optimal set (Zeleny, 1982). However, they did not present a formal methodology that would assist the container terminal operator in the selection of the most preferred berth schedule out of the different schedules found in the Pareto front. Without a formal selection methodology, a significant effort is required for the selection of a good berth schedule within the Pareto front. This issue becomes very noticeable in the berth scheduling problem, where in most real-life instances, the Pareto front is usually in the range of a hundreds (Golias, 2007). This phenomenon is also amplified by the multi-optimal solution space of the problem (Pinedo, 2008). Literature presents that determination of a single solution for multi-objective problems is often performed using methods such as the weighted sum method, utility theory, goal programming, etc (Taboada & Coit, 2008). However, in these methods, the final solution can be highly sensitive to the weights (or costs or penalties) used in the scalarization process. Additionally, in methods such as in the case of the weighted sum method, the weights must be selected by the decision-maker prior to the determination of the optimal solution. Furthermore, even experienced practitioners have difficulty reliably selecting specific weight values even if they are intimately familiar with the problem domain.

This paper presents the application of a recently introduced post-Pareto analysis approach, called the non-numerical ranking preferences method (NRPM), for the analysis of the solutions found in the Pareto front in cases where the decision-maker is uncertain or unable to provide specific weights for each objective function. In this paper we also present an extension of the NRPM where the decision-maker is uncertain on the priorities of the different objective functions. The strength of the former method is that the decision-maker only needs to rank non-numerically, and in order of relative importance, the objective functions and does not have to give specific weight values. The strength of the later method is that the decision-maker does not need to make any decision a-priori and can base his decision on the properties of the resolution space. Both approaches facilitate the selection of a small subset of solutions over the entire solution space of berth schedules, obtained from the solution of the multi-objective berth scheduling problem. We would like to point out that the proposed approach can be applied to other resource allocation and scheduling problems where it is very realistic to think that decision-makers should prioritize the objectives, but cannot mathematically combine them, since the approach used in this paper seems to be one of the most relevant to solve those classes of problems.

The rest of this paper is organized as follows. Section 2 presents an introduction to multiple objective optimization problems. Section 3 describes the post-Pareto analysis method employed in this paper. Section 4 presents the model formulation. A number of experimental results are presented in Section 5 and the last section concludes the paper.

MULTI-OBJECTIVE OPTIMIZATION

Most real-world engineering optimization problems involve the achievement of several objectives, normally conflicting with each other. These problems are called "multi-objective," "multi-criteria," or "vector" optimization problems, and were originally studied in the context of economics. However, scientists and engineers soon realized the importance of solving multi-objective optimization problems, and the development of techniques to model and solve such problems became an important area within operations research. Because of the conflicting nature of their objectives, multi-objective optimization problems do not normally have a single optimal solution,

and in fact, they even require the definition of a new notion or interpretation of "optimum."

A general formulation of a multi-objective optimization problem consists of a number of objectives with a number of inequality and equality constraints. Mathematically, the problem can be written as:

minimize / maximize $\mathbf{f}(\mathbf{x})$ (1)

Subject to:

$$g_j(\mathbf{x}) \le 0 \, j = 1, 2, ..., J \quad (2)$$

$$h_k(\mathbf{x}) = 0 \, k = 1, 2, ..., K \quad (3)$$

where:

$$\mathbf{f}(\mathbf{x}) = (f_1(\mathbf{x}), ..., f_n(\mathbf{x})) \text{ for } i=1, 2, ..., n \quad (4)$$

$g_j(\mathbf{x}) = j^{th}$ inequality constraint evaluated at x (5)

$h_k(\mathbf{x}) = k^{th}$ equality constraint evaluated at x (6)

$f_i(\mathbf{x}) = i^{th}$ objective function evaluated at x (7)

$\mathbf{x} = \{x_1, ..., x_p\}$ is a vector of decision variables
n = number of objectives or criteria to be optimized
p = number of decision variables

In the vector function, $\mathbf{f}(\mathbf{x})$, some of the objectives are often in conflict with others, and some have to be minimized while others are maximized. The constraints define the feasible region X, and any point $\mathbf{x} \in X$ defines a feasible solution. There is rarely a situation in which all the $\mathbf{f}(\mathbf{x})$ values have an optimum in X at a common point $\mathbf{x}$. Therefore, it is necessary to establish a criterion to determine what is considered as an optimal solution, and this criterion is non-dominance.

Thus, solutions to a multi-objective optimization problem are mathematically expressed in terms of non-dominance.

Without loss of generality, in a minimization problem for all objectives, a solution $\mathbf{x}_1$ dominates a solution $\mathbf{x}_2$, if and only if the two following conditions are true:

- $\mathbf{x}_1$ is no worse than $\mathbf{x}_2$ in all objectives, i.e., $f_i(\mathbf{x}_1) \leq f_i(\mathbf{x}_2) \; \forall \; i, \; i \in \{1, 2, .., n\}$
- $\mathbf{x}_1$ is strictly better than $\mathbf{x}_2$ in at least one objective, i.e., $f_i(\mathbf{x}_1) < f_i(\mathbf{x}_2)$ for at least one i.

The optimal solutions to a multi-objective optimization problem are the set of non-dominated solutions and they are usually known as Pareto-optimal set (Zeleny, 1982) or Pareto front. The Pareto front or a representative sub-set can generally be found with the use of a multiple objective evolutionary algorithm. There are two general approaches for the solution of a multi-objective problem. In the first approach the different objectives are combined into a single scalar value by using weighted aggregating functions. These functions are selected according to preferences set by the decision-makers in terms of numerical weights. The complexity and accuracy of this approach though is questionable, since it lies in the proper selection of the weights or utility functions that are used to depict the decision-maker's preferences. In practice, it can be very difficult to precisely and accurately select these weights, even for someone familiar with the problem domain.

In the berth scheduling setup, selecting the appropriate weights for each vessel in order to satisfy contractual agreements between the container terminal operator and the liner shipping company, may be a very cumbersome if not an impossible task (Theofanis et al., 2009). A compromising approach is to solve the problem multiple times using different sets of weights (Imai et al., 2003), but this would require a substantial computational

effort since from the computational complexity theory and depending on the formulation, berth scheduling is NP-hard or NP-complete (Imai et al., 2003, Imai et al., 2005; Papadimitriou & Steiglitz, 1982; Pinedo, 2008).

Alternatively, the later approach involves populating a number of feasible solutions along a Pareto front and the final solution is a set of non-dominated Pareto solutions. For the berth scheduling problem, adopting the latter approach offers a number of advantages. First, the berth scheduling problem can be formulated in a more realistic way, since a number of the container terminal operator objectives can be easily incorporated and identified in the final solution. Second, a multi-objective formulation allows for conflicting constraints to be treated as objectives, an approach that can outperform single objective formulations without a significant sacrifice in terms of performance (Coello Coello, 2000). This observation can be proven very valuable in complex berth scheduling problems where constraints limiting the feasible region of the problem can be viewed as objectives (for example limits on vessel waiting time). Finally, a multi-objective approach provides a wider range of alternatives for the participants in the berth scheduling planning and decision-making processes than its single objective counterpart. We should point out that in terms of optimality of the final solution a multi-objective approach is comparable to its single objective counterpart, since the complexity of the single objective formulation restricts the application of exact solution algorithms.

Post-Pareto Optimality

Once the Pareto front is obtained, the decision-maker has to decide which one of the non-dominated points to choose as the solution to the problem. This follow up step known as post-Pareto analysis helps in the decision-making process. However, post-Pareto analysis can be quite a challenging task since, in the absence of subjective or judgmental information, none of the corresponding trade-offs can be said to be better than the others. Although, several methods for solving multi-objective optimization problems have been developed and studied, little prior work has been done on the evaluation of results obtained in multi-objective optimization. The use of a value function to help the decision-maker identify the most preferred solution in multi-objective optimization problems was suggested in (Korhonen & Halme, 1990). The Greedy Algorithm (GR) was introduced and analyzed in (Venkat et al., 1990) to obtain a sub-set of the Pareto optima from a large set of the Pareto front. The selection of the sub-set was based on maximizing a scalarized function of the vector of percentile ordinal rankings of the Pareto optima within the large set. However, according to problem-specific knowledge, there are regions in the Pareto front which express good compromises and these regions can be identified. These regions are known as the "knee regions" (Das, 1999; Taboada & Coit, 2007). The "knee" is formed by those solutions of the Pareto front, where a small improvement in one objective would lead to a large deterioration in at least one other objective. However, in many multi-objective problems, there exists the case in which the achievement of one objective is more important than the others. This is the case that we examine and present in this paper, and for this; we will introduce the non-numerical ranking preferences method (Taboada & Coit, 2008).

Non-Numerical Ranking Preferences Method

The non-numerical ranking preferences method (NRPM) ranks the objective functions non-numerically and in order of relative importance, without selecting specific numerical weight values for each objective function. Initially, an uncertain weight function is generated based on the decision-maker objective function preferences.

The weight values used are systematically generated using an uncertain weight function and, this uncertain weight function is obtained with the simple information of the decision-maker objective function preferences. Then, possible weight combinations reflecting the decision-makers preferences are generated numerous times from the uncertain weight function. For instance, without loss of generality consider the case in which the first objective is more important than the second objective and the second objective is more important than the third objective: $f_1 \succ f_2 \succ f_3$. Then, random but ranked weights are generated using Monte Carlo simulation methods. These weights are uniformly sampled from the region of interest that satisfies the following: $w_1 > w_3 > w_2$ and $w_1 + w_2 + w_3 = 1$ (Figure 1). For example possible values for the weights in the case $f_1 \succ f_2 \succ f_3$ are: $\frac{1}{2} < w_1 \leq 1$, $\frac{1}{3} < w_2 \leq \frac{1}{2}$ and $0 \leq w_3 \leq \frac{1}{3}$. After obtaining the set of ranked weights, a substantially large set of weights is generated (thousands). Then, each of the weight sets is multiplied by each of the solutions found in the Pareto front as in: $f' = w_1 f_1(\mathbf{x}) + w_2 f_2(\mathbf{x}) + w_3 f_3(\mathbf{x})$. Then, without loss of generality, for minimization multiple objective problems, the solution that yields the minimum value for f' for each weight combination is recorded and gets a counter of 1. At the end, the solutions that have a counter of 1 are those solutions that form the pruned or reduced Pareto front.

Simply explained, in this approach the objectives prioritization adds constraints that effectively remove most of the possible weight combinations, and this leads to a dramatic solution space reduction. The solutions that this method yields have been reported to be those that clearly satisfied the given objective functions preferences (Taboada & Coit, 2008). This procedure is shown in Figure 2 for n objective functions with k solutions in the Pareto front. Without loss of generality we assume a minimization multiple

Figure 1. Weight region for the $f_1 \succ f_2 \succ f_3$ objective function preference

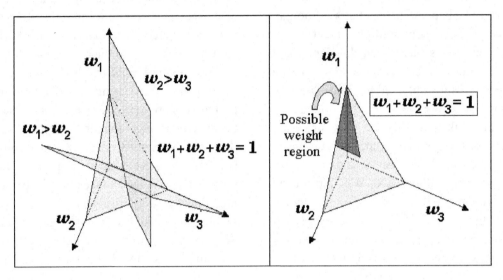

Figure 2. Non-numerical ranking preferences method

Let: $F = \begin{bmatrix} f_{11} & f_{21} & \cdots\cdots & f_{n1} \\ f_{12} & f_{22} & \cdots\cdots & f_{n2} \\ \cdots\cdots & \cdots\cdots & \cdots\cdots & \cdots\cdots \\ f_{1k} & f_{2k} & \cdots\cdots & f_{nk} \end{bmatrix}$,

be the normalized values of each objective function in the Pareto-optimal set.

Also let $f_k = [f_{1k} \quad f_{2k} \quad f_{3k} \quad \cdots\cdots \quad f_{nk}]$

Step 0. Set *PrunedSet*=[ ], *counter*=0, *M*=Simulation length

Step 1. Generate a weight range: $a = [a_1 \quad a_2 \quad a_3 \quad \cdots\cdots \quad a_n]$ so that

$1 \geq a_1 > a_2 > \cdots\cdots > a_n$

Step 2. Generate $W = \begin{bmatrix} w_{11} & w_{12} & \cdots\cdots & w_{1l} \\ w_{21} & w_{22} & \cdots\cdots & w_{2l} \\ \cdots\cdots & \cdots\cdots & \cdots\cdots & \cdots\cdots \\ w_{n1} & w_{n2} & \cdots\cdots & w_{nl} \end{bmatrix}$, based on *a* so that:

$w_{11} > w_{21} > w_{31} > \cdots > w_{nl}, \forall l$ and $w_{11} + w_{21} + w_{31} + \cdots + w_{nl} = 1, \forall l$, where *l* is a large

number (i.e. 10,000)

Step 3. Set *PrunedSet*={*PrunedSet*, $\min_{f_k}(F * W)$}

Step 4. If *counter*=*M* end else set counter=counter+1 and go to Step 1 objectives problem and an objective function relative importance of:

$$f_1 > f_2 > f_3 > \ldots > f_n.$$

Application of NRPM to Scheduling Problems

Scheduling/assignment problems, including project selection and project management, are inherently multi-objective optimization problems since various factors, such as the available budget and resources, the chance of success, and the efficient allocation of the project team/resources, must be considered and optimized simultaneously (Gabriel et al., 2006). The proposed NRPM can be applied to many types of multi-objective scheduling/assignment problems since no requirements are imposed for the problem to be formulated in a particular way, and no requirements are set for the objective function to be differentiable, continuous, linear, separable, or of any particular data-type. The proposed NRPM can be applied to a number of problems for which there is a way to encode and compute the quality of a solution to the problem. The proposed approach can also handle a number of different and simultaneous objectives that include: a) minimization of makespan or total completion time, b) minimization of delays, c) minimization of resources/budget, d) maximization of customer satisfaction, e) maximization of resource utilization etc.

Problem Description And Formulation

Three broad classification schemes of the berth scheduling problem may be specified: a) the discrete and the continuous berthing space, b) the static and the dynamic vessel arrivals, and c) the static and the dynamic vessel handling time (Figure 3). The discrete problem (see for example Imai et al., 1997; Imai et al., 2001; Imai et al., 2003; Hansen et al., 2008; Monaco et al., 2007) views

the quay as a finite set of berths, whereas in the continuous problem studied in (see for example Guan et al., 2002; Guan & Cheung, 2004; Imai et al., 2005; Kim et al., 2003; Moorthy et al., 2006; Park & Kim, 2003) vessels can berth anywhere along the quay. In the static arrival problem all the vessels to be serviced are already in the port, while in the dynamic arrival problem, adopted by the majority of the researchers, not all the vessels to be scheduled for berthing have arrived at the beginning of the scheduling time, although arrival times are known in advance. Finally, in the static handling time problem (see for example Imai et al., 2001; Imai et al., 2003; Hansen et al., 2008), vessel handling time is considered as an input, whereas in the dynamic as a variable (see for example Park & Kim, 2003; Steenken et al., 2004; Golias et al., 2007; Imai et al. 2008).

The problem studied in this paper is the multi-objective discrete and dynamic berth scheduling problem with customer service differentiation (MBSPCS). This problem was initially formulated and solved by Golias et al., (2009), where special attention was given to customer service differentiation by the use of multiple objectives, each portraying a separate customer. This approach provides the port operator with a variety of different berth schedules ranging from a schedule with the best overall berth performance (in terms of the total service time for all the vessels) to a schedule with minimum customer dissatisfaction (in terms of the total service time for the selected preferential customers' vessels). The problem formulation is presented here for consistency:

[MBSPCS]: Minimize
$$\sum_{i \in B} \sum_{j \in V} \sum_{k \in K} (HT_{ij} x_{ijk} + WT_{ij}) \tag{8}$$

Minimize $\sum_{i \in B} \sum_{j \in J_1} \sum_{k \in K} (HT_{ij} x_{ijk} + WT_{ij})$ (9.1)

Minimize $\sum_{i \in B} \sum_{j \in J_2} \sum_{k \in K} (HT_{ij} x_{ijk} + WT_{ij})$ (9.2)

Minimize $\sum_{i \in B} \sum_{j \in J_p} \sum_{k \in K} (HT_{ij} x_{ijk} + WT_{ij})$ (9.p)

Subject to $\sum_{i \in B} \sum_{k \in K} x_{ijk} = 1, \forall j$ (10)

$\sum_{j \in V} x_{ijk} \leq 1, \forall i, k$ (11)

$\sum_{m \neq j \in V} \sum_{h < k \in K} \left(\begin{array}{c} (HT_{im} x_{imh} + y_{imh}) + y_{ijk} \\ -(A_j - S_i) x_{ijk} \geq 0 \end{array} \right), \forall i, j, k$ (12)

$WT_{ij} \geq \sum_{m \neq j \in V} \sum_{h < k \in K} (HT_{im} x_{imh} + y_{imh})$
$+ S_i - A_j - M_{ijk}(1 - x_{ijk}), \forall i, j, (k > 1)$ (13)

$WT_{ij} \geq (S_i - A_j) x_{ijk}, \forall i, j, (k = 1)$ (14)

$x_{ijk} \in \{0,1\}, \forall i, j, k$ (15)

$y_{ijk} \geq 0, \forall i, j, k$ (16)

$WT_{ij} \geq 0, \forall i, j$ (17)

where:

$i = (1, \ldots, I) \in B$ set of berths,
$j = (1, \ldots, T) \in V$ set of vessels,
$k = (1, \ldots, T) \in K$ set of service orders,
$p = (1, \ldots, O) \in P$ set of preferential customers,
J_p = vessels belonging to preferential customer p ($J_p \subseteq V$),
S_i = Time when berth becomes idle for the first time in the planning horizon,
A_j = Arrival time of vessel j,
HT_{ij} = Handling time of vessel j at berth i,

y_{ijk} = Idle time of berth i between departure of vessel j, and the departure of its immediate predecessor

x_{ijk} = 1 if vessel j is served at berth i as the kth vessel, and zero otherwise,

WT_{ij} = waiting time of vessel j served at berth i,

$M_{ijk} = S_i - A_j + HTO_{ijk-1} + \max_{m \neq j} A, \forall i, j, k$,

HTO_{ijk} = Sum of handling times of the first k vessels with the largest handling times at berth i excluding vessel j.

The first objective function (8) minimizes the total of waiting and handling time (also known as vessel service time) for all the vessel and the idle time of the berths, while the second set of objective functions (9.p, p={1, 2, ...O}) minimize the total of waiting and handling time of vessels belonging to preferential customer p. Constraint set (10) ensures that vessels must be served once while constraint set (11) that each berth services one vessel at a time. Constraint set (12) ensures that each vessel is served after its arrival, while constraint set (13) and (14) estimate the waiting time of each vessel (Figure 4). M_{ijk} is a large number that is estimated so that inequality (13) is always feasible.

Computational Experiments

Dataset Description

Different problem instances were developed, where vessels are served with various handling volumes at a multi-user container terminal (MUT) with five and ten berths, with a planning horizon of one and two weeks. For each one of the four berth capacity-planning horizon combinations (i.e. five berths- one and two weeks planning horizon, ten berths-one and two weeks planning horizon) ten different test instances were created. The instances differed in the number of vessels, the vessel arrival and handling times and the number of preferential vessels. The data

Figure 3. Berth scheduling classification schemes based on space and time

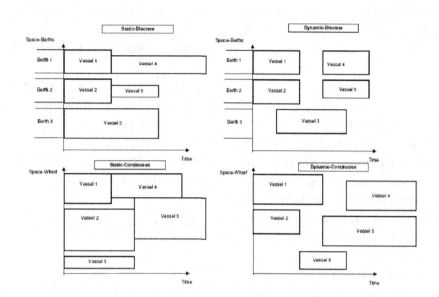

Figure 4. Estimation of wait time for vessel j serviced at berth i as the kth vessel

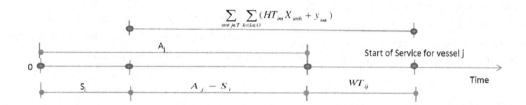

generation process was based on data from two container terminals with similar terminal operating systems (one in Europe and one in the US). The range of variables and parameters considered were chosen according to the data obtained from these two container terminals. In total forty test instances were created. In the dataset used in the experiments, vessel handling volumes (loading and unloading) range from 250 to 4,000 (Twenty-foot Equivalent Units-TEU[1]/vessel), based on a uniform distribution pattern. The handling time of a vessel is dependent on the berth assigned, and is a function of the number of the QCs that may be assigned. We consider that 1 to 3 cranes operate on small sized vessels (<2000 TEU of handling volume), 2 to 4 cranes on medium sized vessels (<3000 TEU of handling volume), and 3-6 on large mother vessels (<4000 TEU of handling volume). The average crane productivity is taken to be 25 TEU/hour. The minimum handling time of a vessel is calculated by dividing the handling volume by the average productivity of a crane multiplied by the maximum number of QCs that may operate on the vessel. At the beginning of the planning horizon availability of berths is calculated using a uniform probability with a minimum of zero and a maximum of 10 hours. Vessel interarrival patterns were based on the scheduled vessel arrivals at the two container terminals over a period of a year. The solution procedure was coded in SciLab 4.1[2] on a Toshiba Satellite Dual Core Intel T2250 with 2GB of RAM.

Results

To evaluate the proposed NRPM two cases of the MBSPCS were considered with one and two preferential customers respectively. The first case considered had the following two objective functions: (a) minimization of total service time for all the vessels (from now on this objective function will be referred to as TST-ALL) and (b) minimization of total service time of vessels belonging to only one preferential customer (TST-one preferential customer). The second case considered had the following three objective functions: (a) minimization of total service time for all the vessels (TST-All), (b) minimization of total service time of vessels belonging to customer A (TST-VCA), and (c) minimization of total service time of vessels belonging to customer B (TST-VCB). In what follows are a presentation and a detailed discussion of the results of the application of the

pruning algorithm (NRPM) after the Pareto front for the test instances was obtained.

Case I: Two Objective Functions

Based on the *p*-customer MBSPCS formulation the problem considering one preferential customer can be formulated as follows:

Single Preferential Customer Problem Formulation

$$\text{Minimize } f_1 = \sum_{i \in B} \sum_{j \in V} \sum_{k \in K} (HT_{ij} x_{ijk} + WT_{ij})$$
(18)

$$\text{Minimize } f_2 = \sum_{i \in B} \sum_{j \in J_1} \sum_{k \in K} (HT_{ij} x_{ijk} + WT_{ij})$$
(19)

Subject to: (10)-(17)

Figure 5 shows the 16 solutions found in the Pareto front for one of datasets before the pruning method was applied. The non-numerical ranking preference method was used to reduce the size of

Figure 5. Pruned solutions of the Pareto front obtained (1 Customer, 5 Berths and 1 Weeks Planning Horizon)

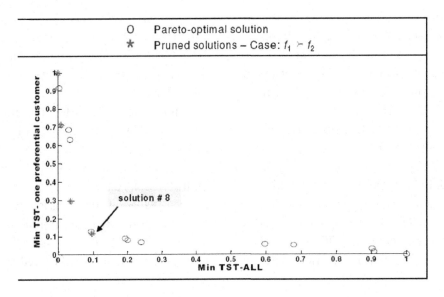

the Pareto front and select one solution for implementation. The importance of the objectives selected to illustrate this example is the case in which $f_1 \succ f_2$, i.e. the minimization of the total service time for all the vessels is more important than the minimization of the total service time of vessels belonging to the preferential customer. These preferences were only selected to demonstrate the pruning process and in practice the objective function preference order is made based on the priorities and goals of the decision maker. The pruned solutions obtained are also shown in figure 5 in red stars reflecting the selected decision-maker's objective function preference ($w_1 > w_2$).

To demonstrate that the pruning method is repeatable and reliable, and that there is no sacrifice for the non-numerically ranking preferences method, ten simulation runs were performed. In each of the ten runs, 10,000 different weights sets were used, randomly selected based on the criterion: $w_1 > w_2$. Table 1 shows the results from the ten simulation runs for the same test instance as in Figure 5. Out of the 16 solutions found in the full Pareto front (shown in Figure 5) only four (solutions 4, 5, 6 and 8) form the pruned Pareto front. The first column in Table 1 shows the solution number while the rest of the columns show the number of times (from now own referred to as counter) that the solution from the pruned Pareto front provided the minimum value of f:
$f' = w_1 f_1(x) + w_2 f_2(x)$ in each simulation run. For example, in the first simulation run solution #8 had the minimum value of f' for 4,998 out of the 10,000 different weight combinations, solution #4 had the minimum value of f' for 3,688 out of the 10,000 different weight combinations etc. The other solutions of the full Pareto front that do not appear on the table had a counter value of zero, meaning that they did not minimize the value of f' for any of the 10,000 weight combinations for any of the 10 different simulations. As can be seen from Table 1, solution #8 is the one that gives the highest counter value for all the 10 different runs and thus, the schedule of this solution can be the

one that may be implemented. Figure 6, shows the full and pruned Pareto front for one test instance for each one of the remaining three berth capacity-planning horizon combinations. Similar to Figure 5, pruned Pareto solutions are shown in red stars while full Pareto solutions are shown in circles. To have comparable units, normalization of the objectives was implemented.

Case II: Three Objective Functions

Based on the p-customer MBSPCS formulation the problem considering two preferential customers can be formulated as follows:

Two Preferential Customer Problem Formulation

$$\text{Minimize } f_1 = \sum_{i \in B} \sum_{j \in V} \sum_{k \in K} (HT_{ij} x_{ijk} + WT_{ij})$$

(20)

$$\text{Minimize } f_2 = \sum_{i \in B} \sum_{j \in J_1} \sum_{k \in K} (HT_{ij} x_{ijk} + WT_{ij})$$

(21)

$$\text{Minimize } f_3 = \sum_{i \in B} \sum_{j \in J_2} \sum_{k \in K} (HT_{ij} x_{ijk} + WT_{ij})$$

(22)

Subject to: (10)-(17)

Figure 7 shows the 71 solutions found in the Pareto front for one test instance. To better visualize the solutions obtained, Figure 7 also shows two different dimensional representations of the same solutions. The non-numerical ranking preference method was used to reduce the size of the found Pareto front and the combination selected to illustrate this example is the case in which $f_1 \succ f_2 \succ f_3$, i.e. the minimization of the total service time is more important than the minimization of the total service time of the first group of the preferential customers, and the minimization of the total service time of the first group of prefer-

11

Table 1. Solutions found in the pruned Pareto set in ten simulation runs (2 customers, 5 berths, and one week planning horizon)

Solution #	Counter on Simulation Run #									
	1	2	3	4	5	6	7	8	9	10
8	5107	4998	4988	5114	5102	4959	5046	5012	5046	5054
4	3688	3717	3735	3659	3687	3778	3705	3704	3664	3659
5	654	695	705	643	654	676	688	712	697	704
6	551	590	572	584	557	587	561	572	593	583

ential customers is more important than the minimization of the total service time of the second group of preferential customers. As with the previous example these preferences were only selected to demonstrate the pruning process. In Figure 7 the 8 pruned solutions are shown in red stars and the Pareto front solutions in blue circles respectively. To have comparable units, normalization of the objectives was implemented.

As with the previous example, the eight solutions obtained are the best solutions that reflect decision-maker's objective function preference ($w_1 > w_2 > w_3$). To again demonstrate that the pruning method is repeatable and reliable, and that there is no sacrifice for the non-numerically rank-

Figure 6. Pareto front and pruned solutions of the Pareto front

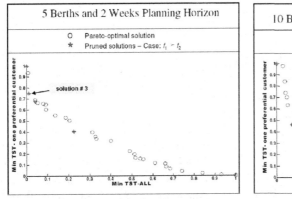

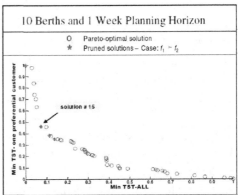

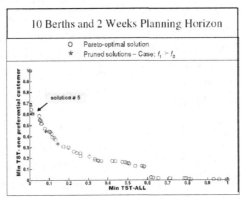

Figure 7. Pruned and Pareto front solutions (2 customers, 5 berths, and 1 week planning horizon)

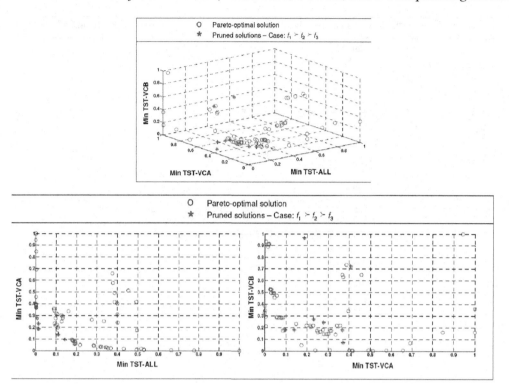

ing preferences method, ten simulation runs have also been performed and in each of the ten runs, 10,000 different weights sets, randomly selected based on the criterion: $w_1 > w_2 > w_3$, were used. Table 2 shows the results for the ten simulation runs. In this table, solutions from the Pareto front that do not appear had a counter value of zero. As seen in Table 2, solution 60 is the one that gives the highest counter value and thus, the schedule of this solution can be the one that may be implemented. Figure 8, shows the full and pruned Pareto front for one test instance from one of the remaining three berth capacity-planning horizon combinations with two preferential customers. Similar to Figure 7, pruned Pareto solutions are shown in red stars while full Pareto solutions are shown in circles.

NRPM Extension to Include Unknown Preferences

From the examples presented in the previous subsection, we can conclude that the NRPM is a strong Post-Pareto optimality method based only on the decision-maker's preferences; that is, the user is only required to specify the ranking of the objective functions instead of giving specific weight values. The resulting pruned Pareto front is a sub-set of the original Pareto front where each solution is potentially the "optimal" solution to a weighted-sum multiple objective problem. In this subsection we show who the proposed NRPM is also applicable in cases where the decision maker is also uncertain or unable to provide the priorities of the different objective functions. In this case the pruning methodology is applied to all the possible combinations of the objective functions preference order. To show how the

Figure 8. Pareto front and Pruned solutions of the Pareto front

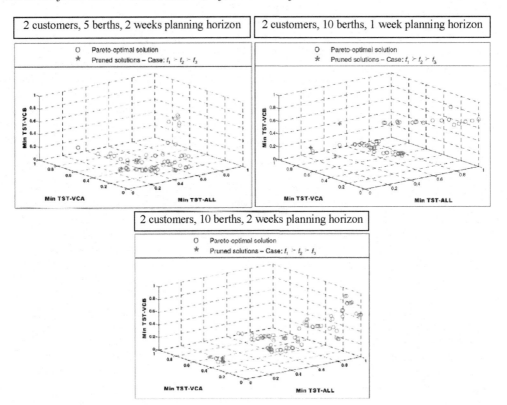

proposed methodology can be applied in this case the NRPM was applied to the forty test instances previously described using all the possible priorities for the objective functions. For example for the problem with the two preferential customers (i.e. three objective functions) six different objective function preference orders will be used. Similar to the computational examples presented in the previous subsection for each one of the possible objective functions priorities ten simulation runs with ten 10,000 different weight sets, randomly selected, were used.

Results for each one test instances with two preferential customers for each one of the four different berth capacity-planning horizons are shown in Tables 3 and 4. For the rest of the test instances similar trends were observed but are omitted due to space limitations. Tables 3 and 4 show the first and the second "*best*" solution (i.e. solution with the first and second largest counter value) found

in the pruned Pareto front for each one of the four test instance, after the NRPM was applied for all the possible objective functions preferences order (i.e. possible different weight order combinations). In both tables the first column presents the berth capacity-planning horizon instance and the second the objective function preference order considered. The rest of the columns show the solution number of the full Pareto front selected for each one of the ten different simulation runs (i.e. the solution that had the largest counter value for the specified weight order shown in the second column). For example, solution 60 and solution 12 are the solutions that give the first and second highest counter value for all the 10 different simulation runs for the problem with five berths capacity and one week planning horizon when the weight order considered is: $w_1 > w_2 > w_3$. For the remaining berth capacity-planning horizon test instances and this weight order the first and the second best solutions found are solutions 2 and 39, solutions 2 and 5, and solutions 1 and 6.

In both tables we observe that as the preferences of the container terminal operator changed (i.e. different weights order) the number of the different "*best*" schedules remained within acceptable limits. For example in Table 3 we observe that for the five berths-one week planning horizon test instance only 3 different solutions (solution 60, 57, and 40) appear as the "*best*" solution irrelevant of the weight order. The same is observed for the remaining test instances where solutions 2 and 4, solution 2, and solutions 6 and 1 are the only first "*best*" solutions obtained for each one of the different weigh orders. Similar results are observed for the second "*best*" solutions shown in Table 4. We should note that, similar to results presented in Table 2, for all the test instances and simulation runs only three to four solutions (out of all the solutions found in the full Pareto fronts) received a significant count (i.e. over 1%) on each simulation run, while the first two solutions accounted for at least 80% of the total counts for each simulation run (i.e. over 8,000 times out of the 10,000 different weight combinations the first two solutions had the minimum value of f').

These results confirm that the proposed methodology can provide a suitable decision environment for the port operator even if the objective functions priorities are difficult to be decided upon. If the NRPM was not applied the terminal operator would have the difficult task of choosing the solution that satisfies most of all of the different objective functions preferences from the full Pareto front. In the case of the pruned Pareto-set this decision becomes straightforward. For example, if the pruning method was not applied to the test instance of the five berths-one week planning horizon and the two preferential customers the terminal operator would have to choose a schedule from 71 different schedules (i.e. the full Pareto set shown in Figure 7). In the case of the pruned Pareto-front this decision becomes more straightforward since the choice is confined between three schedules (solutions 40, 57, and 60-Table 3) if only the first "*best*" solutions are considered or five (solutions 12, 33, 40, 57, and 60-Tables 3 and 4) if both the first and second "*best*" solutions are considered.

We would like to acknowledge that as the number of objective functions increases the different objective function preference combinations also increases but at an exponential rate. In this case the NRPM cannot be applied as is and the decision maker will need to provide priorities in terms of groups of the objective functions without having to prioritize between the objective functions within each group i.e. objective functions f_i

Table 2. Solutions found in the pruned Pareto set in ten simulation runs (2 customers, 5 berths, and one week planning horizon)

	Counter on Simulation Run #									
Solution #	1	2	3	4	5	6	7	8	9	10
60	9218	9211	9222	9184	9212	9282	9229	9200	9226	9242
12	392	423	408	407	359	348	393	394	352	382
59	206	215	195	237	268	217	218	232	242	225
40	157	114	140	146	127	132	132	140	149	127
15	6	8	3	4	8	4	7	13	8	8
10	7	14	12	10	11	6	14	7	6	4
18	6	9	13	9	9	8	4	9	10	6
17	8	6	7	3	6	3	3	5	7	6

and f_2, are more important than objective functions f_3 and f_4, objective functions f_3 and f_4, are more important than objective functions f_5, f_6, and f_7 etc. This would decrease significantly the size of the different objective functions priority combinations and make the methodology presented in this subsection applicable to problems with a large number of objective functions. As a final comment we would like to note that a drawback of the proposed NRPM is that as the number of simulations and weight combinations increase so does the simulation time, making the method less applicable in situations where the problem is

very dynamic and the decision maker is required to select a solution from the Pareto front within a short period of time (i.e. less than one hour).

CONCLUSION

Decision making in container terminal operations involves the need to fulfill multiple, often conflicting, objectives. In this paper we studied the multi-objective berth scheduling problem and provided a methodology for selecting a subset of the feasible/optimal solutions of the problem, suit-

Table 3. First best solution in Pareto set for different objective function preferences

Planning horizon-berth size	Objective Function Preference	Pareto Solution Number									
		1	2	3	4	5	6	7	8	9	10
5 Berths -1 Week Instance	w1>w2>w3	60	60	60	60	60	60	60	60	60	60
	w1>w3>w2	60	60	60	60	60	60	60	60	60	60
	w2>w1>w3	60	60	60	60	60	60	60	60	60	60
	w2>w3>w1	60	60	60	60	60	60	60	60	60	60
	w3>w2>w1	57	40	57	57	57	40	57	57	57	57
	w3>w1>w2	40	40	40	40	40	40	40	40	40	40
5 Berths- 2 Weeks Instance	w1>w2>w3	2	2	2	2	2	2	2	2	2	2
	w1>w3>w2	2	2	2	2	2	2	2	2	2	2
	w2>w1>w3	2	2	2	2	2	2	2	2	2	2
	w2>w3>w1	2	2	2	2	2	2	2	2	2	2
	w3>w2>w1	2	2	2	2	2	4	2	2	2	2
	w3>w1>w2	4	4	4	4	4	4	4	4	4	4
10 Berths- 1 Week Instance	w1>w2>w3	2	2	2	2	2	2	2	2	2	2
	w1>w3>w2	2	2	2	2	2	2	2	2	2	2
	w2>w1>w3	2	2	2	2	2	2	2	2	2	2
	w2>w3>w1	2	2	2	2	2	2	2	2	2	2
	w3>w2>w1	2	2	2	2	2	2	2	2	2	2
	w3>w1>w2	2	2	2	2	2	2	2	2	2	2
10 Berths-2 Weeks Instance	w1>w2>w3	1	1	1	1	1	1	1	1	1	1
	w1>w3>w2	1	1	1	1	1	1	1	1	1	1
	w2>w1>w3	6	6	6	6	6	6	6	6	6	6
	w2>w3>w1	6	6	6	6	6	6	6	6	6	6
	w3>w2>w1	6	6	6	6	6	6	6	6	6	6
	w3>w1>w2	6	6	6	6	6	6	6	6	6	6

Table 4. Second best solution in Pareto set for different objective function preferences

Planning horizon-berth size	Objective Function Preference	Pareto Solution Number									
		1	2	3	4	5	6	7	8	9	10
5 Berths -1 Week Instance	w1>w2>w3	12	12	12	12	12	12	12	12	12	12
	w1>w3>w2	12	12	12	12	12	12	12	12	12	12
	w2>w1>w3	40	40	40	40	59	40	40	40	40	40
	w2>w3>w1	40	40	59	40	40	40	59	40	40	40
	w3>w2>w1	40	57	40	40	40	57	40	40	40	40
	w3>w1>w2	33	33	33	33	33	33	33	33	33	33
5 Berths- 2 Weeks Instance	w1>w2>w3	39	39	39	39	39	39	39	39	39	39
	w1>w3>w2	39	39	39	39	39	39	39	39	39	39
	w2>w1>w3	2	2	2	2	2	2	2	2	2	2
	w2>w3>w1	2	2	2	2	2	2	2	2	2	2
	w3>w2>w1	4	4	4	4	4	2	4	4	4	4
	w3>w1>w2	2	2	2	2	2	2	2	2	2	2
10 Berths- 1 Week Instance	w1>w2>w3	5	5	5	5	5	5	5	5	5	5
	w1>w3>w2	5	5	5	5	5	5	5	5	5	5
	w2>w1>w3	5	5	5	5	5	5	5	5	5	5
	w2>w3>w1	5	5	5	5	5	5	5	5	5	5
	w3>w2>w1	1	1	1	1	1	1	1	1	1	1
	w3>w1>w2	22	22	22	22	22	22	22	22	22	22
10 Berths-2 Weeks Instance	w1>w2>w3	6	6	6	6	6	6	6	6	6	6
	w1>w3>w2	6	6	6	6	6	6	6	6	6	6
	w2>w1>w3	1	1	1	1	1	1	1	1	1	1
	w2>w3>w1	1	1	1	1	1	1	1	1	1	1
	w3>w2>w1	9	9	9	9	9	9	9	9	9	9
	w3>w1>w2	20	20	20	20	20	20	20	20	20	20

able for formulating a preferred berth scheduling policy. This methodology allows the port operator to efficiently evaluate the majority of the feasible berth schedules, and select the ones with a competitive performance for all the objectives in a straightforward manner. The robust approach that was presented, allows the selection of a subset of berth schedules over the entire solution space, by ranking the objective functions non-numerically in order of relative importance, without having to specify weight values. The proposed approach also allows for the selection of a small number of competing schedules to be selected even in the case where the relative importance of the different objective functions cannot be determined. The proposed methodology was evaluated using a multi-objective berth scheduling formulation. Results showed that the method was repeatable and reliable, and a significant decrease in the solution space was obtained without any sacrifice in the objectives' performance. The proposed NRPM can be applied to a number of other scheduling/ assignment problems (including project selection) for which there is a way to encode and compute the quality of a solution to the problem.

ACKNOWLEDGMENT

This material is based upon work supported by the National Science Foundation under Grant No.0538901. Any opinions, findings, and conclusions or recommendations expressed in this material are those of the authors and do not necessarily reflect the views of the National Science Foundation

REFERENCES

Boile, M., Theofanis, S., Golias, M., & Coit, D. (2007). Berth planning by customer service differentiation: A multi-objective approach. In proceedings of the *World Conference on Transport Research (CD-Rom)*, Berkeley, California, 2007.

Branke, J., Deb, K., Dierolf, H., & Osswald, M. (2004). Finding knees in multi-objective optimization. In proceedings of the *8th Conference on Parallel Problem Solving from Nature*, (pp. 722-731), Birmingham, UK.

Coello Coello, A. C. (2000). Treating constraints as objectives for single-objective evolutionary optimization. *Engineering Optimization, 32*(3), 275–308. doi:10.1080/03052150008941301

Das, I. (1999). On characterizing the 'knee' of the Pareto curve based on normal-boundary intersection. *Structural Optimization, 18*(2/3), 107–115.

Gabriel, A. S., Kumar, S., Ordonez, J., & Nasserian, A. (2006). A multiobjective optimization model for project selection with probabilistic considerations. *Socio-Economic Planning Sciences, 40*(4), 297–313. doi:10.1016/j.seps.2005.02.002

Golias, M. M. (2007). *The discrete and dynamic berth allocation problem: Models and algorithms*. Unpublished doctoral disseratation. Rutgers University, New Jersey.

Golias, M. M., Boile, M., & Theofanis, S. (2009). (Manuscript submitted for publication). Berth scheduling by customers differentiation: A multi-objective approach. *Transportation Research Pt. E (Norwalk, Conn.)*.

Golias, M. M., Theofanis, S., & Boile, M. (2007). Berth and quay crane scheduling: A formulation reflecting start and finish of service deadlines and productivity agreements. In *Proceedings of the 2nd Annual National Urban Freight Conference (CD-Rom)*, Long Beach, CA.

Guan, Y., & Cheung, R. K. (2004). The berth allocation problem: models and solution methods. *OR-Spektrum, 26*, 75–92. doi:10.1007/s00291-003-0140-8

Guan, Y., Xiao, W.-Q., Cheung, R. K., & Li, C.-L. (2002). A multiprocessor task scheduling model for berth allocation: Heuristic and worst case analysis. *Operations Research Letters, 30*, 343–350. doi:10.1016/S0167-6377(02)00147-5

Hansen, P., Oguz, C., & Mladenovic, N. (2008). Variable neighborhood search for minimum cost berth allocation. *European Journal of Operational Research, 191*(3), 636–649. doi:10.1016/j.ejor.2006.12.057

Imai, A., Chen, H. C., Nishimura, E., & Papadimitriou, S. (2008). The simultaneous berth and quay crane allocation problem. *Transportation Research Part E, Logistics and Transportation Review, 44*(5), 900–920. doi:10.1016/j.tre.2007.03.003

Imai, A., Nagaiwa, K., & Tat, C.-W. (1997). Efficient planning of berth allocation for container terminals in Asia. *Journal of Advanced Transportation, 31*, 75–94.

Imai, A., Nishimura, E., & Papadimitriou, S. (2001). The dynamic berth allocation problem for a container port. *Transportation Research Part B: Methodological, 35*, 401–417. doi:10.1016/S0191-2615(99)00057-0

Imai, A., Nishimura, E., & Papadimitriou, S. (2003). Berth allocation with service priority. *Transportation Research Part B: Methodological, 37*, 437–457. doi:10.1016/S0191-2615(02)00023-1

Imai, A., Sun, X., Nishimura, E., & Papadimitriou, S. (2005). Berth allocation in a container port: Using continuous location space approach. *Transportation Research Part B: Methodological, 39*, 199–221. doi:10.1016/j.trb.2004.04.004

Imai, A., Zhang, J.-T., Nishimura, E., & Papadimitriou, S. (2007). The berth allocation problem with service time and delay time objectives. *Maritime Economics & Logistics, 9*(4), 269–290. doi:10.1057/palgrave.mel.9100186

Kim, K. H., & Moon, K. C. (2003). Berth scheduling by simulated annealing. *Transportation Research Part B: Methodological, 37*, 541–560. doi:10.1016/S0191-2615(02)00027-9

Korhonen, P., & Halme, M. (1990). Supporting the decision maker to find the most preferred solutions for a MOLP-problem. In proceedings of the *9th International Conference on Multiple Criteria Decision Making (pp. 173-183)*, Fairfax, Virginia.

Li, C.-L., Cai, X., & Lee, C.-Y. (1998). Scheduling with multiple-job-on-one-processor pattern. *IIE Transactions, 30*, 433–445.

Monaco, F. M., & Sammarra, M. (2007). The berth allocation problem: A strong formulation solved by a Lagrangean approach. *Transportation Science, 41*(2), 265–280. doi:10.1287/trsc.1060.0171

Moorthy, R., & Teo, C.-P. (2006). Berth management in container terminal: the template design problem. *OR-Spektrum, 28*(4), 495–518. doi:10.1007/s00291-006-0036-5

Papadimitriou, H. C., & Steiglitz, K. (1982). *Combinatorial optimization: Algorithms and complexity*. Mineola, N.Y: Dover Publications, Inc.

Park, M. Y., & Kim, H. K. A. (2003). A scheduling method for berth and quay cranes. *OR-Spektrum, 25*, 1–23. doi:10.1007/s00291-002-0109-z

Pinedo, M. (2008). *Scheduling: theory, algorithms, and systems-3rd edition*. New York: Springer.

Steenken, D., Voss, S., & Stahlbock, R. (2004). Container terminal operation and operations research – A classification and literature review. *OR-Spektrum, 26*, 3–49. doi:10.1007/s00291-003-0157-z

Taboada, H. (2007) *Multi-objective optimization algorithms considering objective preferences and solution clusters*. Unpublished doctoral disseratation. Rutgers University, New Jersey.

Taboada, H., & Coit, D. W. (2007). Data clustering of solutions for multiple objective system reliability optimization problems. *Quality Technology & Quantitative Management Journal, 4*(2), 35–54.

Taboada, H., & Coit, D. W. (2008). Multiple objective scheduling problems: determination of pruned Pareto sets. *IIE Transactions, 40*(5), 552–564. doi:10.1080/07408170701781951

Theofanis, S., Boile, M., & Golias, M. M. (2009). Container terminal berth planning: Critical review of research approaches and practical challenges. *Journal of the Transportation Research Record*.

Venkat, V., Jacobson, S., & Stori, J. (2004). A post-optimality analysis algorithm for multi-objective optimization. *Computational Optimization and Applications*, *28*, 357–372. doi:10.1023/B:COAP.0000033968.55439.8b

Zeleny, M. (1982). *Multiple criteria decision making*. New York: McGraw Hill Higher Education.

ENDNOTES

[1] One TEU represents cargo capacity of a standard shipping container (20 feet long and 8 feet wide)

[2] Copyright © 1989-2005. INRIA ENPC www.scilab.org

This work was previously published in International Journal of Information Technology Project Management, Volume 1, Issue 1, edited by John Wang, pp. 54-73, copyright 2010 by IGI Publishing (an imprint of IGI Global).

Chapter 2
Optimal Crashing and Buffering of Stochastic Serial Projects

Dan Trietsch
American University of Armenia, Armenia

ABSTRACT

Crashing stochastic activities implies changing their distributions to reduce the mean. This can involve changing the variance too. Therefore, crashing can change not only the expected duration of a project but also the necessary size of its safety buffer. We consider optimal crashing of serial projects where the objective is to minimize total costs including crashing cost and expected delay penalty. As part of the solution we determine optimal safety buffers. They allow for activities that are statistically dependent because they share an error element (e.g., when all durations have been estimated by one person, when weather or general economic conditions influence many activities, etc). We show that under plausible conditions the problem is convex and thus it can be solved by standard numerical search procedures. The purpose of the paper is to encourage software development that will include valid stochastic analysis for scheduling and crashing using current estimates and historical performance records.

INTRODUCTION

Historically, crashing project activities has been associated with CPM, using deterministic activity duration assumptions. By contrast, PERT took into account stochastic activity durations but with few exceptions crashing was not considered. One possible reason for this state of affairs may be that PERT was never a truly effective platform for assessing stochastic activity durations. Baker & Trietsch (2009) list several PERT deficiencies, of which the stochastic independence assumption is the most pernicious. To address this issue, Trietsch (2005) presents the *systemic error model*, which employs a multiplicative stochastic error

DOI: 10.4018/978-1-4666-0930-3.ch002

that is constant for each project but varies across projects. This component of the model represents estimation bias, and it entails positive correlation between the activity durations of each project as compared to the original project schedule. One advantage of the model is that it is straightforward to use historical data to achieve reliable distributions without requiring practitioners to provide three estimates for each activity. That model has recently been validated by field data from two Armenian NGOs (Gevorgyan, 2008). The validation also suggested that the lognormal distribution with a consistent coefficient of variation is useful for modeling activity durations (although in one NGO it was also necessary to account for the Parkinson effect, where activities are often tardy but rarely early). The lognormal distribution is especially convenient if we wish to crash an activity by allocating more capacity to it, because that can be modeled by division of work content by capacity. If both work content and capacity are modeled as lognormal random variables, their ratio is also lognormal. No other widely-used distribution shares this useful property. Furthermore, although the exact distribution of a sum of lognormal variables is unknown, the lognormal distribution itself provides reasonable approximate convolutions (Robb & Silver, 1993).

Those results open the way not only to effective stochastic scheduling but also to modeling and implementing optimal crashing of a stochastic project. Baker & Trietsch (2009) discuss this issue in generic terms, and the purpose of this paper is to explore it in more depth. We do so specifically in terms of a simple but important building block: a serial project. We study optimal or near-optimal crashing of stochastic activities in basic projects with n (not necessarily independent) activities in series, and without intermittent idling. We assume continuous crashing with a linear cost per unit as in classical CPM (Fulkerson, 1961; Kelley, 1961). A due date, D, is given and tardiness is penalized at a proportional rate, P. The objective is to minimize the total cost of crashing plus expected delay penalty. (We refer to this as the *default* objective.) If we define the difference between the due date and the mean completion time as the *project buffer*, then optimal crashing yields optimal project buffers. For this reason we consider the two issues together. Our purpose is to provide a theoretical basis for enhancing project scheduling and control software packages, to handle stochastic analysis properly and without demanding more input from the user than is customary for deterministic analysis.

To review the literature related to stochastic crashing of project activities, the following statements are implied (unless stated otherwise): (1) General PERT networks with statistically independent stochastic activities are addressed. (2) Crashing is continuous. (3) The default objective is pursued (with the "cost of crashing" interpreted according to the context). An alternative, to which we refer explicitly as the *expectation* objective, is to either minimize the expected duration given a crashing budget or achieve a required expected duration most economically (the ability to solve one suffices for the other). The expectation objective is a special case of the default objective, obtained if we set a due date of zero and adjust the penalty rate. Finally, (4) no intentional idling occurs—each activity starts as soon as it becomes feasible. In these terms, our own problem is "serial networks with dependent activity distributions."

Arisawa & Elmaghraby (1972) considered GERT networks where only exclusive-or nodes are allowed (thus excluding general PERT but including the serial case) with an expectation objective, and presented a tractable fractional LP solution. Britney (1976) explicitly addressed both buffers and crashing with a sum of several default objectives as the combined objective, and with possible idling between all activities. His buffers apply to activities one-by-one and planned idling occurs unless the buffer is exceeded. Wollmer (1985) pursued an expectation objective where crashing applies only to activity means. He modeled stochastic variation by discrete random variables, and obtained a convex programming model. Gutjahr, Strauss & Wagner (2000) considered discrete crashing. They solved by a stochastic branch and bound approach that requires extensive simulation and the use of a lower bound instead of the true objective value. Thus they obtained a computationally intensive approximate solution.

In general, it is not necessarily optimal to start all non-critical activities as soon as possible. Usually, one can associate a holding cost with completed activities, and by postponing an activity its holding cost is reduced. Therefore, postponement is mathematically equivalent to negative crashing, and advancement yields positive crashing. Thus, models that deal with the optimal start time of activities are directly relevant to our subject. Ronen & Trietsch (1988) discussed the optimal times to place orders for n project items, where the latest one determines the project's completion time. Highly overlapping results were developed independently by Kumar (1989) and by Chu, Proth & Xie (1993). Hopp & Spearman (1993) addressed the same problem with a step delay penalty function (i.e., with a deadline). Yano (1987, 1987a) analyzed serial supply chains with stochastic activities, with and without planned idling. All these relatively early sources utilize planned buffers to achieve improved reliability and avoid [implicit] project delay penalties.

The planned-buffers idea has been popularized recently and many practitioners find it useful. One of many supportive views of this development was given by Leach (2000), whereas Herroelen, Leus & Demeulemeester (2002), Raz, Barnes & Dvir (2003) and Trietsch (2005a) belong to the select few who presented a more critical viewpoint. The size of the protective buffer in this method is determined, quite arbitrarily, as a constant fraction of the estimated length of the chain leading to the buffer. Leach (2000) suggested the maximum of a buffer based on the traditional independence assumption and the constant fraction. Leach (2003) suggested a buffer based on the sum of the

two elements mentioned before. Trietsch (2005) showed that project activities are likely to be strongly correlated and therefore, if we specify a high service level (e.g., 90%), optimal project buffers should indeed be bounded from below by a fraction of the estimated mean. He also showed how to estimate the means and variances of activity durations by regression. Trietsch (2006) presented an optimality condition for feeding buffers in projects with general PERT networks, without requiring statistical independence. His main insight is that the criticality of the release date (planned start time) of each activity—i.e., the probability the critical path starts there—should be proportional to the relative economic cost of releasing the activity earlier. That economic cost is due to the need to stage various resources in advance. Staging activities are rarely considered explicitly as part of a project network. Instead, they are treated as auxiliary subprojects whose due date is the release date of the activity they support. Nonetheless, they are important (Herroelen & Leus, 2004).

Our primary contribution is solving for cases where activity times are correlated and the variance may change during crashing. Specifically, if the variance decreases with the mean, then more crashing is called for than otherwise; and vice versa if variance increases. Numerical examples demonstrate that the difference can be substantial. Another contribution concerns convexity: if the crashing cost function of each activity is convex and the standard deviation is a convex function of the mean, then we show that the objective function is convex (even though activities may be correlated). For example, if we use the lognormal model for crashing, as suggested by the results of Gevorgyan (2008), the convexity condition that we require here is satisfied.

The remainder of the paper is organized as follows. The next section formulates the models we address. The following section assumes statistical independence without variance effects, to solve the basic model. Then, we add variance effects. Next, we present the main model (with correlation) and derive the convexity result. Another section provides numerical examples. The last section is the conclusion.

MODEL FORMULATIONS

Let a project consist of n activities in series. We denote the duration of activity i by Y_i, where $i = 1,..., n$. Let $F_i(y)$ be the cumulative distribution function (cdf) of Y_i. μ_i denotes the expected value of Y_i (e.g., in weeks) and let $\mu = \Sigma\mu_i$ be the project's expected duration (project parameters have no subscripts in our notation). Similarly, σ_i is the standard deviation of Y_i. C_i is the cost of crashing μ_i by one unit and d_i is the maximal possible crashing at this cost (e.g., if we can reduce μ_i by 0.2 weeks at a cost of \$50, then $d_i = 0.2$ and $C_i = 250\$/wk$). Let $\Delta_i \le d_i$ denote the crashing amount, then the crashing cost is $\Delta_i C_i$. Let the project start at time zero with a due date, D, and a time unit cost (including tardiness penalty) of P per week beyond D; i.e., this cost is given by $P(Y - D)^+$, where $Y = \Sigma Y_i$ and $h^+ = \max\{0, h\}$. The objective is to minimize the expected total cost (TC) of crashing and tardiness,

$$\mathrm{TC} = \sum_{i=1}^{n} C_i\Delta_i + \mathrm{E}[P(Y - D)^+]$$

We refer to the vector of planned crashing amounts, $\{\Delta_i\}$, as the *crashing plan*. Let SL denote the service level, i.e., the probability the path completes in time, then $\mathrm{SL} = F(D)$. As a rule, we use stars to denote optimal values, e.g., SL* is the optimal service level that is associated with the optimal crashing plan, $\{\Delta_i^*\}$. (Although our objective is to find the best crashing plan and project buffer, it is convenient to do so by focusing on SL*.)

In the next three sections we solve three models. *Model 1* assumes that activities are statistically independent and crashing consists of shifting $F_i(y)$ by a constant to the left, thus decreasing μ_i by the crashing amount. We refer to this as *simple crashing*. (All the previous papers that we discussed only address simple crashing.) Another assumption, necessary for convexity, is that the cost of crashing is monotone non-decreasing with Δ_i. *Model 2* is based on Model 1 but allows for the possibility that the distribution may change, and in particular that the standard deviation changes along with the mean. We focus on the case where the standard deviation is a convex function of the mean. *Model 3* generalizes Model 2 by removing the statistical independence assumption.

Model 1: Simple Crashing of Independent Activities

Under simple crashing the variance does not change and the project duration cdf is shifted by the total crashing amount but retains its shape. In our analysis we also assume that the cost per unit of crashing is constant. It is practically immediate to extend this to a case with a non-decreasing crashing cost function, but we omit the details. When C_i is viewed as a function of μ_i (instead of Δ_i), this is equivalent to a non-*increasing* cost function (which is likely if activities are subprojects).

In this and the next section, by the independence assumption, $\sigma^2 = \Sigma\sigma_i^2$. Similarly, since we have $F_i(y)$, we can obtain $F(y)$ by successive convolutions (often the normal approximation may be adequate). For any given crashing plan, we can update $F(y)$ and thus update SL. For any such plan, let $C = P(1 - \mathrm{SL})$. C has a simple economic interpretation: it is the marginal benefit associated with crashing the project further. To see this consider that crashing by an infinitesimal amount δ reduces the delay penalty by $P\delta$ with a probability of $(1 - \mathrm{SL})$, and makes no difference otherwise. So it reduces the expected delay penalty by $P\delta(1 - SL)$. This leads to a necessary and sufficient optimality criterion: Suppose we know $C^* = P(1 - SL^*)$, then any activity with $C_i < C^*$ should be crashed fully, any activity with $C_i > C^*$ should not be crashed at all, and if a k exists such that $C_k = C^*$, then activity k should be crashed by some value between 0 and d_k (inclusive) until SL^* is obtained. A crashing plan that satisfies these conditions always exists, and any such plan is optimal. This is true by convexity, which we prove for a more general case in Section 5. If all the C_i values are distinct, then there is exactly one optimal crashing plan. If we sort all activities by increasing C_i, we can identify an optimal crashing plan by a simple search (we omit further details). We refer to this solution as *Procedure 1*.

The result is essentially identical to the newsvendor model, using C as the "long" cost and $P - C$ as the "short" cost. This interpretation is appropriate because, by definition, $C = P(1 - SL)$ so $P \geq C$ is assured.

Model 2: Crashing with Variance Effects

When crashing is not necessarily simple, the standard deviation of an activity may change during crashing. To illustrate, consider a discrete crashing example: if we ship by air instead of by truck we are likely to achieve a lower mean transport time but a higher variance. In the continuous case, we model that effect by a function, $\sigma_i(\Delta_i)$, whose derivative (when it exists) yields the rate of change of σ_i during crashing. It may be useful to fit such a function even to a discrete case because most activities are either crashed fully or not crashed at all. In the example above, crashing fully would imply switching from truck to air. We would only need a discrete model if that particular transport activity is the one that should be crashed partly. *Model 2* assumes that $\sigma_i(\Delta_i)$ is convex. The same applies to $\sigma_i(\mu_i)$ (because $\Delta_i + \mu_i$ remains constant during crashing). For example, let $\sigma_i(\mu_i) = \sigma_0 + a\mu_i$, where σ_0 is some non-negative value and $a \in R$

but such that if $a < 0$, $\sigma_i \geq 0$ for any feasible μ_i. (If $d\sigma_i/d\mu_i < 0$, e.g., negative a in the example, then the variance increases during crashing.)

The following equation provides two ways to look at the expected penalty, EP (and we switch between them as convenient),

$$EP = P\int_D^\infty (y - D)f(y)dy = P\int_D^\infty [1 - F(y)]dy \tag{1}$$

The right hand side says that EP can be calculated by P times the area between the cdf and 1, from D onwards. Let $Z = (Y - \mu)/\sigma$ be the standardized project duration and let $G(z)$ and $g(z)$ be its cdf and density function (we may refer to these as G and g). Hence $G(z) = F(z\sigma + \mu)$ and $g(z) = \sigma f(z\sigma + \mu)$. A simplifying approximation is to assume that crashing does not change the shape of the final project distribution. In other words, only μ and σ change, while G and g remain the same for any z. This assumption is mild in practice because often we can assume a normal chain distribution, and thus the present assumption would hold. (For the normal distribution we substitute Φ and φ for G and g.) Rewriting Equation 1 in terms of G and g we obtain,

$$EP = P\sigma\int_t^\infty (z - t)g(z)dz = P\sigma\int_t^\infty [1 - G(z)]dz \tag{2}$$

$$\frac{\partial\mu}{\partial\mu_i} = 1 \ ; \quad \frac{\partial\sigma}{\partial\mu_i} = \frac{\partial\sigma}{\partial\sigma_i}\frac{\partial\sigma_i}{\partial\mu_i} \ ;$$

$$\frac{\partial t}{\partial\mu} = \frac{-1}{\sigma} \ ; \quad \frac{\partial t}{\partial\sigma} = \frac{-(D - \mu)}{\sigma} = \frac{-t}{\sigma}$$

here $t = (D - \mu)/\sigma$ is the standardized due date (which, unlike D, may be negative). Under Model 1, σ is constant and crashing reduces EP only by changing t as a function of μ. But here, crashing influences EP in two additional ways: 1) σ multiplies the integral and crashing activity *i* changes it, 2) t is a function of σ. The following basic results play a role,

Using these results and the Leibnitz rule, we obtain

$$\frac{\partial \, \mathrm{EP}}{\partial \mu_i} = P \, \frac{\partial \sigma}{\partial \mu_i} \int_t^\infty [1 - G(z)] \, dz + P \, (1 - \mathrm{SL}) \left(1 + \frac{\partial \sigma}{\partial \mu_i} t \right)$$

and if we group together the elements involving $\partial \sigma / \partial \mu_i$,

$$\frac{\partial \, \mathrm{EP}}{\partial \mu_i} = P \, \frac{\partial \sigma}{\partial \mu_i} \left(\int_t^\infty [1 - G(z)] \, dz + (1 - \mathrm{SL}) \, t \right) + P \, (1 - \mathrm{SL}) \tag{3}$$

Using Equation 2 we can show that

$$\int_t^\infty [1 - G(z)] \, dz + (1 - \mathrm{SL})t =$$
$$\int_t^\infty (z - t) \, g(z) \, dz + (1 - \mathrm{SL})t = \int_t^\infty z \, g(z) \, dz = (1 - \mathrm{SL})\mathrm{E}(Z|Z > t) \tag{4}$$

where the final equality follows by applying Bayes' Rule to the conditional expectation $\mathrm{E}(Z|Z > t)$. That is well-defined only for $1 - \mathrm{SL} > 0$, but any reasonable search procedure stops before violating this condition, and for the normal distribution, in particular, it is always guaranteed. By combining Equations 3 and 4 and considering the cost of crashing we obtain

$$\frac{\partial \, \mathrm{TC}}{\partial \mu_i} = P \, (1 - \mathrm{SL}) \left(1 + \frac{\partial \sigma}{\partial \mu_i} \mathrm{E}(Z \mid Z > t) \right) - C_i \tag{5}$$

where TC is the total cost. Equivalently, the expression yields the equilibrium condition,

$$1 - \mathrm{SL}^* = \frac{C_i}{P \left[1 + \dfrac{\partial \sigma}{\partial \mu_i} \mathrm{E}[Z \mid Z > t^*] \right]} \tag{6}$$

which is achieved at the optimum where the gradient is zero. It should be noted that μ_i decreases as we crash, so when Equation 5 is positive, crashing is beneficial. For Model 2, because $\sigma^2 = \Sigma \sigma_i^2$,

$$\frac{\partial \sigma}{\partial \mu_i} = \frac{\partial \sigma}{\partial \sigma_i} \frac{d\sigma_i}{d\mu_i} = \frac{\sigma_i}{\sigma} \frac{d\sigma_i}{d\mu_i}$$

An important special case is when we approximate the project completion time by a normal variable with $\mu = \Sigma \mu_i$, $\sigma^2 = \Sigma \sigma_i^2$. When this approximation is invoked, we can substitute the appropriate value of $\mathrm{E}(Z|Z > t)$ for the normal distribution in Equation 6. A remarkable feature of the normal distribution is that $(1 - \mathrm{SL})\mathrm{E}(Z|Z > t) = \varphi(t)$. This leads to $\mathrm{E}(Z|Z > t) = \varphi(t)/(1 - \mathrm{SL})$, but $1 - \mathrm{SL} = \Phi(-t)$, and thus, for the normal distribution,

$$1 - \mathrm{SL}^* = \Phi(-t^*) = \frac{C_i}{P \left[1 + \dfrac{\partial \sigma}{\partial \mu_i} \dfrac{\phi(t^*)}{\Phi(-t^*))} \right]} \tag{7}$$

Equation 7 is explicitly circular (and thus requires iterations): we have $1 - \mathrm{SL}$, or $\Phi(-t)$, on both sides of the equation. This circularity appears because we solved $\mathrm{E}(Z|Z > t)$ explicitly. Of course, the same circularity is implicit in Equation 6 for any other distribution as well. We refer to the values

$$M_i = 1 + \frac{\partial \sigma}{\partial \mu_i} \mathrm{E}(Z \mid Z > t) \tag{8}$$

as *modifiers*, because they modify the value of crashing an activity by one unit relative to the simple crashing case. For the normal distribution,

$$M_i = 1 + \frac{\partial \sigma}{\partial \mu_i} \frac{\phi(t)}{\Phi(-t)}$$

If $\partial\sigma/\partial\mu_i \geq 0$ (i.e., the variance decreases during crashing), then $M_i \geq 1$ and the denominator in Equation 6 is guaranteed to be positive; but if $\partial\sigma/\partial\mu_i < 0$, there is no such guarantee. However, the economic interpretation of $M_i \leq 0$ is that the variance effect cancels out the benefit of crashing so in such a case we set $\Delta_i = 0$ (unless negative crashing is allowed). When $C_i/M_i < P(1 - SL)$, it is cost-effective to crash activity i, but notice that M_i is a function of σ. Later, we show that the optimal crashing problem is convex. Therefore, a solution is optimal with $SL = SL^*$ and $\sigma = \sigma^*$ if and only if all activities for which $C_i/M_i < P(1 - SL^*)$ are fully crashed, those for which $C_i/M_i > P(1 - SL^*)$ are not crashed and all other activities are crashed sufficiently to satisfy $C_i/M_i = P(1 - SL^*)$. It can be shown that at most two jobs need to be partially crashed; i.e., there exists an optimal crashing plan with at least $n - 2$ jobs either crashed fully or not at all.

Proposition 1: $\partial\sigma/\partial\mu_i > 0$ *implies more crashing is beneficial than under Model 1 (higher service level); conversely, $\partial\sigma/\partial\mu_i < 0$ calls for less crashing (lower service level).*

In the next section we show that Model 3 (and thus also Model 2) yields a convex total cost function. So we can find an optimal solution by standard non-linear search procedures. We refer to the use of any effective search for this purpose as *Procedure 2*. Procedure 2 can be used as a heuristic even if the convexity conditions of Model 2 do not hold, but in such a case we can only guarantee a local optimum.

Model 3: Positive Dependence Due to Systemic Error

The following model of dependence due to a common random bias element (e.g., by consistent estimation error) had been presented by Trietsch

(2005) and validated by Gevorgyan (2008). Trietsch also showed how to estimate the necessary parameters with minimal input from decision makers: only an estimate of the mean processing time is required and the rest is done by historical regression. Let $\mathbf{X}=\{X_i\}$ be a vector of estimates of $\{Y_i\}$, and note that we treat X_i as a random variable. For convenience we say that the nominal estimate is $e_i = E(X_i)$, and let $V(X_i)$ denote the variance. Systemic error due to common random bias is modeled by the introduction of an additional independent random variable, B, which multiplies $\mathbf{X}$ to obtain the true activity times. We use β and $V_b = \sigma_b^2$ to denote the mean and variance of B. If the true activity times compose the random vector $\mathbf{Y} = \{Y_i\}$, this implies $Y_i = BX_i$. For consistency with the former models, we reserve μ_i and σ_i^2 for the mean and variance of Y_i. In Models 1 and 2 we assumed crashing applies without systemic error, e.g., C_i was the marginal cost of crashing μ_i by one unit. Here, we must recognize that crashing information, by nature, applies to the estimates, e_i, and not directly to μ_i, the true mean. Thus the true crashing cost is bC_i (where b is the realization of B that applies to a particular project). Because we do not know b, however, we use βC_i instead. Whereas knowledge of b would be beneficial in terms of reducing variance, we can indeed reduce μ_i by one unit on average at the marginal cost of βC_i, so the model remains correct. As in Model 1, we assume that the crashing cost is monotone non-decreasing with Δ_i. As in Model 2 we assume that the standard deviation of X_i is a convex function of Δ_i (where Δ_i is interpreted as a planned amount, leading to $B\Delta_i$ in reality).

Because B and $\mathbf{X}$ are independent, $\mu_i = \beta e_i$. But the multiplication by the same realization, b, introduces [positive] dependence between the elements of $\mathbf{Y}$. Specifically, $\sigma_i^2 = \beta^2 V(X_i) + V(X_i) V_b + V_b e_i^2$, and $COV(Y_i, Y_j) = V_b e_i e_j; \forall i \neq j$. We can separate σ_i^2 to two parts, $\beta^2 V(X_i) + V(X_i)V_b$ and $V_b e_i^2$. The former equals $E(B^2)V(X_i)$ and the latter is a special case of $V_{b_i}e_ie_j$. Thus the covariance matrix of **Y** is the sum of a diagonal matrix with elements $V(X_i)E(B^2)$ and a full matrix with elements $V_{b_i}e_ie_j$; $\forall i,j$. The latter can be expressed as the vector product $\{\sigma_b e_i\}\{\sigma_b e_i\}^T$. It follows that $\sigma^2 = E(B^2)\Sigma_{\forall i}V(X_i) + (\sigma_b\Sigma_{\forall i}e_i)^2$. Finally, note that if $B = 1$, we obtain Model 2. If B is deterministic but $\beta \neq 1$, then after correcting for the bias we again obtain an instance of Model 2. Therefore, Model 3 is a generalization of Model 2. The following proposition appeared in Trietsch (2005).

Proposition 2: *Let* $q_1(\mathbf{e}) = E(B^2)\Sigma_{\forall i}V(X_i)$, *and let* $q_2(\mathbf{e}) = (\sigma_b\Sigma_{\forall i}e_i)^2$, *where* $\mathbf{e}=\{e_i\}$, *then*

$$\frac{\max\left\{\sqrt{q_1(\mathbf{e})}, \sqrt{q_2(\mathbf{e})}\right\}}{\sqrt{q_1(\mathbf{e}) + q_2(\mathbf{e})}} \leq \sqrt{q_1(\mathbf{e}) + q_2(\mathbf{e})} \leq \sqrt{q_1(\mathbf{e})} + \sqrt{q_2(\mathbf{e})}.$$

Notice that the central element in the inequality equals σ. By Proposition 2, if we wish to specify a buffer of $k\sigma$ for some $k > 0$, the two approaches provided by Leach (2000) and Leach (2003) provide lower and upper bounds. (There is no theoretical reason to limit ourselves to $k>0$, so we do not limit our analysis to this case. Nonetheless, most project managers are uncomfortable with negative buffers and the low service levels they entail.)

The following lemma, although cast in more general terms, shows that if the square root of each of several additive variance components is convex, then the standard deviation is convex. For this purpose interpret $r()$ as the square root function and $q_k()$ as a variance component.

Lemma 1: Let $q_k(x), k=1,2,...,K$, be K functions from R^m to R and let $r()$ be a monotone increasing function from R to R such that $r^{-1}()$ exists. If

$$r(q_k(\lambda x_1 + (1-\lambda)x_2)) \leq$$
$$r(\lambda q_k(x_1) + (1-\lambda)q_k(x_2)) ; \quad 0 \leq \lambda \leq 1, \forall k$$

for any admissible x_1, x_2 and λ, then

$$r(\Sigma_{\forall k} q_k(\lambda x_1 + (1-\lambda)x_2)) \leq$$
$$r(\lambda\Sigma_{\forall k} q_k(x_1) + (1-\lambda)\Sigma_{\forall k} q_k(x_2)) ; \quad 0 \leq \lambda \leq 1$$

Proof: $r^{-1}()$ is monotone increasing, so by applying it to the K conditions we have

$$q_k(\lambda x_1 + (1-\lambda)x_2) \leq \lambda q_k(x_1) + (1-\lambda)q_k(x_1) ; \quad 0 \leq \lambda \leq 1, \forall k$$

To complete the proof, combine these K inequalities to one and apply $r()$ to the sum. **QED**

Lemma 2: Let σ be a positive convex function of the vector $\{\mu_i\}$, then the expected penalty as a function of this vector is convex.

Proof: From Equation 5 (which applies for Model 3 because we made no independence assumption to derive it) we obtain the gradient of EP,

$$\frac{\partial\text{EP}}{\partial\mu_i} = P(1-\text{SL})\left(1 + \frac{\partial\sigma}{\partial\mu_i}E(Z \mid Z > t)\right)$$

Let $\mathbf{Q}=\{q_{i,j}\}$ be the Hessian of EP, then $q_{i,j}$ is the partial derivative by μ_j of this expression. We have to show that $\mathbf{Q}$ is positive semi-definite (PSD). Note that $d[1-\text{SL}]/dt = -g(t)$, $d[[1-\text{SL}]E(Z|Z>t]/dt = -tg(t)$ (see the last part of Equation 4), and $\partial t/\partial\mu_j = -(1 + t\partial\sigma/\partial\mu_j)/\sigma$. This leads to the following expression for all i,j,

$$q_{ij} = \frac{\partial^2\text{EP}}{\partial\mu_i\partial\mu_j} = \frac{P\,g(t)}{\sigma}\left(1 + t\left(\frac{\partial\sigma}{\partial\mu_i} + \frac{\partial\sigma}{\partial\mu_j}\right) + t^2\frac{\partial\sigma}{\partial\mu_i}\frac{\partial\sigma}{\partial\mu_j}\right)$$
$$+ \frac{P}{\sigma}(1-\text{SL})E(Z \mid Z > t)\frac{\partial^2\sigma}{\partial\mu_i\partial\mu_j}$$

Separate $\mathbf{Q}$ to a sum of two symmetric matrices, $\mathbf{Q}_1$ and $\mathbf{Q}_2$. $\mathbf{Q}_1$ includes the elements multiplied by $Pg(t)/\sigma$. $\mathbf{Q}_2$ includes the remainder. $\mathbf{Q}_1$ is

PSD if $\mathbf{X}^T\mathbf{Q}_1\mathbf{X} \geq 0$ for any vector $\mathbf{X} = (x_1, x_2, \ldots x_n)$ ^{T}. But $Pg(t)/\sigma$ is non-negative so this condition is demonstrated by,

$$\mathbf{X}^T\mathbf{Q}_1\mathbf{X} = \frac{P\ g(t)}{\sigma}\left(\sum_{I=1}^{n} x_i\ \left(1 + t\frac{\partial\sigma}{\partial\mu_i}\right)\right)^2 \geq 0$$

$\mathbf{Q}_2$ is PSD because $P(1 - \mathrm{SL})\mathrm{E}(Z|Z > t)/\sigma$ is non-negative and σ is a convex function of $\{\mu_i\}$. Therefore, as the sum of two PSD matrices, $\mathbf{Q}$ is also PSD. **QED**

Theorem 1: When crashing costs are given by a convex function of the vector $\{\mu_i\}$ and σ is a positive convex function of the same vector then the total cost function is convex.

Proof: By Lemma 2 and the convexity of sums of convex functions. **QED**

Theorem 2: When activities are correlated by a common random bias element, the total cost function is convex.

Proof: We show that this case complies with the conditions of Theorem 1. This requires showing (1) that the crashing cost is a convex function of μ_i and (2) that σ is a positive convex function of the vector $\{\mu_i\}$. However, the vectors $\{\mu_i\}$ and $\{e_i\}$ are proportional to each other, so we can show the conditions in terms of $\{e_i\}$. (1) is true by the conditions we set for C_i (as in Model 1). For (2), using the notation of Proposition 2, we first show that the square root of $q_1(\mathbf{e})$ is convex. $q_1(\mathbf{e})$ is the sum of n elements $\mathrm{E}(B^2)\mathrm{V}(X_i)$, and by invoking Lemma 1 we see that it suffices to show that the square root of $\mathrm{V}(X_i)$ is convex. But this is true by assumption (as in Model 2). The square root of $q_2(\mathbf{e})$ is linear, and thus convex. Therefore, by Lemma 1, $\sigma(\mathbf{e})$—the square root of $q_1(\mathbf{e}) + q_2(\mathbf{e})$—is also convex. **QED**

When there is no common random bias element, our assumptions in this section reduce to those of Model 2, so the convexity result also holds there. As a special case of Model 2, the same applies to Model 1.

NUMERICAL EXAMPLES

Example 1: A project involves 30 exponential activities in series, such that $\mu_i = 10$ ($i = 1,\ldots, 10$) and $\mu_i = 5$ ($i = 11,\ldots, 30$). Activities may be crashed by up to 50% and remain exponential after crashing; e.g., the first 10 activities can be crashed by up to 5 time units each. Let $C_i = 9.8 + (31 - i)0.01$; e.g., $C_1 = 10.1$, $C_{11} = 10$ and $C_{30} = 9.81$.

Solution: Here, Model 2 applies, but we start by solving the problem by Procedure 1 as a heuristic. Observe that the project distribution is approximately normal by the central limit theorem. If we select the cheapest activities to crash, namely activities 11 through 30 (in reversed order), and crash them maximally, then the service level is 0.5 (activity 11, the most expensive crashed activity, implies $\mathrm{SL} = 10/20$ and this is achieved after crashing it ($10\cdot10 + 2.5\cdot20 = 150$). The total cost associated with this solution is 762.9. This crashing plan reduces the variance from 1500 to 1125. But if we crash the first ten activities maximally instead, and thus pay more for crashing but reduce the variance to 750, we obtain the same service level and the objective function is reduced to 721.26. Therefore, selecting activities to crash based on C_i alone is not optimal. Furthermore, the optimal value is 717.11 and it entails a higher service level. It involves crashing all activities to progressively smaller μ_i values as per an arithmetic series with $\mu_1 = 5.326$ and $\mu_{30} = 4.345$ (the maximal crashing constraints are inert). The optimal service level is 57.37%, instead of 50%. Thus it is very important to consider the variance reduction effect and it is also useful to optimize the service level.

The example illustrates Proposition 1: $\partial\sigma/\partial\mu_i > 0$ implies more crashing than Procedure 1 would call for. Example 2 reinforces this point.

Example 2: Let $n = 1$, with an exp(5) activity time distribution, and assume crashing is by switching to another exponential with lower mean. Let $D = 5$, $C = C_1 = 10$ and $P = 20$.

Solution: Due to the memoryless property of the exponential random variable, the expected delay *given* a delay is μ, leading to an un-crashed expected conditional penalty of $5 \cdot 20 = 100$. Multiplying by $1 - SL$ our total expected cost is 36.79. Note that the service level, 0.6321, is already better than 0.5, as Procedure 1 would specify. So it may look like there is no need to consider crashing in this case. Actually, if we could save money by negative crashing (i.e., increasing μ) we might be tempted to check this option instead. However, the true optimal μ in this case is 2.979 (with 3 digits accuracy), leading to a total cost of 31.33 and $1 - SL = 0.1867$ (SL = 0.8133). This high service level is justified because the gain by crashing is much higher than with simple crashing. The objective function is given by

$$TC = C\,(D - \mu) + P\,(1 - SL)\,\mu =$$
$$C\,(D - \mu) + P\exp(-D/\mu)\,\mu$$

Taking the derivative by μ and setting it to zero we obtain

$$C = P\exp(-D/\mu)(1 + D/\mu) =$$
$$P\,(1 - SL)\,(1 + D/\mu) => 1 - SL = \frac{C}{P\,(1 + D/\mu)}$$

which is a special case of Equation 6. Equivalently, the crashing value modifier is given by $M = 1 + D/\mu$. On the one hand, we need a search method to find the exact modification. On the other hand, it is not important to find the exact optimum: The objective function is virtually constant between

2.95 and 3.00 (yielding 31.3333 and 31.3325 respectively, as compared with 31.3318 at 2.979). Furthermore, it changes by less than 0.2% in the range 2.795 to 3.17 (that is, we deviate from optimum by more than 6% but the objective function changes by less than one fifth of a percent).

Similar flatness of the objective function near the optimum often applies for the newsboy objective function when we deviate by a small fraction of σ from optimum.

CONCLUSION

The simplest non-trivial project structure is a serial chain of activities. In this paper we discussed how to crash activities along such chains. We provided convexity conditions—essentially convexity of each activity—that guarantee convexity for the model. We then applied these results to a particular dependence model, the systemic error model (with one systemic error cause), that has been proposed by Trietsch (2005) as an alternative to traditional PERT estimation. That model has been validated by Gevorgyan (2008) in a particular environment. Although further validation would be desirable, the existing evidence is sufficient to demonstrate that at least in some instances the crashing model we presented here can actually be programmed and implemented. Furthermore, when adapted for crashing decisions, the systemic error model entails variance crashing effects of the type we addressed. Specifically, it calls for higher service levels than would be the case without this effect because the variance is reduced along with the mean.

Although we did not cover discrete crashing, we can address it approximately by fitting continuous functions through discrete crashing options, thus obtaining a useful relaxation. In this relaxation, at most two jobs should be partially crashed, so our approach can yield an approximate solution to the discrete crashing problem. It can also serve as the basis of a branch and bound algorithm where branching is performed on the one or two activities that require partial crashing in the continuous relaxation. This problem requires further research, however.

Trietsch (2005a), in addition to a critique of Critical Chain, lists several theoretical challenges that must be addressed before we can build reliable software for project scheduling and control. More specifically, practically every reputable software package in the market, regardless of methodology, is useful for monitoring projects and is thus very useful for important control functions. However, to date, none of the existing methodologies, let alone software packages, can adequately support reliable stochastic scheduling and capacity decisions in advance. The challenge is to provide software that can actually be used at the planning stage and thus make subsequent control easier and cheaper. A necessary condition for that is the availability of reliable stochastic models that do not place onerous requirements on users. Trietsch (2005), Trietsch (2006), Gevorgyan (2008), Baker & Trietsch (2009) and this paper address the bulk of those challenges. We are now practically ready for the next stage: software implementation.

ACKNOWLEDGMENT

I am grateful to Candace A. Yano and to Kenneth R. Baker for useful comments at various stages during the development of this paper.

REFERENCES

Arisawa, S., & Elmaghraby, S. E. (1972). Optimal time-cost trade-offs in GERT networks. *Management Science*, *18*(11), 589–599. doi:10.1287/mnsc.18.11.589

Baker, K. R., & Trietsch, D. (2009). *Principles of sequencing and scheduling*. Wiley.

Britney, R. R. (1976). Bayesian point estimation and the PERT scheduling of stochastic activities. *Management Science*, *22*(9), 938–948. doi:10.1287/mnsc.22.9.938

Chu, C., Proth, J.-M., & Xie, X. (1993). Supply management in assembly systems. *Naval Research Logistics*, *40*, 933–949. doi:10.1002/1520-6750(199312)40:7<933::AID-NAV3220400706>3.0.CO;2-8

Fulkerson, D. R. (1961). A network flow computation for project cost curves. *Management Science*, *7*(2), 167–178. doi:10.1287/mnsc.7.2.167

Gevorgyan, L. (2008). *Project duration estimation with corrections for systemic error*. Unpublished master's thesis. American University of Armenia, Yerevan, Armenia.

Gutjahr, W. J., Strauss, C., & Wagner, E. (2000). A stochastic branch-and-bound approach to activity crashing in project management. *INFORMS Journal on Computing*, *12*(2), 125–135. doi:10.1287/ijoc.12.2.125.11894

Herroelen, W. and R. Leus R. (2004). Robust and reactive project scheduling: A review and classification of procedures. *International Journal of Production Research*, *42*(8), 1599–1620. doi:10.1080/00207540310001638055

Herroelen, W., Leus, R., & Demeulemeester, E. (2002). Critical Chain project scheduling: Do not oversimplify. *Project Management Journal*, *33*(4), 48–60.

Hopp, W. J., & Spearman, M. L. (1993). Setting safety leadtimes for purchased components in assembly systems. *IIE Transactions*, *25*(2), 2–11. doi:10.1080/07408179308964272

Kelley, J. E. (1961). Critical-path planning and scheduling: mathematical basis. *Operations Research*, *9*(3), 296–320. doi:10.1287/opre.9.3.296

Kumar, A. (1989). Component inventory costs in an assembly problem with uncertain supplier lead-times. *IIE Transactions, 21*(2), 112–121. doi:10.1080/07408178908966214

Leach, L. P. (2000). *Critical Chain project management*. Artech House.

Leach, L.P. (2003). Schedule and cost buffer sizing: How to account for the bias between project performance and your model. *Project Management Journal, 2003*(2), 34-47.

Raz, T., Barnes, R., & Dvir, D. (2003). A critical look at Critical Chain project management. *Project Management Journal, 34*(4), 24–32.

Robb, D. J., & Silver, E. A. (1993). Scheduling in a management context: Uncertain processing times and non-regular performance measures. *Decision Sciences, 24*(6), 1085–1108. doi:10.1111/j.1540-5915.1993.tb00505.x

Ronen, B., & Trietsch, D. (1988). A Decision support system for purchasing management of large projects. *Operations Research, 36*(6), 882–890. doi:10.1287/opre.36.6.882

Trietsch, D. (2005). The effect of systemic errors on optimal project buffers. *International Journal of Project Management, 23,* 267–274. doi:10.1016/j.ijproman.2004.12.004

Trietsch, D. (2005a). Why a critical path by any other name would smell less sweet? Towards a holistic approach to PERT/CPM. *Project Management Journal, 36*(1), 27–36.

Trietsch, D. (2006). Optimal feeding buffers for projects or batch supply chains by an exact generalization of the newsvendor result. *International Journal of Production Research, 44,* 627–637. doi:10.1080/00207540500371881

Wollmer, R. D. (1985). Critical path planning under uncertainty. *Mathematical Programming Study, 25,* 164–171.

Yano, C. A. (1987). Planned leadtimes for serial production systems. *IIE Transactions, 19*(3), 300–307. doi:10.1080/07408178708975400

Yano, C. A. (1987a). Setting planned leadtimes in serial production systems with tardiness costs. *Management Science, 33*(1), 95–106. doi:10.1287/mnsc.33.1.95

This work was previously published in International Journal of Information Technology Project Management, Volume 1, Issue 1, edited by John Wang, pp. 30-41, copyright 2010 by IGI Publishing (an imprint of IGI Global).

Chapter 3
A New Technique for Estimating the Distribution of a Stochastic Project Makespan

Yuval Cohen
The Open University of Israel, Israel

Ofer Zwikael
The Australian National University, Australia

ABSTRACT

A critical success dimension in projects is the ability to complete a project within an estimated duration. In that regard, effective project scheduling techniques in an uncertain environment is of interest in many organizations. In this paper, the authors use an analytic approach to analyze the behavior of time duration distributions of projects in stochastic activity networks, and propose a simple computation scheme for approximating their distribution. The findings offer an understanding of the large gap between PERT and simulation results, and the deviation of projects from their intended schedules. In addition to providing theoretical framework, the proposed approach also recommends a simple practical pragmatic technique that computes the time distribution of project duration. This is a simple and handy tool for the project manager that may replace simulation. As a byproduct, the earliest start time distribution for each activity is also estimated.

INTRODUCTION

Scheduling is a core project management area, and finding project's duration (makespan) is one of its important objectives (Kerzner, 2006; PMI,

2008; Zwikael et al., 2006). This paper presents a practical technique that estimates the makespan distribution of a project in a more accurate and reliable way than PERT (Project Evaluation and Review Technique), and is consistent with Monte Carlo Simulation results.

DOI: 10.4018/978-1-4666-0930-3.ch003

One of the most common techniques for project scheduling under uncertainty is PERT, which was originally proposed by Malcolm et al. (1959). While it is still a prevalent planning and controlling tool in project management (Ash & Pittman, 2008; Adler & Smith, 2009), it has been critiqued that PERT provides inaccurate information about the project completion time (e.g., Klingel, 1966; Shogan, 1977; Schonberger, 1981; Dodin, 1985; Schmidt & Grossman, 2000; Dodin, 2006; Hahn, 2008; Kirytopoulos et al., 2008). Alternatively, Monte Carlo simulation has been a practical tool for evaluating the makespan distribution of a stochastic project (e.g., Van Slyke, 1963; Burt & Garman, 1971; Sullivan et al., 1982; Iida, 2000; Demeulemeester & Herroelen, 2002; Kirytopoulos et al., 2008). However, the simulation computational intensity and the time consumed by a simulation, motivated research for searching alternatives (Adlakha & Kulkarni, 1989; Cohen & Zwikael, 2008; Salaka & Prabhu, 2008). While several research directions had been pursued (as discussed in section 1.1.) there is still a need for a practical technique that would replace PERT and would give consistent results with Monte Carlo Simulation.

Alternative Approaches and Their Shortcomings

A common research direction has been to find the likelihood of an activity to become critical (Dodin & Elmaghraby, 1985; Bowman, 1995; Cho & Yum, 1997; Elmaghraby, 2000; Bowman, 2001). Another direction has been to find several possible critical paths (Dodin, 1984; Chen, 2007.)

Iida (2000) identifies three other major research directions for evaluating a project's makespan:

1. Analytical approaches to determine the distribution function of the project duration with diverging complexity (e.g., Hagsrom, 1990; Dodin & Sirvanci, 1990; Dodin, 2006.)

2. Analytical approaches for computing of the bounds on the distribution function of the project duration (e.g., Kleindirfer, 1971; Shogan, 1977; Dodin, 1985; Weiss, 1986; Ludwig et al., 2001.)

3. Analytical approaches for computing of the bounds on the expected project duration (e.g., Elmaghraby, 1967; Lindsey, 1972; Robillard & Trahan, 1976.)

So far, each of the above proposed approaches and techniques have its own shortcomings and consequently have been too complex or unattractive for broad adoption by project mangers.

Starting from the first approach, the computational complexity of the method proposed by Hagstrom (1990) renders it impractical in most cases. Dodin (2006) proposed two distributions approximating two extreme cases: (1) For large parallel activity network the approximation to the distribution limit of infinite number of parallel critical paths is advised. This distribution is known as the Extreme Value (EV) distribution. (2) For more restricted network structure with only one critical path, the series approach of PERT is advised. However, most projects have structures very different than these two extremes. Moreover, Dodin does not explicitly addresses the uncertain risky events causing delays that current practices of risk management take into account while planning and setting the project completion time.

The second approach, of computing the bounds on the distribution, is not sufficient for scheduling decisions. Bounds tightness is hard to measure and tight bounds have different meaning depending on the shape of the distribution tails. Bounds do not allow seeing the whole picture, and to glean some important rules in estimating project duration.

The third approach, of computing of the bounds on the expected project duration is even more problematic. When a contract for executing a project is signed, usually the completion time is set so that a confidence level for completion is well beyond

50%. So knowing only the median or expected project time does not suffice (Elmaghraby, 2005).

This paper suggests an approach will help mitigate/eliminate the shortcomings of the above approaches: its complexity is low, it gives an accurate estimate of the project's makespan probability in chosen points, its precision could be adjusted as desired by adding or subtracting estimation points (complexity is linearly proportional to the number of points). The basic theory for the proposed method is discussed in section 2, including assumptions, notations, calculations, and principles. Section 3 presents the proposed estimation method with an illustrated example. Section 4 discusses validation of the algorithm and the effect of risky events, and section 5 concludes the paper.

THEORETICAL FOUNDATIONS OF THE PROPOSED METHOD

A project includes a set of activities; each has its own duration and predecessor activities. When a certain activity A has several immediate predecessor activities, activity A can start only after the last predecessor is finished. To simplify the discussion assume that all the immediate predecessors started at the same time. So that the early-start time of A is distributed as the maximal duration of its immediate predecessors. While PERT calculations advocate taking the longest expected duration among the predecessors, the distribution of the maximum is different from the distribution of the longest expected activity among the predecessors (David & Nagaraja, 2003), as shown in Equation 1.

Notations:

c_i – The completion time of activity i

$F_i(t) = Pr(c_i < t)$ - Cumulative Distribution Function (cdf) of the completion time of activity i

T_a – The early-start time of activity A

$P(A)$ – The group of immediate predecessors of A

$F^A(t)$ – Cumulative Distribution Function (cdf) of T_a (early-start time of A)

By definition $F^A(t)$ could expressed as $Pr(T_a \leq t)$. By noting that the early-start of any activity A must occur after completing all its immediate predecessors $i \in P(A)$, it follows that:

$$F^A(t) = Pr(T_a \leq t) = Pr((\text{Max } c_i \mid i \in P(A)) < t) \tag{1}$$

Therefore (Kleindorfer, 1971; Dodin, 1985; Dodin, 2006; Dodin & Sirvanci, 1990):

$$F^A(t) = \prod_{i \in P(A)} F_i(t) \tag{2}$$

Further explanation of equation 2 appears in the appendix. Equation 1 is the definition of the of the early start time, but both the distribution and the expected value of Equation 1 are different than those used in PERT (in PERT the distribution of T_a is typically assume to be the distribution of the longest path (having maximal sum of means) leading to it. The distribution of the path is approximated as Normal with expected value as sum of its activity means and variance as sum of activity variances). These differences point to a prominent cause for the PERT inaccuracy: namely the possibility that other activities' duration realizations may dictate the longest path. Subsection 2.1 illustrates the effect of parallelism on the start time of succeeding activities.

Illustrative Example

The example in Figure 1 shows a simple Activities-on-Arcs (AOA) diagram with duration distributions of each activity. Activities A, B, C are uniformly and identically distributed; while activities D, E, F are normally and identically distributed. Activities G, H last 1 time unit and can start at T_1, T_2 respectively. The example il-

Figure 1. An example case study for illustrating the effect of parallel operations

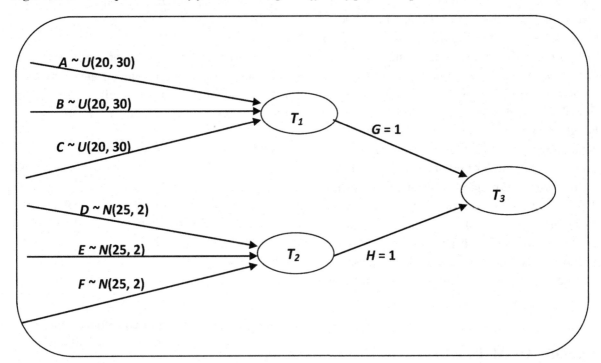

lustrates the shift of the start time distribution that happens in project networks mainly due to parallelism (simultaneous execution of activities).

While computing T_1, T_2, and the Early-start makespan of the example in Figure 1, we shall point to the main effects that determine the actual execution time of projects having stochastic task durations.

Consider tasks: *A, B, C,* and *G*, as depicted in Figure 1. Where *A, B,* and *C* have no predecessors but each precedes T_1 (the start-time of *G*). Tasks *A, B,* and *C* have uniform distribution between 20 and 30 days. According to PERT, the expected durations of activities *A, B, C* is estimated to be 25 days, and therefore PERT assumes that on the average activity *G* starts at the beginning of the 26th day.

Statistically however, *G* starts after the maximum finish time among *A, B,* and *C.* From Order Statistics (David & Nagaraja, 2003) we know that the cumulative distribution of the maximum of *n*

identically distributed variables is $(F(x)^n)$ where $F()$ is the cumulative distribution function and the variable *x* is the duration (uniformly distributed: U[20,30] days). To simplify computations we shall use time units of ten days each. Thus, the variable *x* is uniformly distributed: $x \sim U[2,3]$. Thus, for the example: $F(x) = x - 2$ and the maximal time of the three durations (*A, B, C*) is defined as *y*, and has the following properties:

1. A cumulative distribution of $F(y)=(x - 2)^3$
2. A density of: $f(y)=3(x - 2)^2 f(x) = 3(x - 2)^2$

Since *y* and *x* assume the same values and the same range we were able to replace the $y(dy)$ by $(x)dx$.

An expected value:

$$E[y] = \int_2^3 f(y) \cdot y \, dy = \int_2^3 \left(3(x-2)^2\right) \cdot \left(y\right) dy = \int_2^3 \left(3(x-2)^2\right) \cdot \left(x\right) dx$$

Simplifying the integral and solving we get:

$$E[y] = 3 \int_2^3 (x^2 - 4x + 4) \cdot (x)dx = 3 \int_2^3 (x^3 - 4x^2 + 4x)dx$$

and eventually,

$$= 3 \cdot \left[\frac{x^4}{4} - \frac{4 \cdot x^3}{3} + 2x^2 \right]_2^3 = 3 \cdot \left(\left[\frac{81}{4} - \frac{4 \cdot 27}{3} + 18 \right] - \left[\frac{16}{4} - \frac{4 \cdot 8}{3} + 8 \right] \right)$$
$$= 3 \cdot \left(2.25 - 1.33 \right) = 3 \cdot \left(0.9167 \right) = 2.75$$

Since y is given in units of ten days, the expected duration until T_1 is 27.5 days whereas PERT approach estimate is 25 days. Moreover, the probability of starting activity G after 25 days or less is: $F(2.5)=(x - 2)^3=(2.5 - 2)^3= 0.125$, whereas the probability of starting activity G after 27.5 days or less is: $F(2.75)=(x - 2)^3=(2.75 - 2)^3= 0.422$. In effect, a reasonable estimate for the start time of activity G may be after 28 days, since: $F(2.8)=0.512$ (a little over 50% which is very close to the median).

Figure 2 depicts the distribution function of T_1, T_2 and T_3. Note that while PERT estimation of

T_3 (Figure 1) would be 26 days, Figure 2 shows that the probability of finishing by the end of the 26th day is much less than 10%.

Some Generalizations

This section draws several conclusions from the illustrative example of section 2.1. Each conclusion shall be presented, established and discussed. The following are the conclusions:

1. The median duration ($x=M_n$) for completing $n>1$ simultaneous identical activities (defined by M_n: $[F(x=M_n)]^n = 0.5$) is greater than the individual activity median duration (M: $F(x=M)=0.5$). This is evident from comparing: $[F(x=M_n)]^n = F(x=M) = 0.5$. On the other hand: $[F(x=M_n)] = (0.5)^{1/n} > 0.5$ (for $n>1$) which leads to: $F(x=M_n) > F(x=M)$, and since $F(x)$ is a monotonically increasing function in x, it follows that: $M_n>M$. The calculations in section 2.1 illustrate the same phenomenon for expected values.

2. In comparison to the duration distribution of an individual activity ($F(x)$) - the duration

Figure 2. Distributions of T_1, T_2 and T_3 (see Figure 1)

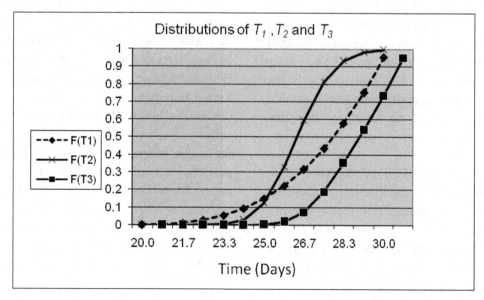

distribution of simultaneous i.i.d. activities ($F(\max\{x_1,...,x_n\}=F(x)^n$) is skewed to the right. This is evident since: $F(x)>F(x)^n$ (for $\forall x$: $0<F(x)<1$). So that the probability of completing all n activities within the first quartile of an individual duration is very small ($(0.25)^n$), and completing within the last few quantiles of an individual duration changes the least (e.g., $(0.99)^n$).

3. The duration of simultaneous activities do not exceed the maximal duration of each of the individual activities. This fact combined with conclusion 2, lead to the inference that variation of the duration to finish simultaneous activities is seriously reduced compared to a single activity.

4. In the presence of independent predecessors segments, the start time cumulative distribution of an AOA node is bounded by the multiplication of the cumulative time distributions of its preceding nodes plus the minimal duration of its immediate predecessors. In case of dependencies, a loose bound could be still achieved by ignoring all the dependencies (choosing to ignore the dependencies which are least likely to be influential.)

5. In large project networks, while moving along the project network the effect of parallelism is propagated, and the distribution typically shifts towards the sum of maximal times along the longest path. This is illustrated in Figure 3. Also, based on conclusion 3, the variance of the makespan is smaller than the sum of the variations along the longest path.

Some papers (e.g., Dodin & Sirvanci, 1990; Dodin, 2006) claim that small project duration tend to be Normally distributed, while the duration of a large project is a very large set of parallel critical paths (each with Normal distributed duration), for which the limiting distribution (for infinite set of parallel paths) is the Extreme Value distribution (which is left-skewed):

$$F(t) = \exp[-e^{-b(t-a)}] \qquad (3)$$

Clearly (see Figure 2 and Figure 3, in pdf and cdf forms) the Normality of small projects' duration is not a good approximation. In the case of large projects the distribution of the paths is not normal either (due to the effects of simultaneous predecessors as shown in sections 2.1, 2.2, and due to bounded durations). So the Extreme Value possesses significant drawbacks for approximating large project durations.

THE PROPOSED ESTIMATION METHOD

In this section, first the main idea and the algorithm are introduced (in Section 3.1) and then the technique used to achieve it is illustrated and explained (in section 3.2). It is assumed that the activity-time distributions are estimated using one of several techniques suggested by other papers (e.g., Malcolm, 1959; Williams, 1992; Ranasinghe, 1994; Chen, 2007; Hahn, 2008). The most common estimating approach is based on PERT and involves estimating (for each activity): optimistic (a), pessimistic (b) and most likely (m) durations. These three points (a, b, m) could either be translated to a triangular distribution, or to a Beita distribution, and give simple approximations for the activity mean ([a+4m+b]/6) and standard deviation ([b-a]/6). The independence between activity durations is a common assumption in the project management literature (activity independence is assumed by all the references of this paper). Moreover, it often happens that dependent activities are consecutive and could be treated as one activity. Accordingly we assumed independent durations. Typically, independent activities are the large bulk of activities while dependency requires

Figure 3. Probability density function of T₃ (see Figure 1)

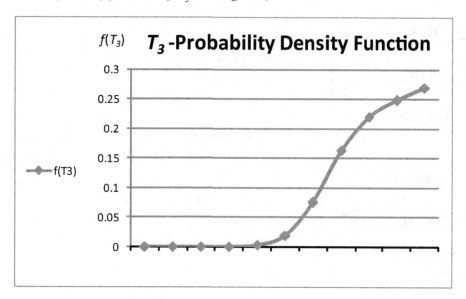

a specific reason to exist (whatever slowed-down activity *x*, would also slow activity *y*).

Equation (2) opens a way to numerically compute the duration of path CDF (*F(x)*) of any AoA node (Or the Early-Start of any AoN node) simply by multiplying the CDFs of the predecessors' completion-time, for desired quantiles. The main remaining issue is to compute the CDF of an activity having its start time distribution.

The Proposed Algorithm

The proposed method progressively computes the median and several desirable quantiles of the start-time of each activity using Equation (2) and the completion-times CDF of the predecessor activities. For getting the CDF of the activity completion time: the start- time distribution is appended to the succeeding activity's distribution.

The main steps of the proposed method are:

1. Order the activities by decreasing number of follower activities (all activities that follow, not only immediate followers). Break ties arbitrarily. Add artificial finish node at the end of the project with zero duration.

2. Set to zero the start-time of activities without predecessors, and compute - using Equation (2) - the start time distribution of their immediate following activities (activities which rely exclusively on the zero start-time activities).

3. For the computed start-time distributions find *y* values for *F(y)* =: 0.5, 0.75, 0.9, 0.95 and 0.99. (i.e., median, third quartile, 90%, 95% and 99%).

4. Find for each successor activity of step 3, the duration percentiles of: 0.5, 0.75, 0.9, 0.95 and 0.99. Add each duration its corresponding start-time duration (with the same percentile). This is based on the well-known fact that summing the medians (50th percentiles) of any two symmetric distributions, yields the median (50th percentile) of their sum. That is, if X and Y are symmetric independent random variables with medians p(X) and p(Y), then Z=X+Y, is symmetric, and adding the values of the two medians, gives the median (50th percentile) for the distribution of their sum: (i.e., p(X)+p(Y)=p(Z) (David & Nagaraja, 2003). While this is accurate for the 50th percentile, as percentiles devi-

Figure 4. An example case study for illustrating the proposed algorithm

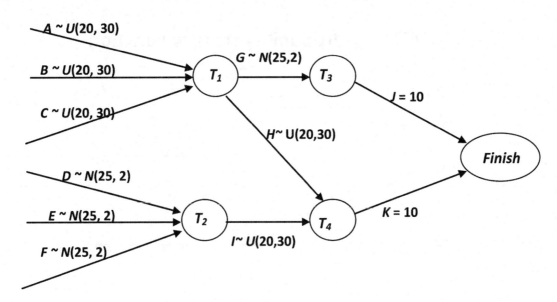

ate from the middle, the computed values become less precise and could be regarded as a conservative upper-bound of the actual distribution.

5. Extrapolate the completion time distributions from step 4
6. Compute - using Equation (2) - the start time distribution of step 5 immediate following activities.
7. If the start-time of the "finish" node is not yet computed go to step 3.

Example for Illustration

We shall illustrate the proposed algorithm on a very simple example

Step-1: Ordering the activities by the number of follower activities, we have: *A, B, C, D, E, F, G, H, I, J, K,*
Step-2: Zero start times are set for: *A, B, C, D, E, F.*

The start-time distributions of T_1 and T_2 are already given in Figure 2 (Table 1, Table 2, and Table 3).

Step-3: Table 1. Calculated values of T_1 and T_2 from Figure 2 (for step 3)

CDF = $F(y)$	0.5	0.7	0.9	0.95	0.99
Start times for T_1: (see Figure 2)	7.8	8.9	9.6	9.9	0.0
Start times for T2: (see Figure 2)	6.3	7.1	8.0	8.5	0.0

Step-4: Table 2. Calculated durations of *G, H* and *I* (for step 4)

CDF = $F(y)$	0.5	0.7	0.9	0.95	0.99
Durations for *G*:	25	26	27.6	28.3	29.6
Durations for *H*:	25	27	29	29.5	29.9
Durations for *I*:	25	27	29	29.5	29.9

Table 3. Calculated completion times of *G, H* and *I* (adding the corresponding start-times from step 3)

CDF = $F(y)$	0.5	0.7	0.9	0.95	0.99
Completion of *G*:	53	55	57.6	58.55	60.1
Completion of *H*:	53	56	59	59.75	60.4
Completion of *I*:	51.2	54	57	58.5	59.9

Step-5: The extrapolation is piecewise linear CDF according to Table 3, and is presented in Figure 5 with the results of step 6.

Step-6: See Figure 5

Step-7: Since the start-time of the "finish" node is not yet computed - **go to step 3**.

For brevity activities *J* and *K* have deterministic durations allowing us to skip steps 3 to 5.

This can be easily verified by noticing that their completion time distribution is just a shift of their starting time distribution (presented in Table 4) by 10 days. Thus, moving directly to step 6 yields the CDF of the project completion time as shown in Figure 5.

Note that PERT calculations will estimate the median project time to be 60 days while Table 5 shows the median is 66 and there is only 2% chance of finishing the project in 60 days. Moreover, for 95% confidence, PERT gives completion time of 68 which is shown to give only 80% confidence.

Iteration 2 - **Step-6:** See Figure 6

VALIDATION AND DISCUSSION

This paper gives a practical tool to practitioners to estimate the distribution of a project duration without running a simulation. The proposed technique is a very simple tool that could be calculated

Figure 5. Calculated probability values for durations of T_3 and T_4 from Figure 2 (for step 6)

	PROBABILITY (To finish by the given duration)					
Duration	Completion CDF of activity G	Activation time of T_3		Completion CDF of activity H	Completion CDF of activity I	Activation time of T_4
(Days)	$F(G)$	$F(T_3)=F(G)$		$F(H)$	$F(I)$	$F(T_4)=F(H)*F(I)$
50	0.23	0.23		0.23	0.43	0.10
51	0.30	0.30		0.30	0.50	0.15
52	0.40	0.40		0.40	0.57	0.23
53	0.50	0.50		0.50	0.63	0.32
54	0.60	0.60		0.60	0.70	0.42
55	0.70	0.70		0.70	0.77	0.54
56	0.78	0.78		0.78	0.83	0.65
57	0.85	0.85		0.85	0.90	0.77
58	0.94	0.94		0.92	0.93	0.86
59	0.97	0.97		0.96	0.96	0.92
60	0.99	0.99		0.99	0.99	0.98
61	0.995	0.995		0.995	0.995	0.990
62	1.00	1.00		1.00	1.00	1.00

Table 4. Summary of 20 validation cases (left tailed chi-square test*)

Network #	No. of activities	D.F.**	Chi-square Observed value	Chi-Square critical value for Alfa=5%	Chi-Square critical value for Alfa=1%
1	10	4	0.346	0.711	0.297
2	10	4	0.274	0.711	0.297
3	12	4	0.258	0.711	0.297
4	12	4	0.164	0.711	0.297
5	13	4	0.421	0.711	0.297
6	13	4	0.223	0.711	0.297
7	14	4	0.095	0.711	0.297
8	14	4	0.232	0.711	0.297
9	15	4	0.074	0.711	0.297
10	15	4	0.431	0.711	0.297
11	16	4	0.189	0.711	0.297
12	16	4	0.097	0.711	0.297
13	17	4	0.134	0.711	0.297
14	17	4	0.033	0.711	0.297
15	18	4	0.235	0.711	0.297
16	18	4	0.164	0.711	0.297
17	19	4	0.036	0.711	0.297
18	19	4	0.227	0.711	0.297
19	20	4	0.133	0.711	0.297
20	20	4	0.214	0.711	0.297

   * Left tailed test is used to reject the hypothesis that the (observed) results of the proposed method are different than the (expected) simulation results.

   **For each net, five comparisons of the estimated vs. the expected value were made for the: 50%, 70%, 90%, 95% and 99% of the project completion time.

by hand or a calculator. This handy tool could be used in risk evaluation and in feasibility studies as a rough tool before committing to a simulation study. The proposed algorithm (from section 3) gives the exact result for the 50% percentile and closely approximates the whole distribution of the project. The main approximation step is the piecewise linear approximation of the CDF function: $F(y)$ (which could be improved by adding calculated points). For validating the proposed method, its results were compared to the results of thousand simulation runs in twenty different project networks (see Table 4). The 20 networks were randomly generated, having 10 to 20 activi-

ties each, with different configurations and random mix of uniform and normal duration distributions. The normal distribution was bounded by 3 standard deviations. This was done for blocking the extreme values that sometime occur and may cause a negative activity time or an unreasonably long duration. A Poisson stream of relatively short delays (single percents of average activity duration) was added to simulate various real life risks and delays. For each project network - the differences in estimating the time distribution points corresponding to 50%, 70%, 90%, 95% and 99% of the project completion time were compared using the chi-square goodness-of-fit test. As shown in

Figure 6. Calculated probabilities for project completion time in the example (Figure 4)

| Duration (Days) | PROBABILITY (t<Duration) | | |
| | Completion CDF of activity J | Completion CDF of activity K | Activation time of *Finish* |
	E(J)	E(K)	F(Finish)=F(J)*F(K)
60	0.23	0.10	0.02
61	0.30	0.15	0.05
62	0.40	0.23	0.09
63	0.50	0.32	0.16
64	0.60	0.42	0.25
65	0.70	0.54	0.38
66	0.78	0.65	0.50
67	0.85	0.77	0.65
68	0.94	0.86	0.80
69	0.97	0.92	0.88
70	0.99	0.98	0.97
71	0.995	0.99	0.985
72	1.00	1.00	1.00

Table 4, all the twenty computed chi-square values were much smaller than the critical values of α=5%, (and in most cases smaller than the values of α=1%), yielding a decisive conclusion that the differences are not significant.

Many projects also face various possible risks yielding unpredicted delays. These risks were not included in the model. However, assuming that risks events are independent of each other, they could be modeled as a compound Poisson process having expected frequency per time unit λ, and expected delay E[d] per event. The longer the project takes the more delays are added. Thus, the delays are directly related to: y = the project duration (without the delays), and the total delay may be approximated by a Normal distribution: $N(y \cdot \lambda \cdot E[d], \sqrt{y \cdot \lambda \cdot E[d]})$. While this subject should be part of future research, these unpredicted delays are another motive for choosing a conservative approach for projects makespan estimation.

CONCLUSION

This paper gives practitioners an easy and practical tool for a estimating the project duration distribution in the presence of task time variability. The effect of parallelism is illustrated and gives a strong support for conservative estimations of project duration. A simple algorithm for estimating the makespan cumulative distribution is presented. The algorithm is based on forward recursive computational approximations and was validated by comparison to simulation results. The technique calculates for each AOA node a piecewise linear approximation of its distribution function. Thus, the accuracy of the proposed technique depends on the number of linear segments in the approximation. While this may be a limitation, the computational complexity of adding a new linear segment to the project distribution function is proportional to the number of nodes. A future extension of this research could be the inclusion of resource consumption, and resource availability limitations. The validation in this paper proves that the approach works for a population of projects, but more studies are needed to validate the proposed approach under various conditions and for variety of project types.

REFERENCES

Adlakha, V. G., & Kulkarni, V. G. (1989). A classified bibliography of rescarch on stochastic PERT Networks: 1966-1987. *INFOR, 27*(3), 272–296.

Adler, R. T., & Smith, L. W. (2009). How organisational cost reporting practices affect project management: the issues of project review and evaluation. *International Journal of Project Organisation and Management, 1*(3), 309–320. doi:10.1504/IJPOM.2009.027541

Ash, C. R., & Pittman, H. P. (2008). Towards holistic project scheduling using critical chain methodology enhanced with PERT buffering. *International Journal of Project Organisation and Management, 1*(2), 185–203. doi:10.1504/IJPOM.2008.022191

Bowman, R. A. (1995). Efficient estimation of arc criticalities in stochastic activity networks. *Management Science, 41*(1), 58–67. doi:10.1287/mnsc.41.1.58

Bowman, R. A. (2001). Due date-based metrics for activity importance in stochastic activity networks. *Annals of Operations Research, 102*(1), 39–48. doi:10.1023/A:1010993713274

Burt, J. M., & Garman, M. B. (1971). Conditional Monte-Carlo: a simulation technique for stochastic network analysis. *Management Science, 18*(3), 207–217. doi:10.1287/mnsc.18.3.207

Chen, S. P. (2007). Analysis of critical paths in a project network with fuzzy activity times. *European Journal of Operational Research, 183*(1), 442–459. doi:10.1016/j.ejor.2006.06.053

Cho, J. G., & Yum, B. J. (1997). An uncertainty importance measure of activities in PERT networks. *International Journal of Production Research, 35*(10), 2737–2770. doi:10.1080/002075497194426

Cohen, Y., & Zwikael, O. (2008). Modelling and scheduling projects using Petri nets. *International Journal of Project Organisation and Management, 1*(2), 221–233. doi:10.1504/IJPOM.2008.022193

David, H. A., & Nagaraja, H. N. (2003). *Order statistics* (3rd ed.). Haboken, NJ: John Wiley and Sons.

Demeulemeester, E. L., & Herroelen, W. S. (2002). *Project scheduling: a research handbook.* Norwell, MA: Kluwer.

Dodin, B. M. (1984). Determining the k most critical paths in PERT networks. *Operations Research, 32*(4), 859–877. doi:10.1287/opre.32.4.859

Dodin, B. M. (1985). Bounding the project completion time distribution in PERT networks. *Operations Research, 33*(4), 862–881. doi:10.1287/opre.33.4.862

Dodin, B. M. (2006). A practical and accurate alternative to PERT. In Josefowska, J., & Weglarz, J. (Eds.), *Perspectives in Modern Project Scheduling* (pp. 3–23). New York: Springer.

Dodin, B. M., & Elmaghraby, S. E. (1985). Approximating the criticality indices of the activities in PERT networks. *Management Science, 31*(2), 207–223. doi:10.1287/mnsc.31.2.207

Dodin, B. M., & Sirvanci, M. (1990). Stochastic networks and the extreme value distribution. *Computers & Operations Research, 17*(4), 397–409. doi:10.1016/0305-0548(90)90018-3

Elmaghraby, S. E. (1967). On the expected duration of PERT type network. *Management Science, 13*(5), 299–306. doi:10.1287/mnsc.13.5.299

Elmaghraby, S. E. (2000). On criticality and sensitivity in activity networks. *European Journal of Operational Research, 127*(2), 220–238. doi:10.1016/S0377-2217(99)00483-X

Elmaghraby, S. E. (2005). On the fallacy of averages in project risk management. *European Journal of Operational Research, 165*(2), 307–313. doi:10.1016/j.ejor.2004.04.003

Hagstrom, J. N. (1990). Computing the probability distribution in PERT networks. *Networks, 20*(2), 231–244. doi:10.1002/net.3230200208

Hahn, E. D. (2008). Mixture densities for project management activity times: A robust approach to PERT. *European Journal of Operational Research, 188*(2), 450–459. doi:10.1016/j.ejor.2007.04.032

Iida, T. (2000). Computing bounds on project duration distributions for stochastic PERT networks. *Naval Research Logistics, 47*(7), 559–580. doi:10.1002/1520-6750(200010)47:7<559::AID-NAV2>3.0.CO;2-9

Kerzner, H. (2006). *Project management: a systems approach to planning, scheduling, and controlling* (9th ed.). Haboken, NJ: John Wiley and Sons.

Kirytopoulos, A. K., Leopoulos, N. V., & Diamantas, V. K. (2008). PERT vs. Monte Carlo simulation along with the suitable distribution effect. *International Journal of Project Organisation and Management, 1*(1), 24–46. doi:10.1504/IJPOM.2008.020027

Kleindorfer, G. B. (1971). Bounding distributions for a stochastic acyclic network. *Operations Research, 19*(7), 1586–1601. doi:10.1287/opre.19.7.1586

Klingel, A. R. (1966). Bias in PERT completion times calculations for a real network. *Management Science, 13*(4), 476–489. doi:10.1287/mnsc.13.4.B194

Ludwig, A., Mohring, R. H., & Stork, F. (2001). A computational study on bounding the makespan distribution in stochastic project nets. *Annals of Operations Research, 102*(1), 49–64. doi:10.1023/A:1010945830113

Malcolm, D. G., Roseboom, J. H., Clark, C. E., & Fazar, W. (1959). Application of a technique for research and development evaluation program. *Operations Research, 7*(5), 646–669. doi:10.1287/opre.7.5.646

PMI Standards Committee. (2008). *A guide to the project management body of knowledge* (4th ed.). Newtown Square, PA: Project Management Institute.

Ranasinghe, M. (1994). Quantification and management of uncertainty in activity durations network. *Construction Management and Economics, 12*, 15–29. doi:10.1080/01446199400000003

Salaka, V., & Prabhu, V. (2008). Project management and scheduling for enterprise integration. *International Journal of Project Organisation and Management, 1*(2), 167–184. doi:10.1504/IJPOM.2008.022190

Schmidt, C. W., & Grossman, I. E. (2000). The exact overall time distribution of a project with uncertain task durations. *European Journal of Operational Research, 126*(3), 614–636. doi:10.1016/S0377-2217(99)00316-1

Schonberger, J. R. (1981). Why projects are ""always" late: a rationale based on manual simulation of a PERT/CPM network. *Interfaces, 11*(5), 66–70. doi:10.1287/inte.11.5.66

Shogan, A. W. (1977). Bounding distributions for a stochastic PERT network. *Networks, 7*(4), 359–381. doi:10.1002/net.3230070407

Sullivan, R. S., Hayya, J. C., & Schaul, R. (1982). Efficiency of the antithetic variate method for simulating stochastic networks. *Management Science, 28*(5), 563–572. doi:10.1287/mnsc.28.5.563

Van Slyke, R. M. (1963). Monte Carlo methods and PERT problem. *Operations Research, 11*(5), 839–860. doi:10.1287/opre.11.5.839

Weiss, G. (1986). Stochastic bounds on distributions of optimal value functions with applications to PERT, network flow and reliability. *Operations Research, 34*(4), 595–605. doi:10.1287/opre.34.4.595

Williams, T. A. (1992). Practical use of distributions in network analysis. *The Journal of the Operational Research Society, 43*(3), 265–270.

Zwikael, O., Cohen, Y., & Sadeh, A. (2006). Nondelay scheduling as a managerial approach for managing projects. *International Journal of Project Management, 24*(4), 330–336. doi:10.1016/j.ijproman.2005.11.002

APPENDIX

Explanation of Equation 2

Most project networks graphically convey the idea that an activity can start only after the completion of all its predecessor activities (it is sufficient to check the completion of all immediate predecessors). Thus, the earliest start time of an activity is its predecessors' largest completion time. That is, the earliest starting time of an activity is the maximal completion time of its immediate predecessors. In AoA networks the time of each node is determined by the largest completion time of the activities of its incoming arcs.

> **Conculsion**: *the time distribution of an AoA node is the time distribution of the maximum of the completion times of its predecessors.*

Since the distribution function $F(.)$ of a maximum of several independent random variables is given by:

$$\Pr(\text{Max}(x_1, x_2, .., x_n) \le t) = \Pr(x_1 \le x,\ x_2 \le x, ..., x_n \le t) =$$

$$= \Pr(x_1 \le t) \cdot \Pr(x_2 \le t) \cdots \Pr(x_n \le t) = F_1(t) \cdot F_2(t) \cdots F_n(t) = \prod_{i=1}^{n} F_i(t)$$

It is the well-known distribution of the maximum taken from the field of "Order Statistics". An adjustment to this equation where the variables x_i ($i=1,2,\ldots,n$) to represent the immediate predecessors of each node yields equation 2.

$$F^A(t) = \prod_{i \in P(A)} F_i(t) \tag{2}$$

That is, Equation 2 expresses the distribution of the maximal time of the predecessors of an AoA node.

This work was previously published in International Journal of Information Technology Project Management, Volume 1, Issue 3, edited by John Wang, pp. 14-27, copyright 2010 by IGI Publishing (an imprint of IGI Global).

Section 2
Requirements Uncertainty and Technological Risks

Chapter 4

The Waterfall Approach and Requirement Uncertainty:
An In-Depth Case Study of an Enterprise Systems Implementation at a Major Airline Company

Huub J. M. Ruël
University of Twente, The Netherlands

Tanya Bondarouk
University of Twente, The Netherlands

Stefan Smink
Sodexo Altys, The Netherlands

ABSTRACT

The Waterfall approach has been the dominant approach for enterprise systems (ES) implementation since the 1970s. It offers ES project managers a simple, step-by-step way to make ES projects manageable and minimize drawbacks. The main criticism of this approach centres on its inflexibility regarding requirement uncertainty. In this article, the authors challenge this criticism. By means of an in-depth case study of a Waterfall approach-based ES implementation project within the maintenance department of one of the world's biggest airline companies, this article will illustrate how it deals with requirements uncertainty and required flexibility in practice.

INTRODUCTION

Enterprise systems (ES) can be defined as con-figurable, off-the-shelf software packages that provide an integrated suite of systems and infor-

DOI: 10.4018/978-1-4666-0930-3 .ch004

mation resources for operational and management processes across a broad range of business activities (Ward et al., 2005). They are intended to support business in the contemporary knowledge-based global economy (De Carvalho & Tanaka, 2008). Enterprise Systems (ES) cover a plethora of subjects that range from Enterprise Resource Planning (ERP), Enterprise Content Management (ECM) and Customer Relationship Management (CRM), to Decision Support Systems and Business Intelligence. It is acknowledged that developing and managing these systems involve dealing with the dynamics of contextual forces (Nandhakumar et al., 2005).

In their review of the studies of enterprise systems implementation, Shanks et al. (2000), Somers and Nelson (2001), Nah et al. (2001), and Umble et al. (2003) show project management, balanced project team, clear goals and objectives, change management, minimum customization, and project champion to be the main critical success factors. All of them stress the importance of ES project management issues as one of the major success factors, a conclusion widely debated in the academic literature on ES implementation and information systems (IS) implementation (Austin & Devin, 2003; Brown, 2004; Kim & Pan, 2006).

ES projects are notorious for their failure rates (Barker & Frolik, 2003; Mendel, 1999; Umble & Umble, 2002), and the question remains, why is project management of ES implementations more difficult than that of other types of IS projects? Jurison (1999) explains that the difficulty is in the nature of the 'product'. The most frequently cited aspects that make managing software projects more difficult are: intangibility of the 'product', complexity of the 'product', and volatility of the requirements. Or in other words, software is invisible, it is difficult to comprehend, and its requirements are under constant pressure to change, making ES project success hard to achieve.

Many project management methodologies and tools have been developed throughout the years that claim to contribute to ES project success, and the importance of project management is fully acknowledged in the literature (White & Fortune, 2002; Somers & Nelson, 2004). Project management is considered a series of activities associated with carrying out a project as effectively as possible (Jurison, 1999, p. 6). Project management aims to anticipate as many of the dangers

and problems as possible and to plan, coordinate, and control the complex and diverse activities of projects to ensure successful completion despite the risks (Lock, 2007). Project management has a long history, but in the modern management literature it was Henry Gantt (1861-1919) who first proposed that an organized approach was needed to manage the complex interrelationships among an enormous number of different tasks performed by many different specialists. He developed the Gantt chart, a way of ordering operations and work which is still widely in use by software project managers to track the progress of projects (Jurison, 1999; Lock, 2007). With the enormous growth in information technology use since the 1970s, a new type of project manager emerged: the IT or software project manager. Unfortunately, this type of project manager need not have project planning or scheduling experience. New project management approaches emerged based on successful manufacturing techniques of mass production, of which the Waterfall approach by Winston Royce (1970) has become a prominent exponent (Lock, 2007). In software project development studies, the Waterfall approach is the one referred to predominantly (Huo et al., 2004; Jiang & Eberlein, 2008).

However, in response to growing environmental uncertainty and flexibility, the Waterfall approach is being criticized for its rigid character (Nerur & Balijepally, 2007). Although we understand the roots of this criticism, we cannot fully agree with it. We still see a lot of potential in the "old" approach and argue that if managed well, this approach can greatly contribute to EIS implementation.

This article aims to contribute to this debate by starting from the assumption that the Waterfall approach in practice is not as ill-suited to the dynamics of ES projects as its critics claim, since it is still the most widely used approach for ES implementation projects (Laplante & Neill, 2004). The leading research question therefore is: how does a Waterfall approach-based ES project cope with requirements uncertainty?

The remainder of the article is organized as follows. First we elaborate on the discussion on the origins and advantages / limitations of the Waterfall approach. After that, we present its main 'rival', the Agile approach, and assess its assumed strengths and weaknesses. Then we introduce our in-depth case study, a Waterfall approach-based ES implementation project in one of the biggest airline companies in the world, present our findings and draw conclusions.

The value of our contribution is two-fold: firstly, this article provides an in-depth case study of a Waterfall approach-based ES project, something that is lacking in the literature. Such an in-depth case study in itself can help to elucidate ES projects for a broader audience. Secondly, this article stimulates the Agile approach supporters to clarify and sharpen the relevance of their criticism towards a plan-driven approach such as the Waterfall approach as we aim to present convincing evidence that the Waterfall approach is well-suited to the dynamics of ES projects.

THE WATERFALL APPROACH TO ENTERPRISE SYSTEMS IMPLEMENTATION: A REVIEW AND ALTERNATIVES

The Waterfall approach was introduced by Winston Royce in 1970, adopted by software project managers and further developed through lessons learned from software projects (Harrison, 2003). Modern project management methodologies, such as PRINCE2 and PMBOK, evolved from the Waterfall approach (Harrison, 2003) and are the most widely used project management methodologies in Europe and North America. The Waterfall approach treats a project as a linear process consisting of a series of basic sequential stages, each of which needs to be formally validated before moving to the next stage, thus reducing the complexity of an ES implementation process (Jurison, 1999; Khalifa, 2000; Huo et al., 2004).

The strength of the Waterfall approach and project methodologies that evolved from it mainly involves the management of each definable stage: planning, executing, testing, and closing. Although the labels for the separate stages of the Waterfall approach can differ per author, the basics still follow the original approach introduced by Royce. The recent literature agrees that ES projects based on this approach typically flow through five stages (Sommerville, 2006; Goedecke, 2007). These are: requirements definition (defining the functionalities), design (translating requirements into an executable format for a software system), coding (turning design into an actual, testable product, i.e. actual programming), system testing (testing whether the actual systems works in accordance with requirements and is accepted by the end-user), and operation (installing the software, training the end-users, setting up support and fixing bugs).

Drawbacks of the Waterfall Approach to ES Projects

Although it is the most mature and widely used form, the Waterfall approach has been increasingly criticised over the years. In sum, the criticism boils down to the following: the Waterfall approach is highly formalized and consists of sequential stages and therefore is not able to control uncertainty and changes in requirements. Requirements uncertainty and change are inherent to ES projects, however, as it is virtually impossible for end-users to list the requirements of the system precisely in advance (Beck, 1999; Khalifa & Verner, 2000; Middleton, 2000; Highsmith & Cockburn, 2001; Huo et al., 2004; Hass, 2007; Nerur & Balijepally, 2007). McConnell (2004) in this respect uses the term *the wicked problem*, a problem for which the requirements of the solution cannot be entirely known before completion. The Waterfall approach's focus on planning incorporates the risk that by the time a system is built, the problem it was supposed to solve has changed; the final result might be in accordance with the initial requirements with hardly any shortcomings, but when the job is done, it turns out to be the 'wrong' software (Austin & Devin, 2003). Parnas and Clements (1986) suggest that even if end-users could know all the requirements at the beginning of a project, there are many other factors that need to be known in advance to build a software system. In addition, 'freezing' the requirements at the beginning of a project, as desired by a Waterfall-based ES project management approach, is an excellent opportunity for end-users to ask for everything they think might be useful, as they realize that they might only get such an opportunity once (Poppendieck & Poppendieck, 2003). Overall, it can be said that a Waterfall-based ES project is mostly concerned with software development; it is less concerned with implementing a product that is accepted by the end-user (Becker, 1999).

An Alternative to the Waterfall Approach: The Agile Approach

As an alternative to the Waterfall approach, a new form of ES project management has emerged since the late 1990s, called the Agile approach (Huo et al., 2004). The first Agile approach-based project management methodologies were introduced by Kent Beck. It took until 2001 before the concept of the Agile approach was formally born. In that year a group of prominent practitioners agreed upon the basic values of the Agile approach as laid down in the *Manifesto for Agile Software Development* (Beck et al., 2001; Highsmith & Cockburn, 2001; Hass, 2007). It basically says that the highest priority is to satisfy the customer through early and continuous delivery of valuable software (Beck et al., 2001). The need for an alternative to the Waterfall approach emerged as various researchers and practitioners believed that nowadays the lessons on which the Waterfall approach is based no longer apply (Harrison, 2003; Olsson, 2008; Veenswijk & Berendse, 2008).

The main philosophy of the Agile approach is well expressed in a quote by Austin and Devin (2003): "The difference between a good and bad system is not how well it meets the requirements you know in advance. Meeting requirements is a necessary but insufficient condition for producing an excellent system. What makes a system great, is details that are not specifiable in advance - aspects that must evolve in the making" (p. 93).

The Agile approach accommodates the volatility of requirements and focuses on collaboration between developer and end-users (Demirkan & Nichos., 2008; Garcia-Crespo et al., 2009; Highsmith & Cockburn, 2001; Huo et al., 2004). According to the Agile *manifesto*, individuals and interactions are valued over processes and tools, and responding to change is valued over following a plan (Beck et al., 2001). The Agile approach deals with unstable and volatile requirements by using the following notable techniques: 1) simple planning, 2) short iteration, 3) earlier releases, and 4) frequent customer feedback (Beck, 1999; Huo et al., 2004). The most commonly used Agile approach-based project management methodologies are SCRUM and eXtreme Programming (XP) (Maurer & Melnik, 2006; Frye, 2008). In conclusion, the Agile approach deals with the drawbacks of the Waterfall approach by focusing on responding to change.

Drawbacks of an Agile Approach to ES Implementation Projects

Obviously, the Agile approach is not immune to criticism either. Opponents, mainly from the Waterfall 'supporters' camp, argue that the Agile method is an attempt by software engineers to legitimize software developers' behavior, which is immediately slinging code and producing something that works instead of delivering something that meets all written requirements (Rakitin, 2001; Austin & Devin, 2003). It is culturally embedded within ES implementation project management that in order to develop quality software you need to progress through a sequential, phased life cycle; therefore, the Agile approach will not be honoured (Harrison, 2003).

According to Agile critics it is impossible to develop realistic estimates of the work effort needed to provide a quote because at the beginning of the project, no one knows the entire scope. Moreover, the risk of scope creep (uncontrolled changes in a project's scope) increases significantly due to the lack of detailed requirements documentation (Stephens & Rosenberg, 2003).

In sum, supporters of the Waterfall approach cannot see how users of the Agile approach expect to build anything that satisfies the customers' or end-users' actual demands, without planning up front and carefully analyzing requirements. Supporters of the Agile approach, however, cannot see the point in spending a large amount of time analyzing requirements because they will change anyway (Austin & Devin, 2003). Some refer to this ongoing debate as the methodology war (Jiang & Eberlein, 2008).

As mentioned in the introduction, this article aims to contribute to this debate by starting from the assumption that the Waterfall approach in practice is not as ill-suited to the dynamics of ES projects as its critics claim, and therefore it is interesting to study how a Waterfall approach-based ES project does cope with requirements uncertainty.

RESEARCH METHODOLOGY

In answering the research question, we chose a case study methodology and, in particular, an in-depth case study. We wanted to obtain detailed insights into how a Waterfall approach-based ES project deals in real life with requirements uncertainty throughout a project. For that reason we selected a typical case (Yin, 2003), an ES project at one of the world biggest airline companies referred to as AirRoyal in this article.

AirRoyal implemented an ES using a Waterfall approach from March to November 2008. We spent eight months on data collection and having access on a full-time basis to the ES project, to project documents, meetings, informal discussions, panels, and round tables. In this way we conducted an in-depth case study, interviewing all project managers and team members. The overwhelming amount of empirical data enabled us to study many different aspects of the EIS implementation in relation to each other and to view the process within its total environment. Consequently, our case study research provided us with a greater opportunity than other available methodologies to obtain a holistic view of a specific research phenomenon (Gummersson, 2000).

The AirRoyal ES implementation project was identified as a typical case because the company itself, the project, and the conditions of the project were representative of ES implementation projects in large organizations. Secondly, it concerned the implementation of an off-the-shelf ES supplied by a third-party supplier, who also had other large airlines as customers. Therefore, the type of project we selected is very likely to be comparable to projects being carried out at large organizations.

As preparation for the actual collection of data, we developed a case study protocol and a database in order to organize and document the raw data. The primary data collection was conducted through semi-structured interviews as well as by direct observation during meetings and interactions with project team members and stakeholders throughout the project. The individual semi-structured interviews with the different project managers were used to obtain perceptions and opinions about the project from different angles as the project unfolded. These data were used for verification and to fill gaps where secondary data about the main features of the methodology used by AirRoyal to execute and manage the ES implementation project were incomplete. All observation notes, interviews and gathered documentation were coded and electronically stored.

In sum, during our eight-month study of the ES project at AirRoyal, we used multiple data collection techniques: document analysis, semi-structured interviews, and direct observations. In this way we adhered to the tactic of Yin (2003) to explore multiple sources of evidence during the data collection process. The use of several data collection methods offers the opportunity for (data) triangulation (Benbasat et al., 1987; Saunders et al., 2007). Or as Yin puts it: "A finding in a case study is likely to be much more convincing and accurate if it is based on several different sources of information" (Yin, 2003, p. 98).

Case Introduction

AirRoyal is an international airline operating worldwide with a fleet of almost 600 aircrafts and more than 90 000 employees. AirRoyal carries passengers and airfreight to more than 250 destinations worldwide, either non-stop or via another airport.

Aircraft maintenance is crucial to AirRoyal, and a sophisticated software system is used in that process, so-called Engineering & Maintenance (E&M) software. In 2006 the business case for purchasing a new E&M software system was approved, a system typically fitting the definition of an ES, and its implementation was planned as a step-wise process requesting sub-implementations for every type of aircraft separately. Our research focused on the first ES project that took place in 2008.

AirRoyal decided not to adopt the ES supplier's project methodology but to use their own methodology, based on the Waterfall approach. AirRoyal planned the ES project as a linear process with sequential stages based on the principles of PRINCE2 and PMBOK. There were two differences in the ES project management approach at AirRoyal compared with the definition of the Waterfall approach taken from the literature. First, the design and coding stages were combined in one, while the literature clearly distinguishes these as two separate stages. Second, a global design was prepared during the requirements definition stage and a detailed design during the design stage, while the literature suggests designing both during the design stage.

FINDINGS

The data gathered from the semi-structured interviews, document analysis, and observations, put down in transcripts, summaries, and field notes, during our eight months of full-time access to the ES project at AirRoyal were analysed step-by-step in such a way that we could describe the full project from day-to-day. We triangulated the data, which enabled us to reconstruct the 'story' of the project as presented in the following section, though very much compressed and therefore focusing on the main 'events' per stage.

The Starting-up and Initiating Project Stage

During the kick-off, all of AirRoyal's ES project stakeholders were present: the project managers, the AirRoyal Information Services department, the AirRoyal Engineering & Maintenance (E&M) business analysts (responsible for defining current requirements), AirRoyal E&M business architects (responsible for designing the final IT landscape) and AirRoyal ES users. From the supplier's side nobody was present at the kick-off. During this event, the participants were informed about the goals and scope of the project, the roles and responsibilities of the participants and the global planning for the project.

After the kick-off, the objectives and scope of the project were evident to the project team members, but a clear view of their responsibilities and the detailed planning of the first stage was lacking, as one of the project team members said:

I had no idea what was expected from me and what the approach would be to achieve the objectives of the first stage. [A project team member]

It was also clear that the project used a Waterfall approach to achieve its objectives (Table 1). The project manager was aware of some of the pitfalls of a Waterfall approach, because during the kick-off the project manager explicitly pointed out the importance of defining realistic requirements within the scope of the project:

Be realistic in requirements; strive for an optimum between dreams and realism in the given timeframe. [The project manager]

The Requirements Definition Stage

The start of the project was the transition from the initiating stage to the requirements definition stage (Table 2). It was clear to the project team members that a number of workshops would be organized to arrive at a final list of requirements, but they did not know what needed to be prepared for these workshops nor their agenda.

To agree on the requirements was a hard and painful process at AirRoyal. After defining the requirements, team members expected them to be evident in the solution, and as such, they found it difficult to accept that some of their requirements were not (yet) included. At the same time,

Table 1. Summary of the starting up and initiating stage

Stage of ES project at AirRoyal	Summary of main 'events'
Starting up and initiating the project	• Initiating document set-up to enable a clear and controlled start of the project and to plan the overall project. • Sharing the project kick-off with all project team members. • Roles and detailed planning of the first stage were not clear to project team members • Project member warned the team of pitfalls of the approach applied [Waterfall].

Table 2. Summary of the requirements definition stage

Stage of ES project at AirRoyal	Summary of main 'events'
Requirements definition stage	• Workshops organized to determine requirements involving the project management, supplier's consultants, AirRoyal's E&M business analysts and architects, and AirRoyal E&M end-users • Business processes as mapped for the 'standard' ES were used to identify the requirements for AirRoyal's ES. • AirRoyal did not prepare any lists of requirements prior to the workshop • Participants perceived this stage as the hardest - to determine the requirements for the business processes of the new ES • The proposed requirements exceeded what was actually needed to achieve the ES project objectives • In general, lengthy and tough discussions were needed, and participants found it difficult to determine what was really required • The supplier's consultants were perceived as not partnering well during the workshops • Based on the requirements (not yet approved), the global design was set up by the supplier. This document proposed an initial design presenting on an abstract level how the requirements would be met • The supplier and AirRoyal ES project management jointly reviewed the global design, and based on this review, the design was refined, and after a hard and painful process, agreement was reached on a number of requirements that would be excluded from the design • Initiating documents were refined based on a clear scope of the project • This stage was formally approved by the project board five months after its start (a two-month delay) • Perceived as a very time-consuming and difficult stage after all, but considered necessary to achieve full involvement and commitment of all project team members

as the project manager remarked, in this way the project team members were involved in the project:

During this stage there were many endless discussions which were time consuming and even causing irritation. I let this happen because these discussions were required to keep all the project team members involved in the project and to get user acceptance in the end. If these people would feel ignored, they would do everything to stall the project and they will spread harmful rumours about the ES which will affect the end-user acceptance. [AirRoyal E&M project manager]

Originally, three months were scheduled to complete this stage, but the definition of the requirements turned out to be a more difficult exercise than expected. One of the project team members noted that some perceived this stage as the most difficult one:

Based on my experience from the previous project I think it was not realistic of the project management to schedule only three months for the requirements definition stage, because we experienced the most difficulties during this stage in the previous project. [A project team member]

The Design and Coding Stage

During this stage the approved global design or solution overview was elaborated, which was based on the AirRoyal E&M requirements and intended for building by the supplier (coding). The kick-off meeting for this design and coding stage (Table 3) took place at AirRoyal, again for all stakeholders. The kick-off was very clear, and the participants were ready to start with this stage, as one of the AirRoyal's ES project team members said:

It is a tight schedule, but the approach feels like a very good way to achieve the desired result. [ES project team member]

The project manager and the project team members were truly satisfied with the translation of their requirements into the detailed design. Their requirements were incorporated as agreed upon in the solution overview, and during the first review it was felt that the design was sufficient to enable them to perform their work effectively and efficiently. When asked why they flagged many issues during the previous workshops although they were satisfied with the incorporated requirements, the project manager had an interesting answer:

On a high level (business process) the list of requirements we formulated was complete and these are incorporated satisfactorily, however the devil is in the detail... [Project manager]

The project manager was sure that once the requirements were implemented on a detailed level, they would find unexpected interrelations and unforeseen issues. He realized that it was almost impossible to identify all potential low-level issues during the requirements definition stage. Therefore, resolving issues was incorporated in the planning of the design and coding stage.

During the final review session, which lasted one week, all the use cases, reports, interfaces and adjusted work instructions were approved (all as separate units), and the team leader Training indicated that the training materials were finished to a previously agreed level. Minor issues were still identified during this session, but not all of them were resolved. Those issues were estimated as representing a marginal risk for the success of the project and could be resolved before system testing started. Based on this information, the project manager wrote the end-stage report, which stated that all the units of the ES were built in accordance with the solution overview, except

Table 3. Summary of the design and coding stage

Stage of ES project at AirRoyal	Summary of main 'events'
Design and coding stage	• The supplier and the ES project management jointly elaborated on the global design, and this elaborated design was built during this stage • Different elements of the global design were elaborated and built in parallel through a number of iterations • First iteration: the supplier builds a prototype of the ES based on the global design for use in the first review session • The supplier and the ES project management jointly reviewed the prototype and evaluated the global design based on this prototype • The ES project management was satisfied with the quality of the first iteration, although many issues were identified on a detailed level • Team leaders were selected to manage the designing and building (resulting from the review sessions) of their assigned element(s) of the entire design • Some of the supplier's team members stayed with the project during designing and building in order to improve communications • The approach towards detailed design worked very well; perfect cooperation between the stakeholders • The second joint review session resulted in an approval of the detailed design, thus the ES was ready to be tested as an integrated system

for some small changes. Based on this end-stage report, the project manager received permission to proceed to the next stage.

The Test Stage

During this stage all designed elements were tested to see whether they worked together correctly and to determine if the system was ready for acceptance by the customer. According to the project manager from the supplier's side:

The system test was done to validate that the ES was ready to be accepted by the customer, it would be poor promotion and the customer's confidence in the ES would drop when numerous no-go items were identified during the acceptance test. [a supplier's side project manager]

The system test took three weeks. Based on the results of this test, the supplier had to carry out revision work to fix all the identified issues up to a level that would be sufficient for the system to undergo the acceptance tests. The criterion for approval to proceed to the acceptance test was defined by the supplier in the test plan. After

two weeks of revision, the identified issues were resolved sufficiently, and approval was given to proceed to the acceptance test.

The acceptance test took two weeks, and various no-go items were identified even though it had passed the system test. These items were related to errors in the system (not detected during the system test), but also to missing functionality.

A major issue was the performance of the ES, however. Based on the result of the acceptance test, the supplier's side project manager said:

We performed the system test at the supplier's site, but when we did the acceptance test at Air-Royal we ran into all kinds of unexpected issues because of the different test environment. Therefore, we decided to execute future system tests at the customer's site. This requires more resources, but then we can be more certain that the ES is ready for customer acceptance and in this way reduce the risk of a possible disappointment by the customer. [Supplier's side project manager]

As mentioned earlier, some missing functionality was identified during the acceptance test. Most of this functionality could not be traced back to the original requirements, or as one of AirRoyal's ES project team members put it:

We simply did not realize that we missed this functionality until we actually carried out all the real-life scenarios with the ES. [AirRoyal's ES project team member]

This functionality was required by AirRoyal, but it did not have a large impact on the project as it concerned some minor changes in the configuration of the ES. (See Table 4)

The Operational Stage

After the ES was accepted, the next and final stage of the implementation was to get the new ES operational (Table 5). This implied the replacement of the old system (so-called site activation). Consequently, the operation stages included two major topics: training of end-users and the transfer process from the old to the new system. The user training process had already been initiated during the requirements definition stage when the initial training development and deployment plans were set up. These plans were included in the overall project planning and recorded in the refined project charter, which was approved by the project board. According to the AirRoyal team leader responsible for training:

Previous projects had significant delays because of training issues, therefore we initiated the training process as early in the project as possible and it was required that the project board was committed to the training plan. [AirRoyal team leader training]

During this project, user training started at the same time as the joint system and acceptance test. The reason for this was according to the AirRoyal team leader responsible for training:

From the start we knew that it would be an immense job to train all these people within six weeks and therefore we decided to take the risk of possible changes in the training material and by doing this gained two additional weeks of training. [AirRoyal team leader training]

After the site activation was completed successfully, the project was ready for the 'go-live' decision. The project board arranged a 'go-live' ceremony which also formed the approval to continue to the next stage. During this ceremony an executive of AirRoyal gave the formal 'go-live' signal, and the old AirRoyal ES system was switched off. The project manager of AirRoyal was very satisfied with the result of this stage as expressed through the following statement:

During the previous stages of this project we had to deviate from the schedule because of various issues, while in contrast, this site activation went extremely smoothly and according to schedule. This shows that it was a long and hard road getting there, but all the effort resulted in a high-quality product. [AirRoyal project manager]

The Closing Stage

During the parallel run and directly after go-live, a transition-to-support team was in place to support the users (Table 6). During the transition-to-support period, a transition manager was ready to manage the support process. The project board received reports at least once a week about the status of this process. The project team was very pleased with the site activation process, as one of the project team members said:

The post go-live support was perfectly arranged, there was always someone to assist the end-users, and issues were resolved very quickly by MXI (the supplier). This, together with the performance of

Table 4. Summary of the test stage

Stage of ES project at AirRoyal	Summary of main 'events'
Test stage	• An installation record was set up to check the versions of the different units built during designing which were integrated into one system • The supplier and AirRoyal defined their test cases (scenarios) and test plan (summary of all the scenarios and the acceptance criteria) which would be used to perform their tests • The system test did not pass the acceptance criteria, and the supplier had to carry out revision work to fix the identified issues • After two weeks the issues were resolved to a sufficient level to pass the acceptance criteria, and approval was given for the acceptance test • AirRoyal performed the acceptance test, this was done in the 'real-life' setting of the ES (including interfaces and 100% accurate data) • Various 'no-go' items were identified during the acceptance test • The 'no-go' items were mainly unexpected issues revealed by the different test environment compared with the system test. Only a few issues were related to missing functionality • A 'no-go' after the acceptance test required a new cycle of system tests and acceptance tests, a decision taken jointly • A month of revision work was required before this joint system and acceptance test could start • The result of the joint system and acceptance test was within the acceptance criteria, and only some minor issues were identified • The ES was accepted by AirRoyal, and approval by the project board to continue to the next stage was given two months behind schedule

Table 5. Summary of the operational stage

Stage of ES project at AirRoyal	Summary of main 'events'
Operational stage	• The two major topics of this stage were user training and site activation • The process of user training was already initiated during the requirements definition stage; the training plan was set up then and included in the project planning • Training material was prepared, and trainers were trained during the design stage; after the test stage, the changes were incorporated • During this stage the training was deployed, and 350 users were trained • When a sufficient level of users were trained, site activation (actual transfer from one system to another) was initiated • The supplier and AirRoyal's project management jointly defined the site activation plan, including the site activation strategy, approach, participants, 'go'/'no-go' criteria, support infrastructure and contingency planning • Old and new systems were running in parallel for a while • Running both systems in parallel was done to compare the performance of the new system with the old one • Only a few issues were identified during the parallel run, and they were mainly related to incorrect data entry by users • After a very smooth site activation and a one-week parallel run, the AirRoyal ES project board arranged a 'go-live' ceremony • The 'go-live' sign was given by a AirRoyal Executive and was perfectly on schedule according to the planning of this particular stage

the ES, resulted in a very good acceptance of the ES by the end-users. [A project team member]

The IT service desk of AirRoyal had already been tested for their ability to provide end-user support.

Finally, an 'end project report' was written, which also listed the lessons learned during this project. The project board reviewed the document and gave approval to close the project down. As a final reflection, the AirRoyal ES project manager stated:

Table 6. Summary of the closing stage

Stage of ES project at AirRoyal	Summary of main 'events'
Closing stage	• Ongoing end-user support was installed The plan for implementing the transition-to-support team and the 'project-exit criteria' was jointly developed by the supplier and AirRoyal's ES project team during the previous stage • The transition-to-support was perfectly organized, was on schedule, and the exit criteria were met four weeks after 'going live' • All project team members were de-charged from the project after the ES project board formally approved the 'end project report' • The project was finished five months later than originally scheduled, nevertheless user acceptance was very high

The project was closed down five months later than originally scheduled, nevertheless the user acceptance was great, and we have learned various useful lessons for carrying out future projects. [The AirRoyal ES project manager]

Comparison of Results with the Drawbacks of the Waterfall Approach

Before evaluating the Waterfall approach, we must emphasize the high quality of the implementation process of ES at AirRoyal. The discussion above shows that every implementation stage resulted in a positive outcome, ranging from the project leader's satisfaction to approval by the board. We clearly observed the evolutionary growth of the implementation quality results. The starting-up stage resulted in warnings given by the project member about the pitfalls of the applied approach [Waterfall]. Then, during the requirements definition stage, the supplier and AirRoyal ES project management achieved a joint revision of the design and agreement on a number of requirements. While designing and coding, the stakeholders acknowledged perfect collaboration that led to an approval of the detailed design and ES's readiness to be tested as an integrated system. The test stage showed that the acceptance level was within the expected criteria. The ES was accepted by Air-Royal and approved by the project board. The closing stage showed a delay of five months, but very high user acceptance.

This illustrates the success of the implementation process at AirRoyal that we definitely attribute to the Waterfall approach the company used.

According to the literature, one of the drawbacks of the Waterfall approach is that it is not able to deal with uncertainty and changes in requirements (occurring from *the wicked problem*; McConnell, 2004) due to its high level of formalization and its sequential stages.

The case of AirRoyal showed that *the wicked problem* does occur in practice, and that requirements do change during an ES project. However, the Waterfall-based ES project was able to deal with *the wicked problem* in practice and with uncertainty and changes in requirements throughout the project. Furthermore, the impact of these requirements changes was not as severe as discussed in the literature. We explain this result as due to the fact that in practice ES projects are not 'built from scratch', and industry standards are available through the supplier that only need some specific adjustments. Therefore, in the AirRoyal case there was some sort of 'back-up' to rely on, a type of knowledge base from earlier cases about how to deal with requirement adjustments.

Another interesting difference between the Waterfall approach as described in the literature and the approach in practice is that a major part of the designing is already included in the requirements definition stage. A rudimentary design is established that describes the final design up to a low level of detail, which is sufficient to convey to the end-users how the requirements will be met. This rudimentary design provides end-users with a better idea of the completeness and correctness of the requirements and allows the incorporation of change in the requirements prior to stage approval. Further design work is done in the coding stage. Therefore, the AirRoyal case study showed that there is space for joint design and coding, and that the design goes through a number of early iterations where adjustments to the requirements can be made, providing end-users with an overview of an early release of the ES.

Another acknowledged drawback of the Waterfall-based ES project management approach is that by freezing requirements at the beginning of the project, end-users tend to ask for everything they think they might need, especially if they believe they will only get 'one shot at it'. Or in other words, there is a risk of an increased scope of a project, well beyond what is necessary to meet a project's overall target. This drawback was observed in the AirRoyal ES project as well. However, in practice it seemed to have a limited impact on the project's success. The explanation for this is again that requirements were prepared in practice on an existing industry standard-based ES from the supplier and not from scratch, something which is not always considered in descriptions of the Waterfall approach in the literature.

The third drawback of the Waterfall approach is that its orientation toward planning means that by the time that building of the system has finished, the problem it is supposed to solve has changed; one might build software with few defects this way, but when it is ready it turns out to be the wrong software. In the AirRoyal ES project this drawback did not emerge. It was not a very smooth process to get the ES implemented, but the acceptance of the ES was very high since it met the end-users' expectations. Moreover, the ES dealt with all the problems it needed to solve.

Overall, the Waterfall approach-based ES project at AirRoyal was able to deal with requirements uncertainty and changes. By including the initial

part of the design stage (rudimentary design) in the requirements definition stage and the remaining part of the design stage (detailed design) in the coding stage, the Waterfall approach includes some of the features that are said to be so special of the Agile approach.

The design process was done in two iterations. After each design step the ES was actually built according to this design, and therefore the building of the ES occurred in two iterations as well. The two design and building iterations resulted in an early release of the ES. Before the design was formally approved, the end-users had already had an opportunity to actually work with a prototype of the ES. The two design and building iterations and the early releases resulting from this allow for more frequent end-user feedback. The initial design part carried out during the requirements definition stage in AirRoyal's ES project permitted more frequent end-user feedback as well.

It can be concluded that a Waterfall approach-based ES project, if well managed, has features that its opponents claim it lacks. By applying these features, a Waterfall approach-based ES project keeps its original focus on planning but is flexible in responding to changing requirements.

CONCLUSION AND DISCUSSION

The main research question in our study was: how does a Waterfall approach-based ES project deal with requirements uncertainty and changes? By means of an in-depth case study, we collected data about an ES project at a major airline company during eight months of full-time access to project meetings, project documentation, and direct observations and by conducting semi-structured interviews with project managers and team members. Through data triangulation and interviewing different stakeholders, we were able to reconstruct the 'story' of the ES project.

The answer to the research question is that a Waterfall approach-based ES project deviates in practice to certain extent from its features as presented in the literature. These deviations include splitting the design stage; one major part is included in the requirements definition stage, and the other part is included in the coding stage. Based on the requirements, a rudimentary design is set up in the former stage that describes the design with a low level of detail, which is sufficient to convey to the end-user how the requirements will be met.

The other part of the system design (detailed design) is included in the coding stage. Thus, in practice a Waterfall approach-based ES project includes a joint (developers plus end-users) design and coding stage, and involves a number of iterations. In this way, adjustments to the requirements can be made and changes included before a final design is approved.

Furthermore, *the wicked problem* does occur in practice, and thus requirements are subject to change in an ES project. However, a Waterfall approach-based ES project does not turn out in practice to be as 'simplistic' and inflexible as opponents of the approach claim. It does include features typical of an Agile approach, such as iterations, early releases, and frequent end-user feedback, though in a more moderate way.

By doing so, a Waterfall approach-based ES project keeps its original focus on planning, but is more flexible in responding to requirements uncertainty and changes. In the case of AirRoyal this turned out to be sufficient and resulted in successful user acceptance of a new ES.

Interestingly, the impact of requirements uncertainty and changes in practice was less than the literature suggests.

The main conclusion of our research is therefore that the 'demise' of the Waterfall approach for ES implementation projects is not imminent. In practice, this approach seemed to be an appropriate one to successfully implement an ES.

Discussion

The question emerges: where do we go from here? If the Waterfall approach seems suitable for ES development and implementation, then what remains of the criticism brought up by its opponents? Abrahamson et al. (2009) state that "Agile system development methods emerged as a response to the inability of previous plan-driven approaches to handle rapidly changing environments". Our in-depth case study presents evidence, however, that a so-called plan-driven approach like the Waterfall approach is more suited for changing environments than claimed by the Agile community.

Perhaps the literature has contributed to the division between the two camps by using labels that do not fully represent reality. Abrahamson (2009) at least acknowledges that there are shortcomings in Agile systems development research, such as a lack of understanding of what constitutes 'agility'.

The same could hold true for research on plan-driven approaches as well, such as what does a term like 'plan-driven' mean? A possible common sense response could be that plan-driven approaches are still designed by humans, and still need human interaction and collaboration for their execution. Therefore, an intriguing question is whether in reality the dividing line between the plan-driven Waterfall and user-oriented Agile approach is more of a sliding scale.

Limitations and Future Research

To ensure the quality of the findings of this research, we carefully followed the prescribed tactics for single case study research. To improve the validity and reliability of this research, the single case was selected very carefully, multiple sources of evidence and multiple viewpoints on the phenomenon were used, and a research protocol was followed. However, there are some limitations that should be noted. The most significant one concerns generalization of the research findings (the external validity), as single case studies form a limited basis for generalizing. In order to strengthen the findings of this research and generalize them, further case studies should be undertaken. Regardless of this limitation associated with the methodology used, this research still provided various useful findings of interest to both academics and practitioners. Although we were able to generalize to the level of a theory as Yin suggests, future cases would be helpful to understand the contingency factors of the Waterfall approach across different sectors and types of organizations.

This research was limited to the investigation of a Waterfall approach-based methodology for ES implementation projects. Future experimental research design might include an Agile approach-based methodology for ES implementation project management. This would provide the opportunity to investigate the effects of an Agile approach on ES implementation success, and would allow for comparisons.

Finally, this research was driven by our curiosity regarding the high failure rate of ES implementation projects. During the literature review, project management was identified as one of the most significant critical success factors. The proposed modifications to the Waterfall approach-based ES implementation methodology as an outcome of this research should result in greater ES implementation success. For that reason, future research is required to verify that the modified approach towards ES implementation project management will actually result in a greater ES implementation success rate.

REFERENCES

Abrahamsson, P., Conboy, K., & Wang, X. (2009). 'Lots done, more to do': The current state of agile systems development research. *European Journal of Information Systems, 18*, 281–284. doi:10.1057/ejis.2009.27

Austin, R., & Devin, L. (2003). Beyond requirements: Software making as art. *IEEE Software, 20*(1), 93–95. doi:10.1109/MS.2003.1159037

Barker, T., & Frolick, M. N. (2003). ERP implementation failure: A case study. *Information Systems Management, 3*, 43–50. doi:10.1201/1078/43647.20.4.20030901/77292.7

Beck, K. (1999). Embrace change with extreme programming. *IEEE Computer*, 70-77.

Beck, K. (2001). *Manifesto for agile software development*. Retrieved August 06, 2008 from http:// www.agilemanifesto.org

Benbasat, I., Goldstein, D. K., & Mead, M. (1987). The case research strategy in studies of information systems. *Management Information Systems Quarterly, 11*(3), 369–385. doi:10.2307/248684

Brown, W. (2004). Enterprise resource planning (ERP) implementation planning and structure: a recipe for ERP success. In J. S. Whiting, J. Ashworth, & D. Mateik (Eds.), *Annual ACM SIGUCCS Conference on User Services 2004* (Vol. 32, pp. 82-86). Baltimore: AMC.

De Carvalho, R. A., & Tanaka, A. K. (2008). Editorial message to a special track on enterprise information systems. In *Proceedings of the Annual ACM symposium on Applied Computing* (Vol. 23). Ceará, Brazil.

Demirkan, H., & Nichos, J. (2008). IT services project management: lessons learned from a case study in implementation. *International Journal of Project Organisation and Management, 1*(2), 204–220. doi:10.1504/IJPOM.2008.022192

Frye, C. (2008). Software *development groups take many routes to agile*. Retrieved August 05, 2008 from www.SearchSoftwareQuality.com

Garcia-Crespo, A., Colomno-Palacios, R., Gomez-Berbis, J. M., & Ruano-Mayoral, M. (2009). A project management methodology for commercial software reengineering. *International Journal of Project Organisation and Management, 1*(3), 253–267. doi:10.1504/IJPOM.2009.027538

Goedecke, D. (2007). The role of the software practitioner in the development of public safety software-intensive systems. In T. Cant (Ed.), *Australian Workshop on Safety Critical Systems and Software and Safety-related Programmable Systems* (Vol. 86, pp. 13-19). Adelaide, SA Australia: Australian Computer Society, Inc.

Gummersson, E. (2000). *Qualitative methods in management research* (2nd ed.). London: Sage Publications Inc.

Harrison, W. (2003). Is software engineering as we know it over the hill? *IEEE Software, 20*(3), 5–7. doi:10.1109/MS.2003.1199629

Hass, K. B. (2007). The blending of traditional and agile project management. *Project Management World Today, 9*(5), 1–8.

Highsmith, J., & Cockburn, A. (2001). Agile software development: The business of innovation. *IEEE Computer, 34*(9), 120–122.

Huo, M., Verner, J., Zhu, L., & Babar, M. A. (2004). Software quality and agile methods. In *Proceedings of the Annual International Computer Software and Applications Conference (COMPSAC 2004)* (Vol. 28, pp. 520-525).

Jiang, l., & Eberlein, A. (2008). Towards a framework for understanding the relationships between classical software engineering and agile methodologies. In P. Kruchten & S. Adolf (Eds.), *The 2008 International Conference on Software Engineering* (Vol. 30, pp. 9-14). Leipzig, Germany: ACM.

Jurison, J. (1999). Software project management: The manager's view. *Communications of the Association for Information Systems, 2*(17), 1–57.

Khalifa, M., & Verner, J. M. (2000). Drivers for software development method usage. *IEEE Transactions on Engineering Management, 47*(3), 360–369. doi:10.1109/17.865904

Kim, H.-W., & Pan, S. L. (2006). Towards a process model of information systems implementation: the case of customer relationship management (CRM). *The Data Base for Advances in Information Systems, 37*(1), 59–76.

Laplante, P. A., & Neill, C. J. (2004). The demise of the waterfall model is imminent and other urban myths. *ACM Queue; Tomorrow's Computing Today, 1*(10), 10–15. doi:10.1145/971564.971573

Lock, D. (2007). *Project Management* (9th ed.). Hampshire, UK: Gower.

Maurer, F., & Melnik, G. (2006). Agile methods: moving towards the mainstream of the software industry. In *Proceedings of the International Conference on Software Engineering, 28*, 1057–1058.

Mendel, B. (1999). Overcoming ERP project hurdles: experts offer tips on avoiding 10 problems that plague many ERP implementation projects. *InfoWorld, 21*(29), 87.

Middleton, P. (2000). Barriers to the efficient and effective use of information technology. *International Journal of Public Sector Management, 13*(1), 85–99. doi:10.1108/09513550010334506

Nah, F. F., Lau, J. L., & Kuang, J. (2001). Critical Factors for Successful Implementation of Enterprise Systems. *Business Process Management Journal, 7*(3), 285–296. doi:10.1108/14637150110392782

Nandhakumar, J., Rossi, M., & Talvinen, J. (2005). The dynamics of contextual forces of ERP implementation. *The Journal of Strategic Information Systems, 14*, 221–242. doi:10.1016/j.jsis.2005.04.002

Nerur, S., & Balijepally, V. G. (2007). Theoretical reflections on agile development methodologies. *Communications of the ACM, 50*(3), 79–83. doi:10.1145/1226736.1226739

Olsson, N. O. E. (2008). External and internal flexibility – aligning projects with the business strategy and executing projects efficiently. *International Journal of Project Organisation and Management, 1*(1), 47–64. doi:10.1504/IJPOM.2008.020028

Parnas, D. L., & Clements, P. C. (1986). A rational design process: how and why to fake it. *IEEE Transactions on Software Engineering*, 1–12.

Parr, A., & Shanks, G. (2000). A model of ERP project implementation. *Journal of Information Technology, 15*, 289–303. doi:10.1080/02683960010009051

Poppendieck, M., & Poppendieck, T. D. (2003). *Lean Software Development: An Agile Toolkit* (1st ed.). Boston: Addison-Wesley Professional.

Rakitin, S. (2001). Manifesto Elicits Cynicism. *IEEE Computer, 34*(12), 4.

Saunders, M., Lewis, P., & Thornhill, A. (2007). *Research Methods for Business Students* (4th ed.). Harlow, UK: Pearson Education Limited.

Shanks, G., Parr, A., Hu, B., Corbitt, B., Thanasankit, T., & Seddon, P. B. (2000). Differences in critical success factors in ERP systems implementation in Australia and China: A cultural analysis. In H. R. Hansen, M. Bichler, & H. Mahrer (Eds.), *The European Conference on Information Systems* (Vol. 8, pp. 537-544). Wienna: Wirtschaftsunivsitat Wien.

Somers, T., & Nelson, K. (2001). The impacts of critical success factors across the stages of enterprise resource planning implementations. In *Proceedings of the Hawaii International Conference of System Sciences, 8*, 1–10.

Sommerville, I. (2006). *Software engineering* (8th ed.). Harlow, UK: Pearson Education.

Stephens, M., & Rosenberg, D. (2003). *Extreme Programming Refactored: The Case Against XP*. USA: APress.

Umble, E. J., Haft, R. R., & Umble, M. M. (2003). Enterprise resource planning: Implementation procedures and critical success factors. *European Journal of Operational Research, 146*, 241–257. doi:10.1016/S0377-2217(02)00547-7

Umble, E. J., & Umble, M. M. (2002). Avoiding ERP implementation failure. *Industrial Management (Des Plaines), 44*(1), 1–25.

Veenswijk, M., & Berensde, M. (2008). Constructing new working practices through project narratives. *International Journal of Project Organisation and Management, 1*(1), 65–85. doi:10.1504/IJPOM.2008.020029

Ward, J., Hemingway, C., & Daniel, E. (2005). A framework for addressing the organisational issues of enterprise systems implementation. *The Journal of Strategic Information Systems, 14*, 97–119. doi:10.1016/j.jsis.2005.04.005

White, D., & Fortune, J. (2002). Current Practice in Project Management - an empirical study. *International Journal of Project Management, 20*, 1–11. doi:10.1016/S0263-7863(00)00029-6

Yin, R. K. (2003). *Case study research Design and Methods* (3rd ed.). London: Sage Publications Inc.

This work was previously published in International Journal of Information Technology Project Management, Volume 1, Issue 2, edited by John Wang, pp. 43-60, copyright 2010 by IGI Publishing (an imprint of IGI Global).

Chapter 5
IT Risk Evaluation Model Using Risk Maps and Fuzzy Inference

Constanţa- Nicoleta Bodea
Academy of Economic Studies - AES, Romania

Maria-Iuliana Dascălu
Academy of Economic Studies - AES, Romania

ABSTRACT

A risk evaluation model for IT projects using fuzzy inference is proposed. The knowledge base for fuzzy processes is built using a causal and cognitive map of risks. This map was specially developed for IT projects and takes into account the typical lifecycle and the risk taxonomy created by the Software Engineering Institute. The model was used to compute the technological risk of an e-testing project. This project was positioned on the middle level of the risk map, implying that the probability of encountering technological difficulties depends on the number of technologies used and their market maturity. A software system for validating the model was also developed.

INTRODUCTION

In a knowledge-based economy, projects are the main method of organizing economic processes. Project owners, project managers, and project teams need to make strategic decisions to achieve a "competitive edge" in the market (Kodama, 2007, p. 2). Perhaps the most important decision to be taken is choosing viable and profitable projects. Investing in a project doomed to fail means wast-

ing money, time, and valuable resources. Factors which increase the chance of project failure are called risks. The degree of risk in projects is generally measured by the amount of money lost. In most projects, risk is quantified in crisp terms, but unfortunately the reality contradicts most forecasts: "Forecasts of cost, demand, and other impacts of planned projects have remained constantly and remarkably inaccurate for decades." (Flyvbjerg, 2006) To get truly useful information in estimating project risk, experts should analyze a distribution, not a punctual value.

DOI: 10.4018/978-1-4666-0930-3.ch005

Identifying, evaluating, prioritizing, and treating risks are complex managerial challenges. Financial risks have been actively managed for a long time (Cumming & Hirtle, 2001). But the variety, number, and interactions between risks are continually increasing.

Operational and strategic risks have intensified due to the failure of control mechanisms in a very dynamic business environment. Under these circumstances, organizations recognize the importance of managing all risks, both standard and new, as many specialists noticed: Clarke and Varma (1999), Liu and Lu (2002) and McGee (2005).

A myriad of organizations (rating agencies, stock exchanges, institutional investors, shareholders, and the corporate governance) exert external pressures on corporate management to analyze risks more systematically and comprehensively. One solution is to adopt the portfolio approach (Nakagawa, Tani, Yasunobu, & Komoda, 2005): management considers the portfolio risk to be the risk to the entire organization. Risk is managed holistically, taking into account the consequences for the entire company.

There is a growing tendency to quantify risk. Risk quantification allows managers to develop "what if" scenarios and make informed decisions. Advances in technology and expertise have made this quantification possible. But despite such advances, there will always be risks that are not easily quantifiable, such as those related to human intervention. There is a continuing effort to quantify portfolio risk based on individual risks and the quantification of interactions. This can be extremely challenging if a high degree of precision is necessary, but this is not usually the case.

Over time and with practice companies become more familiar with risk and more capable of managing it. Some even seek out opportunities to assume risks. Companies understand that informed risk-taking is a means of achieving competitive advantages: "Risk management offers genuine and significant benefits to organizations, their projects and their stakeholders, but these will never be achieved without recognition of the *importance* of managing risk at all levels in the business, matched with operational *effectiveness* in executing risk management in practice." (Hillson, 2005)

IT PROJECTS FROM A RISKS MANAGEMENT PERSPECTIVE

The IT software industry has a high level of risk: "more than 50% of IT projects fail (according to GPM-Association fom project management), 30% of IT projects are stopped before being finished (Standish Group), 50% from IT projects are 90% over-budgeted(Standish Group), the IT project products respect only 40% of the initial specifications (Standish Group)." (Gareis, 2006, p. 275-298)

The growing development of IT technologies requires a permanent improvement of software makers. Because the market demand for IT products is highly dynamic, software developers do not have time to assimilate new technologies and consequently deliver incomplete products. Software quality is the first objective sacrificed. Also, many IT projects are interrupted or experience difficulties that may lead to identity changes. In other words, each IT project is exposed to a wide array of risks.

Many researchers have tried to identify the risk sources of IT projects. Boehm (1991) noticed that the most common IT risks are: project team members are poorly trained, temporary planning and project budgets are not realistic, wrong product features are developed, interfaces are not user oriented, testing in real life situation fails. All these risks can be handled by going through the following phases: risk distribution/evaluation (risk identification, risk analysis, risk prioritization), and risk control (risk treatment plan, risk resolution, risk monitoring). Risk identification and risk assessment should be done as early as possible to minimize negative deviations and to maximize positive results during project development. Miler and Gorski (2004) suggested risks identification using well-known patterns and a systematic approach. A complex pattern for risk identification is also described by Al-Rousan, Sulaiman, and Salam (2008).

Gareis (2006) proposes a slightly different approach to risk management in IT projects. In his view, risk management should contain: risk analysis (risk identification, risk evaluation), planning and performance measures, and risk controls (risks politics control, additional risk analysis, politics for additional risks).

Chris Chapman and Stephen Ward describe a complete methodology for risk management that includes nine phases: concentration, identification, structuring, assignment, assessment, evaluation, planning and administration (Turner, 2004).

Experts at the Software Engineerging Institute (SEI) identify three types of risks in software projects: known, unknown, and unknowable. Known risks are those that one or more project personnel are aware of. Unknown risks are those that could be detected if project personnel were given the right opportunity, cues, and information. Unknowable risks are those that, even in principle, no one can foresee (Carr, Konda, Monarch, Ulrich, & Walker, 1993). Known risks can be evaluated and are the main concern of risk management activities. A classification of known risks was developed by SEI based on a carefully constructed questionnaire. IT risks were organized into three classes: product engineering (the technical aspects of work to be done), development environment (methods, procedures and tools used to create the software product), and program constraints (the contractual, organizational and operational factors that influence the software project).

There are many classifications, methods, and methodologies related to risk management in IT projects. Each project stakeholder chooses the most suitable for his given context. Not all risks have the same impact on IT projects. Also, they do not have the same probability of occurence. Determining the degree of project risk is very important: as soon as the risk is calculated/updated, the project can be started/continued. Even with a brilliant project idea, project success is not guaranteed. Risks are characterized by uncertainty: their quantification can be a difficult process. This is why not all risk quantification methods give correct results. In fact, risk cannot be 100% quantified, but a risk estimate close to reality gives an useful forecast for the attractiveness of an IT project.

RISKS MODELING METHODS

According to the manner in which calculations are carried out, there are analytic and simulation methods for risk modeling. *Analytic methods* require a set of assumptions, especially related to probability distributions. *Simulation methods* require a large number of trials to approximate an answer. They are relatively robust and flexible, can accommodate complex relationships, and depend less on simplifying assumptions and standardized probability distributions. Considering the way in which relationships among variables are represented, there are statistical and structural methods. *Statistical methods* are based on observed statistical qualities of random variables disregarding the cause/effect relationships. *Structural methods* are based on explicit cause/effect relationships. The Casualty Actuarial Society published a research in which characteristics of the above methods were described: the statistical-analytical models are speedy, can be easily replicated, and can use available data; the structural simulation models are flexible, contain complex relationships, and decision processes are driven by scenario examination ("Overview of", 2003). RBC is an example of a statistical-analytical model and DFA is an example of structural simulation model.

Methods used to model risk are usually customized according to the specific risks the company has faced before. There are a myriad of methods that can be used to model risk. Depending on the extent to which they rely on historical data or expert input, they lie in a continuum of different information sources. (Casualty Actuarial Society, 2003) Methods applied to risk modeling are: empirical assessment from historical data, fit parameters from theoretical distribution, extreme value theory, stochastic differential equations, system dynamic simulation, neural networks, regression over variables that affect risk, influence diagrams, Bayesian belief networks, fuzzy logic, direct assessment, preference among bets or lotteries, and the Delphi method.

Although numerous techniques for risk modeling exist, more and more experts are reluctant to use them in making precise risk estimations: "Single-point estimates imply accuracy that is rarely justified in technical projects. Estimates that make risks visible are therefore stated as ranges, or included percentages (plus and minus) to indicate the precision, or specify a probability distribution of expected values" (Kendric, 2003, p. 74). In this context, fuzzy representations are a way of obtaining realistic risk assessments in project management (Chen & Chen, 2006; Kleiner, Rajani, & Sadiq, 2006), within certain limits. A fuzzy approach to risk modeling can be improved by considering causal and cognitive risk mappings (Al-Shehab, Hughes, & Winstanley, 2005). These are diagrams that reflect cause-effect relationships within projects.

AN IT RISK EVALUATION MODEL BASED ON FUZZY LOGIC

The present paper brings a solid contribution to risk management by adapting existent techniques of risk evaluation to IT projects. It proposes a fuzzy model, which has two important stages: risk identification using a database designed by experts,

and risk maps and component development useful in fuzzy inference. The model allows risk quantification by determining the crisp values of risk sources. Due to fuzzy logic mechanisms, the result can be a better approximation of risk. Each stage is thoroughly documented, from fundamentals to a complete example using numerical values.

RISKS IDENTIFICATION USING CAUSAL AND COGNITIVE MAPS

A common approach in project risk identification is to establish the risk sources: management, cost, technology, production, environment, or schedule. The fuzzy model considers risks not only in correlation to their source, but also in correlation to the project lifecycle (Al-Shehab, Hughes, & Winstanley, 2005). "While it is futile to try to eliminate risk, and questionable to try to minimize it, it is essential that the risks taken be the right risks." (Hodge, 2004)

In order to manage risk efficiently, it is useful to create a causal and cognitive map of risks, based on the experience of experts (Al-Shehab, Hughes, & Winstanley, 2005). This map describes the propagation of risk throughout the project: initiation, planning and resource procurement, design and implementation, bug fixing and installation, and maintenance. Risks occurring at a certain point in the project's lifecycle (see Figure 1) will generate other risks in the following phases.

Based on the IT project lifecycle, following risks were identified:

- Environmental risks: unfavorable legislation;
- Management risks (the most important, according to Al Neimat (2009)): unrealistic duration estimation, lack of management experience, poor planning, unclear objectives, poor communication (Rosencrance, 2007), poor quality control, misunderstood overall vision, behind- schedule risk;

Figure 1. IT project lifecycle

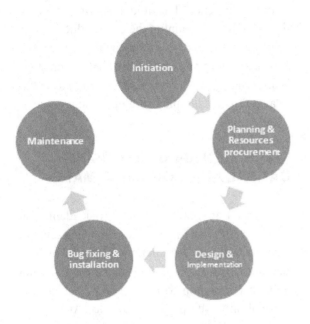

- Financial risks: unrealistic budget estimates, over-budget risk;
- Production & technology (Griffiths, 2009): lack of experienced personnel, poor product quality, unsatisfied client, poor performance;

In addition to creating a risk propagation map (see Figure 2), it is also useful to create a risk register or a risk log, in which each risk identified on the map is assigned a code, a name, a description and a source (type). A fragment of such a register is shown in Table 1. These identified risks are the knowledge base from which fuzzy model rules can be designed. The identified risks are inspired from the SEI taxonomy (Carr, Konda, Monarch, Ulrich, & Walker, 1993) and are adapted to the project context by an experienced project team.

FUZZY INFERENCE CHARACTERISTICS

The proposed model for evaluating risks in IT projects has the typical components of a fuzzy

model (Teodorescu, Zbancioc, & Voroneanu, 2004): input variables, an output variable and fuzzy rules. Although the magnitude of risks depends on many causes (severity of impact – threat intensity, variation in terms of cost and time, probability of impact, susceptibility to change or external influence, degree of independence to other risk factors (Merna & Al-Thani, 2008, p. 11)), the rules used in the current fuzzy risk modelling tool are built on just two parameters: probability of risk occurence and impact on project development. Risks at the first level of the risk map are also influenced by a set of so-called primary causes (Figure 2). The model can be generally stated as: „The more over-budget the project is and the less quality the finished product demostrates, the less satisfied the clients are". The risk located at the highest level of the map was the only one taken into account when stating the model, because of the transitivity principle in risk propagation chains. In fact, the model consists of a set of rules used in defining project risks, which are incorporated into the "Unsatisfied client" risk (see Maintenance level in Figure 2). The model can be used to calculate the value of any risk on the risk map using numerical values for its factors. The model's objective is to determine the project's attractiveness.

Normally, fuzzy models are used in decision-making and they offer two types of answers: the risk can be either accepted or rejected (Hussain, Chang, Hussain, & Dillon, 2006). The proposed model offers only a quantitative value of risk. The decision of accepting or rejecting the risk is taken by the human agent: project manager, risk manager, or any other stakeholder. In conclusion, the output of the developed model is not a form of decision, but an important factor in making a proper decision. The model's components are described next, using fuzzy formalization (Leon, 2008).

Table 1. Fragment of a risk register in IT projects

Risk Code	Risk Name	Risk Description	Risk Type
RSK01	Unfavorable legislation	The legislation does not offer premises to develop such an IT project.	Environment
RSK02	Misunderstood overall vision	Managers do not have enough technical and marketing training.	Management
RSK03	Lack of management experience	Staff members do not gain funding, do not negotiate good prices or work conditions, do not provide training.	Management
RSK04	Unrealistic duration estimation	Deadlines are too optimistic: managers have no experience.	Management
RSK05	Unclear objectives	Developers do not understand the project's objectives. Developers do not know the target group of users.	Management
RSK06	Unrealistic budget estimates	Persons responsible for the estimates have no experience; managers are so determined to win the project that they disregard its real cost.	Financial
RSK07	Poor planning	Planning is not accurate, management is not acting professionally.	Management
RSK08	Poor architecture design	There are no technical specialists in the project team.	Production & Technology
RSK09	Lack of personnel experience	Team members are inexperienced.	Production & Technology
RSK10	Technological difficulties	Identified technologies are new and numerous.	Production & Technology
RSK11	Poor quality control	Managers are too lenient.	Management
RSK12	Poor performance	Software programmers have insufficiently training.	Production & Technology
RSK13	Poor communication	Social interactions between project team members are strained and project managers do not know how to mediate these conflicts.	Management
RSK14	Poor product testing	The technical architecture is not modularized.	Production & Technology
RSK15	Poor product quality	The software does not respect its initial requirements.	Production & Technology
RSK16	Behind-schedule risk	The project is behind schedule.	Management
RSK17	Over-budget risk	The project is behind schedule and extra budget is needed to complete it.	Financial
RSK18	Unsatisfied client	The software owner or buyer does not receive what he expected.	Production & Technology

Table 2. Input variable description in a risk analysis model

Fuzzy Variable Name	Universe of Discourse	Linguistic Grades
P(Rsk)	[0,100] %	VL(very low), L(low),M(medium), H(high), VH(very high)
I(Rsk)	[0, 50]	VL(very low), L(ow),M(medium), H(high), VH(very high)

Model Variables

The model has input and output variables. Input variables can be: input functions and input constants. Input functions take the form:

P(Rsk) = probabily of Rsk occurence
I(Rsk) = impact of Rsk on software project

    where Rsk = considered risk code

    Input functions are described in Table 2 according to fuzzy logic concepts.

    Input constants take the form:

RskCause1 = cause 1 of Rsk occurence
RskCause2= cause 2 of Rsk occurence

where Rsk = considered risk code

    Input constants are defined roughly in the same manner as input functions. The only difference is that the universe of discourse is specific to each identified cause. The model output variable is the value for an identified risk and is denoted as:

V(Rsk) = quantitative value of Rsk, where Rsk = considered risk code; this computed value can be risk probability, risk impact, or a concrete number.

    The output variable is described in Table 3 and graphically represented in Figure 3. In fact, both input and output variables can be graphically represented by fuzzy sets: the value of fuzzy variables is represented on the Ox axis and the value of μ (function of belonging to a fuzzy set) is represented on Oy axis. The "triangles" are fuzzy sets.

Model Rules

The risk evaluation model consists of a set of predefined rules used to determine risk values in IT projects. These inference rules are defined in Table 4. The "and" connective is used to bind conditions of rules. Besides the linguistic values of model variables (VL, L, M, H and VH), some restrictors are used:

- "somewhat"= $\sqrt[3]{\mu}$
- "very"= μ^2

Figure 2. Risk propagation map for IT projects

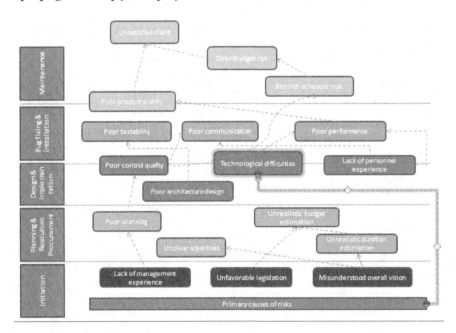

μ is the function showing if a numeric value belongs to a fuzzy set. μ has values between 0 and 1 (a greater value denotes a stronger membership).

Examples of rules are (R1), (R2), (R3):

(R1): *if P(Rsk) is H and I(Rsk) is VH then Rsk is VH*

(R2): *if P(Rsk) is VL and I(Rsk) is VL then Rsk is VL*

(R3): *if P(Rsk) is VH and I(Rsk) is L then Rsk is VH*

The interpretation of rule (R1) is:

If risk Rsk has a high probability of occurence and the impact of this risk is very high, then its value is also very high. (See underlined values in Table 4)

The interpretation of rule (R2) is:

If risk Rsk has a very low probability of occurence and the impact of this risk is very low, then its value is also very low.

The interpretation of rule (R3) is:

If risk Rsk has a very high probability of occurence and the impact of this risk is low, then its value is very high.

APPLYING THE FUZZY MODEL TO EVALUATE RISKS IN AN IT PROJECT FOR E-TESTING

We will validate the fuzzy model for risk evaluation by applying it to an IT project. The project's goal is to create an e-testing adaptive platform suitable for knowledge evaluation in project management. The project's duration is 2 years and the allocated budget is 25,000 EURO. The project is part of a research program that includes the following stages: approach description, assessment of current e-learning systems, evaluation of technical tools used in developing e-learning applications, identification of e-testing role in an e-learning system, identification of e-testing impact on project management knowledge evaluation, development of a project management e-testing module, and software product validation. The software product is complex: artificial intelligence tools

Figure 3. Fuzzy set representation for risk values in IT projects

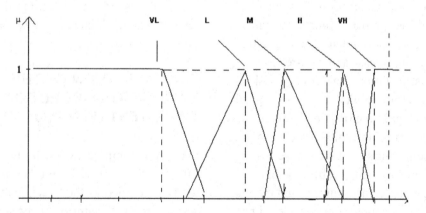

Table 3. Description of output variables in a risk analysis model

Fuzzy Variable Name	Universe of Discourse	Linguistic Grades
V(Rsk)	[0, 10]	VL(very low), L(ow),M(medium), H(high), VH(very high)

Table 4. Inference rules used in technological risk analysis in IT projects

P(Rsk)/ I(Rsk)	VL	L	M	H	VH
VL	VL	somewhat VL	*L*	somewhat M	very H
L	L	L	L	H	VH
M	M	M	M	H	VH
H	H	H	H	very H	VH
VH	*VH*	VH	VH	VH	very VH

Table 5. Technologies used in the E-testing project

No	Technology Name	Technology Description	Market Maturity (years)
1.	WCF	Windows Communication Foundation	3
2.	MsSQL 2008	Microsoft SQL Server 2008	1
3.	Ajax	Asynchronous JavaScript and XML	4
4.	WPF	Windows Presentation Foundation	1
5.	nUnit	Unit-testing framework for C #	4.9
6.	nHibernate	Object Relational Mapping for .NET	2
7.	OWL	Web Ontology Language	3

are needed to obtain adaptive testing or to exploit semantic networks that map project management knowledge. Developing the software product itself is a distinct project with 7 phases: project management, requirements analysis and functional specifications development, estimates, technical portfolio establishment, implementation, testing and documentation, release and post-release.

Since this is an IT project, a major risk in obtaining satisfactory results is "Technological difficulties" (the highlighted risk in Figure 2). The project needs to use the most suitable technologies for developing e-testing systems. Seven technologies are considered, as seen in Table 5. The risk of using them depends on their number and market maturity. These two sources are considered primary sources in the risk map. Technological risk appears in the design and implementation phase and can gain a major importance in the bug fixing phase. Although it does not reflect the overall risk

of the IT project, technological risk is one of the most important risks in any software development activity. This is why we chose it to explain the proposed fuzzy model. Several .Net technologies, database systems, unit testing frameworks or semantic network languages are used.

FORMALIZATION OF THE RISK EVALUATION MODEL FOR THE E-TESTING PROJECT

In order to compute a value for the "Technological difficulties" risk, the number of technologies used is recorded as the "TechNumber" variable and the market maturity of the technologies is recorded as the "TechMaturity" variable. Both variables are defined in Table 6. The inference rules used to determine the effect of changes in

"TechNumber" and "TechMaturity" on the risk value are presented in Table 7.

Membership functions for input variables are illustrated in Figure 4 and 5. Membership functions for the output variable are illustrated in Figure 6.

STEPS IN APPLYING THE RISK EVALUATION MODEL TO THE E-TESTING PROJECT

The fuzzy model transforms the input values to one output value in four steps. To give an example, two numerical values are considered as input values in the risk evaluation model of an e-testing project.

- Insert values for input variables

TechMaturity = 2.7 (the project uses technologies with the average maturity of 2.7 years)
TechNo = 7 (the project uses 7 technologies, as seen in Table 5)

- Classify crisp input values in a suitable fuzzy set so that they gain semantic meaning.

According to Figure 4, the technological maturity can be high and very high. According to Figure 5, the number of technologies can be medium or high.

Establish the membership level of each input value to a fuzzy set; an input value can belong to one or two fuzzy sets, but in a different proportion, named "trust level"; this trust level is the Oy value of the intersection point between input singleton and fuzzy set. (Teodorescu, 2004). The trust level is computed using the following formula:

$$trustLevel_x(A) = b.y + m(x - b.x) \qquad (F1)$$

where a and b are two consecutive points in a fuzzy set, m is the slope of the line determined by these two points, A represents a fuzzy set and x represents an input value.

For TechNo:

Table 6. Fuzzy variables for computing risk in the E-testing project

Fuzzy Variable Name	Variable Type	Universe of Discourse	Linguistic Grades
TechMaturity	input	[0,5] years	VL, L, M, H, VH
TechNumber	input	[0,10] pieces	VL, L, M, H, VH
Technological Difficulties	output	[0,100]%	VL, L, M, H, VH

Table 7. Inference rules for computing "P(Technological Difficulties)" in the E-testing project

Tech Maturity / Tech Number	*VERY LOW*	*LOW*	*MEDIUM*	*HIGH*	*VERY HIGH*
VERY LOW	somewhat M	somewhat M	VL	VL	very VL
LOW	H	H	L	VL	VL
MEDIUM	VH	H	M	*L*	*L*
HIGH	VH	VH	H	*M*	*M*
VERY HIGH	*VH*	VH	VH	*M*	*M*

Figure 4. Membership functions for the "TechMaturity" variable in evaluating E-Testing project risk

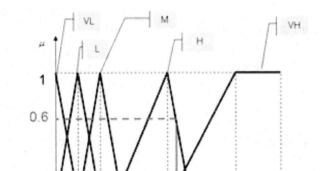

Figure 5. Membership functions for the "TechNumber" variable in evaluating E-Testing project risk

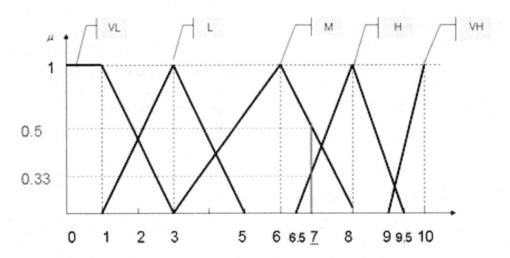

$$trustLevel_7(M) = 0.5$$

$$trustLevel_7(H) = 0.33$$

For TechMaturity:

$$trustLevel_{2.7}(H) = 0.6$$

$$trustLevel_{2.7}(VH) = 0.13$$

The following sentences are considered:

(S1): *"A medium number of technologies are used in the e-testing project."*

(S2): *"A high number of technologies are used in the e-testing project."*

(S3): *"The maturity of the technologies used in the e-testing project is high."*

Figure 6. Membership functions for the "Technological Difficulties" variable in evaluating E-Testing project risk

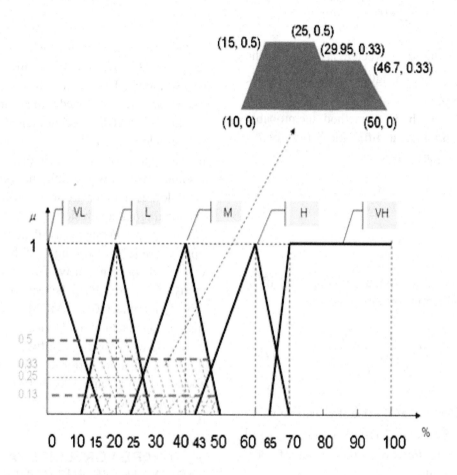

(S4):*"The maturity of the technologies used in the e-testing project is very high."*

According to the trust levels calculated above, (S1) has a 50% truth value, (S2) has 33% truth value, (S3) has a 60% truth value, and (S4) has a 13% truth value.

- Apply inferences rules in 4 stages. The resulting fuzzy sets are cut by a horizontal line. This line is determined by the minimum of the trust levels. Intersections between fuzzy sets and lines are generated: these intersections are usually trapezoidal

in shape. Finally, the reunion of the "cut" fuzzy sets is determined (Figure 6)

- Restrictors (*very*, *somewhat*) are used if necessary.
- Two defuzzification methods are applied to the final fuzzy set. Two similar values for overall risk in the e-testing project should be obtained.

In Centre of Gravity (COG) Defuzzification, the final fuzzy set is decomposed into simple shapes: triangles, rectangles, and trapezoids, as shown in Figure 7. To calculate the probability of risk occurrence, the following formula is used:

$$P(Rsk)_{COG} = \frac{\sum_i center_{fig(i)} area_{fig(i)}}{\sum_i area_{fig(i)}} \qquad (F2)$$

$$P(Rsk)_{MOM} = \frac{0.5 * 15 + 0.5 * 25}{0.5 + 0.5} \Rightarrow P(Rsk)_{MOM} = 20\%$$

where *fig* is the shape vector, $center_{fig(i)}$ is the center of gravity of a figure, and $area_{fig(i)}$ is the area of a figure.

According to the COG method, the probably of the "Technological difficulties" risk for the considered input values is:

$$P(Rsk)_{COG} = \frac{13.33 * 1.25 + 20 * 5 + 28.05 * 2.05 + 38.33 * 5.53 + 47.8 * 0.54}{1.25 + 5 + 2.05 + 5.53 + 0.54} \Rightarrow$$
$$P(Rsk)_{COG} = \frac{16.67 + 100 + 57.7 + 212 + 25.81}{14.37} \Rightarrow$$
$$P(Rsk)_{COG} = 28.68\%$$

In Middle of Maximum (MOM) Defuzzification, the following formula is used:

$$P(Rsk)_{MOM} = \frac{\sum_i locMax_i^x locMax_i^y}{\sum_i locMax_i^y} \qquad (F3)$$

where $locMax_i^y$ is the Oy value of a local maximum (see Figure 8), $locMax_i^x$ is the Ox value of a local maximum and *locMax* is the vector of local maximum points.

According to the MOM method, the probably of the "Technological difficulties" risk for the considered input values is:

The two defuzzification methods reveal similar results (28,68% and 20%). This validates the applied model. The membership function of the output variable is analyzed (see Figure 9) and the conclusion is that the "Technological difficulties" risk has a low probability of occurence for the e-testing project, when the technological maturity is somewhere between high and very high and technologies number are medium-high. This is an encouraging conclusion.

Other experiments can use different values for input variables. According to Table 8, using 9 technologies with maturity of 0.5 years, the probability of occurrence for the technological risk is very high: both COG and MOM indicators show this. For one technology having a high maturity level (it is well-known by software developers), the probability of occurrence of the technological risk is very low: again, both COG and MOM indicators agree.

SOFTWARE FOR RISK EVALUATION BASED ON THE FUZZY MODEL

We used the fuzzy model analyzing technological risk in the e-testing project to develop a risk

Figure 7. COG Defuzzification in the risk evaluation model

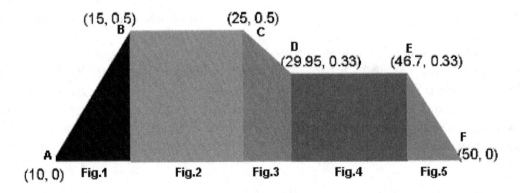

evaluation system. We created a Windows-based application in C#. The interface is intuitive (Figure 9): the end user inserts the number of technologies used and their market maturity and obtains the probability of technological risk occurrence. The system workflow is depicted in Figure 10. Three specific classes (the ones in Figure 11) are used to implement the workflow.

The first class, *FuzzySystem*, contains the inference rules; see the following extract of code:

```
// vectors of trust levels
// vectors elements have values != -1
if and only if x is in the defined
intervals
double[] s = new double[5];double[] t
= new double[5];
// vectors initialization
for (int i=0; i<5; i++){s[i]=-1;}
for (int i=0; i<5; i++){t[i]=-1;}
//inserts x1 (represents technology
maturity)
double x1=x;
// checks if x1 is in the defined
interval
// then,calculates the level of trust
for each of the intervals in which it
is a member
if ((x1<0)||(x1>5))
        Console.WriteLine("Undefined
values: type a value between 0 and
5");
```

Figure 8. MOM Defuzzification in the risk evaluation model

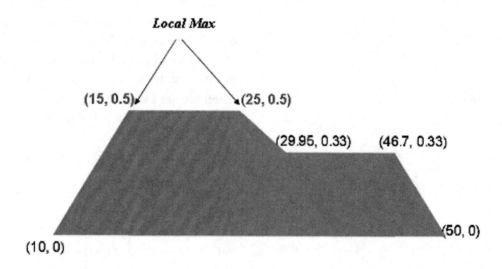

Figure 9. Software product for evaluating technology risk in the E-Testing project

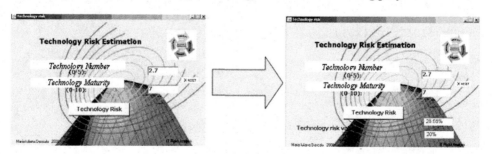

Table 8. Risk model experiments

Tech. maturity	Tech. number	Probability (Tech. Risk): COG	Probability (Tech. Risk): MOM
0.5	9	83.72%	85%
5	1	5%	0%

```
                        else
                        if
(x1<0.5f){
if (x1==0){s[0]=1;}
//It is from: S1 and S2
        s[0]=S1.getLevelOfTrust(x1);
        s[1]=S2.getLevelOfTrust(x1);
        }
else
                if (x1<1){
        if (x1==0.5f){ s[1]=1;}
                        //It is
from: S2 and S3
        s[1]=S2.getLevelOfTrust(x1);
        s[2]=S3.getLevelOfTrust(x1);
}
else
if (x1<1.25){
                        if
(x1==1){s[2]=1;}
        // It is from: S3
        s[2]=S3.
getLevelOfTrust(x1);
}else
        if (x1<1.5f){
        // It is from: S3 and
S4

s[2]=S3.getLevelOfTrust(x1);

s[3]=S4.getLevelOfTrust(x1);
}else
        if (x1<2.5f){
                // It is
from: S4
        s[3]=S4.getLevelOfTrust(x1);
}else           .
```

```
        if (x1<3)
{               if (x1==2.5f){s[3]=1;}
                // It is from: S4 and
S5
        s[3]=S4.getLevelOfTrust(x1);
        s[4]=S5.getLevelOfTrust(x1);
}else
        {if (x1>=4) {s[4]=1;}
                        // It is
from: S5
        s[4]=S5.getLevelOfTrust(x1);
}}
```

The conditional instruction is basically the core of the rule module.

The second class, *FuzzySet*, contains defuzzification methods, union, intersection, restrictor functions; for example, the "somewhat" ($=\sqrt[3]{\mu}$) restrictor is implemented as follows:

```
public FuzzySet somewhatModifier()
{
FuzzySet sol = new FuzzySet();
double nr=0;double
interval,k;FuzzyPoint P1, P2;
for (int i=0; i<fuzzyPoints.Count-1;
i++){
P1 = (FuzzyPoint)fuzzyPoints[i];
P2 = (FuzzyPoint)fuzzyPoints[i+1];
nr = Math.Floor(Math.Abs(P2.y-
P1.y)*10)-1;
interval=(P2.x-P1.x)/(nr+1);
for (double j=P1.x; j<P2.x;
j+=interval){
        k=P2.y+(P2.y-P1.y)*(j-P2.x)/
(P2.x-P1.x);
```

Figure 10. Technological risk evaluation system based on the fuzzy model

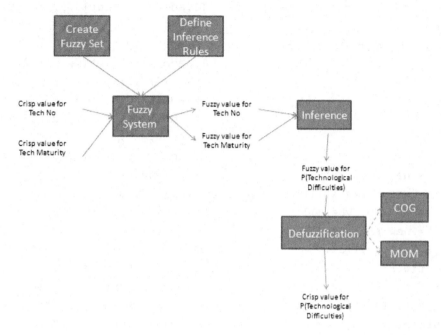

Figure 11. Class diagram for the technology risk evaluation system

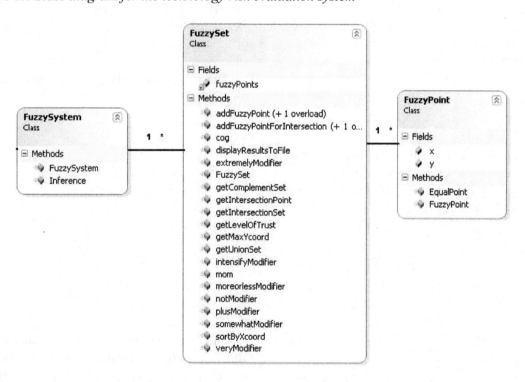

```
        float abcisa=(float)j;
        float ordinate=(float)Math.
Pow(k,0.3);
        sol.addFuzzyPoint(abcisa,ord
inate);}}
        return sol;
}


FuzzySet S1 = new FuzzySet();
FuzzySet S2 = new FuzzySet();
FuzzySet S3 = new FuzzySet();
FuzzySet S4 = new FuzzySet();
FuzzySet S5 = new FuzzySet();
S1.addFuzzyPoint(0, 1);S1.
addFuzzyPoint(0.5f, 0);
S2.addFuzzyPoint(0, 0);S2.
addFuzzyPoint(0.5f, 1);
S2.addFuzzyPoint(1,0);
S3.addFuzzyPoint(0.5f, 0);S3.
addFuzzyPoint(1, 1);
S3.addFuzzyPoint(1.5f,0);
S4.addFuzzyPoint(1.25f, 0);S4.
addFuzzyPoint(2.5f, 1);
S4.addFuzzyPoint(3,0);
S5.addFuzzyPoint(2.5f, 0);S5.
addFuzzyPoint(4, 1);
S5.addFuzzyPoint(5,1);
S1.displayResultsToFile(file, "Tech
Maturity: very low");
S2.displayResultsToFile(file, " Tech
Maturity: low");
S3.displayResultsToFile(file, " Tech
Maturity: medium");
S4.displayResultsToFile(file, " Tech
Maturity: high");
S5.displayResultsToFile(file, " Tech
Maturity: very high");


FuzzySet T1 = new FuzzySet();FuzzySet
T2 = new FuzzySet();
FuzzySet T3 = new FuzzySet();FuzzySet
T4 = new FuzzySet();
```

```
FuzzySet T5 = new FuzzySet();
T1.addFuzzyPoint(0, 1);T1.addFuzzy-
Point(1, 1);
T1.addFuzzyPoint(3, 0);
T2.addFuzzyPoint(1, 0);T2.addFuzzy-
Point(3, 1);
T2.addFuzzyPoint(5, 0);
T3.addFuzzyPoint(3, 0);T3.addFuzzy-
Point(6, 1);
T3.addFuzzyPoint(8, 0);
T4.addFuzzyPoint(6.5f, 0);T4.
addFuzzyPoint(8, 1);
T4.addFuzzyPoint(9.5f, 0);
T5.addFuzzyPoint(9, 0);T5.addFuzzy-
Point(10, 1);
T1.displayResultsToFile(file, "Tech-
nologies Number: very low");
T2.displayResultsToFile(file, "Tech-
nologies Number: low");
T3.displayResultsToFile(file, "Tech-
nologies Number: medium");
T4.displayResultsToFile(file, "Tech-
nologies Number: high");
T5.displayResultsToFile(file, "Tech-
nologies Number: very high");
```

The *FuzzyPoint* class has elements of fuzzy sets:

```
public class FuzzyPoint
{
        public FuzzyPoint(){}
        public float x;
        public float y;
        public bool
EqualPoint(FuzzyPoint p)
                {return x == p.x &&
y == p.y;          }
}
```

The *FuzzySystem* class must be changed to allow other fuzzy systems. A *FuzzySystem* has many *FuzzySets*, and a *FuzzySet* has many *Fuzzy-Points*. To implement the workflow, a number of analytical geometry concepts are applied: line slope, line equation or formula for an intersection point between two lines. All fuzzy set unions or intersections are, in fact, geometric shapes. The software product returns the same results derived from manually calculating the technological risk probability: this proves that the COG and MOM defuzzification models are valid.

Risk analysis can be accomplished manually, but using software speeds up the management process and brings value to project management activities.

CONCLUSION

The proposed model offers an easy-to-use tool for risk evaluation in IT projects. The model relies on fuzzy inference. The knowledge base used by fuzzy rules is built on causal and cognitive maps of risks. The fuzzy model for risk evaluation in IT projects is an innovative instrument which can be used to forecast project failure: stakeholders can save money, time, and effort, without giving up prediction quality. The model was used to develop a software system for evaluating technological risk in an e-testing project, so its applicability is validated. The system can be further extended to evaluate all risks in the proposed IT risks map. Other risks can also be identified.

REFERENCES

Al Neimat, T. (2009). *Why IT projects fail*. Retrieved July 5, 2009 from http://www.projectperfect.com.au/info_it_projects_fail.php

Al-Rousan, T., Sulaiman, S., & Salam Abdul, R. (2008). A risk identification architecture pattern based on bayesian network. *Information Technology, 4*, 1–10.

Al-Shehab, A., Hughes, R. T., & Winstanley, G. (2005). Modelling risks in IS/IT projects through causal and cognitive mapping. *The Electronic Journal of Information Systems Evaluation, 8*, 1–10.

Boehm, B. W. (1991). Software risk management: principles and practices. *IEEE Software, 8*, 32–41. doi:10.1109/52.62930

Carr, M. J., Konda, S. L., Monarch, I., Ulrich, C. F., & Walker, C. F. (1993). *Taxonomy-based risk identification*. Pittsburgh, PA: Software Engineering Institute.

Chen, J.-H., & Chen, S.-M. (2006). *A new method for ranking generalized fuzzy numbers for handling fuzzy risk analysis problems*. Retrieved July 5, 2009 from http://www.atlantispress.com/php/download_paper.php?id=80

Clarke, J. C., & Varma, S. (1999). Strategic risk management: the new competitive edge. *Long Range Planning, 32*(4), 414–424. doi:10.1016/S0024-6301(99)00052-7

Cumming, C., & Hirtle, B. (2001). *The challenges of risk management in diversified financial companies*. Retrieved July 5, 2009 from http://www.capco.com/files/pdf/81/03_FINANCIAL%20CAPITAL/03_The%20challenges%20of%20risk%20management%20in%20diversified%20financial%20companies.pdf

Flyvbjerg, B. (2006). *From Nobel prize to project management: getting risks right*. Retrieved July 5, 2009 from http://flyvbjerg.plan.aau.dk/Publications2006/Nobel-PMJ2006.pdf

Gareis, R. (2006). *Happy projects*. Bucharest, Romania: ASE Press.

Griffiths, M. (2009). *The top five software project risks*. Retrieved July 5, 2009 from http://www.projectsmart.co.uk/top-five-software-project-risks.html

Hillson, D. (2005). *Risk management: important or effective (or both)?* Retrieved July 5, 2009 from http://www.risk-doctor.com/pdf-briefings/risk-doctor12e.pdf

Hodge, B. (2004). *Developing risk management plans.* Retrieved July 5, 2009 from http://www.cs.uwaterloo.ca/~apidduck/CS480/Lectures/RiskMgmt.pdf

Hussain, O. K., Chang, E., Hussain, F. K., & Dillon, T. S. (2006). A fuzzy aproach to risk based decision making. *Lecture Notes in Computer Science, 4278,* 1765–1775. doi:10.1007/11915072_83

Kendric, T. (2003). *Identifying and managing project risk.* New York: AMACOM Div American Mgmt Assn.

Kleiner, Y., Rajani, B., & Sadiq, R. (2006). Failure risk management of buried infrastructure using fuzzy-based techniques. *Journal of Water Supply: Research & Technology - Aqua, 55*(2), 81–94.

Kodama, M. (2007). *Project-based organisation in the knowledge-based society.* London: Imperial College Press.

Leon, F. (2008). *Courses of artificial intelligence.* Retrieved July 5, 2009 from http://eureka.cs.tuiasi.ro/~fleon/curs_ia.htm

Liu, H., & Lu, Y. (2002). From strategic risk measurement to strategic risk management. Retrieved 31 May, 2009 from http://findarticles.com/p/articles/mi_hb6419/is_7_79/ www.chinareview.org/News/manage/image/78105926.doc

McGee Woodward, M. (2005). *Measuring the payoffs of strategic risk management.* Retrieved July 5, 2009 from http://findarticles.com/p/articles/mi_hb6419/is_7_79/ai_n29236259/

Merna, T., & Al-Thani, F. (2008). *Corporater Risk Management.* Hoboken, NJ: John Wiley & Sons.

Miler, J., & Gorski, J. (2004). Risk identification patterns for software projects. *Foundations of Computing and Decision Sciences, 29*(1-2), 115–131.

Nakagawa, T., Tani, S., Yasunobu, C., & Komoda, N. (2005). Business risk management based on a service portofolio approach for an equipment – providing service. In Nardelli, E., & Talamo, M. (Eds.), *Certification and security in inter-organizational e-service* (pp. 85–90). Boston: Springer Boston Press. doi:10.1007/11397427_6

(2003). *Overview of enterprise risk management.* Arlington, VA: Casualty Actuarial Society.

Rosencrance, L. (2007). *Survey: poor communication causes most IT project failures.* Retrieved July 5, 2009 from http://www.computerworld.com/action/article.do?command=viewArticleBasic&articleId=9012758

Teodorescu, H. N., Zbancioc, M., & Voroneanu, O. (2004). *Knowledge based systems. Applications.* Iaşi, Romania: Performantica Press.

Turner, J. R., & Simister, S. J. (2004). *Gower manual for project management.* Bucharest, Romania: Codecs Press.

This work was previously published in International Journal of Information Technology Project Management, Volume 1, Issue 2, edited by John Wang, pp. 79-97, copyright 2010 by IGI Publishing (an imprint of IGI Global).

Section 3
Knowledge Management and Placement of Project Teams

Chapter 6
Knowledge Management in Construction Projects:
A Way Forward in Dealing with Tacit Knowledge

Min An
University of Birmingham, UK

Hesham S. Ahmad
University of Birmingham, UK

ABSTRACT

Knowledge is now becoming the most valuable asset of the construction organisations to gain competitive advantages by improving quality while reducing cost and time of work completion in projects. Knowledge Management (KM) is the most effective way to deal with the intellectual capital of the organisations through facilitating the capturing and sharing of existing knowledge and creating new innovative knowledge. The most useful knowledge in construction projects is tacit knowledge since it includes the people ideas, perceptions and experiences that can be shared and re-used to improve experiences and enhance abilities of employees for problem-solving and decision-making. Many of methods have been adopted to deal with knowledge in the construction organisations, but they are still far from enough, particularly in dealing with tacit knowledge gained from construction projects. This paper presents a methodology for dealing with tacit knowledge efficiently and effectively in construction projects. A case study has been conducted to evaluate the proposed KM method and to test its importance and usefulness in the construction industry.

DOI: 10.4018/978-1-4666-0930-3.ch006

INTRODUCTION

Knowledge management (KM) is now becoming more vital for successful management of construction projects and also as a complement to the business activities of the organisations. With knowledge-based economy increasingly growing, knowledge is becoming an important asset for organisational success among other assets such as capital, materials, machineries, and properties (Kelleher & Levene, 2001; Fong & Wong, 2005). Through successful knowledge capturing, sharing and creation, industrial companies can improve the process of organisational learning to enhance the performance of the organisations and create more possibilities to gain competitive advantages (Li & Gao, 2003; KLICON, 1999; Ahmad & An, 2008).

The current interest in KM has been motivated by the need for continuous changes and improvements to enhance the construction processes (KLICON, 1999). KM has benefited from the remarkable development of computer technology which provides the people with the ability to digitally capture, search and transmit knowledge and electronically contact with other people (Carrillo et al., 2000; Blumentritt & Johnston, 1999). The construction organisations have showed an increased awareness of KM as a necessary prerequisite for improving quality, business performance, efficiency of project delivery, relationships with partners, suppliers and clients and innovations to gain competitive advantages (Egan, 1998; Kamara et al., 2002; Love et al., 2003). KM systems provide end-users with the tools and services necessary to capture, share, re-use, update, and create new experiences and best practices to aid them in processes, such as problem-solving, decision-making and innovation, without having to spend extra time, effort and resources on reinventing solutions that have already been invented elsewhere in the organizations (Ahmad et al., 2007).

In order to encourage the senior management to implement KM in their organisations, many of researches on the relationship between KM and supply chain management have been conducted to demonstrate business benefits and competitive advantages compared to cost of implementation of KM. Davenport et al. (1997) and Robinson et al. (2004) argued that KM has a high positive impact on the performance of the organisations, the speed of learning of new knowledge and technologies and the decision making process in the supply chain. A study conducted by Burgess and Singh (2006) suggested that knowledge, infrastructures and corporate governances can work together to produce the innovations that lead to a desirable improvement of the organisation performance. Carlucci et al. (2004) reviewed the role of KM on the business performance management models, such as the Balance Scorecard (Kaplan & Norton, 1992; Marr & Schiuma, 2001), the Business Excellence Model (EFQM, 1999) and the Performance Prism (Neely et al., 2002), and indicated that KM can be classified into four knowledge asset groups, i.e. knowledge of human resources, management/stakeholder relationships, physical infrastructure and virtual infrastructure. According to Carlucci et al. (2004), this classification will lead to enhancements in competencies, effectiveness and efficiency of organisational processes, business management abilities and business performance, which will finally lead to an increase in value generation for the organisations. The value of intellectual capital can be measured by using methods such as cause-and-effect map that measures contribution of KM initiatives to the strategic objectives of the organisation, evaluation roadmap which is an interactive tool that guides the users to select the most appropriate technique on the basis of a set of structured questions to measure the impact of each KM initiative on the user business performance, cost-benefit checklists that compare costs of each KM initiative to its potential tangible and intangible benefits, and priority matrix that prioritizes KM initiatives of users based on effectiveness and efficiency of performance (Robinson et al., 2004). Verification test is a method that can be applied to determine whether the KM system operates according to the required design and specifications by using questionnaires to collect users' feedback (Lin et al., 2006). Validation test is another method that uses questionnaires to collect users' feedback about the usefulness of the KM systems (Lin et al., 2006). The aim of the previous methods is to evaluate the KM systems by developing measurement rations and benchmarks of the systems (Gupta et al., 2000). Although these methods can help organisations to have better views of the performance and usefulness of their KM systems, there are still no precise ways to evaluate the return on investment in knowledge and the impact of KM on the business performance (Robinson et al., 2004; Carlucci et al., 2004; Chong et al., 2000).

Many of environmental factors such as organisational culture and management support can affect the ability of KM initiatives to deliver desirable results for individuals and organisations (Burgess & Singh, 2006). In order to obtain successful KM systems, the organisations need not only to improve KM processes and technological contents but they also need to enhance the knowledge environment and change the behaviours of employees through practices such as building awareness and cultural acceptability (Davenport et al., 1998). Egbu and Botterill (2002) studied the use of IT-tools for KM in the construction organisations and concluded that IT is more useful for the transmission of explicit knowledge while face-to-face interactions and verbal conversations are more efficient in sharing and transferring tacit knowledge because of the effects from some environmental factors such as the lack of employees awareness of the potential benefits of IT-tools, the lack of a formal strategy to apply the KM system, the short-term nature of projects that cause difficulties with building teams, 'Communities of Practice' and trust among employees, and finally the human nature for preferring familiarity of using the old routines of doing jobs over having to learn new methods of applying and using new technologies. A research carried out by Ahmad and An (2008) suggested that these influential factors can be categorised into a number of groups such as individual factors, organisational factors, technological factors, economical factors, customer factors and regulation factors, which affect the design, implementation and use of KM systems. The study also highlights the importance of management support and the roles of KM teams to maintain and improve the KM systems in the organisations. However, some factors may hinder the process of knowledge coordination and sharing among employees in the different construction projects of the organisation which may cause every project to work as a separated unit. This may cause failure of using knowledge of other projects and learning from past mistakes and experiences (Carrillo et al., 2000). Clear evidences have shown that some individual behaviour (e.g., cultural frictions) can have significant negative effects on the KM process (Davenport & Prusak, 1998). However, by applying procedures such as providing incentives, accepting and rewarding creative errors, providing times and places for learning, meeting and sharing knowledge, and encouraging relationships and trust among employees etc, organisations can reduce the influence of these factors. The environmental factors that may affect the ability of KM methods, tools and activities to deliver desirable outcomes for individuals and organisations are shown in Figure 1 (Davenport & Prusak, 1998; Ahmad & An, 2008).

DATA, INFORMATION, EXPLICIT KNOWLEDGE AND TACIT KNOWLEDGE

Although the terms data, information and knowledge are extremely related, they should not be used interchangeably (Blumentritt & Johnston, 1999; Kakabadse et al., 2001). An useful way to differentiate between these three concepts is by representing them in a hierarchy where knowledge is represented at the top with the most value and

Figure 1. Influence of environmental factors on KM outcomes

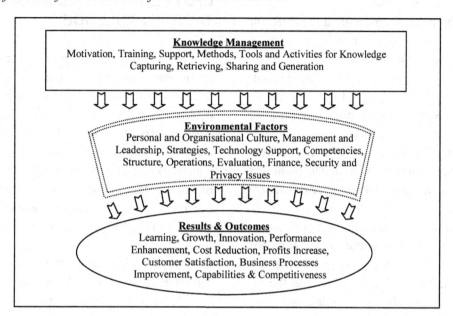

meaning for the end-users, and data is represented at the bottom with the least value and meaning to the end-users but with the most availability and programmability in the organisation (Awad & Ghaziri, 2004; NDR, 2003; Bierly et al., 2000).

Recent literature classifies knowledge into two categories: explicit knowledge and tacit knowledge. This classification helps organisations to identify the types of knowledge with different nature that may need different procedures, tools and methods to be processed and managed (Tserng & Lin, 2004; Lin et al., 2006; Ahmad & An, 2008). Explicit knowledge is the knowledge that can be expressed in formal, systematic languages and shared in the form of scientific formulae, specifications, manuals and such like. Explicit knowledge is easy to be captured, retrieved, shared and used because it can be expressed in words and numbers that can be managed more easily. Tacit knowledge is personal and exists in the individuals' heads and memories in the form of experiences and know-how, which are not easy to be shared and managed (Gore & Gore, 1999; Lin et al., 2006; Nonaka, 2007; Ahmad & An, 2008). However, tacit knowledge has the most valuable type of

contents since it combines information with a person's experiences, skills and understanding, which enables the employees of the organisations to find the best solutions and reduce the possibility of repeating mistakes in their construction activities (Awad & Ghaziri, 2004; Baker et al., 1997; Davenport & Prusak, 1998; Gupta et al., 2000; Tiwana, 1999; Tserng & Lin, 2004). Some of tacit knowledge can be captured, mobilized and turned into explicit knowledge, which would be accessible by others in the organisation to enable the organisation to progress rather than requiring its members to relearn from the same stage all the time (Gore & Gore, 1999). However, a complete tacit explicit split can not be achieved because of the nature of these types of knowledge (Nonaka & Takeuchi, 1995; Inkpen & Dinur, 1998). Therefore, it is useful to understand that the different types of knowledge require different processes, procedures and tools to be managed and dealt with.

Figure 2 illustrates a hierarchy that provides a useful way to understand the differences and relationships among data, information, explicit knowledge and tacit knowledge (Davenport et al., 1998; Probst et al., 2000; Awad & Ghaziri,

2004; Bierly et al., 2000; NDR, 2003). This representation helps to understand the different characteristics and values for different types of contents and how these contents can be transformed from one type to another. Blumentritt and Johnston (1999) suggested that in order to gain competitive advantages, organisations need to enhance the information-knowledge balance through the implementation of IT-based improvements to enhance information management and socially-based mechanisms to enhance knowledge management.

KM systems can be viewed as the development and improvement of information systems that enhance the ability of these systems to manage organisational knowledge, by providing the organisations with the ability to capture, organize, retrieve, analyze, apply, update and share tacit and explicit knowledge (Gupta et al., 2000; Alavi & Leidner, 2001). Data mining tools are important in the KM systems, since they help organisations to transform existing data into more useful shapes of information and knowledge that can be more applicable and available to employees in almost everywhere in the organisation at any time (Gupta et al., 2000).

CHALLENGES OF MANAGING TACIT KNOWLEDGE

As stated earlier in this paper, there are many challenges of the implementation of KM systems in the construction organisations such as the complexity of industry, diversity of work players and adversarial relationships (KLICON, 1999). These challenges become more difficult when dealing with tacit knowledge because individuals normally regard their tacit knowledge as a source of strength and a personal rather than organisational property (Carrillo et al., 2000). The complex nature of tacit knowledge and construction context increase the difficulty for organisations to plan and implement formal KM initiatives. A vast amount of tacit knowledge resides in the heads of individuals who may belong to different specialities, ranging from non-skilled workers to professionals or may belong to different divisions and companies, that cause difficulty for people to collect, share and manage their knowledge within limited time and budget of construction projects (Carrillo et al., 2000).

Studies conducted based on leading construction organisations in the UK showed that the organisations lack the adoption of well formulated

Figure 2. Data, information, explicit knowledge and tacit knowledge

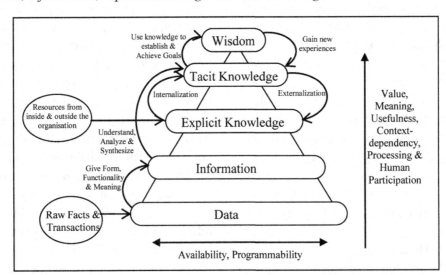

strategies and implementation plans to KM, and a high percentage of them have not appointed a knowledge manager or a team to implement the KM strategy while most of these adopted KM strategies lack the alignment with business strategies of the organisations (Robinson et al., 2004; Robinson et al., 2005). Although construction sector is one of the largest industrial employers in the world, most of this sector consists mainly of small and medium-sized enterprises (SMEs). For example SMEs consist about 96% of the European construction sector and about 99% of the construction sector in the UK (European Commission, 2005; Hari et al., 2005). Most of these SMEs of construction companies may lack the required resources to undertake the additional cost, time and effort of dealing with and managing tacit knowledge. According to empirical studies, small and medium construction companies are less successful in KM implementation than their larger counterparts (Robinson et al., 2004), because they suffer lack of awareness of many important issues associated with knowledge management and its benefits for construction organisations (Hari et al., 2005). Other challenges can come from the fact that managing tacit knowledge may require organisations to apply new management structures and work procedures, which need additional work efforts and time to deal effectively and efficiently with (Carrillo et al., 2000). A survey carried out by Carrillo et al. (2004) indicated that the most significant barrier to KM implementation in the UK construction organisations is the lack of standard work processes such as having too many different procedures to perform similar activities, and the lack of systematic procedures for collecting and reusing lessons learnt and best practices from previous projects. The inflexible hierarchical organisational structures and the existence of too many multi-disciplinary teams in each project can cause more difficulty in managing and using tacit knowledge in the construction organisations (Carrillo et al., 2000). Unrepeated nature of the construction projects is an important challenge to

the management of tacit knowledge. A problem-solution or best practice in a project may confuse other users having similar problems in different projects with different characteristics and contexts. KM systems are designed to help the users to find problem-solutions rather than providing the ultimate solutions for their problems. Fong and Wong (2005) argued that, despite the importance of tacit knowledge in reducing the risk of "reinventing the wheel", it is difficult for people in a project to re-use and re-apply tacit knowledge of other projects. The reason is that it is difficult for employees in a project to understand the context and the reasons for decisions that have been made in other projects simply by using reports or drawings kept after projects' completion.

Although many studies have attempted to select or to develop an appropriate KM strategy for the construction industry, many of the existing KM methods, techniques and tools can only deal with explicit knowledge because the organisations have recognised the importance of documenting explicit knowledge in their projects in the form of drawings, standards, specifications, etc. (Weiser & Morrison, 1998). However, many studies have approved that tacit knowledge is playing the most important role of KM in the organisations, but the role of tacit knowledge and why it seems to be so highly valued and important still needs more research (Burgerss & Singh, 2006). Knowledge generated in construction projects, especially tacit knowledge, can be lost from the company due to many reasons, such as when people with experiences leave the company or when knowledge is saved in unsearchable filing systems (Carrillo et al., 2000). This represents a lost opportunity for the organisation if its competitors succeeded to share and leverage similar knowledge efficiently then they may gain competitive advantages (Zack, 1999).

These challenges and barriers that may affect the successful management of tacit knowledge cause the need for a more coherent and structured approach for utilising tacit knowledge in the construction organisations. Therefore, it is essential to develop a new KM method that can be used as a navigation aid tool to deal with tacit knowledge to satisfy the needs of the industry. This study addresses this problem by developing a methodology that can deal with tacit knowledge more efficiently and effectively. A case study collected from the construction industry was used to demonstrate how the proposed methodology can be used to improve the industry KM performance.

CURRENT METHODOLOGIES OF MANAGING TACIT KNOWLEDGE

Many methods, techniques and tools have been developed, used, reviewed and evaluated in the literature to enhance the management of tacit knowledge and reduce the effect of KM barriers. Examples can include knowledge maps (Lin et al., 2006; Woo et al., 2004), KM models (Abdullah et al., 2002), Activity-Based KM systems (Tserng & Lin, 2004) and Ontology-Based KM systems (Gruber, 1993; KLICON, 1999; El-Diraby & Kashif, 2005). However, these KM techniques need a more structured coherent approach to KM and a better alignment of KM to business goals in the construction organisations.

Nonaka and Takeuchi (1995) suggested that knowledge can be created through continuous interactions between tacit and explicit knowledge to form four modes, Socialization, Externalization, Combination and Internalization (SECI) as shown in Figure 3. It would be a non-stop process to re-create the new knowledge, which everyone in the organisation acts as a knowledge worker. Nonaka (1991) stated that new knowledge always begins with individuals and the individuals' knowledge can be transformed into a valuable organisational knowledge such as when an engineer uses his experience to enhance work processes or provide innovations. The spiral presents the continuous movement between different modes of knowledge creation and the increase of the

spiral radius shows the movement and diffusion of knowledge through organizational levels. *Socialization* is to share or acquire other experiences and tacit knowledge through meetings, direct conversations, observation, practicing and training. For example, an engineer can learn the tacit secrets of solving a problem from an expert or senior engineer in the construction projects (tacit to tacit). *Externalization* is to transform tacit knowledge into explicit knowledge to enable its communication, for example, a senior engineer can translate his tacit knowledge such as experiences, ideas, know-how and perceptions into explicit in the format of reports, specifications, articles, procedures and descriptions that can be easily understood, captured, shared and reapplied (tacit to explicit). *Combination* of various related elements of explicit knowledge to form new explicit knowledge is important in the knowledge creation process because it creates a more useful form of knowledge that is available for other users and contributes to the knowledge base of the organisation. For example, a report can combine explicit knowledge with other related knowledge, which provides more details, analysis and understanding to produce more valuable explicit knowledge available for other employees (explicit to explicit). *Internalization* indicates the process of developing new experiences by learning from, reusing and reapplying the existing explicit knowledge to produce new tacit knowledge that if successfully externalized can help to update and revalidate the existing explicit knowledge. Explicit knowledge that is reapplied by employees can produce new experiences and tacit knowledge (explicit to tacit). These new experiences and tacit knowledge can be shared among individuals through direct contacts (i.e., socialization) to start a new iteration of the continuous spiral.

Li and Gao (2003) studied knowledge creation and its constraints based on the fundamental points of tacit knowledge of Nonaka's SECI model and indicated that the spiral-type model provides an analytical framework for KM activities in business management. However, the study agreed with Polanyi (1996) to further categorise the tacit knowledge into two parts: implicit knowledge and real tacit knowledge. Implicit knowledge is defined as the ability of people to express and articulate knowledge, but they may be unwilling to do so because of specific reasons under certain settings (such as behaviour, culture or organizational style). However, it is of a great value for an organisation to arrange activities to encourage the people to transform implicit knowledge into explicit knowledge through suitable incentive schemes to make this knowledge available and useful for other employees across the organisation (Li & Gao, 2003). According to Planyi (1996), the real tacit knowledge is hard to be communicated among people with different levels of knowledge and it is useless and costly for an organisation to try to organize it for sharing.

McInerney (2002) argued that to effectively manage knowledge and successfully transfer tacit knowledge into explicit accessible formats in any organisation, there should be a clear understanding of the dynamic nature of knowledge. *Explicit knowledge* can be defined as knowledge that has been explained, recorded or documented, while *tacit knowledge* includes the rest of other forms of knowledge that if has not been represented and made explicit, there could be lost opportunities of competitive advantages. However, knowledge can also be a disadvantage to organisations if it is incorrect or misleading, if it is inhibiting or discouraging, or if it is not aligned with or does not satisfy organisation's mission or strategy. Knowledge is considered to be dynamic because it is constantly changing in individuals through experiences and learning, and in organisations through the movement of knowledge to be transferred or shared. Due to the dynamic nature of knowledge, the knowledge stored in the current system repositories need to be ensured that they are updated regularly, as well as keeping knowledge

Figure 3. The SECI model (Nonaka & Takeuchi, 1995)

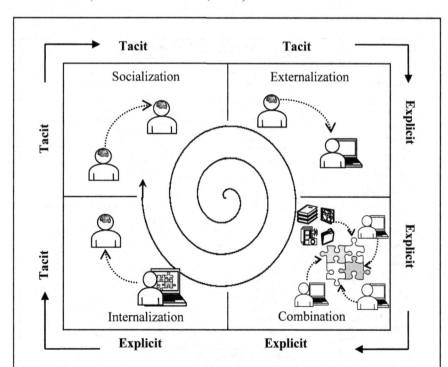

systems flexible enough to deal with continuous updating and changing requirements from all sectors of the organisation. However, instead of investing efforts in the initiatives of extracting knowledge from the employees, it might be more productive for organisations to invest efforts in creating a knowledge culture that encourages employees to learn and share the knowledge, such as establishing small group meeting rooms, conducting on-site seminars, rewarding those who continuously practise learning and who teach others what they know, offering informal "water cooler"-type meeting places throughout the workplace, encouraging trust, dialogue and collaboration among employees, etc. Figure 4 illustrates the interaction of tacit knowledge and explicit knowledge through internal and external processes within and among people in an organisation. The figure provides a graphical representation of a knowledge continuum which shows that a static collection of knowledge is insufficient, but continuous knowledge creation

is essential for knowledge to be used effectively and to keep organisations healthy and innovative.

Although many studies have used the terms of tacit and implicit knowledge synonymously, some other studies have differentiated among three knowledge dimensions, including explicit, implicit and tacit, emphasizing that tacit and implicit knowledge have significant difference and cannot be used interchangeably (Alonderiene et al., 2006; Nickols, 2003; Newman & Conrad, 1999; Bennet & Bennet, 2008). Nickols (2003) introduced a representation that provides a useful way to distinguish among explicit, implicit and tacit knowledge as shown in Figure 5. *Explicit knowledge* consists of knowledge that already has been articulated or codified in the form of text, tables, diagrams, drawings, photos, audios, videos, etc. Therefore, they can be directly and completely captured, re-used or shared, such as documented articles, books, reports, best practices, manuals, specifications and standards (Nickols, 2003; Newman & Conrad, 1999). *Implicit knowledge* is the knowledge that has been

Figure 4. Tacit-explicit knowledge continuum (McInerney, 2002)

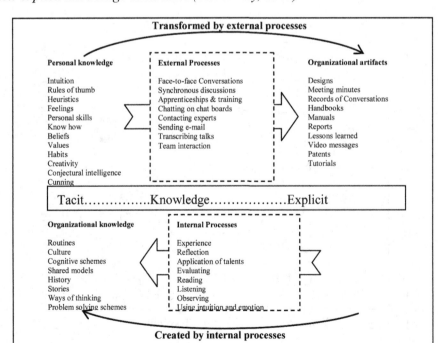

identified that it can be articulated and turned into explicit in the future but has not yet been articulated. This can be caused by some reasons such as if the codification or capturing process has not been completed or even started yet, if the company has not decided to capture this form of knowledge yet or if the company has decided that they do not need to capture this form of knowledge currently. *Tacit knowledge* refers to knowledge that people have, but they cannot articulate, express or transfer to explicit knowledge by using languages, because articulating it will fail to capture its essence (Nickols, 2003; Polanyi, 1997; Alonderiene et al., 2006). Examples include people skills and experiences that cannot be easily described such as how to deal with different people and read the reactions on their faces or the ability and speed to solve problems, provide ideas and innovate.

The research by Bennet and Bennet (2008) discussed the differences and relationships among explicit, implicit and tacit knowledge. *Explicit knowledge* is the knowledge that has been described accurately by words and/or visuals, while *implicit knowledge* is more complicated and not readily accessible. The individuals may not know they have implicit knowledge, but they discover it through questions, dialogues, reflective thoughts, or as a result of an external event. Once this knowledge emerged, the individual can have

the ability to capture it in the form of explicit knowledge or may not have this ability and so the knowledge remains as tacit. *Tacit knowledge* is the knowledge that even if individuals know they have, they still cannot put it into words or visuals that may be useful for others to use and to create new knowledge. Tacit knowledge should be studied in terms of four aspects; embodied, intuitive, affective and spiritual, where each of these aspects represents different tacit knowledge sources with different characteristics as presented in Figure 6 along with explicit and implicit knowledge. *Embodied tacit knowledge* is related to the movement of the body such as knowing a craft or how to use a tool, and the five human senses such as knowing the quality of a material or a finished work from its appearance. This kind of knowledge can be learnt through practicing and behavior skill training, and through time it becomes embedded in memory and retrieved automatically when needed. *Intuitive tacit knowledge* is the knowing that may affect decisions and actions that come from the individuals' sense but the actors cannot explain (unconscious) the reason for taking this action. Intuitive knowledge is developed in the people minds as a result of continuous learning through meaningful experiences that can be built up by practicing making decisions and actions, collecting feedback on these decisions and actions,

Figure 5. Distinguishing among explicit, implicit and tacit knowledge (Nickols, 2003)

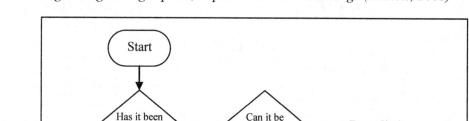

and interpreting the feedback. These practices will help people to develop intuitive skills such as developing the ability to evaluate situations quickly and to predict the consequences of such situations (Klein, 2003). *Affective tacit knowledge* refers to people feelings that may have impact on behaviours, thoughts and responses. Thus affective tacit knowledge is related to other types of knowledge because feelings as a form of knowledge can influence decisions and actions, such as feeling fear or upset that could prevent the decision-maker from taking an action. Finally, *spiritual tacit knowledge* can be described as the animating principles of human life which may affect thoughts and actions such as the moral aspects, the emotional part of human nature and the mental abilities.

To encourage the creation of tacit knowledge and to enhance transferring tacit and implicit knowledge from individuals to the repositories and/or to other individuals, organisations need to use sorts of KM tools, techniques and methods. Building *Communities of Practices (CoPs)* is one of the most widely used techniques to encourage creating and sharing tacit knowledge (Carrillo &

Anumba, 2002; Egbu et al., 2003). An organisation usually have many CoPs where each CoP consists of a group of people (e.g. engineers and experts) who may have different skills, backgrounds and/or experiences, but they share common interests and can collaborate to perform a shared job or task to achieve shared goals (Egbu et al., 2003). A useful way to transfer tacit knowledge among individuals and from individuals into a repository in an organisation is to use some sort of community-based electronic discussions (Davenport et al., 1998). A good practice in projects that may effectively enhance the creation and capturing of tacit knowledge in the form of explicit knowledge is to conduct a *post-project review* at the end of each project (Egbu et al., 2003; Carrillo, 2005). Busby (1999) indicated that the benefit of post-project reviews is that it provides an important learning mechanism that can effectively enhance disseminating tacit knowledge about good practices and problem-solutions, and can also help correcting errors of individuals' knowledge. An effective way to encourage the management of tacit knowledge is to embed KM activities into the work activities of the employees

Figure 6. Continuum of awareness of knowledge sources/contents (Bennet & Bennet, 2008)

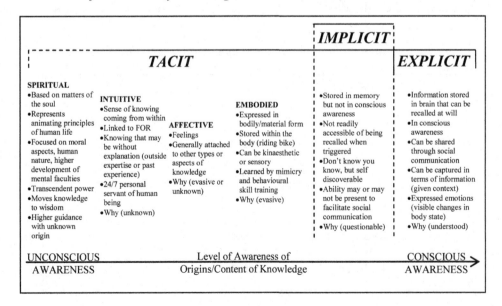

in the construction organisations by making these activities operate as an integral part of individuals' work (Carrillo et al., 2000; Ahmad et al., 2008). For a successful implementation of this method the organisations may need to apply changes to the routine work processes combined with changes of organisational culture and commitment at all organisational levels (Gupta et al., 2000; Ahmad et al., 2008). In this case, dedicated tools and initiatives need to be established to encourage cultural change and enhance knowledge sharing in the organisations (Carrillo et al., 2000). Encouraging relationships, collaborations and interactions through electronic collaborative tools and/or direct face-to-face interactions are very important practices that can be applied to build trust, enhance effective learning and improve knowledge sharing among employees (Egbu et al., 2003; Davenport & Prusak, 1998). A main driver for implementing such KM initiatives is the need to maintain the tacit knowledge of key employees of an organisation (Robinson et al., 2004; Carrillo, 2005).

The following section presents a proposed simple and practical KM method to deal with, manage and exploit tacit knowledge, and to show how this kind of knowledge can be transferred to other types of knowledge such as explicit knowledge. As stated earlier in this paper, tacit knowledge is hard to be captured, formalised and communicated since it is highly personal and only exists in people's heads. In the proposed KM method, electronic knowledge repositories combined with other knowledge sharing and communication tools have been employed, which allow organisations to create, capture, organize, store, disseminate and share tacit knowledge. While most of the previous methods have concentrated on categorising knowledge into two or three types of knowledge and discussing how each type differs from other types in terms of nature, format and characteristics, the proposed method of this research further categorises knowledge into four types of knowledge that require different management procedures and

translate these categories into a practical, comprehensive and structured methodology that helps users from the construction industry to identify the required knowledge resources, processes, methods and tools for managing each type of knowledge, and to satisfy the specific needs and requirements of projects.

A PROPOSED METHOD FOR MANAGING TACIT KNOWLEDGE

As described earlier in section 4, in order to distinguish the differences in nature and processing procedures for the different types of knowledge in an organisation, a KM framework consisting of five components has been developed as shown in Figure 7. The aim of the development of the KM framework is to facilitate understanding, implementing and applying a proposed method for managing knowledge in the construction organisations. The Method is designed to provide a practical way that can enhance handling tacit knowledge and understanding the dynamic nature of knowledge that may result in transformation of knowledge from one type into another more useful and valuable type of knowledge in the organisation.

The proposed KM framework starts with identifying knowledge resources that are available in the organisation, then deciding processing procedures and activities to handle and manage each type of knowledge resources by applying the IT and Non-IT tools that may be required in support to the KM activities. With regard to dynamic nature of knowledge, processing activities help the organisation to transform knowledge to a more useful and valuable shape of knowledge that should be dealt with as a new knowledge resource that need to be managed and maintained in a continuous basis to update, validate and add more value to the knowledge in the organisation. In this study, a KM approach has been developed to provide a better understanding of the different types of knowledge resources and to show how different KM tools, activities and methods are required to deal with the different types of knowledge in the organisation as shown in Figure 8. The proposed KM method also helps the organisations to deal with and manage the new resultant knowledge in a dynamic and continuous basis to update, re-validate, and add value to the knowledge in the repositories of the KM system.

Identifying Knowledge Resources

Obviously, identification of the available types of knowledge resources is important for a successful implementation of a KM system in an organisation.

Figure 7. A proposed framework for managing knowledge

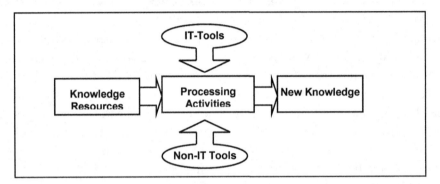

Figure 8. Proposed KM method to simplify tacit knowledge handling

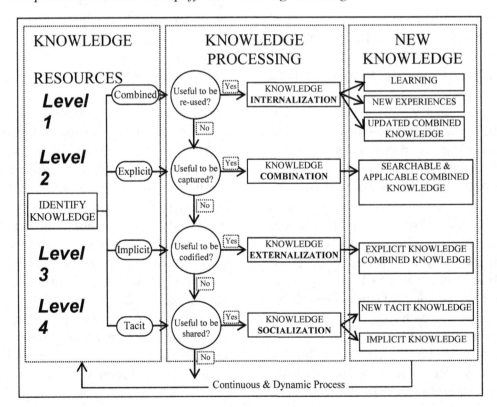

Examples of knowledge resources may include books, organisational documents and individuals' experiences. A useful way to categorize knowledge resources in an organisation is by distinguishing among four levels of knowledge, i.e. combined, explicit, implicit and tacit knowledge as shown in Figure 8. An advantage of this classification is that it differentiates among four types of knowledge with different nature and formats that may require different processing procedures, tools and technologies to be captured, shared and/or re-applied. *Combined knowledge* is the knowledge that can be captured, categorized and adapted in the repositories, which is searchable and available for the end-users of the KM system. This type of knowledge is the product of combining related pieces of knowledge together to produce more valuable and applicable knowledge. *Explicit knowledge* includes the knowledge that can be codified in paper-based and/or electronic-based documents. It can usually be found either inside the enterprise in the form of manuals, specifications, contracts, reports, photos, drawings, and/or organisation's database, or outside the organisation in the form of books, journals, news and regulations. However, this type of knowledge is not usually made available and cannot be easily searched and re-used by end-users of the KM system. But this type of knowledge can be easily transferred from its resources into repositories of a KM system that will make it available and searchable for the end-users of the KM system. *Implicit knowledge* is the part of tacit knowledge that can be easily identified by the organisation and people, which can be transformed and articulated into formats similar to explicit knowledge, for example, experiences, know-how and problem solutions that can be captured into articles, reports, memos and/or other types of electronic or paper-based documents. Although implicit knowledge is more difficult to be stored and formalised and requires more efforts to be managed than explicit knowledge, the implicit knowledge is more valuable and useful for the companies since it includes

people experiences, problem solutions, lessons learnt, best practices and innovations, which may help an organisation to improve its performance of work processes and enhance the quality of its final products. Finally, *tacit knowledge* refers to the rest of knowledge that cannot be captured and turned into explicit knowledge because articulating this type of knowledge may fail to deliver the meaning and the context of influence or because capturing past experiences may oppose privacy, confidentiality and/or security regulations. Additionally, sometimes people may feel that this knowledge is personal that cannot be made available to others across the organisation. Furthermore, organisations cannot capture all the knowledge from their employees since capturing too much knowledge can make the repositories of the KM system overloaded that negatively affects the KM system performance and confuses people, who search for the required knowledge, by having too many choices that makes difficult for them to decide which knowledge is important for making decision of the best problem solution.

Knowledge Processing

At this stage the organisation needs to decide which processing activities are required to process and manage the different types of knowledge for a successful implementation of the KM system. On the basis of the types of the knowledge resources these activities can be categorized into four levels, i.e. knowledge internalisation, knowledge combination, knowledge externalisation and knowledge socialization that need to be dealt with as shown in Figure 8. *Knowledge internalization* includes the activities as described in section 4 that the organisation needs to deal with combined knowledge. The use of technological tools provided by the KM system to retrieve, re-use, evaluate and update the knowledge that previously stored in the repositories are examples of the activities that can be done to process combined knowledge at this processing level. *Knowledge combination* is about managing explicit knowledge by capturing documents, combining related contents, and putting contents into proper formats. This level of knowledge processing may include activities such as digitizing (e.g., Scanning) paper-based documents, reviewing, editing, attaching files, photos and videos, referring to related people, resources and links, categorizing and finally approving knowledge to make it available for the end-users to be searched and re-used. *Knowledge externalization* includes the activities required to capture implicit knowledge and transform it into explicit and combined knowledge. This level of knowledge processing requires people to codify their work experiences, perceptions, know-how and best practices. That may require people of the organisation to prepare reports of problems, solutions, meetings, discussions, innovations and ideas in the projects, and articulate them into explicit formats that can be captured easily in the repositories of the KM system. *Knowledge socialization* includes the processing activities required to deal with tacit knowledge that cannot be captured and stored explicitly in the repositories of the KM system. However, the tacit knowledge may be more useful for the organisation if successfully shared among employees through technological and non-technological tools of the KM system. This would be useful if the combined knowledge is not good enough, outdated or with insufficient details. Thus this method can help the end-users to create new knowledge to edit, combine and add new contents, in other words, more meaning and value, to the previous knowledge base in the repositories of the KM system. Furthermore, the organisation needs to decide which types of explicit knowledge are required and also important for the repositories of the KM system. But, however, capturing too much knowledge in the repositories may waste the organisation's money, time and efforts. Therefore, some shapes of explicit knowledge that may be not useful to the organisation must not be captured or must be removed from the repositories. On the other hand, some knowledge can be made available such as books, manuals and specifications to people from outside the organisation for their use and learning. Finally, through the continuous processes of knowledge identification and processing, new knowledge formats can be identified which require the organisation to apply new methods, tools and activities to capture, share and use them through the KM system.

New Knowledge (Identifying Processing Resultants)

The organisation needs to identify new knowledge produced from the processing of previous knowledge and monitor the usefulness and importance of the new produced knowledge. This will help the organisation to re-validate and add value to the previous contents in the repositories of the KM system.

Knowledge internalization activities aim to help people in re-using combined knowledge to produce new knowledge with more value to the organisation and others. Knowledge internalization can help the end-users to learn new methods, procedures and experiences gained by others by using knowledge searching and retrieval tools. For example, KM systems can help junior engineers to learn faster rather than the need to spend extra time and efforts to learn through the long duration of projects' life cycle. Moreover, re-using combined knowledge of past experiences and best practices can shorten problem-solving and decision-making processes, and enables the end-users to make better decisions while generating new experiences. The new generated experiences and methods can be used to modify, update and re-validate the previous, old contents in the repositories of the KM system. *Knowledge combination* includes activities such as capturing, digitizing, reviewing, combining, categorizing and approving knowledge from inside and outside the organisation, which can help the organisation to transform explicit knowledge into more valuable, searchable and applicable new combined knowledge. Implicit knowledge can be processed through *knowledge externalization* activities to produce new explicit knowledge that can be easily captured, reviewed, categorized, approved and stored in the repositories to make it available for the end-users of the KM system. *Knowledge socialization* tools and activities help people to share tacit knowledge to learn and produce new experiences and knowledge. The end-users can find solutions of problems associated with a project by using tools provided by the KM system such as e-mail, e-discussion etc to search and contact people with the required experiences related to the problems, rather than searching for solutions in the KM system repositories. People interactions and discussions may help to find better solutions adaptable to the special characteristics and contexts of a project than the solutions provided in the repositories of the KM system.

As described in section 4, the organisation can benefit from the dynamic nature of knowledge by planning a continuous process for re-identifying and re-processing the produced new knowledge as shown in Figure 8. This continuous process helps the organisation to update, re-validate and enhance the existing knowledge for use, which also ensures continuous processes of knowledge creation to provide competitive advantages for the organisation. This process is important to check the validity of contents and to remove outdated, incorrect and misleading knowledge from the repositories of the KM system. Identifying the types and importance of the produced new knowledge provides feedback that helps the organisation to recognize the necessary improvements required for KM methods, tools, and activities to successfully manage the new knowledge.

IT-Tools

Information and communication technology plays an increasingly important role in KM systems of the organisations. As described earlier in this paper, the IT tools need to be defined on the basis of four levels of knowledge processing activities, i.e. combined knowledge, explicit knowledge, implicit knowledge and tacit knowledge, in order to provide a better service to the end-users. Developments in information technology have transformed the abilities of the KM systems in the organisations. Figure 9 illustrates some useful IT technologies. For example, at Level 1, combined knowledge can be captured and organised by applying knowledge maps. Knowledge mapping is a technique often adopted by multi-organisations and project-oriented organisations to understand where knowledge resides in their organisations and the nature of its transfer between those who hold it. When applied in this context, knowledge mapping provides the basis for understanding the requirements of individuals and the organisation in order that appropriate mechanisms can be developed reflective of their contextual nature. It is not difficult to understand other techniques described in Figure 9 at Levels 2 and 3. However, it should be noted that tacit knowledge at Level 4 is highly personal and hard to encode. Individuals are the primary repositories of tacit knowledge that, due to its transparent characteristics, is difficult to communicate because such tacit knowledge depends on the experiences of individuals that developed with time in the form of 'know-how' that also depends on mental models, perspectives and beliefs therefore cannot easily be articulated. Therefore, tacit knowledge contains many shapes of knowledge such as descriptions of problems and solutions, experience notes and procedures, ideas, viewpoints and innovations. However, tacit knowledge is difficult to be captured simply by normal tables, but if it is implicit knowledge then it can be captured and stored in forms similar to articles including those attached descriptions, pictures and videos that provide more details and clarifications to the knowledge contents (Ahmad & An, 2008). An effective method to share the real tacit knowledge is through direct and indirect contacts, for example, by using e-messaging,

Figure 9. Technological and non-technological tools that enhance and support KM initiatives and activities

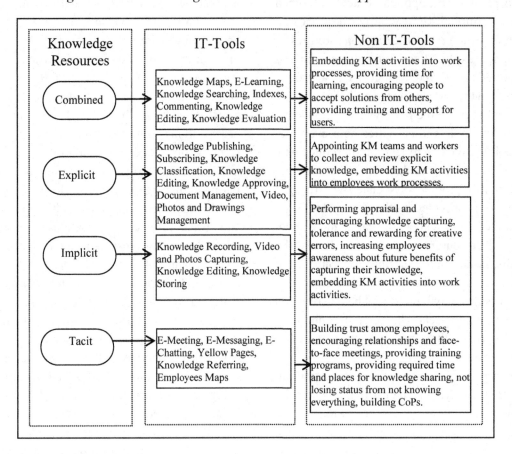

e-chatting and e-meeting. Employee maps and yellow pages provide the people an opportunity to approach the individual experts who have the required knowledge and experiences by providing searchable details about the employees' backgrounds and experiences. However, for a successful implementation and application of IT-tools, the organisation needs to plan and install a compatible hardware and software infrastructure with the specifications required to support the implemented technological tools.

Non-IT Tools

A set of methods and activities need to be developed and established in the organisation in order to enhance the implementation and application and assess the overall performance of the KM system efficiently and effectively. There are many non-IT tools that can be used for successful implementation of the KM system as illustrated in Figure 9. These non-IT tools need to be developed on the basis of processing the four types of knowledge. At the different levels of knowledge processing, an effective application of these non-IT tools is important for capturing and sharing knowledge among individuals. For example, it is important for the organisation to establish the management support, the alignment mechanisms within the organisational strategy and objectives, and the arrangements of cost and time issues to satisfy the needs of customers and deliver the required results. Therefore, the developments of strategies for the implementation and application of KM should set out clear goals, provide plans for activities to be undertaken and determine timeframe and resources required for these activities (Cannon, 1968; Carrillo et al., 2000).

A reward system that may include financial, recognitional and/or developmental incentives to the employees can be very essential to motivate knowledge capturing, sharing and creation in an organisation (Walker, 2001). Examples of recognitional incentives may include providing awards in an organized gatherings to the people who have the most contribution to the KM system and/or presenting their work in an internal newspaper. However, it is recommended to implement organisational and peer-recognition based mechanisms that can be applied through the KM system tools and services, for example, by presenting people's contributions and achievements in the news pages, showing management appreciation for people through the system pages and messages, providing a service were users can publish their own profiles that may include backgrounds, experiences, achievements and published works of the employee, and/or by applying a rating system that enables a user to evaluate the usefulness and importance of a published work or a contribution of an expert in an electronic community system, which will finally provide an indication of the people's contribution to the KM system in terms of frequency of using their work and percentage of positive feedbacks. Finally, methods for evaluating and monitoring the KM system also need to be applied to evaluate the success of the implementation and application processes of the KM system and the effect of the KM system on the organisational performance. It is important to emphasise that the application of a small scale implementation (Prototype) before wide implementation of the KM system tools will help the organisation to collect feedback from the end-users so that the problems and errors of the implemented tools can be found and modifications can be made without wasting money, time and efforts due to large scale implementations.

CASE STUDY

A case study has been carried out to evaluate the proposed KM approach in the UK construction industry. The case study approach aims at providing an example of how the proposed KM model can be used for a successful implementation and application of KM systems and how it can be used to improve the existing ones. It shows how applying the proposed KM model helps to enhance dealing with and managing tacit knowledge in the construction organisation. Evaluation of the proposed KM approach has been conducted by using questionnaire survey to evaluate the usefulness and usability of the proposed KM method. The questionnaires have also been used to evaluate the importance of the different types of knowledge and the importance of the tools required to deal with the different types of knowledge. This shows the importance of classifying knowledge according to the proposed method especially for dealing with tacit knowledge, which was proven by the questionnaire that it is the most valuable type of knowledge to the organisation. In this case, a construction company with more than 7000 employees and many years of experience involving highly sophisticated construction projects was selected as a test site to introduce the proposed KM approach. The company is interested in improving their existing KM system to maintain knowledge and experiences of their senior employees in order to enhance the competitive advantages. Before the proposed KM approach was introduced, an analysis and evaluation were carried out on the feedbacks from end-users of the existing KM system. However, the results showed that there would be a need to improve the existing system by enhancing the way of managing different knowledge resources.

The organisation has adopted a stage-based methodology to implement and enhance the KM system that has been applied in the organisation since the year 2000. Analysis, design, implementation and evaluation of KM system are a cyclic process as shown in Figure 10, where the first iteration related to the implementation of a prototype of a small scale implementation of the KM system or any part of it. The feedback from the evaluation of the prototype provides valuable information and knowledge to modify the design of the system and re-start a wide range implementation of the KM system. Feedback from the implemented KM system provides knowledge for continuous implementation of new KM parts, tools, enhancements and maintenance of the existing system. Data, information and knowledge of 32 previous projects finished before the application of the KM system have been collected and stored to enrich the content of the implemented KM system. The organisation has implemented and applied the KM system according to a procedural process that provides more details to the methodology as shown in Figure 11.

In order to improve the existing KM system performance, a set of technological and non-technological tools, activities and procedures has been planned, implemented and applied as described in section 5. For example, a KM strategy has been established and KM activities, tools and procedures have been chosen to encourage the employees getting involvement with the KM activities across the organisation. Roles of a KM team have been set up to capture, store, categorise, approve, and create new knowledge from the projects. Furthermore, KM activities have been embedded into the routine activities of work processes of the employees. The proposed methods as shown in Figures 7, 8 and 9 have been used to provide the employees with an understanding of the dynamic nature of knowledge in order to keep the KM system and the knowledge contents updated and validated. The proposed method provides guidelines to the organisation to develop and establish detailed plans that introduce and describe the required activities, procedures and tools to manage the different types of knowledge. One of the tasks of the KM team is to assign one or more knowledge workers for each project to capture, digitize, store and categorise any piece of explicit knowledge in a project such as reports, manuals, specifications, correspondences, drawings, email messages, etc. Then the KM team reviews and approves the captured contents and provides levels of authorities that determine the

Figure 10. The cyclic process of analysis, design, implementation and evaluation of KM systems (Ahmad & An, 2008)

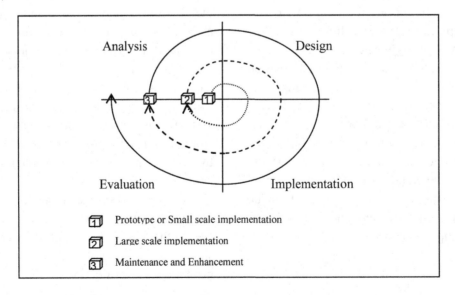

Figure 11. The procedural process of the KM implementation and application

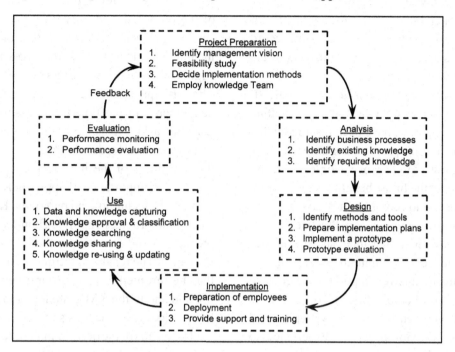

availability of contents for the different end-users. Other responsibilities of the KM team include conducting training programmes, ensuring and encouraging management support, enhancing the awareness of employees about the importance and benefits of the use of the KM system and encouraging the participation of the employees. Conducting training programmes and providing technical and management support to the employees can reduce the time and effort required by employees to learn the new work procedures and methods of applying the KM system.

The organisation has adopted the proposed KM methods, tools and procedures as described earlier in this paper in managing and dealing with the different types of knowledge. For instance, to improve processing *explicit knowledge*, the organisation has further developed its document management system to manage and deal with the different existing formats of documents, drawings and images including paper-based and computer-based documents such as standards, specifications, books, articles and news. To encourage employ-

ees to re-use knowledge from the KM system repositories (*Combined knowledge*), searching tools have been enhanced with more characteristics to refine the results and simplify finding the required knowledge. The knowledge maps have been applied in the KM system to provide a clear idea about the available and missing knowledge in the system repositories and to introduce effective knowledge retrieval and searching tool. In order to encourage people to save their experiences in the KM system repositories (*Implicit knowledge*), training programmes have been conducted to increase the employees' awareness about future benefits of capturing such knowledge. New items that appreciate and award participation and adding to the KM system repositories have been adopted in the performance appraisal system of the organisation. In addition, recording meetings, reporting problems and solutions, and describing procedures, best practices and changing orders during the different stages of projects have also been introduced and embedded in the work processes of the employees. Another practice that has been adopted to encourage the employees to capture projects' implicit knowledge is the application of post projects reviews to review, discuss and record best practices and lessons learnt throughout the life cycle of the projects.

To improve processing *tacit knowledge*, knowledge sharing tools, such as e-messaging, e-chatting and e-discussion tools, have been installed in the organisation. Training programmes have been provided to employees to improve their learning and awareness about the future benefits of these tools. Electronic discussion communities have been encouraged to form Communities of Practices (CoPs) where people with similar interests, specialities and/or experiences can communicate and interact to discuss ideas, answer inquiries and resolve problems. Maps of employees and Yellow pages have been developed to simplify searching and contacting people with appropriate experiences to provide required knowledge for problem-solving and decision-making. Furthermore, user-friendly interfaces of the KM system have been developed to provide the employees with a useful platform of knowledge searching and to deliver a comprehensive idea about the services available in the system. Help-disk services also provide supports to the end-users of the KM system.

In order to evaluate the effect and usefulness of the proposed KM approach, a questionnaire survey has been conducted within the company including members of the knowledge team, knowledge workers and active users of the KM system. The participants include 43 people from different departments and positions in the organisation - representing a 24% response rate. The questionnaire aims to collect feedback from end-users about the usefulness of the improvements to the KM system, the importance of applying KM services through the technological part of the KM system, and the importance of applying non-technological procedures and activities to the KM system performance. The results of the questionnaires show that the new method can encourage employees to use and add to the KM system and to share their knowledge with others as shown in Figure 12.

The results of the questionnaire show that 82% of the end-users believe that the new KM method help employees to use the KM system more efficiently and effectively. The other 18% are not sure if the new approach is useful or think that applying the new method is not useful to improve the performance of the KM system. The main reason described by many respondents is that applying and implementing new KM tools, pro-

Figure 12. Evaluation of the usefulness and importance of the KM method

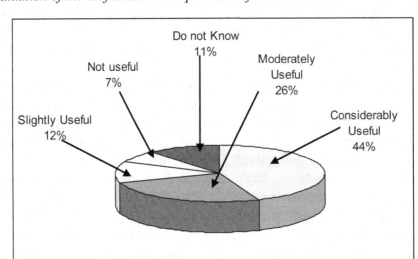

cedures and activities require the organisation to restructure the daily work processes and the employees' roles. This may require the organisation to spend more effort and time to help the employees to learn the new methods and procedures of the improved system. To avoid this problem the organisation should provide training programmes and support to increase the employees' awareness about the future advantages of the application of the KM system and to reduce the time and effort required for employees to learn the new procedures.

The questionnaires also include questions to evaluate the importance of a set of technological tools and non-technological activities categorized according to the four types of knowledge resources as shown in Figure 13. The questionnaires use five levels of rating scales, where 1 stands for less important and 5 stands for most important. The results of the questionnaires have shown that the end-users believe that both technological tools and non-technological activities are important and can work together for a successful implementation and application of the KM system. The results show the highest importance of the technological and non-technological tools in the cases of sharing tacit knowledge and re-using combined knowledge. But in the cases of capturing implicit knowledge and explicit knowledge, the evaluations from the end-users have shown that the

non-technological activities are more important when capturing implicit knowledge, while the technological tools are more important when capturing explicit knowledge. This result shows that more efforts on applying non-technological activities and procedures, such as providing training programmes, support, and awareness etc, are needed to enhance the use of the KM system and encourage the employees to add to the system repositories from their own implicit knowledge.

A set of motivations that may encourage the organisation and employees to apply and use KM systems has also been evaluated in the questionnaires as shown in Figure 14. The motivations have been categorised according to the four types of knowledge resources. Every two motivations have been combined to test the motivations for applying tools and approaches for each type of knowledge, where 1 stands for less important and 10 stands for most important. The results show that the most important motivation to the employees for applying KM tools, methods and approaches is to share and transfer tacit knowledge among employees. The second in importance is the motivation to have the abilities to search and use the combined knowledge in the KM system to learn, innovate and find problem-solutions and best-practice. The lower importance rate for the motivations of capturing implicit knowledge of employees provides an indication that some

Figure 13. Evaluation of the importance of technological tools and non-technological methods

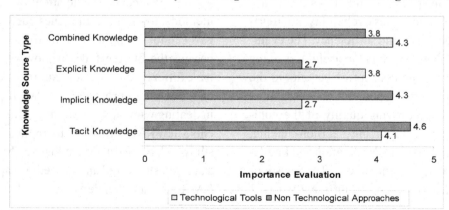

Figure 14.Evaluation of the motivations

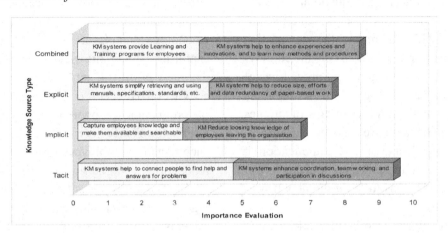

people are unwilling to make their knowledge available to others in the system repositories because they still think that implicit knowledge is personal. The organisation needs to apply more incentives and spend more efforts and time to enhance the awareness of employees about the importance and the future benefits of capturing their own knowledge and making them searchable and applicable for other end-users.

As research work proceeds, another questionnaire survey has been carried out in order to obtain the feedback from end-users regarding the effect of the proposed KM method on the performance by using the KM system. The results from a selected group of end-users show that there is usability and usefulness of the enhancement of the KM system after integrated the proposed KM method. The survey of usability of the system includes system specification issues such as ease of use, comprehensiveness, reliability, appropriateness, applicability and sufficiency. The evaluation of the enhancement in the usefulness of the system covers an assessment of benefits to the end-users, for example, reducing mistakes, time and cost while improving quality of the completed works, and improving decision-making, training, team working, coordination and knowledge maintenance of employees. The questionnaires used five levels of rating scale where 1

stands for strongly disagree and 5 stands for strongly agree. The participant users include four senior engineers with a 15-year experience, two senior engineers with 10-year experience, two project managers with 5-year experience, two junior engineers and two knowledge workers. The weighted average score is 4.63 of usability and 4.58 of usefulness of the KM system, which indicate that the users favourably agree that the proposed KM method has made the existing KM system more feasible and applicable. The results of the evaluation of the KM method are illustrated in Table 1.

CONCLUSION

Although management of construction knowledge has received considerable attention recently, the methods, tools and approaches currently used in KM cannot be applied efficiently and effectively because the different types of knowledge resources have different natures and require different methods, tools and approaches to deal with, particularly in dealing with tacit knowledge. This paper presents a new KM method and its application to a case study in the construction industry, which provides a simple, structured and procedural approach for KM to enhance understanding of the different

Table 1. Results of the evaluation of the KM method

No	Questions	Average Score
System Usability:		
1	Ease of use	4.75
2	Comprehensiveness	4.67
3	Reliability	4.42
4	Appropriateness	4.58
5	Applicability	4.75
6	Sufficiency	4.50
	Weighted average:	4.63
System Usefulness:		
1	Mistakes reduction	4.67
2	Time reduction	4.42
3	Cost reduction	4.50
4	Quality improvement	4.67
5	Decision making improvement	4.75
6	Training	4.42
7	Collaboration	4.58
8	Innovation	4.50
9	Maintaining knowledge of employees	4.67
	Weighted average:	4.58

types of knowledge resources. The proposed KM method adopts different tools and approaches to deal with the different types of knowledge and emphasises the importance of applying non-technological approaches and activities for the successful implementation and application of KM systems. The proposed KM method provides better understanding, dealing with and benefiting from the dynamic nature of knowledge, which helps the organisations to update and validate the knowledge in the repositories of the KM system. The proposed method also provides an approach to review, test and overcome the shortcomings, and enhance the performance of the existing KM systems used in the construction organisations.

The results from the questionnaires conducted in the case study show that the proposed new method has improved the existing KM system, which helps the employees of the organisation to use the KM system more efficiently and effectively. The results also show that applying non-technological approaches and activities are extremely important when dealing with implicit and tacit knowledge.

Tacit and implicit knowledge require more efforts of the organisation to manage than explicit knowledge. But, however, tacit and implicit knowledge provide more value and benefits to the organisation. Therefore, the application of both technological services and non-technological activities and approaches through the KM system to deal with such two types of knowledge is important. An effective way is to apply a set of non-technological activities and approaches to encourage employees to share, capture and create such knowledge and also requires the organisation to provide time and places for employees to learn the new procedures and methods of using the KM system. Furthermore, the organisation may need to enhance the culture that encourage employees to spend time to perform high quality works rather than performing high quantity works with low quality that may cause additional costs and efforts of repeating works and fixing errors in the future.

The proposed KM method motivates a continuous procedure of processing different types of knowledge to produce more valuable shapes of knowledge and erase outdated knowledge, by either deleting them or saving them in other archives, because the existence of outdated knowledge in the repositories of the KM system can be a disadvantage that negatively affects the performance of the end-users. The continuity of such procedures is essential for a successful implementation and application of the KM system.

The research has shown that the most important motivations for applying and improving a KM system are to share and transfer tacit knowledge. Tacit knowledge is complex and hard to be formalised and managed. However, the proposed approach provides the practitioner with a comprehensive technical and social understanding of the nature of tacit knowledge, and identifies areas for improvements, which helps in determining what and how changes can be applied to achieve the desired goals of the organisation. The research also shows that the non-technological tools play important roles in the management of tacit knowledge and the generation of innovation. Effective knowledge management requires a management strategy that allows organisations' management to identify technological and non-technological aspects to manage their intellectual capital in an integrated manner. This study represented an integrated framework that provides a platform to manage different types of knowledge resources in construction organisations and for future multidisciplinary research.

REFERENCES

Abdullah, M. S., Benest, I., Evans, A., & Kimble, C. (2002). Knowledge modelling techniques for developing knowledge management systems. In *Proceedings of the 3rd European Conference on Knowledge Management* (pp.15-25). Dublin, Ireland.

Ahmad, H. S., & An, M. (2008). Knowledge management implementation in construction projects: A KM model for knowledge creation, collection and updating (KCCU). *International Journal of Project Organisation and Management, 1*(2), 133–166. doi:10.1504/IJPOM.2008.022189

Ahmad, H. S., An, M., & Gaterell, M. (2007). Development of KM model to simplify knowledge management implementation in construction projects. In *Proceedings of the 23rd Annual ARCOM Conference, Association of Researchers in Construction Management* (pp.515-516). Belfast, UK.

Ahmad, H. S., An, M., & Gaterell, M. (2008). KM model to embed knowledge management activities into work activities in construction organisations. In *Proceedings of the 24th Annual ARCOM Conference, Association of Researchers in Construction Management* (pp.417-422). Cardiff, UK.

Alavi, M., & Leidner, D. E. (2001). Knowledge management and knowledge management systems: Conceptual foundations and research issues. *Management Information Systems Quarterly, 25*(1), 107–136. doi:10.2307/3250961

Alonderien, R., Pundzien, A., & Krisciunas, K. (2006). Tacit knowledge acquisition and transfer in the process of informal learning. *Problems and Perspectives in Management, 4*(3), 134–145.

Awad, E. M., & Ghaziri, H. M. (2004). *Knowledge management*. Upper Saddle River, NJ: Prentice Hall.

Baker, M., Barker, M., Thorne, J., & Dutnell, M. (1997). Leveraging human capital. *Journal of Knowledge Management, 1*(1), 63–74. doi:10.1108/EUM0000000004581

Bennet, D., & Bennet, A. (2008). Engaging tacit knowledge in support of organizational learning. *Journal of Information and Knowledge Management Systems, 38*(1), 72–94.

Bierly, P., Kessler, E., & Christensen, E. (2000). Organizational learning, knowledge and wisdom. *Journal of Organizational Change Management, 13*(6), 595–618. doi:10.1108/09534810010378605

Blumentritt, R., & Johnston, R. (1999). Towards a strategy for knowledge management. *Technology Analysis and Strategic Management, 11*(3), 287–300. doi:10.1080/095373299107366

Burgess, K., & Singh, P. (2006). A proposed integrated framework for analysing supply chains. *Supply Chain Management: An International Journal, 11*(4), 337–344. doi:10.1108/13598540610671789

Busby, J. S. (1999). An assessment of post-project reviews. *Journal of Project Management, 30*(3), 23–29.

Cannon, J. T. (1968). *Business strategy policy.* New York: Harcourt, Brace and World.

Carlucci, D., Marr, B., & Schiuma, G. (2004). The knowledge value chain: how intellectual capital impacts on business performance. *International Journal of Technology Management, 27*(6/7), 575–590. doi:10.1504/IJTM.2004.004903

Carrillo, P. M. (2005). Lessons learned practices in the engineering, procurement and construction secto. *Engineering, Construction, and Architectural Management, 12*(3), 236–250. doi:10.1108/09699980510600107

Carrillo, P. M., & Anumba, C. J. (2002). Knowledge management in the AEC sector: an exploration of the mergers and acquisition context. *Knowledge and Process Management, 9*(1), 149–161. doi:10.1002/kpm.146

Carrillo, P. M., Anumba, C. J., & Kamara, J. M. (2000). Knowledge management strategy for construction: Key IT and contextual issues. *Construction Informatics Digital Library.* Retrieved from http://itc.scix.net/paper w78-2000-155.content

Carrillo, P. M., Robinson, H., Al-Ghassani, A., & Anumba, C. (2004). Knowledge management in the UK construction: Strategies, resources and barriers. *Journal of Project Management, 35*(1), 46–56.

Chong, C. W., Holden, T., Wilhelmij, P., & Schimdt, R. A. (2000). Where does knowledge management add value? *Journal of Intellectual Capital, 1*(4), 366–380. doi:10.1108/14691930010359261

Davenport, T. H., De Long, D. W., & Beers, M. C. (1997). *Building successful knowledge management projects* (Working paper, Centre for Business Innovation, Ernst & Young).

Davenport, T. H., De Long, D. W., & Beers, M. C. (1998). Successful knowledge management projects. *Sloan Management Review, 39*(2), 43–57.

Davenport, T. H., & Prusak, L. (1998). *Working knowledge: How organizations manage what they know.* Boston: Harvard Business School Press.

EFQM. (1999). *Introducing excellence.* Brussels, Belgium: European Foundation for Quality Management.

Egan, J. (1998). *Rethinking construction: Report of the construction task force on the scope for improving the quality and efficiency of the UK construction industry.* London: Department of the Environment, Transport and the Regions.

Egbu, C., & Botterill, K. (2002). Information technologies for knowledge management: Their usage and effectiveness. *ITcon, 7*, 125–137.

Egbu, C., Kurul, E., Quintas, P., Hutchinson, V., Anumba, C., & Ruikar, K. (2003). *Techniques and technologies for knowledge management.* Retrieved from http://www.knowledgemanagement.uk.net/ resources/WP3%20Interim%20 Report.pdf

EI-Diraby, T. E., & Kashif, K. F. (2005). Distributed ontology architecture for knowledge management in highway construction. *Journal of Construction Engineering and Management, 131*(5), 591–603. doi:10.1061/(ASCE)0733-9364(2005)131:5(591)

European Commission. (2005). ICT and electronic business in the construction industry: ICT adoption and e-business activity in 2005. *Report of the European e-business market watch, e-business sector study in the construction industry.* Retrieved from www.ebusiness-watch.org

Fong, S. W., & Wong, K. (2005). Capturing and reusing building maintenance knowledge: A socio-technical perspective. In Kazi, A. S. (Ed.), *Knowledge Management in the Construction Industry: A Socio-Technical Perspective.* Hershey, PA: IGI Global.

Gore, C., & Gore, E. (1999). Knowledge management: the way forward. *Total Quality Management, 10*(4-5), 554–560.

Gruber, T. R. (1993). A translation approach to portable ontology specifications. *Knowledge Acquisition, 5*(2), 199–220. doi:10.1006/knac.1993.1008

Gupta, B., Iyer, L., & Aronson, J. (2000). Knowledge management: practices and challenges. *Industrial Management & Data Systems, 100*(1), 17–21. doi:10.1108/02635570010273018

Hari, S., Egbu, C., & Kumar, B. (2005). A knowledge capture awareness tool: an empirical study on small and medium enterprises in the construction industry. *Engineering, Construction, and Architectural Management, 12*(6), 533–567. doi:10.1108/09699980510634128

Inkpen, A. C., & Dinur, A. (1998). Knowledge management processes and international joint venture. *Organization Science, 9*(4), 454–468. doi:10.1287/orsc.9.4.454

Kakabadse, N. K., Kouzmin, A., & Kakabadse, A. (2001). From tacit knowledge to knowledge management: Leveraging invisible assets. *Knowledge and Process Management, 8*(3), 137–154. doi:10.1002/kpm.120

Kamara, J., Augenbroe, G., Anumba, C., & Carrillo, P. (2002). Knowledge management in the architecture, engineering and construction industry. *Construction Innovation, 2*(1), 53–67.

Kaplan, R. S., & Norton, D. P. (1992). The balanced scorecard: measures that drive performance. *Harvard Business Review,* (Jan.-Feb.), 71-79.

Kelleher, D., & Levene, S. (2001). *Knowledge management: A guide to good practice.* London: British Standards Institution.

Klein, G. (2003). *Intuition at Work: Why Developing Your Gut Instincts Will Make You Better at What You Do.* New York, NY: Doubleday.

KLICON. (1999). *The role of information technology in knowledge management within the construction industry (Project report of knowledge learning in construction group).* Manchester, UK: University of Manchester, Institute of Science and Technology.

Li, M., & Gao, F. (2003). Why Nonaka highlights tacit knowledge: A critical review. *Journal of Knowledge Management, 7*(4), 6–14. doi:10.1108/13673270310492903

Lin, Y., Wang, L., & Tserng, P. (2006). Enhancing knowledge exchange through web map-based knowledge management system in construction: Lessons learned in Taiwan. *Automation in Construction, 15*(6), 693–705. doi:10.1016/j.autcon.2005.09.006

Love, P., Edum-Fotwe, F., & Irani, Z. (2003). Management of knowledge in project environments. *International Journal of Project Management, 21,* 155–156. doi:10.1016/S0263-7863(02)00089-3

Marr, B., & Schiuma, G. (2001). Measuring and managing intellectual capital and knowledge assets in new economy organisations. In Bourne, M. (Ed.), *Performance Measurement Handbook.* London: GEE Publishing Ltd.

McInerney, C. (2002). Knowledge management and the dynamic nature of knowledge. *Journal of the American Society for Information Science and Technology, 53*(12), 1009–1018. doi:10.1002/asi.10109

NDR. (2003, March). Data, information, and knowledge. *No Doubt Research.* Retrieved from www.nodoubt.co.nz

Neely, A., Adams, C., & Kennerley, M. (2002). *The performance prism: the scorecard for measuring and managing business success.* Financial Times.

Newman, B., & Conrad, K. (1999). A framework for characterizing knowledge management methods, practices, and technologies. In *proceedings of The Knowledge Management Forum in support of The Introduction to Knowledge Management.* West Richland, WA: Spring.

Nickols, F. (2003). *The knowledge in knowledge management.* Retrieved from http://home.att.net/~OPSINC/knowledge_in_KM.pdf

Nonaka, I. (1991). The knowledge-creating company. *Harvard Business Review, 69,* 96–104.

Nonaka, I. (2007). The knowledge-creating company. *Harvard Business Review, 85,* 162–171.

Nonaka, I., & Takeuchi, H. (1995). *The knowledge-creating company: How Japanese companies create the dynamics of innovation.* Oxford, UK: Oxford University Press.

Polanyi, M. (1996). *The tacit dimension.* New York: Anchor Day Books.

Polanyi, M. (1997). Tacit knowledge. In Prusak, L. (Ed.), *Knowledge in Organizations.* Boston: Butterworth-Heinemann.

Probst, G., Raub, S., & Romhardt, K. (2000). *Managing knowledge: Building blocks for success.* West Sussex, England: John Wiley and Sons Ltd.

Robinson, H., Carrillo, P., Anumba, C., & Al-Ghassani, A. (2004). Developing a business case for knowledge management: The IMPaKT approach. *Construction Management and Economics, 22*(1), 733–743. doi:10.1080/0144619042000226306

Robinson, H., Carrillo, P., Anumba, C., & Al-Ghassani, A. (2005). Knowledge management practices in large construction organizations. *Engineering, Construction, and Architectural Management, 12*(5), 431–445. doi:10.1108/09699980510627135

Tiwana, A. (1999). *The knowledge management toolkit: Practical techniques for building a knowledge management system.* Upper Saddle River, NJ: Prentice Hall.

Tserng, H., & Lin, Y. (2004). Developing an activity-based knowledge management system for contractors. *Automation in Construction, 13*(6), 781–802. doi:10.1016/j.autcon.2004.05.003

Walker, D., Wilson, A., & Srikanthan, G. (2001). *The knowledge advantage (K-Adv) for unleashing creativity and innovation in construction industry* (Tech. Rep. No. 2001-004-A). Institute of Construction.

Weiser, M., & Morrison, J. (1998). Project memory: information management for project teams. *Journal of Management Information Systems, 14*(4), 149–166.

Woo, J., Clayton, M. J., Johnson, R. E., Flores, B. E., & Ellis, C. (2004). Dynamic knowledge map: Reusing experts' tacit knowledge in the AEC industry. *Automation in Construction, 13*, 203–207. doi:10.1016/j.autcon.2003.09.003

Zack, M. (1999). Managing codified knowledge. *Sloan Management Review, 40*(4), 45–58.

This work was previously published in International Journal of Information Technology Project Management, Volume 1, Issue 2, edited by John Wang, pp. 16-42, copyright 2010 by IGI Publishing (an imprint of IGI Global).

Chapter 7
Software Project Managers under the Team Software Process:
A Study of Competences Based on Literature

Marcos Ruano-Mayoral
Amvos Consulting, Spain

Ricardo Colomo-Palacios
Universidad Carlos III de Madrid, Spain

Ángel García-Crespo
Universidad Carlos III de Madrid, Spain

Juan Miguel Gómez-Berbís
Universidad Carlos III de Madrid, Spain

ABSTRACT

Despite the clear relevance of the Information and Communications Technologies (ICT) market in world economics and the evident lack of success of software projects, organizations devote little effort to the development and maturity of the software project manager profession. This work analyzes the figure of project manager from the perspective of the Team Software Process (TSP), and it considers the required skills, attitudes and knowledge for a software development project. The basis for the study is the analysis of relevant references from the literature for their subsequent categorization into different competency concepts. The results of the analysis are compared with the contributions which the Guide to the SWEBOK® and the PMBOK® Guide models provide of the profiles of the project manager. The results indicate that the literature relating to the Team Software Process is focused on the definitions of skills and attitudes, and to a lesser extent on knowledge components. The lack of the definition of the components which comprise competency constitutes a challenge for software development organizations

DOI: 10.4018/978-1-4666-0930-3.ch007

that use TSP, whose project managers should confront the task with full capacities, and without the help of established and recognized competencies. The current work attempts to establish the competencies for project managers identified in the literature, in the environment of the use of TSP for software development, using a study based on content analysis.

INTRODUCTION

The software industry has become one of the main streams of development all around the world. In Europe, the ICT market represented 5.74% of the GDP in 2007, and the expected growth for 2008 is 2.9% (EITO, 2007).

Software project management is a relatively recent discipline that emerged during the second half of the 20th century (Kwak, 2005), although most software projects are more concerned with aspects of technology rather than management (de Amescua et al., 2004). The task of managing a software project can be an extremely complex one, drawing on many personal, team and organizational resources (Rose, Pedersen, Hosbond, & Kræmmergaard, 2007). In this scenario, some authors (E.g. Turner & Müller, 2005; Munns & Bjeirmi, 1996) have indicated that the influence of competencies on the success of projects has not been successfully explored, while other authors (E.g. Pinto & Kharbanda, 1995; Skulmoski, Hartman, & DeMaere, 2000; Jiang, 2002; Crawford, 2005) have identified the competencies of project managers applying the competency concept, that is, they have identified the competencies which fundamentally make project managers competent and successful.

In software development projects, Boehm (1981) points out that subsequent to the size of the product, personnel factors have the most important influence on the total effort necessary for the development of a software project, and that personnel characteristics and human resources related activities constitute the most relevant source of opportunities for improving software development (Boehm et al., 2000). On the same issue, some other authors state that inadequate competence verification of software engineers is one of the principal problems when it comes to carrying out any software development project (McConnell, 2003).

In the ICT field, software is a critical element. Failure rates associated with software projects are extremely high, and the personnel included in software development teams is one of the most decisive aspects for projects and their deficiencies (McConnell, 2003). The teams should be comprised of practitioners having heterogeneous education and experience (McConnell, 2003) and human resources management systems should be easily able to identify and assess the engineers' professional training, with the objective of improving the workforce's competence level (Curtis, Hefley, & Miller, 2001). This improvement is one of the key elements of profession models as stated in the 'skills development' component by Ford & Gibbs (1996) and McConnell (2003).

In software engineering, development work is a team activity, and the effectiveness of this teamwork represents a crucial factor for the quality and the success of the entire project (Humphrey, 2006a). Based on this premise, TSP (Team Software Process) originated, aligned with the principles provided by CMM (Capability Maturity Model) and PSP (Personal Software Process), TSP. The main objective of TSP is to provide the fundamental mechanisms so that a development team is able to establish a development process and a plan to define how the work is to be carried out (Humphrey, 2000b). The relevance of TSP is supported by both its integration into the quality framework provided by the SEI (Software Engineering Institute) and the benefits reported by several organizations after its adoption in terms of quality and productivity of engineering teams' improvement (Humphrey, 2000b). For example, *Teradyne* saved 228 engineering hours for every 1000 LOC (lines of code) and reduced the repair costs about 4.5 times the cost of producing the programs in the first place (Humphrey, 2000b).

Given, on the one hand, the importance of software currently in the global economy, and on the other hand, the impact of the maturity initiatives for the software process, from the point of view of the individual (PSP), as well as the development group (TSP), or the organization (CMM), the manager figure of a project in a TSP environment results to be a key element for the process. This article proposes the current study within this scenario, aiming to elucidate whether the TSP literature adequately represents the competencies of these professionals in their distinct environments: skills, attitudes and knowledge.

The remainder of the article is organized as follows. The next section defines the competence paradigm, as well as its components and principal implications. This is followed by the description of the role of the team leader in TSP. The literature regards this role to be similar to that of the software project manager. Subsequently, the article provides the description of the study carried out, and its main findings. Lastly, the article presents the principal conclusions and future work of the study.

THE COMPETENCE PARADIGM

The competence approach to human resources management has a long history. The early Romans already practiced a sort of competence profiling in attempts to detail the attributes of a "good Roman soldier" (Draganidis & Mentzas, 2006). More recently, early 20th century scientific management used the concept of competence (Taylor, 1911), and is well established in the field of human resources management since the middle of the seventies, due to the works by McClelland. McClelland (1973) defined competence as those characteristics that

are found to consistently distinguish outstanding from typical performance in a given job or role.

Competences and competence management has proved to be an extremely relevant area of study. There are several contributions to the field from the academia, the industry and international organizations (such as OECD, EC, and ASEM). Despite the different approaches and objectives of the mentioned initiatives, all of them remark the fact that competences are the key element for the successful development of an individual, in both professional and social environments. From this point of view, Tapio (2004) defines competence as the combination of skills, knowledge, aptitudes and attitudes that, when transferred to a certain task or professional contribution, enable the individual to perform the task efficiently.

However, the fact that the concept of competence has been used in so many areas of research (Bassellier, Horner Reich, & Benbasat, 2001) has lead to an evident confusion that has been named the 'competence pandemonium' (DeHaro, 2004) and furthermore, some authors point out that this misunderstanding has hindered the creation of a cumulative body of knowledge (Marcolin, Compeau, Munro, & Huff, 2000).

Competence is often used in the sense of performance, however, this is not entirely accurate (Bassellier, Horner Reich, & Benbasat, 2001). Nonetheless, competence is a factor that, coupled with motivation, effort and supporting conditions, may have a direct impact on performance (Schambach, 1994). Another approach to competence is the skills-based approach. From this point of view, competence is the fit between an individual and the task to be performed (Davern, 1996). Another component of competence is knowledge, which broadens the definition, considering that the competence is not directly linked to a specific task but is related to the ability to transfer knowledge across tasks (Bassellier, Horner Reich, & Benbasat, 2001).

The impact of the competency paradigm has also had an effect in the Project Management discipline. Diverse organizations have aimed to establish the knowledge necessary for the carrying out of the professional labor of project managers, with initiatives such as the APM Body of Knowledge (Dixon, 2000), the ICB: IPMA Competence Baseline (Caupin, Knopfel, Morris, Motzel, & Pannenbacker, 1999) and the PMBOK Guide (PMI, 2004). Additionally, multiple authors have attempted to establish the competencies of project managers from an empirical viewpoint, generally based on the application of surveys (E.g. McVeigh, 1995; Dinsmore, 1999; Skulmoski, Hartman, & DeMaere, 2000; Jiang, 2002; Crawford, 2005).

Given the range of project types, organizations and researchers can expect a wide variation in the range of project management competences and approaches that may be required (Morris, Crawford, Hodgson, Shepherd & Thomas, 2006). In the IT environment, the literature is saturated with studies concerning the competencies of the professionals of the sector. Studies can be found about the competencies necessary for analysts (Misic & Graf, 2004), chief information officers (Bassellier, Reich & Benbasat, 2001), software engineers (Turley & Bieman, 1995), entry-level IT professionals (McMurtrey, Downey, Zeltmann, & Friedman, 2008) or information systems professionals (E.g. Lee, Trauth, & Farwell, 1995; Wu, Chen & Chan, 2007), to cite some of the most significant cases.

In the concrete environments of software development projects, initiatives concerning the definition and analysis of the competencies of project managers have also been carried out (E.g. Sukhoo, Barnard, Eloff, Van der Poll, Motah, 2005; Rose, Pedersen, Hosbond & Kræmmergaard, 2007). It is without doubt that the importance of maturity models and the characteristics of a team leader for TSP define a field of study which researchers in the field should undertake, with the objective of establishing the competencies of this role with precision.

THE TEAM LEADER ROLE IN TSP

TSP (Team Software Process) was first launched in 1996 by Watts S. Humphrey, aiming at the definition of an operative process to help and support software development teams to consistently perform quality work (Humphrey, 2000b). The approach provided by TSP is aligned and extends the quality strategy developed by Deming and Juran, which also played a crucial role in the development of Capability Maturity Model (CMM) in 1987, and Personal Software Process (PSP) in 1995 (Humphrey, 2000b). PSP, TSP and CMM, as well as People CMM, are integrated into a process maturity framework devised by Humphrey at the beginning of the 1980s (Curtis, Hefley, & Miller, 2001) aimed at the adoption of best quality practices at every level of organizations.

The objective of the TSP is to create a team environment that supports disciplined individual work and builds and maintains a self-directed team (Davis & Mullaney, 2003). To achieve this goal, the TSP is structured in two primary components. The first component is the TSP launch, in which the team reaches a common understanding of the work and the approach adopted (Davis & Mullaney, 2003). By the end of the launch, the team becomes a cohesive and effective working unit, in which all the team members are committed to a plan (Humphrey, 2000b) that balances the needs of the business and customer with a feasible technical solution (Davis & Mullaney, 2003). The second component of the TSP is the team-working and management component. During this process it should be ensured that all team members follow the plan (Humphrey, 2000b) and, therefore, the figure of the team leader becomes crucial.

The team leader is responsible for guiding and motivating the team members, handling customer issues and dealing with management (Humphrey, 2000b). Management expects that the team gets the assigned job done; hence the team leader must be able to follow the schedule with the assigned resources to produce products that meet the stated requirements (Humphrey, 2000b).

The TSP literature does not describe the team leader role as a function of his competencies, but uniquely based on isolated descriptions. Research should examine the peculiarities of the figure with the objective of determining whether the team leader of TSP projects can be differentiated in any way from the descriptions of project managers in the Project Management or Software Engineering literature.

THE STUDY

Taking into account that the source of information for the study was relevant literature, the study carried out is of qualitative character. The said study is centered on the analysis of two of the most relevant books from the TSP literature: (Humphrey, 2000a) and (Humphrey, 2006b). The structure of the qualitative analysis carried out stems from the schemes traditionally used in Sociology and Psychology research. The Austrian psychologists Lazarsfeld and Rosenberg (1957) designed the classic model known as the concept indicator model. Previous authors such as Glaser (1978) contributed models for qualitative exploration, such as those entitled summing indicator concept and comparing indicator concept. Lazarsfeld and Rosember's model, as well as that of Glaser, essentially establishes a structure in which the concept which is the subject of the study, in the current case, the competences, define a series of dimensions, to each of which the researchers associate a series of indicators. The dimensions of a concept are those distinct aspects in which it can be considered, that is, those aspects which represent the components of the concept. Qualitative analysis is an established technique which has previously been used in the literature for the identification of the competencies of IT profes-

sionals (E.g. Todd, McKeen, & Gallupe, 1995; Gallivan, Tuex & Kvasny, 2004).

The focus of the content analysis was the identification of those indicators of the team leader role that are candidates to be mapped to a competence. The researchers carried out the identification of the dimensions and competency indicators by means of the analysis and classification of the occurrence of these in the quoted literature. In order to guarantee the quality of the results, an agreement indicator, Interjudge reliability was obtained, that is, the consistency of measurement obtained when different judges or examiners independently administer the same test to the same individual. In the current case, where three judges were used to verify consistency, the Kappa coefficient obtained was .86, representing statistically significant agreement ($z=6.9$, $p<.01$).

The results of the analysis revealed that the team leader role can be defined as the composition of 4 indicators of knowledge dimension, 13 indicators of skill dimension and 7 indicators of attitude dimension, displayed in Table 1.

An interesting aspect for the analysis of the team leader role is to determine the relative relevance of the different components to the role. In order to do so, the authors performed a frequency analysis of the appearance of the components in the studied literature. The frequency analysis reveals that challenging the team members and using their skills to get the job done are the most relevant skills in team leaders (Figure 1). Additionally, the most demanded attitudes are the will to help the team, labeled as "Job Facilitator", and to consider the different points of view of team members, labeled as "Collaborative leadership" (Figure 2). When considering knowledge components, although they do not present significant differences, team building and risk management have the higher incidence (Figure 3). Lastly, comparing all the components together, in Figure 4, the results of the research demonstrate higher relevance of skills and attitudes against knowledge components.

Table 1. Team leader role components

Dimension	Indicator
Knowledge	**Build and maintain an effective team**
Knowledge	Handle funding issues
Knowledge	Lead risk evaluation and tracking
Knowledge	Participate in the configuration control board
Skill	Maintain team communication
Skill	Identify key issues
Skill	Make objective decisions
Skill	Combine forces
Skill	Work quality as a challenge
Skill	Meeting facilitator
Skill	Establish and maintain discipline
Skill	Enterprise vision
Skill	Promote initiative and creativeness
Skill	Scheduling
Skill	Lead the team effectively
Skill	Being resolute
Skill	Make the team goal oriented
Attitude	Commitment
Attitude	Personality traits
Attitude	Job facilitator
Attitude	Collaborative leadership
Attitude	Do not mind assuming unpopular positions
Attitude	Respect
Attitude	Assuming leadership position

Figure 1. Skill components

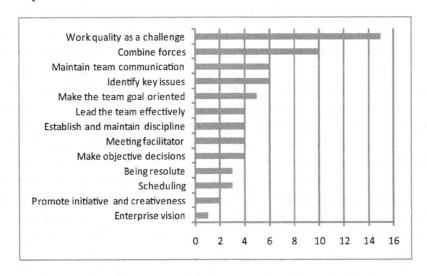

Figure 2. Attitude components

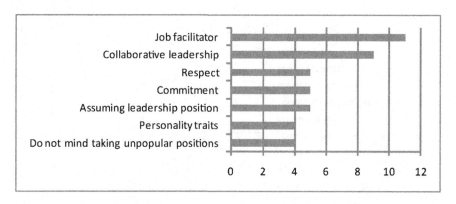

Figure 3. Knowledge components

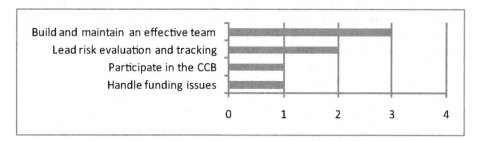

The authors have performed further analysis of the findings they extracted from the studied literature. The question now addressed is the relationship between TSP team leader role definition and two well-known and wide-spread bodies of knowledge such as the *Guide to the Software Engineering Body of Knowledge* (Abran, Bourque, Dupuis, & Moore, 2004) and the *Guide to the Project Management Body of Knowledge* (PMI Standards Committee, 2004). The aim of this comparison is to determine to what extent the TSP literature provides the definition of knowledge. The coverage of the team leader role components compared with the Guide to the SWEBOK® and the PMBOK® Guide is shown in Figure 5 and Figure 6, respectively. The Guide to the SWE-BOK® areas are exclusively matched to knowledge components. However, when considering the PMBOK® Guide areas, matching to knowl-edge and skill components is found. Additionally, no matching from attitude components can be established, neither to the Guide to the SWEBOK® or the PMBOK® Guide, which is consistent with the focus and objectives of both bodies of knowl-edge. Nevertheless, there is a section in the intro-duction of the PMBOK® Guide that mentions skills classified into five areas of expertise that are required for effective project management (PMI Standards Committee, 2004). Taking into account those skills, the matching with the PM-BOK® Guide is wider, but there are interper-sonal skills present in the team leader role which are not present in that section, and there are oth-ers that are less specific and are very task ori-ented.

Examining the matching performed between the competencies identified in the current study and the Guide to the SWEBOK® Knowledge

Figure 4. Team leader role components

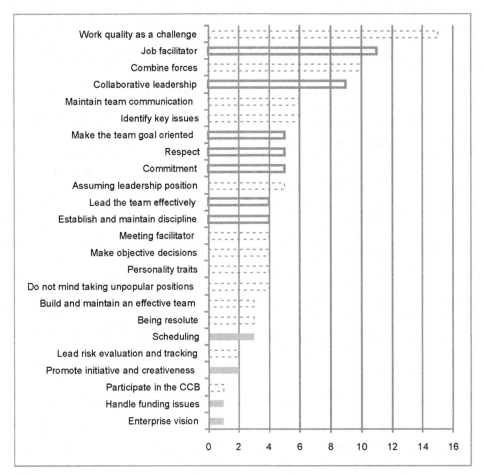

Figure 5. Matching to guide to the SWEBOK®

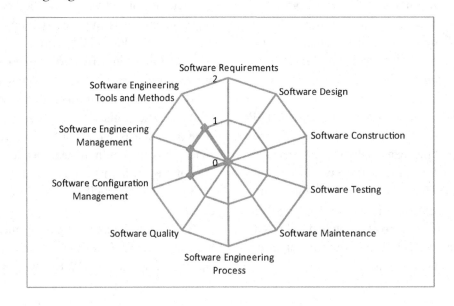

Figure 6. Matching to the PMBOK® guide

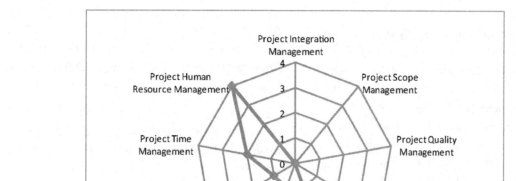

Areas, this study can affirm that the outlining of more technical knowledge relative to software engineering is not sufficiently specified. Taking into account that the team leader generally does not take any other role within TSP projects (Humphrey, 2000b), this circumstance may explain the lack of the definition when referring to this role according to technical competences. Other roles in TSP projects can be undertaken by one person or transferred to more than one during the course of a project.

However, this fact is not able to justify the necessity to know the competency levels of software development project managers in the diverse technical competencies of the discipline in detail. As a result, the authors propose to carry out an empirical study as future work which continues the works of (Acuña & Juristo, 2004) and (Colomo, 2005) in the determination and evaluation of the competencies of the participants in software projects.

Regarding the mapping of the competencies detected in the current work in relation to the areas of the PMBOK® Guide, it can be intuitively established that the principal focus can be found in the necessities of the human resource management of the project manager. Other areas of interest identified are Time Management, and to a lesser extent Risk, Communications, & Cost Management. Initially, it results paradoxical that some of the active areas of the project manager are found neglected by his role, such as in the case of Quality Management or Scope Management, for example. The answer to this paradox may be found in the intrinsic characteristics of the work groups governed by TSP, given that both areas are divided between other roles identified, for example, quality/process manager or plan manager. Thus, the current study deduces that the style of management which TSP adopts is more participative, leaving some of the competencies of the project manager in the hands of the members of the work team.

CONCLUSION AND FUTURE WORK

This article has performed a study of the competential profile of the team leader role in TSP. The study reveals that this role is comprised mainly of skills and attitudes and to a lesser extent of knowledge components. Some of the skills and attitudes identified can be found in 'standard' bodies of knowledge such as the Guide to the SWEBOK® and the PMBOK® Guide, but others are not mentioned in the literature that supposedly defines the software engineering profession. The analysis of the work reveals two types of conclusions. In the first place, and from the technical viewpoint (Software Engineering), the competency levels of the project managers of TSP in relation to the set of competency elements are not established. In the second place, the style of management of TSP permits the team leader to concentrate on aspects such as the management of human resources, delegating some others, such as the management of quality, to team members. As part of a more extensive study, the work has the objective of presenting the analysis of the literature carried out, and in this way, use it as a base for future work.

Taking as a basis the work performed until this moment, future work may consist of identifying the sources to precisely define the unmatched team leader role components using competence as the framework. Effort could also be devoted to extend the same analysis to the other roles present in the TSP. Additionally, and adopting a more classical methodology based on the application of questionnaires, in the future, the authors of this article aim to undertake research for the establishment of the competencies of all of the members in TSP work groups. These initiatives would clearly contribute to the maturity of the software engineering profession under the paradigm presented by Ford & Gibbs (1996) and McConnell (2003).

REFERENCES

Abran, A., Bourque, P., Dupuis, R., & Moore, J. W. (2004). *SWEBOK. Guide to the Software Engineering Body of Knowledge. 2004 Version.* Los Alamitos, CA: IEEE Computer Society

Acuña, S. T., & Juristo, N. (2004). Assigning people to roles in software projects. *Software, Practice & Experience, 34*, 675–696. doi:10.1002/spe.586

Bassellier, G., Horner Reich, B., & Benbasat, I. (2001). Information Technology Competence of Business Managers: A Definition and Research Model. *Journal of Management Information Systems, 17*(4), 159–182.

Boehm, B., Horowitz, E., Madachy, R., Reifer, D., Clark, B. K., Steece, B., et al. (2000). *Software Cost Estimation with COCOMO II.* Upper Saddle River, NJ: Prentice Hall.

Boehm, B. W. (1981). *Software Engineering Economics.* Englewood Cliffs, NJ: Prentice Hall.

Caupin, G., Knopfel, H., Morris, P., Motzel, E., & Pannenbacker, O. (1999). ICB: *IPMA competence baseline.* International Project Management Association, Germany.

Colomo, R. (2005). *A framework for Software Engineers Competence Evaluation.* Ph.D. Thesis. Universidad Politécnica de Madrid, Spain.

Crawford, L. (2005). Senior Management Perceptions of Project Management Competence. *International Journal of Project Management, 23*, 7–16. doi:10.1016/j.ijproman.2004.06.005

Curtis, B., Hefley, W. E., & Miller, S. A. (2001). *People Capability Maturity Model (P-CMM) Version 2.0* (No. CMU/SEI-2001-MM-01). Pittsburgh, PA: Software Engineering Institute.

Davern, M. (1996). *When good fit is bad: the dynamics of perceived fit.* In *Proceedings of the Seventeenth International Conference on Information Systems* (pp. 112-121), Cleveland, Ohio.

Davis, N., & Mullaney, J. (2003). *The Team Software Process (TSP) in Practice: A Summary of Recent Results* (No. CMU/SEI-2003-TR-014): Software Engineering Institute, Pittsburgh, PA.

de Amescua, A., García, J., Velasco, M., Martínez, P., Ruiz, B., & Llorens, J. (2004). A Software Project Management Framework. *Information Systems Management, 21*(2), 78–85. doi:10.120 1/1078/44118.21.2.20040301/80425.11

Dinsmore, P. (1999). *Winning in Business with Enterprise Project Managemen.* New York: Amacom Books.

Dixon, M. (2000). *APM project management body of knowledge* (4th ed.). Peterborough, England: Association for Project Management, Peterborough, UK.

Draganidis, F., & Mentzas, G. (2006). Competency based management: a review of systems and approaches. *Information Management & Computer Security, 14*(1), 51–64. doi:10.1108/09685220610648373

Ford, G., & Gibbs, N. (1996). *A Mature Profession of Software Engineering* (No. CMU/SEI-96-TR-04). Pittsburgh, PA: Software Engineering Institute.

Gallivan, M. J., Tuex, D. P., & Kvasny, L. (2004). Changing patterns in IT skill sets 1988-2003: a content analysis of classified advertising. *ACM SIGMIS Database, 35*(3), 64–87. doi:10.1145/1017114.1017121

Glaser, B. G. (1978). *Theoretical sensivity: advances in the methodology of grounded theory.* Mill Valley, CA: Sociology Press.

Humphrey, W. S. (2000a). *Introduction to the Team Software Process.* Reading, MA: Addison-Wesley.

Humphrey, W. S. (2000b). *The Team Software Process (TSP)* (No. CMU/SEI-2000-TR-023). Pittsburgh, PA: Software Engineering Institute.

Humphrey, W. S. (2006a). *TSP: Coaching Development Teams.* Boston. MA: Addison-Wesley.

Humphrey, W. S. (2006b). *TSP: Leading a Development Team.* Reading, MA: Addison-Wesley.

Jiang, B. (2002). Key Elements of a Successful Project Manager. *Project Management, 8*(1), 14–19.

Kwak, Y. H. (2005). A Brief History of Project Management. In E. G. Carayannis, Y. H. Kwak & F. T. Anbari (Eds.), *The Story of Managing Projects. An Interdisciplinary Approach.* Westport, Connecticut: Praeger Publishers.

Lazarsfeld, P. F., & Rosenberg, M. (1957). *The language of social research: a reader in the methodology of social research.* Glencoe, IL: Free Press.

Lee, D., Trauth, E., & Farwell, D. (1995). Critical Skills and Knowledge Requirements of IT Professionals: A Joint Academic/Industry Investigation. *MIS Quarterly, 19*(3), 313–340. doi:10.2307/249598

Marcolin, B., Compeau, D., Munro, M., & Huff, S. (2000). Assessing User Competence: Conceptualization and Measurement. *Information Systems Research, 11*(1), 37–60. doi:10.1287/isre.11.1.37.11782

McConnell, S. (2003). *Professional Software Development.* Reading, MA: Addison-Wesley.

McMurtrey, M. E., Downey, J. P., Zeltmann, S. M., & Friedman, W. H. (2008). Critical Skill Sets of Entry-Level IT Professionals: An Empirical Examination of Perceptions from Field Personnel. *Journal of Information Technology Education, 7*, 101–120.

McVeigh, C. B. J. (1995). The Right Stuff—Revisited: A Competency Perspective of Army Program Managers. *Program Manager, 24*(1), 30–34.

Misic, M. M., & Graf, D. K. (2004). Systems analyst activities and skills in the new millennium. *Journal of Systems and Software, 71*(1-2), 31–36. doi:10.1016/S0164-1212(02)00124-3

Morris, P. W. G., Crawford, L., Hodgson, D., Shepherd, M. M., & Thomas, J. (2006). Exploring the role of formal bodies of knowledge in defining a profession – The case of project management. *International Journal of Project Management, 24*(8), 710–721. doi:10.1016/j.ijproman.2006.09.012

Munns, A. K., & Bjeirmi, B. F. (1996). The role of project management in achieving project success. *International Journal of Project Management, 14*(2), 81–87. doi:10.1016/0263-7863(95)00057-7

Pinto, J., & Kharbanda, O. (1995). *Successful Project Managers: Leading Your Team to Success.* New York: Van Nostrand Reinhold

PMI Standards Committee. (2004). *A Guide to the Project Management Body of Knowledge (PMBoK Guides)*: Project Management Institute.

Rose, J., Pedersen, K., Hosbond, J. H., & Kræmmergaard, P. (2007). Management competences, not tools and techniques: A grounded examination of software project management at WM-data. *Information and Software Technology, 49*(6), 605–624. doi:10.1016/j.infsof.2007.02.005

Schambach, T. (1994). *Maintaining professional competence: an evaluation of factors affecting professional obsolescence of information technology professionals.* Ph.D. dissertation, University of South Florida.

Skulmoski, G., Hartman, F., & DeMaere, R. (2000). Superior and Threshold Project Competencies. *Project Management, 6*(1), 10–15.

Sukhoo, A., Barnard, A., Eloff, M. M., Van der Poll, J. A., & Motah, M. (2005). Accommodating Soft Skills in Software Project Management. *Issues in Informing Science and Information Technology, 2*, 691–704.

Tapio, S. (2004). *Key competences for lifelong learning: A European reference framework*: European Commission. Directorate-General for Education and Culture, Brussels.

Taylor, F. W. (1911). *The Principles of Scientific Management.* New York: Harper & Brothers.

Todd, P., McKeen, J., & Gallupe, R. B. (1995). The Evolution of IT Job Skills: A Content Analysis of IT Job Advertisements From 1970 to 1990. *MIT Quarterly, 19*(1), 1–27. doi:10.2307/249709

Turley, R. T., & Bieman, J. M. (1995). Competencies of Exceptional an Non-Exceptional Software Engineers. *Journal of Systems and Software, 28*(1), 19–38. doi:10.1016/0164-1212(94)00078-2

Turner, J. R., & Müller, R. (2005). The Project Manager's Leadership Style as a Success Factor on Projects: A Literature Review. *Project Management Journal, 36*(2), 49–61.

Wu, J. H., Chen, Y. C., & Chang, C. (2007). Critical IS professional activities and skills/knowledge: A perspective of IS managers. *Computers in Human Behavior, 23*(6), 2945–2965. doi:10.1016/j.chb.2006.08.008

This work was previously published in International Journal of Information Technology Project Management, Volume 1, Issue 1, edited by John Wang, pp. 42-53, copyright 2010 by IGI Publishing (an imprint of IGI Global).

Chapter 8
Teaching Students How to Effectively Work in Virtual Teams

Sadan Kulturel-Konak
Pennsylvania State University-Berks Campus, USA

Clifford R. Maurer
Pennsylvania State University-Berks Campus, USA

Daniel L. Lohin
Lockheed Martin Corporation, USA

ABSTRACT

This paper, through the voices of two professors and a student, describes an educational experience that exposed students to virtual teams constructed between Information Technology Project Management classes of two branch campuses of the Pennsylvania State University. This experience focused on overcoming the communication problems of virtual teams in order to strengthen team building dynamics. Since working on virtual teams was the first experience for the students, attempts were made to control some aspects of the virtual team environment by eliminating cultural and time differences. The variable to be in focus was the building of trust in a virtual environment. By eliminating all other variables such as time zones, cultural and disciplinary backgrounds, etc., students could experience the efforts required to build trust in a virtual environment. Students were given pre and post experience surveys. The results indicate that initially many students were very apprehensive about virtual teams; however, after completing the course, most students expressed positive attitudes and a general understanding of techniques to work effectively in virtual teams. In addition, almost all teams commented on how important they felt virtual teams would become in the future as digital technology continues to improve.

DOI: 10.4018/978-1-4666-0930-3.ch008

INTRODUCTION

One of the defining characteristics of business in the 21st century is that it is conducted on a global context. Not only are large mega-corporations conducting business on a world wide scale, but also small niche companies can exist because they can serve a small clientele that may be spread out across the world. With a proper organization, corporations may work 24-hour shift although each location works a regular 8-hour shift. In the global business world, the need for people who have skills working in geographically dispersed teams has become very important. Virtual teams in the workplace are becoming increasingly popular. In 1998, the Harvard Business School estimated that over 15 million Americans worked in virtual offices and that number was growing by close to 20% per year (Elkins, 2000).

With the increasing popularity of virtual teams, educators must prepare students for what they will experience after graduation. The exposure to virtual teams is critical for students since virtual teams need to be managed and handled in a different way than regular teams as is noted in the literature (Keyzerman, 2003). Educational experiences must be designed so that they allow team members to work together using technology over the Internet (i.e., computer-mediated communication (CMC)) to communicate with one another in a method which will allow students to solve a problem with minimal to no face-to-face (FtF) contact. Recognizing the role and importance of virtual teams in the global economy, we decided to incorporate a virtual team experience into our classes. In Fall 2005, students from two branch campuses of the Pennsylvania State University were exposed to a semester long project where they worked as virtual teams.

The objective of this paper is to describe a pedagogical experience of introducing students to a virtual team experience in project management. The rest of the paper will first focus on the background of virtual teams. Then, in the Methodology Section, the particular virtual team project will be explained in detail focusing on what kinds of teambuilding activities and project assignments were performed. Finally, findings, discussion, conclusions and the ideas to be included in similar future projects will be presented.

BACKGROUND

The Importance of Virtual Teams in the Global Business and Education

The Internet has created an environment where anyone can be in constant communication with anyone else. Modern logistic supply chain methods, which now permit shipments of goods around the world and allow economic competition with locally manufactured goods, have created a global economy. Many companies that operate globally are not centrally located but have small functional teams spread throughout the world. This global marketplace has brought many benefits as well as a few drawbacks. Global markets allow people all around the world to bring their insight and expertise to a problem (Friedman, 2006). Kock and Nosek (2005) provide an excellent historical view of e-collaboration. Kock (2001) specifically presents e-communication behavior theories. Bergil et al. (2008) extend the knowledge about virtual teams by studying their advantages and disadvantages, and conclude that although virtual teams may not be the unique solution for every organization, their advantages lead them to be a strategically important tool in today's global business. Powell et al. (2004) also review the current literature about virtual teams as well as directions for future research, and they conclude that extensive research is needed to figure out the design characteristics of well working virtual teams.

Studying creativity within different types of teams, Ocker (2005) concludes that people feel more comfortable sharing their ideas in virtual teams. According to Roebuck (2002), virtual teams are also more effective, and the reason stated is that members of the team are capable of focusing on content as opposed to how effectively the people are presenting or how attractive they look. However, as stated earlier, since virtual teams rely significantly on communication technologies, they face more challenges to coordinate members across cultural differences and time zones.

Many distance education courses have been forced to utilize virtual teams due to the nature of the type of education they offer. Previous studies have shown that students in a virtual team environment often perform better work and get better grades than students in a traditional team environment (Coppola et al., 2004). Johnson et al. (2002) discuss how virtual teams are becoming not only better, but also, in some cases, necessary for education. With the rapid rise of students in distance education programs, virtual teams are necessary for students to participate in teamwork. On-line degree programs often rely on videoconferencing and chat rooms to communicate. Nedelko (2007) discusses the different usage of videoconferencing in virtual teams and how videoconferencing eliminates some pitfalls of virtual team environment.

Common Problems Encountered in Virtual Teams

The most common challenge of virtual teams is coordinating the logistics of team work across time, space, and cultures. Worldwide teams are faced with time zone differences that can be disconcerting. Work practices could include differences in approaches to deadlines and uses of confrontation versus diplomacy.

An additional phenomenon of the 21st century is that business projects require multiple disciplines. Bringing a product to market may require interaction among engineering, marketing, manufacturing, and information systems disciplines. Even within what was once considered a single discipline, Information Science,

there may be people involved with specialties in networking, database, system development, support, etc. All of these specialties use specialized terms not understood by those outside the field. Accomplishing complicated organizational tasks requires team work from multi-disciplined, internationally-dispersed people. If this is not achieved, misunderstandings can quickly hinder communication among teams.

Since World War II, a great deal of effort has been focused on how to build teams across disciplines but mainly by focusing on FtF communication. It is only recently that studies have been done on virtual teams. Indeed all of the human interpersonal skills have been developed throughout history on FtF basis. The human psyche has been honed to work on a FtF basis when interacting with others in a collaborative effort. In a regular FtF team meeting, people rely on subtle nonverbal clues like body language, facial expressions, and intonations. They can also see how attentive others are. In a virtual team meeting, however, people don't have these meta-messages. It is more difficult to understand people's thoughts and feelings even if there may be voices over a conference call or multiple typed entries in a "chat room." Therefore, it cannot be assumed because a message is sent, it actually is received and interpreted correctly (Levin & Rad, 2005). Team members should initially invest more time and thought in order to come across fewer difficulties in later stages (Roebuck and Britt). Through their experiments with sophomore level Information Systems students, Lowry et al. (2006) have observed that "FtF communication with CMC support" teams have higher levels of communication quality than "virtual with CMC support" teams.

Team Dynamics in Virtual Teams

Much of the research about virtual teams has centered on how to create efficient teams that can work well with distance between members.

One of the most important aspects of forming virtual teams is the size of the team. Bradner et al. (2005) examine the optimal size of teams. Responses to their survey indicate that members in smaller teams participated more actively and were significantly more aware of the goals when compared with members in larger teams. Bradner et al. (2005) also study the effect of team size by splitting the teams into either small or large groups. The researchers then administer a survey, when the study is over, examining various aspects such as team members' personalities, work roles and the willingness to communicate. Conclusions of the study indicate that smaller teams (nine or fewer members) increase individual participation, knowledge of team mates, levels of commitment, and understanding of the team's goals, and they also reduce the need for formal procedures.

Educators have used a variety of methods to simulate the environment of virtual teams. One method involves giving students an anonymous chat room where no one is allowed to mention who is speaking (Roebuck & Britt, 2002). While this simulation works well in an environment where it is impossible to have students spread out, it is not very realistic. The biggest downfall of this method is that it doesn't simulate a diverse group of people. The students in this simulation are presumably from the same location where cultural and educational differences are probably minimal. Another method uses worldwide teaching collaboration. Johnson et al. (2002) describe a virtual team project in which students are involved from all over the world and actively participate in an environment where a problem needs to be solved. The members of the project are never able to meet one another. The researchers have looked at how conflicts arise and how members of these virtual teams deal with these conflicts. They also have found that it is necessary to modify Tuckman's team development model to an iterative model.

Tuckman (1965) initially defines the team development model as being unidirectional (i.e., flowing through the four stages in only one direc-

tion). These four stages track team development stages from the forming stage when the team first meets and is charged with its duties through the performing stage where every member knows their responsibility, how they are to carry out their responsibility and how their work coordinates with the other members' work. During the forming stage, members are typically seen as individuals looking for a place or position on the team. The storming stage follows and is typically characterized as "the honeymoon is over." Out of the storming stage comes the norming stage where the members begin to accept and understand other members' responsibilities. The final stage, performing, is where it is hoped the highest level of team productivity can occur. Johnson et al. (2002) redefine this model as an iterative model to show that conflict can arise at any stage and may have the effect of the team regressing back to a lower stage, such as from a performing stage back to the forming stage. The modification includes the additional stage of conflict resolution when it occurs. This model is thought to be more appropriate due to the nature of virtual communication and the short time that each team had to finish assignments.

Trust and Leadership in Virtual Teams

Webster's dictionary defines "trust" as: "Assured reliance on the character, ability, strength, or truth of someone or something." Lipnack and Stamps (2000) state that people in all cultures during all ages have been dependent on trust; however, it has become essential in the network age. Jarvenpaa and Leidner (1997) state that the development of trust is based on the personal relationships one has with groups or networks that "share norms of obligation and responsibility." Walther and Ulla (2005) contend that "because of the absence of non-verbal cues in virtual teams," these personal relations cannot be built, and, therefore, members of virtual teams lack trust in their team mates as compared to teams meeting FtF. Much of this research was conducted before the proliferation of such communication techniques as Instant Messaging (IM), etc. When people are expected to use CMC, they are stripped of many of the comforts that they are accustomed to in FtF communication (Levin & Rad, 2005). This is why it is crucial for students to have a solid understanding of how to build trust in virtual teams.

Many studies have been conducted on the performance of teams and how it is related to trust. All of the studies we have examined have shown a positive correlation between trust and the performance of the project (Walther & Ulla, 2005). Trust is critical in any project and needs to be examined. Techniques have been studied to build trust in a timely manner and need to be understood as students learn how to effectively work in virtual teams (Coppola et al., 2004; Walther & Ulla, 2005). Since the communication among virtual team members is almost all task-oriented, developing trust becomes more difficult (Dalton et al., 2002). However, Wilson et al.'s (2006) study shows that the development of trust in virtual teams is not impossible; it just takes a longer time. Malhotra et al. (2007) suggest that using formal norms for communication and establishing guidelines for submissions can create trust in virtual teams. By developing a trust in the "process," virtual team members build a trust in the team. They also suggest making progress explicit. As team members see the progress of all the peers, it helps to build trust that the process is working. All of these things may happen in FtF teams but they must be carefully managed in a virtual team. Then, Malhotra et al. (2007) identify the six effective leadership skills that can be applied to overcome the unique challenges of managing virtual teams. These skills are *i*) establish and maintain trust through the use of communication technology, *ii*) ensure the value of diversity in the team, *iii*) manage virtual work cycle and meetings, *iv*) monitor team success

through the use of technology, *v*) enhance external visibility of the team, and *vi*) ensure individual benefits participating in virtual teams. Similarly, Hunsaker & Hunsaker (2008) provide guidelines to help leading virtual teams more effectively. The guidelines in their paper follow the four stages of a project timeline: pre-project, project initiation, midstream, and wrap-up. By doing so, leaders can more effectively focus on relatively more important issues in each sages of a virtual team project.

Crowston et al. (2007) examine Free/Libre Open Source Software (FLOSS) development teams and how these teams use FtF communication in order to better collaborate. FLOSS projects are primarily managed entirely online. Programs like Concurrent Software Versions (CVS) make this possible by allowing multiple people to contribute to one common goal of a large software application and still provide a formal infrastructure to manage a large project. The interesting thing about FLOSS projects is that while developers are naturally computer savvy, they still clearly find it beneficial to occasionally meet in person. Crowston et al. (2007) also discuss how many of large FLOSS project teams regularly meet in person a few times a year. The paper discusses how this builds unity and trust among the team members which can be beneficial to everyone even when they are online, which is where they spend most of their time collaborating. Crowston et al. (2007) note how many of these software developers use their time to socialize as well as program. So while they do not spend all of their time being productive, the trust that is gained has many intrinsic values that can't be calculated. When a person understands another person, they are much more likely to help the other one out on something like a tricky problem, which benefits the whole team. Talking about one's family or sports is an excellent way of achieving this, but doesn't usually happen in pure online communications.

The Role of Subteams in Virtual Teams

Panteli & Davison (2005) have a valuable pioneer study in exploring the role of subgroups in the communication patterns of global virtual teams. They suggest that team leaders should closely monitor the behaviors of subteams. They also point out the necessity of further research analyzing subteams as parts of virtual teams. The evolving of the subteams in global virtual teams is natural, since companies have branches in geographically dispersed areas and members of virtual teams at one location will form a subteam.

METHODOLOGY

The virtual teamwork in this paper was used at two branch campuses of the Pennsylvania State University. The same Information Technology Project Management course was taught on both campuses by different instructors in Fall 2005, 15-week long semester. The course material included topics of team work and leadership and, therefore, allowed for the discussion of aspects of virtual teams to be included in the syllabus.

Synchronization in Delivering the Course Material

Since the project included two separate classes by two different instructors, we decided using the same content and assignments so that students at both campuses would feel that they were on a par with their peers. The course was delivered using ANGEL, the course management system used university wide, and this allowed the instructors to deliver the same information about their project to students at both campuses. For all the team submissions, template documents were posted so that students would understand expectations clearly.

The class at one campus met once a week on Tuesday evenings while the class at the other campus met twice a week on Tuesday and Thursday afternoons. From previous experience, it was imperative that content be delivered simultaneously and at the same pace for both classes. This was accomplished when the two instructors held weekly status meetings each Monday. While both were allowed to cover the course content in a way that they felt comfortable, the material covered was identical. Other things covered in these meetings were students' reactions to the materials, progress by the teams and any feedback concerning team participation.

Motivation

The degree program we teach aims to prepare leaders for a digital global economy. Each course contains a problem based learning segment that is accomplished as a team effort. Students are exposed to teamwork as incoming freshman and work throughout their academic career in teams. This means that students in this course started with a lot of experience working in teams. Many students have leadership and organization skills. They are ready to face the challenge of virtual teams.

Virtual Team Project- Developing a Project Plan

Subteam and Team Building

Based on research and previous experience, we found that virtual team projects confront students with several new experiences that need to be considered when the project is designed. To help ensure that students have a positive learning experience, we recommend consideration of the following three parameters:

1. The number of unfamiliar team related experiences, such as cultural differences, time zones, language barriers, and corporate cultures/ politics, that the virtual team faces

need to be controlled. By overcoming one variable at a time, the teams can deal with the issues of virtual teams and complete the assignments without being overwhelmed by new variables.

2. The delivery of the materials in each class needs to be in complete alignment. Delivering the material uniformly in all classes gets even more crucial when the project utilizes the Problem Based Learning where students learn the tools to complete the project as the semester progresses.

3. If possible, the subteams should be of equal size. This prevents one site from overruling and dominating the total team because of their majority of team members.

The two undergraduate classes involved in this virtual project were similar in size, and all students were Information Sciences and Technology (IST) majors with junior or senior academic standing. There were 15 students, twelve males and three females, at one campus and 13 students, all males, at the other one. The dominant culture in both locations was American with a few students having influence from Asia and the Middle East. All students in the two classes were involved in the project, and this allowed for four teams of seven people.

Based on the nature of the project and prior experience, it was decided that the virtual team size as seven; therefore, four virtual teams were constructed. Three of the teams were made up of three students from one campus and four from the other. The fourth team had a reverse ratio of the other three teams. The subteams were chosen at each campus separately. At both campuses, students had the opportunity to form nucleus teams (i.e., subteams) with people of their choice. Subteams at both campuses were labeled Subteam 1 through Subteam 4. Subteams were then assigned to virtual teams by their team number. Subteams 1 at both campuses were combined into virtual

team 1, and so on. Random matching of subteams between the campuses provided diverse teams in terms of students' ability and gender. Each subteam was able to work FtF; however, the subteams at different locations only work through CMC which presented a unique challenge for the teams. Subteams in the same location allowed students to work in an environment in which many of them felt comfortable.

The Project Assigned to the Virtual Teams

The problem to be solved by the team concerned a young, growing company that had experienced growth but also recognized that they had problems due to a lack of consistent adaptation of technology within the organization. So, the project assigned to the teams was to prepare a business report for a simulated situation of a company with technology problems within its telephony, network, voicemail, and email systems. Although the students in this project were all from the same discipline, IST, the project could easily be adapted to include business students. In this case, business students would work through the business model aspects of the project while the IST students would focus on technology problems.

The company "hired" the teams to define a project plan that would solve their technology problems. Teams were asked to determine the tradeoffs between different technical solutions and choose the best solution for the company. Note that this project problem can be easily replaced with another one by keeping the virtual team setting similar. The subteams in each campus were assigned to solve specific groups of technology problems. In other words, the responsibility was further broken down by separating the voicemail and telephony to one part of the virtual team and the network and email problems to the other part of the virtual team at the other campus. The entire team was responsible for the budget, resources and overall project plan. It was felt that this split of responsibilities would allow a part of the project to have the look and feel of a traditional team project while still introducing the concept of working in a virtual team for the overall project. Each subteam was required to report on their work as well as their counterpart's work. The teams had to use Microsoft ® Office Project software to document and manage their projects. The software helps students clearly communicate project information to each other and the instructors.

Students were given nine weeks, starting at the sixth week of the semester, to work on their projects. This project was 50% of their course grade. The remaining 50% was earned through class exams, on-line quizzes, homework assignments and class activities. The list of the project assignments, their point values and due dates are given in Table 1. The details of these assignments will be mentioned in later sections.

The Activities Performed in Subteams and Teams

At the beginning of the semester, students filled out a survey, which will be referred to as the entrance survey. They were asked what they thought of virtual teams and if they ever had any prior virtual teamwork experiences. The exact questions of the entrance survey are given in Appendix B. All team members had previous experience of working in traditional teams which meet FtF. However, the entrance survey showed that none had any experience working in a virtual team. It was decided to conduct some activities to familiarize the students with some aspects of team dynamics.

An activity was used to help students cope with problem solving in a team environment while depriving them of one of their senses, and this activity will be mentioned as the "loop" activity in the paper. The activity was conducted separately at each campus. The students lined up shoulder to shoulder all facing in the same direction, and then

Table 1. Project assignments

Project Assignments	Points	%*	Due Date (week)
MOU	10	1.43	4
Contract	10	1.43	4
List of Deliverables	10	1.43	4
Project Charter	15	2.14	7
Activities	25	3.57	N/A
Kickoff Meeting	25	3.57	8
Preliminary Project Plan	25	3.57	9
Statust Review Meeting	25	3.57	11
Weekly Meeting Minutes	25	3.57	each week
Final Report	100	14.29	15
Final Presentation	50	7.14	15
Surveys	30	4.29	15
Total	*350*	*50.00*	

*: represents the percentages by considering the entire course grade.

they were blindfolded. A large single loop of rope was stretched out at their feet allowing six feet for each member of a team of six. This required the blindfolded students to stretch out far enough so that they did not touch the students adjoining them. The assignment was for the team to reach down, pick up the item at their feet and identify it as a length of rope closed into a loop. The team then had ten minutes to move the members of the team so that they formed a perfect square. No member was allowed to let go of the rope or exchange places with another teammate. For this exercise, teams of six were formed at each campus with the remainder of the class assigned as observers. The observers were asked to be sensitive to certain issues given in Appendix A.

The students were also asked to discuss the process that the teams used to develop a solution, such as how did different individuals interact, contribute ideas, lead, follow, create conflict, solve conflict, obtain consensus, etc.? After the activity was over, the teams were asked to record their observations. The instructor then asked how individuals overcame the loss of an important sense, their sight, in this exercise. This dialogue was used to introduce the topic of virtual teams.

The students had previously been exposed to the concepts of personality types using the Myers-Briggs Personality profiles. Myers-Briggs Type Indicator tests were available for us through the University's Career Services. Just as different personality types interact differently in FtF meetings, they also interact differently in virtual meetings. Knowledge of the existence of these different types helps team members understand that others in their team may exhibit different behaviors than their own in a virtual team environment. During the discussions, the individuals' actions and contributions were compared with their personalities. It is the responsibility of all team members to be attuned to their personalities as they begin to appear during the storming stage. Understanding the personality type of each team member and

their strengths and weaknesses can allow teams to utilize team members in their most productive capacity and resolve conflict faster. This is where understanding each other builds trust.

The Assignments

The students were asked to complete several assignments that aided in the development of trust in the virtual teams while establishing early communication. Each team was required to create two documents that defined the relationships between team members and what was expected of them. The first document was a Memorandum of Understanding (MOU). This document sets out the rules of operation for the team. It describes methods of communication, dates and times of meetings, attendance requirements, responsibilities of individuals to the team, etc. It also contains agreements (i.e., code of conduct) describing what would happen if team members do not honor the MOU and their commitments. By requiring this type of document from the team, the instructors were insured that all team members were aware of their responsibilities to their peers. The second document was a Contract that described what the team was responsible for producing during the semester. The Contract lists the team deliverables, individual roles in the project, major milestones, etc. The purpose of this document is to ensure that all team members understood the assignment and their individual roles. These two documents were the first assignment for the team. Students needed to learn how to build trust in early stages of communication. By producing these documents, the team members gained exposure to their teammates and began to build trust. Moreover, instructors were always encouraging participation and were supportive in each phase of the project.

The entire virtual team was also responsible for a Project Charter document, Kickoff and Status Review meetings, an oral presentation and a written document describing the solution. The Project

Charter is a formal document that authorizes the project and includes the formal request document, the preliminary analysis, the project scope document and the project budget. If any third party contracts exist, it will include those as well. The Project Charter should define resources available and a definition of the project manager's role and authority. Finally, any constraints should be clearly defined as well as any assumptions. The purpose of the Kickoff meeting is basically defining the project and its deliverables and establishing a timeline for the project. The Status Review meeting is a work meeting between the project manager and the project team. We had a Status Review meeting in the eleventh week of the semester. All of these included the entire problem, not just the portion assigned to the part of the team at each location. A subteam at each campus was responsible to deliver material representing the entire team's work and accomplishments. Presentations were given at each campus by the representatives of the team at that campus.

Private web spaces were created in ANGEL for each team where only team members and the instructors had access. These sites contained folders for weekly meeting minutes, document templates, drafts of work, etc. All written work was submitted to the team sites so the instructors could monitor the teams' work. The students were allowed to formulate their own method of conducting virtual meetings. As stated before, a portion of the technical aspects of the assignment was the exclusive responsibility of a subteam. Progresses on the subteam assignments were discussed during the weekly team meetings. When team presentations were given during the separate classes members of each team were responsible to report on the progress of the entire project. This required members of a team at one location to report on the progress of the entire team, not just the work done by their subteam.

Weekly meetings were mandatory, and minutes of the meetings were submitted through the private web spaces created in ANGEL as part of their team project grade. This required the members to be knowledgeable and able to discuss relevant details about what their counterparts were doing.

During class, each instructor solicited concerns and issues from the students. The two instructors met weekly to discuss team progress, issues, and course content delivery. Feedback to issues from the minutes and the classroom discussion were formulated and then given back to the students during the next class meeting or through ANGEL. The latter provided the instructors give feedback to students in a personalized way whenever possible.

The teams were also given the opportunity to choose their own project structure. The teams were allowed to choose whether or not they wanted a team leader as well as which member was responsible for handing in assignments. Each of the deliverables for the report was given a set due date, but many of the teams set deadlines within their groups before these due dates so that the members would have time to edit and revise their documents if necessary.

At the end of the semester, when the project was completed, the students also responded to another survey, which will be referred to as the exit survey. At that time, they were given the chance to respond to open-ended questions which allowed the students to provide insight as to what they thought of the project as well as suggestions on making the project better. The students were also expected to evaluate one another in various areas such as how well each of the members worked and if team members failed to accomplish their fair share of work. The questions of the exit survey can be seen in Appendix B, and the details of the responses to the surveys will be discussed in the next section.

FINDINGS AND DISCUSSION

Student responses to the entrance survey showed that many of the students were apprehensive about the concept of virtual teams. More than 70% of the students (20 out of 28) expressed negative feelings before the project began. Many teams were concerned that it would be difficult to keep the project moving forward with the constraints of distance placed between subteams. Many students expressed concerns about controlling the work of their subteam partners at the other location.

When the exit survey was administered, the responses came back significantly different than the entrance survey: more than 75% of the students (22 out of 28) were enthusiastic about virtual teams and felt that they could accomplish goals working in this format. The comparison of entrance and exit surveys can also be seen from Figure 1.

The major problem that many teams frequently faced with in the virtual team setting was that it was easy for subteams to operate in isolation from one another. This was evident in at least two of the teams in the early stages. Many subteams found it easier and more comfortable to just communicate among subteam members and ignore the other subteam in the other campus. In some instances this led to duplication of work as students handed in two parts when only one was

necessary. These teams then had difficulty when it was time to put the parts together. In one instance, a subteam found that it was easier to just finish something on their own rather than to let the subteam from the other campus involved. This created some resentment between the two subteams when one of the subteams found out that they had not been included in the work. There was an attempt to limit these pitfalls by requiring subteam members at each campus to be responsible for reporting on the progress of the work being completed by the subteam members at the other campus. Some subteams tried to meet both virtually and in person, while others chose to only meet virtually.

Many teams that met both virtually and in person as a subteam found it harder to communicate between the different subteams, and this created internal conflicts in the team. The different ways of communication that the teams used can be seen in Table 2. All teams relied on email and IM as their primary communication medium. Most teams included a third method, but the choices were different for each team. One

Figure 1. Student perspectives of virtual teams

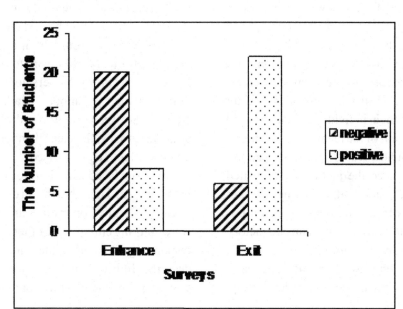

team used phone conferencing and another used the ANGEL Chat. All but one team had many FtF meetings on the subteam level. This implies that even some subteam members in the same campus met in a virtual environment. It is interesting to note that of all the technologies (i.e., IM and email) that the teams used, one is a synchronous communications method (IM) and the other is an asynchronous communications method (email). It appears that IM is used for meetings and email is used to communicate "offline."

The most common complaint mentioned by 13 students was the problem of the lack of mandatory meetings. Many of the teams did not enforce any attendance policy within their teams. This later became a problem as due dates came up and students scrambled to find a time when they could meet. This is similar to much of the research on virtual teams that has been done in the past. Many papers have claimed that virtual teams tend to procrastinate (Walther & Ulla, 2005). Many students felt that they should have set a time once a week when everyone would meet regardless of what needed to be done. It has been shown that virtual team members must communicate regularly in order to be successful (Beise, 2004).

Interestingly, eight students commented that a more detailed code of conduct with well-defined guidelines should be set up at the beginning to deal with non-productive team members. These students mentioned two types of infractions: not handing in deliverables to the team and not attending the pre-set meetings. Many of these eight students felt that their individual grades should be more independent of the team's grade. This is, unfortunately, not how teams in professional life work. In the workplace, the quality of the finished product is all that truly matters. If one member of a team slacks off in certain areas, then missing deadlines and/or producing an unsatisfactory product can penalize the entire team.

Only three students, two from the same team, stated that their team needed more leadership.

Some groups decided not to even use a team leader and rather chose a more ad-hoc method of leadership. This arrangement/format made working on the project much more difficult as there was no authoritative leader to make the final decisions. This caused tension in a few of the teams. One team tried to rotate the leadership among members, and they were pleased with this arrangement. Leadership is crucial in all projects and becomes even more important in virtual teams.

Quite a few students mentioned the necessity of FtF meetings. Many previous studies have shown that trust is usually built more rapidly if the teams meet FtF at least once, usually before the project begins (Levin & Rad, 2005). The beginning stages of the formation of a team are often the most important, and the majority of the trust is built in this stage (Coppola et al., 2004); therefore, it would have been advantageous for a team to meet at least once FtF. In our project, because the two campuses were only approximately 30 miles apart, this would have been feasible, though no team chose to do so. However, students had a thorough understanding of the necessity of FtF communication in brainstorming and decision-making phases of the project.

Many students complained of technical issues such as network outages and software crashing as well as lost files. This showed the students that in a virtual team environment, it is often best to be prepared for technical errors to occur. In virtual teams it is best for members not to expect everything to always go smooth. Bradner et al. (2005) claims that "Technology has the ability to build boundaries as well as tear them down depending on how effectively it is used."

One team faced with significant problems early in the project. The subteams in each campus were having difficulty communicating since members were ignoring emails from other members and not responding. This caused the team to miss their first deadline. In traditional FtF meetings, it is fairly easy to determine whether someone understands what has been said whereas this is not obvious in emails. One of the rules, "Overtly acknowledge you have read one another's message," which was devised and empirically tested by (Walther & Ulla, 2005), is a remedy in this situation.

Many of the team members commented on how important they felt virtual teams would become in the future as digital technology continues to push forward. One of the students even mentioned how the company that they were currently working at utilized virtual teams and web conferencing software to make better use of resources. Another student mentioned an interview at a major corporation where he was asked several questions dealing with his ability to work in virtual teams.

Our findings through entrance and exit surveys showed that many students are now more comfortable with virtual teams after this class project and feel that this experience has been a valuable one. Table 3 shows the student opinions (team based) at the beginning and the end of the project along with the average team project grades. Although

not being statistically significant, there seems a strong correlation between student opinions and project grades. All negative responses in the exit survey were from members of Team 2. All other teams had 100% positive responses. Therefore, together with the fact that Team 2 had the least communication, it indicates a dysfunction that they were not able to overcome in Team 2, and their project grade somehow represented this. We cannot say anything certain about whether this affected their course evaluations since they were anonymously done.

The subteams method, ironically, made the teams more challenging as students were expected to step out of their comfort zones in order to communicate with one another online. The students learned to balance the two types of communications and, in the end, this will be more useful to the workforce. Many of the students also gained a great deal of insight on how they could more effectively manage virtual teams. Even students who are not placed in a virtual team

Table 2. Technology choice

Teams	Communication technologies used				
	Email	IM	Angel	FtF meetings	Phone
			Chat	in subteams	
1	√	√	√	√	
2	√	√			
3	√	√		√	
4	√	√		√	√

Table 3. Student opinion polls and the project grades

Teams	Student Opinions		Average
	Entrance	Exit	Project
	survey	Survey	Grades
1	positive	positive	A
2	negative	negative	C+
3	negative	positive	A-
4	negative	positive	A-

environment in the workplace will find this experience invaluable.

The fact that team members had different class and work schedules created conflicts in scheduling meeting times. Many students had difficulty finding time to meet one another. Most teams did not have the luxury of having all members work at the same time of the day. This made it more difficult for the teams to communicate as effectively as they could have if they all had similar schedules. While this was a drawback, it accurately represents what is often the case in virtual teams. In many cases, some partners may be from other countries and their typical work hours may be on different schedule. Therefore, many students effectively chose to use asynchronous forms of communication, like email, as opposed to synchronous. Email gave the students the ability to send a message to their partners and retrieve messages when it was best for them. For an easy referencing, Table 4 summarizes the main problems teams faced with as well as in which stage of Tuckman's model of the project.

Two topics concerning trust building were given special attention: social communication and behaviors of virtual listeners. In any team environment, social communication between team members builds understanding and familiarizes team members with their teammates' goals and beliefs. This allows a better understanding and therefore develops trust. In virtual teams this socialization must not be omitted because it will be hard to

develop trust without this personal information. In FtF meetings, a speaker can see everyone's reaction to what he/she says, even if there is no response. Without FtF contact, speakers cannot read the body language of their listeners. This requires all listeners to be active listeners; they must exhibit some kind of behavior such as a response to ideas. They must "verbalize" these behaviors in whatever communication method the team has chosen to use (Walther & Ulla, 2005).

CONCLUSION AND FUTURE WORK

Virtual teams in online courses have recently been studied in the literature (Johnson et al., 2002; Clark & Gibb, 2006). Our analysis is one of the few dealing with the virtual team concept not specifically in an online course environment but with subteams from geographically distinct two campuses of the Pennsylvania State University.

Responses to a survey at the end of the course indicate most of the students believe that they have become more comfortable with virtual teams through this exercise. It is also a valuable addition to their education. This experience will be invaluable in their future careers as virtual teams become more prevalent in the work place.

The virtual team project described in this paper was very successful. We will continue to look at new methods of improving it. Student comments reveal that FtF meetings in early stages of the

Table 4. Main problems stated by students through the exit survey

Problems	Tuckman Stages
Lack of meetings between subteams in different locations	all
Lack of mandatory meetings	all
Code of conduct is not comprehensive enough	forming
Lack of leadership	all
Missing FtF meetings	forming
Technical	performing
Scheduling Conflicts	all

project, such as FtF kickoff meetings, should be set up; otherwise, trust is harder to develop and/or easier to lose. Furthermore, in a similar future project, leadership concepts, such as situational leadership (Lee-Kelley, 2002), pre-assigned single or rotated leaders, expectations from a leader, and leadership skills, will receive greater emphasis.

Another area which could be improved is creating teams of members with different experiences. In a real-life team environment, it is highly unlikely that all of the members will have the same major or education level. Many of the team members will graduate from different colleges at different times, and some will have more experience than others. In the study we performed, the class was made up entirely of IST students. All of these students were comfortable using computers at this point as most of them had been learning about computers for at least two years. Another project would have involved numerous majors such as business, accounting, and engineering as in actual corporate situations. Team members don't need to be knowledgeable in many areas, just in their area of expertise to help the team succeed.

While an attempt was made to limit new dimensions in virtual teams in this project, there are some challenges that can be involved in education to better prepare the students for future virtual team work. Once students experienced how to build trust and communicate effectively in virtual teams, their next virtual team project could include students of other universities at different geographical areas. The involvement of additional schools would better simulate the typical work environment. Virtual team members will often be working together with people that are separated by distance as well as cultural boundaries (Bradner et al., 2005).

The professors have come up with a few more areas in which this project could be improved. One method of improving collaboration in the program that the instructors would like to examine is the use of wikis in education. A wiki is an online program that allows users to quickly and easily modify the web page that they are viewing. Anyone that has been given permission can add, delete or change that web page (Bold, 2006). This simplifies the process of collaborating on team projects. This idea would allow users to be able to edit documents and assignments in a more organized fashion. Wikis also track changes which would allow the professors to more closely monitor the team progress and each student's contribution. This program could introduce the students to many new concepts of collaboration software and allow them to collaborate in many new ways that are not possible without this software.

Virtual teams pose a formidable problem to college students. By isolating each of the major parameters of virtual teams (i.e., trust and communications, multi-cultural environments, and major time zone differences), we can focus on teaching any of these parameters. We chose trust and communications since they represented the foundation for the other two. Based on the feedback from the students involved in the project, it can be said that most of the students changed their attitudes from negative to positive toward virtual teams.

REFERENCES

Beise, C. M. (2004). *IT project management and virtual teams*. Paper presented at the 2004 SIGMIS Conference on Computer Personnel Research: Careers, Culture, and Ethics in a Networked Environment.

Bergiel, B. J., Bergiel, E. B., & Phillip, W. B. (2008). Nature of virtual teams: a summary of their advantages and disadvantages. *Management Research News, 31*(2), 99. doi:10.1108/01409170810846821

Bold, M. (2006). Use of wikis in graduate course work. *Journal of Interactive Learning, 17*(1), 5.

Bradner, E., Mark, G., & Hertel, T. D. (2005). Team size and technology fit: participation, awareness, and rapport in distributed teams. *IEEE Transactions on Professional Communication, 48*(1), 68–77. doi:10.1109/TPC.2004.843299

Clark, D. N., & Gibb, J. L. (2006). Virtual team learning: an introductory study team exercise. *Journal of Management Education, 30*(6), 765–787. doi:10.1177/1052562906287969

Coppola, N. W., Hiltz, S. R., & Rotter, N. G. (2004). Building trust in virtual teams. *IEEE Transactions on Professional Communication, 47*(2), 95–104. doi:10.1109/TPC.2004.828203

Crowston, K., Howison, J., Masango, C., & Eseryel, U. Y. (2007). The role of face-to-face meetings in technology-supported self-organizing distributed teams. *IEEE Transactions on Professional Communication, 50*(3), 185. doi:10.1109/TPC.2007.902654

Dalton, M., Leslie, J., Ernst, C., & Deal, J. (2002). *Success for the new global manager: how to work across distances, countries and cultures*. San Francisco, CA: Jossey-Bass.

Elkins, T. (2000). Virtual teams connect and collaborate. *IIE Solutions, 32*(4), 26–32.

Friedman, T. L. (2006). *The world is flat: a brief history of the 21st century*. New York: Farrar, Straus and Giroux.

Hunsaker, P. L., & Hunsaker, J. S. (2008). Virtual teams: a leader's guide. *Team Performance Management, 14*(1/2), 86. doi:10.1108/13527590810860221

Jarvenpaa, S. L., & Leidner, D. E. (1997). *Developing trust in virtual teams*. Paper presented at the 30th Hawaii International Conference on Systems Sciences, Maui, HI.

Johnson, S. D., Suriya, C., Seung Won, Y., Berrett, J. V., & La Fleur, J. (2002). Team development and group processes of virtual learning teams. *Computers & Education, 39*(4), 379–393. doi:10.1016/S0360-1315(02)00074-X

Keyzerman, Y. (2003). Trust in virtual teams. In *Proceedings of Professional Communication Conference (IPCC 2003)* (pp. 391-399). Orlando, FL, USA.

Kock, N. (2001). The ape that used email: understanding e-communication behavior through evolution theory. *Communication of the AIS, 5*(3), 1–29.

Kock, N., & Nosek, J. (2005). Expanding the boundaries of e-collaboration. *IEEE Transactions on Professional Communication, 48*(1), 1–9. doi:10.1109/TPC.2004.843272

Lee-Kelley, L. (2002). Situational leadership: managing the virtual project team. *Journal of Management Development, 21*(5/6), 461–476. doi:10.1108/02621710210430623

Levin, G., & Rad, P. F. (2005). Requirements for effective project communications: differences and similarities in virtual and traditional project environments. Retrieved from www.AllPM.com.

Lipnack, J., & Stamps, J. (2000). *Virtual teams: people working across boundaries with technology*. New York: John Wiley & Sons, Inc.

Lowry, P. B., Roberts, T. L., Romano, N. C., Cheney, P. D., & Hightower, R. T. (2006). The impact of group size and social presence on small-group communication - does computer-mediated communication make a difference? *Small Group Research, 37*(6), 631–661. doi:10.1177/1046496406294322

Malhotra, A., Majchrzak, A., & Rosen, B. (2007). Leading virtual teams. *The Academy of Management Perspectives, 21*(1), 60.

Nedelko, Z. (2007). Videoconferencing in virtual teams. *Business Review (Federal Reserve Bank of Philadelphia), 7*(1), 164.

Ocker, R. J. (2005). Influences on creativity in asynchronous virtual teams: a qualitative analysis of experimental teams. *IEEE Transactions on Professional Communication, 48*(1), 22–39. doi:10.1109/TPC.2004.843294

Panteli, N., & Davison, R. M. (2005). The role of subgroups in the communication patterns of global virtual teams. *IEEE Transactions on Professional Communication, 48*(2), 191–200. doi:10.1109/TPC.2005.849651

Powell, A., Gabriele, P., & Blake, I. (2004). Virtual teams: a review of current literature and directions for future research. *The Data Base for Advances in Information Systems, 35*(1), 6.

Roebuck, D. B. (2002). *Colonel mustard in the library with the knife ... experiencing virtual teaming.* Paper presented at the 67th Annual Meeting of the Association for Business Communication, Cincinnati, OH.

Roebuck, D. B., & Britt, A. C. (2002). Virtual teaming has come to stay--guidelines and strategies for success. *Southern Business Review, 28*(1), 29–39.

Tuckman, B. W. (1965). Developmental sequence in small groups. *Psychological Bulletin, 63*, 384–399. doi:10.1037/h0022100

Walther, J. B., & Ulla, B. (2005). The rules of virtual groups: trust, liking, and performance in computer-mediated communication. *The Journal of Communication, 55*(4), 828. doi:10.1111/j.1460-2466.2005.tb03025.x

Wilson, J. M., Straus, S. G., & McEvily, B. (2006). All in due time: the development of trust in computer-mediated and face-to-face teams. *Organizational Behavior and Human Decision Processes, 99*(1), 16–33. doi:10.1016/j.obhdp.2005.08.001

APPENDIX A: EVALUATION POINTS FOR THE "LOOP" ACTIVITY

The observers were asked to pay attention to any of the following dynamics happening within the team:

- Individual behavior and style
- Participation levels
- Constructive, supportive input ("How can we best approach this...?") versus negative contributions ("This is a stupid game...")
- Natural leaders
- Natural process checkers
- Results driven players
- Compassion and empathy
- Communication skills
- Negotiation skills
- Awareness of process and consensus principles
- Logical and objective assessment of relative values and capabilities
- Integrity
- Awareness of need to preserve mix of team abilities
- Bullying, ganging-up, and defense and reaction to these
- Sexism, racism, prejudice, and defense and reaction to these

APPENDIX B: SURVEY QUESTIONS

Entrance Survey

1. Have you ever worked in a team where you were physically separate from other members of your team (i.e., a virtual team)?
2. If your answer to first question is "Yes", what do you think are the biggest advantages and disadvantages of virtual teams?
3. How comfortable are you while working in teams, face-to-face or virtual?
4. How effective do you feel that virtual teams would work?
5. Are you comfortable with using communication technologies like Instant Messaging and E-mail?

Exit Survey

1. How effective do you feel that your virtual team in this class worked and did you change your idea about virtual team effectiveness? Why or why not?
2. If you were asked in an interview to describe your virtual team experience, how would you response?
3. Would you be willing to work in a virtual team in a work environment? Why or why not?
4. What two things would you change in your own virtual team to make it more effective?
5. How did your team build trust within your virtual team?
6. Please comment on anything about virtual teams rather than the above questions.

This work was previously published in International Journal of Information Technology Project Management, Volume 1, Issue 2, edited by John Wang, pp. 61-78, copyright 2010 by IGI Publishing (an imprint of IGI Global).

Section 4
Acquiring Managerial Experience

Chapter 9
Half–Life of Learning Curves for Information Technology Project Management

Adedeji B. Badiru
Air Force Institute of Technology, USA

ABSTRACT

Learning curves are used extensively in business, science, technology, engineering, and industry to predict system performance over time. Although most of the early development and applications were in the area of production engineering, contemporary applications can be found in all areas of applications. Information technology project management, in particular, offers a fertile area for the application of learning curves. This paper applies the concept of half-life of learning curves to information technology project management. This is useful for predictive measures of information technology system performance. Half-life is the amount of time it takes for a quantity to diminish to half of its original size through natural processes. The approach of half-life computation provides an additional decision tool for researchers and practitioners in information technology management. Derivation of the half-life equations of learning curves can reveal more about the properties of the various curves with respect to the unique life-cycle property of information technology.

INTRODUCTION

An interesting cliché is that if you wait long enough, you'll never have to learn new technology because there will always be a newer and more updated one (Badiru, 2009). Information

DOI: 10.4018/978-1-4666-0930-3.ch009

technology has several unique characteristics that make its management challenging. Some of these characteristics include frequent life cycle changes and uncertainty in the operating environment. Information technology is valuable for effective communication and decision making in an organization (Demirkan & Nichols, 2008; Alter, 1999, 2002; Ross & Beath, 2002). Organizations use information technology (hardware and software) to capture, transmit, store, retrieve, manipulate, or display information. Information technology projects are expected to meet the information processing needs of an organization; therefore, they require communication, cooperation, and coordination among different groups of stakeholders (Badiru, 2008, 2009). Ewusi-Mensah (1997) discussed several critical issues that can lead to the abandonment of information technology projects. Many of such issues involve performance coordination and cost evaluation. The literature contains several applications of learning curves to cost and time estimation (Richardson, 1978).

MOTIVATION

Learning curve analysis offers a viable approach for evaluating information technology projects where human learning and forgetting are involved. With an effective learning curve evaluation, an assessment can be made of how an information technology project meets organizational objectives and maximizes its benefits to the organization. The half-life theory of learning curves introduced by Badiru and Ijaduola (2009) offers one good technique for an accurate assessment. Although a conventional project is defined as one of a kind endeavor with a definite beginning and a definite end, it does contain some repetitive elements when the project or a similar variation is replicated elsewhere. This makes the application of learning curve analysis relevant for the project environment (Badiru, 1995). With this analogy, learning curve analysis can, indeed, be applied to information technology project management. Figure 1 illustrates a conventional curve of the life cycle of information technology project as a function of resource infusion. In reality there will be dips in the curve due to the effects of learning and forgetting phenomena. It is essential to be able to predict locations of such dips so that an accurate assessment of the overall IT performance

can be done when the same IT project is implemented at different locations in an organization. Modern projects have repetitive components that are amenable to learning curves analysis, unlike the traditional era where a project is defined as a unique, one-of-a-kind endeavor.

STAGES OF INFORMATION TECHNOLOGY

Coupled with volatile nature of information technology are other sources of risk and uncertainty that arise as a result of imperfect knowledge of the technology system under consideration. Uncertainty is directly linked to economic loss; therefore, techniques for understanding it and mitigating its impact would be beneficial. Understanding the half-life properties of the learning curves that govern the technology system would be beneficial in achieving overall success of information technology project management. The typical information technology starts from conceptualization through disposal. The expanded stages of information technology are presented below.

- Conceptualization
- Initiation
- Planning
- Requirements analysis
- Design
- Development
- Integration
- Testing
- Implementation
- Operation
- Maintenance
- Phase-out
- Disposal

The impact of learning curves can be seen in each of the several stages above. But the implication of half-life analysis may be most relevant for the stages of design, development, integration,

Figure 1. Information technology project life cycle curve

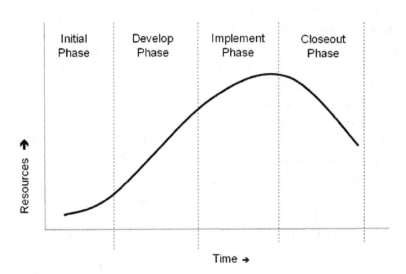

implementation, operation, and maintenance. For the purpose of a concise application of half-life learning curve analysis, we introduce a condensed evaluation model spanning the stages of Design, Evaluation, Justification, and Integration (DEJI). The stages are illustrated with their constituent elements in Figure 2.

TECHNOLOGY LEARNING CURVES AND FORGETTING COMPONENTS

The fact is that the fast pace of technology affects learning curves and the frequent changes of technology degrades learning curves. Thus, specialized analytical assessment of learning curves is needed for information technology project management. Badiru (1995) presents examples of how learning curve changes affect resource work rate analysis in project management. The degradation of learning curves is often depicted analytically by incorporating forgetting components into conventional learning curves as has been shown in the literature over the past few decades (Badiru 1992, 1994; Jaber & Sikstrom, 2004; Jaber et al., 2003; Jaber & Bonney, 1996;

Jaber & Bonney, 2007; Nembhard & Osothsilp, 2001; Nembhard & Uzumeri, 2000; Sule, 1978; Globerson et al., 1998).

HALF-LIFE THEORY OF LEARNING CURVES

As another approach to capturing the essence of forgetting in learning curves, Badiru and Ijaduola (2009) introduced the half-life theory of learning curves. Traditionally, the standard time has been used as an indication of when learning should cease or when resources need to be transferred to another job. It is possible that half-life theory can supplement standard time analysis. The half-life approach will encourage researchers and practitioners to reexamine conventional applications of existing learning curve models. Organizations invest in people, work process, and technology for the purpose of achieving performance improvement. The systems nature of such investment strategy requires that the investment be strategically planned over multiple years. Thus, changes in learning curve profiles over those years become very crucial. Forgetting analysis and half-life

Figure 2. IT project design, evaluation, justification, and integration model

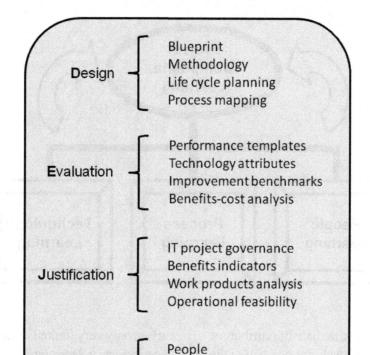

computations can provide additional insights into learning curve changes. Through the application of robust learning curve analysis, system enhancement can be achieved in terms of cost, time, and performance with respect to strategic investment of funds and other organizational assets in people, process, and technology as shown in Figure 3. The predictive capability of learning curves is helpful in planning for integrated system performance improvement.

Formal analysis of learning curves first emerged in the mid-1930s in connection with the analysis of the production of airplanes (Wright, 1936). Learning refers to the improved operational efficiency and cost reduction obtained from repetition of a task. This has a direct impact for training purposes and the design of work. Workers learn and improve by repeating operations.

But they also regress due to the impact of forgetting, prolonged breaks, work interruption, and natural degradation of performance. Half-life computations can provide a better understanding of actual performance levels over time. Half-life is the amount of time it takes for a quantity to diminish to half of its original size through natural processes. Duality is of natural interest in many real-world processes. We often speak of "twice as much" and "half as much" as benchmarks for process analysis. In economic and financial principles, the "rule of 72" refers to the length of time required for an investment to double in value. These common "double" or "half" concepts provide the motivation for half-life analysis.

The usual application of half-life is in natural sciences. For example, in Physics, the half-life is a measure of the stability of a radioactive sub-

Figure 3. Learning components of people-process-technology integration

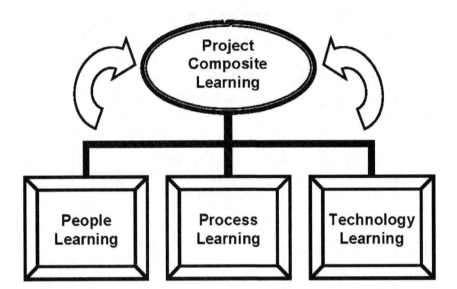

stance. In practical terms, the half-life attribute of a substance is the time it takes for one-half of the atoms in an initial magnitude to disintegrate. The longer the half-life of a substance, the more stable it is. This provides a good analogy for modeling learning curves with the recognition of increasing performance or decreasing cost with respect to the passage of time. The approach provides another perspective to the large body of literature on learning curves. Badiru and Ijaduola (2009) present the following formal definitions:

For learning curves: Half-life is the production level required to reduce cumulative average cost per unit to half of its original size.

For forgetting curve: Half-life is the amount of time it takes for performance to decline to half its original magnitude.

HUMAN-TECHNOLOGY PERFORMANCE DEGRADATION

Although there is extensive collection of classical studies of *improvement* due to learning

curves, only very limited attention has been paid to performance *degradation* due to the impact of forgetting. Some of the classical works on process improvement due to learning include Belkaoui (1986), Camm et al. (1987), Liao (1979), Mazur and Hastie (1978), McIntyre (1977), Nanda (1979), Pegels (1976), Richardson (1978), Smith (1989), Smunt (1986), Sule (1978), Womer (1979, 1981, 1984), Womer and Gulledge (1983), Yelle (1976, 1979, 1983). It is only in recent years that the recognition of "forgetting" curves began to emerge, as can be seen in more recent literature (Jaber & Sikstrom, 2004; Jaber et al., 2003; Jaber & Bonney, 2003, 2007; Jaber & Guiffrida, 2008). The new and emerging research on the forgetting components of learning curves provides the motivation for studying half-life properties of learning curves. Performance decay can occur due to several factors, including lack of training, reduced retention of skills, lapsed in performance, extended breaks in practice, and natural forgetting. The conventional learning curve equation introduced by Wright (1936) has a drawback whereby the cost/time per unit approaches zero as the cumulative output approaches infinity. That is:

$$\lim_{x \to \infty} C(x) = \lim_{x \to \infty} C_1 x^{-b} \to 0$$

Researchers who initially embraced the Wright's learning curve (WLC) assumed a lower bound for the equation such that WLC could be represented as:

$$C(x) = \begin{cases} C_1 x^{-b}, & \text{if } x < x_s \\ C_s, & \text{otherwise} \end{cases},$$

where x_s is the number of units required to reach standard cost C_s. A half-life analysis can reveal more information about the properties of WLC particularly when we consider the operating range of $x_0 < x_s$.

HALF-LIFE DERIVATIONS FOR IT PROJECTS

Learning curves present the relationship between cost (or time) and level of activity on the basis of the effect of learning. An early study by Wright (1936) disclosed the "80 percent learning" effect, which indicates that a given operation is subject to a 20 percent productivity improvement each time the activity level or production volume **doubles**. The proposed half-life approach is the antithesis of the double-level milestone. Learning curve can serve as a predictive tool for obtaining time estimates for tasks that are repeated within a project life cycle. The concept of learning curves is directly applicable to planning and control of information technology projects.

Half-life learning curves analysis is particularly relevant because of the dynamic ever-changing scenarios of information technology applications. A new learning curve does not necessarily commence each time a new technology is implemented since workers can often transfer previous technology skills to technology operations, albeit with new adaptation schemes. The point at which the learning curve begins to flatten depends on the degree of similarity of the new technology to the previous information technology.

Several alternate models of learning curves have been presented in the literature for production-type operations, including *Log-linear model, S-curve model, Stanford-B model, DeJong's learning formula, Levy's adaptation function, Glover's learning formula, Pegels' exponential function, Knecht's upturn model,* and *Yelle's product model.* Many of these are directly applicable to information technology project environments. Levy's technology adaptation function (Levy, 1965) is particularly useful for IT project application. The basic log-linear model is the most popular learning curve model. It expresses a dependent variable (e.g., production cost) in terms of some independent variable (e.g., cumulative production). The model states that the improvement in productivity is constant (i.e., it has a constant slope) as output increases. That is:

$$C(x) = C_1 x^{-b}$$

Where:

$C(x)$ = cumulative average cost of producing x units

C_1 = cost of the first unit

x = cumulative production unit

b = learning curve exponent

The expression for $C(x)$ is practical only for $x > 0$. This makes sense because learning effect cannot realistically kick in until at least one unit ($x \geq 1$) has been produced. For the standard log-linear model, the expression for the learning rate, p, is derived by considering two production levels where one level is double the other. The performance curve, $P(x)$, can be defined as the reciprocal of the average cost curve, $C(x)$. Thus, we have:

$$P(x) = \frac{1}{C(x)},$$

which will have an increasing profile compared to the asymptotically declining cost curve. In terms of practical application, learning to drive is one example where maximum performance can be achieved in relatively short time compared to the half-life of performance. That is, learning is steep, but the performance curve is relatively flat after steady state is achieved. The application of half-life analysis to learning curves can help address questions such as the ones below:

- How fast and how far can system performance be improved?
- What are the limitations to system performance improvement?
- How resilient is a system to shocks and interruptions to its operation?
- Are the performance goals that are set for the system achievable?

Half-life of the Log-Linear Model

Figure 4 shows the basic log-linear model, with the half-life point indicated as $x_{1/2}$. The half-life of the log-linear model is computed as follows: Let:

C_0 = Initial performance level

$C_{1/2}$ = Performance level at half-life

$$C_0 = C_1 x_0^{-b} \quad \text{and} \quad C_{1/2} = C_1 x_{1/2}^{-b}$$

But $C_{1/2} = \frac{1}{2} C_0$

Therefore, $C_1 x_{1/2}^{-b} = \frac{1}{2} C_1 x_0^{-b}$, which leads to

$x_{1/2}^{-b} = \frac{1}{2} x_0^{-b}$, which, by taking the $(-1/b)^{\text{th}}$ exponent of both sides, simplifies to yield the follow-

ing expression as the general expression for the standard log-linear learning curve model,

$$x_{1/2} = \left(\frac{1}{2}\right)^{-\frac{1}{b}} x_0, \quad x_0 \geq 1$$

where $x_{1/2}$ is the half-life and x_0 is the initial point of operation. We refer to $x_{1/2}$ (Figure 3) as the ***First-Order Half-Life***. The ***Second-Order Half-Life*** is computed as the time corresponding to half of the preceding half. That is:

$$C_1 x_{1/2(2)}^{-b} = \frac{1}{4} C_1 x_0^{-b},$$

which simplifies to yield:

$$x_{1/2(2)} = (1/2)^{-2/b} x_0,$$

Similarly, the **Third-Order Half-Life** is derived to obtain:

$$x_{1/2(3)} = (1/2)^{-3/b} x_0,$$

In general, the ***k^{th}-Order Half-Life*** for the log-linear model is represented as:

Figure 4. Profile of Basic Learning Curve with Half-Life Point

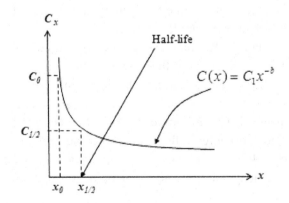

$$x_{1/2(k)} = (1/2)^{-k/b} x_0,$$

HALF-LIFE COMPUTATIONAL EXAMPLES

This section uses examples of log-linear learning curves with b=0.75 and b=0.3032 respectively to illustrate the characteristics of learning which can dictate the half-life behavior of the overall learning process. Knowing the point where the half-life of each curve occurs can be very useful in assessing learning retention for the purpose of designing, evaluating, justifying, and integrating new information technology. For $C(x) = 250x^{-0.75}$, the First-Order half-life is computed as:

$$x_{1/2} = (1/2)^{-1/0.75} x_0, \quad x_0 \geq 1$$

If the above expression is evaluated for $x_0 =$ 2, the first-order half-life yields $x_{1/2} = 5.0397$; which indicates a fast drop in the value of *C(x)*. *C(2) =148.6509* corresponding to a half-life of 5.0397. Note that *C(5.0397) = 74.7674,* which is about half of 148.6509. The conclusion from this analysis is that if we are operating at the point *x=2,* we can expect the curve to reach its half-life decline point at *x=5*. For $C(x) = 240.03x^{-0.3032}$, the First-Order half-life is computed as:

$$x_{1/2} = (1/2)^{-1/0.3032} x_0, \quad x_0 \geq 1$$

If we evaluate the above function for $x_0 = 2$; the first-order half-life is $x_{1/2} = 19.6731$. For a simple example of possible application scenario, consider a case where an IT technician can install new IT software in three computers every four hours. At this rate, it is desired to compute how long it would take the technician to install the same software in five computers. We know, from the information given, that we can write the proportion three computers is to four hours as the proportion that five computers is to *x* hours, where *x* represents the number of hours the technician would take to install software in five computers. This gives the following ratio relationship:

$$\frac{3 \; computers}{4 \; hours} = \frac{5 \; computers}{x \; hours},$$

which simplifies to yield *x* = 6hours, 40 minutes. Now consider a situation where the technician's competence with the software installation degrades over time for whatever reason. We will see that the time requirements for the IT software installation will vary depending on the current competency level of the technician. Half-life analysis can help to capture such situations so that an accurate work time estimate can be developed.

Several models and variations of learning curves are used in practice. Models are developed through one of the following approaches:

1. Conceptual models
2. Theoretical models
3. Observational models
4. Experimental models
5. Empirical models

ALTERNATE LEARNING CURVE MODELS

The S-Curve Model: The S-Curve (Towill & Cherrington, 1994) is based on an assumption of a gradual start-up. The function has the shape of the cumulative normal distribution function for the start-up curve and the shape of an operating characteristics function for the learning curve. The gradual start-up is based on the fact that the early stages of production are typically in a transient state with changes in tooling, methods, materials, design, and even changes in the work force. The basic form of the S-Curve function is:

$$C(x) = C_1 + M(x + B)^{-b}$$

$$MC(x) = C_1\left[M + (1 - M)(x + B)^{-b}\right]$$

Where:

$C(x)$ = learning curve expression
b = learning curve exponent
$M(x)$ = marginal cost expression
C_1 = cost of first unit
M = incompressibility factor (a constant)
B = equivalent experience units (a constant).

Assumptions about at least three out of the four parameters $\left(M, B, C_1, \text{and } b\right)$ are needed to solve for the fourth one. Using the $C(x)$ expression and derivation procedure outlined earlier for the log-linear model, the half-life equation for the S-Curve learning model is derived to be:

$$x_{1/2} = (1/2)^{-1/b}\left[\frac{M(x_0 + B)^{-b} - C_1}{M}\right]^{-1/b} - B$$

Where:

$x_{1/2}$ = half-life expression for the S-Curve Learning Model
x_0 = initial point of evaluation of performance on the learning curve

In terms of practical application of the S-Curve, consider when a worker begins learning a new task. The individual is slow initially at the tail end of the S-Curve. But the rate of learning increases as time goes on, with additional repetitions. This helps the worker to climb the steep-slope segment of the S-Curve very rapidly. At the top of the slope, the worker is classified as being proficient with the learned task. From then on, even if the worker puts much effort into improving upon the task,

the resultant learning will not be proportional to the effort expended. The top end of the S curve is often called the slope of **diminishing returns.** At the top of the S-Curve, workers succumb to the effects of *forgetting* and other performance impeding factors. As the work environment continues to change, a worker's level of skill and expertise can become obsolete. This is an excellent reason for the application of half-life computations.

The Stanford-B Model: Tthe Stanford-B model is represented as:

$$UC(x) = C_1\left(x + B\right)^{-b}$$

Where:

$UC(x)$ = direct cost of producing the xth unit
b = learning curve exponent
C_1 = cost of the first unit when $B = 0$;
B = slope of the asymptote for the curve;
B = constant $\left(1 < B < 10\right)$.

This is equivalent units of previous experience at the start of the process, which represents the number of units produced prior to first unit acceptance. It is noted that when $B = 0$, the Stanford-B model reduces to the conventional log-linear model. The general expression for the half-life of the Stanford-B model is derived to be:

$$x_{1/2} = (1/2)^{-1/b}(x_0 + B) - B$$

Where:

$x_{1/2}$ = half-life expression for the Stanford-B Learning Model
x_0 = initial point of evaluation of performance on the learning curve

Badiru's Multi-Factor Model: Badiru (1994) presents applications of learning and forgetting curves to productivity and performance analysis.

One example presented used production data to develop a predictive model of production throughput. Two data replicates are used for each of ten selected combinations of cost and time values. Observations were recorded for the number of units representing double production levels. The resulting model has the functional form below and the graphical profile shown in Figure 5.

$$C(x) = 298.88x_1^{-0.31}x_2^{-0.13}$$

Where:

$C(x)$ = cumulative production volume
x_1 = cumulative units of Factor 1
x_2 = cumulative units of Factor 2
b_1 = First learning curve exponent = -0.31
b_2 = Second learning curve exponent = -0.13

A general form of the modeled multi-factor learning curve model is:

$$C(x) = C_1 x_1^{-b_1} x_2^{-b_2}$$

and the half-life expression for the multi-factor learning curve was derived to be:

$$x_{1(1/2)} = (1/2)^{-1/b_1} \left[\frac{x_{1(0)} x_{2(0)}^{b_2/b_1}}{x_{2(1/2)}^{b_2/b_1}} \right]^{-1/b_1}$$

$$x_{2(1/2)} = (1/2)^{-1/b_2} \left[\frac{x_{2(0)} x_{1(0)}^{b_1/b_2}}{x_{1(1/2)}^{b_2/b_1}} \right]^{-1/b_2}$$

Where:

$x_{i(1/2)}$ = half-life component due to Factor i (i=1, 2)
$x_{i(0)}$ = initial point of Factor i (i=1, 2) along the multi-factor learning curve

Knowledge of the value of one factor is needed to evaluate the other factor. Just as in the case of single-factor models, the half-life analysis of the multi-factor model can be used to predict when the performance metric will reach half of a starting value.

DeJong's Learning Formula: DeJong's learning formula is a power function which incorporates parameters for the proportion of manual activity in a task. When operations are controlled by manual tasks, the time will be compressible as successive units are completed. If, by contrast, machine cycle times control operations, then the time will be less compressible as the number of units increases. DeJong's formula introduces as incompressible factor, M, into the log-linear model to account for the man-machine ratio. The model is expressed as:

$$C(x) = C_1 + Mx^{-b}$$

$$MC(x) = C_1 \left[M + (1-M)x^{-b} \right]$$

Where:

Figure 5. Bivariate model of learning curve

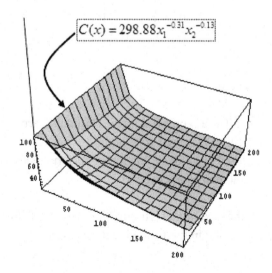

$$C(x) = 298.88x_1^{-0.31}x_2^{-0.13}$$

$C(x)$ = learning curve expression
$M(x)$ = marginal cost expression
b = learning curve exponent
C_1 = cost of first unit
M = incompressibility factor (a constant)

When $M=0$, the model reduces to the log-linear model, which implies a completely manual operation. In completely machine-dominated operations, $M=1$. In that case, the unit cost reduces to a constant equal to C_1, which suggests that no learning-based cost improvement is possible in machine-controlled operations. This represents a condition of high incompressibility. This profile suggests impracticality at higher values of production. Learning is very steep and average cumulative production cost drops rapidly. The horizontal asymptote for the profile is below the lower bound on the average cost axis, suggesting an infeasible operating region as production volume gets high. The analysis above agrees with the fact that no significant published data is available on whether or not DeJong's learning formula has been successfully used to account for the degree of automation in any given operation. Using the expression, *MC(x)*, the marginal cost half-life of the DeJong's learning model is derived to be:

$$x_{1/2} = (1/2)^{-1/b} \left[\frac{(1-M)x_0^{-b} - M}{2(1-M)} \right]^{-1/b}$$

Where:

$x_{1/2}$ = half-life expression for the DeJong's learning curve marginal cost model
x_0 = initial point of evaluation of performance on the marginal cost curve

If the C(x) model is used to derive the half-life, then we obtain the following derivation:

$$x_{1/2} = (1/2)^{-1/b} \left[\frac{Mx_0^{-b} - C_1}{M} \right]^{-1/b}$$

Where:

$x_{1/2}$ = half-life expression for the DeJong's learning curve model
x_0 = initial point of evaluation of performance on the DeJong's learning curve

Levy's Technology Adaptation Function: As mentioned earlier, Levy's adaptation model is perhaps most relevant for information technology application. In this case, reference to production rate is analogous to technology yield measurement. Recognizing that the log-linear model does not account for leveling off of production rate and the factors that may influence learning, Levy (1965) presented the following learning cost function:

$$MC(x) = \left[\frac{1}{\beta} - \left(\frac{1}{\beta} - \frac{x^{-b}}{C_1} \right) k^{-kx} \right]^{-1}$$

Where:

β = production index for the first unit;
k = constant used to flatten the learning curve for large values of x.

The flattening constant, *k*, forces the curve to reach a plateau instead of continuing to decrease or turning in the upward direction. The half-life expression for Levy's learning model is a complex non-linear expression derived as shown below:

$$(1/\beta - x_{1/2}^{-b}/C_1)k^{-kx_{1/2}} = 1/\beta - 2[1/\beta - (1/\beta - x_0^{-b}/C_1)k^{-kx_0}]$$

Where:

$x_{1/2}$ = half-life expression for the Levy's learning curve model

x_0 = initial point of evaluation of performance on the Levy's learning curve

Knowledge of some of the parameters of the model is needed to solve for the half-life as a closed form expression.

Glover's Learning Model: Glover's learning formula (Glover, 1966) is a learning curve model that incorporates a work commencement factor. The model is based on a bottom-up approach which uses individual worker learning results as the basis for plant-wide learning curve standards. The functional form of the model is expressed as:

$$\sum_{i=1}^{n} y_i + a = C_1 \left(\sum_{i=1}^{n} x_i \right)^m$$

Where:

y_i = elapsed time or cumulative quantity;
x_i = cumulative quantity or elapsed time;
a = commencement factor;
n = index of the curve (usually 1+b);
m = model parameter.

This is a complex expression for which half-life expression is not easily computable. We defer the half-life analysis of Levy's learning curve model for further research by interested readers.

Pegel's Exponential Function: Pegels (1976) presented an alternate algebraic function for the learning curve. His model, a form of an exponential function of marginal cost, is represented as:

$$MC(x) = \alpha a^{x-1} + \beta$$

where α, β, and a are parameters based on empirical data analysis. The total cost of producing x units is derived from the marginal cost as follows:

$$TC(x) = \int \left(\alpha a^{x-1} + \beta \right) dx = \frac{\alpha a^{x-1}}{\ln(a)} + \beta x + c$$

where c is a constant to be derived after the other parameters are found. The constant can be found by letting the marginal cost, total cost, and average cost of the first unit to be all equal. That is, $MC_1 = TC_1 = AC_1$, which yields:

$$c = \alpha - \frac{\alpha}{\ln(a)}$$

The model assumes that the marginal cost of the first unit is known. Thus,

$$MC_1 = \alpha + \beta = y_0$$

Mathematical expression for the total labor cost in Pegel's start-up curves is expressed as:

$$TC(x) = \frac{a}{1-b} x^{1-b}$$

Where:

x = cumulative number of units produced;
a, b = empirically determined parameters.

The expressions for marginal cost, average cost, and unit cost can be derived as shown earlier for other models. Using the total cost expression, TC(x), we derive the expression for the half-life of Pegel's learning curve model to be as shown below:

$$x_{1/2} = \left(\tfrac{1}{2} \right)^{-1/(1-b)} x_0$$

Knecht's Upturn Model: Knecht (1974) presents a modification to the functional form of the learning curve to analytically express the observed divergence of actual costs from those predicted by learning curve theory when units produced exceed 200. This permits the consideration of non-constant slopes for the learning curve model. If UC_x is defined as the unit cost of the xth unit, then it approaches 0 asymptotically as x increases. To avoid a zero limit unit cost, the basic functional form is modified. In the continuous case, the formula for cumulative average costs is derived as:

$$C(x) = \int_0^x C_1 z^b dz = \frac{C_1 x^{b+1}}{(1+b)}$$

This cumulative cost also approaches zero as x goes to infinity. Knecht alters the expression for the cumulative curve to allow for an upturn in the learning curve at large cumulative production levels. He suggested the functional form below:

$$C(x) = C_1 x^{-b} e^{cx}$$

where c is a second constant. Differentiating the modified cumulative average cost expression gives the unit cost of the xth unit as shown below. Figure 6 shows the cumulative average cost plot of Knecht's upturn function for values of C_1=250, b=0.25, and c=0.25.

$$UC(x) = \frac{d}{dx}\left[C_1 x^{-b} e^{cx}\right] = C_1 x^{-b} e^{cx}\left(c + \frac{-b}{x}\right).$$

The half-life expression for Knecht's learning model turns out to be a nonlinear complex function as shown below:

$$x_{1/2} e^{-cx_{1/2}/b} = \left(\tfrac{1}{2}\right)^{-1/b} e^{-cx_0/b} x_0$$

Where:

$x_{1/2}$ = half-life expression for the Knecht's learning curve model
x_0 = initial point of evaluation of performance on the Knecht's learning curve

Given that x_0 is known, iterative, interpolation, or numerical methods may be needed to solve for the half-life value.

Yelle's Combined Technology Learning Curve: Yelle (1979) proposed a learning curve model for products by aggregating and extrapolating the individual learning curve of the operations making up a product on a log-linear plot. The model is expressed as shown below:

$$C(x) = k_1 x_1^{-b_1} + k_2 x_2^{-b_2} + \cdots + k_n x_n^{-b_n}$$

where

$C(x)$ = cost of producing the xth unit of the product;
n = number of operations making up the product;
$k_i x_i^{-b_i}$ = learning curve for the ith operation.

Aggregated Learning Curves: In comparing the models discussed in the preceding sections, the deficiency of Knecht's model is that a product-specific learning curve seems to be a more reasonable model than an integrated product curve. For example, an aggregated learning curve with 96.6% learning rate obtained from individual learning curves with the respective learning rates of 80%, 70%, 85%, 80%, and 85% does not appear to represent reality. If this type of composite improvement is possible, then one can always improve the learning rate for any operation by decomposing it into smaller integrated operations. The additive and multiplicative approaches of reliability functions support the conclusion of impracticality of Knecht's integrated model. Jaber and Guiffrida (2004) presented an aggregated form of the WLC where some of the items produced are defective and require reworking. The quality learning curve that they provide is of the form:

Figure 6. Knecht's cumulative average cost function for c_1=250, b=0.25, and c=0.25

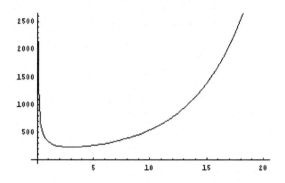

$$t(x) = y_1 x^{-b} + 2r_1 \left(\frac{p}{2}\right)^{1-\varepsilon} x^{1-2\varepsilon}$$

Where y_1 is the time to produce the first unit, r_1 is the time to rework the first defective unit, p is the probability of the process to go out-of-control ($p <<1$), and b is the learning exponent of the reworks learning curve. The variable $t(x)$ has three behavioral patterns, for $0 < b < ½$ (Case I), $b = ½$ (Case II), and $½ < b < 1$ (Case III). Assuming no production error, we computed the half life for $t(x)$ for case 1 as:

Case I: $x_{1/2} = \left(\frac{1}{2}\right)^{-\frac{1}{b}} x$ and $x_{1/2} = \left(\frac{1}{2}\right)^{-\frac{1}{1-2\varepsilon}} x$

Case II: $t(x) = y_1 x^{-b} + 2r_1 \left(\frac{p}{2}\right)^{1-\varepsilon} x^{1-2\varepsilon}$ reduces to

$t(x) = y_1 x^{-b} + t(x) = y_1 x^{-b} + 2r_1 \sqrt{\frac{p}{2}}$, where

$2r_1 \sqrt{\frac{p}{2}}$ is the lower bound, or the plateau of the learning curve.

Case III: The behavior of $t(x)$ follows that of the WLC: monotonically decreasing as cumulative out put increases. It is noted that Jaber and Guiffrida (2008) assumed that the percentage defective reduces as the number of interruptions to restore the process increases. They found that $t(x)$ could converge to

the WLC as the learning curve exponent becomes insignificant.

Figure 7 shows some of the possible profiles of the forgetting curve. Profile (a) shows a case where forgetting occurs rapidly along a convex curve. Profile (b) shows a case where forgetting occurs more slowly along a concave curve. Profile (c) shows a case where the rate of forgetting shifts from convex to concave along an S-curve.

The profile of the forgetting curve and its mode of occurrence can influence the half-life measure. This is further evidence that the computation of half-life can help distinguish between learning curves, particularly if a forgetting component is involved. The combination of the learning and forgetting functions presents a more realistic picture of what actually occurs in a learning process. The combination is not necessarily as simple as resolving two curves to obtain a resultant curve. The resolution may particularly be complex in the case of intermittent periods of forgetting. Figure 8 shows representations of periods where forgetting occurs and the resulting learn-forget profile.

APPLICATION FOR INFORMATION TECHNOLOGY TRAINING PROGRAMS

Formal training programs should be an essential part of any organization's strategy for project management. Many projects have been known to fail due to a lack of consistency of practice. With a unified training approach, there is a better assurance that technology work processes are carried out consistently. But the training must take into account the points of degradation of the capabilities of workers. Learning curves are traditionally used for diagnostic and planning purposes in installed operations. The premise of this paper is that learning curves analysis, learn-forget modeling, and half-life analysis can be used proactively to

Figure 7. Profiles of learning decline curves

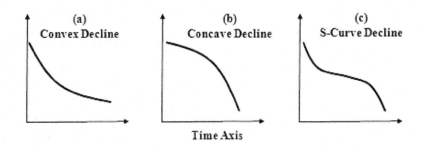

design or enhance information technology training programs, thereby improving overall systems effectiveness. There are two aspects of justifying training programs: effectiveness and efficiency of the training program. Effectiveness refers to the benefits that an organization derives from training the workforce to meet organizational objectives. Efficiency refers to the process of determining the resources required for the training versus the expected output. In this process, it is essential to provide the resources required at the right time, in the right form, and in the right quantity. An understanding of the half-life characteristics of the learning process can make the resources allocation process more effective.

In practice, there is a lack of structured approach to ensuring training effectiveness and efficiency. Sawhney et al. (2004) presents a structured model training. The model is adapted for Figure 8 to show where learning curve analysis may be important and how half-life analysis can be incorporated for a streamlined training process incorporating learning curve analysis, forgetting analysis, and half-life analysis as well as a cross-training component.

The first phase is to assess the alignment of the training program to the organizational strategic goals in light of the learning curve impact. Phase 2 involves specific design of the training program with recognition of the learn-forget phenomenon. Phase 3 addresses training implementation with respect to the limit of the learning effect, half-life

properties of learning, and the limit of retention. Phase 4 finalizes the process with training enhancement activities. This can involve resource realignment, output evaluation, and risk mitigation for the subsequent rounds. Cross training, as illustrated in Figure 9, is an effective strategy to combat the debilitating effect of forgetting.

CONCLUSION

Degradation of performance occurs naturally either due to internal processes or externally imposed events, such as extended production breaks. For productivity assessment purposes, it may be of interest to determine the length of time it takes a production metric to decay to half of its original magnitude. For example, for career planning strategy, one may be interested in how long it takes for skills sets to degrade by half in relation to current technological needs of the workplace. The half-life phenomenon may be due to intrinsic factors, such as forgetting, or due to external factors, such as a shift in labor requirements. Half-life analysis can have application in intervention programs designed to achieve reinforcement of learning. It can also have application for assessing the sustainability of skills acquired through training programs. Further research on the theory of half-life of learning curves should be directed to topics such as the following:

Figure 8. Resolution of learn-forget performance curves

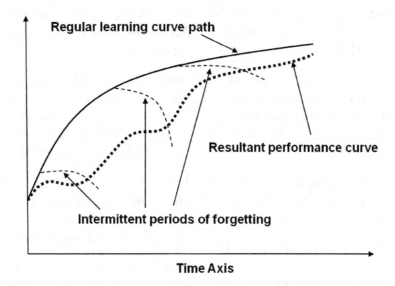

Figure 9. Incorporation of learning, forgetting, and half-life analysis into IT project training

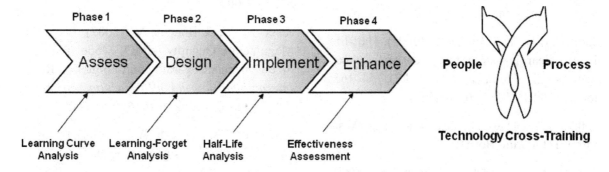

- Half-Life Interpretations
- Training and Learning Reinforcement Program
- Forgetting Intervention and Sustainability Programs

In addition to the predictive benefits of half-life expressions, they also reveal the ad-hoc nature of some of the classical learning curve models that have been presented in the literature. We recommend that future efforts to develop learning curve models should also attempt to develop the corresponding half-life expressions to provide full operating characteristics of the models. Readers are encouraged to explore half-life analysis of other learning curve models not covered in this paper.

REFERENCES

Alter, S. (1999). *Information systems: A management perspective* (3rd ed.). Reading, MA: Addison-Wesley.

Alter, S. (2002). *Information systems: Foundation of e-business* (4th ed.). Upper Saddle River, NJ: Prentice Hall.

Badiru, A. B. (1992). Computational survey of univariate and multivariate learning curve models. *IEEE Transactions on Engineering Management, 39*(2), 176–188. doi:10.1109/17.141275

Badiru, A. B. (1994). Multifactor learning and forgetting models for productivity and performance analysis. *The International Journal of Human Factors in Manufacturing, 4*(1), 37–54. doi:10.1002/hfm.4530040105

Badiru, A. B. (1995). Incorporating learning curve effects into critical resource diagramming. *Project Management Journal, 26*(2), 38–45.

Badiru, A. B. (2008). *Triple C model of project management: Communication, cooperation, and coordination.* Boca Raton, FL: CRC Press.

Badiru, A. B. (2009). *STEP project management: Guide for science, technology, and engineering Projects.* Boca Raton, FL: CRC Press.

Badiru, A. B., & Ijaduola, A. (2009). Half-life theory of learning curves for system performance analysis. *IEEE Systems Journal, 3*(2), 154–165. doi:10.1109/JSYST.2009.2017394

Belkaoui, A. (1986). *The Learning Curve.* Westport, CT: Quorum Books.

Camm, J. D., Evans, J. R., & Womer, N. K. (1987). The unit learning curve approximation of total cost. *Computers & Industrial Engineering, 12*(3), 205–213. doi:10.1016/0360-8352(87)90014-3

Demirkan, H., & Nichols, J. (2008). IT services project management: lessons learned from a case study in implementation. *International Journal of Project Organisation and Management, 1*(2), 204–220. doi:10.1504/IJPOM.2008.022192

Ewusi-Mensah, K. (1997). Critical issues in abandoned information systems development projects. *Communications of the ACM, 40*(9), 74–80. doi:10.1145/260750.260775

Globerson, S., Nahumi, A., & Ellis, S. (1998). Rate of forgetting for motor and cognitive tasks. *International Journal of Cognitive Ergonomics, 2*(1), 181–191.

Glover, J. H. (1966). Manufacturing progress functions: An alternative model and its comparison with existing functions. *International Journal of Production Research, 4*(4), 279–300. doi:10.1080/00207546508919983

Jaber, M. Y., & Bonney, M. (1996). Production breaks and the learning curve: The forgetting phenomena. *Applied Mathematical Modelling, 20*(3), 162–169. doi:10.1016/0307-904X(95)00157-F

Jaber, M. Y., & Bonney, M. (2003). Lot sizing with learning and forgetting in setups and in product quality. *International Journal of Production Economics, 83*(1), 95–111. doi:10.1016/S0925-5273(02)00322-5

Jaber, M. Y., & Bonney, M. (2007). Economic Manufacture Quantity (EMQ) Model With Lot Size Dependent Learning and Forgetting Rates. *International Journal of Production Economics, 108*(2), 359–367. doi:10.1016/j.ijpe.2006.12.020

Jaber, M. Y., & Guiffrida, A. L. (2004). Learning curves for processes generating defects requiring reworks. *European Journal of Operational Research, 159*(3), 663–672. doi:10.1016/S0377-2217(03)00436-3

Jaber, M. Y., & Guiffrida, A. L. (2008). Learning curves for imperfect production processes with reworks and process restoration interruptions. *European Journal of Operational Research, 189*(1), 93–104. doi:10.1016/j.ejor.2007.05.024

Jaber, M. Y., Kher, H. V., & Davis, D. (2003). Countering forgetting through training and deployment. *International Journal of Production Economics, 85*(1), 33–46. doi:10.1016/S0925-5273(03)00084-7

Jaber, M. Y., & Sikstrom, S. (2004). A numerical comparison of three potential learning and forgetting models. *International Journal of Production Economics, 92*(3), 281–294. doi:10.1016/j.ijpe.2003.10.019

Knecht, G. R. (1974). Costing, technological growth, and generalized learning curves. *Operational Research Quarterly, 25*(3), 487–491.

Levy, F. K. (1965). Adaptation in the production process. *Management Science, 11*(6), B136–B154. doi:10.1287/mnsc.11.6.B136

Liao, W. M. (1979). Effects of learning on resource allocation decisions. *Decision Sciences, 10*(1), 116–125. doi:10.1111/j.1540-5915.1979.tb00011.x

Mazur, J. E., & Hastie, R. (1978). Learning as accumulation: A reexamination of the learning curve. *Psychological Bulletin, 85*(2), 1256–1274. doi:10.1037/0033-2909.85.6.1256

McIntyre, E. V. (1977). Cost-volume-profit analysis adjusted for Learning. *Management Science, 24*(2), 149–160. doi:10.1287/mnsc.24.2.149

Nanda, R. (1979). Using learning curves in integration of production resources. In *Proceedings of 1979 IIE Fall Conference* (pp. 376-380).

Nembhard, D. A., & Osothsilp, N. (2001). An empirical comparison of forgetting models. *IEEE Transactions on Engineering Management, 48*(1), 283–291. doi:10.1109/17.946527

Nembhard, D. A., & Uzumeri, M. V. (2000). Experiential learning and forgetting for manual and cognitive tasks. *International Journal of Industrial Ergonomics, 25*(3), 315–326. doi:10.1016/S0169-8141(99)00021-9

Pegels, C. C. (1976). Start-up of learning curves - some new approaches. *Decision Sciences, 7*(4), 705–713. doi:10.1111/j.1540-5915.1976.tb00714.x

Richardson, W. J. (1978). Use of learning curves to set goals and monitor progress in cost reduction programs. In *Proceedings of 1978 IIE Spring Conference* (pp. 235-239).

Ross, J. W., & Beath, C. M. (2002, winter). Beyond the business case: New approaches to IT investments. *MIT Sloan Management Review*, 51-59.

Smith, J. (1989). *Learning curve for cost control.* Norcross, GA: Industrial Engineering and Management Press.

Smunt, T. L. (1986). A comparison of learning curve analysis and moving average ratio analysis for detailed operational planning. *Decision Sciences, 17*(1), 23–35.

Sule, D. R. (1978). The effect of alternate periods of learning and forgetting on economic manufacturing quantity. *AIIE Transactions, 10*(3), 338–343.

Towill, D. R., & Cherrington, J. E. (1994). Learning curve models for predicting the performance of advanced manufacturing technology. *International Journal of Advanced Manufacturing Technology, 9*(3), 195–203. doi:10.1007/BF01754598

Womer, N. K. (1979). Learning curves, production rate, and program costs. *Management Science, 25*(4), 312–219. doi:10.1287/mnsc.25.4.312

Womer, N. K. (1981). Some propositions on cost functions. *Southern Economic Journal, 47*(2), 1111–1119. doi:10.2307/1058169

Womer, N. K. (1984). Estimating learning curves from aggregate monthly data. *Management Science, 30*(8), 982–992. doi:10.1287/mnsc.30.8.982

Womer, N. K., & Gulledge, T. R. Jr. (1983). A dynamic cost function for an airframe production program. *Engineering Costs and Production Economics, 7*(1), 213–227. doi:10.1016/0167-188X(83)90015-0

Wright, T. P. (1936). Factors affecting the cost of airplanes. *Journal of the Aeronautical Sciences, 3*(2), 122–128.

Yelle, L. E. (1976). Estimating learning curves for potential products. *Industrial Marketing Management, 5*(2), 147–154. doi:10.1016/0019-8501(76)90037-7

Yelle, L. E. (1979). The learning curve: Historical review and comprehensive survey. *Decision Sciences, 10*(2), 302–328. doi:10.1111/j.1540-5915.1979.tb00026.x

Yelle, L. E. (1983). Adding life cycles to learning curves. *Long Range Planning, 16*(6), 82–87. doi:10.1016/0024-6301(83)90011-0

This work was previously published in International Journal of Information Technology Project Management, Volume 1, Issue 3, edited by John Wang, pp. 28-45, copyright 2010 by IGI Publishing (an imprint of IGI Global).

Chapter 10
Critical Behavioral Competencies for IT Project Managers:
What Are They? How Are They Learned?

Hazel Taylor
University of Washington, USA

Jill Palzkill Woelfer
University of Washington, USA

ABSTRACT

What behavioral competencies do experienced IT project managers apply when facing critical situations in their projects, and how have they developed those competencies? In this paper, the authors answer these questions. The authors interviewed 23 experienced IT project managers from 11 organizations, focusing on critical situations that they now managed differently from their earlier, novice, practices, and on how they had learned to develop these different approaches. The authors discuss a variety of management development and training interventions. They use a thematic analysis to identify the key competencies being applied and learning methods experienced by this set of managers. Results suggest that IT project managers are drawing on a different set of competencies from those required for project management in other industries. Additionally, this paper reveals the importance of informal learning channels, often involving project experiences, for the development of IT project management competencies.

DOI: 10.4018/978-1-4666-0930-3 .ch010

INTRODUCTION

Information Technology (IT) projects have an unenviable reputation for poor performance, with well-publicized failures (Drummond, 1996; Lyytinen, Mathiassen, & Ropponen, 1998) and regular reports of major cost and schedule over-runs (Standish Group, 2001). There is, however, evidence that an experienced project manager, with the right project tools and methodology, can increase the likelihood of a successful project (Cooke-Davies, 2002; Sauer, Gemino, & Reich, 2007; Standish Group, 2001). Thus, there is increasing interest and emphasis within research and practice on the need to develop and manage the performance of IT project managers.

While organizations make substantial investments in the development of their functional and line managers, through the provision of general management development initiatives including formal management and leadership training programs, performance appraisals, 360-degree feedback, and management coaching, less support is provided for development of *project* managers (El-Sabaa, 2001). Indeed, surveys of project managers reveal that few organizations provide specific project management training (Carbone & Gholston, 2004), with the result that project managers are often promoted to their positions based on the technical expertise they have demonstrated in prior projects (Matsuo, Wong, & Lai, 2008; Nellore & Balachandra, 2001) and must develop their project management skills through on-the-job experience (Matsuo et al., 2008) or by taking commercial training programs on their own initiative (El-Sabaa, 2001).

The increasing move towards project-based work in organizations, coupled with the on-going problems in IT project performance, suggest that attention to the development of key knowledge, skills and abilities in project managers could be a fruitful avenue for organizations looking to improve their IT project performance. However, identifying the right focus for training and develop-ment efforts for IT project managers is critical if organizations are to get the project performance results they expect from their personnel developmental initiatives.

In this study, we focus on identifying key behavioral competencies that experienced IT project managers apply in critical situations during their management of projects, and we explore the avenues by which these managers have developed these competencies in the course of their careers. By examining both the critical competencies that experienced managers are applying and how they have acquired these competencies, we are able to provide recommendations on effective development and training programs for the next generation of IT project managers. Two key objectives of this study were 1) to determine those competencies that are critical for IT project management; and 2) to identify avenues of learning these competencies that organizations can utilize for improved facilitation of training for less-experienced project managers.

LITERATURE REVIEW

Project Management Skills

Project management is a complex process requiring a multi-dimensional set of knowledge, skills and abilities covering the technological and business domains of the project, specific management and project management skills, and interpersonal and communication skills (Kerzner, 2001). Research investigating generic project management skills across a range of industries has highlighted the need for technical, leadership, teamwork and client relationship skills (Brill, Bishop, & Walker, 2006; Kaulio, 2008; Turner & Müller, 2006), as well as identifying the importance of emotional competencies such as self-management, resilience and self control (Dainty, Cheng, & Moore, 2003; Dainty, Cheng, & Moore, 2004; Turner & Müller, 2006). As noted by Crawford and Gaynor (1999), these studies have been primarily survey-based, seeking respondents' opinions on the key knowledge and skill requirements of project managers working in many industries.

The IT project context has certain unique features, including high levels of uncertainty and technical complexity, a primary focus on conceptual, rather than physical, work, lower levels of continuity of project personnel from one project to the next, and a myriad group of organizational stakeholders, all of which compound the management of IT projects. Additionally, many IT project managers must assume both internal and external roles, managing the in-house project team as well as building and maintaining the relationship with the organization's clients (Langer, Slaughter, & Mukhopadhyay, 2008; Matsuo et al., 2008; Webber & Torti, 2004). Thus, we might expect that the specific skills required for effective IT project performance may differ somewhat from the generic skills described above.

Some studies have suggested sets of knowledge, skills and abilities that are important for information systems (IS) professionals in general. Lee, Trauth and Farwell's (1995) study is one of the seminal works in this area. Drawing from the perceptions of a broad range of IS and business managers and consultants about the skill requirements of IS professionals, Lee et al. concluded that the necessary skills fell into four groups: technology management skills; business functional skills; interpersonal skills; and technical skills. More recently, also examining competencies of IT professionals in general, Bassellier and Benbasat (2004) found that business competence, defined as organization-specific knowledge together with interpersonal and management knowledge was a key skill for IT professionals whose work involves substantial contact with business clients.

While these studies of the knowledge, skills and abilities required of IS and IT personnel provide some insight into specific requirements for IT project managers, their focus is on IS professionals in general, who might include project managers, but also include project team members, IS department managers and support staff, and IS consultants. Only a handful of studies have focused directly on the specific set of knowledge, skills and abilities that are particularly relevant to IT project managers. Jiang, Klein, and Margulis (1998) looked at whether skills previously specified as important for systems analysts were also important for IT project managers, and identified directing, managing and information seeking as key skills. A subsequent study by Jiang, Klein, and Chen (2001) focused on the importance of leadership skills for successful project outcomes, reinforcing the importance of the team leadership competency.

More recently, Langer, Slaughter, and Mukhophyay (2008), in a study of IT outsourcing managers noted that, while hard skills such as technology and domain expertise were necessary, soft skills related to managing tasks, self, career, peers, subordinates, superiors and clients were more important for this set of project managers. Finally, Napier, Keil, and Tan (2009) conducted a repertory grid study of 19 IT project managers to elicit their perceptions of the differences between more and less successful project managers. Napier et al. derived nine skill categories from their interviews: client management, communication, general management, leadership, personal integrity, planning and control, problem solving, systems development, and team development.

In addition to these empirical research studies, there is also an extensive professional literature providing prescriptive guidelines for best practice in project management. In the United States, the Project Management Institute (2004) provides a series of professional certifications based on standards set out in its Project Management Body of Knowledge (PMBOK). The PMBOK sets out nine knowledge areas that are claimed to encompass the sum of knowledge recognized as good practice in the project management profession. In addition to these detailed knowledge areas, PMBOK also notes that effective project management requires an understanding of the application area, the project environment, general management knowledge and skills, and interpersonal skills. In the United Kingdom, the Association for Project Management (APM), reflecting concerns that the PMBOK had too narrow a focus on delivering projects to the specified scope, schedule and budget, developed its own APM BOK, offering a greater breadth of knowledge areas, including contextual, technological, commercial and general management topics (Morris, 2001).

While the knowledge base provided in the field's BOKs provides a foundation of declarative knowledge for the profession, the ability of a project manager to selectively apply the relevant parts of the knowledge in a particular project context, using appropriate skills, is a complex competency, not adequately encapsulated in a body of knowledge alone (Boyatzis, 1982; Spencer & Spencer, 1993). The skills identified in the empirical research discussed earlier relate to these competencies, but researchers have used varying approaches to defining their skills categories, and the categories themselves are often couched in broad, generic terms that provide insufficient detail on the specific competencies required for the project management job. Thus we turn now to the job competency literature for insight into the specific competencies that might support effective IT project management performance.

Project Management Competencies

A job competency is an underlying characteristic of a person that is demonstrated through the person's behavior, and can lead to more effective job performance (Boyatzis, 1982; Spencer & Spencer, 1993). A set of competencies for a particular job comprises the foundational knowledge and skills in the area, together with the necessary behaviors to apply the knowledge and skills effectively in the job context. These competencies can be changed through training and behavior modeling (Burke

& Day, 1986; Pescuric & Byham, 1996; Taylor, Russ-Eft, & Chan, 2005), although some are more difficult to change than others.

Building on the knowledge standards in the PMBOK, the PMI has developed a framework of project management competencies (Project Management Institute, 2002), specifying three dimensions of competency required for effective project management performance. These dimensions comprise the declarative knowledge required (that is, the nine knowledge areas of the PMBOK), the procedural knowledge needed to apply the declarative knowledge (performance standards for each knowledge area), and the behavioral competencies necessary to support effective project management performance. For example, a project manager demonstrating declarative knowledge would be able to explain what a project plan is; the manager has procedural knowledge if she knows how to develop a project plan; and finally, she can demonstrate competency by using appropriate behaviors to ensure all stakeholders are involved and fully engaged in developing the project plan. The competency framework is comprehensive and the declarative and procedural knowledge competencies are generally accepted as essential components of any project manager's skill set. However, the 19 behavioral competencies, shown in the left hand column of Table 1, have been adapted from general managerial competencies listed in the competency dictionary developed by Spencer and Spencer (1993), and have not been empirically tested for their specific applicability to project management work.

There is still little *empirical* research into the question of the specific behavioral competencies required by project managers to do their jobs (Morris, 2001). One particularly useful program of research in the construction industry (Dainty et al., 2004; 2005) has led to the development of an empirically derived competency model, reporting a more tightly focused group of 12 core competencies, shown in the center column of

Table 1. Behavioral competencies for project managers (*Expanded definition encompassing Bassellier and Benbasat's (2004) business competence)

Project Management Institute (2002)	Dainty et al. (2004; 2005)	Definitions for the current study derived from Spencer & Spencer (1993)
Self control	Composure/self control	Maintains control over emotions and avoids negative actions under stress
Team leadership	Team leadership	Leads others in a team; is able to develop the sense of team purpose and direction to achieve team goals
Directiveness/assertiveness	Directiveness/assertiveness	Shows ability to make others comply with own wishes through direction, setting of performance standards, and confrontation of non-performance
Achievement orientation	Achievement orientation	Sets own standards for excellence in works and strives to meet them
Analytical thinking	Analytical thinking	Systematically understands situations by breaking them into smaller parts in a step-by-step causal way
Flexibility	Flexibility	Is able to adapt to and work effectively with a variety of situations, individuals, or groups
Teamwork & cooperation	Teamwork & cooperation	Works cooperatively as part of a team and fosters teamwork
Initiative	Initiative	Is proactive in taking action to avoid problems or create opportunities
Information seeking	Information seeking	Actively seeks out in-depth information through research and with others
Conceptual thinking	Conceptual thinking	Builds a larger understanding of a situation by identifying patterns that are not obviously related, seeing the larger picture
Impact & influence	Impact & influence	Demonstrates ability to influence others to support own agenda
Customer service orientation	Focus on client needs	Focuses efforts on understanding and meeting the client's needs
Interpersonal understanding		Is sensitive to, listens to, and wants to understand other people
Relationship building		Works to build relationships with people who are, or might someday be, useful in achieving work-related goals
Developing others		Shows the intent to teach others or foster their work development
Organizational awareness		Understands the organizational structure and power relationships in own and client organizations; understands business impact of IT and IT projects*
Self confidence		Expresses confidence in ability to deal with challenging situations and in handling failures constructively
Concern for order, quality and accuracy		Strives to maintain or increase order in the work situation
Organizational commitment		Is able and willing to align with the needs, priorities and goals of the organization

Table 1, that are regarded as critical for effective construction project management performance. Dainty et al. note that two of these competencies – self control and team leadership – were the most predictive of effective construction project management performance. We have not found empirical work testing the applicability of these competencies to IT project managers, and while it seems reasonable to assume that the Dainty et al. (2004, 2005) set of skills would be required, some may not be so important for IT projects, while additional competencies from the PMI list may be more important in the IT project context.

In particular, as noted earlier, IT project managers are often required to play an especially strong client relationship role (Langer et al., 2008; Matsuo et al., 2008; Webber & Torti, 2004), which requires extensive organization-specific knowledge (Bassellier & Benbasat, 2004). The organization-specific knowledge aspect of Bassellier and Benbasat's business competence category is broader than the definition of organizational awareness competence derived from Spencer and Spencer's (1993) competency dictionary, which refers simply to an understanding of the power relationships in the organization. Bassellier and Benbasat's (2004) definition also encompasses an understanding of organizational structure and the business impact of IT projects. Since IT project management work typically requires significant interaction with clients and other stakeholders in the organization, this broader view of organizational awareness is likely to be an important aspect of the necessary competencies, and we adopted the expanded definition shown in the right hand column of Table 1 for the organizational awareness competency.

The behavioral competencies outlined in the PMI's competency framework, together with Bassellier and Benbasat's business competence, provide a starting point for examining skills required for IT project management. However, it is likely that some of the required competencies are industry and role-specific (Dainty et al.,

2005; Morris, 2001) and so further investigation of the requirements for effective performance in the IT field is required. We do not yet know which aspects of the competency framework are essential for IT project managers. Thus, one aim of the current research was to investigate which skills experienced IT project managers regard as critically important components of their project management toolkit.

IT Project Management Skill Development

Understanding the specific skills required for effective IT project management is only the first step. We also need to learn about how best to support the development of project managers in these areas. Two surveys of experienced project managers across a range of industries report that very few organizations have implemented in-house training development programs in the project management area, relying instead on on-the-job experience to develop their project managers (Carbone & Gholston, 2004; Conger, 2004). Indeed, there has been a somewhat unquestioning assumption in industry that project managers can be promoted based on their technical ability and that they will somehow absorb the necessary project management skills during their time on projects in a more technical capacity (Carbone & Gholston, 2004; Matsuo et al., 2008; Nellore & Balachandra, 2001). Yet managerial and inter-personal skills are generally rated of higher importance than technical skills for project managers across all industries (El-Sabaa, 2001). This is of particular concern in the IT arena because, as noted earlier, the expectation that IT project managers will manage both the internal team and external client relationships of the project means that managerial skills are likely to be essential for effective performance.

While organizations may not be initiating project management training, the dramatic increase in project managers holding the PMI

Project Manager Professional certification noted by Gray and Larson (2008) – from fewer than 3,000 in 1996 to over 200,000 in 2005 – suggests that individual project managers are taking an increasingly proactive approach to their own professional development. The extensive training and certification opportunities provided by professional associations such as the PMI and the APM can address the development of the declarative knowledge base that will provide the foundational knowledge required for project managers (Morris, 2001). However, as Crawford (2005) revealed in a very interesting study comparing project managers' knowledge of the standards encompassed in professional bodies of knowledge such as the PMBOK with their supervisors' perceptions of their job performance, a high level of declarative knowledge is not sufficient to guarantee superior performance as judged by the supervisors.

As Crawford's (2005) study suggests, ensuring that potential IT project managers receive project management training, either through their organizations or their own initiative, will provide a foundational level of knowledge, but the development of procedural skills and behavioral competence typically requires a more situated learning approach, embodying practice, feedback and reflection (Eraut, 2000). Cicmil (2006), drawing on Dreyfus and Dreyfus' (1986) model, sets out conceptually the typical progress of expertise development in project management from novice, through advanced beginner, competent performer, proficient performer, and finally expert. Practitioners at the novice and advanced beginner levels rely initially on generalized rules derived from a foundation body of knowledge such as PMBOK. With more experience, the practitioners advance to the competent performer level, where they understand the importance of the project context and are able to exercise judgment about how and when to apply the rules. Finally, at proficient performer and expert levels, practitioners take a holistic approach, displaying high levels of competence in their decision-making, exercising judgment in a

highly reflective manner, and tailoring their approach to each project context. This progression is demonstrated empirically in Matsuo, Wong, and Lai's (2008) study of career progression of IT project managers and consultants in six Japanese IT firms. Matsuo et al.'s findings reinforce the picture of IT project managers' development occurring simply through experience gained on increasingly large and complex projects, with little reference to any organizational support for career planning and training.

While it seems clear that development of high levels of expertise in project management requires experience through exposure to many project situations, this does not mean that project managers should be left to develop these levels of proficiency through a haphazard, trial-and-error process. As McCall Jr. (2004) notes, "People don't automatically learn from experience." The challenge for organizations is to provide support to ensure that project managers do in fact learn as much as they can from their normal work experiences (Davies & Easterby-Smith, 1984). Indeed, the typical interventions for developing general management and leadership skills in employees do include both formal training programs to develop the declarative knowledge foundation for key competencies and on-going developmental support initiatives aimed at building on this foundation and supporting continuous individual development of the procedural knowledge and behavioral competencies necessary to be an effective performer in the job (McCauley & Hezlett, 2001). Formal management training programs cover a range of generic knowledge and skills, such as general management knowledge and interpersonal skills, believed to be important for managers to understand. On-going developmental practices, such as 360-degree feedback, coaching and mentoring, modeling and apprenticeship, and communities of practice, are aimed at supporting employees in their continuous development in the workplace, and are particularly useful for supporting change in behaviors and transforming understanding in order to guide future action. In particular, apprenticeship opportunities coupled with support and feedback to encourage reflection and sense-making of the leadership apprenticeship are regarded as valuable approaches for leadership development (Day, 2001; Kempster, 2006).

The prior research discussed above does suggest that organizations are not providing their potential project managers with specific project management training in the foundational knowledge area. It might also seem that project managers are expected to be completely autonomous in developing the necessary project-specific procedural knowledge and competencies to further their careers, but most of the required competencies discussed earlier are similar to generic management competencies rather than being specific to the project management job. Thus organizations may rely on more general management and leadership interventions to provide the necessary development training for their project managers, and this is an area that has not been explored.

The Current Study

The research reviewed above has highlighted a framework of knowledge, skills and behavioral competencies that are required for project managers, but it is still unclear which aspects of this framework are of critical importance for effective IT project management. In addition, we know little about how best to support project managers in developing the required competencies. Thus in the present study, we focused both on exploring the skills that experienced IT project managers regard as critically important components of their project management toolkit, and how they developed these skills during their careers. Our key objectives were to discover which competencies were critical for IT project management and to understand how individual learning from project experiences can best be facilitated. We used the following questions to guide our investigation:

- Which of the skills that experienced project managers have gained during their career do they see as critically important for their project success?
- How have experienced project managers learned these key skills?
- What management developmental interventions (such as training programs, coaching, and mentoring) have managers experienced and how have these contributed to their learning?

METHODOLOGY

This research was an in-depth, multiple case study investigation, with the objective of exploring individual IT project managers' learning. The nature of the study is exploratory and descriptive, because, while there is plenty of literature on learning and development of generic management and leadership skills, little attention has been paid to the challenges of developing specific IT project management competencies. The PMI's project manager competency development framework (2002) with the expanded definition of organizational awareness, shown in Table 1, provided an initial research model.

Sample

We used a two-stage purposive sampling approach to identify experienced IT project managers for this study. Eleven organizations representing wide variation in terms of type of organization (both specialist IT firms and organizations with IT departments carrying out internal projects) and type of IT project (for example, software development, package implementation, infrastructure upgrades, and internet and intranet projects) were invited to participate. Within each organization, we identified key informants at the CIO, program executive, or senior project manager level and sought nominations from these key informants of one or two expert project managers within their firm. We then used a snowball approach to seek further participants from the initial set of nominated project managers.

In total, we interviewed 23 project managers from the eleven organizations. The respondents were experienced project managers, ranging from 5 to 30 years of experience with an average of just less than 14 years. 10 respondents held Bachelor's degrees, 10 had Masters degrees, and three held technical degrees or certificates. The ages of the respondents ranged from 20-29 to over 60, with 10 respondents in the 40-49 age group and 5 respondents in the 50-59 age group. Gender was evenly split (13 male and 10 female). They had typically worked for several different companies during their project management careers, and drew their learnings from across their experiences with these different companies. The respondents had wide experience across a range of project types, including in-house development, web development, infrastructure upgrades, and customized package implementation work, with varying team sizes, budgets and durations, and reported experience working on a low of 5 to a high of 120 projects during their careers.

Data Collection Procedures

The semi-structured interviews with individual project managers relied largely on the critical incident method (Flanagan, 1954), which has been demonstrated to be effective in surfacing tacit knowledge and in getting beyond respondents' espoused theories (in the present case, about what and how they have learned) to reveal actual practice (in the present case, practice about actual learning) (DuBois, 2002; Klein, Calderwood, & MacGregor, 1989; Taylor, 2005). Interviews lasted approximately 45-60 minutes. Interviews were tape recorded with the permission of the participants and transcribed. The transcripts

were returned to participants for checking and confirmation.

We provided the interview guide to participants ahead of time, because we believed that they would be able to give more meaningful responses if they had time to reflect on the questions. While the guide explained our purpose in seeking critical situations in the project manager's experience that had contributed to his or her learning, we were careful not to seed the guide with any specific skills or competencies, in order to ensure that we captured the respondent's actual practice, rather than prompting espoused theories about practice. In addition to collecting basic demographic data and details about project experience, the interviews covered three main areas. In the first part, we encouraged respondents to focus on key incidents in their more recent projects where they had applied knowledge or skills differently from the way they would have approached these incidents early in their careers. We examined these incidents with the respondents to understand what skills were now being applied and what, specifically, these experienced project managers now do differently from what they did earlier in their careers. The second stage of the interviews focused on how the respondents learned the key skills they had identified. Again, we focused respondents on identifying the specific learning events that first triggered a change in the way they approached the area under discussion. Finally, we asked project managers about a variety of interventions that are used by organizations to develop and improve personnel performance. For each intervention we discussed respondents' experience with the intervention, and how helpful it had been in terms of their overall development as a project manager.

After thirteen interviews had been completed, we conducted a preliminary analysis, following the procedures described in more detail below. We were surprised to find from this initial analysis that the predominant learning method reported for all competencies was reflection on experience, and that formal training was rarely identified, even with respect to the concern for order, quality and accuracy competency, which relies heavily on declarative and procedural knowledge about project management methodologies. This finding might have reflected the lack of organizational support for project managers' training, but, when we examined the management development initiatives, most of the project managers had participated in training that would be expected to be relevant for the critical learnings that they described. Moreover, most of the project managers reported that they found these management development initiatives at least somewhat useful. However, we realized that in many cases we could not tell whether the formal training had occurred before or after the critical learning experience.

In order to address this gap, we modified the interview protocol to incorporate the capture of an event history calendar - a timeline of key events. Event history calendars draw on autobiographical memory research, and have been shown to enable respondents to reconstruct the time sequence of past events more completely and accurately, thus usefully augmenting the critical incident method to maximize the quality of retrospective reports (Belli, 1998). In the remaining ten interviews, we first established the respondent's timeline of key career events, and then asked the respondents to locate their critical learning experiences and management development initiatives on their career timeline.

Analysis Procedures

The initial research model, derived from the PMI's project manager competency development framework (Project Management Institute, 2002), provided support for an interpretive prior-research-driven thematic analysis well grounded in the data (Boyatzis, 1998; Miles & Huberman, 1994; Ritchie & Spencer, 1994; Spencer & Spencer,

1993). The analysis proceeded in three stages, corresponding to the three research questions that guided our investigation. We first extracted the key learnings identified by each project manager as critical elements in their efforts to ensure project management success, and derived a definition for these learnings, couched in the participant's own words. Respondents typically spoke of three or four key learnings that they had found critical, providing a total of 89 learnings from this set of project managers. We used the framework of competencies shown in Table 1 to categorize the learnings into the underlying competencies that they reflected. Just over two-thirds of the key learnings encompassed more than one competency, which is typical in this kind of competency research (Spencer & Spencer, 1993). One respondent identified a competency related specifically to IT technical expertise, which was not covered by the PMI framework, although it is included in the Spencer and Spencer competency dictionary and was also identified as a critical skill in one (Langer et al., 2008) of the three prior studies on IT project managers' skills. Thus we expanded the framework to 20 competencies, with 182 instances of these competencies.

For the second question, examining how managers had learned their critical skills, we allowed the categories of methods of learning to emerge naturally from the data, resulting in seven learning methods, as shown in Table 2.

For the third question about the developmental interventions experienced by the respondents, we summarized those interventions experienced by each participant, and their perceptions of the usefulness to their overall development. Finally, for the ten interviews with event history timelines, we plotted the occurrences of training and critical learning experiences on a timeline in order to determine the sequence of events.

Table 2. Learning methods and number of respondents learning with each method

Learning method	No. of PMs learning a critical skill with method (out of 23)
Reflection on experience	23
Observation of other PMs	11
Formal training	8
Coach or mentor	8
Performance feedback	6
Communities of practice	2
Independent learning	2

Table 3. Critical learnings and number of respondents describing at least one learning related to competencies

Competency (as defined in Table 1)	Number of critical learnings linked to the competency (out of a total of 89 learnings)	Number of PMs describing at least one learning linked to the competency (out of a total of 23 PMs)
Team leadership	29	19
Concern for order, quality and accuracy	28	17
Relationship building	16	13
Impact & influence	14	11
Organizational awareness	13	9
Achievement orientation	9	7
Flexibility	8	7
Focus on client needs	7	7
Interpersonal understanding	7	7
Initiative	7	6
Teamwork & cooperation	9	5
Information seeking	8	5
Directiveness/assertiveness	6	5
Analytical thinking	7	4
Self confidence	4	4
Developing others	4	3
Self control	2	2
Organizational commitment	2	2
Conceptual thinking	1	1
IT technical knowledge	1	1

RESULTS

Critical Competencies and Learning Methods

Table 3 shows the number of critical learnings linked to each competency, and the number of project managers describing at least one learning related to each competency. Five of the competencies in Table 3 were evident in skills described by more than one third of the project managers in the present study, namely team leadership; concern for order, quality and accuracy; relationship building; impact and influence; and organizational awareness. The remaining competencies could be identified in less than one third of the respondents, suggesting that these areas are of lesser importance for most IT project managers

The two competencies containing the most critical learnings were team leadership, with 29 related learnings and mentioned by 19 of the 23 respondents, and concern for order, quality and accuracy, with 28 related learnings and mentioned by 17 of the 23 respondents. These two competencies together can be seen as representing the key dimensions of project management skills, as described by E2:

Hard skills get you into the business. Soft skills keep you in the business.

Similarly, G2 commented:

It's easy to learn hard skills, [but] it's really hard to put those to use in a practical environment without the soft skills and a real understanding of why are you doing these things. Because you can go through the mechanics, you can give somebody a step by step 'here's what you do' but projects just never quite go that way and people never respond very well to that.

The team leadership competency was an area that respondents regarded as critically important and on which they focused much on-going energy in honing their skills. As shown in Table 4, the primary learning method here, and the only learning method for eight of the respondents, was reflection on experience. Six respondents also commented that observation of peers and senior project managers had guided them in their own practice, with three of these noting that such observations helped them learn what not to do. Five respondents described getting feedback from a superior or coaching from a mentor as the trigger for their reflection on experience and subsequent learning. One respondent described applying a formal training on team leadership in her practice.

Not surprisingly, the concern for order, quality and accuracy competency relies heavily on declarative and procedural knowledge about project management methodologies. Ten of the 17 managers reporting a skill related to this competency actually described two critical skills in their toolkit both drawing on this competency, suggesting that concern for order was a foundational project management skill for these respondents. More surprising was how these respondents reported learning about these foundational skills (see Table 4). Only seven of the 17 managers described formal training as the primary learning method, and all except one of these managers described supplementing their formal learning with at least one other approach, including extensive reflection on their experience, observation of other project managers, interaction in communities of practice, independent learning, and being coached. The remaining ten managers described learning skills related to the concern for order competency by reflection on experience, supplemented by performance feedback and mentoring (four managers), observation of other project managers (three managers), and interaction in communities of practice (one manager).

A further three competencies – relationship building, organizational awareness, and impact and influence – were mentioned by at least nine of the 23 respondents. The primary learning method for these three competencies was reflection on experience, with triggers for learning sometimes provided by mentors, performance feedback or observation of other project managers. The relationship building and impact and influence competencies were linked, in that nine of the 16 relationship building learnings were also coded to impact and influence, with the managers describing the need to build relationships on a continuous basis in order to have impact and influence to promote the needs of their projects. A 'currency' theme was apparent in some of the respondents' approaches to their relationship building and

their actions to develop impact and influence. For example, B1 commented:

I [used] to assign work based on authority and position. Now, I work completely through influence ... It's the idea of finding a "currency". I have to very subtly work with people and have them do something because it's the right thing to do, because they need to do it. So it's not direct; it's very subtle. I have to trade experience, knowledge and skill to get work accomplished.

Table 4. Methods reported for acquiring each competency (Note: Some respondents reported multiple methods for learning critical skills)

Competency (as defined in Table 1)	Reflection on experience	Observation of other PMs	Formal training	Coach or mentor	Performance feedback	Communities of practice	Other
Team leadership	14	6	1	3	1	-	-
Concern for order, quality and accuracy	13	6	7	2	2	2	1
Relationship building	12	2	-	2	1	-	-
Impact & influence	9	1	-	2	1	-	-
Organizational awareness	8	1	-	2	-	1	-
Achievement orientation	6	2	-	4	-	-	-
Flexibility	6	-	-	-	2	-	1
Focus on client needs	6	1	-	1	-	-	-
Interpersonal understanding	5	2	-	1	-	-	-
Initiative	5	2	-	1	-	-	1
Teamwork & cooperation	6	-	-	1	1	-	-
Information seeking	6	2	-	1	-	-	-
Directiveness /assertiveness	4	1	-	2	-	-	-
Analytical thinking	3	2	1	-	1	-	1
Self confidence	4	1	-	1	-	-	-
Developing others	3	1	1	-	-	-	-
Self control	2	1	-	-	-	-	-
Organizational commitment	2	-	-	-	-	-	-
Conceptual thinking	-	-	-	-	1	-	-
IT technical knowledge	1	-	-	-	-	-	-

Respondent B5 noted:

Identify all the stakeholders and involve them early, be proactive ... a lot of it's relationships ... I've kind of viewed it as a bank account - you make deposits when you help somebody and withdrawals when you need help.

The organizational awareness competency was identified in 13 critical learnings described by nine respondents. These respondents displayed a keen sense of looking beyond the immediate concerns of the project to address the wider business goals. Considering the overall business goals was of paramount importance for I1:

The first question has to be, 'are we creating business value?' And then the second question should be, 'what role can project management play in that?' Sometimes that first question doesn't get adequately addressed, and if it did, sometimes project management wouldn't actually be the answer.

Similarly, B6 commented:

The first thing I look at when I look at creating a solution ... is more at what the business can become actively engaged in. ... If a solution is designed and developed, it should be able to encompass the broadest possible benefit as opposed to just looking at what's being done on a day-to-day basis.

Management Development Initiatives

In the final portion of the interviews we examined what formal learning opportunities the respondents had experienced, and how useful they found these learning occasions. We have seen that, except for the concern for order, quality and accuracy competency, respondents overwhelmingly identified reflection on experience as the primary learning mechanism for their critical skills, and even though

formal training was important for the concern for order competency, reflection on experience also played a big part in the respondents' descriptions of their skill development here. We were interested to compare respondents' perceptions of the learning mechanisms that had been effective for their critical skills development with their views on the usefulness of their organizations' development interventions.

As can be seen from Table 5, the respondents had experienced a wide range of training interventions. All except two respondents had participated in formal project management training, most of which was either provided in-house or paid for by their employers. While this training was generally regarded as useful, three who had studied at least some of the Project Management Institute training materials commented that they had not found the material particularly helpful. I1 explained:

They've gotten so focused on instituting project management practices that they've sometimes lost sight of the fact that ultimately what we're all trying to do here is to create value for our organizations and project management can be a pathway to doing that, it can be one part of that, but it is a means to an end, not the end itself.

It is also interesting to note that while 16 of the 17 respondents who identified skills related to the concern for order competency had received formal project management training, only seven of these 16 attributed learning their skill to their formal training, even though they may have found the formal training useful. For example, H1 commented about the project management training she received early in her career:

Having the foundation of the training just gives you tools, it gives you processes, it gives you fundamentals to work with so that you aren't floundering in the dark so much.

Table 5. Development interventions experienced by respondents

Development intervention	Number of respondents (out of 23) reporting experience with the intervention
Formal project management training	21
Other management training	22
Performance appraisals	22
Participating in communities of practice	22
Coaching or mentoring	22
360-degree feedback	18

Yet, when describing how she learned her skills related to the concern for order, quality and accuracy competency, she referred only to learning by reflecting on her experiences on the job. Notably, she added, when commenting about the project management training:

But don't think that training necessarily makes you a good project manager. I think that you need to get out and get the experience.

Twenty-two of the 23 respondents had also received a variety of other management trainings, including general management, leadership, team building, conflict and negotiation, interpersonal, intercultural and presentation skills, and these trainings were generally described as very helpful. Looking at the 19 project managers who identified team leadership as a critical skill, all except one had experienced formal management training related to leadership, team building, conflict and negotiation, or intercultural skills – all types of training which might be expected to contribute to a manager's overall team leadership skill development. However, even though these managers generally commented that their various management trainings had been useful – for example J1 commented: *"those are the kind of the building blocks that you need to be a good project manager"* - only one cited formal training as a major learning method for her team leadership skills. Other than reflection on experience, having a coach or mentor was highly valued by those who had the opportunity to work with someone in this role, as was the opportunity to observe other project managers in action, although in four cases, such observation of other project managers led to a learning about what not to do.

DISCUSSION

It is interesting to compare the competencies identified in this study of IT project managers (in Table 3) with the competencies identified by Dainty et al. (2004, 2005) for construction project managers (in Table 1). Three of the five most frequently mentioned competencies in the present study – concern for order, quality and accuracy; relationship building; and organizational awareness – do not appear in Dainty et al.'s set. Additionally, Dainty et al. found self control and team leadership were the most predictive competencies for effective performance of construction managers, and while team leadership was the most frequently mentioned competency in the present study, self control was only identified in critical learnings described by two project managers. These results suggest that IT project managers may be drawing on quite a different skill-set from construction managers.

The two most highly mentioned competencies found in the present study – team leadership and concern for order, accuracy and quality - correspond to two types of training - management and project management - that were experienced by almost all of our respondents. Yet the formal trainings the project managers received did not feature prominently in their descriptions of learning methods for these competencies. Those managers who did mention formal project management training as a learning method for the concern for order competency typically described two or three additional experiential methods for their development in this skill, while reflection on experience was the primary learning method for team leadership skills.

We were surprised at the disconnect between the positive evaluations of organization-initiated training experiences and the lack of mention of these training experiences in the methods of learning identified by respondents for their critical skills. As noted in the Methodology section, we thought initially that our interview protocol may have contributed to this disconnect, so for the final ten respondents, we anchored the learnings described during the interview against the career timeline, providing an opportunity for the respondents to recall events such as training that occurred at the same time as the learning incident. The timelines revealed that the provision of specific project management training often did not occur until later in the respondent's career, most likely after the manager had already acquired the skills experientially, thus providing a possible explanation for the disconnect related to project management training. General management training was usually provided in a timely fashion early in the managers' careers and so might have been expected to feature more highly in the methods of learning. However, the critical learnings described by the respondents typically came from quite recent projects, even though their project management careers spanned decades, suggesting that a key underlying competence of these project managers may be related to the ability to build on early formal training and engage in on-going learning throughout their careers.

Indeed, we were struck by the descriptions from some respondents of the extent of their self motivation for learning and their active reflection on their experiences. Two managers described their practice of maintaining a journal, while a third described his own reflective practices: *"I make a mindmap and notes for myself."* Respondent B6 commented that he actively sought out developmental assignments in a spirit of continuous learning: *"Even if you crash and burn, which I have as well, you learn why."* And B5 commented: *"I believe I'm still learning, and probably always will be. If I ever think I've learned it all I think I'll be in trouble."*

IMPLICATIONS FOR RESEARCH AND PRACTICE

The first key objective for this study was to identify specific competencies that are important for IT project managers and the results presented here have identified a set of competencies largely different from those previously found to be important for construction project managers. Thus these results provide some support for the argument that project management competencies are industry-specific (Morris, 2001). Additionally, some competencies from the PMI competency framework (Project Management Institute, 2002) – team leadership, concern for order, quality and accuracy, relationship building, impact and influence, and organizational awareness - appear to be more important for IT project managers than other competencies. While the current study is exploratory and further work is required to substantiate these findings, organizations would be wise to proceed cautiously before assuming that project management skills in one practice arena can be automatically translated into relevant skills in another area.

Further research is also needed to examine which of the competencies are predictive of superior performance, and a follow-up study is under way to develop a validated competency model for IT project managers. Such a model can be used to aid selection and training and development decisions, as well as for career planning and performance management.

The second objective of the study – how IT project managers have learned their skills and competencies - related to the question of how organizations can best support the development of project managers throughout their careers. Clearly, the inter-relationship between training events and subsequent learning is a complex one requiring further in-depth research, but it seems evident that different kinds of support are required as the project manager advances through the stages of expertise development described earlier, of novice through competent performer to expert (Cicmil, 2006; Dreyfus & Dreyfus, 1986). We speculate that while formal training alone is not enough to foster the development of a particular skill, it may provide the necessary foundation for subsequent experiential learning to occur. It is particularly of concern that the group of project managers in the present study, for the most part, did not receive specific formal project management training early in their careers so that they had a basis from which to develop. Without a solid foundation of the basic declarative knowledge relevant to the profession, practitioners are left to gain their knowledge and expertise in a haphazard and trial-and-error fashion, which exposes the organization to risks of poor project management performance through lack of basic skills, and can also result in managers reaching relatively high levels in the organization while still having significant gaps in their basic project management knowledge. Thus organizations could well benefit substantially, in terms of project performance, by instituting early formal project management training for potential project managers in order to provide the necessary foundation for their future development.

Finally, as noted earlier, even with the foundational declarative knowledge in place, procedural knowledge and behavioral competence are more likely to develop in a situated learning environment, where trainees have the opportunity to practice the skills that have been addressed in the formal situation and to get feedback and reflect on their practice (Eraut, 2000). The project managers in the current study were striking for the depth of their reflections and persistence in seeking out learning opportunities. Thus, organizations wishing to foster project management skills in their personnel may find that developing a supportive environment and encouraging self reflective practices such as journaling and a life-long learning attitude could be a productive development route for junior project managers. In addition, organizations would be well advised to plan formal trainings and developmental assignments that are supported with apprenticeship or mentoring relationships between senior and junior project managers and constructive feedback on performance.

ACKNOWLEDGMENT

This research was funded in part by the Institute for Innovation in Information Management (I3M) at The Information School, University of Washington, under the Transfer of Learning Across IT Projects project.

REFERENCES

Bassellier, G., & Benbasat, I. (2004). Business competence of information technology professionals: Conceptual development and influence on IT-business partnerships. *Management Information Systems Quarterly, 28*(4), 673–694.

Belli, R. F. (1998). The structure of autobiographical memory and the event history calendar: Potential improvements in the quality of retrospective reports in surveys. *Memory (Hove, England), 6*(4), 383–406. doi:10.1080/741942610

Boyatzis, R. E. (1982). *The competent manager: A model for effective performance.* New York: Wiley.

Boyatzis, R. E. (1988). *Transforming qualitative information: Thematic analysis and code development.* Thousand Oaks, CA: Sage.

Brill, J. M., Bishop, M. J., & Walker, A. E. (2006). The competencies and characteristics required of an effective project manager. *Educational Technology Research and Development, 54*(2), 115–140. doi:10.1007/s11423-006-8251-y

Burke, M. J., & Day, R. R. (1986). A cumulative study of the effectiveness of managerial training. *The Journal of Applied Psychology, 71*(2), 232–246. doi:10.1037/0021-9010.71.2.232

Carbone, T. A., & Gholston, S. (2004). Project manager skill development: A survey of programs and practitioners. *Engineering Management Journal, 16*(3), 10–16.

Cicmil, S. (2006). Understanding project management practice through interpretative and critical research perspectives. *Project Management Journal, 37*(2), 27–37.

Conger, J. A. (2004). Developing leadership capability: What's inside the black box? *The Academy of Management Executive, 18*(4), 136–139.

Cooke-Davies, T. (2002). The "real" success factors on projects. *International Journal of Project Management, 20*(3), 185–190. doi:10.1016/S0263-7863(01)00067-9

Crawford, L. (2005). Senior management perceptions of project management competence. *International Journal of Project Management, 23*(1), 7–16. doi:10.1016/j.ijproman.2004.06.005

Crawford, L., & Gaynor, F. (1999). Assessing and developing project manager competence. In *Proceedings of the 30th Annual Project Management Institute 1999 Seminars & Symposium*, Project Management Institute, Sylva, NC.

Dainty, A. R. J., Cheng, M.-I., & Moore, D. R. (2003). Redefining performance measures for construction project managers: An empirical evaluation. *Construction Management and Economics, 21*(2), 209–218. doi:10.1080/0144619032000049737

Dainty, A. R. J., Cheng, M.-I., & Moore, D. R. (2004). A competency-based performance model for construction project managers. *Construction Management and Economics, 22*(8), 877–886. doi:10.1080/0144619042000202726

Dainty, A. R. J., Cheng, M.-I., & Moore, D. R. (2005). A comparison of the behavioral competencies of client-focused and production-focused project managers in the construction sector. *Project Management Journal, 36*(2), 39–48.

Davies, J., & Easterby-Smith, M. (1984). Learning and developing from managerial work experiences. *Journal of Management Studies, 21*(2), 169–183. doi:10.1111/j.1467-6486.1984.tb00230.x

Day, D. V. (2001). Leadership development: A review in context. *The Leadership Quarterly, 11*(4), 581–613. doi:10.1016/S1048-9843(00)00061-8

Dreyfus, H. L., & Dreyfus, S. E. (1986). *Mind over machine: The power of human intuition and expertise in the era of the computer.* New York: Free Press.

Drummond, H. (1996). The politics of risk: trials and tribulations of the Taurus project. *Journal of Information Technology, 11*(4), 347–357.

DuBois, D. A. (2002). Leveraging hidden expertise: Why, when, and how to use cognitive task analysis . In Kraiger, K. (Ed.), *Creating, implementing, and managing effective training and development: State-of-the-art lessons for practice* (pp. 80–114). San Francisco, CA: Jossey-Bass.

El-Sabaa, S. (2001). The skills and career path of an effective project manager. *International Journal of Project Management, 19*(1), 1–7. doi:10.1016/S0263-7863(99)00034-4

Eraut, M. (2000). Non-formal learning and tacit knowledge in professional work. *The British Journal of Educational Psychology, 70*(1), 113–136. doi:10.1348/000709900158001

Flanagan, J. C. (1954). The critical incident technique. *Psychological Bulletin, 51*(4), 327–358. doi:10.1037/h0061470

Gray, C. F., & Larson, E. W. (2008). *Project management: The managerial process* (4th ed.). New York: McGraw Hill Irwin.

Jiang, J. J., Klein, G., & Chen, H.-G. (2001). The relative influence of IS project implementation policies and project leadership on eventual outcomes. *Project Management Journal, 32*(3), 49–55.

Jiang, J. J., Klein, G., & Margulis, S. (1998). Important behavioral skills for IS project managers: The judgments of experienced IS professionals. *Project Management Journal, 29*(1), 39–43.

Kaulio, M. A. (2008). Project leadership in multi-project settings: Findings from a critical incident study. *International Journal of Project Management, 26*(4), 338–347. doi:10.1016/j.ijproman.2007.06.005

Kempster, S. (2006). Leadership learning through lived experience: A process of apprenticeship. *Journal of Management & Organization, 12*(1), 4–23.

Kerzner, H. (2001). *Project management: A systems approach to planning, scheduling, and controlling* (7th ed.). New York: John Wiley.

Klein, G. A., Calderwood, R., & MacGregor, D. (1989). Critical decision method for eliciting knowledge. *IEEE Transactions on Systems, Man, and Cybernetics, 19*(3), 462–472. doi:10.1109/21.31053

Langer, N., Slaughter, S. A., & Mukhopadhyay, T. (2008). Project managers' skills and project success in IT outsourcing. In *Proceedings of the 29th International Conference on Information Systems*, Paris.

Lee, D. M. S., Trauth, E. M., & Farwell, D. (1995). Critical skills and knowledge requirements of IS professionals: A joint academic/industry investigation. *Management Information Systems Quarterly, 19*(3), 313–340. doi:10.2307/249598

Lyytinen, K., Mathiassen, L., & Ropponen, J. (1998). Attention shaping and software risk - A categorical analysis of four classical risk management approaches. *Information Systems Research, 9*(3), 233–255. doi:10.1287/isre.9.3.233

Matsuo, M., Wong, C. W. Y., & Lai, K.-H. (2008). Experience-based learning of Japanese IT professionals: A qualitative research. *The Journal of Strategic Information Systems, 17*(3), 202–213. doi:10.1016/j.jsis.2008.03.001

McCall, M. W. Jr. (2004). Leadership development through experience. *The Academy of Management Executive, 18*(3), 127–130.

McCauley, C. D., & Hezlett, S. A. (2001). Individual development in the workplace. In Anderson, N., Ones, D. S., Sinangil, H. K., & Viswesvaran, C. (Eds.), *Handbook of Industrial, Work & Organizational Psychology* (pp. 313–335). London: Sage.

Miles, B. M., & Huberman, A. M. (1994). *Qualitative Data Analysis: An Expanded Sourcebook* (2nd ed.). London: Sage.

Morris, P. W. G. (2001). Updating the project management bodies of knowledge. *Project Management Journal, 32*(3), 21–30.

Napier, N. P., Keil, M., & Tan, F. B. (2009). IT project managers' construction of successful project management practice: A repertory grid investigation. *Information Systems Journal, 19*(3), 255–282. doi:10.1111/j.1365-2575.2007.00264.x

Nellore, R., & Balachandra, R. (2001). Factors influencing success in integrated product development (IPD) projects. *IEEE Transactions on Engineering Management, 48*(2), 164–174. doi:10.1109/17.922476

Pescuric, A., & Byham, W. C. (1996). The new look of behavior modeling. *Training & Development, 50*(7), 24–31.

Project Management Institute. (2002). *Project manager competency development (PMCD) framework*. Newton Square, PA: Project Management Institute.

Project Management Institute. (2004). *A guide to the project management body of knowledge (PMBOK Guide)* (3rd ed.). Newton Square, PA: Project Management Institute.

Ritchie, J., & Spencer, L. (1994). Qualitative data analysis for applied policy research . In Bryman, A., & Burgess, R. G. (Eds.), *Analyzing qualitative data* (pp. 173–194). London: Routledge. doi:10.4324/9780203413081_chapter_9

Sauer, C., Gemino, A., & Reich, B. H. (2007). The impact of size and volatility on IT project performance. *Communications of the ACM, 50*(11), 79–84. doi:10.1145/1297797.1297801

Spencer, S. M., & Spencer, L. M. (1993). *Competence at work: Models for superior performance*. New York: John Wiley.

Standish Group. (2001). *Extreme CHAOS*. The Standish Group International Inc.

Taylor, H. (2005). A critical decision interview approach to capturing tacit knowledge: Principles and application. *International Journal of Knowledge Management, 1*(3), 25–39.

Taylor, P. J., Russ-Eft, D. F., & Chan, D. W. L. (2005). A meta-analytic review of behavior modeling training. *The Journal of Applied Psychology, 90*(4), 692–709. doi:10.1037/0021-9010.90.4.692

Turner, J. R., & Müller, R. (2006). *Choosing appropriate project managers: Matching their leadership style to the type of project*. Newton Square, PA: Project Management Institute.

Webber, S. S., & Torti, M. T. (2004). Project managers doubling as client executives. *The Academy of Management Executive, 18*(1), 60–71.

This work was previously published in International Journal of Information Technology Project Management, Volume 1, Issue 4, edited by John Wang, pp. 1-19, copyright 2010 by IGI Publishing (an imprint of IGI Global).

Chapter 11
Questioning the Key Techniques Underlying the Iterative and Incremental Approach to Information Systems Development

Angus G. Yu
University of Stirling, UK

ABSTRACT

The iterative and incremental development (IID) approach is widely adopted in information systems development (ISD) projects. While the IID approach has played an important role the management of many ISD projects, some of the key techniques have not received critical appraisal from the academic community. This paper aims to fill the gap and examines three such techniques through a case study. First of all, the gap between the theory of user participation and the reality of user's lack of real influence on design and development is explored. The author proposes the concept of "participatory capture" to explain the side effect of user participation. Secondly, the assumption that evolutionary prototyping converges to a successful design is questioned. Thirdly, the side effect of the timeboxing technique is considered. The paper suggests that the IID approach represents the learning approach as categorized in Pich et al. (2002) and it might be ineffective in dealing with the significant uncertainties in ISD projects.

INTRODUCTION

The iterative and incremental development (IID) approach has long been proposed as a solution to the so-called "software crisis" (Larman & Basili,

2003). Indeed, the concept can be traced back to the seminal paper by Royce (1970). While IID has been built into a number of recent and current information systems development (ISD) methodologies, some of the key techniques have not received critical appraisal from the academic community.

DOI: 10.4018/978-1-4666-0930-3.ch011

This paper aims to fill the gap. Through a case study, the author explores the research question: to what extent might IID help or hinder successful ISD project management? The paper starts with a brief survey of the IID literature, highlighting three key techniques for further examination. The case study project is then described followed by discussions of the IID techniques. The nature of the IID approach is then briefly discussed within the scheme of project management approaches categorized by Pich et al. (2002). The last section outlines conclusions and further research questions.

THE IID APPROACH

The IID approach is not designed by a single source. Rather it has come "independently from countless unnamed projects and the contributions of thousands" (Larman and Basili, 2003). At the simplest level, the IID approach refers to a way of developing information systems that emphasizes a number of techniques including user participation, incremental evolution and time-boxed iteration. The approach is shared by a number of ISD methodologies, including Rapid Application Development (RAD, see Eva, 2001; Martin, 1991), Dynamic systems development methodology (DSDM, see Stapleton, 1997), SCRUM (Schwaber, 1995), Rational Unified Process (Kruchten, 2000), eXtreme Programming (Beck, 2000) and various other "agile" methodologies (Highsmith, 2000; Lin & Shao, 2000). IID has been construed as the way to overcome the weaknesses of the "Waterfall Model", or "the sequential process" (Kruchten, 2000). The IID approach recognizes that requirements cannot be "frozen". It thus dispels the misconception about the need for complete requirements before design and development. IID also acknowledges the inseparability of design and development. At a theoretical level, IID advocates a flexible, social constructive approach to product management,

unlike the traditional planning-based approach (Koskela & Howell, 2002b). Koskela and Howell (2002a) examine SCRUM in particular and concluded that it is based on "alternative theories of planning, execution and control".

While the IID-based methodologies may represent a step forward in the thinking of information system development, they have not always been successful in resolving ISD project challenges. Despite the proclaimed intention of the IID proponents to address system development failures, the rate of failures has remained high (see e.g. Charette, 2005; Goulielmos, 2004). There could be multiple explanations to account for this lack of success. One is that "effective" methods are not applied (see Humphrey, 1998 for such a discussion in the context of software engineers' practices) or applied incorrectly (see Highsmith, 2002 for an example of incorrect use of timeboxing). Another possibility is that there might be fundamental weaknesses with the IID approach itself. Many publications and training courses have been made available to practitioners based on the first explanation (Humphrey, 1998). This article, however, critically examines the possible weaknesses of the IID approach itself. Three key techniques are identified that are common to IID-based ISD methodologies, namely user participation, evolutionary prototyping, and timeboxing, each is briefly outlined below.

User Participation

User participation, also loosely referred to as "user involvement", is central to IID. Martin (1991) emphasizes the need for user involvement during Joint Application Design workshops. Stapleton (1997) describes it as "absolutely vital". Of DSDM's nine principles, three are about user involvement. Of course, the so-called traditional systems development approach also involves users, as acknowledged by Stapleton (1997). The question is not if users should be involved, rather it is which users and how they are to be involved.

Before addressing the question of which users to be involved in IS development, it is necessary to be clear as to who the users are. There is some terminology confusion in the literature. In this article the terms client, user and customer are defined as follows. A client pays for developing a system and typically owns and operates the system if successfully developed. A client usually interacts with one or more suppliers that are typically external commercial companies. There is usually some written contractual agreement between a client and a supplier. A user of a system is someone who is expected to use the system. There may be internal users inside the client organization or external users who are not part of the client organization but are allowed to access the system (e.g. for online shopping). A customer is someone the client organization serves in its business operations. Customers are typically external users.

Of the multitude of users, there is the question of the "right users" to be involved during system development (Beynon-Davies et al., 1997). In addition, there is the question of how users should be involved. The two questions are related. If the "right" users are limited to a concentrated small number, they might be more fully involved than otherwise. It has also been suggested that "user involvement" should be differentiated from "participatory design" (Beynon-Davies et al., 1997). In this article, a more inclusive term "user participation" is used to reflect active user involvement during both requirements planning and system design phases.

Though strongly advocated in the IS literature, user participation has not always been associated with successful systems design and development (Cavaye, 1995; Hwang & Thorn, 1999; McKeen et al., 1994). Lynch and Gregor (2004) suggest that system design success depends on the level of user influence, which may be minimal despite user participation. Research has shown that, under the rhetoric of user participation, the reality of developer-user relation is problematic. Beath and

Orlikowski (1994) reveal that, despite the emphasis of user participation in "joint development", users are portrayed as "naïve, technically unsophisticated, and parochial" while developers are seen as "more knowledgeable, more professional, and more corporate-minded". Such contradictions are likely to undermine interactions between users and developers. Communication barriers make iterative processes less open and less productive. As a result, user participation may not lead to much user influence on system design (Lynch & Gregor, 2004). Further, Howcroft and Wilson (2003) depict "the antagonistic relations between end-users (employees) and sponsors of the system (managers)" with developers in between, thus highlighting the "paradoxical nature of user participation". The case study further contributes to the literature on user participation, exploring the causes of possible difficulties identified through the case study.

Evolutionary Prototyping (EP)

EP is one of the key IID techniques. Though problems have been identified with prototyping, including poor design, poor documentation and increased difficulties to manage and control (Alavi, 1984; Avison & Fitzgerald, 2003; Baskerville & Stage, 1996; Gordon & Bieman, 1995) most researchers consider it necessary to embrace the technique. While some prototypes are of the "throw-away" type, an evolutionary prototype aims to grow into a full system. Thus the key assumption underlying evolutionary prototyping is the converging argument, as described by Highsmith (2000):

... a project that begins with a divergence between the customer's and the developer's views of the product. During each successive cycle, the stakeholders learn more about each other's view of the feature sets. ... as this learning takes place, the difference narrows until the final product emerges to satisfy both the customer's and developer's requirements. (p86)

Martin (1991) suggested that a prototype "should become the final system". Thus EP is assumed to converge and converge to success. If a solution does not meet client requirements, the implicit option is continued prototyping, which incurs additional cost and delays and may or may not be acceptable to the client from a project management perspective. It is not surprising that the available evidence supporting the technique seems to be mainly based on views from the developer (e.g. Gordon & Bieman, 1995) rather than those of the client. The case study presented in this article questions the converging argument.

Timeboxing

Timeboxing is a technique that plans for time and resources rather than functionality in order to achieve delivery deadlines (Avison & Fitzgerald, 2003). A timebox is a timeframe within which a system must be constructed. There are usually three main justifications for timeboxing. The first is the 80:20 rule, i.e. 80% of a system's function can be completed in 20% of time allocated (Zahniser, 1995), The second justification is to overcome "creeping functionality" (Martin, 1991). The concern is that prototyping may lead users or developers to adding functionality "in an uncontrolled fashion". The third justification is that it can be used as a motivating technique for project team members to achieve deadlines. Timeboxing has been adopted in DSDM (Stapleton, 1997) and many other agile methodologies (Larman, 2004).

Berger and Beynon-Davies (2004) suggested that timeboxing is impractical and unacceptable to some clients where 100% of business needs are mandatory. Apart from that and some concerns about developers' burnout (Nørbjerg, 2002), timeboxing has received little attention in academic literature. This article gives a critical assessment of the technique based on the case study from the client perspective.

RESEARCH METHOD AND THEORETICAL FRAMEWORK

The purpose of the article is to examine the possible link between the IID approach and poor IS project performance. The method of case study is appropriate for such an explorative and explanatory article (Yin, 1994). The case reported here is about a project the author participated as a test manager and thus as a full project member (Adler, 1987). Thus the author is equipped with tacit and contextual knowledge of the project that may be otherwise difficult to acquire. Such knowledge is valuable for interpretation of people, events and outcomes of typically complex IS projects. The author tries to make sense of a situation using "a mixture of events, anecdotes, views and attitudes of those observed…" (Mintzberg, 1973, p226), and perhaps most importantly documentary evidence from the project. The author believes that the case is "revelatory" (Beynon-Davies et al., 2000; Yin, 1994) in highlighting a number of key issues with the IID approach. The observations available for analysis represent the author's interpretations of the project under study. The author does not claim to be totally bias-free but relies on available project documents to keep a sense of objectivity. In presenting the case details, all companies names have been anonymized.

The article presents the case study and discussions within the principal-agent (PA) framework (Eisenhardt, 1989). Müller and Turner (2005) provide an excellent introduction of the PA theory within the context of project management. The PA framework is helpful in explaining contractual behaviours when the contracting parties are assumed to have potentially diverting interests. In this article, the perspective is primarily that of the client's. This is necessary if a project's success is judged according to its value contribution to the client (Yu et al., 2005). It is within the PA framework that the hypothesis of "participatory capture" is introduced in the "Discussions" section.

THE WEBSHOP PROJECT

The WebShop Project was carried out by one of the large utility companies in the UK (coded as UKOne) from April 2000 to March 2001. Like any sizable IT project, it can be described from a number of different perspectives. In this article, the focus is on the use of an IID-based methodology to develop the "look & feel" or the user interface of the WebShop, an online shopping system. The project is outlined first with its background and organization followed by a description of supplier selection and development progress for the user interface.

Project Background

At the time when the WebShop Project was initiated, UKOne's core business was to serve nearly 5 millions energy customers with electricity and gas. In addition, UKOne had a chain of over 100 retail stores selling domestic appliances and consumer electronics throughout the UK. The retail stores marketed energy related products and services. Some retail shops also had facilities to enable energy customers to pay their bills. The idea was that energy customers' attention could be turned into consumer goods sales opportunities. Likewise, customers coming into the shops for consumer goods would be exposed to marketing campaigns for energy sales and services. Thus retail and energy offerings were to complement each other.

The WebShop Project was initiated to implement a similar complementary strategy online. The project had two main parts. One was to establish the necessary technical infrastructure and the other to develop the online WebShop system. The system was to enable energy customers to submit meter readings, view and pay bills as well as purchasing goods like fridges, cookers and TVs. The project was championed by OneSub, UKOne's subsidiary responsible for both the retail and energy services.

The Project was planned for completing all three workstreams (Retail, Energy Services and Customer Services) in six months. The initial estimated budget was £2million, covering the costs of the infrastructure hardware, system software, bespoke software and integration with other internal systems. Even though the Energy Services workstream was taken out of the scope half way through the project, the final project cost came to nearly £3million. The project was closed after a delay of five months. Four months after the WebShop system went live, it was withdrawn from the Internet.

Project Organization

The Client's E-Business Project Director acted as the client sponsor. Within the Client, three related but separate teams were holding stakes in the outcome of the project. The first was the Marketing Team responsible for customer capture and services. The second was the Retail Team responsible for selling domestic appliances and consumer electronics. The third was the Energy Team responsible for energy sales and services. Accordingly, there were three project workstreams, each supported by one or two product manager(s) from within the business teams. Among other things, their roles were to specify business processes, agree functional specifications, carry out acceptance testing and "sign off" the system. The product managers reported directly to the project sponsor.

A prime contractor (SLC) managed the project on a "Time & Materials" basis by supplying core project team members including the Project Manager, Workstream Team Leaders and the Test Manager. SLC was awarded the contract because of its overall systems maintenance contract with UKOne and its excellent understanding of UKOne's existing systems and data. However SLC lacked a pool of technically skilled and qualified personnel for software development. Therefore,

SLC subcontracted software development to external suppliers. Two suppliers were envisaged to participate in software development, one for graphic design, providing the "look & feel" part of the system, and the other for "backend functions". NQ and another supplier were chosen to fulfil the roles respectively. This case study only focuses on the interface development NQ was contracted for.

Selecting and Contracting NQ

NQ, a company with 250 employees and with offices in London, New York and San Francisco, was selected via a process of proposal, review and referencing. There was no evidence of competition in the selection process. Instead, NQ was selected as a "design partner" in the spirit of partnership. With its impressive presentation and a well-versed proposal to OneSub and SLC, NQ seemed to be capable and experienced. In the presentation, NQ proposed a delivery methodology based on RAD (Martin, 1991), featuring techniques including joint workshops, prototyping and timeboxing.

The selection decision was made jointly by OneSub and SLC shortly after NQ's presentation and a contract was awarded accordingly. The contract was between SLC and NQ on a "Time & Materials" basis. Since the contract between OneSub and SLC was on the same basis, it meant that OneSub had an interest to manage NQ closely. The contract clearly specified NQ's services to comprise of activities including design, build, testing and integration. To carry out these activities, different types of resources were estimated in terms of hours, and each resource type had an hourly rate specified. This gave an estimated total cost. One important clause in the contract is related to the possibility of exceeding the cost estimate:

[NQ] shall not without the Client's prior written consent exceed these estimates. Accordingly, on becoming aware that these estimates will be exceeded [NQ] will notify the Client and, once these estimates have been reached, [NQ] will be entitled to suspend provision of the Services until it receives the Client's written consent to continue.

This clause suggests that if the cost estimate is reached before the promised activities are completed, the client is given a choice of accepting what is developed or allowing the development to continue with an increased budget. As it turned out, SLC had to accept unfinished deliverables from NQ and used internal resources for further development.

Design and Development Progress

In line with the four phases of the RAD lifecycle (Martin, 1991), the development phases of the "look & feel" of the WebShop can be outlined as:

- Requirements planning.
- User design through rapid prototyping.
- Developing web pages for a demonstration.
- Integrating the design into the website for further testing and eventual launch.

Shortly after Phase 2, the project manager reported to the client that the signed off "look & feel" had been confirmed as "excellent" by all reviewing parties. However, by the end of Phase 3, there was a demonstration to an independent client audience who had not participated in the project in the first place. The demonstration resulted in an issue with "High" impact being logged in the risk register that the client had a "dislike" of the design. Exactly why the client reviewers disliked the design is not recorded but the log warns that if "there is a requirement to modify the layout this will affect all pages – and will require substantial rework". There were urgent discussions among the project sponsor, SLC and the suppliers. However, it was too late to have any substantial change. The project simply proceeded to incorporate the design into the website for further development and the eventual launch.

The Use of IID Techniques

By choosing NQ as the developer, SLC accepted the IID-based delivery methodology. Prior to this project, SLC used a traditional lifecycle approach to manage systems development. SLC employees were experienced and knowledgeable in the traditional system development with clear ideas for the need of detailed documented requirements. Detailed requirements were drafted in the requirements planning phase before NQ was contracted. Once NQ brought its IID-based methodology into the project, the requirements documents were set aside in favour of the IID techniques.

The stakeholders were well represented during the design process. In addition to internal users, external potential customers were consulted. The key internal users were middle-level project managers. Other internal users were also available for testing. All internal users were appointed by management, and therefore were in the category of "representative participation" (Mumford, 1983). External potential users were engaged in usability testing through a marketing agency. The engagement was on a consultative basis (Mumford, 1983).

A total of 8 initial iterations took place in less than a month through joint design workshops and frequent email communications. Afterwards, the prototype "look & feel" was "signed off". This was followed by webpage development. The webpages were signed-off individually, though NQ complained at the time about the slow sign-off process.

The project also used timeboxing aggressively to manage the project scope. Half way through the project, it was realised that it would have been impossible to complete the whole project by the initial deadline. It was decided to split the system into two releases. Release 1 was to include 32 out of the total 75 initially planned user interface screens and necessary Customer Services functions. Release 2 was to include the Energy Services functions. Following the concept of timeboxing, Release 1 was to be delivered by the initial deadline. However, it was implemented until the closure of the project with a delay of five months. Release 2 was not attempted within the project.

DISCUSSIONS

In this section, the suitability of RAD to the interface design is discussed first. The attention is then turned to examining the key RAD techniques of user participation, evolutionary prototyping and timeboxing. Finally, the IID approach is considered within project management framework using the scheme proposed by Pich et al. (2002).

Suitability of RAD for the Project under Study

The RAD methodology has generally been considered suitable for small to medium-sized projects that are interface-intensive (Berger & Beynon-Davies, 2004; Howard, 1997; Osborn, 1995). In the WebShop Project, the RAD method was only applied to the design of the user interface. At least this part of the project might be justified as meeting the "interface intensive" criterion. The issue of the development size is less easy to establish. The WebShop Project had an initial budget of £2million, increased to £3million. This is small compared with the £10million project reported by Berger & Beynon-Davies (2004). Project budget, however, is a poor measure for the project size or complexity. This is due to the fact that a project spends on acquiring hardware, system software as well as coding, testing and project management. In the case of the WebShop Project, only around 18% of the total project expenditure was spent on NQ for designing and developing the user interface while around 30% on the backend functions. The project expenditure does not accurately reflect the actual effort for two additional reasons. One is that the client's internal staff time is not always charged to the project. Secondly, varying labour rates makes cross-project comparisons difficult. Bearing in mind these limitations, the user interface part of the WebShop Project can be considered as a small to medium-sized development endeavour. Therefore, the RAD methodology seems suitable for its design and development, at least according to the criteria given by RAD proponents.

User Participation

Reviews of literature have shown that positive correlation of user participation and system success accounts for around 36% to 37% of the case studies (e.g. Cavaye, 1995). The WebShop interface design provides a striking example that active user participation may somehow lead to a "disliked" design. In the WebShop Project, at least to the project team the "right" users (both knowledgeable middle managers and front-line staff) were closely involved in design, development and testing. The project also encouraged an atmosphere of client-supplier partnership so that communications could be open and honest. Why should such consciously practised user participation lead to a design that would be "disliked" by internal users who had not participated in the project? Multiple explanations are possible. Most of the explanations to date are behaviour-based, attributing to groupthink or other types of problematic user-developer communications (Cavaye, 1995; Gallivan & Keil, 2003; Lynch & Gregor, 2004). However, such explanations, apart from urging caution and more training, are difficult to be effectively applied to real world projects. This article proposes a hypothesis of "participatory capture" as an alternative explanation based on the principal-agent (PA) framework. As a hypothesis it is inherently speculative. It is presented here in the hope of contributing to an alternative solution for resolving developer-user communication problems highlighted in the relevant literature.

The concept of "participatory capture" is analogous to "regulatory capture" proposed by Laffont & Tirole (1990). In studying government regulation of industries, Laffont & Tirole proposed a principal-agency-agent model, in which the government (the Congress in their paper) acts as the principal, the regulatory bodies as the agency and the industry as the agent. While the agency should regulate the agent according to rules and regulations set by the principal, Laffont and Tirole successfully demonstrated that the agency may suffer from "regulatory capture" and act in collusion with the agent and hide information from the principal. Therefore, regulatory capture is an undesirable side-effect of the regulatory process. Likewise, the intended consequence of a user participation process is for users to influence a system design to better meet their needs. A possible side effect of the process, however, is that users may lose the ability to assess the resultant design independently and critically. The author thus proposes an analogous concept of "participatory capture" as a result of participation. Figure 1 illustrates the two types of capture.

In the context of the WebShop project, Figure 1 may be interpreted as follows. The principal is the client organization (OneSub). The agency is the prime contractor (SLC) and the agent is the subcontractor (NQ). The representatives of the principal are those OneSub employees who participated in the design. While NQ (the agent) had the main responsibility of developing the user interface, the agency (SLC) had a supervisory or regulatory responsibility on behalf of the principal to manage NQ. In this sense, SLC was expected to have a "regulatory effect" on NQ. However, project reporting is not easy to reflect project reality (Thompson et al., 2007). What is worse, as an agency, SLC had an incentive to report good progress on the project. Otherwise there could have been a risk of the project being more closely scrutinized (Snow et al., 2007) or even cancelled. As a result, SLC may have hidden

Figure 1. Regulatory capture and participatory capture

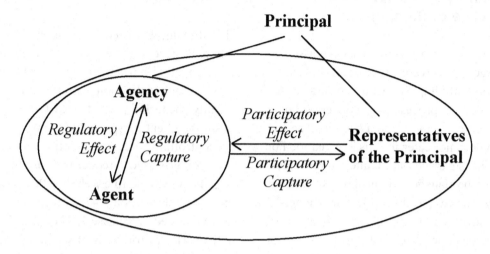

information from or put a positive interpretation on any progress on behalf of NQ (the agent) to OneSub (the principal). In this way, SLC may be said to have suffered from "regulatory capture". At the same time, the representatives from OneSub were expected to provide open and honest inputs to the design process, which would be the desired "participatory effect". However, the representatives did not disagree openly with the biased report from the prime contractor, which led to the "disliked" design to be discovered too late. The failure of the representatives to report the poor design could be due to a number of reasons. Firstly, they might have genuinely agreed with SLC that the design was "excellent", thus failed to take a critical stand. Or secondly, they may have been sceptical about the design but did not voice any concern for the sake of a good working relationship with the project manager. Or thirdly they may not have liked the design but did not state their views openly since they felt partly to blame due to the joint design process. In the second and the third instances, they can be said to have suffered from "participatory capture".

The desire to increase user influence for better design (Lynch & Gregor, 2004) and the risk of participatory capture present a dilemma. On the one hand, a user may be blamed for not effecting sufficient influence on a design. On the other hand, the more the user exerts influence, the more likely the user is "captured", and therefore loses the ability to assess the resultant design independently and critically. Either of the scenarios can lead to poor design.

A question can be asked as for how a client can effectively participate and not to lose the critical viewpoint. The case study provides one possible answer. In the WebShop Project, the client realised that the design did not quite meet its requirements through a demonstration to a group of managers not involved in the design process. In other words, one way for the client to retain a critical viewpoint is to keep a group of users from participation. However, issues remain regarding when the new users should see a design and how their feedback can be incorporated into a design without their suffering from participatory capture next time around. Since any critique implies a suggestion for improvement, which if adopted, has the potential to "capture" the critic, it is hypothesised here that participatory capture is inherent in participation. This hypothesis will benefit from empirical testing in ISD projects and other participatory contexts.

Evolutionary Prototyping and the Practice of Signing Off

The evolutionary prototyping process is assumed to converge and converge to success (Highsmith, 2000). The WebShop Project demonstrated that the evolutionary process may converge, but it may not always converge to a success. The IID approach does not cater for this eventuality. For small projects carried out by internal resources, the risk may be managed within the organizational boundary. For any sizable project with external suppliers involved, the financial implications of abandoning a poor design and starting again can be significant. Who should bear the cost of such a re-start? Would any manager, whether from the client, the prime contractor or the subcontractor, admit responsibility and therefore the liabilities? Such questions proved too hard to resolve in the WebShop Project. Though the issue was raised and recorded, the project team had no option but to carry on with a design the client "disliked".

During prototyping and user design process in the WebShop Project, client representatives were required to "sign off" prototype outputs. The sign-off practice has been acknowledged to be useful for obtaining a user decision (Avison & Fitzgerald, 2003). However, exactly what a sign-off means in terms of design quality is not clear. Wiegers (1999) discussed the vague meaning of signing off within the context of requirements management. There was the same problem with sign-offs in the WebShop project. Since the signed-off artefacts were prototypes, they could not have embodied 100% of the requirements. Yet, how could the missing elements have been communicated from the client to the supplier if the artefacts had been signed off? Signing off a prototype is thus to be a contradiction. What is worse, signing off is likely to have aggravated the participatory capture effect. Further research is needed to assess the practice of user signing-off and its consequences on user-developer interactions and design process.

Timeboxing

Timeboxing was used aggressively in the Web-Shop Project. Despite the assurance given by McConnell (1996) about timeboxing having no positive or negative impact on functionality and quality, the technique had at least three problems from the client perspective. One is that, instead of controlling "creeping functionality" (Martin, 1991), it was used to reduce system functionality significantly. When the WebShop Project was split into two releases, only 43% of interface screens were retained in Release 1. The other 57% were left to a later project, clearly adding cost to the client in the long run and delaying the planned system benefits. Secondly, timeboxing did not deal with the complex and interrelated nature of software components. A web system cannot be broken down "as finely as the developer desires" (Chen & Heath, 2001). Thus it was possible to leave behind a separate workstream, but it was not possible to separate customer services entirely from the retail part in the WebShop system. In other words, the required application could only be divided within constraints. Thirdly, there was the problem of quality. In NQ's proposal document, system testing was specifically promised. However, NQ carried out only a limited amount of testing since a full system testing at the end of each design iteration was deemed not quite possible due to the lack of other fully developed components. It turned out that NQ's html pages were not compatible with Netscape browsers. NQ refused to carry out further work without extra funding when the pre-budgeted time had been used up. The lesson was that quality was "de-scoped" as well as functions due to timeboxing. Such use of timeboxing is also observed by Berger and Beynon (2004), who record attempts "to descope development work in order to meet timeboxed deadlines".

The net result was that timeboxing was a direct cause of the poor design with fewer functions and worse quality than promised. The fact that the WebShop Project involved external suppliers made the loss of features and quality particularly visible. McConnell (1996) warned that the use of timeboxing is only suited to internal projects. This may well be the case for internal control purpose, but from the value-centred viewpoint (Yu et al., 2005), external projects are not necessarily any different from internal ones. The loss of features and quality usually means the loss of value to the client organization. At the same time, timeboxing may not reduce the client's cost in a proportionate manner. Therefore, it is a technique that may suit the supplier rather than the client.

The supplier-centred perspective of the timeboxing technique is clearer if it is contrasted with normal practices of a commercial transaction. When a client goes to the market, the important considerations are functions (scope), quality, price (cost) and time as acknowledged widely in the ISDMs and PM literature (e.g. Bittner & Spence, 2006). What the client usually likes to "box" in first, however, is functions and quality, and then to choose the right price and delivery time if relevant. While it does happen when a client fixes a budget first, it is usually expected that a product will meet a minimum level of functions and quality in the first place. It is unlikely that a client would be willing to fix the price upfront and accept a product whatever its functions and quality. The timeboxing technique says nothing about ensuring a certain level of functions and quality. In the face of uncertainties in IS development, it is understandable from the supplier's viewpoint, but is likely to damage the client's interest.

The IID Approach in a Project Management Context

It has been generally acknowledged that IS development methodologies (ISDMs) and project management frameworks (PMFs, e.g. PMBOK by PMI, 2004) serve different purposes: ISDMs for product development and PMFs for managing an overall project (Marchewka, 2006). How do the two fit together? One view is that ISDMs can be

embedded in PMFs (Marchewka, 2006) without incompatibilities (Charbonneau, 2004). How does the IID approach reconcile with the cost target and time deadline of a typical project? The standard answer is to use the timeboxing technique. However, as discussed earlier, timeboxing only helps time and cost targets, it sacrifices functions and quality. To improve functions and quality, more iterations are required, thus demanding more time and budget. A project lifecycle is therefore likely to be dictated by the progress of the product development lifecycle, or end with a product with less functions and quality. In the former case, if a project exceeds its budget and still ends with a product with its value exceeding the cost, the project might be considered as a partial success (Yu et al., 2005). In the latter case, the project may produce a product with so little value that it does not even cover the project cost, thus rendering the project a failure (Yu et al., 2005).

However, the assumption that having more iterations will improve a system "incrementally" must be questioned. Iterations may result in a "converged" solution, meaning that the involved users no longer wish to add or take anything away. However, a converged solution might not meet the client's requirements as demonstrated by the case study in this article. When a design does not meet the client's requirements in some fundamental ways, merely having more iterations is not enough to improve the design. What is required may be a re-design, requiring a substantial amount of time and cost. When no one is willing to assume such liabilities, the project becomes out of control and runs the risk of failure. The IID approach does not seem to plan for the ultimate risk of developing a product not meeting a client's requirements.

How can this ultimate risk be addressed? It is commonly known that a late change to product development is costly (Beck, 2000). It follows that the later a change is introduced, the higher the cost, and the less likely the change will be implemented. While the IID approach hopes to address this concern by the techniques of early user involvement and prototyping, there are good reasons that late changes are sometimes inevitable due to communication barriers and, as the case study in this article suggests, participatory capture. In the meantime, it is recognised that the IID approach deals with technical issues and the risk of not developing a satisfactory product is more appropriately addressed within the project management framework.

Beyond IID

Following the issues raised in this article, it is useful to relate IID to the classification scheme for project management approaches proposed by Pich et al. (2002). According to Pich et al., there are three approaches to project management:

- The instructionist approach: pre-specifying and triggering actions based on signals;
- The learning approach: conducting new planning in the middle of a project;
- The selectionist: the pursuit of multiple candidate solutions until the best can be identified.

In software development, the Waterfall Model might be said to follow the "instructionist approach". This has long been recognised as not suitable for software development (Larman & Basili, 2003). IID, on the other hand, is effectively taking the learning approach. As Pich et al. (2002) point out, learning can be "time consuming, psychologically difficult, and often resisted". The observations from this case study suggest that the IID approach, while it may be an improvement on the instructionist approach, is ineffective in dealing with the significant uncertainties in ISD projects and is ultimately costly for the client. It is suggested that the costs and benefits of different approaches including the selectionist approach be examined in order to develop more effective ISD project management frameworks. This will require rethinking of the client-supplier relationship and a re-examination of the project management theory for information systems development.

CONCLUSION AND FURTHER RESEARCH QUESTIONS

The WebShop Project was not technologically innovative. By the year 2000, there were many sophisticated retail websites on the Internet. Yet its user interface design was not a success from the client's viewpoint. While there might be a number of possible explanations including poor co-ordination of the suppliers and less than perfect application of the IID techniques, the design failure may be attributed at least partly to the IID techniques. Firstly, user participation assumes that user input directs the design and development. In reality, however, users can be in a weak position to effect real influence on the design process due to problematic client-developer-user relations and communications (Beath & Orlikowski, 1994; Cavaye, 1995; Howcroft & Wilson, 2003; Lynch & Gregor, 2004) and possibly due to participatory capture as discussed. Secondly, the IID approach rightly emphasizes the need to deal with changes but assume that a converged solution will emerge at the end of iterations. While a converged solution may emerge, there is no guarantee that it meets with client requirements. Due to time and other resource constraints, an unsatisfactory converged solution may well be accepted by the client due to the lack of choice and thus contributes to the risk of project failure. Thirdly, while timeboxing is useful in prioritizing certain functionality and delivering early results, it does not consider adequately the loss of value to the client due to reduction of product functionality and quality.

This article does not suggest that the IID approach and the associated techniques are of no value to ISD projects. Rather, there seem to be gaps between the IID approach that focuses on product development and project management frameworks that have to balance product value (functionality and quality) with project cost and time. The article raises a number of further research questions, especially the phenomenon of participatory capture. The practice of signing off prototypes should be critically assessed for its possible contribution to participatory capture and possibly other effects in system design and development. Another important issue to be addressed is how to manage the risk of an evolutionary process converging to an unsatisfactory design. The developer-biased timeboxing technique should be re-assessed to see how the needs of the client and the supplier can be suitably balanced. It is suggested that the costs and benefits of different approaches including the selectionist approach be examined in order to develop more effective ISD project management frameworks.

REFERENCES

Adler, P. A. (1987). *Membership roles in Field Research*. Newbury Park, CA: Sage.

Alavi, M. (1984). An Assessment of the Prototyping Approach to Information-Systems Development. *Communications of the ACM, 27,* 556–561. doi:10.1145/358080.358095

Avison, D. E., & Fitzgerald, G. (2003). *Information systems development methodologies, techniques and tools*. (3rd ed.) London: McGraw-Hill.

Baskerville, R. L., & Stage, J. (1996). Controlling prototype development through risk analysis. *MIS Quarterly, 20,* 481–504. doi:10.2307/249565

Beath, C. M., & Orlikowski, W. J. (1994). The Contradictory Structure of Systems Development Methodologies: Deconstructing the IS-User Relationship in Information Engineering. *Information Systems Research, 5,* 350–377. doi:10.1287/isre.5.4.350

Beck, K. (2000). *Extreme programming explained: embrace change*. Reading, MA: Addison-Wesley.

Berger, H., & Beynon-Davies, P. (2004). Issues Impacting on the Project Management of a RAD Development Approach of a Large, Complex Government IT Project. *Pacific Asia Conference on Information Systems (PACIS)*, 8th-11th July, 2004. Shanghai, China.

Beynon-Davies, P., Mackay, H., & Slack, R. (1997). User Involvement in Information Systems Development: the problem of finding the 'right' user. *European Conference on Information Systems*. Cork: Cork Publishing Ltd.

Beynon-Davies, P., Mackay, H., & Tudhope, D. (2000). 'It's lots of bits of paper and ticks and post-it notes and things…': A Case Study of a Rapid Application Development Project. *Journal of Information Systems, 10,* 195–216. doi:10.1046/j.1365-2575.2000.00080.x

Bittner, K., & Spence, I. (2006). *Managing Iterative Software Development Projects*. Addison-Wesley.

Cavaye, A. L. M. (1995). User participation in system development revisited. *Information & Management, 28,* 311–323. doi:10.1016/0378-7206(94)00053-L

Charbonneau, S. (2004). *Software Project Management - A Mapping between RUP and the PMBOK*. Retrieved April 28, 2008, from http://www.ibm.com/developerworks/rational/library/4721.html.

Charette, R. N. (2005). *Why Software Fails*. Retrieved April 28, 2008, from http://www.spectrum.ieee.org/sep05/1685.

Chen, J. Q., & Heath, R. (2001). Building Web Applications. *Information Systems Management, 18,* 68–79. doi:10.1201/1078/43194.18.1.20010101/31266.8

Eisenhardt, K. M. (1989). Agency Theory - An Assessment and Review. *Academy of Management Review, 14*, 57–74. doi:10.2307/258191

Eva, M. (2001). Requirements acquisition for rapid applications development. *Information & Management, 39*, 101–107. doi:10.1016/S0378-7206(01)00082-9

Gallivan, M. J., & Keil, M. (2003). The user-developer communication process: a critical case study. *Information Systems Journal, 13*, 37–68. doi:10.1046/j.1365-2575.2003.00138.x

Gordon, V., & Bieman, J. (1995). Rapid Prototyping: Lessons Learned. *IEEE Software, 12*, 85–95. doi:10.1109/52.363162

Goulielmos, M. (2004). Systems development approach: transcending methodology. *Information Systems Journal, 14*, 363–386. doi:10.1111/j.1365-2575.2004.00175.x

Highsmith, J. (2000). *Adaptive Software Development*. New York: Dorset House.

Highsmith, J. (2002). What is agile software development? Retrieved October 4, 2008, from http://www.pyxis-tech.com/agilemontreal/docs/WhatIsAgileSoftwareDevelopment.pdf.

Howard, A. (1997). A new RAD-based approach to commercial information systems development: the dynamic system development method. *Industrial Management & Data Systems, 97*, 175–177. doi:10.1108/02635579710785456

Howcroft, D., & Wilson, M. (2003). Paradoxes of participatory practices: the Janus role of the systems developer. *Information and Organization, 13*, 1–24. doi:10.1016/S1471-7727(02)00023-4

Humphrey, W. S. (1998). *Why Don't They Practice What We Preach?* Retrieved April 28, 2008, from http://www.sei.cmu.edu/publications/articles/practice-preach/practice-preach.html.

Hwang, M. I., & Thorn, R. G. (1999). The effect of user engagement on system success: A meta-analytical integration of research findings. *Information & Management, 35*, 229–236. doi:10.1016/S0378-7206(98)00092-5

Koskela, L., & Howell, G. (2002a). The theory of project management: explanation to novel methods. *Proceedings of IGLC-10.*

Koskela, L., & Howell, G. (2002b). The underlying theory of project management is obsolete. *Proceedings of the PMI Research Conference.*

Kruchten, P. (2000). *The rational unified process an introduction.* (2nd ed.) Reading, MA: Addison-Wesley.

Laffont, J. J., & Tirole, J. (1990). The Politics of Government Decision-Making - Regulatory Institutions. *Journal of Law Economics and Organization, 6*, 1–31.

Larman, C. (2004). *Agile and iterative development: A Manager's Guide*. Reading, MA: Addison-Wesley.

Larman, C., & Basili, V. R. (2003). Iterative and Incremental Development: A Brief History. *IEEE Computer, 36*, 47–56.

Lin, W. T., & Shao, B. B. M. (2000). The relationship between user participation and system success: a simultaneous contingency approach. *Information & Management, 37*, 283–295. doi:10.1016/S0378-7206(99)00055-5

Lynch, T., & Gregor, S. (2004). User participation in decision support systems development: influencing system outcomes. *European Journal of Information Systems, 13*, 286–301. doi:10.1057/palgrave.ejis.3000512

Marchewka, J. T. (2006). *Information Technology Project Management*. New Jersey: Wiley.

Martin, J. (1991). *Rapid Application Development*. New York: Macmillan Publishing.

McConnell, S. (1996). *Rapid Development: Taming Wild Software Schedules*. Redmond, WA: Microsoft Press.

McKeen, J. D., Guimaraes, T., & Wetherbe, J. (1994). The Relationship Between User Participation and User Satisfaction: An Investigation of Four Contingency Factors. *MIS Quarterly, 18*, 427–451. doi:10.2307/249523

Mintzberg, H. (1973). *The Nature of Managerial Work*. New York: Harper & Row Publishers.

Müller, R., & Turner, J. R. (2005). The impact of principal-agent relationship and contract type on communication between project owner and manager. *International Journal of Project Management, 23*, 398–403. doi:10.1016/j.ijproman.2005.03.001

Mumford, E. (1983). *Designing Participatively: Participative Approach To Computer Systems Design*. Manchester: Manchester Business School.

Nørbjerg, J. (2002). Managing incremental development: combining flexibility and control. *Proceedings of the Tenth European Conference on Information Systems*, 229-239.

Osborn, C. (1995). SDLC, JAD, and RAD: Finding the Right Hammer. Retrieved April 28, 2008, from faculty.babson.edu/osborn/cims/rad.htm#SDLCvsJADvsRAD.

Pich, M., Loch, C., & De Meyer, A. (2002). On Uncertainty, Ambiguity and Complexity in Project Management. *Management Science, 48*, 1008–1023. doi:10.1287/mnsc.48.8.1008.163

PMI. (2004). *A Guide to the Project Management Body of Knowledge*. (3rd ed.) Project Management Institute.

Royce, W. (1970). Managing the Development of Large Software Systems. *Proceedings of IEEE WESCON*; 1-9.

Schwaber, K. (1995). The Scrum Development Process. Retrieved April 28, 2008, from www.controlchaos.com/old-site/scrumwp.htm.

Snow, A. P., Keil, M., & Wallace, L. (2007). The effects of optimistic and pessimistic biasing on software project status reporting. *Information & Management, 44*, 130–141. doi:10.1016/j.im.2006.10.009

Stapleton, J. (1997). *Dynamic Systems Development Method: The Method In Practice*. London: Addison-Wesley.

Thompson, R. L., Smith, H. J., & Iacovou, C. L. (2007). The linkage between reporting quality and performance in IS projects. *Information & Management, 44*, 196–205. doi:10.1016/j.im.2006.12.004

Wiegers, K. E. (1999). Customer Rights and Responsibilities. Retrieved April 28, 2008, from www.processimpact.com/articles/customer.html.

Yin, R. K. (1994). *Case study research: Design and methods*. London: Sage.

Yu, A. G., Flett, P. D., & Bowers, J. A. (2005). Developing a value-centred proposal for assessing project success. *International Journal of Project Management, 23*, 428–436. doi:10.1016/j.ijproman.2005.01.008

Zahniser, R. (1995). Timeboxing For Top Team Performance. Retrieved April 28, 2008, from www.belizenorth.com/articles/TIMEBOX.htm

This work was previously published in International Journal of Information Technology Project Management, Volume 1, Issue 1, edited by John Wang, pp. 15-29, copyright 2010 by IGI Publishing (an imprint of IGI Global).

Chapter 12
Processes in R&D Collaboration

Sanne Bor
Hanken School of Economics, Finland

Kees Boersma
VU University Amsterdam, The Netherlands

ABSTRACT

This paper examines the process leading to a formalised co-operation. A comparative case study of Research and Development (R&D) collaborations illustrates how, during the process of formalising, the creation of shared understanding of the co-operation is supported or hindered. When participants are involved in setting goals, writing work plans, and creating the rules for the co-operation, each participant will have a better understanding of their relationship with others, their own role and responsibility and those of the others. In this study, the authors identify five possible factors that encourage or discourage the partners to use the process of formalising for the purpose of sensemaking.

INTRODUCTION

In this paper, we investigate the process and management of formalising collaboration between research partners in Research and Development (R&D) networks. We especially look at how this process can be used to create a shared understanding of collaboration and to create an understanding for each participant concerning their relationships, roles and responsibilities.

In recent years, inter-organisational R&D collaboration has grown rapidly as is evident from the longitudinal study by Hagedoorn and his colleagues (Hagedoorn, 2002; Hagedoorn & Kranenburg, 2003; Roijakkers & Hagedoorn, 2006). These collaborative networks have become increasingly important for both the innovation process and for the competitive advantage of companies and the economy in general (Chiesa & Manzini, 1998; Leydesdorff & Etzkovitz, 1996). Although inter-organisational R&D networks offer considerable potential, they also introduce new questions concerning management and organising (e.g., Provan, Fish, & Sydow, 2007). The partners in the collaboration need to create a shared understanding of what their collaboration is about,

DOI: 10.4018/978-1-4666-0930-3.ch012

what expectations each partner has, and how to work and make decisions together. This is needed in project teams in general (Demirkan & Nichols, 2008), but when partners come from different organisations it becomes even more important.

So far, the literature on inter-organisational R&D networks has focused mainly on collaboration between companies (see Grandori and Soda (1995) for an extensive overview of this literature). Far less attention has been given to collaboration between research institutes or between research institutes and companies. Some exceptions of this are Chompalov, Genuth, and Shrum (2002), Mothe and Quélin (2000), and Tijssen and Korevaar (1997).

This paper presents an in-depth empirical study of two Information Technology (IT) enabled R&D networks which have been funded as Networks of Excellence by the European Commission. This study seeks to respond to the need voiced for example by Provan et al. (2007) for empirical and reflexive investigation into collaborative networks.

This paper is structured as follows: first we introduce and explain the two core concepts used in the paper: *formalisation* and *sensemaking*. After this, we explain how the study on which the paper is built has been conducted. Following this we present the results of our empirical study. We start with a description of how the formalisation process unfolds in the two cases. As part of the formalisation process we discuss initiation and goal setting, member selection/recruitment, content development, rules for co-operation and management/decision making structure. After this we discuss the differences between the cases and how this impacts sensemaking and we identify potential factors that encourage/discourage participants to use/from using the formalisation process for the purpose of sensemaking. We then present our final conclusions and discuss possible directions for future research.

NETWORK FORMALISATION AS A SENSEMAKING PROCESS

If the partners in a collaborative network are to be effective in their collaboration, they need to create a shared understanding of the collaboration. In an inter-organisational setting in which the participants have commitments to both their own organisation and the network, a shared understanding is even more important. A shared understanding of the expectations of each partner concerning the desired outcomes, how to work together and how decisions are made is essential in preventing frustration, demotivation or even conflict. In more positive terms, it encourages participants in a collaborative network to be effective, supportive and motivated to work together. In this paper, the concept of *sensemaking* (Weick, 1995) is used to refer to the process of creating this shared understanding. According to Weick (1995), sensemaking is at its simplest "the making of sense" (p.4) and it has the following seven properties: (1) it is grounded in identity construction; (2) it is retrospective; (3) it enacts sensible environments; (4) it is social; (5) it is ongoing; (6) it is based on extracted cues; and (7) it is based on plausibility rather than accuracy.

As discussed in this paper, the formalisation process of R&D collaboration is understood as the process through which collaboration becomes or is made formal. The process results, for example, in a contract, rules, procedures, or work plans. The concept of formalisation is closely related to the concept of institutionalisation (e.g., DiMaggio & Powel, 1983; Scott, 2001). Institutionalisation, however, refers to the setting of both formal and informal rules, procedures, and acceptable ways of acting. As we look at the formal side, we have chosen to focus on formalisation instead of institutionalisation.

Vlaar, Van den Bosch, and Volberda (2007) argue that inter-organisational management researchers have become increasingly interested in the concept of formalisation and its outcomes. So far, however, much inter-organisational network research focuses only on the very outcome of formalisation, taking certain formal arrangements as a sign that the process has taken place (see Chompalov et al. (2002) for an example) or describing the type of outcome of the formalisation process as predictably based on relational or other variables (e.g., Grandori, 1997).

Following the arguments made by Vlaar, Van den Bosch, and Volberda (2006), we do not look at the outcomes of the process as such, but rather at how and when the formalisation process supports sensemaking. Vlaar et al. (2006) propose four mechanisms through which formalisation contribute to sensemaking. Firstly, they propose that the formalisation process helps to focus the attention of the partners. Their attention becomes focused when they clarify "whether there are decisions that need to be made and what those decisions may consist of, and by demarcating what is allowed, expected, acceptable and possible, and what is not" (Vlaar et al., 2006, p. 1623). Secondly, it is proposed that the formalisation process helps to articulate, deliberate on, and reflect upon issues concerning the network as these issues need to be put on paper. Thirdly, the formalisation process helps to provoke and maintain interaction as the participants have committed themselves to creating the end-product of the process. Fourthly, it is suggested that the formalisation process reduces the impact of individual biases and judgment errors; in that it helps in uncovering and eliminating incompleteness and inconsistencies in the information the partners have about each other and their collaboration.

In the formalisation process of inter-organisational networks, the participants thus most importantly use the process to make sense of what it is that they can do as a collective. That means that one would expect more co-operation between the members in the network. Furthermore,

when the formalisation process is used as a sensemaking process, we expect the participants to identify themselves with the network more. That is, belonging to the network is part of the identity of the participants.

RESEARCH METHODOLOGY AND RESEARCH DESIGN

The empirical research employed for this paper is a multiple-case study designed for comparison, whereby the cases have been selected using a replication logic (Yin, 1994, 2003). The main goal is to compare the processes of formalisation in order to locate factors that may influence how this process supports or hinders sensemaking. In this sense the case study has been carried out to improve our theoretical understanding (Eisenhardt, 1989).

Based on an analysis of about 50 consortium agreements gathered from networks that have been successful in their application for Network of Excellence (NoE) funding from the European Commission (EC), we have chosen to study *Sci-Net* and *TechStar* in-depth. The original names of the cases will not be used in the paper for the purposes of confidentiality. These networks are of similar size, have similar degrees of experience in applying for EC funding, and function in the same broad field of research. Furthermore, these NoEs have similar external demands on the needed outcomes of their formalisation process, as these outcomes are set by the EC.

However, the two cases differ in network configuration and earlier research into networks has shown that the shape of a network is not a neutral phenomenon (Swan & Scarbrough, 2005; Ibarra, Kilduff, & Tsai, 2005). The network configuration has consequences for the way in which the network functions and can be managed and governed. As it is proposed sensemaking through the formalisation process relies heavily on the communication between the participants in the network, the network configuration can be expected to have a great influence. Evan (1966) identifies three basic types of network configuration:

- The star network model, which is sometimes also called a wheel network model (see Figure 1). In this star network model all participants connect to one another through one central participant (in networks-terms called the broker).
- The all-channel network model, also sometimes called full-graph model (see Figure 2). In this model each participant connects to all other participants with a direct line.
- The chain network model (see Figure 3). In this model the participants connect to a maximum of two other participants, creating a chain.

The cases presented in this paper represent an all-channel network, SciNet, and a star network model TechStar. No chain network model was found in the 50 consortium agreements analysed and for that reason could not be included.

The data we gathered for each case include interview data and documents (see Table 1 for a detailed overview). The interview data concerns ten telephone interviews with management team members (executive group/executive committee/etc.). We used a semi-structured interview scheme and each interviews lasted between 30 and 45 minutes. The interview scheme included questions concerning personal histories, building the network and decisions and decision-making processes in the management team while the consortium was running. The interviews were audio-taped and transcribed.

The documents include, most importantly, the consortium agreement. This agreement is the contract between the partners describing the or-

Figure 1. A star network model

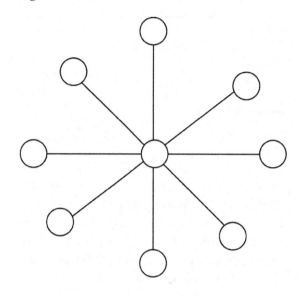

Figure 2. An all-channel network model

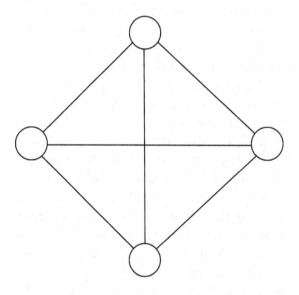

Figure 3. A chain network model

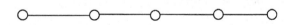

Table 1. Overview data gathered in case studies

Consortium Type of data	*SciNet*	*TechStar*
Interviews	6 interviews, in total 219 minutes	4 interviews, in total 144 minutes
Documents	Consortium agreement Expression of interest Technical annex Webpage	Consortium agreement Expression of interest Technical annex Webpage

ganisation and management structures and rules and details the various rights and obligations of the members of the consortium. The secondary data also include the Expression of Interest submitted to the EC by each of the cases. Furthermore, the secondary data include the technical annex to the contract with the EC, which describes the organisational structures and further details the work and the division of work within the consortium. Finally, the secondary data include documents and information available on the websites of the cases. This varies highly between the cases, ranging from mere description to reports and plans written for the EC.

The data and information gathered where prepared and entered into NVivo, a computer program assisting the storing, coding and retrieval of qualitative data. The data were then further prepared by coding them on five broad themes. The themes we coded were network history, initial network development, development of work plans, development of consortium agreement and network structure. This coding had the purpose of data reduction (Coffey & Atkinson, 1996). After this the data were retrieved and analysed based on the themes and then further coded on the properties of sensemaking. This coding was done with the purpose of data complication (Coffey & Atkinson, 1996) and to make them accessible for the purpose of this paper.

THE PRACTICE OF FORMALISATION WITHIN TWO NETWORKS OF EXCELLENCE

The NoE funding scheme of the European Commission has the purpose of "…strengthening excellence by tackling the fragmentation of European research, where the main deliverable is a durable structuring and shaping of the way that research is carried out on the topic of the network…" (European Commission, 2002). The rules set out and advice given by the EC concerning applications for NoE funding (for example in European Commission, 2002; FP6 Instruments Task Force, 2003; the core-contract and so on) give an institutional framework for those applying. They prescribe aspects like the general aim and objective, the specific components to be included, the type of members, aspects considered important for a coherent management-framework and specific activities to be undertaken by the management of a NoE.

The Networks of Excellence go through four steps of formalising. First, they write an 'Expression of Interest', a draft of what the co-operation could be about and who would be included. Second, after the publication of the call for proposals by the EC, a proposal needs to be written. This proposal includes a 'Joint Programme of Activities (the content of the collaboration), a list of participants and the connections built between them to do the research, a description of a coherent management framework, a description of how the 'excellence' will be spread and the length and costs of the co-operation. Third, the contract with the EC is negotiated. This contract includes a finalised version of the management framework and a list of participants and also a 'technical annex' (the final content and timetable of the co-operation with specified deliverables). Fourth, a consortium agreement needs to be drawn up. This is the agreements between the co-operating partners, defining the network, its structure and the co-operation rules and procedures.

From the analysis, we identified five main aspects of the process of formalising the Networks of Excellence. These five are (1) initiation and goal-setting, (2) member selection/recruitment, (3) content development, (4) rules for co-operation, and (5) management/organisation structure. Below we describe how these processes took place in the two cases.

Initiation and Goal-Setting

In *SciNet,* the idea of starting a network and applying for funding came from one person, who discussed the idea with a few people in her own and another institute. The institute of the initiator was willing to fund the preparation stage of the network. One of the interviewees explained this as follow:

(The initiating institute) made a clear, let's say, institutional decision, that they wanted this network of excellence (...) and they were willing to support it upfront (...) without any funding from the commission.

In *SciNet,* interviewees point out that for the development of the strategic, broad lines, the people came together in a series of face-to-face meetings.

I was there for (...) three or four meetings to set it all up, which gradually defined through discussion the shape of and content of this.

And another interviewee remembered:

If I remember well, we had two or three meetings in (place name) before applying (...) and sometimes there was some fight between the partners because of course we have to divide the [work], we have to choose the topics, we have to decide the way of functioning, the name of the clusters, where each partner will go, what we can share and so on, and that was not so easy.

Through these meetings the participants slowly found a shared understanding. As one of the interviewees states:

(...) then over time, from all these discussions, in the beginning a bit reluctantly, but then more and more openly, common ground was found.

In the case of *TechStar,* the idea for the co-operation also came from one person. From the interviews it does not become clear how other participants were involved in the development of the goals, but one of the interviewees tells:

Well, the thing was initiated by (name co-ordinator) and he got in touch with some of the people he knew reasonably well, so I was one, and (...) we discussed the idea with (name co-ordinator).

Member Selection / Recruitment

From the interviews conducted in *SciNet* it becomes clear that the people from the initiating institute made a list of people/groups/institutes they wanted to participate. These people were contacted by email and phone and invited to participate to the development of a NoE.

We were invited to cooperate or to begin to write the application, by (name co-ordinator), and he invited about 20 different groups base on people he thought were likely to contribute to it in constructive ways.

The people who reacted positively and were willing to participate were invited to develop the idea of the network in face-to-face meetings.

In *TechStar* the search for partners went in rounds. First the closest colleagues were asked to join. And these then helped thinking of other partners. One interviewee explains it as follow:

So there was some point, information from (name co-ordinator) that we should try to include more people in the network. So then we sent him feedback for new, possible members. Then later there was a discussion that maybe it was getting too big, maybe get a bit smaller, and we discussed in the same way, we discussed how we could make it smaller without people getting annoyed. So these sort of more key decisions were made by (name co-ordinator) in the end.

Another interviewee tells that potential partners were chosen based on research area. As one interviewee explains it:

It [the selecting of potential partners] was based on their area of work. One thing we tried to do was include as far as possible all different [areas].

Content Development

In *SciNet*, the content was discussed per cluster. The participants of each cluster worked together to define what the cluster would do. One of the interviewees describes this process as cluster co-ordinators and their deputies drawing together the different individuals from the participating institutes.

Then people drew together the collaborators within the work of each cluster to define what is known as work packages, would define milestones and deliverables.

And then we started to write the application, I mean the cluster co-ordinator together with the

participants in different clusters. And that was a tough thing!

One of the interviews point out that the content development was done through email. However, there were major disagreements when more personal communication was used.

(...) each cluster worked independently and that was per email and occasionally, there where we were really in disagreement, we had telephone calls.

The coordinator combined the different Joint Programmes produced by the research lines. The coordinator and its institute wrote and included the parts of the document and work packages concerning organisation, management, etc. were written and added by the coordinator and its institute. The draft proposal was then sent to all participants for comments and ideas for further development. These were then integrated and the final proposal was sent to the EC.

In *TechStar*, the writing of the proposal was mainly done by the co-ordinator. One of the interviewees describes the process as follows:

It tended to be (name of co-ordinator) doing the writing. (Name of the co-ordinator) did, I must say, most of the work and that was how it went in the end. That (name of the co-ordinator) did most of the work and we, we amended it, changed it a bit as he wrote. So it was, it was an e-mail process, we met rarely, if ever, and that was the way it worked.

The contributions by other partners are referred to as 'writing their bit' or commenting on circulated drafts. As one interviewee put it:

Well of course I have provided my bit so to speak.

From the Joint Programme of Activities it becomes clear that 'my bit' means that each representative of a member organisation is responsible for a specified part of the research, and wrote what the member organisation would do and with which budget.

Rules for Co-Operation

In the case of *SciNet,* the initiating institute's lawyers and administrators developed the draft consortium agreement. This draft was then circulated among the members. When the draft was circulated, difficulties arose especially over issues relating to patenting. One of the interviewees describes it as follows:

They (the initiating institute) wanted to convert it in principle into a (...) development for applied research (...) and were very strict on patenting all this. (...) that was really in contrast to the open policies of most European universities. And that caused, at least initially that caused really a major, major problem. And then really we brought it to the point and said that either the (initiating institute) now follows what we have in mind or we change the coordination.

After this intervention and backup from the EC, the cooperation started working again. As the interviewee continues by stating:

And that was also then the standpoint the Commission took. And that then worked miraculous. And all of a sudden things then worked. (...) And then (the initiating institute) wrote with comments from all other universities the consortium agreement and that was then finally accepted.

Furthermore, the contract plays an important role in the co-operation. As can be understood from the quote below:

There is a legal agreement which does underlie a lot of work that we do.

In the *TechStar* network, however, the consortium agreement was written and dealt with by the initiator/coordinator. The interviewees reported that they had neither read nor discussed the agreement. As one interviewee put it:

I don't think any of us have had a look at the consortium agreement.

The consortium agreement also does not play a major role in the consortium:

I think we try to do this in a less structured way, so more by effectively doing. (...) We have not really tried to connect things in a very formal way.

Management/Organisation Structure

In the case of *SciNet,* the management and organisation structure had been emerging out of the initial face-to-face discussions. The initiating institute then asked particular individuals to become coordinators/deputy coordinators of the major lines of research agreed upon. These coordinators together with the deputy coordinators were asked to develop a Joint Programme of Activities with the people that had indicated an interest in that research area. As described by one interviewee:

I was there [in the face-to-face meetings] where we more clearly defined what we were going to do. And we started then to write the application. And I was then asked whether I want to be the cluster co-ordinator with another person and I agreed to do that.

In the case of *TechStar,* only the co-ordinator was in the beginning involved with management tasks. During the process of contract negotiations with the EC, however, difficulties arose between the EC representative and the coordinator. As one interviewee describes it:

(During the negotiations, the coordinator) collaborated closely with the person in Brussels that was followed by trouble after the first meeting we had where the EC official was there as well." And he continues, *"(...) for reasons not known to me, they did not get along for a while. (...) And that (after the first meeting) is when (the coordinator) asked me to step into a management role, which I offered to him to get the [negotiations] going again.*

The EC official then suggested that this person become the coordinator, but the person refused. Instead, he suggested that they would form a management team. The coordinator and the person then discussed the matter together and decided on the people to be asked to join this management team. When the members of the management team were clear and the management team had been formed, the other partners were informed about this decision and asked if there were major objections to this decision. As no one spoke against this decision, the coordinator rewrote the consortium agreement to include a management group. As an interviewee points out:

The reason for that probably is that even in a small network like this one it is hard to persuade everybody to come to meetings or even sometimes respond to e-mails. (...) The one way of making decisions more efficiently was to elect an executive group and have that group take most of the decisions, if not all the decisions.

In order to put this statement into perspective, the decisions the interviewee talks about concern what to do with spare money, where meetings are to be held and other organisational and administrational decisions. Most of the budget was decided on forehand and the content is decided by the individual members. As one interviewee points out:

We do not plan the science (...) we are scientists ourselves and we hate being told what to do.

DIFFERENCES IN THE FORMALISATION PROCESS

The two cases can be seen as two extremes with regard to use of the formalisation process for the purpose of sensemaking, see for an overview Table 2. *SciNet* is an example in which the members participate in the various steps of the process and in interaction with one and other to make sense of their collaboration, the different partners, and the relationships in which they are engaged. In *TechStar*, the sensemaking by the participants involved is limited as they have no way of knowing how the different members reflect upon the co-operation and what the possible shared perspectives may be because they only see the results that have been processed by the co-ordinator during the formalisation process.

POTENTIAL FACTORS

As such big differences exist between the two cases, we in this section will discuss what the potential factors are that encourage or discourage the partners to use/from using the formalisation process for the purpose of sensemaking. From the data we identify the following five potential factors.

First, and foremost, network configuration during the formalisation process may encourage/discourage the use of mechanisms, which would support sensemaking. In the all-channel model chosen by the initiator of *SciNet*, the participants all communicated with one another both via email and face-to-face. All of them focused their attention at the same time on the same issues and through the shared discussions they articulated, deliberated and reflected upon these issues together. This means that all partners have been stimulated in gaining a good understanding of the viewpoints and ideas of the other participants. In the star model as used by the initiator of *TechStar*, most communication went through her/him, and he/she became

Table 2. Overview of the differences

	SciNet	TechStar
Initiation and strategic content	Idea developed with a few, got institutional support for face-to-face meetings with all potential members	Idea and strategic content mainly from co-ordinator, but discussed and developed further with a close colleagues over email
Member selection/recruitment	Initiators made a list and invited those on the list to join. Those interested became members.	Invited close colleagues, these invited even closer colleagues, based on getting the whole area covered, too many and the number should be reduced
Management/ organisation structure	Structure developed during initial face-to-face meetings, management team members selected by initiators based on expertise, management team members to co-ordinate sub-parts	Initially only co-ordinator, later management team based on who is available and co-operative, management team members to help co-ordinator make decisions, co-ordination of sub-parts left to each member
Content development	Management team members co-ordinated, development by all members participating in a particular part, mainly by email, when needed by telephone.	Each member writing 'their bit', co-ordinator compiling and writing most, circulation of drafts and commenting to co-ordinator.
Rules for co-operation	Strict rules concerning participation, developed by lawyers of initiating institute, representatives of others interfered, additions and changes were made.	Rules exist for the sake of EC, co-ordinator developed and knows what is in the agreement, others expected not to ever have read the agreement.

a knowledge-broker. This means that although everybody read and commented upon the drafts circulated, no one except the coordinator knew where the different ideas came from. So, only the coordinator knew about the ways in which each participant articulated, deliberated and reflected upon the possibilities of the collaboration. All other partners obtained only a processed version that was articulated, deliberated and reflected upon by the coordinator only. The possibility that the participants were not able to realise the potential of the collaboration will therefore be very high.

Second, the better the partners know about one another, the less they seem to utilise the potential of the formalisation process for sensemaking. In *SciNet,* the interviewees pointed out that the partners chosen knew up to about half of the other partners at the outset. Hence, he formalisation process, supported through all the different mechanisms, determines whether the potential for collaborating with all these different partners will be explored. In *TechStar,* at first only the close friend-colleagues of the coordinator were asked to join and they were also the first participants to

be included. At first glance, this strategy might have given the participants the idea that they knew what was going on, because they trusted the initiator who was similar and like-minded. At the same time, however, it discouraged the partners from seeing the potential of the formalisation process in terms of sensemaking while creating an unintended false feeling of 'we know who we are' where this may not be the case.

Third, and very much connected to the second point, the more participants work within the same/ similar discipline, the less they may realise the potential of the formalisation process for sensemaking. In *SciNet,* the collaboration focused on building a bridge between two lines of research in a field that was previously split. The need to explain and argue for one's perspective and the reactions of others on the articulated views supported the participants to gain an understanding of the different vocabulary, ways of working, preferences, and perspectives of 'the others'. In *TechStar*, however, the partners worked within similar disciplines having similar research backgrounds. The perceived need for clarifying and putting in an effort to understand 'the other', as was the case in *SciNet*, did not exist in *TechStar*. This discouraged the partners from using the formalisation process to reduce individual biases and judgment-errors and led to inconsistencies and incompleteness in the participants' understanding of the collaboration.

Fourth, the more independent the partners are of one another within the collaboration, the less they may realise the potential of the sensemaking process during the formalisation. In *SciNet*, the partners were highly dependent on one another to create a coherent Joint Programme of Activities. Thus the partners try to find the possible areas on which to work together, as one interviewee explained:

We hear what each other person is doing or thinking of doing and we come up with areas where we can work together.

In *TechStar*, the dependence is lower as each group works locally, and topics groups were defined for the purpose of discussion and learning. The groups thus were not working together as such, but reporting results and discussing ideas. This also is reflected in the following statement of an interviewee:

We don't plan the science because we leave that to the individual scientist. We are scientists ourselves and we hate being told what to do.

Fifth, there were differences in how the participants who we interviewed reflected upon the formalisation process and outcomes. In *SciNet*, this process is seen as very positive though demanding, whereas in *TechStar* the formalisation process is seen as unnecessary and bureaucratic. Also, when it comes to the outcomes of the process of formalisation, the interviewees in *SciNet* reflect positively, describing the contract and agreement as rules that help in understanding what is expected

from them, how they can work together with others and how decisions can be made. Interviewees in *TechStar* reflected rather negatively on the formalisation demands, explaining that their research would have been done in the same way without the contract and agreement and that the demands are burdensome. This leads us to consider that a positive attitude toward the formalisation process and the outcomes thereof enables participants to see the formalisation process as an opportunity to gain understanding, whereas a negative attitude would discourage them from using this process for sensemaking.

CONCLUSION AND FURTHER RESEARCH

In this paper we have analysed the formalisation process of two Networks of Excellence. The case of *SciNet* was an example in which the members actively used the formalisation process to make sense of the cooperation, the other members and their own role. The case of *TechStar* was an example in which this did not happen during the formalisation process. We identified five potential factors that may influence how the sensemaking mechanisms in the formalisation process are utilised or not utilised for the purpose of sensemaking. These five aspects contribute to the theoretical discussion on the formalisation process as a sensemaking function. First, the network configuration chosen for the formalisation process seems highly important for the way in which participants make sense of the collaboration. Secondly, the extents to which partners already know one another have the potential to influence the perceived need and thus utilisation of the formalisation process. Thirdly, the similarity of the partners potentially influences the perceived need and utilisation of the mechanisms. Fourthly, the dependence of the partners on one another may impact the perceived need and utilisation of the mechanisms and fifthly, the attitude towards formalisation of the partners can influence the perceived need for and utilisation of the mechanisms for sensemaking.

The practical implications of the results are mainly that research managers and those involved in formalisation processes of innovation and IT-based R&D collaboration should consider how they encourage or discourage sensemaking during the process of formalising.

In future research it may be advisable to investigate the consequences of utilising or not utilising the mechanisms in the formalisation process for the purpose of sensemaking. This would provide more insight into the importance of sensemaking for the collaboration and its outcome. Also, research may focus specifically on the potential factors identified, as the importance of the factors could not be evaluated though this research.

ACKNOWLEDGMENT

The authors would like to thank Pekka Linna and the anonymous reviewers for their insightful comments which helped to improve the paper significantly. An earlier version of this article was presented at the EuroMOT 2008 conference held in Nice, France from 17.9.2008-19.9.2008.

REFERENCES

Chiesa, V., & Manzini, R. (1998). Organizing for technological collaborations: a managerial perspective. *R & D Management, 28*(3), 199–212. doi:10.1111/1467-9310.00096

Chompalov, I., Genuth, J., & Shrum, W. (2002). The organization of scientific collaborations. *Research Policy, 31*(5), 749–767. doi:10.1016/S0048-7333(01)00145-7

Coffey, A., & Atkinson, P. (1996). *Making sense of qualitative data: Complementary research strategies*. London: Sage.

Demirkan, H., & Nichols, J. (2008). IT services project management: lessons learned from a case study in implementation. *International Journal of Project Organisation and Management, 1*(2), 204–220. doi:10.1504/IJPOM.2008.022192

DiMaggio, P. J., & Powell, W. W. (1983). The iron cage revisited: institutional isomorphism and collective rationality in organizational fields. *American Sociological Review, 48*, 147–160. doi:10.2307/2095101

Eisenhardt, K. M. (1989). Building theories from case study research. *Academy of Management Review, 14*(4), 532–550. doi:10.2307/258557

European Commission. (2002). *FP6 instruments: Implementating the priority thematic areas of the sixth framework programme*. Luxembourg: Office for Official Publications of the European Communities.

Evan, W. M. (1966). The organization-set: Toward a theory of interorganizational relations. In Thompson, J. D. (Ed.), *Approaches to organizational design* (pp. 173–191). Pittsburgh, PA: University of Pittsburgh Press.

FP6 Instruments Task Force. (2003). *Provisions for implementing networks of excellence: Background document*. Luxembourg: Office for Official Publications of the European Communities.

Grandori, A. (1997). An organizational assessment of interfirm coordination modes. *Organization Studies, 18*(6), 897–925. doi:10.1177/017084069701800601

Grandori, A., & Soda, G. (1995). Inter-firm networks: Antecedents, mechanisms and forms. *Organization Studies, 16*(2), 183–214. doi:10.1177/017084069501600201

Hagedoorn, J. (2002). Inter-firm R&D partnerships: An overview of major trends and patterns since 1960. *Research Policy, 31*(4), 477–492. doi:10.1016/S0048-7333(01)00120-2

Hagedoorn, J., & van Kranenburg, H. (2003). Growth patterns in R&D partnerships: An exploratory statistical study. *International Journal of Industrial Organization, 21*(4), 517–531. doi:10.1016/S0167-7187(02)00126-1

Ibarra, H., Kilduff, M., & Tsai, W. (2005). Zooming in and out: connecting individuals and collectivities at the frontiers of organizational network research. *Organization Science, 16*(4), 359–371. doi:10.1287/orsc.1050.0129

Leydesdorff, L., & Etzkovitz, H. (1996). Emergence of a Triple Helix of University-Industry-Government Relations. *Science & Public Policy, 23*, 279–286.

Mothe, C., & Quélin, B. (2000). Creating competencies through collaboration: The case of EUREKA R&D consortia. *European Management Journal, 18*(6), 590–604. doi:10.1016/S0263-2373(00)00052-9

Provan, K. G., Fish, A., & Sydow, J. (2007). Interorganizational networks at the network level: A review of the empirical literature on whole networks. *Journal of Management, 33*(3), 479–516. doi:10.1177/0149206307302554

Roijakkers, N., & Hagedoorn, J. (2006). Inter-firm R&D partnering in pharmaceutical biotechnology since 1975: Trends, patterns, and networks. *Research Policy, 35*(3), 431–446. doi:10.1016/j.respol.2006.01.006

Scott, R. W. (2001). *Institutions and Organizations* (2nd ed.). Thousand Oaks, CA: Sage.

Swan, J., & Scarbrough, H. (2005). The politics of networked innovation. *Human Relations, 58*(7), 913–943. doi:10.1177/0018726705057811

Tijssen, R. J. W., & Korevaar, J. C. (1997). Unravelling the Cognitive and Interorganisational Structure of public/private R&D Networks: A Case of Catalysis Research in the Netherlands. *Research Policy, 25*, 1277–1293. doi:10.1016/S0048-7333(96)00908-0

Vlaar, P. W. L., Van den Bosch, F. A. J., & Volberda, H. W. (2006). Coping with problems of understanding in interorganizational relationships: Using formalisation as a means to make sense. *Organization Studies, 27*(11), 1617–1638. doi:10.1177/0170840606068338

Vlaar, P. W. L., Van den Bosch, F. A. J., & Volberda, H. W. (2007). On the evolution of trust, distrust, and formal coordination and control in interorganizational relationships: Toward an integrative framework. *Group & Organization Management, 32*(4), 407–429. doi:10.1177/1059601106294215

Weick, K. E. (1995). *Sensemaking in organizations*. Thousand Oaks, CA: Sage.

Yin, R. (1994). *Case study research: Design and methods* (2nd ed.). Beverly Hills, CA: Sage.

Yin, R. (2003). *Case study research: Design and methods* (3rd ed.). Thousand Oaks, CA: Sage.

This work was previously published in International Journal of Information Technology Project Management, Volume 1, Issue 3, edited by John Wang, pp. 1-13, copyright 2010 by IGI Publishing (an imprint of IGI Global).

Section 5
Project Outcomes and Conception of Success

Chapter 13

The Role of User Review on Information System Project Outcomes:
A Control Theory Perspective

Jack Shih-Chieh Hsu
National Sun Yat-Sen University, Taiwan

Houn-Gee Chen
National Taiwan University, Taiwan

James Jiang
University of Central Florida, USA

Gary Klein
University of Colorado, Colorado Springs, USA

ABSTRACT

The effect of user participation on system success is one of the most studied topics in information systems, yet still yields inconclusive results. Contingency-based concepts attempt to resolve this issue by providing a plausible explanation which indicates that users can only generate expected results when there is a need for users to participate in the development process. As a different approach, this study adopts a mediating perspective and asserts that influence due to the effectiveness of participation determines the final outcomes. Based on control theory, and viewing user participation in reviews as one kind of control, we propose that the influence users can generate through participation determines project outcomes. Data collected from 151 information systems personnel confirms the relationships and that an ability to achieve quality interactions among developers and users heightens the achievement of user influence.

DOI: 10.4018/978-1-4666-0930-3.ch013

INTRODUCTION

After decades of study, the effect of user participation on information system (IS) success is still not well understood (Markus & Mao, 2004). Users vary widely as information systems are recognized as any software designed to provide information to support job duties. User participation, representatives of the target user group assuming active roles and responsibilities, is believed to improve user acceptance of the new system, reduce resistance to implementation, and increase satisfaction with the final product (Hwang & Thorn, 1999). However, inconsistent results of empirical studies hint at the need to reevaluate methodological and theoretical approaches to examining the impact of user participation. Among theoretical advances, contingency theory receives significant attention. Contingency theory models have been confirmed that show the effect of user participation on development outcomes is moderated by desired involvement, complexity, design environment, development stage, task interdependence, and user expertise. In whole, researchers conclude that user participation can generate the desired improvements only when sharing crucial information about system functionality.

Ravichandran and Rai argue that instead of understanding the direct relationship between user participation and development outcomes, researchers should shift their focus to exploring how the development process is influenced by user representatives (Ravichandran & Rai, 2000). Their assertion implies that, in addition to understanding the contingent effect, there is a need to reinvestigate the effectiveness of participation through an influence lens. Indeed, the level of influence users can generate through participation may be more important than participation itself (Lynch & Gregor, 2004). Participation can be viewed as effective only when users generate significant influence (Markus, 1983). Only when user voices are heard and taken seriously by developers will the final product better fit user needs and requirements. To do this, users must not just participate; they must exert some form of control over the process.

The application of control theory to user participation requires that stakeholders have active roles during the information system development (ISD) process. Users are a primary stakeholder in the application of controls (Kirsch, Sambamurthy, Ko & Purvis, 2002). When outcomes are measurable, users can adopt outcome control mechanisms to insure the ISD meets the predefined schedule and cost. When behavior is observable, granting users the authority to review work carried out by the developers insures that the final product will better meet business needs. These studies on controls provide a solid foundation for understanding which control tactics can be exercised under what conditions. However, they also raise some interesting questions. In particular, how does the user effect the design process by exercising control and does the exercise of control generate the expected effect?

Based on control theory and the user participation research stream, this study aims at understanding how users can influence the system development outcomes through participating in and exercising control of the development process. We target a plausible explanation for the inconsistent results yielded by past user engagement literature. We assert that in addition to types of participation or the timing of the participation, the influence exhibited by effective participation is important. Based on this assertion, we hypothesize that the effect of user participation on project performance is fully mediated by user influence. However, the controls must be done in an effective fashion, so it is additionally expected that the positive impacts of participation can be enlarged when users and developers interact in a high quality manner. That is, the total influence the users generate through control activities is determined by the quality of interaction between users and developers.

The research results contribute to user participation and project control research by showing how users can affect project performance through control activities. In the following sections, we first review prior literature that serves as the basis of the hypotheses and research model. In the methodology section, measurement construction and data collection are described. The fourth section includes data analysis. Finally, a discussion of implications with conclusions, limitations, and future research direction conclude the paper.

THEORETICAL BACKGROUND AND HYPOTHESES DEVELOPMENT

Control theory-based research in ISD projects focuses on managerial control, referring to the project leader's attempts to influence subordinates to behave in accordance with team goals (Henderson & Lee, 1992). Such control can be formal or informal. Informal control relies on social or personal strategies. Formal control is a performance strategy based on the evaluation of outcome and behavior. Rewards are based on the extent that participants meet the desired outcome and/or follow the predefined procedure. Existing policies, mechanisms, task characteristics, role expectations, and project related knowledge dictate which control mechanisms should be adopted. Moreover, a control portfolio contains different control mechanisms that may change at the various stages in a development project.

In addition to managers, users can also play a role in ISD control through participating in the development process (Kirsch, et al., 2002). Users can exercise informal controls by putting peer pressure on developers or exert influence through their organizational roles. They can also exercise controls through reviewing or jointly developing project plans, being present in meetings, reviewing or approving progress reports, reviewing ISD technical documents, evaluating requirement documents, and being present when developers report progress to the user community.

The control activities users conduct are similar to the user participation concept. According to Barki and Hartwick, user participation includes three dimensions: hands-on activities, responsibilities, and IS-user relationships (Barki & Hartwick, 1994). Responsibility means the user has to take charge of one or more tasks in a project or assume accountability for portions of overall project success. User-IS relationships refer to the communication and influence between user and IS personnel, including defined activities such as formal reviews. Hands-on activities represent the physical design or task related activities performed by users. Users generate influence when they participate in the ISD process by performing the listed activities. They can also control the development process by assuming responsibility or performing periodic reviews. In this study, we argue that user reviews, one dimension of user participation, provide users a means to provide input and control outcomes.

The model derived from control theory is shown in Figure 1. User reviews form the control activities performed by the participating user. User reviews may tend to have a direct influence on the measures of success, both on the product quality as measured by software responsiveness, and project performance, which is considered to be a composite of traditional project success measures to include cost, time, and scope. The reviews will serve to create influence on the part of the user that should serve as a mediator in the relationship to success. Interactions between users and developers can serve as a moderator of the relationship between user review and influence such that influence is heightened when interaction is of high quality. Interaction quality is determined as productive communication activity between the user and ISD team.

Two project outcomes were included in this study to represent ISD success: responsiveness (of the resulting system) and project performance.

Figure 1. Research model

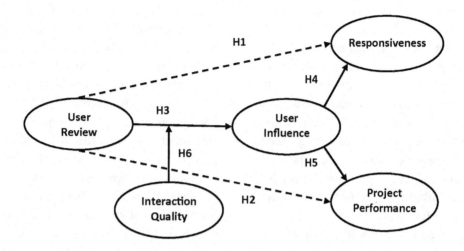

Information system project managers often have to balance these two outcomes of product quality and process completion in an environment more complex and dynamic than in other contexts (Schwalbe, 2007). Previous studies find that user participation has a positive impact on system quality (Hsu, Chan, Liu & Chen, 2008). System responsiveness is one component of system quality that considers the extent that a system meets current needs of the user and can be adjusted to meet changing needs (Bevan, 1999). To increase system responsiveness, traditional wisdom emphasizes the importance of obtaining actual user needs. It is important for users and developers to exchange their knowledge and expertise to clarify actual requirements in the early development stage. However, even when actual needs can be identified or obtained from users; these needs may not be incorporated into the final system by developers (Markus & Mao, 2004). Users should take control through review and approval of work done by developers during the development process to ensure their needs are incorporated into the final product. Therefore, we hypothesize that:

H1: *User review has a positive effect on responsiveness.*

Participation leads to better group performance (Aladwani, Rai &Ramaprasad, 2000). Many projects cannot adhere to predefined schedules or budgets because development teams fail to identify serious problems in the early stages. In fact, many systems are first presented to end users or senior managers during testing or even implementation stages, in which case flaws and inappropriate functions are first identified in these late stages. The rework cost for flaws found in the later stages is much higher (40 to 100 times) than in the early stages (Boehm & Turner, 2003). To reduce unnecessary cost, flaws should be identified and corrected as early as possible.

User review can serve as a control tool to monitor system development and identify potential flaws from the business perspective. Granting users the authority to review the system periodically allows inappropriate system functions to be fixed earlier. This better allows the project to adhere to the predefined schedule and budget. In addition, periodic user review and approval of work done by the IS staff provides feedback that allows developers to understand whether the project is still on the right track. User opinions help pull a problematic system development back on track. Therefore, we hypothesize that

H2: *User review has a positive effect on project performance.*

User participation was originally viewed as a user and developer "cooperatively involved to the extent that the activities of each facilitate the attainment of the ends of the others" (Swanson, 1974). It can also be viewed as a mutual influence process. That is, users exercise their influence in persuading system developers to comply with their requirements just as the technical specialists exercise their influence to constrain the system within technical feasibility.

User influence is the extent to which members of an organization affect decisions related to the final design of an information system (Robey, Farrow & Franz, 1989). In early system development contexts, users were not involved in the system development directly and could only exercise influence through the analyst. After the user participation concept came under study, influence came to be viewed as the outcome of user participation behaviors. Ives & Olson (1984) treated user influence as the degree of participation and categorized six degrees of participation which range from no involvement to involvement by strong control. Since users can only exercise their direct influence through participating in the development process, no influence can be found when there is no participation. Therefore, we hypothesize that

H3: *User review has a positive effect on user influence.*

Saleem (1996) concluded that influential user participation is critical for system success. Acceptance and satisfaction increase when users see the value of their participation, that is, by generating influence. However, participating in an ISD development process doesn't generate influence automatically. It is possible that users can participate in the system development without generating any influence. For example, developers may not react to the user requests sincerely when users simply perform "sign-off" duty at each stage. Developers may also be reluctant to comply when there are conflicts between users and developers.

Whether users can generate influence depends on to the extent that users' voices are heard and taken seriously by developers (Swanson, 1974). Project outcomes can be improved only when user inputs are taken seriously and incorporated into the system design. This implies that project outcomes are determined by user influence instead of user participation. Therefore, we expect that the variance of system outcomes explained by user participation increases after including user influence in the model. Likewise, influence will be more effective as participation increases. Thus, user influence mediates the effect from participation to project outcomes.

H4: *The relationship between user review and system responsiveness is mediated by user influence.*

H5: *The relationship between user review and project performance is mediated by user influence.*

Contingency based theories, such as social influence theory, indicate that the magnitude of influence generated from activities or messages is contingent on environmental factors. In this study, we view interaction quality as a moderator of the relationship between user participation and user influence and argue that users can generate more influence under high quality interaction, a recognized success factor in project management (Karlsen, Graee & Massaoud, 2008).

Early user participation research emphasizes the importance of effective interaction or communication between users and developers (Swanson, 1974). More information related to system development can be exchanged under effective communication and high quality interaction (Gallivan & Keil, 2003). Empirical studies support this concept by showing that high quality interaction between users and IS developers generates positive impacts, such as obtaining user support, as well as eliminates negative impacts, such as avoiding and resolving conflicts (Jiang, Klein & Chen, 2006). When users and developers interact in a high quality manner, it is easier for developers to take opinions and suggestions from users seriously and, therefore, users can generate more influence on the system development process. In contrast, when the interaction quality is low, conflicts exist and inputs from users are possibly ignored by developers. Therefore, we hypothesize that

H6: *The magnitude of user review impact on user influence is increased under high conditions of interaction quality.*

RESEARCH METHODS

The sample requires individuals familiar with an IS project in terms of process and outcome characteristics. For that reason, the target sample was IS project managers who are members of the Project Management Institute (PMI). The survey asked questions about recently completed projects on which they were leaders. Due to the responsibilities of their position and expressed knowledge by choice of their professional society, the target should have the necessary experience and knowledge to respond to questions about the project. A package, including a cover letter and questionnaire about participation and project outcomes, was sent to 1000 randomly selected members of the target population. All respondents were assured that their responses would be kept confidential. A total of 152 returned the questionnaire. One returned instrument was unusable due to omissions. Table 1 summarizes important characteristics of the projects and organizations.

User review refers to the reviewing behaviors and activities that the representatives of user groups perform in the system development process. The measurement considers whether users review and approve development work as part of the project process. A total of four items were adapted to measure user reviewing activities: users formally approved work done by the IS staff, users formally reviewed work done by IS staff, users were informed of progress and/or problems, and users signed a formalized agreement (Barki

Table 1. Organization and project characteristics

Variables	Categories	Number	Percent
Industry type	Service Manufacturing Education	115 34 2	76% 23% 1%
Number of IS employees	< = 10 11-50 51-100 101-500 > 500	9 18 17 38 69	6% 12% 11% 25% 46%
Average Team Size	< = 7 8-15 16-25 > = 26	40 63 30 18	26% 42% 20% 12%
Average Project duration	< =1 year 1 - 2 years 2 - 3 years 3 - 5 years >= 6 years	83 52 10 4 2	55% 34% 7% 3% 1%
Total sample size: 151			

& Hartwick, 1994). Likert-type scales (from 1 to 5), with anchors ranging from "not at all" to "to a large extent" were used for each question.

User influence refers to the extent to which members of an organization affect decisions related to the final design of an information system. A total of three items adopted from Hartwick and Barki (1994) were used to measure the influence that users generate during the development process: how much influence did users have in decision making, to what extent were users' opinions about this system actually considered by developers, how much personal influence did users have. Likert-type scales (from 1 to 5), with anchors ranging from "none at all" to "a great extent" were used for the questions.

IS-user interaction quality refers to the extent of productive interaction between users and IS developers during the system development. A total of four items adapted from Nidumolu (1995) cover completeness of training provided to users, quality of communication between developers and users, expressed user feelings of participation in project, and overall quality of interaction with users. Likert-type scales (from 1 to 5), with anchors ranging from "very poor" to "very good" represented the rating of delivery on each item.

Software responsiveness refers to the extent that the developed system meets user needs. A total of three items adapted from Nidumolu (1995) cover the ability to customize output to meet user needs, range of outputs that can be generated, difficulty of adapting software to changes in business and overall long term flexibility. Likert-type scales (from 1 to 5), with anchors ranging from "very poor" to "very good" were used to evaluate the delivery of each item.

Project performance refers to the extent that project team accomplishes system development tasks efficiently and effectively. A total of seven items adapted from Henderson and Lee, (1992) were used to measure project performance: the project adhered to the original schedule, the project adhered to the original budget, the project met the intended scope, tasks were completed efficiently, project goals were met, the expected amount of work was completed, and completed work was of high quality. Likert-type scales (from 1 to 5), with anchors ranging from "strongly disagree" to "strongly agree" were used for all questions to represent whether the project manager perceived the item to have been accomplished during their most recently completed project.

In this study, partial least squares (PLS) analysis was used to test item reliability, convergent validity, and discriminant validity (Hulland, 1999). Individual item reliability can be examined by observing the factor loading of each item. As shown in table 2, all factor loadings are significant using t-statistics and are higher than the recommended 0.7 (Hulland, 1999). The item-total correlations (ITC) are also higher than the recommended cut-off value of 0.3. Individual item reliability is assured in this study.

Convergent validity should also be examined because more than two indicators were used to measure each construct. We used composite reliability (CR) of constructs and average variance extracted (AVE) by constructs to evaluate convergent validity (Fornell & Larker, 1981). Convergent validity is assured since composite reliability of all constructs is higher 0.7 and the AVE values are all greater than 0.5. Lastly, as table 2 and 3 show, the correlations between pairs of constructs are below 0.8 and the square root of AVE is higher than each corresponding correlation coefficient (Chin, 1998). These properties indicate that the measures of constructs are sufficiently distinct from each other and discriminant validity is assured.

HYPOTHESES TESTING

The structural model was also tested with PLS with the results shown in Figure 2, which clearly

Table 2. Validity and reliability

Constructs	Indicators (abbreviated)	Factor Loadings	t-statistics*	ITC
User Influence *CR: 0.87; AVE: 0.69*	Decision making	0.80	14.91	0.59
	Opinions considered	0.83	21.90	0.55
	Personal influence	0.87	25.63	0.69
Interaction Quality *CR: 0.92; AVE: 0.74*	Training provided	0.71	13.49	0.56
	Quality communication	0.88	39.62	0.75
	Perceived participation	0.90	42.64	0.79
	Overall interaction quality	0.93	70.19	0.84
User Review *CR: 0.88; AVE: 0.66*	Approving works	0.76	13.96	0.51
	Reviewing works	0.87	27.04	0.71
	Informed of progress	0.91	55.36	0.82
	Sign formal agreement	0.70	9.78	0.53
Project Performance *CR: 0.91; AVE: 0.60*	Adhere to schedule	0.80	21.68	0.68
	Adhere to cost	0.78	16.53	0.67
	Met scope	0.78	19.19	0.62
	Efficient task completion	0.79	17.48	0.72
	Met project goals	0.75	14.82	0.69
	Work completed	0.78	19.48	0.70
	High quality of work	0.74	13.41	0.67
Responsiveness *CR: 0.90; AVE: 0.69*	Ability to customize output	0.73	9.65	0.51
	Range of output generated	0.86	20.56	0.76
	Difficulty of SW changes	0.81	14.97	0.70
	Overall responsiveness	0.91	62.79	0.78

* all significant at $p < 0.05$ CR is composite reliability, AVE is average variance extracted, ITC is item-total correlation

Table 3. Descriptive statistics and correlation matrix

Constructs	Mean	M2	M3	M4		UR	IQ	UI	R	PP
User Review (UR)	3.64	0.95	-0.43	-0.38		**0.83**				
Interaction Quality (IQ)	3.50	0.86	-0.46	-0.09		0.54	**0.86**			
User Influence (UI)	3.76	0.83	-1.13	1.70		0.52	0.44	**0.81**		
Responsiveness (R)	3.66	0.75	-0.06	-0.31		0.27	0.47	0.34	**0.77**	
Project Performance (PP)	3.65	0.77	-0.26	-0.59		0.29	0.52	0.41	0.41	**0.83**

M2: Standard Deviation; M3: Skewness; M4: Kurtosis; The diagonal line of correlation matrix represents the square root of the average variance extracted shows the mediating effect of user influence. Relationships between user review and system responsiveness and between user review and project performance are not significant. Examination of the correlations in Table 2 shows that a relationship between user review and each dependent variable exists, but user influence alone explains more of the variation and becomes the only significant input to both dependent variables. This indicates that user influence is a full mediator in the model. However, user review is crucial in explaining influence, so that user review is considered crucial in the overall model in terms of explaining how influence is generated. Thus, H1 and H2 are not supported, but H3, H4 and H5 are supported.

For H6, a moderated multiple regression (MMR) approach was adopted to test the moderating effect of interaction quality. The MMR approach includes three steps and emphasizes the R-square change instead of the significance level of the interaction term (Carte & Russell, 2003). Coefficients and R-square obtained from three regression steps (model 0, 1, and 2), using PLS, are shown in Table 4. Model 0 establishes the significance of the independent variable in explaining the dependent variable. Model 1 then introduces the moderating variable to the relationship to examine its influence in addition to user review. Since both are significant, model 2 tests the interaction term of user review and interaction quality. The R-square difference between model 1 and model 2 is significant at the 0.05 level, which indicates a significant moderating effect of interaction quality on the relationship between user review and user influence. H6 is supported.

As shown in Table 4, the coefficient of the interaction term is negative, indicating that there is not much influence of interaction quality when user review is already high. However, user review is greatly assisted in pushing for higher influence when user review is minimal. To advance understanding of the moderating role of interaction quality, relationships between user review and user influence under high, middle, and low interaction quality are provided in figure 3. When user review is low, more influence is generated when interaction quality is high. As user review increases, influence is larger to start and need not be assisted as fully by the quality of interaction.

DISCUSSION

User participation has long been studied in information systems research, but a consistent conclusion hasn't been reached. Most research focused

Figure 2. Path analysis

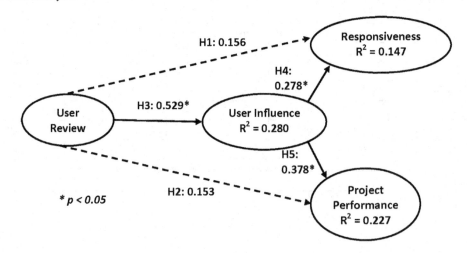

Table 4. Moderating effect of interaction quality

	Model 0	Model 1	Model 2
User Review (UR)	0.529 **	0.385 **	0.336 **
Interaction Quality (IQ)		0.254 **	0.227 **
UR * IQ			*-0.161 **
R²	0.280	0.322	0.344
R² Difference		0.042 **	*0.022 **
Note: *: p < 0.05; **: p < 0.01			

on whether the user physically participated or was psychologically involved in the ISD process, and whether that leads to success (Barki & Hartwick, 1994). Theories to support the arguments include participative decision making theory, planned organizational change theory, and contingency theory (Markus & Mao, 2004). Previous evidence shows that although user participation in decision making and other aspects of the development process leads to higher user satisfaction, the effect is moderated by the need to participate. Contingent participation is often tested with varying results on success measures (Jiang, et al., 2006).

This study provides an explanation for the inconsistent and wide-ranging results of past research. The mediating effect of user influence shows that taking action does not necessarily result in the expected outcome. The key spirit of participation is to generate influence, action itself is not sufficient. Moreover, how much influence the user can generate depends on the interaction quality between users and developers. Positive relationships between user review and influence are found under all levels of interaction quality, which implies user review is a major source of user influence. However the moderating effect of interaction quality shows that users generate different level of influence under different levels of interaction quality, with the most gains made when user review activities are less. This illus-

Figure 3. Moderating effect of interaction quality

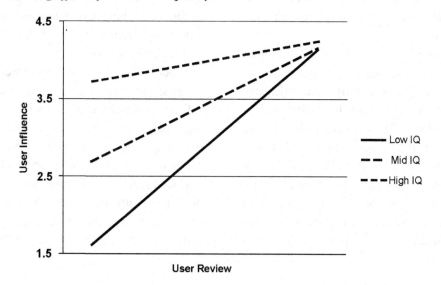

trates the importance of maintaining a high quality relationship when users do not actively conduct formal reviews. From the users' perspective, it is important to maintain a good relationship with developers so that developers consider the input of users seriously to improve the outcomes of the ISD.

This study advances our understanding of user participation by introducing the role of the user in IS development from a control perspective. Based on past research aimed at determining which control mechanisms should be taken under what situation, we show how a particular control mechanism (user reviews) can affect project outcomes. Results show that incorporating user reviews in the development process is critical for project success from two perspectives. First, system responsiveness, a crucial quality metric, can be improved by assuring the final system product can satisfy certain user and maintenance needs. Second, user reviews help point out inadequate design earlier in the life cycle. Catching problems earlier keeps development work on the right track and helps development teams adhere to schedule and budget. Moreover, a fully mediated effect of user influence implies that ineffective controls that do not generate influence are a waste of time and should be avoided. To insure control activities generate expected benefits, it is important to maintain a high interaction quality between users and developers.

Although users generate more influence under high interaction quality, this advantage diminishes with increasing review activity. User influence reaches its peak with intensive participation, regardless the level of interaction quality. In any power situation, the sum of influence that both parties possess is fixed (Markus, 1983). The maximum influence users can exert through reviews cannot break the upper limits. The diminishing trend implies that intensive user review can mitigate the negative effect caused by low interaction

quality. However, the final decision should take the cost of user participation into account. Users are forced to leave their regular work to review the developed outcome which reduces productivity in other functional areas.

Much of this result may be due to a reduction in conflict. Barki and Hartwick (1994) found a negative relationship between influence and conflict. The negative relationship indicates that conflict can be reduced when users generate influence. However, the exercise of influence does not always generate a positive impact on project process and outcome. For example, users hostile to the system could wield their influence to sabotage the system. The exercise of power also risks issues with power. Researchers who adopted a power perspective found that the exercise of user influence, similar to the exercise of power, generates resistance and unwanted conflict (Robey, et al., 1989). Thus, the literature provides both encouragement and warnings about generating influence. Interaction quality and partnering agreements may serve to help mitigate any negative effects and accentuate the benefits of participation via reviews (Jiang, et al., 2006).

As with any survey research, limitations exist to this study. First, common method variance may bias the result when both independent and dependent variables were collected from a single respondent. Future researchers are encouraged to collect data from different respondents and also other cultures to extend the external validity of the model. Secondly, only one dimension of user participation (user review) serves to represent control activities in this study. Other control activities might yield different results, and should according to contingency considerations. Similarly, only responsiveness of the software is considered as product quality - other dimensions may not yield the same results. Future research should include other control mechanisms and aspects of quality. Lastly, whether users can exert influence might also depend on their power position within the organization (Lynch & Gregor, 2004). Other contextual factors absent in this study may also affect the ability of users to exercise their influence during information system development. Future research should study the effect of user influence under differing contexts.

CONCLUSION

We proposed and confirmed that users can help control projects with their influence generated through review activities. The moderating role of interaction quality is also examined. The model expands on previous research which typically was unable to explain the nature of the relationships between participation and success. Future work should consider the intermediary variables that might exist in making a development project a success. Both control theory and contingency theory indicate that the overly simplistic models in past work are not adequate to describe the nature of the relationships.

Information system project managers should consider the impact potential of increasing the importance of user reviews. User reviews provide an increase to certain aspects of software quality and to the completion goals of the project. The development approach selected will dictate the timing of reviews, with a waterfall approach allowing for scheduled reviews at crucial checkpoints and prototyping approaches requiring more ad hoc reviews based on completed features. In addition, the importance of considering the comments of the user seriously shows in the impact of influence. Should users feel that their evaluations are ignored, there is not much value to the reviews. Lastly, interaction quality is important when user review activities are less, indicating that the development team members must foster productive discussions with the users when reviews are not effective. At least a few team members should be

trained in conflict resolution and other effective communication techniques.

REFERENCES

Aladwani, A. M., Rai, A., & Ramaprasad, A. (2000). Formal participation and performance of the system development group: the role of group heterogeneity and group-based rewards. *The Data Base for Advances in Information Systems*, *31*(4), 25–40.

Barki, H., & Hartwick, J. (1994). Measuring user participation, user involvement, and user attitude. *MIS Quarterly*, *18*(1), 59–82. doi:10.2307/249610

Bevan, N. (1999). Quality in use: meeting user needs for quality. *Journal of Systems and Software*, *49*(1), 89–96. doi:10.1016/S0164-1212(99)00070-9

Boehm, B. W., & Turner, R. (2003). *Balancing agility and discipline: A guide for the perplexed*. Upper Saddle River, NJ: Addison-Wesley.

Carte, T. A., & Russell, C. J. (2003). In pursuit of moderation: nine common errors and their solutions. *MIS Quarterly*, *27*(3), 479–501.

Chin, W. W. (1998). The partial least squares approach to structural equation modeling. In G. A. Marcoulides (Ed.) *Modern methods for business research* (pp. 295-336). Mahwah, NJ: Lawrence Erlbaum Associates.

Fornell, C., & Larcker, D. (1981). Evaluating structural equation models with unobservable variables and measurement error. *JMR, Journal of Marketing Research*, *18*(1), 39–50. doi:10.2307/3151312

Gallivan, M. J., & Keil, M. (2003). The user-developer communication process: a critical case study. *Information Systems Journal*, *13*(1), 37–68. doi:10.1046/j.1365-2575.2003.00138.x

Hartwick, J., & Barki, H. (1994). Explaining the role of user participation in information use. *Management Science*, *40*(4), 440–465. doi:10.1287/mnsc.40.4.440

Henderson, J. C., & Lee, S. (1992). Managing I/S design teams: a control theories perspective. *Management Science*, *38*(6), 757–777. doi:10.1287/mnsc.38.6.757

Hsu, J. S. C., Chan, C. L., Liu, J. Y. C., & Chen, H. G. (2008). The impacts of user review on software responsiveness: moderating requirements uncertainty. *Information & Management*, *45*(4), 203–210. doi:10.1016/j.im.2008.01.006

Hulland, J. (1999). Use of partial least squares (PLS) in strategic management research: a review of four recent studies. *Strategic Management Journal*, *20*(2), 195–204. doi:10.1002/(SICI)1097-0266(199902)20:2<195::AID-SMJ13>3.0.CO;2-7

Hwang, M. I., & Thorn, R. G. (1999). The effect of user engagement on system success: a meta-analytical integration of research findings. *Information & Management*, *35*(4), 229–236. doi:10.1016/S0378-7206(98)00092-5

Ives, B., & Olson, M. H. (1984). User involvement and MIS success: a review of research. *Management Science*, *30*(5), 586–603. doi:10.1287/mnsc.30.5.586

Jiang, J. J., Klein, G., & Chen, H. G. (2006). The effects of user partnering and user non-support on project performance. *Journal of the Association for Information Systems*, *7*(1), 68–88.

Karlsen, J. T., Graee, K., & Massaoud, M. J. (2008). The role of trust in project-stakeholder relationships: a study of a construction project. *International Journal of Project Organisation and Management*, *1*(1), 105–118. doi:10.1504/IJPOM.2008.020031

Kirsch, L. J., Sambamurthy, V., Ko, D. G., & Purvis, R. L. (2002). Controlling information systems development projects: the view from the client. *Management Science*, *48*(4), 484–498. doi:10.1287/mnsc.48.4.484.204

Lynch, T., & Gregor, S. (2004). User participation in decision support systems development: influencing system outcomes. *European Journal of Information Systems*, *13*(2), 286–301. doi:10.1057/palgrave.ejis.3000512

Markus, M. L. (1983). Power, politics, and MIS implementation. *Communications of the ACM*, *26*(6), 430–444. doi:10.1145/358141.358148

Markus, M. L., & Mao, J. Y. (2004). Participation in development and implementation - updating an old, tired concept for today's IS contexts. *Journal of the Association for Information Systems*, *5*(11-12), 514–544.

Nidumolu, S. (1995). The effect of coordination and uncertainty on software project performance: residual performance risk as an intervening variable. *Information Systems Research*, *6*(3), 191–219. doi:10.1287/isre.6.3.191

Ravichandran, T., & Rai, A. (2000). Quality management in systems development: an organizational system perspective. *MIS Quarterly*, *24*(3), 381–415. doi:10.2307/3250967

Robey, D., Farrow, D. L., & Franz, C. R. (1989). Group process and conflict in system development. *Management Science*, *35*(10), 1172–1191. doi:10.1287/mnsc.35.10.1172

Saleem, N. (1996). An empirical test of the contingency approach to user participation in information systems development. *Journal of Management Information Systems*, *13*(1), 145–166.

Schwalbe, K. (2007). *Information technology project management* (5th ed.). Boston: Course Technology.

Swanson, E. B. (1974). Management information systems: appreciation and involvement. *Management Science, 21*(2), 178–188. doi:10.1287/mnsc.21.2.178

This work was previously published in International Journal of Information Technology Project Management, Volume 1, Issue 1, edited by John Wang, pp. 1-14, copyright 2010 by IGI Publishing (an imprint of IGI Global).

Chapter 14
Using Realist Social Theory to Explain Project Outcomes

Michael J. Cuellar
North Carolina Central University, USA

ABSTRACT

In researching IS phenomena, many different theoretical lenses have been advanced. This paper proposes the use of Margaret Archer's Morphogenetic Approach to Analytical Dualism (MAAD) as a social theoretic approach to explain why social phenomena may occur in a case study. This paper provides a brief overview to MAAD, providing a description of its tenets and methodology for use in an empirical study. As an example, the author applies MAAD to the implementation of Lotus Notes in the Alpha consulting organization as reported by Orlikowski (2000). This approach shows that the differential success of the implementation efforts in the different organizations was due to the diverse cultures and possible experiences with technology found in those organizations. This example shows that the use of this social theory can provide explanatory purchase where social phenomena are involved. For practitioners, it suggests that structural analysis at the beginning of a project may provide direction as to how to make the project more successful.

INTRODUCTION

In the study of project management, it is often desired to discover why a project succeeded or failed. While the definition of project success may be disputed, it is commonly defined in the textbooks as occurring when a project produces the desired deliverables on time, on budget and with the proper quality (Brewer & Dittman, 2010; Gray & Larson, 2008; Kerzner, 2009; Schwalbe, 2007). However many times these goals are not met. The CHAOS study of the Standish Group has documented much of the issues of information systems project management (Rubenstein, 2007) in that many projects fail to deliver anything at all and many fail to achieve one or all of the goals of a successful project.

Two characteristics of projects stand out as important to be considered in the study of their success. The first characteristic is that they are designed to be change activities. Projects are commonly defined as an activity with a defined lifespan, an established objective, cross-functional involvement and novel objectives (Gray & Larson, 2008; Schwalbe, 2007). The novel objectives

DOI: 10.4018/978-1-4666-0930-3.ch014

described in the definition indicate that projects are designed to bring something to pass that has not existed before. That new something may be an information technology artifact, a redesigned work system or the implementation of technology into a business process. In all these cases, change is involved. In information systems, we can consider the process in two phases: development of the IT artifact and then its implementation in an organization. In the first phase, the IT artifact is brought into existence, a change from conception to reality. In the second phase, business processes are changed to incorporate the IT artifact.

Second, the definition tells us that those projects, especially information technology projects, are social activities in that they usually have cross-functional involvement. It is not an individual activity but one in which groups of people interact either in harmony or in conflict. In developing an information system groups of developers and users interact to bring the IT artifact into existence. Similarly, when an artifact is implemented into an organization, the developers and users interact to create a new business system that incorporates the artifact. The resultant artifact or implementation of an artifact is rarely that which is intended by any one of the parties. Rather, it is usually the outcome of the negotiated interactions between the parties.

Thus, the study of project success or failure (outcomes) requires an approach that considers the social aspects of change. In the field of sociology, one of the major concerns has been the issue of creating a general model of change in social structures. The question is asked that if we have a social structure such as a culture, division of labor, organizations etc. how do those structures come into existence and how do they change over time? In particular, how do actors and agencies interact with the structures to produce such change and under what circumstances does it occur? This type of questions seems to be very useful for information systems research. If we consider such things as business processes (whether they involve technology artifacts or not) as social structures, then social theory, the use of theoretical frameworks to study and interpret social structures and phenomena (Wikipedia, 2009), could be one way that we can analyze project interactions to explain how the project generated the results that it did.

Social theory has typically been implicit within information systems analysis. That is project results have been analyzed without explicitly considering the context or how social structures might have affected project results. However, recently, research has been done which explicitly attempts to apply Giddens' Structuration theory (ST) (Jones & Karsten, 2008; Jones, Orlikowski, & Munir, 2004) to a wide variety of situations in the IS literature (Jones & Karsten, 2008). Jones and Karsten (2008) indicate that ST has been used in a variety of ways. First, it has been taken as a "given" and used to offer insights on IS phenomena and applying it in general to the phenomena in question. A second way it has been used it to provide a "background" to the analysis and focus on certain aspects of it. A third, smaller group has focused on Giddens' later writings to emphasize certain concepts. Additionally, it has subjected to reinterpretation within the IS field manifesting in variants such as Adaptive Structuration Theory (DeSanctis & Poole, 1994) and Duality of Technology (Orlikowski, 1992).

While ST has been widely utilized in the IS literature, it has been subject to a number of criticisms. For example, in general sociology it has been criticized for an a-historicity in its model of relations between structure and agency (Archer, 1995). Because of its melding of structure and agency, analysis can only take place in the "now". Examination of the effects of previous structures is ruled out since different people than those here constituted them present. Another issue is the over-privileging of agency with respect to structure. Since social structures are regularized social practices, they do not exist until instantiated by actors. Thus they have no relatively enduring existence apart from the actors. Therefore, while they actors draw upon them to inform their practice, they cannot have any causal influence over the actors. Given that structures do not endure apart from actions of the actors, ST has a tendency to direct toward the immediate moment of interaction (Stones, 2001).

The handling of technology within ST has also been problematic. Rose, Jones, and Truex (2005) claim that ST unduly privileges human agency which causes technology to vanish into being simply "an occasion for structuring". As dealt with in Orlikowski (2000), information technology is held to be a non-actor. It is treated as a multi-faceted tool from which users select features to be employed in structuring the organizations. In Orlikowski (2005), she seems to recognize this and advocates that we need to look at "different conceptual treatments of human and technological agencies" (p. 185). She recognizes a difference between human and technological agency preferring to call the latter "technological performativity" of settings.

Because of these issues, it seems to make sense to look at another form of social theory that might avoid these criticisms and might be able to assist us in examining project outcomes. One such theory is Archer's Morphogenetic Approach to Analytical Dualism (MAAD) (Archer, 1988, 1995). The purpose of this paper is to provide a description of MAAD and to provide an illustration of how it applies to the explanation of information systems project outcomes. This theory as shall be seen below resolves many of the issues associated with ST. As opposed to the a-historicity of ST, MAAD specifically includes time into the analysis in the form of the Morphogenetic Cycle that will be explained below. Similarly, structure and agency are held apart analytically in a dualism rather than the conflationary duality used by ST. Thus neither structure nor agency is privileged. Finally, IT artifacts can find a place as a material structure within the framework of MAAD thus allowing it to be introduced into the analysis. Stones

(2001) has indicated that MAAD also provides us with a series of middle and macro concepts that "precise and linked quite carefully with issues of ontology" (p. 178).

The contribution of this paper is to show how MAAD offers the capability of providing explanatory insights beyond the approaches employed by other social theories. This paper therefore seeks to describe MAAD and to demonstrate how it can be used to explain project outcomes by means of a secondary case study. MAAD is a general social theory developed specifically to assist in identifying why change in social structures occurred or did not occur and thus seems to be ideal for use in analyzing project outcomes. The rest of the paper describes Archer's theory and then show how it applies to analysis of a case of project escalation.

A DESCRIPTION OF MAAD

This section describes the basic tenets of Archer's Morphogenetic Approach to Analytical Dualism (MAAD). It describes the basic components of MAAD: structures, agencies and the morphogenetic cycle. For further study of MAAD and how it has been applied to the IS field, please see Appendix A.

Components: Material and Ideational Structures

Social structures are considered to be emergent properties of relationships between social entities that as such are irreducible to those entities, relatively autonomous in their influence and relatively enduring. They are considered emergent in that they arise from interactions between agencies. Structures have properties that allow them influence the world around them. Structures pre-date any particular set of individuals and thus can be only reproduced or transformed by social action (Archer, 1995, p. 168).

Structures are considered to be of two types: material structures and ideational structures (or culture). Material structures consist of relationships between individuals, and other material structures. In material structures, the relationships are between role-positions rather than incumbents of those positions. In a marriage relationship, for example, husband and wife are role positions that exist independently of who the husband and wife are. Thus the existing material structure pre-exists any social interaction based on or conditioned by it and every change or elaboration of the structure post-dates the interaction. Thus every couple marrying reproduces or transforms the existing marriage structure. Any transformation of the structure post-dates the interaction of the agents.

Ideational structures (also called cultures or cultural systems) are logical relationships between propositions. Cultural systems are extracted from the sum total of existing "intelligibilia" which roughly corresponds with Popper's World Three (Archer, 1988). These propositions stand in objective logical relationship with each other. For example, some propositions might be A: "all men are created equal", B; "in Christ, all men are equal", C: "black men are not socially equal to white men" and D: "blacks should be subservient to whites." If these four propositions are part of the cultural system, propositions A and B are complementary to each other as are C and D. However propositions A and B are contradictory to C and D. As logical relationships, the cultural system is independent of any society or cultural group that holds it. Should no group espouse it, it still can exist in the accumulated cultural library of the society where it can be extracted and advocated for.

Components: Agency

Agencies are groups of social actors going through the same life experiences. These social actors in turn are derived from Persons who assume roles within the Agency. Persons are viewed as reflexive agents. They can examine their current existence and circumstances and decide to continue or discontinue their existing situation. Actors derive from a relationship between the people and the agency. A person is born and socialized within a particular agency. As s/he comes to maturity, s/he can choose to take a role as an actor within that agency or seek to move to a different agency. Actors are thus a particular social identity taken on by a person as their role within an agency.

There are two kinds of agencies: primary and corporate. Primary agents are simply collectivities of individuals sharing a life experience. They are not organized and have neither leadership nor a message to articulate. A corporate agent is a group of persons who have organized to take action. They have a set of roles and leadership that articulates a message and seeks to execute an action as a group.

These agencies have different distributions of resources (wealth, sanction or expertise). This distribution either enables or disables the agencies for undertaking desired projects.

Components: Morphogenetic Cycle

The link between the structures and the agencies in terms of defining how structural change occurs is the morphogenetic cycle (see Figure 1 in the Appendix). Previous cycles have created a particular set of existing structures and distributions of resources as the result of prior cycles which condition the actions of existing agencies creating opportunity costs to intended actions which in turn create material and ideational interests which create situational logics of action (structural conditioning). As the agencies act to achieve their interests (Social Interaction), agencies and resources are redistributed this in turn changes the balance of power leading to the reproduction or transformation of structures (Morphostasis/ Morphogenesis).

This cycle is an analytical distinction rather than an ontological one. Action is constantly go-

Figure 1. Archer (1998)'s MST model of social action (p.376)

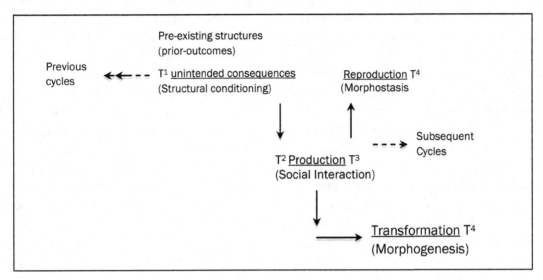

ing on and there is no static point. However, it is possible to abstract from reality salient features of societal change actions that are desired to be analyzed. These situations can be analyzed by means of this device. We will now look at each phase in more detail.

Structural Conditioning

Phase I of the morphogenetic cycle, Structural Conditioning is the result of the actions of previous agents. The "first order effects" of these actions are the conditions in which the agents find themselves. These conditions have three effects on agents: 1) they enable certain actions and discourage or penalize others; 2) they create certain opportunity costs for pursuing certain actions; 3) they also allocate various distributions of resources among the agents. These various conditions create a vested interest in the agent of either preserving or changing the status quo.

Conditioning also provides "direction guidance" (Archer, 1995, p. 213). The properties of the structures and cultures that exist interact to provide this guidance. These properties can be required by the nature of their relationship (e.g.,

employer-employee, manager-team member, husband-wife) in that they cannot exist without the other. Or their relationships can be contingent, only incidentally related (e.g., all people of a certain age). Additionally, the relationship between the properties can be one of coherence or contradiction. Coherence means that the role relationships of a material structure or the propositions support each other and are not in contradiction. Where contradictions exist, these are "fault lines" which can be exploited to create change in the structures. Contradictions can also be created by proposals for change in the social structures. Where an existing set of structures is in the ascendency, a group can create a contradiction by advocating for a new structure to replace the old ones. Archer calls this coherence or contradiction a "second order effect" (Archer, 1995, p. 215) as they arise from the first order effects described above.

These interactions give rise to "situational logics" (Archer, 1995, pp. 216-218). Where the relationships between elements of a structure are necessary and where they are compatible with each other, agents are motivated by their vested interests and opportunity costs of change to protect the existing structures. Similarly, where relationships are necessary but are incompatible with each other, those in power are motivated to compromise in order to retain their structure. Where relationships are not essential to the structure and are incompatible, it is possible to seek to directly eliminate the incompatibility either to preserve the status quo or to create revolutionary change. Lastly, where the structures are not required but are compatible, it fosters an attitude of opportunism: to create new potentials by exploiting new capabilities to increase the capabilities of the agents.

Social Interaction

Phase 2 of the morphogenetic cycle, social interaction, begins when one or more agencies decide to make an effort to effect change or maintain the status quo according to their situational logics, creating environmental pressures. This shapes the context for all actors. Other agencies react to these pressures. As the agencies interact, the various agents constrain and enable each other and the various agencies are redefined over time. The net result is that at the end of the process, there is realignment of the relationships between the agents with regard to size, constituency, and resource allocation. The original resource (management sanction, wealth and expertise) distribution that existed at the time of structural condition is now redistributed among the realigned agencies.

Transformation

In this final phase, transformation or social elaboration, the effects of the social interaction in the previous phase are worked out. This is accomplished by transactions between the realigned agents carried out by means of exchange and power. This works out by engaging one of three different types of interaction: confluence of desires, where all parties are agreed on the course of action; reciprocal exchange, where each gives something in exchange for a gain in another area; and power-induced compliance, where the will

of one agent is forced on the others. The agents' ability to enact their desired situation logic is based on their access to resources. This interaction of the agents with their resource levels creates their bargaining power, which in turn determines their ability to carry out the actions that they desire per their situational logic.

Bargaining power however is a necessary but not sufficient condition for the definition of an exchange because a transaction requires us to consider the bargaining power of each participant in the exchange to determine a successful transaction. This leads to the concept of negotiating strength. Depending on the resources possessed and needed by each partner, the negotiating power of an agent will vary. Where one agent is dependent on another for certain resources, the transaction will tend to be transacted in terms of power while where the resource requirements are evenly distributed, it will tend to be more of an exchange.

This negotiating strength then is exerted by Corporate Agents who seek to enact their desired social state in methods derived from their situational logic. Where negotiating strength is relatively equal, the new social arrangements are negotiated. Where there is a disparity in strength, the new social arrangements can be imposed by power. Whichever is the case, the resulting social/cultural structure is not predictable.

In the next section, the paper describes a methodology for how to apply this approach in IS research and then uses it in an example secondary case study.

A METHODOLOGY FOR USING ARCHER'S SOCIAL THEORY IN IS RESEARCH

Archer describes a basic process for doing explanatory research (Archer, 1995). This explanation takes the form of "analytic histories". In these histories, we describe the morphogenetic cycle that occurred for the social phenomenon under study. We describe the structural conditions that existed and how these impacted the agencies in play during the sequence. The agencies, structures, vested interests, situational logics and resource distributions should be examined. Next, we describe the interaction that occurred and how the agencies changed and realigned during the cycle. Changes in resource distributions should be examined. Finally, we discuss the changed bargaining power of the agencies, which led to changes in negotiating strength and power relationships. Then we should describe the nature of the negotiations over the form of the structures that took place and why the resulting structures took the form that they did.

MAAD and this methodology are most appropriate for use in the study of change activity: why a social structure changed as it did or did not change. Research questions focused around change are the indicators of the appropriateness of this approach. Questions such as why the project did not generate a usable artifact, or one at all; why did the implementation fail or succeed; why did the attitudes of the project team sour over the course of the project; why is the resource profile of the system as it is are all appropriate questions as they address the question of the change in social structures at macro levels. Questions directed at the individual level of analysis and other non-social issues such as the proper technical design of an artifact are counter-indicative for use of this methodology.

The sections below describe a set of steps to operationalize the use of MAAD for a case study.

Identification of the Structure under Analysis

The first step in the process should be the identification of the social structure under analysis. If the research objective is to understand why software was allowed to develop with a flawed design concept, the target social structure is the either the IT artifact or the design specification. If the object of analysis were an implementation, the structure would be the business process or processes that would be changed as a result of the implementation activity. The research question should be framed as why did the structure either change as it did (development) or why did the organization change as it did or not change (implementation).

Data Collection

In the data collection phase of the study, one objective is to collect as much information about the pre-existing structural conditions as is possible. In the case of the retrospective studies undertaken where the project is complete, it relies in large part on the memories of participants and analysis of documentary evidence. Therefore, it is better to collect data as the project is moving forward, if at all possible. There the researcher can observe and perform data collection of structural conditions before interaction begins without relying on participant memories. Data should be collected about existing social structures such as organizations, work systems (Alter, 2006), belief systems and values. Groups involved in the project should be recorded for possible identification as agencies. Effort should be made to identify the organization if any of the group and what agenda the group may have in regards to this project. The resources (expertise, wealth and sanction) possessed by the group should be identified as well. The past history of the agency interactions should be gathered as this leads to identification of the agency vested interest and situational logic.

Then the history of the project should be gathered or observed from the various agencies. Attention should be paid to how support, resource alignment and group membership changed over the course of the interaction between the agencies. How the interaction was started should be documented, e.g. the CIO determined that Lotus

Notes should be used in the organization. The reactions of the various agencies including the splintering or combining of agencies, the motivation of primary agencies to be corporate agencies should be noted. No reaction is just as much of a reaction and violent protests and strikes.

Finally the negotiations surrounding the resulting form of the social structure should be recorded. Was it a negotiation or was it imposed? What was the ultimate result of the negotiations? What were the bargaining chips possessed by each agency? Were these chips desired by other agencies? If so, by how much?

Analysis

The first step in the analysis is the examination of the existing structure under analysis. Where are the incompatibilities/contradictions within the structure? This analysis identifies the potential leverage points for morphogenetic activity. Then the agencies are defined, their resource allocations, whether they are primary or corporate agencies in terms of the change initiative under consideration and their vested interests. From this analysis and from the structural analysis, the situational logics of each agency can be defined. Then the history of the agential interactions is analyzed with particular interest in the strategies/tactics that allowed the successful/unsuccessful realignment of agencies and resources. Finally a power analysis that analyzes the bargaining power and negotiating strength and the negotiating tactics used by each agency in the elaboration of a new social structure is performed. From this analysis, the causal factors in the success/failure of the change effort can be extracted and recommendations for future attempts at similar activities can be extracted.

EXAMPLE CASE STUDY

To demonstrate the capability of this methodology, this section reviews the "Alpha" case study (Orlikowski, 2000). This case was chosen, as it is a prominent case study that was used to demonstrate the "practice lens" enhancement to structurational analysis. Additionally, it possesses sufficient detail that a morphogenetic analysis can be performed. By performing this reanalysis, the strengths of MAAD can be displayed compared to that of structurational analysis. This case also includes the reaction of three different agencies to a technology implementation initiative; one successful, one unsuccessful and one partially successful. This provides the opportunity to the show the methodology analyzing a success as well as failure.

One of the limitations of secondary study analysis is that the data is collected for a different purpose and presented only to support the existing analysis. Thus some of the data that would be collected is not presented in the case study. While all the information desired is not found in the published article, enough exists to provide a demonstration of the results of the process. Thus when data is needed that is not found in the published case, it has been interpolated or drawn from other studies and inserted into the morphogenetic analysis.

This case concerns Alpha, a large multinational consulting organization with offices around the world. In the late 1980s, the CIO of the organization determined that Lotus Notes would provide the organization with valuable capabilities to allow the consultants to collaborate through the use of Email and enable knowledge sharing throughout the organization. This knowledge sharing would enable the organization to avoid the costs of "reinventing the wheel" on each engagement and thus allow the company to achieve a competitive advantage through the reduction of cost and improvement of service. He therefore purchased thousands of licenses of Notes and had his technology organization install it in all offices as rapidly as possible to achieve the benefits as rapidly as possible. In this activity, the benefits of Notes were quickly achieved in the technology group; however the use Notes was largely rejected in the consulting organization with most using it only nominally and some using the system for personal productivity. The question here is why were the disparate results achieved despite implementation of the same package in the same organization.

Structure under Analysis

The structure under analysis in this case is the work processes of the consultants and technology support personnel in building a solution for their customers. The CIO sought to change this function by using Lotus Notes to increase collaboration and information sharing between them.

Structural Conditions at the Start of the Cycle

Agencies

In looking at this project, we can identify three agencies: the CIO, the technology group and the consultants. While little information is provided about him in the published case, we know that the CIO was in a newly established position within the company and was given responsibility for the global use of information technology. The extent of his resources is not completely known, but we do know that he controlled the 40 person technology group, had enough budget to purchase several thousand licenses of Notes, but had no sanction to set policy for the use of technology with the consultant group. That is he could control the technology purchased and used but could not mandate a particular utilization of the technology. The technology group consisted of 40 people reporting to the CIO. They set corporate technology standards and supported the corporate infrastructure. They had technical backgrounds and were career programmers or computer support staff. Their resources largely came from the CIO. The case does not provide much information about the backgrounds of the consultants. We do

know that they had the primary call on resources in the organization. They set their own policy on the use of technology with their group. Little information is provided about the consultants, but it is apparent that many of the consultants were skeptical about technology in general.

Structures

There were several social structures identified in the case. Within the company culture, there were different standards applied to different groups. The consultants were held to a standard that required them to bill their time to clients. It was unthinkable for them to take time that could be billed and use it for something that could not be billed. As one consulted noted, "[s]eniors and managers never have nonchargeable hours. It's just not done" (Orlikowski, 2000, p. 416). Additionally, they had an "up or out" career path. They would get promoted to the next step (senior, manager, partner) at the appropriate time or they would have to leave the company. Since, they had a normal pyramid relationship, this lead to a highly competitive and individualistic struggle for those positions. In fact, the culture of the consultants was such that they believed that they needed to hold on to information so as to maximize the competitive advantage in the race for promotion. As one manager put it, "[sharing information] is not in our culture ... People hide information because it gives them and edge" (p. 417). Lastly, the consultants considered themselves to be paid to manage relationships not transfer information. The technology group was held to a different standard. They were not regarded as consultants and therefore did not have to bill their time out nor were they subject to the rigid promotion timing of the consultant group. Additionally, they had a culture of cooperation with each other in order to solve problems.

Situational Logic

These structures were all consistent with each other as applied to the various agencies. The consultants' structures focused on the idea of generating high amounts of revenue, and building consultants that could build their own competence and their own book of business. Thus the Darwinian approach of weeding out the less fit for this environment was complementary to the other structures in place at Alpha. The CIO's vision therefore was at a various with these structures and therefore introduced what is called a competitive contradiction in MAAD terminology: he introduced a concept at variance to the prevailing culture. Rather than sustain the existing competitive culture, he unwittingly introduced a variant concept that consultants should work together to produce better solutions for customers in a cooperative manner, a profoundly counter-cultural concept within the Alpha consultancy. The consultants presumably had a vested interest in maintaining the status quo to protect their investment in the large effort they had put into their careers. The CIO had a vested interest in proving his value to the organization. The consultants therefore adopted a strategy of preservation regarding their work processes while the CIO had and elimination strategy with regard to their processes seeking to change them with his new ones.

Within the technology group, his concept was not counted as counter-cultural as that was the way that they worked. While, the information about them is sketchy, we know that they already had a cooperative customer support culture in which they helped each other. Thus the CIO's vision was a necessary complementarity with their existing culture. That is it supported and expanded their existing structure. Assuming that the technology group members had a vested interest in maintaining their culture and the CIO had the vested interest in proving his value by implementing notes as described above, a necessary complementarity existed between for them. The structures that existed were required for the CIOs vision to succeed and therefore were necessary. The Notes functionality was a complement to this structure of the existing work processes of the technology group.

We see now that the CIO had a found a receptive group in the technologists where an situational logic existed to preserve their culture and Notes fit well as a complementary technology for that purpose. On the other hand, the CIO presented a profoundly competitive contradiction to the existing culture of the consultant organization.

Interaction

The details of the interaction are limited in the case as presented. We do not know what occurred when Notes was introduced to the technology organization. However, we do know that after the technology organization had accepted the technology and was using it, it was introduced to the consultant organization. The case indicates to us that the consultants received training on the software in classes. However in those classes, no attempt was made to relate Notes to the consultants' business process. The classes were technical and abstract. The introduction of the technology resulted in a split within the consultants' agency between those who chose not to make limited use of the technology and those who used it for personal productivity. Insufficient information is provided to make a definitive declaration as to why this split occurred, but it seems that those who resisted the technology completely were those who were technology skeptics while those who adopted it for personal use may have had a higher technology background. Resource allocations did not appear to change as a result of this interaction.

Structural Elaboration

In the technology organization, the CIO had wealth in terms of the budget, the sanction to force the issue but did not have the expertise to do it. The technologists had the expertise but not the budget or the sanction to adopt it. Both acting on their situation logic of necessary complementarity agreed on the adoption and combining their resources soon achieved a harmonious adoption of the technology within their organization.

However, in the consultant organization, in attempting to implement his elimination strategy to resolve the competitive contradiction, he ran into trouble. While he possessed the resources to determine what technology would be used, he did not have the sanction to enforce use. Bargaining power is based on having something that the other wants. The method by which he chose to introduce the Notes technology did not convince the consultant organization that Notes was anything that they wanted or needed. In effect, they were left to themselves to determine the use of the technology. The introduction effort was did not generate any desire in the technology skeptic consultant organization for the software. In fact, they viewed the Notes technology as being able to do things they had no desire to do and was therefore a "solution in search of a problem" (p. 416). Negotiating strength is predicated on the resource allocation between the agencies. The agency which has more wealth expertise and/or sanction to enact their situation logic along with bargaining power has more negotiating strength. In this case, the CIO had no sanction to enforce usage of Notes in the manner in which he desired it. He had therefore had insufficient negotiating strength to persuade the consultants to do more than minimally use the software let alone force them to use it.

With the less technology skeptic consultants, the CIO was also unable to enact his project but they did adopt the software to a certain extent. Similarly with them, his vision of cooperative work and knowledge sharing between the consultants fell on deaf ears for the same reasons as with the technology skeptics. However, these consultants found that the software could be used consonant with their structures of competitive individuality. They saw that the software could increase their

competitive advantage by automating their existing work, relieving them of manual activities. Thus these consultants saw in the Notes technology something that they wanted. Therefore the CIO had more negotiating strength and thus was able to achieve more adoption of the system in this group. This example shows the unintended consequences of an implementation effort. The CIO was attempting to implement his vision of cooperative work, which was rejected by the consultants. However some seeing value chose to enact a different vision of the use of the software.

What Could the CIO Have Done to Be Successful?

The CIO's vision of Alpha utilizing Notes as a tool for knowledge sharing was such a counter cultural concept that it is difficult to conceive of how the CIO could have succeeded in his project. To have achieved his goal, the culture of the consulting organization would have to have been more like that of the technology organization which would have been a fundamental structural change. This would have changed his initiative from one that causes a competitive contradiction to one of complementarity. However this type of morphogenetic change would require the identification and exploitation of a contradiction in the structures, which is not evident in the description of the case, or a fundamental change in the external environment which would cause a contradiction to occur between the existing structure and organizational survival.

DISCUSSION AND LIMITATIONS

As discussed above, this approach is limited by the nature of the data provided. The data was collected and reported to support a structurational practice lens analysis and reported as such. Therefore it lacks the richness of information that data collected for a morphogenetic analysis would have. The fact that the results do not vary too dramatically from that reported by Orlikowski can be partially attributed to this fact. A full original case analysis subject to analysis from both sides would be needed to display the difference in analysis. Nevertheless, this paper shows the power and capabilities of morphogenetic analysis.

What is important to observe here is that MAAD provides, as Stones (2001) points out, the macro- and meso- level concepts to provide the "explanatory engine" for the results whereas structurational analysis provides only "sensitizing" capabilities for the analysis. This refers to concepts such as contradictions/coherence, vested interests, situational logics, bargaining power and negotiating strength. These concepts are held to "emerge" from the interaction of "lower level" entities. For example, as agencies interact with the existing set of structures, they develop vested interests in retaining or changing them. This is one of the features that is enabled by the dualistic conception of structure and agency that is explicitly denied by structuration theory (Archer, 1995). Thus we see in the morphogenetic approach that following the interaction of the agencies the emergence of the entities, which explains why the results occurred. This is opposed to the original structurational analysis, which, denying the concept of emergence, only featured the researcher's opinion based on the evidence.

These concepts also allow the researcher to maintain the balance between structures and agencies to ensure that we avoid emphasis on one or the other as is seen in structurational analysis with its focus on the immediate moment (Stones, 2001). Through the morphogenetic cycle and the methodological approach that traces the change activity from structural conditioning through interaction and elaboration, we can take into consideration the effects of previous actions and projects on the project under analysis and how they constrain the actions of the actors and then consider how the agencies interacted with themselves and other structures which result in changed relationships

and resource realignments which lead to the rationale for the elaboration of structures.

The more structured approach to analysis of the change activity provided by MAAD guides the researcher into an understanding of the dynamics and relationships involved in the morphogenetic cycle. It provides a structural framework that guides the researcher's analysis along a path leading to explanation. In this example, the methodology described here also indicates for the researcher the types of data that is needed to be collected to perform the analysis. It then leads them through the process of doing structural analysis. This analysis showed that the CIO possessed few resources to empower him to command implementation and that cultural situation was such that the consultants would oppose implementation. The interaction analysis showed that the consultant agency split into two separate agencies: those who limited their use and those who adopted it for personal productivity. And finally, the elaboration analysis showed why the CIO failed in his goal with the consultants but was partially successful with the technology group.

MAAD explains but doesn't predict. The methodology described here allows the researcher to explain the outcome of the project but it doesn't facilitate the prediction of results. As illustrated by the unintended consequences of this project where we saw that the consultants agency split into two agencies during interaction, events may occur beyond what we can see on the basis of structural conditioning. Similarly, the results of this study are the results of an interpretive qualitative study and therefore are corrigible and subject to revision based on the acquisition of new knowledge. Therefore the explanatory results of any study must be compared to that of other studies to identify causal factors for a phenomenon that transcend the current case.

Orlikowski (2000) describes a view of the technological structure as being enacted by recurrent social practices of a community of users as they work with a technology artifact. It therefore focuses on what the users do with a certain technology in everyday practices. This seems to be due to the conception that structures, in structuration theory, are intangible things that are drawn on to guide actor behavior and to instantiate practices. In morphogenetic analysis, structures are considered to be real things. That is, following its critical realist (Bhaskar, 1979; Mingers, 2004) foundations, MAAD views structures as things having an existence separate from people and their conceptions of it. IT artifacts therefore can participate in structures. We may therefore consider that since information systems replace human actors in the performance of business processes (Kogut & Zander, 1992), that information systems may be viewed as actors themselves in those processes. The technology artifact placed into a work system performs work delegated to it by human actors and often includes in it decision rules which decide how the data is to be processed. This artifact may assume more or less of the process as determined by the human actors. In some processes such as payroll processing or health care claims processing where the process involves manipulation of information, the artifact may perform almost all of the process; the humans providing only input and exception handling of the data. At the other end where the artifact only monitors the results of a process such as manufacturing plant-monitoring system, the artifact may perform only a data collection or process analysis function. Given that they generally not capable of analyzing and changing their own behavior, we may consider then non-reflexive actors in social structures. This concept should be subject to further development.

For practitioners, while morphogenetic analysis doesn't predict results and can't anticipate unintended consequences, it can provide guidance for project leaders and sponsors as to the advisability of projects or suggested approaches. For, example in the case analyzed here, had a structural conditioning analysis been performed, it would have been seen that the consultants had vested interests and situational logic geared toward maintaining the status quo. This information would have allowed the CIO to select different goals or to enhance his rollout process to sell the value of the software to the consultants to bring more of them into the camp of those who used it for personal productivity. In other situations, the project leader can use structural conditioning analysis as a way to identify whether preliminary material structural change is needed prior to a project (Sarker & Lee, 2003) or whether ideational structures need to be modified by processes of socializing or teaching change (Huy, 2001) prior to beginning a project.

CONCLUSION

This secondary study has shown that using Archer's MAAD social theory allows explanatory purchase for identifying reasons for differential adoption of technology in the Alpha consulting organization. It has shown that social structures, both ideological and material, should be considered in the development of explanations for phenomena. In particular, it places focus on the reasons for why structural change occurred or did not occur and therefore is useful for examining cases where the introduction or use of information systems caused changes in social structures such as business processes, organizations or culture.

REFERENCES

Alter, S. (2006). *The work system method connecting people, processes and it for business results*. Larkspur, CA: Larkspur Press.

Archer, M. (1998). Realism and morphogenesis. In Archer, M., Bhaskar, R., Collier, A., Lawson, T., & Norrie, A. (Eds.), *Critical realism essential readings*. London: Routlege.

Archer, M. S. (1982). Morphogenesis versus structuration: On combining structure and action. *The British Journal of Sociology, 33*(4), 455–483. doi:10.2307/589357

Archer, M. S. (1988). *Culture and agency, the place of culture in social theory*. New York: Cambridge University Press.

Archer, M. S. (1995). *Realist social theory: The morphogenetic approach* (1st ed.). New York: Cambridge University Press. doi:10.1017/CBO9780511557675

Archer, M. S. (2000). *Being human the problem of agency*. New York: Cambridge University Press. doi:10.1017/CBO9780511488733

Archer, M. S. (2003). *Structure, agency and the internal conversation*. New York: Cambridge University Press.

Bhaskar, R. (1979). *The possibility of naturalism* (1st ed.). Brighton, UK: The Harvester Press Limited.

Brewer, J., & Dittman, K. (2010). *Methods of it project management* (1st ed.). Upper Saddle River, NJ: Prentice Hall.

Cuellar, M. J. (2007). *A realist social theory of information systems*. Paper presented at the AMCIS 2007, Keystone, CO.

de Vaujany, F.-X. (2008). Capturing reflexivity modes in is: A critical realist approach. *Information and Organization, 18*, 51–72. doi:10.1016/j.infoandorg.2007.11.001

DeSanctis, G., & Poole, M. S. (1994). Capturing the complexity in advanced technology use: Adaptive structuration theory. *Organization Science, 5*(2), 121–147. doi:10.1287/orsc.5.2.121

Gray, C., & Larson, E. (2008). *Project management: The managerial process* (4th ed.). New York: McGraw-Hill.

Huy, Q. N. (2001). Time, temporal capability and planned change. *Academy of Management Review, 36*(4), 601–623. doi:10.2307/3560244

Jones, M., & Karsten, H. (2008). Gidden's structuration theory and information systems research. *Management Information Systems Quarterly, 32*(1), 127–157.

Jones, M., Orlikowski, W. J., & Munir, K. (2004). Structuration theory and information systems: A critical reappraisal. In Mingers, J., & Willcocks, L. (Eds.), *Social theory and philosophy for information systems* (pp. 297–328). Chichester, UK: John Wiley & Sons.

Kerzner, H. (2009). *Project management* (10th ed.). Hoboden, NJ: John Wiley & Sons.

Kogut, B., & Zander, U. (1992). Knowledge of the firm, combinative capabilities and the replication of technology. *Organization Science, 3*(3), 383–397. doi:10.1287/orsc.3.3.383

Mingers, J. (2004). Real-izing information systems: Critical realism as an underpinning philosophy for information systems. *Information and Organization, 14*, 87–103. doi:10.1016/j.infoandorg.2003.06.001

Mutch, A. (2002). Actors and networks or agents and structures: Towards a realist view of information systems. *Organization, 9*(3), 477–496. doi:10.1177/135050840293013

Mutch, A. (2007). Concerns with "Mutual constitution": A critical realist commentary. In Stahl, B. C. (Ed.), *Issues and trends in technology and human interaction* (pp. 230–244). Hershey, PA: IGI Global.

Orlikowski, W. J. (1992). The duality of technology: Rethinking the concept of technology in organizations. *Organization Science, 3*(3), 398–427. doi:10.1287/orsc.3.3.398

Orlikowski, W. J. (2000). Using technology and constituting structures: A practice lens for studying technology in organizations. *Organization Science, 11*(4), 404–428. doi:10.1287/orsc.11.4.404.14600

Orlikowski, W. J. (2005). Material works: Exploring the situated entanglement of technological performativity and human agency. *Scandinavian Journal of Information Systems, 17*(1), 183–186.

Rose, J., Jones, M., & Truex, D. (2005). Sociotheoretic accounts of is: The problem of agency. *Scandinavian Journal of Information Systems, 17*(1), 133–152.

Rubenstein, D. (2007). Standish group report: There's less development chaos today. *Software Development Times on the Web*. Retrieved from http://www2.sdtimes.com/content/article.aspx?ArticleID=30247

Sarker, S., & Lee, A. S. (2003). Using a case study to test the role of three key social enablers in erp implementation. *Information & Management, 40*, 813–829. doi:10.1016/S0378-7206(02)00103-9

Schwalbe, K. (2007). *Information technology project management* (5th ed.). New York: Thomson.

Stones, R. (2001). Refusing the realism-structuration divide. *European Journal of Social Theory, 4*(2), 177–197. doi:10.1177/13684310122225064

Volkoff, O., Strong, D. M., & Elmes, M. B. (2007). Technological embeddedness and organizational change. *Organization Science, 18*(5), 832–848. doi:10.1287/orsc.1070.0288

Wikipedia. (2009). Social theory. *Wikipedia*. Retrieved October 31, 2009, from http://en.wikipedia.org/wiki/Social_theory

APPENDIX A: REFERENCE WORKS ON MAAD

For those who wish to gain a deeper understanding of MAAD and to see how it has been applied within the IS field, this reference list is provided.

1. Archer (1988, 1995, 2000, 2003) are reference literature from the sociological discipline. The first two books describe MAAD as applied to culture and then generally to social structures. The last two deal with internal conversation theory
2. Archer (1982) provides an interesting critique of structuration theory from the MAAD perspective.
3. Alastair Mutch has done some significant work with both critical realism and with MAAD in the information systems field
   a. Mutch (2002) provides a useful distinction between Actor-Network Theory and MAAD
   b. Mutch (2007) compares MAAD with ST
4. Cuellar (2007) provides an overview of MAAD and how it may be applied to the IS field
5. Volkoff, Strong, and Elmes (2007) is the first, although flawed, use of MAAD in IS. It is not a true application of Archer's theory as it does not use the critical realism underpinnings.
6. de Vaujany (2008) has applied Archer's later investigations into Internal Conversation Theory (Archer, 2000, 2003) to the IS field.

This work was previously published in International Journal of Information Technology Project Management, Volume 1, Issue 4, edited by John Wang, pp. 38-52, copyright 2010 by IGI Publishing (an imprint of IGI Global).

Chapter 15
Runaway Information Technology Projects:
A Punctuated Equilibrium Analysis

M. Keith Wright
University of Houston, USA

Charles J. Capps III
Sam Houston State University, USA

ABSTRACT

This paper presents an in-depth insider's case study of a "runaway" information systems (IS) project in a U.S. State government agency. Because such projects are politically sensitive matters and often obscured from public view, details of how such projects operate are not well understood. This case study adds new details to the body of knowledge surrounding IS project escalation and de-escalation. The authors' resulting project narrative details how this project went out of control for so long, raising important questions for future research in theory development for both IS project escalation and de-escalation. The paper argues that a punctuated equilibrium approach to analyzing "runaway" IS projects are a more fruitful area to explore than are "stage models."

INTRODUCTION

Information Systems (IS) project failure is a costly problem, and it is well known that failing projects can seem to take on a life of their own without adding business value (Zmud, 1980; DeMarco, 1982; Abdel-Hamid & Madnick, 1991; Johnson, 1995). A study of over 8,000 IS projects by Johnson (1995) revealed that only 16 percent were completed on time and within budget. The most studied projects are those that wasted hundreds of millions of dollars, and attracted lots of press. Examples are the FBI Trilogy project (Knorr, 2005; US GAO, 2006), the California Motor Vehicles Driver Licensing System (Bozman, 1994), and the Denver airport baggage handling system (Montealegre & Keil, 2000). These cases of IS projects going wildly over time and budget are called "runaways" (Glass, 1998; Mann, 2003). The management behavior that underlies runaway

DOI: 10.4018/978-1-4666-0930-3.ch015

projects resembles what psychologists have called "escalation of commitment to a failing course of action" (Brockner, 1992; Keil, 1995). IS project de-escalation, on the other hand, has been defined as the reverse of this process (Keil & Robey, 1999; Montealegre & Keil, 2000; Royer, 2003; Heng et al., 2003) (see Table 1).

The literature surrounding both project escalation and de-escalation have suggested four general types of determinant factors of project commitment: project, psychological, social, and organizational (For a good review of this see Newman & Sabherwal, 1996). However because only a handful of in-depth case studies have been published in this area (Newman & Sabherwal, 1996; Montealegre & Keil, 2000; Pan et al., 2006a; Pan et al., 2006b), little is known about the interaction effects of these factors. This is a view shared by luminaries in the field of IS project escalation (Staw, 1997; Mahring & Keil, 2008). Because we feel that improved understanding of IS project escalation will increase the chance of discovering effective counter-measures, we decided to examine the case presented here.

The paper is organized as follows. First is a literature review of both IS project escalation and de-escalation -- including perspectives from psychology, information systems, and organizational behavior. Second we present the (unpublished) case of a runaway IS project in a U.S. State agency, we call the Workers Compensation Commission (WCC). This project lasted over eighteen years, and was particularly resistant to attempts to substantially redirect or stop it, despite the presence of many of the de-escalation triggers mentioned in the IS literature (see Table 1.) Third, our paper discusses the limits of the ability of existing theory to describe the WCC case. The paper concludes with a summary of the resulting important unanswered research questions raised by our analysis. We stop short of offering a new process model for IS project escalation or de-escalation, but argue that the punctuated equilibrium theory (Eldredge & Gould, 1972) of organizational change offers a promising overarching framework for future important research in these areas. Punctuated equilibrium models have their roots in biology (Eldredge & Gould, 1972) but are increasingly being proposed in the organizational sciences (e.g., Tushman & Anderson, 1986; Mokyr, 1990; Gersick, 1991).

LITERATURE REVIEW

The roots of both project escalation and de-escalation research can be traced to psychology and organizational science. The literature suggests four general types of determinant factors of project commitment: *project, psychological, social, and organizational* (Newman & Sabherwal, 1996; Keil & Robey, 1999; Pan et al., 2006).

Project factors are its costs and benefits as perceived by management. Projects are seen prone to escalation when they involve a large potential payoff, when they require a long-term investment before substantial gain, and when setbacks are perceived as temporary surmountable problems (Keil, 1995; Keil, Man, & Rai, 2000).

Table 1. Proposed information system project de-escalation triggers

Recognizing unambiguous negative feedback	Garland and Conlon (1998); Ross and Staw (1993); Montealegre and Keil (2000)
Clarifying the magnitude of the problem	Rubin and Brockner (1975); Brockner (1992)
Separation of duties	Barton et al. (1989)
Redefining the problem	Tversky and Khaneman (1981); Montealegre and Keil (2000)

Psychological factors are those that cause managers to believe the project will eventually be successful (Brockner, 1992). These include the manager's previous experience, the degree to which the manager feels personally responsible for the project (Newman & Sabherwal, 1996, p. 28) and cognitive biases (Tversky & Kahneman, 1981).

One line of psychological research suggests that managers may engage in a kind of "self-justification" behavior in which they tend to commit additional resources to a project rather than to end it and admit their earlier decisions incorrect (Whyte, 1986; Staw & Ross, 1987; Ross & Staw, 1993). This line of research, known as self-justification theory (SJT), is grounded in Festinger's (1957) theory of cognitive dissonance.

Another line of psychological research known as "prospect theory" focuses on the cognitive biases that influence human decision making under uncertainty. Prospect theory posits that people choose between risk averse and risk seeking behavior depending on how a problem is "framed" (Tversky & Kahneman, 1981). Research has shown that people exhibit risk seeking behavior when choosing between, on the one hand, a sure loss (e.g., the initial loss on the investment resulting from a de-escalated project) and, on the other hand, a small chance for a large gain (e.g., a successful project outcome) combined with a large chance of a large loss (e.g., a failed project) (Tversky & Khaneman, 1981). Derived from prospect theory is the so-called "sunk cost" effect in which decision makers exhibit a tendency to "throw good money after bad" (Garland & Conlon, 1998). This research suggests that sunk costs may influence decision makers to adopt a negative frame, thereby promoting risk seeking (IS project escalation) behavior.

Another psychological theory related to IS project management decisions is approach-avoidance theory (Rubin & Brockner, 1975; Brockner, 1992). Approach-avoidance theory has been applied to the problem of IS project escalation, where it has been suggested there is a natural tendency for IS projects to escalate because their "driving" forces usually outweigh "restraining" forces (Pan et al., 2006). One of these driving forces "the completion effect" suggests the motivation to achieve a goal increases as an individual gets closer to that goal (Garland & Conlon, 1998). The completion effect may be particularly germane to software projects, which frequently exhibit the so-called "90% complete" syndrome (DeMarco, 1982; Garland & Conlon, 1998).

Social factors have also been said to promote IS project escalation (Newman & Sabherwal, 1996; Pan et al., 2006). These factors include competitive rivalry with other social groups, the need for external justification, and norms for consistency (Brockner et al., 1979; Hirschhem, Klein, & Newman, 1991). Projects are prone to escalation when competitive rivalry exists between the decision-making group and another social group, when external stakeholders believe the project will be successful, or when norms of behavior favor persistence (Ross & Staw, 1993). One social determinant of commitment is "the desire not to lose face or credibility with others" (Staw & Ross, 1987, p. 55). This concept of "face saving" is grounded in self-justification theory (Whyte, 1986; Staw & Ross, 1987; Ross & Staw, 1993) and has been discussed in the IS project de-escalation literature (Montealegre and Keil, 2000).

Organizational factors include the structural and political factors that form the "ecosystem" of a project. These are particularly relevant to understanding the events that transpired during our case study of the WCC. Of particular importance in our case is what organization theory calls the "agency effect" defining the agency relationship as "a contract under which one or more persons (the principal(s)) engage another person (the agent) to perform some service on their behalf which involves delegating some decision authority to the agent" (Jensen & Meckling, 1986). Furthermore, agency relationships may exist between different levels within a firm's hierarchy (Jensen & Meckling, 1986). Agency theory predicts that goal incongruence between principal and agent creates a situation in which the agent acts in a self-interested manner, rather than acting in the best interests of the principal. The concept of information asymmetry is central to all principal-agent models; agents are assumed to have private information to which the principal cannot freely gain access (Baiman, 1990). Further, agents are presumed to be work-averse. This combination of information asymmetry and work aversion promotes the agent's self-interested behavior. The agency problem is likely to occur in IS projects because software's invisible nature contributes to information asymmetry (DeMarco, 1982; Abdel-Hamidand & Madnick, 1991). Agency theory may also be used to explain IS project de-escalation (Montealegre & Keil, 2000).

Information systems researchers (for example Keil, Mann, & Rai, 2000) have referred to several other organizational factors relevant to our case study that may affect commitment to an IS project. These are top management's knowledge of information technology (Vitale et al., 1986), information intensity of the organization's value chain (Johnston & Carrico, 1988) and maturity of the IS function (Sabherwal & King, 1992). Other organizational factors identified in the literature about IS project escalation and de-escalation include top management support for the project, administrative inertia in the organization, and the extent to which the project is institutionalized or the extent to which it seems strategic (Johnston & Carrico, 1988).

Recent work on IT project de-escalation suggests projects may be resistant to de-escalation because of organizational "inertia" which causes long periods of organizational "equilibrium" that are difficult to disrupt because of the constancy of the "deep structure" of the organization (Gersick, 1991; Pan et al., 2006). This line of research has suggested that organizations may be unable to change substantially unless forced by a crisis

(Tushman & Romanelli, 1985). In a number of industries, it has been observed that long periods of unsuccessful "incremental" organizational changes tend to be interrupted by short periods of "radical" changes called "revolutionary periods" (Abernathy & Utterback, 1978; Utterback, 1994). This pattern has been called "punctuated equilibrium," a term that originated in biology (Eldredge & Gould, 1972) and subsequently was adopted in the management literature (e.g., Tushman & Anderson, 1986; Mokyr, 1990). According to punctuated equilibrium theory, organizations tend towards "equilibrium" -- due to the permanence of the "deep structure" of the organization. According to Anderson and Tushman (1990, p. 161), "The *deep structure* of an organization consists of its "alliances, associations and co operations with interlocking interests."

Tushman and Romanelli (1985, p. 176) define this "deep structure" as follows: ... " it can be described by five facets: (1) core beliefs and values regarding the organization, its employees, and its environment; (2) products, markets, technology and competitive timing; (3) the distribution of power; (4) the organization's structure; and (5) the nature, type and pervasiveness of control systems."

Gersick (1989) argues that sunk costs occurring during periods of equilibrium, along with fear of losing control over one's situation if the equilibrium ends; contribute heavily to the human motivation to avoid significant system change. Other organizational research has discussed the inertial constraints of obligations among stakeholders inside and outside a system. As Tushman and Romanelli (1985, p. 177) suggested, "even if a system overcomes its own cognitive and motivational barriers against realizing a need for change, the 'networks of interdependent resource relationships and value commitments' generated by its structure often prevent its being able to change."

This analysis complements Tushman and Romanelli's (1985, p. 179) identification of "performance pressures . . . whether anticipated or actual as the fundamental agents of organizational reorientation." Tushman, Newman, and Romanelli (1986) described as typical the scenario of an organization falling into serious trouble before responding by replacing its top management. They found that "externally recruited executives are more than three times more likely to initiate frame-breaking change than existing executive teams… Failures caused by inappropriate deep structures are destined to elude the (misdirected) efforts of current system members to correct them. Unless such failures kill the system, they command increasing attention and raise the likelihood that newcomers will either be attracted or recruited to help solve the problems. The newcomer has the opportunity to see the system in an entirely different context than incumbent members, and he or she may begin problem solving on a new path."

We trust the preceding literature review demonstrates the extreme complexity of the study of information system (IS) project escalation and de-escalation. Existing research has demonstrated the presence of many important factors that affect commitment to a failing IS project. We feel this research has been appropriately guided by the assumption that IS projects live in organizations comprised of many goal directed individuals whose purposes may be incompatible. In this context an IS project emerges within an organizational ecosystem but often develops its own identity. It is a search for detailed descriptions of a runaway IS project and its organizational ecosystem that determined our choice of research methods.

RESEARCH METHOD

To encompass the complexity of organizational research, our approach assumed a simple learning and description role rather than a hypothesis testing one. This qualitative approach has been effectively used elsewhere (Sutton, 1987; Isabella, 1990; Ancona, 1990; Pettigrew, 1990; Elsbach & Sutton, 1992; Orlikowski, 1993). Our data col-

lection and presentation method resembles that of the "ethnographic confessional" approach used by Schultze (2000). (See also Agar, 1986; Marcus & Fischer, 1986; Atkinson & Hammersley, 1994; Van Maanen, 1995).

We selected our research site in the fall of 2004. From press accounts, we identified a U.S. State government agency involved with health insurance claims. The health insurance industry is known for the "information intensity of its value chain" (See Johnston & Carrico, 1988) and is thus a likely birthplace of a runaway IS project. The agency, we call the Workers Compensation Commission (WCC), was well known for being one of the most inefficient of its kind in the U.S. The principal investigator (PI) approached the agency's Director of Internal Audit with a request to collect data on a troubled IS project. In response, the PI received permission to collect data on a WCC software development project called the *WEBCOMP* project. (All proper names of projects or organizations used in this paper are pseudonyms.) The agency Commissioner had recently asked Internal Audit to monitor the project. A formal internal audit of the project was not however in the department's audit charter that year.

The PI received permission to collect data on the project with the understanding the data might be used for published academic research. However, in return, the PI, a certified information systems auditor, was asked to perform the project monitoring function for the Internal Audit Director. He introduced the PI to the organization as a part-time information systems auditor with permission to monitor the *WEBCOMP* project. The PI's role was a double-edged sword: the resulting visibility and legitimacy made gaining access to internal documents, auditors and technical staff easy. However, access at the managerial level was more difficult. By 2004, the status of the project as troubled had long ago become an albatross for management. The PI interacted primarily with three other groups in addition to the Internal Audit Department. One was the software development team, including contractors. Second was the project management team including the agency Commissioner, the agency Director, the manager of IT Services and her three subordinates. The third was the computer system administrators.

The PI was in the field over an eight-month period, from December 2004 to mid-July 2005. He was at the agency during business hours on the three days per week when WEBCOMP project meetings were held. While in the field, he conducted twenty-eight semi-structured, interviews in his office supplied by the agency (see interview questions listed in Table 2). The interviewees included project staff, internal auditors, project management, and agency management. All interviews were one on one and each interviewee was assured of complete confidentiality.

Reliability was increased by using the narratives from one subject to confirm or contradict others (Miles, 1979). The PI did not attempt to privilege one story over another. During interviews and meetings, the PI took hand-written notes, which he recorded on his laptop during the day. He was always cognizant of the trade-off between writing more detailed descriptions of events -- and observing interactions with people in the field and tended to err on the side of seeking encounters with people.

While in the field, to corroborate interview data, the PI collected a variety of historical documents including memos, outsourcing contracts, staff resumes, internal project documentation, public reports, and presentations to congressional committees. Throughout his fieldwork, the PI was engaged in data analysis. He had lunch with the Internal Audit Director once a week to make sense of current project events, identify themes and gaps in the data, and to strategize how to fill those gaps. The PI submitted weekly reports and recommendations to the Internal Audit Director about the project.

After the PI left the field, data were collected via newspaper accounts and public web site postings. Telephone interviews with remaining staff were also conducted -- after explaining that we were conducting academic research.

As a first step in post-field data analysis, the authors analyzed project antecedent conditions and the project outcome. Then a detailed project history was created in narrative form from 1990 to 2008. Next, we organized the narrative into the major events that framed management commitment to the project. This approach involved reanalyzing events in terms of the commonly held determinant factors of project commitment as revealed in the literature review. These included project, structural, social, psychological, and political factors. This type of protocol analysis has described similar case studies (Montealegre & Keil, 2000; Pan et al., 2006). We performed three iterations of this analysis before event descriptions were established. The results were then presented to an appropriate manager at the state agency for his corroboration of the events, which he provided at the time of this case writing, summer 2009.

Table 2. Interview questions

What is your role in the WEBCOMP project?
Can you take me through the project history?
What is the next project milestone on which you are working?
What is your estimate of the probable date you will achieve this milestone?
Is there anything that I or anyone else can do to help you achieve this milestone?
Is there anything else you would like to share?

RESULTS

Case Summary

Appendix A narrates in depth the critical factors that our data suggests determined management commitment to a series of related failed IS projects at the Workers Compensation Commission (WCC) from 1990 to 2008. In general, the narrative data suggests that ineffective state IT governance resulted in over $27 million wasted on these projects. Because these projects all aimed at the same underlying business problem, we collectively called these the Workers Compensation System (WCS) project. The WCS project was born in a politically charged environment, and quickly became institutionalized. This likely made the project resistant to attempts to de-escalate it for over sixteen years. Our review of WCC personnel records revealed that low salary structures probably contributed to the State's inability to hire qualified staff (see Appendix A, Events 7, 10, 12) and diminished the agency's belief in the eventual success of the project.[1] This lack of perceived organizational self-efficacy combined with extreme political pressure encouraged project shortcutting, which resulted in insufficient requirements capture and then extensive rework (Events 2, 5, 7, 9, 11). Furthermore, parallel project tasks were attempted when obvious dependencies existed (Event 8). Finally, our data suggests the project was poorly monitored. Because of this complex set of political and structural factors, the project was officially de-escalated in 2007, after sixteen years -- by partial abandonment (Event 26).

DISCUSSION

Goal Incongruence

Our data suggests an important determinant of management commitment to the Workers Compensation Systems (WCS) project was extreme

goal incongruence among the project stakeholders. As mentioned earlier, the study of goal incongruence in IS projects has been framed in "agency theory" (Jensen & Meckling, 1986) which suggests an "agency relationship" may exist between different levels of a firm's hierarchy. On one level, our data indicated goal incongruence between those of WCC staff and those of the State's IT governing bodies. The State's goal, we assume, was to efficiently process workers compensation claims. However, the WCC goal was likely something else. As explained earlier, the WCC staff did not seem to believe the WCS project was feasible, given the organizational factors present at that time. Many agency staff seemed to make project decisions based mainly on self-interest rather than on project interests. WCC staff seemed committed to the WCS project only to the extent it would increase skills that they could then apply on some other -- possibly successful -- project. For example, some of the later WCS project "make-or-buy" decisions seemed to be based on the belief that the best way to learn a technology is to develop it from scratch, rather than to buy an off-the-shelf solution (Event 12).

Risk Aversion

An important determinant of management commitment to the WCS project suggested by our data was risk aversion. These included political risk ("face saving") and monetary risk (Ross & Staw, 1993; Montealegre & Keil, 2000). Our narrative suggests that the inability of the WCC managers to "save face" may have been a key reason for the runaway escalation of the WCS project. For example, it was very difficult for the State's IT governance bodies to save face, because they were responsible for approving all expenditures throughout the long series of failed projects. Corroborating this interpretation was our principal investigator's interview with the State Auditor's Office (SAO) (Event 22). During the interview, one of the SAO staff let it slip that, due to a fundamental lack of independence; the State's audit function was "completely corrupted."

However, the ability to "save face" -- and thus avoid political risk – seemed to change markedly after the transfer of the WCS project management from the Workers Compensation Commission (WCC) to the Department of Insurance (DI). For the first time in the project's long history, business requirements analysts were in control of disbursements from the WCS technical project budget. These non-technical DI business managers could "save face" by blaming the former WCC technical managers for the project failures (Event 21, 24, 25). Furthermore, seen in the light of "face saving" behavior, we assume the only way the Governor's office could "save face" was to adopt the Sunset Commission's recommendation to eliminate WCC in 2007.

Another important risk aversion behavior our data indicated was that of Corp2 – a project contractor. This finding is consistent with other examples of major contractors resisting project de-escalation (Ross & Staw, 1993; Montealegre & Keil, 2000). Just prior to the WCS de-escalation, Corp2 was actively engaged in a bid for an $863 million contract with an agency in the same state, the Information Resources Department (IRD) (Events 25, 26). That project was to "streamline the information technology operations of 27 state agencies" including WCC (Event 26). Corp2 resistance to de-escalating the WCS project may have dropped when Corp2 won the DIR contract (Event 26). If so, the finding is consistent with the idea of the "enfranchising stakeholders" as a de-escalation trigger (Montealegre & Keil, 2000). However, it is not strong support for this trigger, because we have no direct data explaining why Corp2 received the new $863 million contract, especially given the company's long association with the notorious WCS project. Thus, we believe a promising specific area for future research in IS project escalation would be to examine the role of industry lobbyists in the awarding of U.S. State IS contracts. More generally, our preceding discus-

sion of risk aversion suggests a need for a better understanding of optimal risk sharing structures in U.S. State IT governance.

The Role of Collective Belief

An important determinant of management commitment to an IS project is termed "collective belief" in the eventual success of the project (Royer, 2002). However, the way in which this operated in the WCC case runs counter to that reported in Royer (2002). Royer (2002) found that "collective belief" in the eventual success of the project was a primary determinant of continued project commitment. Yet, throughout the WCS project, there were widespread doubts about the inherent ability of the WCC to complete this project successfully. These doubts contributed to a downward spiral of events, the most critical of which was probably to have bought the original software (COMPASS) system, which quickly gained the reputation of not meeting the business requirements (Event 2). However, the WCS project continued half-heartedly for years, with constant staff turnover. Historical documents and interviews with WCC managers indicated that the general perception was the project was greatly under funded from the beginning. Our interviews with technical staff suggested they saw no way to gain from *any* behavior in their project role despite their own individual best efforts because management incompetence or inadequate legislative funding would prevent the project from ultimately succeeding. These either staff members seemed to expect that management would ignore ideas for improvement because they would not be understood or thought too expensive.

Contributing to the apparent pessimism surrounding the WCS project may have been the lack of personal accountability for it. Historical documents indicated no one person outside the Governor had complete responsibility for the project. Our interviews also indicated that no one might have had sufficient formal accountability for the project: project problems were usually blamed on some structural factor out of the interviewee's control. For example, WCC managers blamed the project failings on the legislature for a salary structure that did not support hiring qualified technical people (Event 4). In turn, technical staff blamed business analysts for not doing requirements correctly, and blamed management for incompetence. The requirements analysts blamed the requirements shortcomings on the legislature for writing bad law (Events 5, 9, 10, 11). These results contradict Royer (2002) and suggest that a promising area for future research would be the effects of management experience and organizational structure on the perception of management self-efficacy. This is a view shared by Mahring and Keil (2008) and has been dealt with tangentially in the following works: Kahn (1990), Arkes (1991), Boulding, Morgain, and Staelin (1997), Schmid and Calantone (2002), and Whyte and Fassina (2007).

Project Institutionalization

A critical determinant of IS project commitment discussed in the literature is the degree to which IS projects are "institutionalized" (Johnston & Carrico, 1988; Pan et al., 2006). Institutionalized projects have also been referred to as "mission critical" (Mahring & Keil, 2008) or those of "high business criticality" (Pan et al., 2006). Our WCS project narrative supports the idea that the project was institutionalized from the beginning because WCS was strongly linked to WCC's mission (Events 1, 5). However, our case does not clearly support prior research on project de-institutionalization as a trigger for de-escalation (see Table 1). According to Ross and Staw (1993), "De-escalation can be facilitated when an organization de-institutionalizes a project, removing it from the core of the firm either by moving it physically away from the central location of the company or by emphasizing its peripheral nature." In this case, however it is not clear if the WCS project was ever deinstitutionalized (Event 26).

Redefining the Problem

An important IS project de-escalation "trigger" is called "redefining the problem" (Montealegre & Keil, 2000). Our data suggest there were four major WCS project redefinitions, all aimed at the same underlying business problem – the efficient processing of workers compensation claims. The original 1990 project definition was simply to use the COMPASS system purchased from another state (Event 1). The first redefinition was to modify the COMPASS system to fit existing business processes better (Event 4). The second redefinition was to replace COMPASS with the *WEBCOMP* system – a web based system to be developed from scratch (Event 7). This involved reengineering the WCC business processes. The third redefinition happened after the Department of Insurance (DI) replaced the WCS project management team (Event 21). This re-definition was to convert COMPASS feature by feature to a web based system (Event 23). This involved a substantial reinstatement of the original WCC business processes. However, it was only the fourth redefinition that produced de-escalation. That definition focused on publicly redefining the underlying business problem to be mainly the expensive Corp3 contract - the maintenance contract for the original COMPASS system (Event 25). The technical solution then became simple and twofold: use the source code of the COMPASS system as the basis of a requirements document and then convert that code, feature by feature, to run on cheaper PC based servers rather than on the more expensive mainframe.

However, as of this writing, it is likely the actual original business problem underlying all the WCS project incarnations – namely, the efficient handling of workers compensation claims -- has yet to be addressed (Event 26). Thus, our data suggest the fourth and last project re-definition was used mainly for political purposes ("face saving") rather than to address real business problems. This finding suggests that another promising area for future research on IS project de-escalation would be to identify the conditions under which project redefinitions address underlying business problems rather than politics.

Limits of Current Theory

In brief, our previous discussion of the WCC case discussed how aspects of this case relate to some of the critical determinants of management commitment to IS projects proposed in the psychology and organizational behavior sciences literature. This literature has offered convincing but disjointed evidence of certain such determinants. In an effort to integrate and frame these disjointed theoretical contributions, the IS literature has contributed primarily by offering "stage" models of both escalation (Staw & Ross, 1987; Mahring & Keil, 2008) and de-escalation (Montealegre & Keil, 2000). Such models are based on a limited number of case studies.

For example, Staw and Ross (1987) proposed a model (see Table 3) which is based on the analysis of British Columbia's decision to host the 1986 World's Fair (Ross & Staw, 1986), where it was observed that escalation began because of project-related factors and then was reinforced by psychological, then social, and finally organizational factors. However, that model is not well supported in subsequent case research (Ross & Staw, 1993; Newman & Sabherwal, 1996). Subsequent research suggested the sequencing of those factors is not that simple. For example Ross and Staw (1993) applied the model to the analysis of the Shoreham Nuclear Power Plant case, and concluded that the "contextual influences

Table 3. Staw and Ross (1987) model of IS project escalation

Phase 1: Promise of Future Outcomes
Phase 2: Receipt of Questionable Outcomes
Phase 3: Receipt of Highly Negative Outcomes

became a very powerful force in the Shoreham case in ways the model would not predict" (Ross & Staw, 1993, pp. 722-723). Newman and Sabherwal (1996) applied the Staw and Ross model to the CENTCO case, an inventory control and materials management system in a large North American firm. They found that "project and structural determinants are crucial in obtaining initial commitment for the IS project: social and structural determinants influence whether commitment is withdrawn, and psychological and project determinants influence escalation of commitment" (Newman & Sabherwal, 1996, p. 45).

The WCC case presented in this paper suggests that political factors were the most important project influences on both escalation and de-escalation throughout the long project. This result together with those of Ross and Staw (1993) and Newman and Sabherwal (1996) suggest that temporal sequencing of different types commitment determinates may not be a fruitful way to develop a general theory of IS project escalation or de-escalation. This is a view shared by leading researchers in project escalation theory. For example, Mahring and Keil (2008) concluded that the Staw and Ross model "fails to provide an understanding of the dynamics of escalation. It does not explain what really distinguishes one phase from another or what triggers the movement from one phase to another" (Mahring & Keil, 2008, p. 242).

In an effort to suggest a more general model of IS project escalation Royer (2002) proposed an eight-phase model (see Table 4) based on two cases. Additionally, Royer cautioned that one of the two cases grounding the model "did not seem to include the relentless phase and the other included successive identical phases" (Royer 2002, p. 6). Furthermore, Mahring and Keil (2008, p. 243) critiqued Royer's model as an improvement over the Staw and Ross model in that it ncludes transitions triggers. However, the Royer model blurs the distinction between escalation and de-escalation.[ii]

Table 4. Royer (2002) model of IS project escalation

Phase 1: Birth of the idea
Phase 2: Organization of project
Phase 3: Implementation
Phase 4: Blindly going on
Phase 5: Relentlessness
Phase 6: Diagnosis
Phase 7: Verification
Phase 8: Implementation of withdrawal

Table 5. Mahring and Keil (2008) model of IS project escalation

Antecedent Condition: Project framing
Phase1: Drift → problem emergence
Phase2: Unsuccessful incremental adaptation, → increased visibility
Phase3: Rationalized continuation→imminent threat
Outcome: De-escalation

The Royer (2002) model is also problematic in application to our WCC case because it is difficult to determine the periods in which the model can be applied. In the case of WCC, it is arguable how many "projects" there were. One could argue there were at least four -- corresponding to the four major case "periods" (See Figure 1). On the other hand, because all these projects were intimately related, aimed at the same underlying business problem, and governed by the same state authorities, one could argue that the Royer model should be applied as if there was only one long project, not four shorter ones.

In an effort to encompass more complexity than that of the Royer (2002) model, Mahring and Keil (2008) proposed a three phase model of escalation, where "catalysts" promote escalation within each phase and "transition triggers" push the process from one phase to the next (see Table 5). In that model, proceeding the period of escalation is an "antecedent condition" which encompasses the rationale for the project and how it is viewed. The first escalation phase called "drift" is when the project continues to consume resources as ambiguity concerning the project charter is resolved. "Problem emergence" then triggers the shift to the second phase, "unsuccessful incremental adaptation." During this phase, there is a continued "mismatch between underlying problems and attempted remedies." Together, these two "catalysts" produce continued escalation

that triggers the third phase, "rationalized continuation." When rationalizations lose their credibility, an imminent threat to project continuation triggers project de-escalation, which is modeled as the outcome of the process of escalation.

The Mahring and Keil model, although offering a better description of the WCC case than any other stage models, fails to capture the political complexity of the WCC case. Furthermore, it is again difficult to determine the period in which the model can be applied. This is because the model, as that of Royer (2002) focuses on a "project" rather than on the underlying business problem. Another limitation of applying the Mahring and Keil model to the WCC case is their model does not distinguish between a project that is successfully de-escalated and one that is unsuccessfully de-escalated. In our view a successful de-escalation is one in which the underlying business requirements either disappear -- because of non-project related factors -- or the project is redirected in such a way that it eventually meets its original business requirements. Our data suggest that the WCS project was not de-escalated successfully, because the underlying business problem remained after the project was substantially abandoned (Event 26).

In brief, the existing stage models found in our literature search do not capture the complexity of cases like the WCS, which seem to undulate back and forth -- creating and stopping projects, only to revive them again (See Pan et al., 2006). This difficulty lies in the over simplicity of such

Figure 1. WCC Projects Timeline

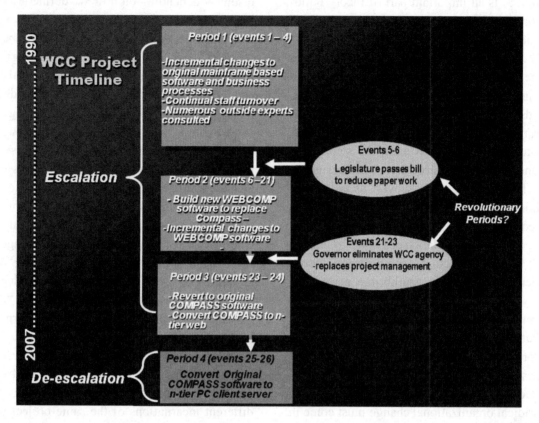

"stage" models. These models struggle with the assumption that individual systems of the same type develop along the same path and in "forward" directions. One reason for this, as Gersick (1988) points out, is that the development of such stage models "seeks commonalities in the outcomes of project decisions but dismiss individual project differences as noise" (Gersick, 1991, p. 16).

Other research has supported this idea that stage models may not be particularly useful as a framework for studying organizational change and IS project management (Rubin & Brockner, 1975; Tushman & Romanelli, 1985; Gersick, 1991; Stubbart & Smalley, 1999; Pan et al., 2006).

Project Life Cycle as Punctuated Equilibrium

Our discussion thus far suggests that better theories of IS project escalation and de-escalation should allow for common decision/event categories, and for infinite variety in the individual systems' particular solutions. Punctuated equilibrium theory may offer some insight here. In a punctuated equilibrium framework runaway IS projects can generally be viewed as recurring cycles of long periods of organizational equilibrium followed by shorter periods of disequilibrium. Seen in this light, an IS project tends toward escalation equilibrium because of the stability of the organization's "deep structure." In general, "deep structure" may be thought of as the "design of the playing field and the rules of the game" (Gersick, 1991, p. 16). More specifically, deep structure is the set of fundamental "choices an organization has made including the basic parts into which its units will be organized and the basic activity patterns that will maintain its existence…Deep structures are highly stable because the trail of choices made rules many options out. Identifying these sets of choices is an important part of theory building for specific punctuated equilibrium models" (Gersick, 1991).

The equilibrium period -- comparable to a "game in play" -- consists of maintaining and carrying out these choices. Within equilibrium periods, the organization's deep structure remains the same. "Human systems in equilibrium may look turbulent enough to mask the stability of the underlying deep structure. A project group may choose implicitly to subvert its task, or an organization may commit to a strategy it is not well equipped to accomplish, resulting in patterns of overt conflict, vacillation or failure" (Gersick, 1991, p. 16). Punctuated equilibrium theory predicts that during an equilibrium period, the only type of organizational change possible is an "incremental" one. One likely to be unsuccessful if what is really needed is a "radical" change -- of the sort that an IS project de-escalation has been suggested to be (Pann et al., 2006).

According to "punctuated equilibrium" theory, any radical organizational change must come in short periods of "disequilibrium." Transition from equilibrium to disequilibrium occurs because of events called "critical," "radical," or "revolutionary" (Gersick, 1991). The difference between the incremental organizational changes in equilibrium periods and the revolutionary changes in disequilibrium periods is like the difference between changing the game of football by moving the goal posts versus changing it by removing them. Only the first kind of change leaves the game's deep structure intact. Thus punctuated equilibrium theory predicts that an organization's deep structure must be dismantled, leaving the system temporarily disorganized, before fundamental organizational changes can be accomplished (Gersick, 1991).

The data we were able to capture during our study of the WCS case does not permit description here of a completely satisfactory punctuated equilibrium model of IS project escalation. Nevertheless, the theory does offer one of two interesting

results -- depending on how we define the deep structure of the WCC. For example, under one interpretation, the WCS case can be described as four periods of "equilibrium" corresponding to the four periods seen in Figure 1. Project escalation can then be said to have occurred in periods one through three, with de-escalation occurring only in period four. The "disequilibrium" periods can be described as Events 5-6 and 21-23. These two periods could reasonably be described as what Gersick would call "revolutionary" because each resulted in a complete shakeup of the WCS project management at the agency level. However, our data does not let us conclude whether or not agency level organization should be termed the true "deep structure" of the WCS project. Nevertheless, it seems more reasonable to assume that the "deep structure" included the State level IT governance bodies including the Governor's office, the State Legislature, and the State Auditor's Office.

Seen in this light, the WCS case can be described as one long period of equilibrium in which different incarnations of the same project were unsuccessful "incremental" attempts to solve the underlying business problem. In this light, it seems more reasonable to assume the WCS project is today still slowly escalating and is thus not adequately addressing the underlying business problem. Therefore, an entirely reasonable expectation from such a punctuated equilibrium analysis is that the WCS project will continue escalating until the election of a new Governor, or a radical realignment of the State Legislature.

CONCLUSION

In conclusion, many insights emerge from this study. Our research supports the prior research illustrating that after a considerable effort has been invested in an IS project, powerful forces can result in escalation. These include "completion effects" (Garland, 1990), "deaf effects" (Events 16, 17) (Cuellar et al., 2006), "mum effects" (Events 16,

18) (Smith & Keil, 2003), "face saving" behavior (Events 22-26) (Staw & Ross, 1987) and biased belief updating (Boulding et al., 1997; Snow & Keil, 2002; Snow et al., 2007; Thompson, Smith, & Iacovou, 2007). Secondly, this WCC case supports the idea escalation is a complex gradual process that is difficult to capture with a temporal process model. Third our results suggest project escalation should be expected to occur in most large IS projects and that when it does, it will do so in a manner consistent with that of an organization in "equilibrium."

Thus, the importance of employing solid project monitoring and control techniques cannot be overstated (Wright & Capps, 2008). The relationship between control practices and the escalation process is a promising area for future research (See also Kirsch, 1997; Mahring, 2002; Kirsch, 2004; Tiwana & Bush, 2007). Another promising area for research would be to go beyond the results of Mahring (2002) and Kirsch (2004) to explore further, whether the constitution and effectiveness of project governance is inversely related to escalation. For example, it would be of interest to explore if the organization's ability to adapt control practices to the dynamic nature of complex projects reduces the likelihood of escalation periods. The relationship between escalation and the requirements determination process is another possible area for future research (See Kirsch & Haney, 2006).

Our analysis suggests it is more important to study why information systems organizations are repeatedly ineffective in addressing business problems than it is to study why they do not respond to problems at all. This suggests that future models of the escalation/de-escalation process should focus less on "projects" and more on the life cycle of the underlying business problem. This study raises the following specific research questions:

1. What are the most important set of organizational choices forming the "deep structure" of an information systems (IS) project organization?

2. Are U.S. State government IS projects prone to escalation and resistant to de-escalation?

3. How can large organizations be structured to prevent projects from escalation and make them more amenable to de-escalation?

4. What are the factors governing when IS project redefinitions are used mainly for political purposes rather than to address real business problems?

5. What are the factors governing when an IS project can be de-escalated without "revolutionary" organizational change?

6. How do IS projects function during revolutionary periods?

7. How do IS project revolutionary periods conclude?

8. How is an organization's perception of its self-efficacy related to IS project escalation?

9. What are the factors that determine the believability of management reports about project progress?

There are at least three basic limitations of this study. The first is the production of its project narrative (See Appendix) which depended on the personal judgment of the principal investigator and authors. The narrative contains some conjecture about what actually happened during periods where data were not readily available. Although the narrative covers eighteen years, our principal investigator (PI) was only available for direct observation from 2004-2005. Second, because the PI was viewed by the Workers Compensation Commission (WCC) organization as an auditor, he may have been threatening to management. This may have caused management to be less than candid in their responses to interview questions. Third, the PI was able to interview primarily only project management at the WCC agency level, not at the state level. Thus, there are no interview data from the state level IT governance bodies. Because of these limitations in research methods, we cannot propose a new general process model of either project escalation or de-escalation. However, we believe future study of U.S. State IT governance practices could help produce such a new important model, given more of a grounded theory approach to model development (Glaser & Strauss, 1967; Martin & Turner, 1986; Orlikowski, 1993).

Despite the limitations of our research approach, we believe this paper contains some important contributions to research in both IS project escalation and de-escalation. First, the case is based on a rarely published type of in-depth ethnographic perspective (See Agar, 1986; Atkinson & Hammersley, 1994). Next, because the Workers Compensation System (WCS) project took on a misleading political identity, it would have been extremely difficult for any outsider to analyze this case. Project failure is a sensitive subject, and therefore one is seldom allowed access for in-depth case studies. As a result, one must seize single case opportunities (Herriott & Firestone, 1983; Yin, 2003). Furthermore, single cases have been recognized as an accepted way to motivate research questions and to illustrate conceptual constructs that would otherwise be harder to measure (Siggelkow, 2007, p. 21-22). Clearly more IS project management longitudinal case studies are needed -- with an aim of generating an explanatory theory of project escalation and de-escalation cycles. We believe additional insights can come from organization theory and organizational behavior models (See Sutton, 1987; Ancona, 1990; Isabella, 1990; Pettigrew, 1990; Elsbach & Sutton, 1992; Shenhar, 1998; Cule & Robey, 2004). Moreover, there is a need for the IS audit and academic community to join hands in conducting future academic research in government IS projects. Surveys of IS auditors concerning the frequency, circumstances and characteristics of similar projects could be most helpful. Furthermore, the Information Systems Audit and Control Association have supported this type of survey research (See Keil & Robey, 1999). The outsourcing literature (Tiwana & Bush, 2007)

may give further guidance in this area, and we hope our paper offers a small contribution as well.

REFERENCES

Abdel-Hamid, T., & Madnick, S. E. (1991). *Software project dynamics: an integrated approach.* Upper Saddle River, NJ: Prentice Hall.

Abernathy, W., & Utterback, J. M. (1982). Patterns of industrial innovation. In Tushman, M., & Moore, W. (Eds.), *Readings in the Management of Innovation* (pp. 97–108). Boston: Harvard.

Agar, M. H. (1986). *Speaking of ethnography.* Thousand Oaks, CA: Sage.

Ancona, D. (1990). Outward bound: strategies for team survival in an organization. *Academy of Management Journal, 33*(2), 334–365. doi:10.2307/256328

Anderson, P., & Tushman, M. L. (1990). Technological discontinuities and dominant designs. *Administrative Science Quarterly, 35,* 604–633. doi:10.2307/2393511

Arkes, H. R. (1991). Costs and benefits of judgment errors: implications for de-biasing. *Psychological Bulletin, 110,* 486–498. doi:10.1037/0033-2909.110.3.486

Atkinson, P., & Hammersley, M. (1994). Ethnography and participant observation. In Nenzin & Lincoln (Eds.), *Handbook of Qualitative Research* (pp. 248-261). Thousand Oaks, CA: Sage.

Baiman, S. (1990). Agency research in managerial accounting: a second look. *Accounting, Organizations and Society, 4,* 341–371. doi:10.1016/0361-3682(90)90023-N

Barton, S. L., Duchon, D., & Dunegan, K. J. (1989). An empirical test of Staw and Ross's prescriptions for management of escalation of commitment behavior. *Decision Sciences, 20,* 532–544. doi:10.1111/j.1540-5915.1989.tb01565.x

Boulding, W., Morgan, R., & Staeiin, R. (1997). Pulling the plug to stop the new product drain. *JMR, Journal of Marketing Research, 34*(1), 164–116. doi:10.2307/3152073

Bozman, J. S. (1994). *California kills failed $ 44M project*. Computerworld.

Brockner, J. (1992). *The escalation of commitment to a failing course of action: toward theoretical progress*. New York: Wiley and Sons.

Brockner, J., & Rubin, J. (1985). *Entrapment in escalating conflicts: a social psychological analysis*. New York: Springer.

Brockner, J., Shaw, M., & Rubin, J. (1979). Factors affecting withdrawal from an escalating conflict: quitting before it's too late. *Journal of Experimental Social Psychology, 15*, 492–503. doi:10.1016/0022-1031(79)90011-8

Cuellar, M., Keil, M., & Johnson, R. (2006). The deaf effect response to bad news reporting in IS projects. *EService Journal, 5*(1), 75–97. doi:10.2979/ESJ.2006.5.1.75

Cule, P., & Robey, D. (2004). A dual-motor, constructive process model of organizational transition. *Organization Studies, 25*(2), 229–260. doi:10.1177/0170840604040037

Demarco, T. (1982). *Controlling software projects*. New York: Yourdon Press.

Drummond, H. (1998). Is escalation always irrational? *Organization Studies, 19*(6), 911–929. doi:10.1177/017084069801900601

Eldredge, N., & Gould, S. (1972). Punctuated equilibria: an alternative to phyletic gradualism. In Schopf, T. J. (Ed.), *Models in paleobiology* (pp. 82–115). San Francisco, CA: Freeman, Cooper and Co.

Elsbach, K. D., & Sutton, R. I. (1992). Acquiring organizational legitimacy through illegitimate actions: a marriage of institutional and Impression Management Theories. *Academy of Management Journal*, 699–738. doi:10.2307/256313

Festinger, L. A. (1957). *Theory of Cognitive Dissonance*. Evanston, IL: Row, Peterson.

Firestone, H. R. (1983). Multisite qualitative policy research: optimizing description and generalizability. *Educational Researcher, 12*, 14–19.

Garland, H., & Conlon, D. E. (1998). Too close to quit: the role of project completion in maintaining commitment. *Journal of Applied Social Psychology, 28*(22), 2025–2048. doi:10.1111/j.1559-1816.1998.tb01359.x

Gersick, C. (1989). Marking time: Predictable transitions in task groups. *Academy of Management Journal, 32*, 274–309. doi:10.2307/256363

Gersick, C. (1991). Revolutionary change theories: A multilevel exploration of the punctuated equilibrium paradigm. *Academy of Management Review, 16*(1), 10–36. doi:10.2307/258605

Glaser, B. G., & Strauss, A. L. (1967). *The Discovery of grounded theory: strategies for qualitative research*. New York: Aldine Publishing Company.

Glass, R. L. (1998). *Software runaways*. Upper Saddle River, NJ: Prentice-Hall.

Heng, T. B., & Wei, K. (2003). De-escalation of commitment in software projects: who matters? What matters? *Information & Management, 41*, 99–110. doi:10.1016/S0378-7206(03)00030-2

Hirschheim, R., Klein, H. K., & Newman, M. (1991). Information systems development as social action: theoretical perspective and practice. *Omega, 19*(6), 587–608. doi:10.1016/0305-0483(91)90009-I

Isabella, L. A. (1990). Evolving interpretations as a change unfolds: how managers construe key organizational events. *Academy of Management Journal, 33*(1), 7–41. doi:10.2307/256350

Jensen, M. C., & Meckling, W. H. (1986). Theory of the firm: managerial behavior, agency costs, and ownership structure. In Barney, J. B., & Ouchi, W. G. (Eds.), *Organizational Economics* (pp. 214–275). San Francisco, CA: Jossey-Bass.

Johnson, J. (1995). Chaos: the dollar drain IT project failures. *Application Development Trends, 2*(1), 41–47.

Johnston, H. R., & Carrico, S. R. (1988). Developing capabilities to use information strategically. *Management Information Systems Quarterly, 12*(1), 37–48. doi:10.2307/248801

Kahn, W. A. (1990). Psychological conditions of personal engagement and disengagement at Work. *Academy of Management Journal, 33*(4), 692–724. doi:10.2307/256287

Keil, M. (1995). Pulling the plug: Software project management and the problem of project escalation. *Management Information Systems Quarterly, 19*(4), 421–447. doi:10.2307/249627

Keil, M., Mann, J., & Rai, A. (2000). Why software projects escalate: an empirical analysis and test of four theoretical models. *Management Information Systems Quarterly, 24*(4), 631–664. doi:10.2307/3250950

Keil, M., Rai, A., Mann, J., & Zhang, G. P. (2003). Why software projects escalate: the importance of project management constructs. *IEEE Transactions on Engineering Management, 50*, 251–261. doi:10.1109/TEM.2003.817312

Keil, M., & Robey, D. (1999). Turning around troubled software projects: an exploratory study of the de-escalation of commitment to failing courses of action. *Journal of Management Information Systems, 15*(4), 63–87.

Kirsch, L. J. (1997). Portfolios of control modes and IS project management. *Information Systems Research, 15*, 374–395. doi:10.1287/isre.1040.0036

Kirsch, L. J. (2004). Deploying common systems globally: the dynamics of control. *Information Systems Research, 15*(4), 374–395. doi:10.1287/isre.1040.0036

Kirsch, L. J., & Haney, M. H. (2006). Requirements determination for common systems: turning a global vision into a local reality. *The Journal of Strategic Information Systems, 15*(2), 79–104. doi:10.1016/j.jsis.2005.08.002

Knorr, E. (2005). Anatomy of an IT disaster: How the FBI blew it. *Infoworld.com*.

Mahring, M. (2002). *IT project governance*. Stockholm, Sweden: Economic Research Institute (EFI).

Mahring, M., & Keil, M. (2008). Information technology project escalation: a process model. *Decision Sciences, 39*(2), 239–272. doi:10.1111/j.1540-5915.2008.00191.x

Mann, J. (2003, August 4-5). Preventing runaway IT projects: protecting auditors from entrapment. In *Proceedings of Americas Conference on Information Systems*, Tampa, FL.

Marcus, G. E., & Fischer, M. M. J. (1986). *Anthropology as cultural critique: an experimental moment in the human sciences*. Chicago: University of Chicago Press.

Martin, P. Y., & Turner, B. A. (1986). Grounded theory and organizational research. *The Journal of Applied Behavioral Science, 22*(2), 141–157. doi:10.1177/002188638602200207

Miles, M. (1979). Qualitative data as attractive science: the problem of analysis. *Administrative Science Quarterly, 24*, 590–601. doi:10.2307/2392365

Mokyr, J. (1990). *The lever of riches*. Oxford, UK: Oxford University Press.

Montealegre, R., & Keil, M. (2000). De-Escalating information technology projects: lessons learned from the Denver international airport. *Management Information Systems Quarterly*, *24*(3), 417–447. doi:10.2307/3250968

Newman, M., & Sabherwal, R. (1996). Commitment determinants to information systems development: a longitudinal investigation. *Management Information Systems Quarterly*, *20*, 23–54. doi:10.2307/249541

Orlikowski, W. J. (1993). CASE tools as organizational change: investigating incremental and radical changes in systems development. *Management Information Systems Quarterly*, *17*(3), 309–340. doi:10.2307/249774

Pan, S. L., Pan, S. C., Newman, M., & Flynn, D. (2006a). Escalation and de-escalation for commitment to information systems projects: insights from a project evaluation model. *European Journal of Operational Research*, *17*(3), 1139–1160. doi:10.1016/j.ejor.2005.07.009

Pan, S. L., Pan, S. C., Newman, M., & Flynn, D. (2006b). Escalation and de-escalation for commitment: a commitment transformation analysis of an e-government project. *Information Systems Journal*, *16*, 3–21. doi:10.1111/j.1365-2575.2006.00209.x

Pettigrew, A. M. (1990). Longitudinal field research on change: theory and practice. *Organization Science*, *1*(3), 267–292. doi:10.1287/orsc.1.3.267

Ross, J., & Staw, B. M. (1986). Expo86: An escalation prototype. *Administrative Science Quarterly*, *3*(1), 274–297. doi:10.2307/2392791

Ross, R. J., & Staw, B. M. (1993). Organizational Escalation and Exit: Lessons from the Shoreham Nuclear Power Plant. *Academy of Management Journal*, *36*(4), 701–732. doi:10.2307/256756

Royer, I. (2002). *Escalation in organizations: The role of collective belief*. Denver, CO: Academy of Management Conference.

Royer, I. (2003). Why bad projects are so hard to kill. *Harvard Business Review*, 49–56.

Rubin, J., Brockner, J., Small-Weill, S., & Nathanson, S. (1980). Factors affecting entry into psychological traps. *The Journal of Conflict Resolution*, *25*, 405–426. doi:10.1177/002200278002400302

Rubin, J. Z., & Brockner, J. (1975). Factors affecting entrapment in waiting situations: The Rosencrantz and Guildenstern Effect. *Journal of Personality and Social Psychology*, *31*, 1054–1063. doi:10.1037/h0076937

Sabherwal, R., & King, W. R. (1992). Decision Processes for developing strategic Apps of IS: A contingency approach. *Decision Sciences*, *23*(4), 917–943. doi:10.1111/j.1540-5915.1992.tb00426.x

Schmidt, J. B., & Calantone, R. J. (2002). Escalation of commitment during new product development. *Journal of the Academy of Marketing Science*, *30*(2), 103–118. doi:10.1177/03079459994362

Schultze, U. (2000). A confessional Account of an Ethnography about Knowledge Work. *Management Information Systems Quarterly*, *24*(1), 3–41. doi:10.2307/3250978

Shenhar, A. J. (1998). From theory to practice: Toward a typology of project management styles. *IEEE Transactions on Engineering Management*, *45*, 33–48. doi:10.1109/17.658659

Siggelkow, N. (2007). Persuasion with case studies. *Academy of Management Journal*, *50*(1), 20–24.

Smith, H., & Keil, M. (2003). The reluctance to report bad news on troubled software projects: a theoretical model. *Information Systems Journal*, *13*(1), 69–95. doi:10.1046/j.1365-2575.2003.00139.x

Snow, A. P., & Keil, M. (2002). The challenge of accurate software project status reporting: A two-stage model incorporating status errors and reporting bias. *IEEE Transactions on Engineering Management, 49,* 491–504. doi:10.1109/TEM.2002.807290

Snow, A. P., Keil, M., & Wallace, L. (2007). The effects of optimistic and pessimistic biasing on software project status reporting. *Information & Management, 44*(2), 130–141. doi:10.1016/j.im.2006.10.009

Staw, B. M. (1997). The escalation of commitment: an update and appraisal. In Shapira, Z. (Ed.), *Organizational Decision Making* (pp. 191–215). Cambridge, UK: Cambridge University Press.

Staw, B. M., & Ross, J. (1987). Behavior in escalation situations: antecedents, prototypes and solutions. In Staw, B. M., & Cummings, L. L. (Eds.), *Research in Organizational Behavior* (pp. 39–78). Greenwich, CT: JAI Press.

Stubbart, C., & Smalley, R. (1999). The deceptive allure of stage models of strategic processes. *Journal of Management Inquiry, 8*(3), 273–287. doi:10.1177/105649269983005

Sutton, R. I. (1987). The process of organizational death: disbanding and reconnecting. *Administrative Science Quarterly, 32*(4), 542–569. doi:10.2307/2392883

Thompson, R. L., Smith, H. J., & Iacovou, C. L. (2007). The linkage between reporting quality and performance in IS projects. *Information and Management, 44,* 196-205.

Tiwana, A., & Bush, A. A. (2007). A comparison of transaction cost, agency, and knowledge-based predictors of IT outsourcing decisions: A U.S.-Japan cross cultural field study. *Journal of Management Information Systems, 24*(1), 259–300. doi:10.2753/MIS0742-1222240108

Tushman, A. A. (1986). Technological discontinuities and organizational environments. *Administrative Science Quarterly, 31,* 439–465. doi:10.2307/2392832

Tushman, M., & Romanelli, E. (1985). Organizational evolution: A metamorphosis model of convergence and reorientation. In Cummings, L. L., & Staw, B. M. (Eds.), *Research in organizational behavior* (pp. 171–222).

Tushman, M. L., Newman, W. H., & Romanelli, E. (1986). Convergence and upheaval: Managing the unsteady pace of organizational evolution. *California Management Review, 29*(1), 29–44.

Tversky, A., & Kahneman, D. (1981). The Framing of Decisions and the Psychology of Choice. *Science, 211,* 453–458. doi:10.1126/science.7455683

US GAO. (2006). *Weak controls over trilogy project led to payment of questionable contractor costs and missing assets, GAO Report to Congressional Requesters.* Washington, DC: Government Accountability Office.

Utterback, J. M. (1994). Radical innovation and corporate regeneration. *Research Technology Management, 37*(4), 10–18.

Van Maanen, J. (1995). An end of innocence: The ethnography of ethnography. In *Representation in Ethnography* (pp. 1–35). Thousand Oaks, CA: Sage.

Vitale, I. B., & Beath, C. M. (1986). Linking information technology and corporate strategy: an organizational view. In *Proceedings of the Seventh International Conference on Information Systems,* San Diego, CA (pp. 265-276).

Whyte, G. (1986). Escalating commitment to a course of action: a reinterpretation. *Academy of Management Review, 11*(2), 311–321. doi:10.2307/258462

Whyte, G., & Fassina, N. E. (2007). Escalating commitment in group decision making. In *Proceedings of the Academy of Management*, Philadelphia.

Wright, M. K., & Capps, C. J. (2008). Information technology customer service: 'Best Practices' processes for operations. *Journal of Applied Business Research, 24*(3), 63–76.

Yin, R. K. (2003). *Case study research: design and methods* (3rd ed.). Thousand Oaks, CA: Sage.

Zmud, R. W. (1980). Management of large software efforts. *Management Information Systems Quarterly, 4*, 45–55. doi:10.2307/249336

ENDNOTES

[1] This was also reported to be a basic problem with another eGovernment project, the FBI Trilogy case (Knorr, 2005; US GAO, 2006).

[2] This critique resulted from the fact that the last two phases of the Royer model of escalation resembled the first phase of Montealegre and Keil model of de-escalation (See Table 4.)

APPENDIX

Determinants of Commitment to the Workers Compensation System (WCS) Project

Table 1a.

Event 1: (1990) New system proposed The Workers Compensation Commission (WCC) was created by 1990 legislation, which eliminated the State Industrial Accident Board. The new agency's mission provided for no-fault income replacement benefits and medical care for workers injured on the job and unable to earn their pre-injury wage. WCC was created to administer key parts of the system including delivery of benefits to injured workers, and to regulate and train all system participants. The mission of the new agency was data processing intensive.	**Antecedent** ← **Condition**
The Industrial Accident Board was an agency notoriously inefficient in handling of workers comp claims. This created a politically critical need for a new information system, the Workers Compensation System (WCS).	Political factors
The WCS software development project was put under financial control of an interagency governance committee.	Structural factors
Instead of developing the WCS from scratch, the new agency bought *COMPASS*, a software system from another state. This was thought to be the least expensive option.	Project factors
The legislature initially funded this acquisition project at $3 million -- a relatively modest amount compared to well-known IT project failures. For example, the FBI's Trilogy project was funded for over $500M (US GAO 2006).	Cost
Event 2: (1991) Requirements problems identified	**Commitment determinants**
Within a year, the new agency WCC was also unable to handle workers compensation claims efficiently. As a result, a data entry backlog was accumulating rapidly.	Structural factors
The agency was quickly getting a reputation for inefficiency.	Political factors
Event 3 (1991): Governance board intervenes ineffectively	**Commitment determinants**
In response, the agency project governing body appointed a statewide task force to study how to alleviate that backlog. The task force was headed by an IT auditor from the State Auditor's Office (SAO) and staffed with two computer specialists from the Comptroller's Office. However, in clear contrast to the commonly accepted audit principal of "separation of duties," this task force was headed by an employee of the same agency that had originally approved the *COMPASS* purchase—the SAO.	Structural factors
Instead of recommending a de-escalation action, the task force found that the agency (WCC) had made "significant progress" in using automation to fulfill its mission and recommended proceeding with the *COMPASS* acquisition and conversion.	Social factors
Event 4 (1991-1998): Incremental unsuccessful efforts to address requirements shortcomings of the *COMPASS* software	**Commitment determinants**
During this eight-year period of relative equilibrium, there were several incremental changes to the *COMPASS* project charter and the *COMPASS* software. This period also saw a replacement of the agency director. These adaptations nevertheless did not enable the agency to alleviate the work backlog; and the *COMPASS* conversion project "muddled along with an insufficient annual budget, and insufficient salaries." (Software development manager interview, January 2005).	Project factors
The agency (WCC) work backlog steadily increased over this eight-year period.	Structural factors
Local newspapers repeatedly cited the agency (WCC) as one of the least efficient of its kind. In 1992 one of the WCC commissioners resigned amid fraud allegations.	Political factors
$1,000,000/yr.	Cost
Event 5: (1999) Legislation to reduce agency paperwork (*BPI*) passed	**Commitment determinants**

continued on following page

Table 1a. Continued

In 1999, The State Legislature passed a bill requiring WCC to "reduce its paper work." This law resulted in a new WCC project known as the *Business Process Improvement Initiative, or BPI* project. The *BPI* requirements gathering project was placed under control of a WCC agency user group. The BPI related software development was placed under control of the WCC IT department. WCC planned to replace *COMPASS* with a new system to be developed from scratch. WCC planned to reengineer their business processes such that *COMPASS* could no longer be used.	Structural factors
The legislature appropriated $2.5 million for the WCC to redesign its business processes, and plan for the replacement of the mainframe that hosted the old system, which was *COMPASS*.	Cost
Event 6: (2000) Little progress on business process initiative (*BPI*) reported. *COMPASS* use continues.	**Commitment determinants**
The only progress for the first two years of the *BPI* was a plan to replace the mainframe that hosted *COMPASS*. As public discontent with the agency mounted, the WCC agency Commission appointed a new agency director. This was the third such director since WCC inception. Local newspapers reported that the appointment was equivalent to "a fox being put in charge of the hen house." A former insurance industry lobbyist, the new director had presided over a related agency during the 1990s, when it was beleaguered by criticism from consumers, workers, the Legislature, Ralph Nader and an investigation by the State District Attorney.	Political factors
Event 7: (2001) New software development contract with Corp1 signed for new web based system (*WEBCOMP*)	**Commitment determinants**
Instead of simply planning to convert *COMPASS* to a cheaper hardware platform, WCC managers planned to replace *COMPASS* with a new web site to be known as *WEBCOMP*. The new web site was to be developed from scratch by a combination of WCC employees and outside contractors. Internal project plans had expanded to five "Tiers" (or software releases). Tier 1 was to provide essential requirements needed only for medical providers. Tier 2 was to add the essential participant requirements. Mainframe replacement was pushed back into Tier 5 – after complete *COMPASS* replacement by *WEBCOMP*. Tier 1 was to complete in February 2003, Tier 2 in August 2003 and Tier 5 in 2007.	Project factors
Agency managers blamed WCC's high operating costs on the Corp3 contract and *COMPASS* software inadequacies. (Corp3 housed and operated the mainframe that hosted *COMPASS*.) WCC managers assumed the legislature wanted a new public web site for the agency. They hoped that the web would distribute to the field offices (and the public) much of the data entry formerly done at WCC's central site	Political factors
WCC managers planned for *WEBCOMP* -- the State's most technically complex "eGovernment" facility to date. The new software was to be written in the JAVA programming language. *WEBCOMP* was to be directed by staff that had no prior large-scale web site development experience. Software development began using only former *adabase natural* programmers with no experience or training with JAVA and web security technologies.	Structural factors
$5,000,000/yr. for five years includes hardware and software.	Cost
Event 8: (2000-2004) *WEBCOMP* Software development stalls	**Commitment determinants**
The original *WEBCOMP* release plan called for a direct cutover from the old *COMPASS* mainframe system to the new web-based system. However, that plan would have pushed back the first release of the *WEBCOMP* web site to a politically unacceptable late date, so it was scrapped and replaced by a plan to run *COMPASS* and *WEBCOMP* initially in parallel.	Political factors
The new *WEBCOMP* database had to be initialized with years of old *COMPASS* data. After three years, this data migration project was still not complete. Technical staff was overwhelmed with new technology learning curves. During this period of relative equilibrium, the software development team missed several release dates and had extensive personnel turnover. To hasten software development, Corp1 recommended the agency buy a business rules expert system tool. However, this proved to be a costly delay. The decision to use *COMPASS* and *WEBCOMP* in parallel during the system cutover proved fatal. During the parallel phase, these two systems were to have separate but redundant databases. This meant the two databases had to be in real time synchronization, which later proved impossible.	Project factors
When the first version of the new website was released to the public, the agency help desk was overwhelmed with calls, but the new release could not be backed out.	Political factors

continued on following page

Table 1a. Continued

Programmer's morale became quite low. "Tools don't work." "No one understands this project as a whole." (Technical staff interviews 2005)	Psychological factors
Event 9: (2003) Governance board (QAT) intervenes ineffectively	**Commitment determinants**
The project governing body -- the Quality Assurance Team (QAT)-- hired a local software project management consulting company to evaluate the project That report indicated only that improper quality control was the reason for a dispute between Corp1 and the agency over the *WEBCOMP* requirements.	Structural factors
$75,000	Cost
Event 10: (2003) Agency (WCC) software development manager replaced	**Commitment determinants**
In 2003, both the business requirements group and the software development group were put under a single manager.	Project factors
The new software development manager had no prior IT experience, education, or a college degree.	Psychological factors
The new software development manager had been the former head of the *WEBCOMP* business requirements group. Before that, she had been a WCC branch office clerical staff member for several years. She was young, attractive, quit witted, and considered an agency up and comer, heroic for accepting the technical management responsibility for the troubled project, despite lacking a technical background.	Social factors
Event 11: (2003) New ineffective contract for re-work of *WEBCOMP* requirements definition signed	**Commitment determinants**
A revised list of WCS requirements was written by Corp2, which had recently bought Corp1. Within a few weeks, there was a dispute over problems with Corp2's contract performance including a lack of promised architecture documents.	Project factors
$300,000	Cost
Event 12: (2003-2004) New time and materials contracts for *WEBCOMP* development signed	**Commitment determinants**
Because of the dispute over Corp2's contract performance, it was terminated. The software development manager replaced that contract with several individual time and materials contracts. Each contract was for an individual with experience in a needed web technology. Each such person was named a development team lead. There were fifteen WCC employees assigned to these teams, bringing the total development team size to about thirty people. The state IS project governing boards approved all these new contracts. Because WCS was now taking a much more active role in project management, a *WEBCOMP* project steering committee was formed This consisted of six WCC department heads, including the Internal Audit manager and the WCC director. Technical team decides to write a web security system from scratch rather than to use the one that comes off the shelf with Java. Software development stalls.	Structural factors
The WCC software development manager hired an original Corp1 employee to be project manager. This employee had resigned when Corp2 bought Corp1, having no prior web development experience.	Social factors
$100 / hr. average for each of the twelve contractors	Cost
Event 13: (2004) WCC's statutory time limit review nears	**Commitment determinants**
In 2004, the State Sunset Commission, began its first and only review of WCC, and within a few months, issued its report to the Governor. (According to law, the Sunset Commission reviews each state agency's performance at regular intervals. Unless the agency can justify its continuance, the Governor eliminates it.) The report contained a number of possible recommendations. One of its recommendations was to "improve WCC's web site to be more customer friendly." Another was to eliminate WCC and transfer its function to another state agency, the Department of Insurance (DI).	Structural factors
WCC managers perceived the report as confusing and contradictory.	Social factors
Agency morale decreased. "What's the point in finishing this project? ...we are just going to be eliminated." (Technical staff interviews 2005)	Psychological factors

continued on following page

Table 1a. Continued

Event 14: (July 2004) WCC replaces its director again	Commitment determinants
In an effort to repair its public image, the WCC Board replaced the agency director who had been with the agency since 1991 working in various management positions.	Political factors
Event 15: (Sept. 29 2004) New agency director issues misleading press release	Commitment determinants
In one of his first public acts, the new agency director issued a misleading press release. Following is an excerpt: "For the first time in (the State), workers injured on the job can report the injury to the WCC via the Internet. The online reporting…. was launched as part of the Commission's *WEBCOMP* system. We are tremendously pleased to achieve this milestone…Injured workers still have the option of submitting a paper copy of the …form"	Political factors
It was true that the *WEBCOMP* web site had advanced to the point where injured workers could submit an injury report to the agency remotely from a home computer or a branch office kiosk. However, the public was not told that, after such a remote report was submitted, WCC workers at headquarters had to re-enter it manually into both the *COMPASS* and *WEBCOMP* databases.	Project factors
Event 16: (2003-2005) WCC Internal Audit Department gets more involved with the project	Commitment determinants
In 2004, WCC the Internal Audit Director resigned and a staff auditor was named the new Director of Internal Audit. Although the new Internal Audit Director wanted to conduct a formal internal audit of the WCS project, the agency Commissioner would not allow it. Therefore, the new audit director had to settle for only monitoring the project. Our principal investigator (PI) agreed to perform that function.	Structural factors
Old Internal Audit reports revealed that the previous WCC audit director had been aware of serious problems with the *WEBCOMP* project but never raised the issue with management. (There were suspicions that the previous audit director had compromised audit independence by developing a personal friendship with the WCC software development manager.)	Social factors
The new audit director cautioned our principal investigator (PI) that, although the Internal Audit department reported directly to the agency Commissioner, he felt the audit department's power minimal. The WCC Director had recently prohibited a previous auditor from attending software development team meetings because "he was delaying project progress". Thus, the audit director asked our PI to keep a low profile.	Political factors
The new audit director did also not have an IT background.	Psychological factors
Event 17: (Jan. 2005) Principal investigator (PI) begins field work	Commitment determinants
The audit directory introduced the principal investigator (PI) to the agency director as an expert technical project advisor. Although he was polite, and expressed hope that the team would eventually turn around, the troubled project, the agency director did not seem interested in discussing the project. Next, the audit director introduced the PI to the software development manager who blamed the WCS project troubles on low state salaries and unscrupulous contractors.	Social factors
The PI began attending weekly project meetings. The agency was planning an upcoming release of the *WEBCOMP* web site, but was waiting for the defect list to shrink instead of grow each week.	Project factors
Event 18: (Feb. 2005) WCC software development manager staged a failed software demonstration	
Stakeholders from throughout the State were invited to the *WEBCOMP* demonstration, which was advertised to be "live." The demonstration did not go well: the effects of several obvious system crashes were projected onto a large screen in front of a large audience.	Political factors
The hardware, data, and software were not the actual *WEBCOMP* equipment, but a "one of" configuration of staged data processed on a laptop computer.	Project factors
Event 19: (Mar. – Jul. 2005) Whistle blown on the WCS project	Commitment determinants

continued on following page

Table 1a. Continued

In March of 2005, our principal investigator (PI) gave the Internal Audit Director an initial evaluation of the troubled WCS project. The report cautioned that the *WEBCOMP* project was probably technically infeasible and that the contractors were not bearing a reasonable level of the development risks. In July, the PI issued the final monitoring report to the new audit director. Because the PI could find no written plan that clearly described the remaining work to be done, expected costs, or predicted when the work would complete; his report recommended that all funding for the WCS software development project be stopped. The Internal Audit Director then resigned and took a job with an unrelated state agency. The PI then left the field, and continued following the project on the agency websites, newspaper accounts, and phone interviews with staff left behind at the agency.	Structural factors
The *WEBCOMP* project continued unchanged for a few more months before it finally collapsed.	Project factors
Most WCC managers then believed that the Governor would eliminate the agency within a few weeks, transferring its authority to new management in another state agency.	Psychological factors
The *WEBCOMP* project's economic cost exceeded $27,000,000 over the previous six years, with little to show for the money. Most of it had been spent on time and materials contracts, which specified no project deliverables, except time sheets and progress reports. More than $1,000,000 had been spent on hardware (made by Corp2) that had become merely "shelf-ware."	Cost
Event 20: (August 2005) *WECOMP* website ineffectively updated, causes more problems	**Commitment determinants**
In August 2005, the software development team updated the *WEBCOMP* website again.	Project factors
This new web site caused a flood of help desk calls, so the release was backed out.	Political factors
Event 21: (Sept 2005) Governor eliminates WCC agency. Transfers control of WCS project to the Department of Insurance (DI)	**Commitment determinants**
DI is located in another part of the same city as the old agency WCC. This new division of the other agency is called the Division of Workers Compensation (DWC). DI replaced all the former WCC software development managers.	Structural factors
Event 22: (Dec. 2006) The State Auditor's Office (SAO) begins "independent audit" of the *WEBCOMP* project.	**Commitment determinants**
In 2006, the Department of Insurance (DI) asks the SAO to perform a contracts audit of the *WEBCOMP* project. In regards to that audit, the PI agreed to an SAO interview in return for permission to interview SAO staff regarding all WCS contracts. The SAO public report issued weeks later recommended redirecting the WCS project and terminating the time and materials contracts.	Political factors
Event 23: (Jan. 2006) The new WCS project management team at the Department of Insurance (DI) disagrees over project direction	**Commitment determinants**
In early 2006, the Department of Insurance eliminated the *WEBCOMP* project, and replaced it with a new very broad project charter. The new project was called once again, the "Business Project Improvement" (*BPI2*) project. Although the DI may have intended to de-escalate the WCS project, it in essence escalated it by planning to convert the entire *COMPASS* system to a web based system. Following is an excerpt from the new *BPI2* charter. "It would be necessary to change the project's scope significantly to improve the likelihood of meeting project timeframes with the amount appropriated to the project… By migrating all applications from the mainframe to a web-based environment by the end of this biennium, DI will reduce expenses related to mainframe maintenance in its current operating budget."	Project factors
At that time, because former WCC employees, now part of DI's DWC was physically located in a different building across town from DI, planners may have been unaware that the DWC did not have the sufficient web infrastructure for such a web project, such as enough systems administrators, firewalls, servers, load balancers, etc.	Structural factors
Event 24: (2006) New management team lacks confidence in project turnaround	**Commitment determinants**

continued on following page

Table 1a. Continued

Later in 2006, public reports indicated a lack of confidence in the eventual success of the BPI2 project. Following is an excerpt: "During the last quarter of 2006, DWC staff began processing accumulated proof of Coverage data. Unfortunately, its rejection rate for this data was 40%. Without a reliable method to correct the rejected data, the Division discontinued processing." .	Political factors
DI managers, originally intending to deescalate the WCS project, realized they had mistakenly escalated the project by planning to convert all of the *COMPASS* functionality to the web.	Structural factors
Event 25: (2007) Project redefined and legitimized	**Commitment determinants**

Having identified the problems with the WCS software they had inherited from WCC, DI managers explored more alternatives, and then proposed the adoption of a partial abandonment strategy. Key to this decision was a redefinition of the essential business problems which then proclaimed that the underlying problems were caused, not by the lack of a comprehensive web site, but rather the following three things:
    1. lack of a document scanning and storage system;
    2. an unstable private computer network infrastructure; and
    3. the expensive mainframe maintenance contract with Corp3.
As a result, DI managers decided to abandon plans for web based processing of workers compensation claims.
	Structural factors

The technical team planned simply to port the *COMPASS* system to much cheaper PC based hardware.	Project factors
Event 26: (2007) Project de-escalated	
In mid 2007, DI managers announced that the *BPI* project, originally chartered in 2000, was completed successfully. Following is an excerpt from a public report to the State IT governance body the Quality Assurance Team (QAT) published Sept 30, 2007. "The Division successfully completed all major aspects of the migration of *COMPASS* functionality to the new computing environment. The mainframe was disconnected on September 30 2007..." Because the *BPI* project was then "closed," DI managers no longer had to report to the QAT and thus there was no traceable subsequent public funding for it. Nor was there any public reporting required for it. Nor was their any further mention of the completely abandoned *WEBCOMP* project. Much of the original *WEBCOMP* system vision does not exist today, and the DWC's web site presence is minimal. However, there is an "informal" DWC project called "getting to the web." DWC still does not have workflow software, a shortcoming which puts it years behind the technology used in health insurance companies. Moreover, DWC still relies heavily on the converted, but outdated *COMPASS* system. DI managers declined to comment on the division's recent cost and return to work performance. However in 2008 the former WCC Internal Audit Director told the principal investigator in an interview that DWC still has the reputation of not been able to efficiently handle comp claims, and that as a result, the DWC director was replaced again in 2008. Much of the original agency's (WCC) data management responsibility has been transferred to the Information Resources Department of (IRD) after Corp2 won a new $863 million contract with the State. This contract, stemming from 2005 legislation mandating consolidation of the State data centers, was touted as a way to improve the agency's data security, and standardize the systems; saving $178 million over the life of the contract. However, in November 2008, citing recent data losses and service problems, the Governor halted the contract and notified Corp2 that it had "breached its contractual duties and obligations to the State." However, a State Representative, who supported the 2005 legislation, said the project has achieved its broad goals of improving state data processing services. "What we didn't foresee is the contractor not being able to meet the terms of the contract."	←Outcome

This work was previously published in International Journal of Information Technology Project Management, Volume 1, Issue 4, edited by John Wang, pp. 53-79, copyright 2010 by IGI Publishing (an imprint of IGI Global).

Section 6
Implementation of IT Projects for Commercial Environment, Agencies, and Governments

Chapter 16

Service–Oriented Architecture Adoption:
A Normative Decision Model for Timing and Approach

Andrew P. Ciganek
UW-Whitewater, USA

Marc N. Haines
Ictect, Inc., USA

William (Dave) Haseman
UW-Milwaukee, USA

ABSTRACT

Service-oriented architecture (SOA) have been adopted by organizations in a wide variety of industries, however, best practices have still yet to mature. This article, which is part of a larger study on SOA, develops a normative decision model introducing key factors that influence the timing and approach of adopting a SOA. The decision model is based on the results of multiple case studies of organizations that had either employed or were considering implementing a service-oriented architecture project. The results indicate that there are four main areas an information technology (IT) manager needs to assess to determine when and how to move towards a SOA: the maturity of relevant standards, the technology gap, the organizational gap, and the nature of the benefits expected from a SOA. Analyzing these results suggest that differences in the business environment need to be considered in the decision of when and how an IT manager should pursue the move to a service-oriented architecture.

INTRODUCTION

Organizations are often searching for best practices to follow as guidance before adopting technologies. Oftentimes, especially with novel or innovative technologies, such practices either do not exist or are not readily accessible. Without best practices or exemplars of successful adoptions in hand, organizations struggle facing a sometimes steep and daunting learning curve. In some of those instances, these challenges that are faced ultimately lead to failure. A service-oriented architecture (SOA) is one of those recent technology

DOI: 10.4018/978-1-4666-0930-3.ch016

approaches that have received a wide amount of attention regarding its advantages, such as its ability to improve the flexibility of an organization's technology architecture and utilizing an approach that is based on open, cross-platform standards. Despite these benefits, there are many organizations worldwide that have been reluctant to adopt (Sholler, 2008). This unwillingness by organizations is in sharp contrast to the many predictions that SOA would be pervasive in industry by now. The objective of this research is to further examine the process organizations follow in pursuit of a SOA adoption to gain a deeper understanding of this surprising reluctance amongst organizations. The primary contribution of this research is that we present a normative decision model, based on the results of multiple case studies, which can guide information technology (IT) managers to determine their approach and timing of moving towards a SOA.

To develop an understanding of the challenges that organizations face pursing a SOA project, interviews took place with multiple individuals from eight organizations that either employed a project utilizing Web services or were considering developing a SOA based on Web services. Data was collected during a period of time when adoption of SOA was not commonplace and reasonably could be perceived among organizations as either a novel or innovative technology. Based on those interview results, we developed a normative decision model containing key considerations for organizations in the process of moving towards a SOA based on Web service standards. We next present a literature review for this research to provide further background for a SOA followed by a discussion of the research methodology. We then identify four key areas that an IT manager should consider in determining when and how to move to SOA, based on case evidence. The paper concludes with a discussion of its limitations and proposed future work.

LITERATURE REVIEW

The technology of interest in this research is a service-oriented IT architecture. The researchers chose this particular technology to develop a decision-making framework for because many experts had anticipated SOA to be widespread in industry by today, but this has yet to occur. For example, the widely cited Gartner 2008 hype cycle for emerging technologies (Fenn et al., 2008) expected Web services to be viewed as fairly mature and reaching the "plateau of productivity," with SOA reaching the "slope of enlightenment". Despite these predictions and the wide attention that SOA has received in the trade press, best practices for SOA are not commonplace (Gootzit et al., 2008). It is true that SOA adoption overall is increasing, but it is occurring at a pace much slower than initially anticipated (Sholler, 2008). Part of this hesitance might be attributed to the lack of formal best practices identified in the academic literature for IT managers to follow.

A SOA is best described as a means for building software applications that use available services in a network (Papazoglou, 2008). It is a way to both organize and utilize distributed capabilities under the control of different ownership domains (MacKenzie, Laskey, McCabe, Brown, & Metz, 2006; Tang & Cheng, 2006, 2007). Although a SOA supports various communication protocols, protocols based on open standards are commonly used in modern SOA implementations (Erl, 2006; Papazoglou, 2008). Most large SOAs will provide access to services with a mix of technologies that are not necessarily based on the WS-*[1] standards. Thus, open standards are not the only way that a SOA may be implemented. Web services based on WS-* standards, however, are at the core of the integration products of the major vendors, including IBM, SAP, and Oracle. Furthermore, recent industry surveys suggest that WS-* standards remain the prevalent underlying technology standard for the major SOA platforms (Sholler,

2008). The major feature that differentiates SOA with Web services from prior attempts of distributed computing (e.g., using CORBA) is both the level of standardization that has been achieved and the ubiquitous acceptance of these standards by the major vendors and service providers. Consequently, our focus is on SOAs realized with Web services.

According to the World Wide Web Consortium (W3C), Web services are software systems designed to support interoperable machine-to-machine interaction over a network with an interface described in a machine-processable format (namely, Web Services Description Language [WSDL]) (Haas & Brown, 2004). External or disparate systems interact with Web services in a manner prescribed by its description using SOAP messages, which are typically conveyed using Hypertext Transfer Protocol (HTTP) with an eXtensible Markup Language (XML) serialization along with other Web-related standards. The last component of a SOA framework is a service registry, which is used to publish and discover Web services based on the Universal Description Discovery & Integration (UDDI) standard. A SOA utilizes Web services to become accessible and be applied in a Web-based environment.

METHODOLOGY

A multiple case research strategy was utilized to give greater insight into the complex nature of adopting of a service-oriented architecture. The focus of this research, which is part of a larger study on SOA, is to provide direction for IT managers through the development of a normative decision model. A theoretical framework and a detailed analysis of the case findings are described further in Ciganek et al. (2009). Since the adoption of a SOA is a recent event in which substantial scientific theory has not yet been established, but can be observed in a real-life context, a multiple case

study approach is appropriate. The transcripts from each of the case interviews were analyzed following a rigorous process based on the procedures outlined by Strauss and Corbin (1998) and ideas presented in Eisenhardt (1989) and Yin (1994).

Research Design

The goal of this research was to obtain greater insight into the decision making and approach that organizations take when pursing the adoption of a SOA. As a result, a multiple case design was more appropriate than examining an individual case. The advantage that a multiple case design offers is that it allows for cross-case analyses, which forces investigators to look beyond initial impressions and see evidence through multiple perspectives (Eisenhardt, 1989).

The research process, including data collection and data analysis, followed a research protocol that identified the overall research goals, data collection sources and procedures (i.e., interview instrument), and the data analysis process. The research protocol, interview transcripts, and all other documents produced during data collection and analysis were stored in a secure online repository shared among the researchers. The qualitative analysis tool NVivo 2.0 (Richards, 2002) was used to administer and support the analysis of our research documents.

Case and Participant Selection

Each of the organizations chosen to participate in the study are major national organizations in their respective industries in the United States and had either already implemented a project utilizing Web services or were considering developing a SOA based on Web services. Eight organizations with varying levels of SOA adoption and industry characteristics were purposefully selected to provide contrasting results, though the availability of such organizations was limited during the time of data collection. A minimum of two participants were selected for each case and were identified based on the recommendations of our contact person at each organization. At least one individual that was interviewed had technical expertise with respect to designing and implementing SOA (e.g., an IS analyst) while another participant was interviewed separately that had managerial responsibility for the SOA projects and a broader business perspective (e.g., a vice-president of information systems). In sum, we interviewed seventeen individuals in eight participating organizations during the spring of 2004 and spring of 2005. Table 1 summarizes each organization interviewed.

Data Collection

The interviews with individuals from the eight organizations lasted on average forty-five minutes and all but three interviews were conducted face-to-face. The three interviews with organization F3 were conducted over the phone. A semi-structured interview document guided the interview process. This document included eight open-ended questions to ensure consistency among all interviews and addressed the firm's organizational and IT background, the perspective and involvement of the interviewee, current SOA initiatives, expected benefits, the key challenges, long-term solutions and temporary workarounds, as well as key lessons learned in dealing with a SOA.

Every interview was voice recorded and subsequently transcribed. Summaries of the transcripts were then created by the researchers and provided the participants with the chance to make corrections, such as elaborating upon important details or requesting that sensitive information be removed. After this process was complete, a summary description for each case was produced by the researchers. Each case summary was then independently interpreted by each of the three researchers.

Data Analysis

The case summaries that were produced for each of the interview transcripts, which were reviewed by each participant, were the inputs for our data analysis. There were three primary steps in the analysis process: 1) the preparation of data sources, 2) the open coding and category development, and 3) the development of relationships and the resulting theoretical model. Figure 1 illustrates the analysis process. The data analysis process followed the steps outlined by Strauss & Corbin (1998). The details of this process and data findings (Table 2) are described in greater detail in Ciganek et al. (2009).

NORMATIVE DECISION MODEL

There are four main areas an IT manager needs to assess to determine when and how to move towards a SOA: the maturity of relevant standards, the technology gap, the organizational gap, and the nature of the benefits expected from a SOA. Due to the importance of standards for SOA based on Web services, the assessment of maturity and acceptance of these standards play a critical role. Therefore, we included standards assessment as a key area relevant for the SOA decision. Furthermore, the principles of SOA need to be implemented using some set of technologies that are suitable for a SOA (i.e., Web services). While it is critical, it cannot be assumed that the current technical environment in an organization supports these SOA related technologies. This technology gap is therefore included as the second main assessment area.

Our case evidence suggests that the move to a SOA entails some organizational changes, whether it is IT or business function related. It cannot be assumed that an organization's current business processes and structures would support these

Table 1. Case overview (Ciganek et al., 2009)

Label	Description
F1	F1 is in the financial industry and has applications utilizing Web services that have been operational for over a year. This organization is primarily a provider as opposed to a consumer of services and its stated goal is to convert all of its existing applications, which range from mainframe to web applications, to fit a SOA based on Web services. These systems all pass XML messages, which use industry standards (IFX and OFX) when possible. Web services are currently not published in a public registry, and initially Web-services were only available internally within the firewall or through a virtual private network (VPN). More recently the WS-Security standard was leveraged to secure some Web services. Its primary motivation to move towards a SOA based on Web services was to provide a standard platform for development, provide a method for integration of the various systems, and support its desire to reuse code.
F2	This organization is also in the financial industry and has many applications in production that employ "pre-Web services" XML-based messaging, but has a limited adoption of actual Web services. Prior to the introduction of Web services, the organization developed its own standard for formatting XML messages similar to SOAP within its own firewall and considered this home-grown architecture to be service-oriented, albeit not based on open standards.
F3	F3 is in the financial industry and operates as an application service provider and licenses the financial software it develops. While some industry standards exist (e.g., OFX and IFX), they do not provide all the data required in some of their existing applications. While the architectural structure could be converted to a SOA model, the IT management believes that the cost of conversion currently outweighs its benefits. The real drive for change will occur when the organization's key customers or partners start demanding functionality delivered through standard Web services.
F4	This organization is also in the financial industry and its primary role is to serve as the facilitator of business-to-business communications between consumers and financial services vendors. These vendors represent significant players in the financial industry and they exert great influence over the protocols by which communication takes place. The organization does not currently have a SOA or any applications that utilize Web services. While it sees a number of benefits related to Web services, it is only delivering what its business partners demand. If its business partners were to require Web services, it would meet those requirements.
M1	M1 is a manufacturing organization and is currently putting integration structure in place to facilitate moving to a SOA. One application is currently Web services-enabled, and plans exist to interface the HR package with existing systems and the portal project using Web services. XML over HTTP was previously used to feed information to the existing portal, but the portal vendor has discontinued this feature. The call center application package is Web services-enabled, which may provide an opportunity to employ Web services.
M2	This organization is another manufacturing organization. The organization is currently in the middle of a large project of implementing an ERP system worldwide. The organization has been involved in a small project using Web Services but has not embarked on a larger scale SOA effort. It sees Web Services as providing an opportunity to reduce latency (providing real time data and inventories with all its partners), therefore allowing for cutting costs. It is concerned that SOA and Web services may currently offer more hype than real functionality and is waiting until it can demonstrate a good cost benefit for using the technology before applying Web services on a larger scale.
R1	R1 is a large retailer and has two major IT divisions: corporate IT and retail locations. Its corporate efforts include a lot of legacy COBOL applications running on mainframes, with all new work being developed on the J2EE platform. One Web service application has been developed to interface with a third party system. A second application interfaces to an interactive voice response (IVR) system. Its second effort is related to supporting the organization's many retail locations. The approximately 1,000 retail locations use a single IT model, which is based on the Microsoft Windows platform. A major Web service project in this area is in the "proof-of-concept" stage that will be used to communicate inventory demands between the retail locations and the corporate location.
H1	H1 is an intermediary in the health care industry. It connects customers with suppliers for long-term health care products. Historically it has interacted with business partners using EDI, first through VANs and now primarily through HTTPS. It also has some experience transferring XML over HTTP. Essentially all IT is based on the Microsoft Windows platform and most applications are custom developed in-house. It currently is developing its first Web services with a supplier to transmit data in real time. It sees Web services as a solution to provide interoperability and move from a batch mode, which is typical of its EDI, to real-time interactions. The health care industry is a highly fragmented industry that is traditionally slow to adopt any new technology. As a technology leader in the long-term health care industry, this organization faces the challenge of convincing business partners of the value of moving to Web services that can be leveraged in a SOA.

Figure 1. Data analysis process (Ciganek et al., 2009)

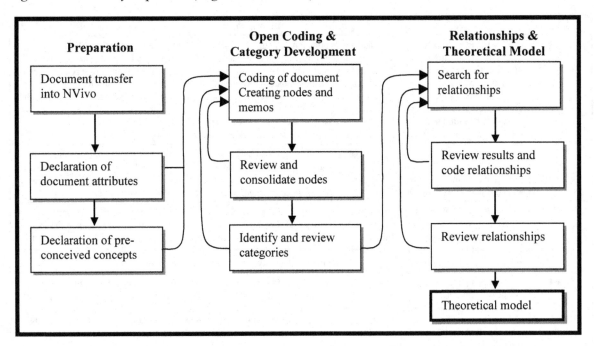

changes. Consequently, assessing this potential organizational gap is a key assessment area. Finally, SOA initiatives can only move forward with adequate leadership and funding. A key element in obtaining both is to convincingly demonstrate the benefits of a SOA. Thus, the benefits assessment is the fourth key assessment area.

We next discuss each assessment area in further detail, including a decision flow representing the key questions that need to be asked and possible actions. These individual assessments are then aggregated into a normative decision model. The desired outcome is a decision regarding the adoption of a SOA that outlines the timing, scale, and usage pattern. The key question is not so much if SOA is being adopted, but when and how it makes sense to move "mindfully" towards a SOA, given the specific organizational characteristics and the business environment (Swanson & Ramiller, 2004).

Standards Maturity Assessment

The availability of mature and widely accepted standards is an important cornerstone for implementing a standards-based SOA. Standards apply to different layers of the system stack. Web services can currently be considered a key enabling technology for realizing a SOA based on open standards. Therefore, the standards development related to Web services is a crucial aspect for SOA projects. The core Web services standards (SOAP, WSDL) can be considered fairly mature, and key standards related to security (WS-Security) have reached broader acceptance. However, some other standards that are important for the commercial use of Web service are still in the process of reaching maturity. One example is the standards addressing reliable messaging (WS-Reliability vs. WS-Reliable Messaging). This is an issue that all organizations implementing Web services have to deal with.

However, the question of whether the relevant standards are sufficiently mature or not needs to also include the payloads exchanged in the messages. The standards governing the XML payloads exchanged in Web service interactions are often industry specific (i.e., IFX in the financial industry or MIMO for mortgages). Consequently, the timing of moving towards a SOA hinges to some extent on whether such standards exist. For example, a participant from organization M1 identified the absence of industry payload standards as the main reason why they are hesitant from exposing functionality as a Web service since it is not clear which format would be appropriate for its potential business partners. On a similar issue, a participant from organization M2 stated that payload definitions are a primary challenge because current industry standards are immature and too basic to be useful. The participant additionally stated that their organization did not have sufficient influence to provide the payload definitions to its business partners. The participant felt that this type of leadership must come through an industry consortium to gain widespread acceptance.

If sufficiently mature payload standards exist, a key foundation for moving forward with a SOA is given. If such standards do not exist or are not mature enough, an IT decision maker needs to evaluate the ability of the organization to set such a standard internally and possibly also externally. In some industries, "big players" have the ability to coerce their customers or suppliers into using their specifications and can lead the standards development. If this is not an option, companies can collaborate in standardization organizations or industry groups to advance the development of standards relevant for their SOA. This obviously takes time and can be a reason for limiting or delaying the move towards a SOA (see Figure 2).

Technology Gap Assessment

Organizations will usually move towards a SOA based on an existing IT infrastructure and set of applications. In fact, one of the frequently touted benefits of SOA is the ability to reuse functionality residing in existing applications. This functionality can, of course, only be reused if it is exposed as a service, typically an XML Web service inter-

Table 2. Interview guide (Ciganek et al., 2009)

1. How are you involved in IT initiatives that involve Web services? Provide a brief overview of the current IT infrastructure, including key technology platforms and major applications. Independent from Web services, what are the major objectives that IT tries to accomplish? How do they relate to overall business objectives?
2. Please provide us with an overview of current IT initiatives that involve Web services. This may include a summary of the technology platforms and tools used for development, the usage patterns of Web services (provider/consumer, internal/external), the project scope, and the project status (exploration, planning, testing, production).
3. Based on your personal involvement and experience with Web services, choose a key project of the projects mentioned above (even if it is only an exploratory or planned project) and describe it in more detail. This description may include further information about the motivation, the technology and tools used in the project, the current status, and timeline.
4. What do you see as the key benefits of Web services? What are other important impacts that Web services has on software development, the IT infrastructure, and perhaps the organization as a whole?
5. What are the key challenges encountered in the process of adopting Web services? Please describe the technological or organizational challenges you encountered.
6. What do you see as important steps that need to be taken or issues that need to be resolved to overcome the challenges mentioned above?
7. What solutions has your organization developed to – at least temporarily – handle the shortcomings of current Web services? This may include workarounds and custom solutions, as well as decisions to not adopt Web services at this point in time
8. If you were to give some advice to a senior manager who was considering the adoption of Web services technology, what would be the three most important lessons you have learned in the process of evaluating, developing, or using Web services?

Figure 2. Standards maturity

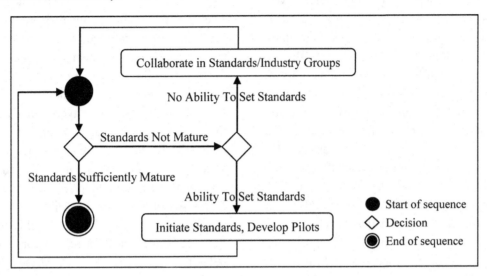

face. This functionality requires the availability of technology that effectively provides service interfaces and the ability to consume services. Packed applications (e.g., enterprise systems) frequently play a central role in the IT landscape of organizations. The vendors of these applications play an important role in either promoting or inhibiting the development of a SOA. The evidence collected in our cases suggests that the lack of appropriate application programming interfaces (APIs) in major applications can be a significant obstacle to moving to a SOA. As one participant stated, "The way the […] tool is designed you're kind of forced […] to use certain architectures, and that's how the Web services end up in there." The incorporation of Web services in development tools and having them the preferred API for integration in packaged applications are important factors that influence organizations to adopt Web services, almost to the point that developers may sometimes feel required to use them. While the use of Web services does not necessarily result in a SOA, the availability of standards-based service interfaces helps to close the technology gap and arguably makes the move to a SOA easier.

Essentially all major vendors have incorporated Web services APIs and tools to expose functional-ity into their latest offerings. If a vendor offers this functionality but the currently installed version of the software does not, a plan for transitioning to a more current version of the software needs to be developed. This applies to the applications themselves as well as the tools to develop applications. In the case of custom and some packaged applications, the custom development of APIs may not be avoided, but then a tool set that sufficiently supports Web services and other SOA related technologies needs to be available. If an organization requires time to bridge the technology gap, it can consider implementing only a SOA pilot and wait with a full scale SOA adoption until tools and applications provide the necessary support (see Figure 3).

Organizational Gap Assessment

Several of the participants indicated that there is what could be best described as "changes in mindset" involved in pursuing a service-oriented application architecture. The literature describe this type of behavior as a "mindshift" (D. J. Armstrong & Hardgrave, 2007) and may likely have significant implications on the type of expertise needed for a SOA project. There are also considerations to introduce new organizational roles and structures to support the SOA efforts (i.e., service librarian). The move to a SOA entails both changes in business functions as well as changes within the IT organization to be effective (see Figure 4). Participants indicated that issues of ownership and governance of services need to be resolved before a full scale SOA deployment can take place. If these issues are not addressed, the manageability of the services can become a problem and consequently impede agility, one of

the main benefits associated with a SOA. Changing organizational structures requires time and may delay SOA adoption on a larger scale.

Benefits Assessment

One of the key challenges that emerged in our cases was the lack of external demand for interfaces implemented with Web services and the availability of an external service "ecosystem" that could be leveraged for creating composite

Figure 3. Technology gap

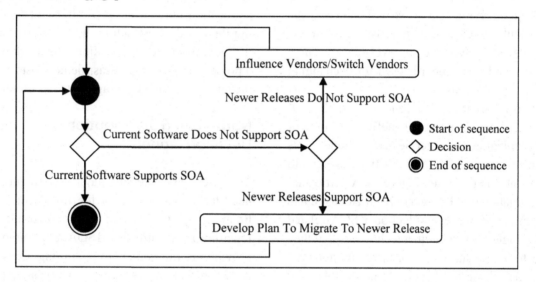

Figure 4. Organizational gap

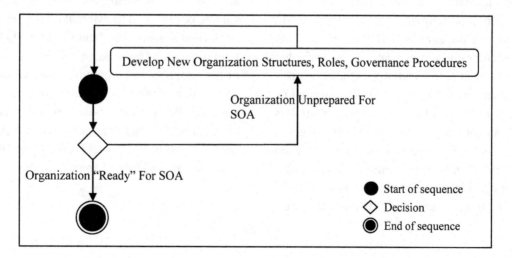

applications within a SOA. Also there were also few expectations that a SOA would result in new business models and services for external business partners, so the focus for justifying investments in SOA was largely internal. One participant suggested, "There are no blind dates in Web services," emphasizing that "old fashioned face-to-face agreements" are currently the only way an exchange with a partner occurs. However, the case evidence suggests that this picture may quickly change once a critical mass of services becomes available. This opinion was best illustrated by one participant who stated that "rather than being in mentality of 'If we build it, they will come' [it is] 'If they come, we will build it." This is particularly relevant in industries where a few "big players" have leverage over their business partners and the standards used for exchanging business documents.

If no apparent external benefits exist, the ROI needs to focus on internal benefits. For some of the organizations we interviewed this benefit was clearly not large enough to justify investing into a SOA at this time (see Figure 5). A participant from organization H1 stated that their customers may simply view the introduction of SOA-related technologies as just another technology that they need to adopt that does not have any apparent immediate business benefits. The challenge of associating a SOA to immediate business benefits was also stated by participants in organization R1. In addition, a participant from organization M2 revealed that the current ROI for a SOA is not sufficient for rapid adoption, as a service-oriented approach doesn't offer anything for their organization that cannot be attained within the current IT architecture, despite their architecture being less flexible and probably more costly in the long run.

Successful SOA proof-of-concept or even pilot implementations on a smaller scale are usually a good, if not necessary, tool to get buy-in from the stakeholders and advance necessary organizational adjustments. This approach, utilized by participants in this study, is similar to the business process re-engineering efforts of the 1980's and 1990's in which organizations sought the "low hanging fruit", or projects that are most likely to achieve a desirable result (e.g., cost savings, code reduction) to establish justification and support for subsequent, more extensive projects (Stoddard & Jarvenpaa, 1995). Current project funding practices also emerged as an inhibiting factor to make the initial step towards a SOA, as some organizations require business units sponsoring the first project leveraging a SOA to take on not only the costs for the SOA-based business application, but also the up-front cost for developing the SOA infrastructure. In this case, a clear mandate from the organizational leadership and a process to share the infrastructure costs across the enterprise can encourage SOA development.

Normative SOA Adoption Decision Model

The outcomes of the four major assessment areas need to be aggregated for the final decision to be made by an IT manager. The final decision regarding a standards-based SOA adoption should provide information about the timing, the scale, and usage pattern (see Figure 6). The usage pattern relates to whether services are mainly provided and consumed internally, consumed from external source, or provided to external consumers.

Although some key benefits of a SOA, particularly reuse of services, increases with the scale of the adoption and the number of services that are available, the first move towards a SOA in our cases has typically been a proof-of-concept or pilot implementation, usually with the purpose to assess and bridge the technology gap and provide clearer evidence of some benefits.

RELEVANCE FOR PRACTICE

This research has relevance because it presents several best practices to guide IT managers in their approach and timing of moving towards a SOA. These practices are tailored towards an organization's overall preparedness for moving towards a SOA, which may vary from one organization to the next. There has been an increase in the research that has examined service-oriented IT architecture, particularly related to technical issues. Despite this attention, the predictions of widespread adoption of SOA by organizations have yet to be fulfilled and there is a role for additional academic research in this area. Consequently, this research deals with a current topic on a leading edge practice, which has been encouraged by eminent IS researchers (Benbasat & Zmud, 1999; Lyytinen, 1999; Markus & Saunders, 2007). We identify a normative decision model for examining the timing and approach

Figure 5. Benefits

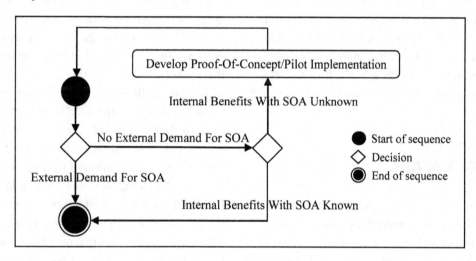

Figure 6. SOA decision-making process

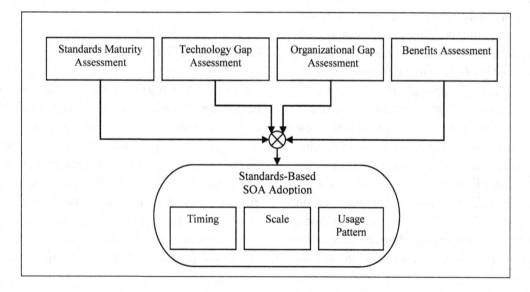

of adopting a SOA. The outcomes of this study can be applied to conduct further research on both SOA adoption and on the challenges of pursing these types of projects.

Our results indicate that there are four main areas an IT manager needs to assess to determine when and how to move towards a SOA: the maturity of relevant standards, the technology gap, the organizational gap, and the nature of the benefits expected from a SOA. IT managers should first seek to understand their overall preparedness before moving towards a SOA, and then consider these findings for guidance, which are based on the experiences of eight organizations from varying industries. Given the lack of best practices that exist in the current academic literature for organizations moving towards a SOA, this research should have particular appeal for IT managers.

LIMITATIONS AND FUTURE RESEARCH

The normative decision model presented in this research is based on the experiences of eight organizations in multiple industries at a single point in time. It is possible to generalize from case study findings to theory, but as Lee and Baskerville (2003) reveal, the resulting theory may have limited generalizability beyond the examined cases. Every organization is different and the approach that they take to pursue a SOA may very well be unique. The significance of the factors that influence the timing and approach of adopting a SOA may also change over time as organizations benefit from the lessons learned from other firms and their own learning curves. For example, variables that were not revealed or deemed unimportant in the case analyses discussed in Ciganek et al. (2009) might later become significant. An investigation of inter-coder reliability was not performed as part of the larger study on SOA. Although inter-coder reliability is occasionally reported in case-based

research, the appropriateness of this measure has been challenged (Armstrong, Gosling, Weinman, & Marteau, 1997). As part of our larger study on SOA, however, every research document produced were coded and reviewed by multiple researchers independently and combined during face-to-face sessions. This process aided in minimizing the impact that personal biases might have had in the case summaries and allowed additional perspectives to be introduced.

Future research is necessary to either validate or refine our normative decision making model. This model could also be validated using a larger quantitative survey which incorporates the four main areas an IT manager needs to assess to determine when and how to move towards a SOA that were identified in this study. Utilizing an additional methodology to examine our results would generate a more detailed representation of those factors that influence how and when an organization should move towards a SOA. Not only will an examination of the decision-making process of IT managers over multiple points in time aide in the understanding of relevant factors, it will also provide insights into the change management practices that may take place during these transitions. A longitudinal study may also provide additional insights into the process of a SOA adoption.

CONCLUSION

This article, which is part of a larger study on SOA, develops a normative decision model introducing key factors that influence the timing and approach of adopting a SOA. This decision model is based on the insights gained from interviews with multiple individuals from eight organizations that either employed a project utilizing Web services or were considering developing a SOA based on Web services. Analyzing the results, IT managers should first seek to understand their overall preparedness before moving towards a SOA, and then consider the findings from this research as guidance to aide in making "mindful" adoption decisions (Swanson & Ramiller, 2004).

The results of this research only reflect the experiences of the organizations that were examined at a single point in time. Every organization is different and the approach that they use to pursue a SOA may very well be unique. In addition, the significance of the factors that influence the timing and approach of adopting a SOA may change over time. As a result, additional research is necessary to either validate or refine our normative decision making model.

REFERENCES

Armstrong, D., Gosling, A., Weinman, J., & Marteau, T. (1997). The place of inter-rater reliability in qualitative research: An emprical study. *Sociology, 31*(3), 597–606. doi:10.1177/0038038597031003015

Armstrong, D. J., & Hardgrave, B. C. (2007). Understanding mindshift learning: The transition to object-oriented development. *Management Information Systems Quarterly, 31*(3), 453–474.

Benbasat, I., & Zmud, R. W. (1999). Empirical research in information systems: The practice of relevance. *Management Information Systems Quarterly, 23*(1), 3–16. doi:10.2307/249403

Chwelos, P., Benbasat, I., & Dexter, A. S. (2001). Research report: Empirical test of an EDI adoption model. *Information Systems Research, 12*(3), 304–321. doi:10.1287/isre.12.3.304.9708

Ciganek, A. P., Haines, M. N., & Haseman, W. D. (2009). Service-Oriented Architecture Adoption: Key Factors and Approaches. *Journal of Information Technology Management, 20*(3), 42–54.

DePietro, R., Wiarda, E., & Fleischer, M. (1990). The context for change: Organization, technology, and environment. In Tornatzky, L. G., & Fleischer, M. (Eds.), *The Process of Technological Innovation* (pp. 151–175). Lanham, MD: Lexington Books.

Eisenhardt, K. M. (1989). Building theories from case study research. *Academy of Management Review, 14*(4), 532–551. doi:10.2307/258557

Erl, T. (2006). *Service-Oriented Architecture: Concepts, Technology, and Design.* Upper Saddle River, NJ: Prentice Hall.

Fenn, J., Drakos, N., Andrews, W., Knox, R. E., Tully, J., Ball, R. J. G., et al. (2008). *Hype Cycle for Emerging Technologies 2008* (Gartner No. G00159496).

Fichman, R. G. (1992). *Information Technology Diffusion: A Review of Empirical Research.* Paper presented at the Proceedings of the Thirteenth International Conference on Information Systems, Dallas, TX.

Gootzit, D., Phifer, G., Valdes, R., Drakos, N., Bradley, A., Harris, K., et al. (2008). *Hype Cycle for Web and User Interaction Technologies 2008* (Gartner No. G00159447).

Haas, H., & Brown, A. (2004). *Web services glossary.* Retrieved February, 2009 from http://www.w3.org/TR/ws-gloss/

Iacovou, C. L., Benbasat, I., & Dexter, A. S. (1995). Electronic data interchange and small organizations: Adoption and impact of technology. *Management Information Systems Quarterly, 19*(4), 465–485. doi:10.2307/249629

Kwon, T. H., & Zmud, R. W. (1987). Unifying the fragmented models of information systems implementation. In Boland, R. J., & Hirschheim, R. A. (Eds.), *Critical Issues in Information Systems Research* (pp. 252–257). New York: John-Wiley.

Lee, A. S., & Baskerville, R. L. (2003). Generalizing generalizability in information systems research. *Information Systems Research, 14*(3), 221–243. doi:10.1287/isre.14.3.221.16560

Lyytinen, K. (1999). Empirical research in information systems: On the relevance of practice in thinking of IS research. *Management Information Systems Quarterly, 23*(1), 5–28. doi:10.2307/249406

MacKenzie, C. M., Laskey, K., McCabe, F., Brown, P. F., & Metz, R. (2006). *Reference Model for Service Oriented Architecture 1.0 (Committee Specification soa-rm-cs)*. OASIS.

Markus, M. L., & Saunders, C. (2007). Looking for a few good concepts… and theories… for the information systems field. *Management Information Systems Quarterly, 31*(1), iii–vi.

Papazoglou, M. P. (2008). *Web Services: Principles and Technology*. Harlow, England: Pearson.

Premkumar, G., Ramamurthy, K., & Crum, M. R. (1997). Determinants of EDI adoption in the transportation industry. *European Journal of Information Systems, 6*(2), 107–121. doi:10.1057/palgrave.ejis.3000260

Richards, L. (2002). *Using NVivo in Qualitative Research*. London: Sage Publications.

Sholler, D. (2008). *2008 SOA User Survey: Adoption Trends and Characteristics* (Gartner No. G00161125).

Stoddard, D., & Jarvenpaa, S. (1995). Business process redesign: Tactics for managing radical change. *Journal of Management Information Systems, 12*(1), 81–107.

Strauss, A., & Corbin, J. (1998). *Basics of Qualitative Research: Techniques and Procedures for Developing Grounded Theory* (2nd ed.). Thousand Oaks, CA: Sage Pulications.

Swanson, E. B., & Ramiller, N. C. (2004). Innovating mindfully with information technology. *Management Information Systems Quarterly, 28*(4), 553–583.

Tang, Q. C., & Cheng, H. K. (2006). 2007). Optimal strategies for a monopoly intermediary in the supply chain of complementary web services. *Journal of Management Information Systems, 23*(3), 275–307. doi:10.2753/MIS0742-1222230310

Yin, R. K. (1994). *Case Study Research* (2nd ed., *Vol. 5*). Thousand Oaks, CA: Sage Publications.

Zhu, K., Kraemer, K. L., Xu, S., & Dedrick, J. (2004). Information technology payoff in e-business environments: An international perspective on value creation of e-business in the financial services industry. *Journal of Management Information Systems, 21*(1), 17–54.

ENDNOTE

[1]   WS-* refers to a set of standards that include SOAP, WSDL, UDDI, and other Web services related standards typically prefixed with WS-, such as WS-Security or WS-BPEL.

This work was previously published in International Journal of Information Technology Project Management, Volume 1, Issue 2, edited by John Wang, pp. 1-15, copyright 2010 by IGI Publishing (an imprint of IGI Global).

Chapter 17

Issues in Electronic Procurement Project Implementation in Local Government

Rugayah Hashim
Universiti Teknologi MARA, Malaysia

ABSTRACT

Implementing an e-procurement system is a challenge for local government; however, lessons learned through the identification of these challenging issues allow local government ICT project managers to checklist these issues and ensure a successful e-procurement system rollout in their respective organization. For this study, qualitative research design and analyses were used to identify and rank the emergent issues. Through pattern-coding analyses of the interview transcriptions, twelve key issues emerged to be found as the common barriers of successful e-procurement rollout. In this regard, the author's research is significant given that the return of investment is crucial to a local government's administrative functions as well as for effective and efficient service delivery.

INTRODUCTION

In keeping up with globalization, the Malaysian government has allocated substantial amount for Information and Communication Technology (ICT) in the country's annual budget. Recognizing the potential of ICT in enhancing public service delivery, the current policy initiatives advocated by a developing nation like Malaysia, must increase the need for competitive advantage in a restrictive economic environment through administrative modifications (Abdullah, 2004). Furthermore, driven by the need to acquire, manage and distribute information, the last decade have seen a massive growth in ICT investments by both public and private institutions. Besides enhancing Malaysia's competitiveness, the public delivery system must be improved simply because the citizens demand it. Consequently, the public sector delivery system has the entire nation and the population as its clientele. Therefore, the civil servants, particularly at the local government level

DOI: 10.4018/978-1-4666-0930-3 .ch017

must be able to deliver every facet of service to the people in their respective constitutions (Karim, 1999, 2003).

To realize an electronically driven government, an in-depth understanding of the specific issues relating to e-procurement implementation is essential for the establishment of appropriate principals and effective approaches. In fact, in the implementation of the e-government and e-procurement initiatives, many issues and challenges to both initiatives are inter-related. These include issues and challenges pertaining to information security, establishment of a comprehensive, widespread and affordable telecommunications infrastructure as well as adequate education and training which encompass not only government employees but the masses as well (Karim, 1999, 2003; Karim & Khalid, 2003; Croom & Brandon-Jones, 2007). Each individual issue is important in its own context because of the multiple impacts which inordinately affect the organization and implementation of ICTs within it. Subsequently, effective management of ICT and e-procurement across the board can only take place when a more comprehensive understanding of the myriad of issues is achieved (Ward, 1995; Beaumaster, 2002).

For this paper, the local governments of the state of Selangor were the focus of this study. Of the 14 states in Malaysia, Selangor is the only one that has achieved the status of a developed state as of August 29, 2005. Being the leader in economic development, Selangor plays a major role in making Malaysia's Vision 2020 a reality. Henceforth, the paper will showcase the emergent issues on e-procurement implementation in the local governments of Selangor, Malaysia.

E-PROCUREMENT IN MALAYSIA

Prior to 2000, e-procurement was one of the pilot projects under the e-government flagships of the Multimedia Super Corridor (MSC). The MSC is Malaysia's multimedia utopia encompassing both a physical area and a paradigm shift for creating value in the Information Age (Karim & Khalid, 2003). Most e-initiatives were started at the federal level, therefore, once the initiatives are up and running, the state and local governments will then be directed to implement the same systems used at the federal level. The Malaysian scene for e-procurement (EP) is very slow to pick up. At the federal government level, e-procurement started in 2000 with the registration of suppliers and central contract (APEC, 2006), then direct purchase in 2002. Subsequently, the module of quotation and tender went live in 2003 (APEC, 2006). Nevertheless, it is important to note that in Malaysia, the e-procurement system is better known as e-*Perolehan* which is managed by the Treasury Department, Ministry of Finance, Malaysia (Karim & Khalid, 2003). *E-Perolehan* streamlines the federal government's procurement activities so as to improve the quality of service it provides by allowing suppliers to present their products on the Internet. "The suppliers' product catalogue is then converted into the form of an electronic catalogue" which can be viewed anywhere, anytime (ePerolehan, 2009). Hence, the problem whether e-procurement would have a successful run at the local government level as it had been at the federal and state levels was the gap researched in this paper.

IMPORTANCE OF E-PROCUREMENT

The development of the Internet offers increasing opportunity for electronic commerce which has attracted much attention from businesses, not only to get connection with others and make a profit from their product/service, but also to reduce the costs of internal and external operational procedures such as purchasing or procurement (Croom & Johnston, 2003; Croom & Brandon-Jones, 2007). Procurement is a very critical task because it is a matter not only for making a profit, but also for staying in business in a highly competitive environment (Neef, 2001; Pushman & Alt, 2005; Kheng & Al-Hawamdeh, 2002; Gansler et al., 2003; Davila et al., 2002; Carayannis & Popescu, 2005). Liao et al. (2003) pointed out that in the government sector, procurement is sometimes the source of corruption, scandal and abuse of public resources. Besides inadequately qualified personnel, "transparency" of the procurement environment becomes another source of problems in the procurement procedure.

Electronic procurement is one area where governments can reduce inefficiencies in their service provision. Every level of government is involved in purchasing or procuring and most local governments in Malaysia still use the traditional purchase order method which is a slow and antiquated process requiring multiple levels of bureaucracy for almost any purchasing decisions. These methods satisfy the goal of increased public accountability, but increase the cost of procurement. Definitely, this system has worked and will continue working for most local governments but in a dragging manner. Thus, by incorporating technology, purchasing will be made easier, cheaper and more accountable through streamlined electronic procurement, that is, a digital or electronic paper trail is recorded at every level of the transaction (Guijarro, 2009; Olsson, 2008; Garson, 2003; Kirby & Wagner, 1999). However, for the Selangor local government organizations, they have been slow to implement technology to improve the procurement process. If the Selangor local governments delay implementing e-procurement, they would have difficulty in interfacing with the federal government agencies as well as the vendors or suppliers listed in the *ePerolehan*'s e-catalogue.

Electronic procurement processes exist, formally or informally, in every organization that acquires information and communication technologies. Procurement involves all aspects of ICT acquisition such as competitive bidding, purchasing equipment and services, and evaluation of implemented systems. Part of the complication of ICT procurement in particular is that the acquisition of ICTs is not just about the purchase and use of hardware and software, it is also inherently tied to the acquisition of a variety of services, support personnel, intellectual properties, and any items that have either a direct or indirect effect on information and communication technologies (Croom & Brandon-Jones, 2007; Puschmann & Alt, 2005). The ICT procurement process is interdisciplinary and in most circumstances, involves everyone in an organization – IT staff, purchasing, legal, and financial employees, not to mention a number of end users from all departments across the organization and its planning and implementation procedures (Puschmann & Alt, 2005; Panayiotou et al., 2003). This multi-dimensional aspect makes e-procurement especially complex in relation to an organization's traditional purchasing practices (Neef, 2001). This complexity, in conjunction with the huge number of available products and services, and the speed with which new products are introduced to the market, makes the area of e-procurement an extremely intricate and volatile process area (Croom & Brandon-Jones, 2007; Puschmann & Alt, 2005; Garson, 2003; Gansler et al., 2003; Croom & Johnston, 2003; Lyne, 1996).

Literature surrounding this domain is relatively scarce for the Malaysian scene. Aside from the many prescriptions and guidelines for actually carrying out the procurement processes, much of what is available speaks primarily on major trends like cost-benefit analysis of ICT and specific procurement practices in a particular, individual organization. Essentially, the procurement of information and communication technology (ICT) consists of budgeting for ICTs and the ultimate acquisition of ICTs. The early literature in this area in essence discussed procurement as a set of alternatives for ICT acquisition, the first of which is internal information and communication technology appropriation. At its most fundamental level, this means that each individual municipality must take care of all the budgeting, cost-benefit analysis, ICT selection, purchasing and implementation on its own. The second alternative, known as external, is the contracting out of all, or a significant portion of all ICT equipment and services for a given municipality (Kraemer & King, 1977).

Most of these early discussions were based on the need for an organization to achieve economies of scale with regard to their ICT processes. To have an internal procurement process meant that the organization could provide ICT services for it and still achieve a great cost-benefit ratio than contracting out would allow. In the 1960s and 1970s in the United States, only the larger local governments could afford the luxury of internal procurement. For smaller municipalities the economies of scale were much smaller and they had to contract out to external agencies that could provide ICT services for them at a substantially lower cost than they could achieve by doing it themselves (Kraemer & King, 1977). Much of this situation changed in the early 1980s with the arrival of the technology scene in the form of the microcomputer or PC (Personal Computer), which created an environment where most ICT processes could be provided internally by the local government. Even with this technological boost, there still remained the problem of contracting-out factor. The hardware had become much more cost effective for a locality to own but in many cases some of the operations (like network management) continued to exist beyond the fiscal grasp and expertise level of the organization. Currently, contracting out still occurs for the provision of certain ICT services.

More recent literature with regard to ICT procurement discusses the process of acquiring ICT equipment and services but it refers mostly to the state and federal levels of government. This discussion provides an overview of the bidding and contracting process, which is often defined in statutes and regulations. According to Beaumaster (2002), this aspect of the procurement process creates special problems for the management of ICTs by the local government administrators.

Most of the procurement regulations require the acceptance of minimum bids for equipment and services, which meet proposal guidelines. The procedures are often quite slow and stretch out over a number of planning cycles. In this environment, it is difficult to handle system and software upgrades, which are an integral part of today's information technologies. As in the earliest stages of information and communication technology (ICT) procurement, the area of cost-benefit analysis remains a prominent concern. Many of the problems with ICT implementation that local governments face today are drawn from the history of a strict cost-benefit approach to the development of information systems (Guijarro, 2009; Carayannis & Propescu, 2005). Over time, the level of concern and frustration that managers have developed with regard to ICT acquisitions have grown substantially. Their main consideration has become a question of how ICT can best be made to work efficiently and economically, and deliver the expected benefits. This view often comes from unrealistic expectations of technology, ignorance of the systems, and excessive expense. Unfortunately, these issues have taken focus away from other important issues, which come into play (Ward, 1995).

Local governments must look on the acquisition of information and communication technologies as an investment decision, which necessarily requires careful evaluation of the risks as well as the benefits. As Kraemer and King (1977) pointed out, ICT acquisitions entail future costs, which go far beyond initial procurement decisions. There must necessarily be a substantial commitment to future upgrades, operating expenses, software and personnel. Typical cost-benefit analysis of an ICT investment does not fully realize the implications of the ICT procurement process. ICT investments cannot be calculated the same as other capital investments, that is, by using internal rates of return or net present values to determine whether to invest in specific systems or not. According to Ward (1995), this method only works when the costs and benefits can be accurately predicted over the life cycle of the system and since the actual life cycle is extremely hard to determine, it is very difficult to evaluate ICTs on a financial basis alone.

In order to effectively evaluate (in an appropriate manner) ICT investments, it is necessary to secure a more holistic view of the process – taking into consideration infrastructure investments, personnel investments and, incremental capacities (Ward, 1995; Karim, 2003; Garson, 2003; Gansler et al., 2003). Part of the problem with quantifying the benefits of ICT lies in the inability to convert the many "intangibles" of information and communication technologies into financial figures (Beaumaster, 2002; Demirkan & Nichols, 2008). In effect it is really not possible to quantify all of the benefits of ICT nor does it make sense to try and force these types of quantitative measures on those that are not quantifiable. Parker (1988), in Information Economics, provides an analysis technique specifically for ICT, which takes into account possible IT applications and then justifies five basic techniques for evaluation. They maintained the traditional cost-benefit analysis and added to it the following techniques:

- Value linking (improvement and performance)
- Value acceleration (improvements in time use)
- Value restructuring (productivity through organizational change)
- Innovation evaluation (the value of new processes and practices).

This approach is one of the more creative of the limited offerings in the literature on this area and provides a better way of interpreting the long-term values of ICT for an organization. Thus, to determine the tangible benefits of ICT, they must be broken down into distinct divisions, which represent the types of technology categories.

Parker et al. (1988) provided three main ways in which ICT systems benefits accrue:

i. Substitutive – replacing people power with machine power. This approach is generally driven by economic factors with the ultimate goal of improving efficiency.

ii. Complementary – improving productivity and personnel effectiveness by providing new ways to perform tasks through ICT.

iii. Innovative – increasing a competitive edge by creating new applications for ICT. In this particular model, the authors provided a way of looking at ICT acquisitions, which provides for a view which is neither purely based on efficiency, nor solely on innovation. Instead, they provide a framework where integration between cost-benefit analysis and innovative evaluation is possible depending on organization needs and directives.

Nevertheless, Information and communication technology (ICT) has been and will continue being the catalyst for the new source of economic wealth. ICT has become the generally accepted umbrella term for a rapidly expanding range of equipment, applications, services and basic technologies that process information (Harper & Utley, 2001). Many industries and specific organizations have successfully implemented numerous ICTs and as a result, enjoy great competitive advantages, while others have not.

Henceforth, for this study, the concept of local government will actually consists of the twelve municipalities or local agencies and nine land/district offices (LDO) within the state of Selangor, Malaysia as shown in Table 1.

RESEARCH DESIGN

Most research projects on ICT or information systems are quantitatively analyzed, thus the findings missed out on the important insights

Table 1. The 12 Selangor local government organizations

	LOCAL COUNCILS (12)
1.	Shah Alam City Council
2.	Subang Jaya Municipal Council
3.	Petaling Jaya Municipal Council
4.	Ampang Jaya Municipal Council
5.	Klang Municipal Council
6.	Kajang Municipal Council
7.	Selayang Municipal Council
8.	Sepang Municipal Council
9.	Kuala Langat District Council
10.	Hulu Selangor District Council
11.	Kuala Selangor District Council
12.	Sabak Bernam District Council

into information technology phenomena (Myers & Avison, 2002). This was also noted by Paré (2002) where there is now a growing tradition of using qualitative research approaches to study information technology phenomena (e.g., Nelson et al., 2000; Romm & Pliskin, 1997; Trauth & Jessup, 2000; Wixon & Ramey, 1996). Hence, this paper germinated from qualitative analyses where interviews were the main method of data collection. Rigor was established through Eisenhardt's (1989) framework. The interviews were divided into two phases:

- Phase 1 – involved the use of a structured survey guide. Seven local government entities were identified based on the close proximity (easy access and short distance) to the researcher's base. The seven were: Petaling Land/District Office, Petaling Jaya Municipal Council (MPPJ), Subang Jaya Municipal Council (MPSJ), Shah Alam City Council (MBSA), Ampang Jaya Municipal Council (MPAJ), Klang Municipal Council (MPK) and the Kuala Selangor Land/District Office. Only the department head of the respective ICT Department of each local government body was interviewed. After analyzing the interview transcriptions, it was found that the land and district offices (LDOs) do not

have the autonomy to make decisions any decisions pertaining to ICT, let alone on implementing an e-procurement system. The Selangor state ICT Center controls the LDOs ICT units. With that outcome, it was resolved that a second phase of repeat interviews would give in-depth and rich data through the use of a semi-structured interview guide.

- Phase 2 – The analyses of the seven interview transcriptions provided the improvements necessary to construct a semi-structured interview guide. The guide included open-ended questions that would allow the researcher to probe into pertinent areas. This time, all the ICT heads are interviewed. In between interviews, the transcriptions have to be analyzed immediately. The process ends once saturation has been reached.

As for data analysis, pattern coding was employed for the dissection of interview transcriptions. According to Miles and Huberman (1994), coding is analysis; therefore, the examination of issues was also the preliminary step in this study's analysis through the identification and naming of the issues (open coding) that emerged. It is important to highlight that a data table was created to avoid duplication of data as well as to make sense of the data collected and segregated. In simple terms, the data table acts as an inventory for each categorization of issues. Furthermore, the data table ensured that the researcher is not swamped by the accrued data. In addition, Miles and Huberman (1994) advocated that the analyzing of data is to "*dissect them meaningfully, while keeping the relations between the parts intact*". Hence codes act as tags or labels for assigning units of meaning to the descriptive information. Codes are usually attached to the words, phrases, sentences or whole paragraphs, connected or unconnected to a specific setting, thus they take the form of a straightforward category label or a more complex one (Miles & Huberman, 1994). Also, codes give embedded meaning to the significance of the phenomenon being studied.

For this study, the conventional way of allocating codes was done by inductively going through the transcripts line by line within a paragraph (Strauss & Corbin, 1990) and marking the coherent words, phrases, sentences or whole paragraphs that hold significant meanings to the research problem. The next step is to divide them into issues (themes or gestalts) and sub-issues at different levels of analysis. These issues would presumably recur with some regularity throughout the rest of the cases being analyzed.

As an illustration, pattern (or descriptive) coding was applied to this research where each issue was given three-character alphabets inferred from the words themselves, for example 'leadership' is coded as 'LDR'. Pattern coding has been a support d by Miles and Huberman (1994, p. 57) as *"an analogue to the cluster-analytic and factor-analytic devices used in statistical analyses"* but being *"even more inferential and explanatory"* among other codes used in analyzing qualitative data. Besides allowing for the easy identification of the three-character acronyms given for each issue, a coded segment of the interview transcripts *"illustrates an emergent leitmotiv or pattern that can discern the relationships between the themes"*. In addition, pattern coding *"pulls together a lot of material into more meaningful and parsimonious units of analysis"* (Miles & Huberman, 1994, 57).

FINDINGS

Twelve key issues emerged from the analyses of the interview transcriptions as shown in Table 2. The issues are ranked according to the number of times they are commonly referred in the interviews.

Thus, the most problematic issue faced by the Selangor local government executives with regard to e-procurement implementation is the interdepartmental coordination issue, followed by orga-

nizational directives and the existing legacy systems. Three issues were ranked fourth, which are organizational support, written procedures and planning model. Yet again three issues were ranked fifth and they are organizational ICT expertise, organizational culture and individual support. In the sixth place are leadership and strategic planning, while two issues were ranked in the seventh place – individual ICT expertise and finance/budgeting issues. In the eighth place was internal and external politics, while standardization issues were ranked in the ninth place, followed by timeframe and scheduling matters. Finally, human resource and adequate staffing were ranked eleventh and twelfth respectively.

LIMITATIONS OF RESEARCH

Every research project is limited in some way or another and this research too has its limitations. A major limitation of this study is the choice of qualitative analysis as the research approach. Aside from the lengthy timeframe required for the face-to-face interviews, the transcriptions of the taped interviews, data analyses and data interpretation require a lot of time too. Furthermore, repeated interviews have to be conducted to ensure that rich and in-depth data are collected. Though the use of the interview guide aided the interviews, observations of the local government environment – the offices - required unbiased and unprejudiced record of the events, that is, accurate and complete data. In addition, observation generally is limited to descriptions of what happens in small groups of people, which also limits the ability to generalize the results (Neuman, 2003; O'Sullivan et al., 2008).

Since specific cases – the local governments within the state of Selangor were concentrated on; this limitation also applies to research based on the case study or focus group techniques. The element of biasness introduced by the investigator in the collection and analysis of the data remains a threat.

Table 2. ICT implementation in the selangor local governments

No.	Issues (Themes)
1.	Interdepartmental Coordination
2.	Organizational Directives
3.	Existing system / Legacy system
4.	Organizational Support, Written Procedures, Planning Model
5.	Organizational ICT Expertise, Organizational Culture, Individual Support
6.	Leadership, Strategic Planning
7.	Individual ICT Expertise, Finance/Budgeting Issues
8.	Internal and External Politics
9.	Standardization
10.	Timeframe and Scheduling
11.	Human Resource
12.	Adequate staffing

Also, according to Newman (2003), "it is difficult to generalize findings from either a case study or results of a focus group. Even if participants in a focus group are selected randomly from some population, the size of the sample is usually too small to warrant generalization".

DISCUSSION AND CONCLUSION

The findings of this study showed that twelve mainstream issues emerged from the interviews with the local government representatives with regard to the success (or failure) of implementing e-procurement in their respective entity. The first one ranked and oft-mentioned by the interviewees was interdepartmental coordination. This can be explained by the fact that for local government administrators, implementing an e-procurement system is actually a directive from the federal/central government, and as such coordination and communication between and among government agencies are considered problematic. Moreover, this issue relates to the degree an organization is able to coordinate its ICT implementation process across departments. With the rise in use of personal computers (PCs), information systems management has become increasingly decentralized. In the district offices and local councils, this often means that ICT planning, procurement and, implementation may not be coordinated across departments thus perpetuating duplication, lack of standardization, and other problems.

The second issue was organizational directives. This issue is also related to interdepartmental coordination. However, for the local government administrators, this issue refers to their missions, objectives, and plans. Internal or in-house directives serve as guidelines for future plans and actions of the organization and they must be strategically defined to facilitate effective ICT implementation within a local government entity only. If a directive is received from the federal government for immediate implementation of a certain system, most times smaller municipalities would not be able to accommodate such a request because of limited resources from hardware, software and trained personnel. The existence of legacy systems is also a major issue for the local governments of Selangor. Since budget is limited, most of the ICT systems are not as up-to-date as those at the federal government departments, and therefore, compatibility issues arise. Compatibility issues refer to the ability to interact, communicate and, share information across networks and between software. Without systems and software compatibility data exchange would be impossible, hence, it is very important that newly proposed systems be compatible with existing systems and that compatibility be addressed early on in the planning process.

The fourth issues raised were organizational support, written procedures and planning model. It is a known fact that successful and effective implementation of ICTs relies on the ability of an organization to change and adapt in order to exploit the uses of advanced technologies. This issue refers to an organization's predilection toward supporting strategic vision and planning at all levels, which in turn will allow it to make use of rapidly changing technologies (Demirkan & Nichols, 2008). In the case of the Selangor local governments, there is obvious lack of organizational support because of weak leadership. In addition, the lack of a written procedure hinders the smooth implementation of any information system. Usually, written procedures are state or federal mandates which affect local government with regard to ICT planning, procurement, and implementation as this involves specific or internal policies that must be applied to the locality. This issue includes fiscal concerns, contracts, vendors, suppliers and other external consultants. Since, there is hardly a formal written procedure for most information systems implemented at the local government organization, therefore it follows that any ICT planning model is also absent.

The sixth issues that came next were leadership and strategic planning. Leadership relates to various levels of helmsman-ship within the organization with regard to ICT implementation. One of the problems with technology and the workplace is that not everyone is ready or willing to become part of a technologically based workforce. In many situations, leadership from managers and co-workers can help to enhance

effective implementation of ICTs. Managers especially can promote ICT implementation by example. Also, pressure for quick solutions to very complex ICT problems served to work against strategic planning in organizations. The successful implementation of information and communication technologies in an organization depends heavily on the strategic analysis of organization needs and objectives. Organizations, which do not make use of formalized planning with regard to ICT, may find themselves without direction in a rapidly changing environment.

Two issues emerged as seventh ranked; individual ICT expertise and finance or budgeting issues. The issue of individual ICT expertise refers to the level of ICT skill of each employee. It is typical for a locality to employ individuals with a very diverse range of ICT competence. It is also typical that some of these individuals will have a willingness and desire to learn more about technology and how to use specific ICTs, and others will be quite resistant to adapting to new technologies. This was obviously true for most local government organizations located in sub-urban and rural areas of Selangor. Once they are in a comfort zone, it is very difficult for the ICT managers to re-engineer certain processes particularly for e-procurement applications. As for budgetary concerns, ICTs are expensive at a number of levels including fiscal issues. Fiscal concerns for ICT require definition and measurement of operating costs, investment costs, and the possible/achieved benefits of technologies (Gansler et al., 2003). In the case of the Selangor local governments, their annual budget is limited, thus, implementing an expensive and complicated system such as an e-procurement system puts a heavy burden on the administrators to seek for extra funding. The issue of funding, on one hand, is linked to internal and external politics. This issue is inherent in any organizational activity and e-procurement implementation is no different. State government executives and ICT professionals alike must recognize and address the political ramifications of ICT implementation within their organization and the external environment. Technological activities in general are political by nature and the constant interferences from internal and external parties further aggravate the successful implementation of a system (Heeks, 2006).

The ninth issue that emerged was the standardization of ICT elements such as hardware, software, data and procedures. Without some standards, planning for future ICT uses and acquisitions would prove nearly impossible. Setting standards within an organization can be problematic enough – standardization between organizations can prove impossible (Beaumaster, 2002). Standards make communication possible and lend consistency and efficiency to information systems. Standardization is made substantially more difficult due to the ICT industry itself and its own standardization problems. Standardization issues are related to existing and legacy systems within all three tiers of government.

Timeframe and scheduling are also problematic to e-procurement implementation in local government. With mandates and directives from the federal government, the time given is usually very short. Since the local government entities do not have the necessary infrastructure or people to implement such a complicated system, the project is definitely doomed for failure. Finally, the eleventh and twelfth issues on the list are human resource and adequate staffing. Though these issues could mean the same, the difference is in the level of ICT skill and experience of the staff deployed to work on the e-procurement system. For the former, these are issues related to the management process of human resources. A well-designed organization runs on carefully developed general procedures with relevant and skilled personnel to meticulously plan, manage and ultimately use ICTs for better productivity and performance. This is one of the most important issue areas and in many cases one that is ignored. Relating this to the Selangor local authorities requisitions for more staff is filled with bureaucratic bumps and

may take years before a staff is acquired. Meanwhile, they have to make do with what they have and this hinders the immediate implementation of any system. Consequently, the need for adequate staffing will result in feasible and effective system implementation. Furthermore, adequate staffing is a quantity and quality issue where the number of qualified staff is crucial to the success of running any ICT-based system.

As a conclusion, it can be deduced that the local governments of Selangor (Municipalities and, Land and District Offices) are not ready to have such a sophisticated system such as the e-procurement system unless the twelve issues are resolved beforehand. Once these issues are sorted out, the implementation and adoption of e-procurement at the local government level of Selangor would be easily attained.

ACKNOWLEDGMENT

The author acknowledges the Editor-in-Chief of the journal, Professor John Wang, and the anonymous reviewers for their indispensable input that improved the paper significantly. Also, to UiTM and the Selangor local government ICT administrators for their cooperation and support in realizing this study.

REFERENCES

Abdullah, A. B. (2004). *Keynote address – Managing the national economy in challenging times: Enhancing the delivery systems and mechanism.* Kuala Lumpur, Malaysia: National Institute of Public Administration (INTAN).

APEC (Asia-Pacific Economic Cooperation). (2006, September 5-6). *Final report on APEC services or transparency in procurement and e-procurement*, Ha Noi, Vietnam. Retrieved from http://www.apec.org/apec/publications/free-downloads/06_cti_ gpeg_transparency[1].pdf

Beaumaster, S. (1999). *IT implementation issues in local government: An analysis.* Unpublished doctoral dissertation, Blacksburg, VA.

Beaumaster, S. (2002). Local government IT implementation issues: A challenge for public administration. In *Proceedings of the 35th Hawaii International Conference on System Sciences (HICSS-35'02).*

Carayannis, E. G., & Popescu, D. (2005). Profiling a methodology for economic growth and convergence: learning from the EU e-procurement experience for central and eastern European countries. *Technovation, 25,* 1–14. doi:10.1016/S0166-4972(03)00071-3

Croom, S., & Brandon-Jones, A. (2007). Impact of e-procurement: Experiences from implementation in the UK public sector. *Journal of Purchasing and Supply Management, 13,* 294–303. doi:10.1016/j.pursup.2007.09.015

Croom, S., & Johnston, R. (2003). E-service: enhancing internal customer service through e-procurement. *International Journal of Service Industry Management, 14*(5), 539–555. doi:10.1108/09564230310500219

Davila, A., Gupta, M., & Palmer, R. J. (2002). *Moving procurement systems to the internet: The adoption and use of e-procurement technology models* (Tech. Rep. No. 1742). Retrieved March 22, 2003, from http://ssrn.com/abstract=323923

Demirkan, H., & Nichols, J. (2008). IT services project management: lessons learned from a case study in implementation. *International Journal of Project Organisation and Management, 1*(2), 204–220. doi:10.1504/IJPOM.2008.022192

ePerolehan. (2009). *ePerolehan, the official portal for Malaysian government procurement.* Retrieved from http://home.eperolehan.gov.my/

Gansler, J. S., Lucyshyn, W., & Ross, K. M. (2003). *Digitally integrating the government supply chain: E-procurement, e-finance, and e-logistics.* College Park, MD: University of Maryland.

Garson, G. D. (2003). *Public information technology: Policy and management issues.* Hershey, PA: IGI Global.

Guijarro, L. (2009). ICT standardization and public procurement in the United States and in the European Union: Influence on e-government deployment. *Telecommunications Policy, 33,* 285–295. doi:10.1016/j.telpol.2009.02.001

Harper, G. R., & Utley, D. R. (2001). Organizational culture and successful information technology implementation. *Engineering Management Journal, 13*(2), 11–15.

Heeks, R. (2006). *Implementing and managing eGovernment: An international text.* London: Sage.

ILBS – International Law Book Series. Laws of Malaysia. (2003). *Local government act 1976 (Act 171) & subsidiary legislation: As at 25th July 2003.* Kuala Lumpur, Malaysia: Direct Art Company.

Karim, M. R. A. (1999). *Reengineering the public service: leadership and change in an electronic age.* Kuala Lumpur, Malaysia: Pelanduk Publications.

Karim, M. R. A. (2003). Technology and improved service delivery: Learning points from the Malaysian experience. *International Review of Administrative Sciences: Creating Self-Confident Government* (p. 69, 191). London: Sage.

Karim, M. R. A., & Khalid, N. (2003). *E-government in Malaysia.* Kuala Lumpur, Malaysia: Pelanduk.

Kheng, C. B., & Al-Hawamdeh, S. (2002). The adoption of electronic procurement in Singapore. *Electronic Commerce Research, 2,* 61–73. doi:10.1023/A:1013388018056

Kirby, C., & Wagner, A. (1999). The ideal procurement process: The vendor's perspective. *Gaylord Information Systems*. Retrieved from http://www.ilsr.com/vendor.htm

Kraemer, K. L., & King, J. L. (1977). *Computers and local government: Volume 1, a manager's guide.* New York: Praeger.

Liao, S. H., Cheng, C. H., Liao, W. B., & Chen, I. L. (2003). A Web-based architecture for implementing electronic procurement in military organizations. *Technovation, 23*(6), 521–533. doi:10.1016/S0166-4972(02)00006-8

Lyne, C. (1996). Strategic procurement in the new local government. *European Journal of Purchasing & Supply Management, 2*(1), 1–6. doi:10.1016/0969-7012(95)00022-4

Mayer-Schonberger, V., & Lazer, D. (Eds.). (2007). *Governance and information technology: From electronic government to information government.* Cambridge, MA: MIT Press.

Miles, M. B., & Huberman, A. M. (1994). *Qualitative data analysis: An expanded source book* (2nd ed.). Thousand Oaks, CA: Sage.

Neef, D. (2001). *e-Procurement: From strategy to implementation.* Upper Saddle River, NJ: Prentice Hall.

Neuman, W. L. (2003). *Social research methods: Qualitative and quantitative approaches* (5th ed.). Boston, MA: Allyn and Bacon.

O'Sullivan, E., Rassel, G. R., & Berner, M. (2008). *Research methods for public administrators* (5th ed.). New York: Pearson-Longman.

Olsson, N. O. E. (2008). External and internal flexibility – aligning projects with the business strategy and executing projects efficiently. *International Journal of Project Organisation and Management, 1*(1), 47–64. doi:10.1504/IJPOM.2008.020028

Panayiotou, N. A., Gayialis, S. P., & Tatsiopoulos, I. P. (2003). An e-procurement system for governmental purchasing. *International Journal of Production Economics, 90*, 79–102. doi:10.1016/S0925-5273(03)00103-8

Puschmann, T., & Alt, R. (2005). Successful use of e-procurement in supply chains. *International Journal of Supply Chain Management, 10*(2), 122–133. doi:10.1108/13598540510589197

Seneviratne, S. J., & Garson, G. D. (Eds.). (1999). *Information technology and organizational change in the public sector.* Hershey, PA: IGI Global.

Stangor, C. (2004). *Research methods for the behavioral sciences* (2nd ed.). New York: Houghton Mifflin.

Vlach, J. (2007). *Public-private partnership as a basis of the development of public procurement.* Bratislava, Slovakia: Transparency International Slovensko. Retrieved July 20, 2009, from http://www.icoste.org/Roundup1105/Vlach1105.pdf

Ward, J. (1995). *Principles of information systems management.* New York: Routledge.

Yong, J. S. L. (2003). *E-Government in Asia: Enabling public service innovation in the 21st century.* Singapore: Times Edition.

This work was previously published in International Journal of Information Technology Project Management, Volume 1, Issue 3, edited by John Wang, pp. 59-70, copyright 2010 by IGI Publishing (an imprint of IGI Global).

Chapter 18
Establishing Preconditions for Spanning the Boundaries in Public Private IT Megaprojects

Roman Beck
Johann Wolfgang Goethe University, Germany

Oliver Marschollek
Johann Wolfgang Goethe University, Germany

Robert Wayne Gregory
Johann Wolfgang Goethe University, Germany

ABSTRACT

Inter-organizational cooperations between public and private partners, called public private partnerships (PPP), are increasingly gaining more importance concerning renewal, standardization, and optimization of the information technology (IT) infrastructure of public sector organizations. Reasons for this trend include the search for partners with necessary technological and innovative knowledge of sourcing IT and the identification of cost-saving potentials. Unfortunately, IT-PPP-cooperations are particularly susceptible to failure due to the clash of different cultures. Divergent understandings, expectations, and pressure from the relevant stakeholders hinder a working partnership. Therefore, in this exploratory, qualitative single-case study from the German TollCollect IT megaproject, the authors draw on findings from boundary spanning literature to explain how establishing preconditions for boundary spanning and actively bridging the gap between the partners, moderated by external stakeholder support, affects the formation of mutual trust and success of an IT-PPP-megaproject.

DOI: 10.4018/978-1-4666-0930-3.ch018

INTRODUCTION

Public sector organizations are continuously searching for opportunities of optimizing the effectiveness and efficiency of their administrative processes. These information-based processes, such as the request for a valid identification card, are the core business of public administration work. Carrying out these processes requires special administrative, regulatory, and legal know-how. Hence, outsourcing the provision of these services to a private sector agent (Dibbern, Goles, Hirschheim, & Jayatilaka, 2004) is no valid option for public sector organizations due to the knowledge gap of private industry of public structures and the responsibility of public administration to deliver administrative services to the citizens themselves (Hodge & Greve, 2007). However, the increasing demand for delivering innovative information technology (IT)-based services to citizens and the lack of technological and innovative know-how on the public side requires the exchange and cooperation with private companies to acquire the necessary IT resources. For these reasons, involving the sourcing of necessary technological know-how and IT infrastructure optimization of public sector organizations, the public administration often enters into technological alliances with private industry partners, called public private partnerships (PPP) (Reijniers, 1994). Considering the necessity of cooperation, PPPs allow for an opportunity for long-term, strategic cooperation focused on innovation using the core competences of both sides (Trafford & Proctor, 2006). Furthermore, this approach creates the possibility of realizing cost reductions, sharing risks, and raising new financial models for the public administration. In addition, PPPs are also gaining importance in IT megaprojects since increasingly public infrastructure projects are large IT projects rather than brick and mortar infrastructure projects as in the past (Brooks, 1987; Venugopal, 2005). IT megaprojects are unique, innovative multibillion-dollar investments which are affected by political and public stakeholders (Davies, Gann, & Douglas, 2009; Flyvbjerg, Bruzelius, & Rothengatter, 2005) and often do not meet the desired goals (Flyvbjerg et al., 2005; Nelson, 2007). Although the number of research contributions on IT project management practices in a purely private context (Cule, Schmidt, Lyytinen, & Keil, 2000; Kappelman, McKeeman, & Zhang, 2006; Sumner, Bock, & Giamartino, 2006) and success factors in the context of PPPs is increasing (Jacobsen & Choi, 2008; Jost, Dawson & Shaw, 2005; Trafford et al., 2006), we still have a lack of understanding of how IT-PPP-megaprojects can be successfully turned around in case of a failing course of action.

Hence, we conducted an exploratory, qualitative single-case study of the German TollCollect case to analyze how this IT-PPP-megaproject, which was on the verge of failure, finally succeeded. Preliminary research results and the initial setting of the project were already discussed in Beck and Möbs (2006). TollCollect is the German satellite-based toll collecting system for heavy trucks. With more than €3 billion of revenue streams per year and €2 billion costs for development and installation of the system, the TollCollect project is not only the single-largest PPP project ever carried out in Germany, but also the largest IT development project in Europe in the years from 2002 to 2005. Public and private partners in this project had to cope with challenges that gradually led to an initial breakdown of cooperation. However, this downturn was stopped by spanning the boundaries and reestablishing the partnership through the formation of trust between public and private parties leading to a successful implementation of the TollCollect system. Therefore, this case offered an interesting opportunity to answer the following research question: "How can the establishment of preconditions for boundary spanning and boundary spanning activities themselves reestablish a working partnership in IT-PPP-megaprojects?"

Public private cooperation requires bridging the gap of different cultural environments. Recent research on public private megaprojects has extended the external view of ongoing difficulties during their realization (Flyvbjerg et al., 2005) concerning project performance, budget and on-time delivery to an internally-focused view of actual practices in the light of project design and culture (van Marrewijk, Clegg, Pitsis, & Veenswijk, 2008). The cultural distance in these partnerships necessitates the exploration of boundary spanning practices for establishing a working partnership. Boundary spanning in this context deals with understanding, acknowledging, and respecting the different interests, values, norms, expectations, and regulations of the different cultural environments (Williams, 2002). Organizational research so far has focused on spanning the boundaries within organizations, between organizations, and between organizations and their environment (Leifer & Delbecq, 1978; Santos & Eisenhardt, 2005). Prior information systems (IS) research has mainly concentrated on evaluating the effects of the use of IT for boundary spanning in organizations and collaborations in offshoring projects (Levina & Vaast, 2006, 2008). Furthermore, prior PPP research has already shed light on the role and behaviors of boundary spanning managers during the establishment of PPPs (Noble & Jones, 2006). However, considering ongoing difficulties during the realization of IT-PPP-megaprojects, we still need to know how to reestablish a working partnership for turning around IT-PPP-megaprojects in case of a failing course of action. In addition, concerning the use of boundary spanning activities, there is little research on the necessary preconditions for the effective installation of boundary spanners on the organizational level. Therefore, we also studied the necessary preconditions to contribute to the boundary spanning literature.

The remainder of this paper is structured as follows. The following section discusses boundary spanning as a theoretical foundation. The next section presents our selected research methodology, employing the grounded theory method (GTM). After a brief introduction to the case, we explain the results from our theory-building case analysis and present the emerged model of boundary spanning in the context of IT-PPP-megaprojects. The final section of the paper presents the theoretical and practical contributions and provides directions for future research.

THEORETICAL BACKGROUND

As we started searching for theoretical support during the data analysis, we found insights in the extant literature on antecedents of boundary spanning, boundary spanning activities and trust formation, as well as the role of management during this process. Boundary spanning has already been analyzed on various levels (individual, team and organizational level) and in different disciplines (e.g., management and IS literature). On an individual level, boundary spanning literature concentrated so far on evaluating the functions (Aldrich & Herker, 1977), characteristics (Tushman, 1977), and the antecedents of boundary spanning roles (Tushman & Scanlan, 1981). Furthermore, empirical studies on an individual level of analysis focused on the differentiation of boundary spanning roles (Friedman & Podolny, 1992) and the individual skills, competencies and behaviors of boundary spanners (Williams, 2002). More recent literature explores boundary spanning on a team level of analysis, identifying the effects of the cultural orientation of team members on boundary spanning (Golden & Veiga, 2005). A further main focus of boundary spanning literature on a team level of analysis is the identification of factors influencing team member engagement in boundary spanning (Marrone, Tesluk, & Carson, 2007) and the exploration of the effects of antecedents on team boundary spanning behavior (Joshi, Pandey, & Han, 2009). Moreover on an organizational level, management literature has developed a model of boundary spanning activities to explain the relation between organizations and their environment (Leifer et al., 1978) and explored how boundary spanning activities affect organizational dynamics between different organizational settings (Robertson, 1995). On the other hand, IS literature has focused on how the use of IT facilitates working across boundaries in joint cooperations (Levina & Vaast, 2005; Pauleen & Yoong, 2001) and how IT can help to deteriorate boundaries within organizations (Levina et al., 2006). Furthermore, IS literature has analyzed how country and organizational contexts affect boundaries and status differences in IS development projects (Levina, 2006; Levina et al., 2008) and how different types of IS affect IT's role in boundary spanning activities (Lindgren, Andersson, & Henfridsson, 2008). PPP literature has extended these research results by examining the roles and behaviors of boundary-spanning managers during the establishment of PPPs (Noble et al., 2006). However, our research concentrates on exploring the organizational preconditions and the necessary task-oriented boundary spanning activities for reestablishing a working partnership in IT-PPP-megaprojects in case of a failing course of action which was one of the main emerging issues during our data collection and analysis.

Public sector organizations are dependent on specialized private companies for achieving operational efficiency and effectiveness, reducing financial deficits, and acquiring the necessary technological resources (Robertson, 1995). These technological alliances between public and private parties are based on formal contracts, providing the legal framework for cooperating, which are often accomplished in the form of a PPP. However, formal contracts are not able to cover every possible risk scenario. Therefore, successful public private collaboration comprises more than designing an explicit contract and dealing with legal restrictions. It is also about managing the informal aspects of the relationship such as mutual trust (Grimsey & Lewis, 2002). Prior PPP research has already

confirmed that mutual trust affects the success of PPP projects (Jacobsen et al., 2008; Jost et al., 2005). Consequently, underpinning divergences between the parties in a PPP are obstacles for the establishment of a successful partnership such as divergent expectations and interests which are anchored in their different cultural backgrounds (Reijniers, 1994).

Collaboration between public and private partners is often used to realize IT megaprojects (Clegg, Pitsis, Rura-Polley, & Marosszeky, 2002; Flyvbjerg et al., 2005) while their success strongly depends on the management ability how to deal with conflicting interests (Flyvbjerg et al., 2005). Conflicting interests in a PPP are anchored in different socio-cultural environments (van Marrewijk, 2007). Bridging these different interests, managers in a PPP need to have an unprejudiced view and understand the different motivation of the participating parties which is the foundation for an unbiased relationship (Williams, 2002). Besides, boundary spanning activities depend on expertise about different socio-cultural backgrounds which encompasses, among others, the knowledge of project management approaches and goals from the private side and regulatory as well as legal restrictions from the public side (Lindgren et al., 2008). Finally, the basic precondition for enforcing changes between public and private parties is formal power enabling the management of PPPs to give instructions and directions to the participating parties in this kind of partnership (Bloomfield & Coombs, 1992). Forming a cooperation between public and private parties however does not necessarily indicate that employees working for the partnership are disciplinary and functionally assigned to the new partnership and that they need to follow instructions from the management in charge.

Overcoming organizational boundaries can be achieved by boundary spanners who are individuals mediating between groups separated by location, hierarchy or function and sharing their expert knowledge (Pawlowski & Robey, 2004;

Wenger, 1998). In order to create an environment of trust and understanding between public and private parties, boundary spanners need to protect the parties from external pressure (e. g., public and political) and have to foster information exchange within and across teams (Leifer et al., 1978). Achieving transparency between the parties and guaranteeing the security of not being blamed for failure during the realization of a joint project fosters open communication. In this case, open communication about group-specific knowledge supports a learning environment and enables the possibility of aligning different interests which is one of the main factors for the success of PPPs (Lindgren et al., 2008).

Accordingly, shared goals and a mutual understanding level the way for the development of trust and belief in PPP success (Williams, 2002). Trust is the psychological state in which an individual accepts the vulnerability relying on positive expectations of the intentions of others concerning their behavior (Rousseau, Sitkin, Burt, & Camerer, 1998). Important obstacles for the establishment of a trust-based partnership are diverging interests and cultural differences (Rosenau, 1999). The reestablishment of the partnership through trust formation can only be achieved by resolving discrepancies in mutual understanding, meeting the expected outcome conditions of the project and reinforcing trust (Kim, Dirks, & Cooper, 2009; Williams, 2002). Hence, the necessary precondition for successfully managing IT-PPP-megaprojects is the establishment of a working partnership in which the partners cooperate with a single vision of project outcomes (Levina et al., 2005). Building upon prior IS research; we analyze boundary spanning phenomena at the inter-organizational level integrating the views of both, the private and public side. One of our core categories, trust formation, emerged from our analysis following GTM which we explain in more detail in the following section.

METHODS

We entered the field without any preconceived concepts or frameworks in mind, focusing on understanding failure in IT-PPP-megaprojects and how these projects can be successfully turned around which currently is not explored sufficiently. Therefore, we conducted an exploratory, qualitative, interpretive single-case study using a GTM approach which is predestined for under-researched areas. This methodological approach can be used for discovering deep insights and understandings of the underlying structures and the context of phenomena (Hughes & Jones, 2003). By invitation of one of the leading corporations responsible for the development of TollCollect, we gained access to primary data, consisting of 12 qualitative expert interviews with leading managers of the public and the private side in the TollCollect project, and secondary data, including extensive documentation of the historical development of toll collection on German highways. The interviews were the primary basis for our interpretative, qualitative single-case study (Walsham, 1995a, 1995b; Yin, 2003) of the German TollCollect case. On average, the interviews lasted from 52 minutes to 3 hours and 45 minutes each. The interviewees were carefully selected according to their role in the project, their position in the hierarchy, and affiliation to the project's stakeholders, discovering insights of the project from a dyadic perspective (public and private side). All interviews were tape-recorded and transcribed which resulted in 1003 recorded audio minutes and 246 pages of transcriptions. Secondary material was analyzed to enable further comparisons and triangulation of findings. In addition, an analysis of press articles that appeared during the time period of the project was conducted for triangulation purposes. The first semi-structured interviews were held in an open-ended fashion and were conducted in May 2006. Following the GTM technique 'theoretical sampling', these initial interviews were first openly coded and analyzed, identifying discrete concepts and categories to guide subsequent data collection and analysis efforts. For coding purposes, the software Atlas.ti (Muhr, 2008) was used. Over time, the core categories started to emerge from the data and our analytical efforts became more focused. The last semi-structured interviews with a more specific focus on the core themes were conducted in June 2007. Besides, emphasis was also given to investigator triangulation, meaning that we conducted the analysis in a group of multiple researchers. The first analysis phase of open coding generated a list of approximately 330 descriptive and partly overlapping codes. Triangulation and conceptualization efforts (following the constant comparison method) led to the consolidation of the codes, constantly comparing the data according to similarities and differences and assigning multiple data incidents to a common meaning.

Following GTM (Glaser, 1978; Glaser & Strauss, 1967), our model was driven by the analysis of the case study, constant comparison with extant literature, and evaluation of secondary data. The extant literature solely served as guide or sensitizing device for constant comparisons to support the conceptualization process. Our initial data collection and analysis steps focused on generating concepts and categories. Over time, we reached a point of theoretical saturation (Eisenhardt, 1989) and started to integrate our findings (Glaser, 1978). Our data collection and analysis efforts were deeply intertwined with each other. Initial analysis results were already generated in the second half of 2007. As the analysis was intensified especially during the first half of 2009, the core categories emerged from the data. During our analysis, we used the extant literature as slices of data to be compared with primary and secondary data. Furthermore, we analyzed the case among multiple researchers to triangulate their different perspectives. The process of conceptualizing continued in a similar way. After identifying the indicators for the concepts in the data, we compared literature on boundary span-

ning related to our findings and aligned it with them. In addition, we used the extant literature as guide for enhancing the theoretical foundation of our research model. Using the extant literature as sensitizing device, we were able to develop the concepts of "boundary spanning activities" and "trust formation" and their relations to "preconditions of boundary spanning activities", as well as even identify new concepts which also emerged from the data (i. e., external stakeholder support). The result of our research is a model of establishing the necessary preconditions for spanning the boundaries in public private IT megaprojects.

THE GERMAN TOLLCOLLECT CASE

As often when 'innovation on demand' is ordered, the German TollCollect IT megaproject (www.tollcollect.de) was prone to high risks and potential project failure from the very beginning. The idea of building an automatic toll collecting system for heavy trucks was first born in 1994 by federal government. In November 1998, the official political announcement was made to build a toll collecting system for the German autobahn for heavy trucks. This announcement triggered the interest of a large number of multi-national companies. Subsequently, several commercial syndicates emerged to join the necessary core competencies for this project such as telematics, automobile know-how, experience with toll collection, as well as bearing the financial risk. After a long and difficult commercial tendering procedure beginning in December 1999, the German Federal Ministry of Transport engaged the private companies Deutsche Telekom, DaimlerChrysler Financial Services and the French freeway operator Cofiroute as the executing syndicate 'Toll-Collect' in September 2002. Both, the tendering procedure and project realization were influenced by several law suits filed by competing bidders during the tendering procedure and the European Union during the realization. These law suits were a major obstacle for TollCollect concerning the start of operations.

'TollCollect' is the joint venture company which was founded for the cooperation with the German Federal Ministry of Transport. Not only were the private companies within TollCollect involved in this project, but also several suppliers which were for example providing parts of the technical infrastructure. Besides the numerous players on the private side, the stakeholders on the public side consisted of politics, the German Federal States, and the European Union which also were involved in project realization. The initiators of TollCollect in Germany had the ambitious goal to design and develop the first satellite-based toll collecting system in the world, based on the global system for mobile communications (GSM) standard and the satellite-based global positioning system (GPS). The project was carried out in cooperation between public and private partners and eventually started operating on January 1st, 2005.

The system's infrastructure is formed by over 600,000 on-board-units installed into European trucks (which had to be updatable via GSM) and 300 enforcement bridges overarching the autobahn for an effective controlling. The on-board-unit (OBU) is a fat client for collecting traffic data records as well as sending the mileage data accumulated to the central TollCollect accounting system. The enforcement bridges are equipped with cameras and scales embedded into the autobahn for a visual control of the trucks, weight control, and for counting the number of axles. If a truck is not logged into the TollCollect system then an automatic check against the German license plate register (or registers from other European countries) is made to identify the owner and send a ticket. The TollCollect system was designed to automatically detect and charge the use of a defined roadway system depending on the emission class, weight, and number of axles of a truck. An automatic, satellite-based as well as a manual, terminal-based booking functionality was required. Although the completion was delayed

several times, finally the implementation of the toll collecting system succeeded on January 1st, 2005 (Rehring, 2006).

The initial problems resulted from mismatching divergent understandings and expectations between public and private parties which eventually caused the termination of the formal contract between TollCollect and the German Federal Ministry of Transport and a rising public interest. Although TollCollect was officially disengaged, the chief executive officers of Deutsche Telekom and DaimlerChrysler were still trying to achieve a mutual consent directly with the German chancellor. TollCollect developed an amended project realization concept and hence publicly announced the successful renegotiation of the formal contract with the German chancellor on March 1st 2004. The new project realization concept contained a possible project start for January 1st 2005 with a technical solution that provided only a reduced number of features. The remaining set of functionalities should be implemented in a second roll out phase by January 1st 2006. After the successful renegotiation, TollCollect replaced their top management from DaimerChrysler with leading managers from Deutsche Telekom and changed the operative leadership of project realization to Deutsche Telekom. Overcoming the initial divergent understandings and expectations of the different fields of practice contributed to reestablish a working partnership. However, before boundary spanning and reestablishment of a working partnership was possible, TollCollect had to make a radical change in its leadership and management style as we will illustrate in the following section.

CASE ANALYSIS

Preconditions for Boundary Spanning

Since the project faced tremendous difficulties due to grown distrust and miscommunication, before any boundary spanning activity could have been applied successfully the right preconditions had to be in place which was illustrated by a member of the new management team:

Taking over the operative leadership of the project, we discovered a situation of reciprocal finger-pointing and resistance of starting over new. Before restarting the project and fulfilling our mission, this attitude had to be changed which was one of our hardest challenges.

In the case of TollCollect, that meant establishing an unbiased relation between the new TollCollect management and the public stakeholders, acquiring expertise in public administration areas of practice, as well as the power to enforce changes. These preconditions played an important role for successfully bridging the divide between the parties.

The change in leadership became ultimately necessary because of the deterioration of mutual trust. The relation between the parties needed to be reestablished due to divergent understandings and expectations. Consequently, reestablishing the relationship was only possible by a radical change which was stated by a leading manager of the public side:

TollCollect had started a complete reengineering of project structures which included a drastic replacement of human resources. This was the basic precondition for a project restart because we still believed that the old management had not communicated every emerging problem.

Establishing an unbiased relationship by changing the management showed the public authorities TollCollect´s willingness to complete the project successfully. The formation of the management team was related to different governance issues such as the mediation of a basis for mutual trust, representing the interests of both parties, and finally having access to the informal

network of all stakeholders (Cross & Prusak, 2002; Friedman et al., 1992). Hence according to our analysis, it was necessary from both sides of the PPP to establish a management team without a tainted relationship. Consider the following remark of a leading manager from the public side which illustrates the atmosphere in the project at that point of time:

The change in management was inevitable for achieving project´s goals because mutual trust was deteriorated. Replacing people who had not communicated the ongoing problems openly had a signaling effect for the renewal of the relation.

The new managers were chosen due to their experience and qualification as successful crisis managers in other projects. Furthermore, TollCollect became aware of the necessity to install a management team which was familiar with the cultural background and administrative requirements of the public partner. In addition, the management team also needed to be aware of the processes and governance structures on the private side, identifying the key people who are necessary for realizing the project successfully which was revealed by a leading manager of TollCollect:

After the decision to form a new management team, we knew that we needed somebody who can deal with our public partner because we were not able to realize the project without their support. At the same time, this person needed to be knowledgeable about the specialties of private industry and have the necessary insider know-how.

The change of the management team also initiated a change in the communication style to open and timely exchanges. This change empowered them to align the formerly divergent expectations and take into account political constraints articulated by public stakeholders. Soon after the installation of the new management, mutual understanding and respect for the achievements were bridging the divide between the public and private party, as a leading manager from TollCollect remarked:

The new management carefully avoided further confrontations with public authorities, intensified open communication, solved the technical complexity of the project, and finally fostered the emergence of a team spirit between the parties.

The familiarity of the new management with decision-making processes within public authorities, as well as their open communication style, enabled them to bridge the initial divide between the parties as a crucial precondition for reestablishing the relationship which is confirmed by IS literature (Pawlowski et al., 2004; Wenger, 1998). The integration of knowledge about both participating fields of practice allowed for the establishment of a collaborative environment and the foundation for information exchange (Lindgren et al., 2008). Furthermore, the TollCollect management introduced and cultivated a new participatory leadership model to strengthen a common understanding among the project team members. Enforcing a shift in the relation between management and employees as well as to all stakeholders was necessary for finally delivering the toll collecting system. The use of formal power in this case supported that the employees within TollCollect now were identifying with the project, for example by installing clear governance and responsibility structures and requiring the employees to report every single problem immediately. These management actions convinced the employees of their importance for the success of the project. The concept of formal power has already been identified as an important factor for the change of behavior in management and IS literature (Bloomfield et al., 1992; Jasperson, Carte, Saunders, Butler, Croes, & Zheng, 2002). However, in our analysis 'formal power' plays an important role for establishing the preconditions for boundary spanning. Aligning different interests could only be achieved by first underlining

the importance of every employee, component supplier as well as the public authorities for the success of the project. In doing so, a mentality change took place that fostered also the emergence of a cooperative culture with stakeholders outside of TollCollect, as remarked by a leading manager from the private side:

The expertise and experience as well as the formal position enabled the new management team to change the way of collaborating within the syndicate, with component suppliers, and public authorities.

Boundary Spanning Activities

Changing the management team and starting a shift in the working culture of the project, the primary task of the new management team now was strengthening the initial euphoria and motivation of all participants within TollCollect. Reestablishing a working partnership through the formation of mutual trust as well as belief in project success was determining the future course of action of the project which was stated by a leading manager of the private side:

At that point of time, most of the people working for TollCollect were still motivated to continue the realization of the project, although they had sacrificed their free-time and family life for the project and their effort was always judged as failure by the public media. The continuous external influence exacerbated strengthening the belief in project success.

After setting the preconditions for the formation of mutual trust by triggering the establishment of the organizational preconditions for boundary spanning, the new management had to shield their employees from the enormous public pressure. It was important to allow for an open, even critical discussion of problems while guaranteeing that nobody will be fired or even be blamed publicly. In doing so, the TollCollect team was able to work on problem solutions in spite of the constant external pressure. Creating a shielded environment for resolving difficulties in the realization of TollCollect, as well as managing the alignment of interests can be regarded as the central boundary spanning activities, as the following statement illustrates:

Due to the project status and the situation between the parties, political influence had to be shielded away. In order to relieve the blockades of talking openly about technical problems, political discussions as well as media cover stories had been kept away from developers and engineers.

After creating a safe environment, openly talking about technical, managerial, and legal problems was enforced by the new managers. Protecting the cooperating parties from external pressure as well as fostering mutual exchange of information facilitated the collaboration. Comparing organizational and IS research results from an inter-organizational, purely private context with our findings, we identified similar boundary spanning activities in a public private environment (Leifer et al., 1978). Furthermore, we found great fit in the data that "shielding from external influences" was the primary boundary spanning activity that had to be conducted to mediate between the parties. In addition, open communication to all stakeholders created a situation of total transparency concerning project status. Only a joint approach could avoid another breakdown of cooperation which was confirmed by a leading manager from TollCollect:

Total transparency and engaging every single person working for the project was the only solution for project success. Furthermore, explaining that everyone was important for achieving the overall goal gave further motivation to the participants.

Total transparency and fostering open communication was not only important for solving technical, managerial and legal problems within the private syndicate, but also for managing the relation to the public side. Openness about the current status of project realization and additional open discussions with further stakeholders from all kinds of public administrations reinforced the formation of mutual trust. This was stated by a leading manager on the public side:

In-time project realization was only possible if the relationship was based on openness. Technical problems as well as obstacles in negotiations with the different stakeholders had to be communicated internally before the media publicly announced it.

Openly communicating group-specific knowledge between the parties caused a learning atmosphere and was the basis for the start of renegotiating the formal and informal contract. Shifting the organizational culture within the project towards open communication and close coordination enabled TollCollect to avoid misunderstandings of mutual expectations, for example by setting up a joint testing procedure together with the German Federal Ministry of Transport. Consider the following remark of a leading manager from the private side:

Agreeing on a joint testing scope between TollCollect, the German Federal Ministry of Transport, and the independent system reviewer supported the development of mutual trust and belief in the success of the project.

Divergent understandings and expectations which initially led to frustrations culminating into massive trust decline could have been prevented in this newly instantiated environment. Bridging the gap between the parties by openly sharing expectations and understandings improved the formation of trust and created the basis for the alignment of interests, team building and admitting compromises. Our findings aggregate prior research results from an individual perspective on boundary spanning capabilities to a task-oriented, organizational view on boundary spanning activities (Williams, 2002). Aligning divergent interests ultimately enabled TollCollect to realize the project successfully, as a manager from TollCollect mentioned:

The new shared understanding between the parties was driven by open communication and a joint motivation concerning project realization. Finally, political constraints concerning technical requirements were not carved in stone anymore. Both parties had realized that only mutual compromises would lead to project success.

The Moderating Role of External Stakeholder Support

Boundary spanning activities had a positive impact on the formation of trust. For example, the creation of total transparency by openly communicating to the public side supported the belief in the success of the project. However as explained before, this open communication culture would have not been possible without shielding TollCollect from external influences. In addition to the activities of the new management team for shielding the employees of TollCollect, the German Federal Ministry of Transport strengthened this influence in the public which was stated by a leading manager from the private side:

The German Federal Ministry of Transport was the determining authority for us because we always sensed a serious interest in realizing the project on their side. The publicly stated belief of the minister in project success reassured us to continue reporting even critical issues openly.

The support of the top management of the industry syndicate partners, the main leaders from politics as well as other external stakeholders (e.g., transport associations) strengthened the influence of boundary spanning activities, as illustrated before. Therefore, external stakeholder support had a

positive moderating effect on the relation between boundary spanning activities and the formation of trust within the project. The importance of the effect of top management support has already been shown in other studies (Ragu-Nathan, Apigian, Ragu-Nathan, & Tu, 2004). Not only that Toll-Collect now had unlimited financial and human resources, but also top management attention from the German Minister of Transport as well as the chief executive officers of Deutsche Telekom and DaimlerChrysler positively influenced the partnership. For example, the German Federal Ministry of Transport operatively accompanied negotiations with local police and border patrols responsible to enforce the autobahn toll together with TollCollect. The external support facilitated the cooperation between the parties because negotiations became easier which was stated by leading managers of TollCollect:

The German Minister of Transport was the first one to draw a toll ticket which underlined his belief and trust in the successful realization of the project. This caused positive media cover stories which developed even more belief as well as efforts inside the syndicate and trust in the general public.

Moreover, transport associations also strengthened the effect of boundary spanning activities on trust formation. Mutual trust had not only deteriorated between TollCollect and the public authorities but also towards the general public. Fostering open communication and revealing the technical complexity as well as spending high amounts of efforts on solving these problems, the transport associations were convinced of the seriousness of TollCollect's top management. Therefore, they intensified the implementation of OBUs in their trucks and publicly announced that the system now really worked. Announcements like the aforementioned once supported the formation of mutual trust, as a manager from TollCollect commented:

Third party communication and the public announcement of the transport associations that the IT solution was working without interruptions initiated a breakthrough in mutual belief of project success.

Trust Formation

Setting the preconditions for boundary spanning and conducting boundary spanning activities between the parties positively contributed to the formation of mutual trust. The shift in the culture of the partnership, for example by open communication, triggered a growing mutual understanding for a joint approach. Public and private parties started to recognize that this project can only be realized jointly by making compromises which was illustrated by a leading manager from the private side:

The growing mutual understanding initiated a process of rethinking the different perspectives of the different parties. It became clear to both of them that clinging to formal procedures and regulations will not be the solution for the success of the project. Regular meetings for discussing open issues and mutual compromises were identified as the appropriate measures for solving inherent problems within the partnership.

Bridging the gap by open communication in a shielded environment and aligning divergent interests gradually restored the credibility of Toll-Collect. In addition, several public tests proved the stability of the IT solution and fostered the belief in project success which was corroborated by a leading manager of TollCollect:

TollCollect delivered several public tests with users from various transport companies to reassure the internal as well as the external stakeholders of

project success. The communication of test results and the public demonstration finally contributed to restore the credibility of TollCollect.

Communicating not only problems but also capabilities of the different employees working for TollCollect initiated a growing network for knowledge exchange within the project. The participants recognized that besides managerial and technical capabilities within TollCollect also the support of the public partner was crucial for project realization. Joining the different fields of practice into a shared understanding of this IT-PPP-megaproject and a working partnership strengthened trust formation which was stated by a leading manager of TollCollect:

Identifying the key people within TollCollect which had the knowledge for integrating the different parts of the IT solution and developing a shared understanding with the public authorities supported the development of mutual trust between all parties involved.

Emerged Model of Boundary Spanning in PPPs

As a result of the analysis, we present the emerged model of boundary spanning between public and private parties for reestablishing a working partnership in IT megaprojects in Figure 1.

The formation of trust in the analyzed TollCollect case was highly influenced by boundary spanning activities which have been adapted to the PPP context and were not directly applicable. First, the necessary preconditions had to be created in order to exercise boundary spanning activities effectively. This is an important yet underresearched relation in literature. Especially in already troubled projects with a failing course of action, it is necessary to level the setting for boundary spanners. In the case of IT-PPP-megaprojects, this includes knowledge from the business as well as politics and public administration

Figure 1. Boundary spanning in public private IT megaprojects for reestablishing a working partnership

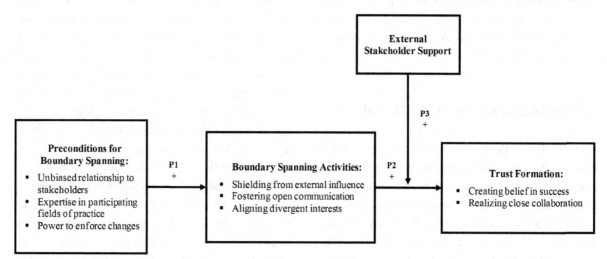

world, apart from an unbiased relationship for a restart and the organizational precondition to exercise power, for example, to enforce a cultural shift in the working behavior.

While boundary spanning outcomes are characterized by mutual understanding, open communication, and the formation of a cooperative culture, boundary spanning activities are purposefully applied capabilities that enable boundary spanners to bridge the divide between contrary parties. As illustrated in our case analysis, these preconditions for boundary spanning were ultimately crucial for the execution of boundary spanning activities. Hence, we propose:

Proposition 1: Effective boundary spanning activities in public private IT megaprojects depend on the establishment of organizational preconditions, including unbiased relationships, relevant expertise, and formal power.

Subsequently, we explained in our case analysis how boundary spanning activities contributed to the formation of mutual trust. Here again, the IT-PPP-megaproject setting has to be taken into account. Besides establishing an open discussion

culture with the public client (e.g., allowing for total transparency by the exchange of information), all kinds of communication channels to other stakeholders need to be orchestrated while protecting the project team from too much external influence. Therefore, we propose:

Proposition 2: Boundary spanning activities in public private IT megaprojects, including shielding from external influence, fostering open communication, and aligning divergent interests, have a positive effect on trust formation, expressed through belief in success and close collaboration.

In addition, our analysis illustrates the moderating effect of external stakeholder support on the relationship between boundary spanning activities and trust formation. The support of the German Federal Minister of Transport as well as top management attention of the private parties and exemplarily transport associations strengthened the effect of boundary spanning activities on trust formation. This caused the creation of belief in project success and initiated even closer collaboration between all parties involved which supported trust formation. Hence, we propose:

Proposition 3: External stakeholder support in public private IT megaprojects strengthens the effect of boundary spanning activities on trust formation.

DISCUSSION AND CONCLUSION

Though TollCollect went through several difficulties during establishing the partnership in a commercial tendering procedure and realizing the project, it finally was implemented successfully and evaluated as a success story by all stakeholders and the general public. However, terminating the formal contract in midterm of the project was essential to reestablish a working partnership between public and private parties which was only possible due to bridging the divide between the different cultural environments. In order to achieve project realization successfully, replacing the management team in charge was an initial starting point for the reestablishment of the relation to the client and to establish organizational preconditions for spanning the boundaries between the parties. Installing a management team with an unprejudiced view and understanding of the different motivation of the participating parties was a crucial precondition for reestablishing an unbiased relationship with the stakeholders. In addition, TollCollect recognized that bridging the gap would only be possible choosing managers who are familiar with the specialties and regulations of the public side, as well as the processes and governance structures of the private side. Finally, enforcing a shift in the preconditions for cooperating, the use of formal power was the basic precondition for enforcing changes in the working mentality, for example by requiring the employees to report every single problem immediately. Increasing the identity of the employees with the project and having the formal power to install a clear governance and responsibility structure allowed the establishment of the organizational preconditions for boundary spanning. Boundary

spanning literature so far has either concentrated on an individual level of analysis on individual capabilities and the roles of boundary spanners (Aldrich et al., 1977; Friedman et al., 1992; Tushman, 1977; Tushman et al., 1981; Williams, 2002) and on team level of analysis on cultural effects and antecedent conditions influencing team boundary spanning (Golden et al., 2005; Joshi et al., 2009; Marrone et al., 2007). Our case study extended the findings of antecedent conditions for boundary spanning on an organizational level of analysis identifying an 'unbiased relationship to the stakeholders', 'expertise in participating fields of practice', and 'power to enforce changes' as the necessary organizational preconditions for reestablishing a working partnership in IT-PPP-megaprojects.

In addition to identifying the necessary preconditions for boundary spanning in a public private environment, we also identified the necessary boundary spanning activities for bridging the divide between public and private cultural backgrounds. In order to start a shift in the working culture of the project and to reestablish the initial euphoria and motivation of all participants, shielding the employees from the enormous public pressure was necessary for allowing for an open, even critical discussion of problems. Achieving transparency within TollCollect and its interaction with the stakeholders by open communication enabled a shift in the working culture towards more coordination and joint decision-making which finally created a deep understanding of mutual expectations. The initial divergent understandings and expectations were finally aligned by openly sharing and communicating mutual expectations which improved the formation of trust and created the basis for the alignment of interests, team building and admitting compromises. Prior research on boundary spanning activities focused so far on the relation between organizations and their environment (Leifer et al., 1978; Robertson, 1995). Our findings though aggregate prior research results from an individual perspective on boundary spanning capabilities to a task-oriented, organizational view on boundary spanning activities, identifying the determining boundary spanning activities in a public private environment.

Prior IS literature so far has focused on the use of IT for boundary spanning (Levina et al., 2005, 2006; Lindgren et al., 2008; Pauleen et al., 2001) and how country and organizational contexts affect boundaries and status differences in IS development projects (Levina, 2006; Levina et al., 2008). PPP literature has extended these research results by examining the roles and behaviors of boundary-spanning managers during the establishment of PPPs (Noble et al., 2006). However, our research concentrated on exploring the organizational preconditions and the necessary task-oriented boundary spanning activities for reestablishing a working partnership in IT-PPP-megaprojects.

Our developed model provides a substantial theoretical contribution to the area of reestablishing a working partnership by boundary spanning in IT-PPP-megaprojects, especially in the area of enabling boundary spanning activities and establishing the organizational preconditions for boundary spanning. The generalizability of our findings is restricted to the PPP domain. However, megaprojects also occur in the private sector and are equally prone to failure such as the Channel Tunnel project (Flyvbjerg et al., 2005). Although our case study was conducted in a PPP environment, the Channel Tunnel example indicates that our findings can probably be applied to the realm of non-PPP IT projects (Nelson, 2007). Furthermore to get an even more holistic view of phenomena in IT-PPP-projects, adding the insights from a user and political perspective to a managerial perspective would allow even more details of the specifications of relationship management and governance structures within IT-PPP-projects.

Besides the theoretical contribution, we also offer practical advice. The challenge for practitioners in an IT-PPP-megaproject is to establish and maintain mutual trust as well as shielding an established relationship from external influences.

In prior literature, spanning the boundaries between different cultural and organizational fields has been referred as the necessary precondition for successfully managing IT projects (Levina et al., 2005). Our analysis shows how important the organizational preconditions for boundary spanning and boundary spanning activities themselves are for the establishment of mutual understanding and the successful management of expectations for succeeding in IT-PPP-megaprojects. Taking the aforementioned into account, an initial failing course of action, expectations´ violation, and termination of contracts in IT-PPP-megaprojects could be avoided by constant relationship management and the introduction of adequate governance structures adapted to a public private environment. Future research may investigate in detail instruments and methods for establishing a relationship management, governance structures as well as adequate leadership styles for constantly maintaining a working partnership in IT-PPP-megaprojects.

ACKNOWLEDGMENT

The authors thankfully appreciate the vital participation of the practitioners in this research. This work was developed as part of a research project at Johann Wolfgang Goethe University Frankfurt. We are indebted to and gratefully acknowledge the financial support of ISPRAT e.V. Any opinions, findings, conclusions, or recommendations expressed in this paper are those of the authors and do not necessarily reflect the views of ISPRAT e.V. or its supporting partners.

REFERENCES

Aldrich, H., & Herker, D. (1977). Boundary spanning roles and organization structure. *Academy of Management Review*, 2(2), 217–230. doi:10.2307/257905

Beck, R., & Möbs, A. (2006). The public hand and it mega-projects: Lessons from the german tollcollect case. In *Proceedings of the Inaugural (First) International Research Workshop on IT Project Management (IRWITPM 2006)*, Milwaukee, WI.

Bloomfield, B. P., & Coombs, R. (1992). Information technology, control, and power: The centralization and decentralization debate revisited. *Journal of Management Studies, 29*(4), 459–484. doi:10.1111/j.1467-6486.1992.tb00674.x

Brooks, F. P. (1987). No silver bullet: Essence and accidents of software engineering. *Computer, 20*(4), 10–19. doi:10.1109/MC.1987.1663532

Clegg, S. R., Pitsis, T. S., Rura-Polley, T., & Marosszeky, M. (2002). Governmentality matters: Designing an alliance culture of inter-organizational collaboration for managing projects. *Organization Studies, 23*(3), 317–337. doi:10.1177/0170840602233001

Cross, R., & Prusak, L. (2002). The people who make organizations go - or stop. *Harvard Business Review, 80*(6), 104–112.

Cule, P., Schmidt, R., Lyytinen, K., & Keil, M. (2000). Strategies for heading off is project failure. *Information Systems Management, 17*(2), 65–73. doi:10.1201/1078/43191.17.2.20000301/31229.8

Davies, A., Gann, D., & Douglas, T. (2009). Innovation in megaprojects: Systems integration at london heathrow terminal 5. *California Management Review, 51*(2), 101–125.

Dibbern, J., Goles, T., Hirschheim, R., & Jayatilaka, B. (2004). Information systems outsourcing: A survey and analysis of the literature. *The Data Base for Advances in Information Systems, 35*(4), 6–102.

Eisenhardt, K. M. (1989). Building theories from case study research. *Academy of Management Review, 14*(4), 532–550. doi:10.2307/258557

Flyvbjerg, B., Bruzelius, N., & Rothengatter, W. (2005). *Megaprojects and risk, an anatomy of ambition* (3rd ed.). New York: Cambridge University Press.

Friedman, R. A., & Podolny, J. (1992). Differentiation of boundary spanning roles: Labor negotiations and implications for role conflict. *Administrative Science Quarterly, 37*(1), 28–47. doi:10.2307/2393532

Glaser, B. G. (1978). *Theoretical sensitivity*. Mill Valley, CA: The Sociology Press.

Glaser, B. G., & Strauss, A. L. (1967). *The discovery of grounded theory: Strategies for qualitative research*. Chicago: Aldine Publishing Company.

Golden, T. D., & Veiga, J. F. (2005). Spanning boundaries and borders: Toward understanding the cultural dimensions of team boundary spanning. *Journal of Managerial Issues, 17*(2), 178–197.

Grimsey, D., & Lewis, M. K. (2002). Accounting for public private partnerships. *Accounting Forum, 26*(3), 245–270. doi:10.1111/1467-6303.00089

Hodge, G. A., & Greve, C. (2007). Public-private partnerships: An international performance review. *Public Administration Review, 67*(3), 545–558. doi:10.1111/j.1540-6210.2007.00736.x

Hughes, J., & Jones, S. (2003). Reflections on the use of grounded theory in interpretive information systems research. In *Proceedings of the 11th European Conference on Information Systems (ECIS 2003)*, Naples, Italy.

Jacobsen, C., & Choi, S. O. (2008). Success factors: Public works and public-private partnerships. *International Journal of Public Sector Management, 21*(6), 637–657. doi:10.1108/09513550810896514

Jasperson, J. S., Carte, T. A., Saunders, C. S., Butler, B. S., Croes, H. J. P., & Zheng, W. (2002). Review: Power and information technology research: A metatriangulation review. *Management Information Systems Quarterly, 26*(4), 397–459. doi:10.2307/4132315

Joshi, A., Pandey, N., & Han, G. (2009). Bracketing team boundary spanning: An examination of task-based, team-level, and contextual antecedents. *Journal of Organizational Behavior, 30*(6), 731–759. doi:10.1002/job.567

Jost, G., Dawson, M., & Shaw, D. (2005). Private sector consortia working for a public sector client - factors that build successful relationship: Lessons from the uk. *European Management Journal, 23*(3), 336–350. doi:10.1016/j.emj.2005.04.012

Kappelman, L. A., McKeeman, R., & Zhang, L. (2006). Early warning signs of it project failure: The dominant dozen. *Information Systems Management, 23*(4), 31–36. doi:10.1201/1078.10580 530/46352.23.4.20060901/95110.4

Kim, P. H., Dirks, K. T., & Cooper, C. D. (2009). The repair of trust: A dynamic bilateral perspective and multilevel conceptualization. *Academy of Management Review, 34*(3), 401–422.

Leifer, R., & Delbecq, A. (1978). Organizational/ environmental interchange: A model of boundary spanning activity. *Academy of Management Review, 3*(1), 40–50. doi:10.2307/257575

Levina, N. (2006). Collaborating across boundaries in a global economy: Do organizational boundaries and country contexts matter? In *Proceedings of the 27th International Conference on Information Systems*, Milwaukee, WI.

Levina, N., & Vaast, E. (2005). The emergence of boundary spanning competence in practice: Implications for implementation and use of information systems. *Management Information Systems Quarterly, 29*(2), 335–363.

Levina, N., & Vaast, E. (2006). Turning a community into a market: A practice perspective on information technology use in boundary spanning. *Journal of Management Information Systems, 22*(4), 13–37. doi:10.2753/MIS0742-1222220402

Levina, N., & Vaast, E. (2008). Innovating or doing as told? Status differences and overlapping boundaries in offshore collaboration. *Management Information Systems Quarterly, 32*(2), 307–332.

Lindgren, R., Andersson, M., & Henfridsson, O. (2008). Multi-contextuality in boundary-spanning practices. *Information Systems Journal, 18*(6), 641–661. doi:10.1111/j.1365-2575.2007.00245.x

Marrone, J. A., Tesluk, P. E., & Carson, J. B. (2007). A multilevel investigation of antecedents and consequences of team member boundary-spanning behavior. *Academy of Management Journal, 50*(6), 1423–1439.

Muhr, T. (2008). *Atlas.Ti - the knowledge workbench, scientific software development*, Berlin.

Nelson, R. R. (2007). It project management: Infamous failures, classic mistakes, and best practices. *MIS Quarterly Executive, 6*(2), 67–78.

Noble, G., & Jones, R. (2006). The role of boundary-spanning managers in the establishment of public-private partnerships. *Public Administration, 84*(4), 891–917. doi:10.1111/j.1467-9299.2006.00617.x

Pauleen, D. J., & Yoong, P. (2001). Relationship building and the use of ict in boundary-crossing virtual teams: A facilitator's perspective. *Journal of Information Technology, 16*(4), 205–220. doi:10.1080/02683960110100391

Pawlowski, S. D., & Robey, D. (2004). Bridging user organizations: Knowledge brokering and the work of information technology professionals. *Management Information Systems Quarterly, 28*(4), 645–672.

Ragu-Nathan, B. S., Apigian, C. H., Ragu-Nathan, T. S., & Tu, Q. (2004). A path analytic study of the effect of top management support for information systems performance. *Omega, 32*(6), 459–471. doi:10.1016/j.omega.2004.03.001

Rehring, E. (2006). Germany's tolling success. *Traffic World, 270*(6), 14.

Reijniers, J. J. A. M. (1994). Organization of public-private partnership projects, the timely prevention of pitfalls. *International Journal of Project Management, 12*(3), 137–142. doi:10.1016/0263-7863(94)90028-0

Robertson, P. J. (1995). Involvement in boundary-spanning activity: Mitigating the relationship between work setting and behavior. *Journal of Public Administration: Research and Theory, 5*(1), 73–98.

Rosenau, P. V. (1999). Introduction: The strengths and weaknesses of public-private policy partnerships. *The American Behavioral Scientist, 43*(1), 10–34.

Rousseau, D. M., Sitkin, S. B., Burt, R. S., & Camerer, C. (1998). Not so different after all: A cross-discipline view of trust. *Academy of Management Review, 23*(3), 393–404.

Santos, F. M., & Eisenhardt, K. M. (2005). Organizational boundaries and theories of organization. *Organization Science, 16*(5), 491–508. doi:10.1287/orsc.1050.0152

Sumner, M., Bock, D., & Giamartino, G. (2006). Exploring the linkage between the characteristics of it project leaders and project success. *Information Systems Management, 23*(4), 43–49. doi:10.1201/1078.10580530/46352.23.4.20060901/95112.6

Trafford, S., & Proctor, T. (2006). Successful joint venture partnerships: Public-private partnerships. *International Journal of Public Sector Management, 19*(2), 117–129. doi:10.1108/09513550610650392

Tushman, M. L. (1977). Special boundary roles in the innovation process. *Administrative Science Quarterly, 22*(4), 587–605. doi:10.2307/2392402

Tushman, M. L., & Scanlan, T. J. (1981). Boundary spanning individuals: Their role in information transfer and their antecedents. *Academy of Management Journal, 24*(2), 289–305. doi:10.2307/255842

van Marrewijk, A. (2007). Managing project culture: The case of the environ megaproject. *International Journal of Project Management, 25*(3), 290–299. doi:10.1016/j.ijproman.2006.11.004

van Marrewijk, A., Clegg, S. R., Pitsis, T. S., & Veenswijk, M. (2008). Managing public-private megaprojects: Paradoxes, complexity, and project design. *International Journal of Project Management, 26*(6), 591–600. doi:10.1016/j.ijproman.2007.09.007

Venugopal, C. (2005). Single goal set: A new paradigm for it megaproject success. *IEEE Software, 22*(5), 48–53. doi:10.1109/MS.2005.135

Walsham, G. (1995a). The emergence of interpretivism in is research. *Information Systems Research, 6*(4), 376–394. doi:10.1287/isre.6.4.376

Walsham, G. (1995b). Interpretive case studies in is research: Nature and method. *European Journal of Information Systems, 4*(2), 74–81. doi:10.1057/ejis.1995.9

Wenger, E. (1998). *Communities of practice: Learning, meaning, and identity*. New York: Cambridge University Press.

Williams, P. (2002). The competent boundary spanner. *Public Administration, 80*(1), 103–124. doi:10.1111/1467-9299.00296

Yin, R. (2003). *Case study research - design and methods*. Thousand Oaks, CA: Sage Publications.

This work was previously published in International Journal of Information Technology Project Management, Volume 1, Issue 4, edited by John Wang, pp. 20-37, copyright 2010 by IGI Publishing (an imprint of IGI Global).

Chapter 19
Development of M–Government Projects in a Developing Country:
The Case of Albania

Silvana Trimi
University of Nebraska - Lincoln, USA

Kozeta Sevrani
University of Tirana, Albanaia

ABSTRACT

This paper is a qualitative study regarding m-government in a developing country in Eastern Europe with a poor infrastructure and a democratic history—Albania. To understand why m-government is unavoidable and necessary for Albania, the authors provide an overall picture of the country's current telecommunication infrastructure, which explains some of the current e-government initiatives, and their level of implementation success and barriers to progress. In addition, this paper presents possible benefits of m-government for Albanians, along with possible future applications, challenges, and issues in their implementation.

INTRODUCTION

The Internet has tremendously transformed the way business organizations conduct activities. Since the 1990s, public sector organizations have also been applying the Internet and other information and communication technologies (ICTs) in innovative ways to conveniently and economically deliver services to and engage citizens, a set of practices known as electronic government (e-government). Improved transparency, speed, and efficiency through e-government increase trust and reduce perceptions of corruption, in the eyes of the citizens and businesses. Governments also save money by dealing with people via automated online systems rather than face to face or on the phone (The Economist, 2008), integrating and innovating services, and improving employees' productivity by connecting them to the central database.

DOI: 10.4018/978-1-4666-0930-3.ch019

However, many e-government projects, even when designed successfully, have been either canceled or not fully utilized because of the lack of users' awareness and/or lack of technological access to these services, a problem quite prevalent in countries with poor telecommunication infrastructure. An explosion in the use of mobile technologies (m-technologies) and wireless networks, especially in countries where wired infrastructure is non-existent or poor, has encouraged and enabled governments to complement e-government services with m-government applications. M-technology for many developing or undeveloped countries can be the major or the only conduit to provide online government services to citizens, businesses, and government employees, thus removing infrastructure constraints.

In this paper we examine the difficult process of implementing e-government services and the necessity of the m-government project in an infrastructure and democracy history poor country, Albania. We selected Albania as the study target because of its unique historic characteristics. Even though Albania is a European country, fifty years of centrally planned economy under a severe communist dictatorship has left the country far behind other European countries, both economically and politically. Wanting and intending to become a member of the European Union (EU), the Albanian government has been working very hard to overcome many challenges such as poor public service infrastructures, high levels of corruption and bureaucracy, and immature democracy culture.

Even though an impressive progress has been made in building the country's IT infrastructure, the wired telecommunication infrastructure still remains poor and Internet access is one of the lowest in Europe (less than 1%). Therefore, very few users can access e-government services. On the other hand, mobile telecommunication has a high penetration rate. Over 90% of all Albanian territory is covered by wireless networks and over 75% of the population owns cellular phones. Thus, delivering online government services through mobile devices (m-government applications) would be more plausible for Albania. M-government applications can help Albanian government to: (1) provide service access and convenience to citizens and businesses as Albania has poor wired telecommunication infrastructure, poor transportation infrastructure, and difficult terrains; (2) alleviate some of the current problems, such as corruption and a low level of transparency, thus increasing trust and efficiency; and (3) increase efficiency and effectiveness of government employees, by allowing them to have access to the information needed in real-time and update records on the spot. Therefore, Albanian government not only should start designing and building m-government applications, but it should make them a priority since e-government is still at early stages and synergy between the two can be explored and duplications avoided.

In this paper, we used a qualitative study to understand the unavoidable major project toward m-government, possible benefits and barriers, and provide suggestions on the type of applications that would be needed and work the best for Albania. We interviewed many key individuals: employees of different service providers (wired and wireless), government officials who are currently involved in the early planning stage of m-government (different ministries and the National IT Strategy Agency), IT professionals who manage e-government projects, business people, and some citizen users. Also, we obtained relevant government documents and statistics. The results of this research are provided in this paper as follows: first, we provide an overview of the unique characteristics of Albania and its current state of telecommunication (wired and wireless) infrastructure; second, we describe e-government initiatives undertaken by the Albanian government; third, we present the rationale for m-government as an immediate goal for the Albanian government, providing some suggestions of m-government applications that can benefit Albanian government and citizens; and finally, what should and can be done in the near future.

OVERVIEW

Country Background

Albania is a small country located across the Adriatic Sea from Italy, bordered by Montenegro and Kosovo on the North, Republic of Macedonia on the East, and Greece on the South. The population of Albania itself is approximately 3.17 million. Albania is a low income country with the lowest per capita income in Europe ($2927 as of 2008). In 1990, after the fall of the most totalitarian communist government in the world, that ruled the country for 40 years, Albania started the process of reforms towards a democratic form of government. As Albania struggled to develop a market economy and the necessary supporting infrastructures, the Western donor community began providing massive support in the form of humanitarian aid, financial support, technical assistance, and capacity building. The country has made significant progress since its transition from a communist regime toward a democratic form of government with a market-based economy. The economic structure has shifted from agriculture and industries to services and construction. Albania has a high GDP growth rate of around 6% per year.

EU has initiated the Electronic South Eastern Europe (eSEE), whose goal is helping SEE countries prepare for integration into EU (eSEEurope Initiative, 2002). Eager to join EU, Albania signed (in mid-June 2006) the European Union (EU)'s Stabilization and Association Agreement in 2006 and is working very hard to comply with its directives. Because of great potential of ICT in providing the stability, cohesion, and integration of the Union, EU has established a comprehensive strategy for ICT and standards development for all of its members to follow. Thus, all national IT strategies and infrastructure development in Albania are carefully designed based on these EU directives and standards. The following section

describes the Albanian progress in ICT infrastructure as a result of these efforts and strategies as well as deficiencies which need to be overcome.

IT Infrastructure in Albania

Regulations: The development and use of ICT is one of the highest priorities for the Albanian government as they are important for economic growth and improvement of quality of life for Albanians, and helping with the goal of joining EU in the near future. The Albanian government has been investing an average of 6% of its GDP in IT for the last four years, which is greater than not only the average of EU countries (about 2.5%) but also that of most of other countries in the SEE region (Cullen International, 2007). In 2003, the government of Albania developed the National Strategy of ICT for addressing issues such as bridging digital divide, continued development of telecommunication infrastructure, and defining mechanisms for creating legal and fiscal frameworks for implementing e-governance, e-education and e-commerce.

The beginning point of the reform in the telecommunication sector was the opening of the market for competition (opening up to private firms), encouraging private investments through privatization, gradual market liberalization, and improvement of the regulatory framework (policies and laws). As a result, the Albanian government currently is quite advanced in the process of privatization compare to the majority of former communist or socialist countries in the SEE region. Before the reforms, there was only one and wholly state-owned telecommunication company in the country (Albtelecom). However, today, out of all telecommunication companies, the government owns only 24% of Albtelecom and 12.6% of AMC, one of the three wireless providers.

The ICT market has been fully liberalized since January 2005. However, only rural local networks and services have been fully liberalized (there are 55 local and regional private telecommunication operators). Telecommunication service in urban areas remains closed to competition because no licensing framework has been defined for this segment. Full liberalization and privatization of the ICT sector is needed for further positive impacts on the development of telecommunication infrastructure, increase accessibility (penetration), improve quality of service, and reduce cost.

Service providers: there is one fixed (landline) telephone service provider (Albtelecom), which is also the only backbone operator (fiber optic, that covers the entire territory of Albania); three mobile service providers (AMC, Vodafone and Eagle Mobile); and 33 Internet Service Providers (ISPs).

Accessibility: The penetration rate of *fixed* (landline) telephony is still very low, only about 11.2% of the population, or 34% of households, which is the lowest in the SEE region (UN E-government Survey, 2008). This is mainly a result of poor wired infrastructure (limited number of lines in the country) but also partially because of the slow process of liberalization of national services.

On the other hand, the penetration rate for *wireless* telephony is one of the highest among SEE countries. However, even though about 90% of population in Albania is covered with the service (2G), the cost of service is one of the highest in the SEE region. Again, liberalization, through increased competition and additional investments, is needed to lower prices and improve the quality of service. According to Harvard International Review (Hathaway-Zepeda, 2006), a 10% decrease in the average annual cost of mobile services would increase mobile communication technology diffusion by 5%. Thus, recent price reductions in Albania, especially for the medium and high usage

baskets (respectively 27% and 19%, and 18% for low usage) (Cullen International, 2007), increased the penetration rate for wireless phone service from 52% in 2006 to 77% currently (which is eight times the penetration rate of the fixed lines).

Broadband: Even though broadband service has been the fastest growing segment in the SEE telecommunication market, with an average increase rate of 4.43% in 2006, Albania has the lowest broadband penetration rate at below 1% (for both fixed and wireless services) (Cullen International, 2007) even though there is a fiber optic backbone that covers the entire Albanian territory.

As for *mobile* internet access, it is almost non-existent with the exception of a wireless access from a cell phone to a laptop (through wireless cards) provided by Eagle Mobile company. Most of mobile service in Albania is GSM (2G). Therefore, mobile phones are used for voice and data (SMS) communication. The Albanian government has liberalized and will soon start licensing the 3.5 GHz spectrum for WiMAX, GSM 4, and 3G technologies. In 2009, the Albanian mobile phone services market will be enlarged with a WiMAX system. It is a good solution for Albania because of its limited wired infrastructure, rugged terrain, and the lower costs of WiMAX in comparison to the wired solution. With the introduction and development of these new technologies and infrastructures, the Albanian government is targeting to reach 20% in broadband penetration by mid 2009.

RESEARCH METHODOLOGY

For policy and program evaluation research, the most used methodology is the qualitative research. Our study's purpose is to evaluate the m-government in Albania: to ascertain why m-government is unavoidable and necessary, what stage of m-government the country is currently at, what are some of the challenges and issues for designing and implementing m-government applications, and what are some possible future m-government applications. To get answers to these questions, we interviewed a number of key individuals that are presently involved with e-government, from government officials (policy makers, government project managers, IT users) to service providers' administrators, and end users (business managers and individuals). In addition, we used government documents and statistics, which were provided by the government officials we interviewed. We took written notes or recorded the interviews (where and when we were given the permission from the interviewees). The interviews were open-ended but structured around the research questions presented earlier in the paper. We chose one representative from each group interviewed (policy makers, e-government project manager, service providers' managers, business and individual users) as the spokesperson to reconcile differences in opinions and ideas in the group. The findings and conclusion of this qualitative research are provided in the rest of this paper.

E-GOVERNMENT INITIATIVES AND PROJECTS IN ALBANIA

E-government is defined as application of ICTs by governments for better access and delivery of services to citizens, enhanced interaction with citizens and businesses, empowerment of citizens, and improved efficiency of government operations (Lee, Tan, & Trimi, 2005). E-government brings significant benefits in the form of effectiveness and efficiency, transparency and democracy. E-government, in any country, goes through the following phases: (1) infrastructure building (broadband network); (2) integration – leverage the infrastructure within the public sector while simultaneously changing the public service processes; and (3) transformation – totally reforming and innovating the e-government services by taking

advantage of ICT. Recognizing the importance of the e-government and its prerequisites (building the infrastructure, policies and regulations, capacity development, and applications and content), the Albanian government, with the help and the support of foreign aid and donor governments, has made tremendous progress towards e-government. These efforts have improved Albania's ranking, among 182 countries, in readiness for e-government from being in the 102th place in 2005 to the 86th in 2008 (UN e-Government Survey, 2008).

Progress made in the first stage, building the infrastructure in Albania, was described in the previous section. The Albanian government is now working for the second phase, integration of IT in public sectors while changing its services. Integration can be done: (1) vertically, between agencies at different levels of government; and (2) horizontally, between agencies at the same level and/or inclusion of other stakeholders such as the private sector. E-government projects in Albania include both. We interviewed key officials in the Council of Ministers, Ministry of Finance, and National IT Strategy Agency, who are directly involved in the e-government development in Albania. We will describe the major e-government projects based on the classifications of the e-government service: government to citizens (G2C), government to businesses (G2B), government to government (G2G), and internal efficiency and effectiveness (IEE) (Lee et al., 2005).

- **G2B/G2C:** In 2006, the Albanian government started the *Millennium Challenge Account Threshold Program*. This two-year threshold project for $13.85 million with the Millennium Challenge Corporation (MCC), implemented with the support of the U.S. Agency for International Development (USAID), aims to reduce corruption, alleviate the "informal" economy, and improve the investment climate through IT-based solutions, and technical and legal assistance (Millennium

Challenge Corporation, 2009). The project includes:

1 Digitization of *Tax Administration.* The primary goal of this program is to reduce corruption in the tax policy and administration. This part of the program has been effective as currently all five major tax declarations for e-filing, including monthly declaration of Value Added Tax (VAT), personal income tax withholdings, health and social insurance contributions, estimated profits tax, and the annual profit tax declaration, are available online. There were 600,000 hits in the first 20 days of the site's operation.

2 *Public Procurement.* The main goal of this program is to realize transparency in procurement processes of the government and reduce corruption. The e-Procurement System, an electronic government procurement system open to businesses, has listed thus far over $17 million worth of procurement. After developing a public awareness campaign, the Procurement Advocate's Office immediately received and successfully investigated 39 complaints by bidders involving government procurements. This indicates the increased transparency and accountability involving public procurement.

3 *Business Registration's* goal is to decrease corruption in Business Entry and Registration and increase its effectiveness by speeding up the process. Since its implementation in September 2007, The National Registration Center has processed more than 30,000 new applications, created a fully accessible e-database of all registered businesses (110,000) in Albania, and completed scanning and indexing of all registration files for legal entities and

self-employed individuals contained in the Albanian business registry. Application windows are located throughout Albania, thus a business can complete all registration procedures locally. Since business registration complies with international standards, business registration and commercial registry information are fully accessible to foreign business partners as well as to Albanian users. The registration process now takes only one day, a far cry from 47 days previously. This system has tremendously increased the efficiency and transparency, and has lowered corruption (cut the red tape and tax evasion).

- **G2G/IEE:** To reform public administration and civil service, the government established the Inter-Ministerial Board for *Institutional and Public Administration Reform* and has initiated the following projects:

1 *Treasury System Project,* funded by the World Bank and the Ministry of Finance (MoF). Designed and implemented to improve efficiency, transparency, and accountability of MoF treasury functions, it provides the capability to capture and process all government financial transactions, both payments and revenue collection at the source, and enables these to be managed in accordance with budgets and spending authorities. The treasury system was modernized first by restructuring processes. Thus, during Phase I, completed in 2003, computer-based solutions were developed to replace existing manual procedures and implemented a new budget structure. In Phase II, completed in 2006, an integrated financial management system was implemented. These were followed

by building a technical infrastructure. Thus, servers and networking equipment were installed at MoF and 36 Treasury District Offices throughout Albania (vertical integration). During Phase III, also completed at the end of 2006, a Wide Area Network (WAN) infrastructure for MoF was built to connect all district offices, headquarters of various agencies and external institutions, such as Customs, Bank of Albania, Social Insurance Institute, and Health Insurance Institute (horizontal integration).

2 *Government Electronic Network (Gov-Net),* established a high-speed and secure fiber network (GovNet) that connects together all governmental ministries and agencies. The purpose of this project is to build up a secure and centrally-managed e-mail system, securely and reliably connect all central government offices and agencies through an Intranet, and provide voice over IP (VoIP) to main government institutions.

In the first phase, which started in September 2004, a virtual private network (VPN) and a high-speed fiber optic network were created for electronic data collection, exchange, and utilization at the central government level. It interconnected 17 ministries and the Council of Ministers. The second phase's objective, started in 2007, is to expand the network by including other government institutions such as the Albanian Parliament, prefectures, and other government agencies. An intranet will be established to improve the accessibility and communication among ministries, and to implement an integrated solution for web-publishing and document management for public government web-portals (G2C) and internal intranet system (G2G).

Table 1 summarizes all e-government applications in Albania based on their types and goals. As clearly evident, Albania has made much progress in developing e-government.

M-GOVERNMENT IN ALBANIA

M-government utilizes wireless and mobile technologies to provide services to citizens, businesses, and government units. M-government complements e-government but does not replace it since at the current level of technology development mobile devices lack the ability to transfer large volumes of data at high speed. Nevertheless, ease of use of mobile devices, low cost of ownership and use, timely and personalized delivery of information, and very often the-only-communication technology available, has made m-government to be a very important add-on to e-government, and sometimes the only alternative available to governments to reach and interact with citizens (Trimi & Sheng, 2008). Since mobile communication penetration in undeveloped and developing countries is much higher than fixed-lines penetration, wireless internet and technology are a cheaper, better, and very often, the only choice for citizens.

In addition, m-government can help increase transparency and democracy in a speedier manner which is particularly important for less developed and apt to corruption countries.

Potentials and Benefits of M-Government

While the Albanian government has been working hard and has successfully implemented some e-government projects, not many citizens and/or even businesses can access such services. As previously mentioned, fixed-line infrastructure is still very poor, particularly in rural areas, and therefore, internet access is either scarce or very costly for the majority of population. With the exception of internet cafés in major cities, there

Table 1. E-government projects implemented in Albania

Type of E-government	Projects	Goals
G2B/G2C	•*Tax Digitalization* - E-filing of VAT, personal income tax, health and social insurance contribution, annual profit tax	- Decrease corruption - Reduce errors
	•*Public Procurement* - electronic government procurement system opened to businesses	- Increase transparency - Decrease corruption
	•*Business Registration* - Business entry and registration	- Decrease corruption - Increase efficiency
G2G/IEE	•*Treasury System* - Capture and process all government financial transaction	- Increase efficiency - Increase transparency - Increase accountability
	•*Government Electronic Network (GovNet)* - Build government Intranet - Provide VoIP	- Increase efficiency - Secure communication - Central, high security database

are no internet centers or kiosks that can offer services to the general population in other more remote areas. In addition, PC penetration is very low, at only 1.7% in 2006. As for businesses, the majority of Albanian firms are small or very small family businesses. Micro, small, and medium enterprises account for 99% of private enterprises and contribute more than 75% of Albanian GDP. Their use of ICT is almost non-existent.

On the other hand, when it comes to wireless technology, the majority of the population and businesses have access with a penetration of around 80%. Therefore, the best and perhaps the only way to serve citizens and businesses by offering timely and locality-based information and to perform transactions would be m-government applications. M-government applications will help decrease the digital divide by lowering entry barriers in e-services for citizens and businesses. M-government services will save people time and money by avoiding trips to and long queues in government offices, which is particularly important for rural and geographically remote places. Getting information and performing transactions online lowers or eliminates bribery of government officials and employees, thus decreases the corruption and bureaucracy. M-government will

help in fostering democracy by allowing citizens to participate in government decision-making through polling and transparent interactions.

Many Albanians travel abroad frequently, either for doing business, leisure, or visiting relatives (more than one third of population has immigrated, mostly to other European countries). M-government will offer convenience and more freedom and mobility to citizens, particularly business people, by allowing them to have access to government services and pay their dues on-time, anytime anywhere, even when they are out of the country.

In addition, m-government will provide services to those who are unwilling to access public services through the fixed internet. Since the majority of Albanians own mobile phones, they are more comfortable in using m-technology, which is easier to learn (compare to wired technology) and therefore more likely to be used, especially from older and less educated citizens, thus making m-government applications accessible from a wider base of population (Ghyasi & Kushchu, 2004; Kushchu & Borucki, 2004). M-government applications and technologies will also help increase efficiency and effectiveness of government (internal efficiency and effectiveness - IEE) itself by connecting previously unconnected areas and provide information and services on-the-spot to mobile government employees and enforcement officers.

From the platform-building point of view (infrastructure and applications), Albania has two advantages regarding m-government: first, it is in the early stages of design and implementation of e-government and therefore every change can and should be made by considering mobile technology; second, Albania is a very small country and its geographic proximity makes wireless infrastructure easier, faster, and cheaper to build compare to wired, thus overcoming the country and social digital divide access issue. For example, WiMAX is a great choice and Albania, as previously discussed, has already started to build it in 2009.

Lastly, m-government applications must be designed to be interoperable between countries thus helping the realization of true globalization. All SEE countries, including Albania, have followed European guidelines and standards of eSEE for e-government applications. Through standardization, EU countries are making certain that they can collaborate, access/exchange information, and join forces in the war against criminals and terrorism. Applications such as designing mID cards, can be developed which will be recognized, read, and can access the same central database in any country in EU.

Suggestions for M-Government Applications for Albania

Even though, as discussed above, m-government applications would be very advantageous for Albania, currently, there is no m-government service offered in Albania. Moreover, the general attitude of some of the officials (those we interviewed) is that it may be too early to think of m-government when e-government is still at the beginning stage. However, being at the beginning stages of e-government, Albania could be in an advantageous position because it can incor-

porate m-technologies from the planning stage of e-government, thus potentially discovering a synergy between e- and m-government and also avoid any unnecessary duplication of services, e.g., mobile communication to field workers can be taken over by m-government (Cilingir & Kushchu, 2004). Therefore, m-government development should be done in parallel with and to complement e-government projects. Reviewing some of the m-government applications of the developed countries (Trimi & Sheng, 2008), we suggest the following m-government projects to be considered by the Albanian government:

- **mG2G:** providing tools to field workers to do their job better and make government employees more mobile, thus improving effectiveness and efficiency. These applications would be very beneficial in Albania, because they would help in decreasing crime and corruption, and also increasing transparency. To avoid paying taxes, many small ghost businesses operate by bribing government officers to misreport their business activities. A field inspector can inspect such businesses and their activities, and send data on the spot. Some mG2G applications that can be developed are:
  - Field inspectors can use handheld devices to:
    - Complete surveys
    - Submit data to home offices
  - Enforcement units (police, parking officers, etc.) can use handheld devices to:
    - Connect remote units with central databases to access information about licenses, plates, criminal records history by police, inspectors, surveyors, etc.
    - Parking enforcement officers can use m-units to scan a VIN and print parking tickets immediately

- **mG2C/mG2B:** providing services to individuals and businesses to:
  - *Deliver information (one way transactions)* quickly, remotely, cheaply. Tremendous migration of population to urban areas and increase of the living standard after the fall of communism in Albania have made big cities very chaotic, with crowded pedestrians and traffic jams. On the other hand, Albania has a very mountainous geography, bad road infrastructure, which makes it difficult, time-consuming, and expensive for rural citizens to travel to the cities, for either selling their products or to receive government services. Economy is growing and new jobs and opportunities are being created. Citizens need to be informed of such opportunities and government and businesses need to find the best candidate chosen from as large a pool of people as possible. For this, keeping information flowing to citizens is very important. Government is also working hard to transform Albania into a true democratic country and join EU. Many new laws and legislation are being approved on the daily basis and citizens need to be aware and abide to them. To achieve this level of information diffusion and improve the quality of life for all Albanians, the following applications could be very useful:
    - Provide instant information about traffic conditions, accidents, market prices (to farmers, fishermen), etc.
    - Notifications of parking restrictions, natural disasters, or homeland security threats
    - Send SMS for taxes due, appointment reminders, birthday wishes
    - Judicial and legal systems: send information to citizens (for example, about new law); polling results, etc.
    - Information about employment opportunities
  - *Perform transactions (two-way, interactive).* Banking infrastructure has tremendously improved in Albania. Now many citizens and majority of business owners have bank cards. However, the majority of payments by citizens are done by cash and bank cards are used mostly at ATM rather than for payment. Albanians are not comfortable with the current levels of security and privacy of payment systems. Thus, for those citizens who either do not have or do not want to use credit cards, service providers, banks, and the government can cooperate to make it easy for citizens to pay for various transaction or taxes through mobile service providers. Thus, we suggest the following applications:
    - Pay taxes (both citizens and businesses)
    - Pay traffic or parking violation tickets
  - *E-democracy/e-participation (two-way, enhanced):* Albania is still a young democratic country with numerous problems of the past and present. Although much progress has been made, citizens are not happy with the level of corruption, lack of transparency, and the speed of progress toward an advanced country. Albanians love politics, to be involved and be heard in government decision-making. M-government applications

can be used to engage citizens in the democratic decision-making process through e-polling, m-voting, communication with the government; fight the crime and corruption (sending information and complains); and increase transparency. Therefore, we suggest the following applications:

- Polling (SMS)
- mVoting
- Citizens can send SMS about corrupt government employees and evaluate governmental services
- Report criminal offenses or emergency assistance needs

Obviously, the above-described m-government applications require technological (hardware and software) and human resource investments. The Albanian government should continue to work closely with EU, the World Band, and other donor nations for funding and technical support. M-government applications suggested for Albania are summarized in Table 2.

DISCUSSION

While remaining the poorest country in Europe, Albania has made tremendous progress toward market economy and democracy. Recognizing the importance of ICT in the country's and society's development and having the drive to become an EU member country, the Albanian government has developed strategies, frameworks and guidelines, and has initiated many projects to build an IT infrastructure and e-government applications. Thus, there already are e-government applications being successfully used by government employees, some businesses and citizens. However, the majority of these services are out of reach for most citizens and small businesses.

High costs of fixed internet access and the scarcity of access devices (PCs) in Albania, as well as the currently high and fast increase penetration rate of mobile technology, dictate the urgent need for developing m-government application projects to provide services to citizens and businesses. M-technologies are easier to use, and can be used anywhere, at anytime. They also help decrease digital divide in fragile democratic countries, such as Albania, where the internet can be a catalyst to increase public participation in democracy (the have-/well-educated people will have even louder and more effective voices while the majority goes unheard). Implementing m-government applications in Albania will improve the quality of government services provided to the public, increase government employee efficiency, decrease corruption, and enhance democracy.

Being at the beginning of e-government transformation, the Albanian government can enhance e-government services with m-government ones, the synergy between the two can be achieved, while avoiding duplication of services. On the other hand though, there are many challenges that still need to be overcome. First, applications need to be *designed on what users need and want*. Collecting users' feedback can be difficult and may take time, since many users in Albania are not familiar with many government services in general, let alone the online services. Second, public *awareness and education* will also take time and efforts. Currently, the Albanian government is working on the "e-school" project, which intends to provide internet access and education in all middle and high schools. The purpose of this project is not only to improve general education of the young generation but also increase public awareness of the internet and its services through families' exposure to their children's school projects and homework. Third, *financing* is always a big issue for poor countries like Albania. Realizing the importance of m-government, Albanian government should put a high priority on its development and awareness, with continued

Table 2. Suggested m-government applications for Albania

Types of M-government	Applications	Goals
mG2B/mG2C	•*Deliver Information (one way)* - Information about traffic, market prices (to farmers), natural disasters etc.	- Convenience - Improve efficiency
	•*Perform Transactions (two way, enhancement)* - Pay taxes (citizens, businesses) - Pay traffic or parking violation	- Convenience - Improve efficiency - Increase transparency
	•*E-democracy/E-participation (two way, enhancement)* - Polling - Voting - Report corruptions - Report criminal offenses - Emergency assistance	- Increase democracy - Increase transparency - Convenience
mG2G/mIEE	•*Field Inspectors* - Submit inspection data to main office - Complete survey	- Improve efficiency - Reduce errors - Increase transparency
	•*Enforcement Units* (police, parking officers etc.) - Get information on the spot from a central database about licenses, criminal records etc. - Scan VIN and print parking ticket on the spot; enter data to a central database on the spot	- Improve efficiency - Decrease crime and errors - Increase transparency

efforts to find financial support from international agencies and donor countries. Fourth, *privacy and security* concerns: privacy of citizens may be an issue because it is not only citizens who, through technology, get more information about government, but also governments get a great deal of information about people, with or without their consent. M-government applications are especially vulnerable for security and privacy issues due to the nature of the mobile technology. This could be a bigger concern in ex-communist countries such as Albania, with the worst history in collecting and misusing private information of the citizens. It will take a long time not only for the governments to change their culture and create privacy policies, but also for the citizens to heal from their mistrust of the government and to fully understand the concept of information security and their privacy rights. Strong regulations and legislations are preconditions that are immediately needed. Considering all these, we feel that the

Albanian government should immediately start working on m-government development.

CONCLUSION

To increase the quality, accessibility, and efficiency of public services to citizens, and citizens' participation in decision making, governments around the world are increasingly offering more services online. However, governments may spend a vast amount of money in developing e-government programs only to observe that their citizens do not fully utilize them. This can be due to a lack of understanding of the needs of people they serve, inadequate technology infrastructure, inadequate delivery of services, content accessibility, usefulness and accuracy, lack of marketing, and lack of trust and confidentiality.

The Albanian government, as the poorest nation in Europe, has made an impressive stride toward e-government projects. However, the severely limited fixed-line infrastructure has hampered any significant utilization of e-government services. It is especially true for rural area residents who simply cannot afford the relatively expensive internet service and costly computer equipment. Thus, the Albanian government should immediately start to plan and initiate m-government projects, to offer quality services to all of its citizens, wherever they are (in the most remote areas, or even abroad), increase their participation in decision making, thus improving transparency, decreasing corruption, enhancing democracy, and overall, increasing the citizens' quality of life.

This paper makes a contribution in detailing how unique political, historic, social, and economic conditions of a country affect the e- and m-government implantation project. This paper could have been more valuable if similar data/information could have been collected from other developing countries and present a comparative study. However, this type of qualitative research requires social capital which allows access to key government and service provider employees, and also government documents. Thus, such a comparative study will require a collaborative research with colleagues in several countries. That is the goal of the authors.

REFERENCES

Cilingir, D., & Kushchu, I. (2004). E-government and m-government: concurrent leaps by Turkey. *mGovLab*. Retrieved August 30, 2009, from http://www.mgovernment.org/resurces/mgovlab_dcik.pdf

Cullen International. (2007, November 30). *Country comparative report: supply of services in monitoring of South East Europe – telecommunications services sector and related aspects.*

Ghyasi, F. A., & Kushchu, I. (2004). m-Government: cases of developing countries. *mGovLab*. Retrieved October 22, 2008, from http://www.mgovernment.org/resurces/mgovlab_afgik.pdf

Hathaway-Zepeda, T. (2006). fall). Disconnected: taxing mobile phones in the developing world. *Harvard International Review*, 32–35.

Kushchu, I., & Borucki, C. (2004). Impact of mobile technologies on government. *mGovLab*. Retrieved October 22, 2008, from http://www.mgovernment.org/resurces/mgovlab_ikcb.pdf

Lee, S., Tan, X., & Trimi, S. (2005). Current practices of leading e-government countries. *Communications of the ACM, 48*(10), 99–104. doi:10.1145/1089107.1089112

Millennium Challenge Corporation. (2009). *Threshold quarterly report August 2008*. Retrieved June 18, 2009, from http://www.mcc.gov/documents/qsr-albania.pdf

Stability pact – eSEEurope initiative. (2002). Stability pact – eSEEurope initiative. *eSEEurope agenda for the development of the information society, a cooperative effort to implement the information society in South Eastern Europe.* Retrieved October 30, 2008, from http://www.eseeuropeconference.org/agenda.pdf

The Economist. (2008, February 14). A special report on technology and government. 3-18.

Trimi, S., & Sheng, H. (2008). Emerging trends of m-government. *Communications of the ACM, 51*(5), 53–58. doi:10.1145/1342327.1342338

UN E-government survey. (2008). *From e-government to connected governance.* Retrieved November 3, 2008, from http://unpan1.un.org/intradoc/groups/public/documents/UN/UNPAN028607.pdf

This work was previously published in International Journal of Information Technology Project Management, Volume 1, Issue 3, edited by John Wang, pp. 46-58, copyright 2010 by IGI Publishing (an imprint of IGI Global).

Compilation of References

Abdel-Hamid, T., & Madnick, S. E. (1991). *Software project dynamics: an integrated approach*. Upper Saddle River, NJ: Prentice Hall.

Abdullah, A. B. (2004). *Keynote address – Managing the national economy in challenging times: Enhancing the delivery systems and mechanism*. Kuala Lumpur, Malaysia: National Institute of Public Administration (INTAN).

Abdullah, M. S., Benest, I., Evans, A., & Kimble, C. (2002). Knowledge modelling techniques for developing knowledge management systems. In *Proceedings of the 3rd European Conference on Knowledge Management* (pp.15-25). Dublin, Ireland.

Abernathy, W., & Utterback, J. M. (1982). Patterns of industrial innovation. In Tushman, M., & Moore, W. (Eds.), *Readings in the Management of Innovation* (pp. 97–108). Boston: Harvard.

Abrahamsson, P., Conboy, K., & Wang, X. (2009). 'Lots done, more to do': The current state of agile systems development research. *European Journal of Information Systems, 18*, 281–284. doi:10.1057/ejis.2009.27

Abran, A., Bourque, P., Dupuis, R., & Moore, J. W. (2004). *SWEBOK. Guide to the Software Engineering Body of Knowledge. 2004 Version*. Los Alamitos, CA: IEEE Computer Society

Acuña, S. T., & Juristo, N. (2004). Assigning people to roles in software projects. *Software, Practice & Experience, 34*, 675–696. doi:10.1002/spe.586

Adlakha, V. G., & Kulkarni, V. G. (1989). A classified bibliography of research on stochastic PERT Networks: 1966-1987. *INFOR, 27*(3), 272–296.

Adler, P. A. (1987). *Membership roles in Field Research*. Newbury Park, CA: Sage.

Adler, R. T., & Smith, L. W. (2009). How organisational cost reporting practices affect project management: the issues of project review and evaluation. *International Journal of Project Organisation and Management, 1*(3), 309–320. doi:10.1504/IJPOM.2009.027541

Agar, M. H. (1986). *Speaking of ethnography*. Thousand Oaks, CA: Sage.

Ahmad, H. S., An, M., & Gaterell, M. (2007). Development of KM model to simplify knowledge management implementation in construction projects. In *Proceedings of the 23rd Annual ARCOM Conference, Association of Researchers in Construction Management* (pp.515-516). Belfast, UK.

Ahmad, H. S., An, M., & Gaterell, M. (2008). KM model to embed knowledge management activities into work activities in construction organisations. In *Proceedings of the 24th Annual ARCOM Conference, Association of Researchers in Construction Management* (pp.417-422). Cardiff, UK.

Ahmad, H. S., & An, M. (2008). Knowledge management implementation in construction projects: A KM model for knowledge creation, collection and updating (KCCU). *International Journal of Project Organisation and Management, 1*(2), 133–166. doi:10.1504/IJPOM.2008.022189

Al Neimat, T. (2009). *Why IT projects fail*. Retrieved July 5, 2009 from http://www.projectperfect.com.au/info_it_projects_fail.php

Aladwani, A. M., Rai, A., & Ramaprasad, A. (2000). Formal participation and performance of the system development group: the role of group heterogeneity and group-based rewards. *The Data Base for Advances in Information Systems, 31*(4), 25–40.

Alavi, M. (1984). An Assessment of the Prototyping Approach to Information-Systems Development. *Communications of the ACM, 27*, 556–561. doi:10.1145/358080.358095

Alavi, M., & Leidner, D. E. (2001). Knowledge management and knowledge management systems: Conceptual foundations and research issues. *Management Information Systems Quarterly, 25*(1), 107–136. doi:10.2307/3250961

Aldrich, H., & Herker, D. (1977). Boundary spanning roles and organization structure. *Academy of Management Review, 2*(2), 217–230. doi:10.2307/257905

Alonderien, R., Pundzien, A., & Krisciunas, K. (2006). Tacit knowledge acquisition and transfer in the process of informal learning. *Problems and Perspectives in Management, 4*(3), 134–145.

Al-Rousan, T., Sulaiman, S., & Salam Abdul, R. (2008). A risk identification architecture pattern based on bayesian network. *Information Technology, 4*, 1–10.

Al-Shehab, A., Hughes, R. T., & Winstanley, G. (2005). Modelling risks in IS/IT projects through causal and cognitive mapping. *The Electronic Journal of Information Systems Evaluation, 8*, 1–10.

Alter, S. (1999). *Information systems: A management perspective* (3rd ed.). Reading, MA: Addison-Wesley.

Alter, S. (2002). *Information systems: Foundation of e-business* (4th ed.). Upper Saddle River, NJ: Prentice Hall.

Alter, S. (2006). *The work system method connecting people, processes and it for business results*. Larkspur, CA: Larkspur Press.

Ancona, D. (1990). Outward bound: strategies for team survival in an organization. *Academy of Management Journal, 33*(2), 334–365. doi:10.2307/256328

Anderson, P., & Tushman, M. L. (1990). Technological discontinuities and dominant designs. *Administrative Science Quarterly, 35*, 604–633. doi:10.2307/2393511

APEC (Asia-Pacific Economic Cooperation). (2006, September 5-6). *Final report on APEC services or transparency in procurement and e-procurement*, Ha Noi, Vietnam. Retrieved from http://www.apec.org/apec/publications/free-downloads/06_cti_ gpeg_transparency[1].pdf

Archer, M. (1998). Realism and morphogenesis. In Archer, M., Bhaskar, R., Collier, A., Lawson, T., & Norrie, A. (Eds.), *Critical realism essential readings*. London: Routlege.

Archer, M. S. (1982). Morphogenesis versus structuration: On combining structure and action. *The British Journal of Sociology, 33*(4), 455–483. doi:10.2307/589357

Archer, M. S. (1988). *Culture and agency, the place of culture in social theory*. New York: Cambridge University Press.

Archer, M. S. (1995). *Realist social theory: The morphogenetic approach* (1st ed.). New York: Cambridge University Press. doi:10.1017/CBO9780511557675

Archer, M. S. (2000). *Being human the problem of agency*. New York: Cambridge University Press. doi:10.1017/CBO9780511488733

Archer, M. S. (2003). *Structure, agency and the internal conversation*. New York: Cambridge University Press.

Arisawa, S., & Elmaghraby, S. E. (1972). Optimal time-cost trade-offs in GERT networks. *Management Science, 18*(11), 589–599. doi:10.1287/mnsc.18.11.589

Arkes, H. R. (1991). Costs and benefits of judgment errors: implications for de-biasing. *Psychological Bulletin, 110*, 486–498. doi:10.1037/0033-2909.110.3.486

Armstrong, D. J., & Hardgrave, B. C. (2007). Understanding mindshift learning: The transition to object-oriented development. *Management Information Systems Quarterly, 31*(3), 453–474.

Armstrong, D., Gosling, A., Weinman, J., & Marteau, T. (1997). The place of inter-rater reliability in qualitative research: An empirical study. *Sociology, 31*(3), 597–606. doi:10.1177/0038038597031003015

Ash, C. R., & Pittman, H. P. (2008). Towards holistic project scheduling using critical chain methodology enhanced with PERT buffering. *International Journal of Project Organisation and Management*, *1*(2), 185–203. doi:10.1504/IJPOM.2008.022191

Atkinson, P., & Hammersley, M. (1994). Ethnography and participant observation. In Nenzin & Lincoln (Eds.), *Handbook of Qualitative Research* (pp. 248-261). Thousand Oaks, CA: Sage.

Austin, R., & Devin, L. (2003). Beyond requirements: Software making as art. *IEEE Software*, *20*(1), 93–95. doi:10.1109/MS.2003.1159037

Avison, D. E., & Fitzgerald, G. (2003). *Information systems development methodologies, techniques and tools.* (3rd ed.) London: McGraw-Hill.

Awad, E. M., & Ghaziri, H. M. (2004). *Knowledge management.* Upper Saddle River, NJ: Prentice Hall.

Badiru, A. B. (1992). Computational survey of univariate and multivariate learning curve models. *IEEE Transactions on Engineering Management*, *39*(2), 176–188. doi:10.1109/17.141275

Badiru, A. B. (1994). Multifactor learning and forgetting models for productivity and performance analysis. *The International Journal of Human Factors in Manufacturing*, *4*(1), 37–54. doi:10.1002/hfm.4530040105

Badiru, A. B. (1995). Incorporating learning curve effects into critical resource diagramming. *Project Management Journal*, *26*(2), 38–45.

Badiru, A. B. (2008). *Triple C model of project management: Communication, cooperation, and coordination.* Boca Raton, FL: CRC Press.

Badiru, A. B. (2009). *STEP project management: Guide for science, technology, and engineering Projects.* Boca Raton, FL: CRC Press.

Badiru, A. B., & Ijaduola, A. (2009). Half-life theory of learning curves for system performance analysis. *IEEE Systems Journal*, *3*(2), 154–165. doi:10.1109/JSYST.2009.2017394

Baiman, S. (1990). Agency research in managerial accounting: a second look. *Accounting, Organizations and Society*, *4*, 341–371. doi:10.1016/0361-3682(90)90023-N

Baker, K. R., & Trietsch, D. (2009). *Principles of sequencing and scheduling.* Wiley.

Baker, M., Barker, M., Thorne, J., & Dutnell, M. (1997). Leveraging human capital. *Journal of Knowledge Management*, *1*(1), 63–74. doi:10.1108/EUM0000000004581

Barker, T., & Frolick, M. N. (2003). ERP implementation failure: A case study. *Information Systems Management*, *3*, 43–50. doi:10.1201/1078/43647.20.4.20030901/77292.7

Barki, H., & Hartwick, J. (1994). Measuring user participation, user involvement, and user attitude. *MIS Quarterly*, *18*(1), 59–82. doi:10.2307/249610

Barton, S. L., Duchon, D., & Dunegan, K. J. (1989). An empirical test of Staw and Ross's prescriptions for management of escalation of commitment behavior. *Decision Sciences*, *20*, 532–544. doi:10.1111/j.1540-5915.1989.tb01565.x

Baskerville, R. L., & Stage, J. (1996). Controlling prototype development through risk analysis. *MIS Quarterly*, *20*, 481–504. doi:10.2307/249565

Bassellier, G., & Benbasat, I. (2004). Business competence of information technology professionals: Conceptual development and influence on IT-business partnerships. *Management Information Systems Quarterly*, *28*(4), 673–694.

Bassellier, G., Horner Reich, B., & Benbasat, I. (2001). Information Technology Competence of Business Managers: A Definition and Research Model. *Journal of Management Information Systems*, *17*(4), 159–182.

Beath, C. M., & Orlikowski, W. J. (1994). The Contradictory Structure of Systems Development Methodologies: Deconstructing the IS-User Relationship in Information Engineering. *Information Systems Research*, *5*, 350–377. doi:10.1287/isre.5.4.350

Beaumaster, S. (1999). *IT implementation issues in local government: An analysis.* Unpublished doctoral dissertation, Blacksburg, VA.

Beaumaster, S. (2002). Local government IT implementation issues: A challenge for public administration. In *Proceedings of the 35th Hawaii International Conference on System Sciences (HICSS-35'02)*.

Beck, K. (1999). Embrace change with extreme programming. *IEEE Computer*, 70-77.

Beck, K. (2000). *Extreme programming explained: embrace change*. Reading, MA: Addison-Wesley.

Beck, K. (2001). *Manifesto for agile software development*. Retrieved August 06, 2008 from http:// www.agilemanifesto.org

Beck, R., & Möbs, A. (2006). The public hand and it mega-projects: Lessons from the german tollcollect case. In *Proceedings of the Inaugural (First) International Research Workshop on IT Project Management (IRWITPM 2006)*, Milwaukee, WI.

Beise, C. M. (2004). *IT project management and virtual teams*. Paper presented at the 2004 SIGMIS Conference on Computer Personnel Research: Careers, Culture, and Ethics in a Networked Environment.

Belkaoui, A. (1986). *The Learning Curve*. Westport, CT: Quorum Books.

Belli, R. F. (1998). The structure of autobiographical memory and the event history calendar: Potential improvements in the quality of retrospective reports in surveys. *Memory (Hove, England)*, 6(4), 383–406. doi:10.1080/741942610

Benbasat, I., Goldstein, D. K., & Mead, M. (1987). The case research strategy in studies of information systems. *Management Information Systems Quarterly*, 11(3), 369–385. doi:10.2307/248684

Benbasat, I., & Zmud, R. W. (1999). Empirical research in information systems: The practice of relevance. *Management Information Systems Quarterly*, 23(1), 3–16. doi:10.2307/249403

Bennet, D., & Bennet, A. (2008). Engaging tacit knowledge in support of organizational learning. *Journal of Information and Knowledge Management Systems*, 38(1), 72–94.

Berger, H., & Beynon-Davies, P. (2004). Issues Impacting on the Project Management of a RAD Development Approach of a Large, Complex Government IT Project. *Pacific Asia Conference on Information Systems (PACIS)*, 8th-11th July, 2004. Shanghai, China.

Bergiel, B. J., Bergiel, E. B., & Phillip, W. B. (2008). Nature of virtual teams: a summary of their advantages and disadvantages. *Management Research News*, 31(2), 99. doi:10.1108/01409170810846821

Bevan, N. (1999). Quality in use: meeting user needs for quality. *Journal of Systems and Software*, 49(1), 89–96. doi:10.1016/S0164-1212(99)00070-9

Beynon-Davies, P., Mackay, H., & Slack, R. (1997). User Involvement in Information Systems Development: the problem of finding the 'right' user. *European Conference on Information Systems*. Cork: Cork Publishing Ltd.

Beynon-Davies, P., Mackay, H., & Tudhope, D. (2000). 'It's lots of bits of paper and ticks and post-it notes and things…': A Case Study of a Rapid Application Development Project. *Journal of Information Systems*, 10, 195–216. doi:10.1046/j.1365-2575.2000.00080.x

Bhaskar, R. (1979). *The possibility of naturalism* (1st ed.). Brighton, UK: The Harvester Press Limited.

Bierly, P., Kessler, E., & Christensen, E. (2000). Organizational learning, knowledge and wisdom. *Journal of Organizational Change Management*, 13(6), 595–618. doi:10.1108/09534810010378605

Bittner, K., & Spence, I. (2006). *Managing Iterative Software Development Projects*. Addison-Wesley.

Bloomfield, B. P., & Coombs, R. (1992). Information technology, control, and power: The centralization and decentralization debate revisited. *Journal of Management Studies*, 29(4), 459–484. doi:10.1111/j.1467-6486.1992.tb00674.x

Blumentritt, R., & Johnston, R. (1999). Towards a strategy for knowledge management. *Technology Analysis and Strategic Management*, 11(3), 287–300. doi:10.1080/095373299107366

Boehm, B. W. (1981). *Software Engineering Economics*. Englewood Cliffs, NJ: Prentice Hall.

Boehm, B. W., & Turner, R. (2003). *Balancing agility and discipline: A guide for the perplexed.* Upper Saddle River, NJ: Addison-Wesley.

Boehm, B., Horowitz, E., Madachy, R., Reifer, D., Clark, B. K., Steece, B., et al. (2000). *Software Cost Estimation with COCOMO II.* Upper Saddle River, NJ: Prentice Hall.

Boehm, B. W. (1991). Software risk management: principles and practices. *IEEE Software, 8,* 32–41. doi:10.1109/52.62930

Boile, M., Theofanis, S., Golias, M., & Coit, D. (2007). Berth planning by customer service differentiation: A multi-objective approach. In proceedings of the *World Conference on Transport Research (CD-Rom)*, Berkeley, California, 2007.

Bold, M. (2006). Use of wikis in graduate course work. *Journal of Interactive Learning, 17*(1), 5.

Boulding, W., Morgan, R., & Staeiin, R. (1997). Pulling the plug to stop the new product drain. *JMR, Journal of Marketing Research, 34*(1), 164–116. doi:10.2307/3152073

Bowman, R. A. (1995). Efficient estimation of arc criticalities in stochastic activity networks. *Management Science, 41*(1), 58–67. doi:10.1287/mnsc.41.1.58

Bowman, R. A. (2001). Due date-based metrics for activity importance in stochastic activity networks. *Annals of Operations Research, 102*(1), 39–48. doi:10.1023/A:1010993713274

Boyatzis, R. E. (1982). *The competent manager: A model for effective performance.* New York: Wiley.

Boyatzis, R. E. (1988). *Transforming qualitative information: Thematic analysis and code development.* Thousand Oaks, CA: Sage.

Bozman, J. S. (1994). *California kills failed $44M project.* Computerworld.

Bradner, E., Mark, G., & Hertel, T. D. (2005). Team size and technology fit: participation, awareness, and rapport in distributed teams. *IEEE Transactions on Professional Communication, 48*(1), 68–77. doi:10.1109/TPC.2004.843299

Branke, J., Deb, K., Dierolf, H., & Osswald, M. (2004). Finding knees in multi-objective optimization. In proceedings of the *8th Conference on Parallel Problem Solving from Nature,* (pp. 722-731), Birmingham, UK.

Brewer, J., & Dittman, K. (2010). *Methods of it project management* (1st ed.). Upper Saddle River, NJ: Prentice Hall.

Brill, J. M., Bishop, M. J., & Walker, A. E. (2006). The competencies and characteristics required of an effective project manager. *Educational Technology Research and Development, 54*(2), 115–140. doi:10.1007/s11423-006-8251-y

Britney, R. R. (1976). Bayesian point estimation and the PERT scheduling of stochastic activities. *Management Science, 22*(9), 938–948. doi:10.1287/mnsc.22.9.938

Brockner, J. (1992). *The escalation of commitment to a failing course of action: toward theoretical progress.* New York: Wiley and Sons.

Brockner, J., & Rubin, J. (1985). *Entrapment in escalating conflicts: a social psychological analysis.* New York: Springer.

Brockner, J., Shaw, M., & Rubin, J. (1979). Factors affecting withdrawal from an escalating conflict: quitting before it's too late. *Journal of Experimental Social Psychology, 15,* 492–503. doi:10.1016/0022-1031(79)90011-8

Brooks, F. P. (1987). No silver bullet: Essence and accidents of software engineering. *Computer, 20*(4), 10–19. doi:10.1109/MC.1987.1663532

Brown, W. (2004). Enterprise resource planning (ERP) implementation planning and structure: a recipe for ERP success. In J. S. Whiting, J. Ashworth, & D. Mateik (Eds.), *Annual ACM SIGUCCS Conference on User Services 2004* (Vol. 32, pp. 82-86). Baltimore: AMC.

Burgess, K., & Singh, P. (2006). A proposed integrated framework for analysing supply chains. *Supply Chain Management: An International Journal, 11*(4), 337–344. doi:10.1108/13598540610671789

Burke, M. J., & Day, R. R. (1986). A cumulative study of the effectiveness of managerial training. *The Journal of Applied Psychology, 71*(2), 232–246. doi:10.1037/0021-9010.71.2.232

Burt, J. M., & Garman, M. B. (1971). Conditional Monte-Carlo: a simulation technique for stochastic network analysis. *Management Science, 18*(3), 207–217. doi:10.1287/mnsc.18.3.207

Busby, J. S. (1999). An assessment of post-project reviews. *Journal of Project Management, 30*(3), 23–29.

Camm, J. D., Evans, J. R., & Womer, N. K. (1987). The unit learning curve approximation of total cost. *Computers & Industrial Engineering, 12*(3), 205–213. doi:10.1016/0360-8352(87)90014-3

Cannon, J. T. (1968). *Business strategy policy.* New York: Harcourt, Brace and World.

Carayannis, E. G., & Popescu, D. (2005). Profiling a methodology for economic growth and convergence: learning from the EU e-procurement experience for central and eastern European countries. *Technovation, 25*, 1–14. doi:10.1016/S0166-4972(03)00071-3

Carbone, T. A., & Gholston, S. (2004). Project manager skill development: A survey of programs and practitioners. *Engineering Management Journal, 16*(3), 10–16.

Carlucci, D., Marr, B., & Schiuma, G. (2004). The knowledge value chain: how intellectual capital impacts on business performance. *International Journal of Technology Management, 27*(6/7), 575–590. doi:10.1504/IJTM.2004.004903

Carrillo, P. M., Anumba, C. J., & Kamara, J. M. (2000). Knowledge management strategy for construction: Key IT and contextual issues. *Construction Informatics Digital Library.* Retrieved from http://itc.scix.net/paper w78-2000-155.content

Carrillo, P. M. (2005). Lessons learned practices in the engineering, procurement and construction secto. *Engineering, Construction, and Architectural Management, 12*(3), 236–250. doi:10.1108/09699980510600107

Carrillo, P. M., & Anumba, C. J. (2002). Knowledge management in the AEC sector: an exploration of the mergers and acquisition context. *Knowledge and Process Management, 9*(1), 149–161. doi:10.1002/kpm.146

Carrillo, P. M., Robinson, H., Al-Ghassani, A., & Anumba, C. (2004). Knowledge management in the UK construction: Strategies, resources and barriers. *Journal of Project Management, 35*(1), 46–56.

Carr, M. J., Konda, S. L., Monarch, I., Ulrich, C. F., & Walker, C. F. (1993). *Taxonomy-based risk identification.* Pittsburgh, PA: Software Engineering Institute.

Carte, T. A., & Russell, C. J. (2003). In pursuit of moderation: nine common errors and their solutions. *MIS Quarterly, 27*(3), 479–501.

Caupin, G., Knopfel, H., Morris, P., Motzel, E., & Pannenbacker, O. (1999). ICB*: IPMA competence baseline.* International Project Management Association, Germany.

Cavaye, A. L. M. (1995). User participation in system development revisited. *Information & Management, 28*, 311–323. doi:10.1016/0378-7206(94)00053-L

Charbonneau, S. (2004). *Software Project Management - A Mapping between RUP and the PMBOK.* Retrieved April 28, 2008, from http://www.ibm.com/developerworks/rational/library/4721.html.

Charette, R. N. (2005). *Why Software Fails.* Retrieved April 28, 2008, from http://www.spectrum.ieee.org/sep05/1685.

Chen, J.-H., & Chen, S.-M. (2006). *A new method for ranking generalized fuzzy numbers for handling fuzzy risk analysis problems.* Retrieved July 5, 2009 from http://www.atlantispress.com/php/download_paper.php?id=80

Chen, J. Q., & Heath, R. (2001). Building Web Applications. *Information Systems Management, 18*, 68–79. doi:10.1201/1078/43194.18.1.20010101/31266.8

Chen, S. P. (2007). Analysis of critical paths in a project network with fuzzy activity times. *European Journal of Operational Research, 183*(1), 442–459. doi:10.1016/j.ejor.2006.06.053

Chiesa, V., & Manzini, R. (1998). Organizing for technological collaborations: a managerial perspective. *R & D Management*, *28*(3), 199–212. doi:10.1111/1467-9310.00096

Chin, W. W. (1998). The partial least squares approach to structural equation modeling. In G. A. Marcoulides (Ed.) *Modern methods for business research* (pp. 295-336). Mahwah, NJ: Lawrence Erlbaum Associates.

Cho, J. G., & Yum, B. J. (1997). An uncertainty importance measure of activities in PERT networks. *International Journal of Production Research*, *35*(10), 2737–2770. doi:10.1080/002075497194426

Chompalov, I., Genuth, J., & Shrum, W. (2002). The organization of scientific collaborations. *Research Policy*, *31*(5), 749–767. doi:10.1016/S0048-7333(01)00145-7

Chong, C. W., Holden, T., Wilhelmij, P., & Schimdt, R. A. (2000). Where does knowledge management add value? *Journal of Intellectual Capital*, *1*(4), 366–380. doi:10.1108/14691930010359261

Chu, C., Proth, J.-M., & Xie, X. (1993). Supply management in assembly systems. *Naval Research Logistics*, *40*, 933–949. doi:10.1002/1520-6750(199312)40:7<933::AID-NAV3220400706>3.0.CO;2-8

Chwelos, P., Benbasat, I., & Dexter, A. S. (2001). Research report: Empirical test of an EDI adoption model. *Information Systems Research*, *12*(3), 304–321. doi:10.1287/isre.12.3.304.9708

Cicmil, S. (2006). Understanding project management practice through interpretative and critical research perspectives. *Project Management Journal*, *37*(2), 27–37.

Ciganek, A. P., Haines, M. N., & Haseman, W. D. (2009). Service-Oriented Architecture Adoption: Key Factors and Approaches. *Journal of Information Technology Management*, *20*(3), 42–54.

Cilingir, D., & Kushchu, I. (2004). E-government and m-government: concurrent leaps by Turkey. *mGovLab*. Retrieved August 30, 2009, from http://www.mgovernment.org/resurces/mgovlab_dcik.pdf

Clark, D. N., & Gibb, J. L. (2006). Virtual team learning: an introductory study team exercise. *Journal of Management Education*, *30*(6), 765–787. doi:10.1177/1052562906287969

Clarke, J. C., & Varma, S. (1999). Strategic risk management: the new competitive edge. *Long Range Planning*, *32*(4), 414–424. doi:10.1016/S0024-6301(99)00052-7

Clegg, S. R., Pitsis, T. S., Rura-Polley, T., & Marosszeky, M. (2002). Governmentality matters: Designing an alliance culture of inter-organizational collaboration for managing projects. *Organization Studies*, *23*(3), 317–337. doi:10.1177/0170840602233001

Coello Coello, A. C. (2000). Treating constraints as objectives for single-objective evolutionary optimization. *Engineering Optimization*, *32*(3), 275–308. doi:10.1080/03052150008941301

Coffey, A., & Atkinson, P. (1996). *Making sense of qualitative data: Complementary research strategies.* London: Sage.

Cohen, Y., & Zwikael, O. (2008). Modelling and scheduling projects using Petri nets. *International Journal of Project Organisation and Management*, *1*(2), 221–233. doi:10.1504/IJPOM.2008.022193

Colomo, R. (2005). *A framework for Software Engineers Competence Evaluation*. Ph.D. Thesis. Universidad Politécnica de Madrid, Spain.

Conger, J. A. (2004). Developing leadership capability: What's inside the black box? *The Academy of Management Executive*, *18*(4), 136–139.

Cooke-Davies, T. (2002). The "real" success factors on projects. *International Journal of Project Management*, *20*(3), 185–190. doi:10.1016/S0263-7863(01)00067-9

Coppola, N. W., Hiltz, S. R., & Rotter, N. G. (2004). Building trust in virtual teams. *IEEE Transactions on Professional Communication*, *47*(2), 95–104. doi:10.1109/TPC.2004.828203

Crawford, L., & Gaynor, F. (1999). Assessing and developing project manager competence. In *Proceedings of the 30th Annual Project Management Institute 1999 Seminars & Symposium*, Project Management Institute, Sylva, NC.

Crawford, L. (2005). Senior Management Perceptions of Project Management Competence. *International Journal of Project Management*, *23*, 7–16. doi:10.1016/j.ijproman.2004.06.005

Croom, S., & Brandon-Jones, A. (2007). Impact of e-procurement: Experiences from implementation in the UK public sector. *Journal of Purchasing and Supply Management*, *13*, 294–303. doi:10.1016/j.pursup.2007.09.015

Croom, S., & Johnston, R. (2003). E-service: enhancing internal customer service through e-procurement. *International Journal of Service Industry Management*, *14*(5), 539–555. doi:10.1108/09564230310500219

Cross, R., & Prusak, L. (2002). The people who make organizations go - or stop. *Harvard Business Review*, *80*(6), 104–112.

Crowston, K., Howison, J., Masango, C., & Eseryel, U. Y. (2007). The role of face-to-face meetings in technology-supported self-organizing distributed teams. *IEEE Transactions on Professional Communication*, *50*(3), 185. doi:10.1109/TPC.2007.902654

Cuellar, M. J. (2007). *A realist social theory of information systems.* Paper presented at the AMCIS 2007, Keystone, CO.

Cuellar, M., Keil, M., & Johnson, R. (2006). The deaf effect response to bad news reporting in IS projects. *EService Journal*, *5*(1), 75–97. doi:10.2979/ESJ.2006.5.1.75

Cule, P., & Robey, D. (2004). A dual-motor, constructive process model of organizational transition. *Organization Studies*, *25*(2), 229–260. doi:10.1177/0170840604040037

Cule, P., Schmidt, R., Lyytinen, K., & Keil, M. (2000). Strategies for heading off is project failure. *Information Systems Management*, *17*(2), 65–73. doi:10.1201/1078/43191.17.2.20000301/31229.8

Cullen International. (2007, November 30). *Country comparative report: supply of services in monitoring of South East Europe – telecommunications services sector and related aspects.*

Cumming, C., & Hirtle, B. (2001). *The challenges of risk management in diversified financial companies.* Retrieved July 5, 2009 from http://www.capco.com/files/pdf/81/03_FINANCIAL%20CAPITAL/03_The%20challenges%20of%20risk%20management%20in%20diversified%20financial%20companies.pdf

Curtis, B., Hefley, W. E., & Miller, S. A. (2001). *People Capability Maturity Model (P-CMM) Version 2.0* (No. CMU/SEI-2001-MM-01). Pittsburgh, PA: Software Engineering Institute.

Dainty, A. R. J., Cheng, M.-I., & Moore, D. R. (2003). Redefining performance measures for construction project managers: An empirical evaluation. *Construction Management and Economics*, *21*(2), 209–218. doi:10.1080/0144619032000049737

Dainty, A. R. J., Cheng, M.-I., & Moore, D. R. (2004). A competency-based performance model for construction project managers. *Construction Management and Economics*, *22*(8), 877–886. doi:10.1080/0144619042000202726

Dainty, A. R. J., Cheng, M.-I., & Moore, D. R. (2005). A comparison of the behavioral competencies of client-focused and production-focused project managers in the construction sector. *Project Management Journal*, *36*(2), 39–48.

Dalton, M., Leslie, J., Ernst, C., & Deal, J. (2002). *Success for the new global manager: how to work across distances, countries and cultures.* San Francisco, CA: Jossey-Bass.

Das, I. (1999). On characterizing the 'knee' of the Pareto curve based on normal-boundary intersection. *Structural Optimization*, *18*(2/3), 107–115.

Davenport, T. H., De Long, D. W., & Beers, M. C. (1997). *Building successful knowledge management projects* (Working paper, Centre for Business Innovation, Ernst & Young).

Davenport, T. H., De Long, D. W., & Beers, M. C. (1998). Successful knowledge management projects. *Sloan Management Review*, *39*(2), 43–57.

Davenport, T. H., & Prusak, L. (1998). *Working knowledge: How organizations manage what they know.* Boston: Harvard Business School Press.

Davern, M. (1996). *When good fit is bad: the dynamics of perceived fit.* In *Proceedings of the Seventeenth International Conference on Information Systems* (pp. 112-121), Cleveland, Ohio.

David, H. A., & Nagaraja, H. N. (2003). *Order statistics* (3rd ed.). Haboken, NJ: John Wiley and Sons.

Davies, A., Gann, D., & Douglas, T. (2009). Innovation in megaprojects: Systems integration at london heathrow terminal 5. *California Management Review, 51*(2), 101–125.

Davies, J., & Easterby-Smith, M. (1984). Learning and developing from managerial work experiences. *Journal of Management Studies, 21*(2), 169–183. doi:10.1111/j.1467-6486.1984.tb00230.x

Davila, A., Gupta, M., & Palmer, R. J. (2002). *Moving procurement systems to the internet: The adoption and use of e-procurement technology models* (Tech. Rep. No. 1742). Retrieved March 22, 2003, from http://ssrn.com/abstract=323923

Davis, N., & Mullaney, J. (2003). *The Team Software Process (TSP) in Practice: A Summary of Recent Results* (No. CMU/SEI-2003-TR-014): Software Engineering Institute, Pittsburgh, PA.

Day, D. V. (2001). Leadership development: A review in context. *The Leadership Quarterly, 11*(4), 581–613. doi:10.1016/S1048-9843(00)00061-8

de Amescua, A., García, J., Velasco, M., Martínez, P., Ruiz, B., & Llorens, J. (2004). A Software Project Management Framework. *Information Systems Management, 21*(2), 78–85. doi:10.1201/1078/44118.21.2.20040301/80425.11

De Carvalho, R. A., & Tanaka, A. K. (2008). Editorial message to a special track on enterprise information systems. In *Proceedings of the Annual ACM symposium on Applied Computing* (Vol. 23). Ceará, Brazil.

de Vaujany, F.-X. (2008). Capturing reflexivity modes in is: A critical realist approach. *Information and Organization, 18*, 51–72. doi:10.1016/j.infoandorg.2007.11.001

Demarco, T. (1982). *Controlling software projects*. New York: Yourdon Press.

Demeulemeester, E. L., & Herroelen, W. S. (2002). *Project scheduling: a research handbook*. Norwell, MA: Kluwer.

Demirkan, H., & Nichols, J. (2008). IT services project management: lessons learned from a case study in implementation. *International Journal of Project Organisation and Management, 1*(2), 204–220. doi:10.1504/IJPOM.2008.022192

Demirkan, H., & Nichols, J. (2008). IT services project management: lessons learned from a case study in implementation. *International Journal of Project Organisation and Management, 1*(2), 204–220. doi:10.1504/IJPOM.2008.022192

DePietro, R., Wiarda, E., & Fleischer, M. (1990). The context for change: Organization, technology, and environment. In Tornatzky, L. G., & Fleischer, M. (Eds.), *The Process of Technological Innovation* (pp. 151–175). Lanham, MD: Lexington Books.

DeSanctis, G., & Poole, M. S. (1994). Capturing the complexity in advanced technology use: Adaptive structuration theory. *Organization Science, 5*(2), 121–147. doi:10.1287/orsc.5.2.121

Dibbern, J., Goles, T., Hirschheim, R., & Jayatilaka, B. (2004). Information systems outsourcing: A survey and analysis of the literature. *The Data Base for Advances in Information Systems, 35*(4), 6–102.

DiMaggio, P. J., & Powell, W. W. (1983). The iron cage revisited: institutional isomorphism and collective rationality in organizational fields. *American Sociological Review, 48*, 147–160. doi:10.2307/2095101

Dinsmore, P. (1999). *Winning in Business with Enterprise Project Managemen*. New York: Amacom Books.

Dixon, M. (2000). *APM project management body of knowledge* (4th ed.). Peterborough, England: Association for Project Management, Peterborough, UK.

Dodin, B. M. (1984). Determining the k most critical paths in PERT networks. *Operations Research, 32*(4), 859–877. doi:10.1287/opre.32.4.859

Dodin, B. M. (1985). Bounding the project completion time distribution in PERT networks. *Operations Research, 33*(4), 862–881. doi:10.1287/opre.33.4.862

Dodin, B. M. (2006). A practical and accurate alternative to PERT. In Josefowska, J., & Weglarz, J. (Eds.), *Perspectives in Modern Project Scheduling* (pp. 3–23). New York: Springer.

Dodin, B. M., & Elmaghraby, S. E. (1985). Approximating the criticality indices of the activities in PERT networks. *Management Science, 31*(2), 207–223. doi:10.1287/mnsc.31.2.207

Dodin, B. M., & Sirvanci, M. (1990). Stochastic networks and the extreme value distribution. *Computers & Operations Research, 17*(4), 397–409. doi:10.1016/0305-0548(90)90018-3

Draganidis, F., & Mentzas, G. (2006). Competency based management: a review of systems and approaches. *Information Management & Computer Security, 14*(1), 51–64. doi:10.1108/09685220610648373

Dreyfus, H. L., & Dreyfus, S. E. (1986). *Mind over machine: The power of human intuition and expertise in the era of the computer*. New York: Free Press.

Drummond, H. (1996). The politics of risk: trials and tribulations of the Taurus project. *Journal of Information Technology, 11*(4), 347–357.

Drummond, H. (1998). Is escalation always irrational? *Organization Studies, 19*(6), 911–929. doi:10.1177/017084069801900601

DuBois, D. A. (2002). Leveraging hidden expertise: Why, when, and how to use cognitive task analysis. In Kraiger, K. (Ed.), *Creating, implementing, and managing effective training and development: State-of-the-art lessons for practice* (pp. 80–114). San Francisco, CA: Jossey-Bass.

EFQM. (1999). *Introducing excellence*. Brussels, Belgium: European Foundation for Quality Management.

Egan, J. (1998). *Rethinking construction: Report of the construction task force on the scope for improving the quality and efficiency of the UK construction industry*. London: Department of the Environment, Transport and the Regions.

Egbu, C., Kurul, E., Quintas, P., Hutchinson, V., Anumba, C., & Ruikar, K. (2003). *Techniques and technologies for knowledge management*. Retrieved from http://www.knowledgemanagement.uk.net/ resources/WP3%20Interim%20Report.pdf

Egbu, C., & Botterill, K. (2002). Information technologies for knowledge management: Their usage and effectiveness. *ITcon, 7*, 125–137.

EI-Diraby, T. E., & Kashif, K. F. (2005). Distributed ontology architecture for knowledge management in highway construction. *Journal of Construction Engineering and Management, 131*(5), 591–603. doi:10.1061/(ASCE)0733-9364(2005)131:5(591)

Eisenhardt, K. M. (1989). Agency Theory - An Assessment and Review. *Academy of Management Review, 14*, 57–74. doi:10.2307/258191

Eisenhardt, K. M. (1989). Building theories from case study research. *Academy of Management Review, 14*(4), 532–550. doi:10.2307/258557

Eldredge, N., & Gould, S. (1972). Punctuated equilibria: an alternative to phyletic gradualism. In Schopf, T. J. (Ed.), *Models in paleobiology* (pp. 82–115). San Francisco, CA: Freeman, Cooper and Co.

Elkins, T. (2000). Virtual teams connect and collaborate. *IIE Solutions, 32*(4), 26–32.

Elmaghraby, S. E. (1967). On the expected duration of PERT type network. *Management Science, 13*(5), 299–306. doi:10.1287/mnsc.13.5.299

Elmaghraby, S. E. (2000). On criticality and sensitivity in activity networks. *European Journal of Operational Research, 127*(2), 220–238. doi:10.1016/S0377-2217(99)00483-X

Elmaghraby, S. E. (2005). On the fallacy of averages in project risk management. *European Journal of Operational Research, 165*(2), 307–313. doi:10.1016/j.ejor.2004.04.003

El-Sabaa, S. (2001). The skills and career path of an effective project manager. *International Journal of Project Management, 19*(1), 1–7. doi:10.1016/S0263-7863(99)00034-4

Elsbach, K. D., & Sutton, R. I. (1992). Acquiring organizational legitimacy through illegitimate actions: a marriage of institutional and Impression Management Theories. *Academy of Management Journal*, 699–738. doi:10.2307/256313

ePerolehan. (2009). *ePerolehan, the official portal for Malaysian government procurement*. Retrieved from http://home.eperolehan.gov.my/

Eraut, M. (2000). Non-formal learning and tacit knowledge in professional work. *The British Journal of Educational Psychology, 70*(1), 113–136. doi:10.1348/000709900158001

Erl, T. (2006). *Service-Oriented Architecture: Concepts, Technology, and Design*. Upper Saddle River, NJ: Prentice Hall.

European Commission. (2002). *FP6 instruments: Implementating the priority thematic areas of the sixth framework programme*. Luxembourg: Office for Official Publications of the European Communities.

European Commission. (2005). ICT and electronic business in the construction industry: ICT adoption and e-business activity in 2005. *Report of the European e-business market watch, e-business sector study in the construction industry*. Retrieved from www.ebusiness-watch.org

Eva, M. (2001). Requirements acquisition for rapid applications development. *Information & Management, 39*, 101–107. doi:10.1016/S0378-7206(01)00082-9

Evan, W. M. (1966). The organization-set: Toward a theory of interorganizational relations. In Thompson, J. D. (Ed.), *Approaches to organizational design* (pp. 173–191). Pittsburgh, PA: University of Pittsburgh Press.

Ewusi-Mensah, K. (1997). Critical issues in abandoned information systems development projects. *Communications of the ACM, 40*(9), 74–80. doi:10.1145/260750.260775

Fenn, J., Drakos, N., Andrews, W., Knox, R. E., Tully, J., Ball, R. J. G., et al. (2008). *Hype Cycle for Emerging Technologies 2008* (Gartner No. G00159496).

Festinger, L. A. (1957). *Theory of Cognitive Dissonance*. Evanston, IL: Row, Peterson.

Fichman, R. G. (1992). *Information Technology Diffusion: A Review of Empirical Research*. Paper presented at the Proceedings of the Thirteenth International Conference on Information Systems, Dallas, TX.

Firestone, H. R. (1983). Multisite qualitative policy research: optimizing description and generalizability. *Educational Researcher, 12*, 14–19.

Flanagan, J. C. (1954). The critical incident technique. *Psychological Bulletin, 51*(4), 327–358. doi:10.1037/h0061470

Flyvbjerg, B. (2006). *From Nobel prize to project management: getting risks right*. Retrieved July 5, 2009 from http://flyvbjerg.plan.aau.dk/Publications2006/Nobel-PMJ2006.pdf

Flyvbjerg, B., Bruzelius, N., & Rothengatter, W. (2005). *Megaprojects and risk, an anatomy of ambition* (3rd ed.). New York: Cambridge University Press.

Fong, S. W., & Wong, K. (2005). Capturing and reusing building maintenance knowledge: A socio-technical perspective. In Kazi, A. S. (Ed.), *Knowledge Management in the Construction Industry: A Socio-Technical Perspective*. Hershey, PA: IGI Global.

Ford, G., & Gibbs, N. (1996). *A Mature Profession of Software Engineering* (No. CMU/SEI-96-TR-04). Pittsburgh, PA: Software Engineering Institute.

Fornell, C., & Larcker, D. (1981). Evaluating structural equation models with unobservable variables and measurement error. *JMR, Journal of Marketing Research, 18*(1), 39–50. doi:10.2307/3151312

FP6 Instruments Task Force. (2003). *Provisions for implementing networks of excellence: Background document*. Luxembourg: Office for Official Publications of the European Communities.

Friedman, R. A., & Podolny, J. (1992). Differentiation of boundary spanning roles: Labor negotiations and implications for role conflict. *Administrative Science Quarterly, 37*(1), 28–47. doi:10.2307/2393532

Friedman, T. L. (2006). *The world is flat: a brief history of the 21st century*. New York: Farrar, Straus and Giroux.

Frye, C. (2008). Software *development groups take many routes to agile*. Retrieved August 05, 2008 from www.SearchSoftwareQuality.com

Fulkerson, D. R. (1961). A network flow computation for project cost curves. *Management Science, 7*(2), 167–178. doi:10.1287/mnsc.7.2.167

Gabriel, A. S., Kumar, S., Ordonez, J., & Nasserian, A. (2006). A multiobjective optimization model for project selection with probabilistic considerations. *Socio-Economic Planning Sciences, 40*(4), 297–313. doi:10.1016/j.seps.2005.02.002

Gallivan, M. J., & Keil, M. (2003). The user-developer communication process: a critical case study. *Information Systems Journal*, *13*, 37–68. doi:10.1046/j.1365-2575.2003.00138.x

Gallivan, M. J., Tuex, D. P., & Kvasny, L. (2004). Changing patterns in IT skill sets 1988-2003: a content analysis of classified advertising. *ACM SIGMIS Database*, *35*(3), 64–87. doi:10.1145/1017114.1017121

Gansler, J. S., Lucyshyn, W., & Ross, K. M. (2003). *Digitally integrating the government supply chain: E-procurement, e-finance, and e-logistics*. College Park, MD: University of Maryland.

Garcia-Crespo, A., Colomno-Palacios, R., Gomez-Berbis, J. M., & Ruano-Mayoral, M. (2009). A project management methodology for commercial software reengineering. *International Journal of Project Organisation and Management*, *1*(3), 253–267. doi:10.1504/IJPOM.2009.027538

Gareis, R. (2006). *Happy projects*. Bucharest, Romania: ASE Press.

Garland, H., & Conlon, D. E. (1998). Too close to quit: the role of project completion in maintaining commitment. *Journal of Applied Social Psychology*, *28*(22), 2025–2048. doi:10.1111/j.1559-1816.1998.tb01359.x

Garson, G. D. (2003). *Public information technology: Policy and management issues*. Hershey, PA: IGI Global.

Gersick, C. (1989). Marking time: Predictable transitions in task groups. *Academy of Management Journal*, *32*, 274–309. doi:10.2307/256363

Gersick, C. (1991). Revolutionary change theories: A multilevel exploration of the punctuated equilibrium paradigm. *Academy of Management Review*, *16*(1), 10–36. doi:10.2307/258605

Gevorgyan, L. (2008). *Project duration estimation with corrections for systemic error*. Unpublished master's thesis. American University of Armenia, Yerevan, Armenia.

Ghyasi, F. A., & Kushchu, I. (2004). m-Government: cases of developing countries. *mGovLab*. Retrieved October 22, 2008, from http://www.mgovernment.org/resurces/mgovlab_afgik.pdf

Glaser, B. G. (1978). *Theoretical sensivity: advances in the methodology of grounded theory*. Mill Valley, CA: Sociology Press.

Glaser, B. G. (1978). *Theoretical sensitivity*. Mill Valley, CA: The Sociology Press.

Glaser, B. G., & Strauss, A. L. (1967). *The discovery of grounded theory: Strategies for qualitative research*. Chicago: Aldine Publishing Company.

Glaser, B. G., & Strauss, A. L. (1967). *The Discovery of grounded theory: strategies for qualitative research*. New York: Aldine Publishing Company.

Glass, R. L. (1998). *Software runaways*. Upper Saddle River, NJ: Prentice-Hall.

Globerson, S., Nahumi, A., & Ellis, S. (1998). Rate of forgetting for motor and cognitive tasks. *International Journal of Cognitive Ergonomics*, *2*(1), 181–191.

Glover, J. H. (1966). Manufacturing progress functions: An alternative model and its comparison with existing functions. *International Journal of Production Research*, *4*(4), 279–300. doi:10.1080/00207546508919983

Goedecke, D. (2007). The role of the software practitioner in the development of public safety software-intensive systems. In T. Cant (Ed.), *Australian Workshop on Safety Critical Systems and Software and Safety-related Programmable Systems* (Vol. 86, pp. 13-19). Adelaide, SA Australia: Australian Computer Society, Inc.

Golden, T. D., & Veiga, J. F. (2005). Spanning boundaries and borders: Toward understanding the cultural dimensions of team boundary spanning. *Journal of Managerial Issues*, *17*(2), 178–197.

Golias, M. M. (2007). *The discrete and dynamic berth allocation problem: Models and algorithms*. Unpublished doctoral disseratation. Rutgers University, New Jersey.

Golias, M. M., Theofanis, S., & Boile, M. (2007). Berth and quay crane scheduling: A formulation reflecting start and finish of service deadlines and productivity agreements. In proceedings of the *2nd Annual National Urban Freight Conference (CD-Rom)*, Long Beach, CA.

Golias, M. M., Boile, M., & Theofanis, S. (2009). (Manuscript submitted for publication). Berth scheduling by customers differentiation: A multi-objective approach. *Transportation Research Pt. E (Norwalk, Conn.)*.

Gootzit, D., Phifer, G., Valdes, R., Drakos, N., Bradley, A., Harris, K., et al. (2008). *Hype Cycle for Web and User Interaction Technologies 2008* (Gartner No. G00159447).

Gordon, V., & Bieman, J. (1995). Rapid Prototyping: Lessons Learned. *IEEE Software*, *12*, 85–95. doi:10.1109/52.363162

Gore, C., & Gore, E. (1999). Knowledge management: the way forward. *Total Quality Management*, *10*(4-5), 554–560.

Goulielmos, M. (2004). Systems development approach: transcending methodology. *Information Systems Journal*, *14*, 363–386. doi:10.1111/j.1365-2575.2004.00175.x

Grandori, A. (1997). An organizational assessment of interfirm coordination modes. *Organization Studies*, *18*(6), 897–925. doi:10.1177/017084069701800601

Grandori, A., & Soda, G. (1995). Inter-firm networks: Antecedents, mechanisms and forms. *Organization Studies*, *16*(2), 183–214. doi:10.1177/017084069501600201

Gray, C. F., & Larson, E. W. (2008). *Project management: The managerial process* (4th ed.). New York: McGraw Hill Irwin.

Griffiths, M. (2009). *The top five software project risks*. Retrieved July 5, 2009 from http://www.projectsmart.co.uk/top-five-software-project-risks.html

Grimsey, D., & Lewis, M. K. (2002). Accounting for public private partnerships. *Accounting Forum*, *26*(3), 245–270. doi:10.1111/1467-6303.00089

Gruber, T. R. (1993). A translation approach to portable ontology specifications. *Knowledge Acquisition*, *5*(2), 199–220. doi:10.1006/knac.1993.1008

Guan, Y., & Cheung, R. K. (2004). The berth allocation problem: models and solution methods. *OR-Spektrum*, *26*, 75–92. doi:10.1007/s00291-003-0140-8

Guan, Y., Xiao, W.-Q., Cheung, R. K., & Li, C.-L. (2002). A multiprocessor task scheduling model for berth allocation: Heuristic and worst case analysis. *Operations Research Letters*, *30*, 343–350. doi:10.1016/S0167-6377(02)00147-5

Guijarro, L. (2009). ICT standardization and public procurement in the United States and in the European Union: Influence on e-government deployment. *Telecommunications Policy*, *33*, 285–295. doi:10.1016/j.telpol.2009.02.001

Gummersson, E. (2000). *Qualitative methods in management research* (2nd ed.). London: Sage Publications Inc.

Gupta, B., Iyer, L., & Aronson, J. (2000). Knowledge management: practices and challenges. *Industrial Management & Data Systems*, *100*(1), 17–21. doi:10.1108/02635570010273018

Gutjahr, W. J., Strauss, C., & Wagner, E. (2000). A stochastic branch-and-bound approach to activity crashing in project management. *INFORMS Journal on Computing*, *12*(2), 125–135. doi:10.1287/ijoc.12.2.125.11894

Haas, H., & Brown, A. (2004). *Web services glossary*. Retrieved February, 2009 from http://www.w3.org/TR/ws-gloss/

Hagedoorn, J. (2002). Inter-firm R&D partnerships: An overview of major trends and patterns since 1960. *Research Policy*, *31*(4), 477–492. doi:10.1016/S0048-7333(01)00120-2

Hagedoorn, J., & van Kranenburg, H. (2003). Growth patterns in R&D partnerships: An exploratory statistical study. *International Journal of Industrial Organization*, *21*(4), 517–531. doi:10.1016/S0167-7187(02)00126-1

Hagstrom, J. N. (1990). Computing the probability distribution in PERT networks. *Networks*, *20*(2), 231–244. doi:10.1002/net.3230200208

Hahn, E. D. (2008). Mixture densities for project management activity times: A robust approach to PERT. *European Journal of Operational Research*, *188*(2), 450–459. doi:10.1016/j.ejor.2007.04.032

Hansen, P., Oguz, C., & Mladenovic, N. (2008). Variable neighborhood search for minimum cost berth allocation. *European Journal of Operational Research*, *191*(3), 636–649. doi:10.1016/j.ejor.2006.12.057

Hari, S., Egbu, C., & Kumar, B. (2005). A knowledge capture awareness tool: an empirical study on small and medium enterprises in the construction industry. *Engineering, Construction, and Architectural Management*, *12*(6), 533–567. doi:10.1108/09699980510634128

Harper, G. R., & Utley, D. R. (2001). Organizational culture and successful information technology implementation. *Engineering Management Journal*, *13*(2), 11–15.

Harrison, W. (2003). Is software engineering as we know it over the hill? *IEEE Software*, *20*(3), 5–7. doi:10.1109/MS.2003.1199629

Hartwick, J., & Barki, H. (1994). Explaining the role of user participation in information use. *Management Science*, *40*(4), 440–465. doi:10.1287/mnsc.40.4.440

Hass, K. B. (2007). The blending of traditional and agile project management. *Project Management World Today*, *9*(5), 1–8.

Hathaway-Zepeda, T. (2006). fall). Disconnected: taxing mobile phones in the developing world. *Harvard International Review*, 32–35.

Heeks, R. (2006). *Implementing and managing eGovernment: An international text*. London: Sage.

Henderson, J. C., & Lee, S. (1992). Managing I/S design teams: a control theories perspective. *Management Science*, *38*(6), 757–777. doi:10.1287/mnsc.38.6.757

Heng, T. B., & Wei, K. (2003). De-escalation of commitment in software projects: who matters? What matters? *Information & Management*, *41*, 99–110. doi:10.1016/S0378-7206(03)00030-2

Herroelen, W. and R. Leus R. (2004). Robust and reactive project scheduling: A review and classification of procedures. *International Journal of Production Research*, *42*(8), 1599–1620. doi:10.1080/00207540310001638055

Herroelen, W., Leus, R., & Demeulemeester, E. (2002). Critical Chain project scheduling: Do not oversimplify. *Project Management Journal*, *33*(4), 48–60.

Highsmith, J. (2000). *Adaptive Software Development*. New York: Dorset House.

Highsmith, J. (2002). What is agile software development? Retrieved October 4, 2008, from http://www.pyxis-tech.com/agilemontreal/docs/WhatIsAgileSoftwareDevelopment.pdf.

Highsmith, J., & Cockburn, A. (2001). Agile software development: The business of innovation. *IEEE Computer*, *34*(9), 120–122.

Hillson, D. (2005). *Risk management: important or effective (or both)?* Retrieved July 5, 2009 from http://www.risk-doctor.com/pdf-briefings/risk-doctor12e.pdf

Hirschheim, R., Klein, H. K., & Newman, M. (1991). Information systems development as social action: theoretical perspective and practice. *Omega*, *19*(6), 587–608. doi:10.1016/0305-0483(91)90009-I

Hodge, B. (2004). *Developing risk management plans*. Retrieved July 5, 2009 from http://www.cs.uwaterloo.ca/~apidduck/CS480/Lectures/RiskMgmt.pdf

Hodge, G. A., & Greve, C. (2007). Public-private partnerships: An international performance review. *Public Administration Review*, *67*(3), 545–558. doi:10.1111/j.1540-6210.2007.00736.x

Hopp, W. J., & Spearman, M. L. (1993). Setting safety leadtimes for purchased components in assembly systems. *IIE Transactions*, *25*(2), 2–11. doi:10.1080/07408179308964272

Howard, A. (1997). A new RAD-based approach to commercial information systems development: the dynamic system development method. *Industrial Management & Data Systems*, *97*, 175–177. doi:10.1108/02635579710785456

Howcroft, D., & Wilson, M. (2003). Paradoxes of participatory practices: the Janus role of the systems developer. *Information and Organization*, *13*, 1–24. doi:10.1016/S1471-7727(02)00023-4

Hsu, J. S. C., Chan, C. L., Liu, J. Y. C., & Chen, H. G. (2008). The impacts of user review on software responsiveness: moderating requirements uncertainty. *Information & Management*, *45*(4), 203–210. doi:10.1016/j.im.2008.01.006

Hughes, J., & Jones, S. (2003). Reflections on the use of grounded theory in interpretive information systems research. In *Proceedings of the 11th European Conference on Information Systems (ECIS 2003)*, Naples, Italy.

Hulland, J. (1999). Use of partial least squares (PLS) in strategic management research: a review of four recent studies. *Strategic Management Journal*, *20*(2), 195–204. doi:10.1002/(SICI)1097-0266(199902)20:2<195::AID-SMJ13>3.0.CO;2-7

Humphrey, W. S. (1998). *Why Don't They Practice What We Preach?* Retrieved April 28, 2008, from http://www.sei.cmu.edu/publications/articles/practice-preach/practice-preach.html.

Humphrey, W. S. (2000a). *Introduction to the Team Software Process*. Reading, MA: Addison-Wesley.

Humphrey, W. S. (2000b). *The Team Software Process (TSP)* (No. CMU/SEI-2000-TR-023). Pittsburgh, PA: Software Engineering Institute.

Humphrey, W. S. (2006a). *TSP: Coaching Development Teams*. Boston. MA: Addison-Wesley.

Humphrey, W. S. (2006b). *TSP: Leading a Development Team*. Reading, MA: Addison-Wesley.

Hunsaker, P. L., & Hunsaker, J. S. (2008). Virtual teams: a leader's guide. *Team Performance Management, 14*(1/2), 86. doi:10.1108/13527590810860221

Huo, M., Verner, J., Zhu, L., & Babar, M. A. (2004). Software quality and agile methods. In *Proceedings of the Annual International Computer Software and Applications Conference (COMPSAC 2004)* (Vol. 28, pp. 520-525).

Hussain, O. K., Chang, E., Hussain, F. K., & Dillon, T. S. (2006). A fuzzy aproach to risk based decision making. *Lecture Notes in Computer Science, 4278*, 1765–1775. doi:10.1007/11915072_83

Huy, Q. N. (2001). Time, temporal capability and planned change. *Academy of Management Review, 36*(4), 601–623. doi:10.2307/3560244

Hwang, M. I., & Thorn, R. G. (1999). The effect of user engagement on system success: a meta-analytical integration of research findings. *Information & Management, 35*(4), 229–236. doi:10.1016/S0378-7206(98)00092-5

Hwang, M. I., & Thorn, R. G. (1999). The effect of user engagement on system success: A meta-analytical integration of research findings. *Information & Management, 35*, 229–236. doi:10.1016/S0378-7206(98)00092-5

Iacovou, C. L., Benbasat, I., & Dexter, A. S. (1995). Electronic data interchange and small organizations: Adoption and impact of technology. *Management Information Systems Quarterly, 19*(4), 465–485. doi:10.2307/249629

Ibarra, H., Kilduff, M., & Tsai, W. (2005). Zooming in and out: connecting individuals and collectivities at the frontiers of organizational network research. *Organization Science, 16*(4), 359–371. doi:10.1287/orsc.1050.0129

Iida, T. (2000). Computing bounds on project duration distributions for stochastic PERT networks. *Naval Research Logistics, 47*(7), 559–580. doi:10.1002/1520-6750(200010)47:7<559::AID-NAV2>3.0.CO;2-9

ILBS – International Law Book Series. Laws of Malaysia. (2003). *Local government act 1976 (Act 171) & subsidiary legislation: As at 25th July 2003*. Kuala Lumpur, Malaysia: Direct Art Company.

Imai, A., Chen, H. C., Nishimura, E., & Papadimitriou, S. (2008). The simultaneous berth and quay crane allocation problem. *Transportation Research Part E, Logistics and Transportation Review, 44*(5), 900–920. doi:10.1016/j.tre.2007.03.003

Imai, A., Nagaiwa, K., & Tat, C.-W. (1997). Efficient planning of berth allocation for container terminals in Asia. *Journal of Advanced Transportation, 31*, 75–94.

Imai, A., Nishimura, E., & Papadimitriou, S. (2001). The dynamic berth allocation problem for a container port. *Transportation Research Part B: Methodological, 35*, 401–417. doi:10.1016/S0191-2615(99)00057-0

Imai, A., Nishimura, E., & Papadimitriou, S. (2003). Berth allocation with service priority. *Transportation Research Part B: Methodological, 37*, 437–457. doi:10.1016/S0191-2615(02)00023-1

Imai, A., Sun, X., Nishimura, E., & Papadimitriou, S. (2005). Berth allocation in a container port: Using continuous location space approach. *Transportation Research Part B: Methodological, 39*, 199–221. doi:10.1016/j.trb.2004.04.004

Imai, A., Zhang, J.-T., Nishimura, E., & Papadimitriou, S. (2007). The berth allocation problem with service time and delay time objectives. *Maritime Economics & Logistics, 9*(4), 269–290. doi:10.1057/palgrave.mel.9100186

Inkpen, A. C., & Dinur, A. (1998). Knowledge management processes and international joint venture. *Organization Science, 9*(4), 454–468. doi:10.1287/orsc.9.4.454

Isabella, L. A. (1990). Evolving interpretations as a change unfolds: how managers construe key organizational events. *Academy of Management Journal*, *33*(1), 7–41. doi:10.2307/256350

Ives, B., & Olson, M. H. (1984). User involvement and MIS success: a review of research. *Management Science*, *30*(5), 586–603. doi:10.1287/mnsc.30.5.586

Jaber, M. Y., & Bonney, M. (1996). Production breaks and the learning curve: The forgetting phenomena. *Applied Mathematical Modelling*, *20*(3), 162–169. doi:10.1016/0307-904X(95)00157-F

Jaber, M. Y., & Bonney, M. (2003). Lot sizing with learning and forgetting in setups and in product quality. *International Journal of Production Economics*, *83*(1), 95–111. doi:10.1016/S0925-5273(02)00322-5

Jaber, M. Y., & Bonney, M. (2007). Economic Manufacture Quantity (EMQ) Model With Lot Size Dependent Learning and Forgetting Rates. *International Journal of Production Economics*, *108*(2), 359–367. doi:10.1016/j.ijpe.2006.12.020

Jaber, M. Y., & Guiffrida, A. L. (2004). Learning curves for processes generating defects requiring reworks. *European Journal of Operational Research*, *159*(3), 663–672. doi:10.1016/S0377-2217(03)00436-3

Jaber, M. Y., & Guiffrida, A. L. (2008). Learning curves for imperfect production processes with reworks and process restoration interruptions. *European Journal of Operational Research*, *189*(1), 93–104. doi:10.1016/j.ejor.2007.05.024

Jaber, M. Y., Kher, H. V., & Davis, D. (2003). Countering forgetting through training and deployment. *International Journal of Production Economics*, *85*(1), 33–46. doi:10.1016/S0925-5273(03)00084-7

Jaber, M. Y., & Sikstrom, S. (2004). A numerical comparison of three potential learning and forgetting models. *International Journal of Production Economics*, *92*(3), 281–294. doi:10.1016/j.ijpe.2003.10.019

Jacobsen, C., & Choi, S. O. (2008). Success factors: Public works and public-private partnerships. *International Journal of Public Sector Management*, *21*(6), 637–657. doi:10.1108/09513550810896514

Jarvenpaa, S. L., & Leidner, D. E. (1997). *Developing trust in virtual teams*. Paper presented at the 30th Hawaii International Conference on Systems Sciences, Maui, HI.

Jasperson, J. S., Carte, T. A., Saunders, C. S., Butler, B. S., Croes, H. J. P., & Zheng, W. (2002). Review: Power and information technology research: A metatriangulation review. *Management Information Systems Quarterly*, *26*(4), 397–459. doi:10.2307/4132315

Jensen, M. C., & Meckling, W. H. (1986). Theory of the firm: managerial behavior, agency costs, and ownership structure. In Barney, J. B., & Ouchi, W. G. (Eds.), *Organizational Economics* (pp. 214–275). San Francisco, CA: Jossey-Bass.

Jiang, l., & Eberlein, A. (2008). Towards a framework for understanding the relationships between classical software engineering and agile methodologies. In P. Kruchten & S. Adolf (Eds.), *The 2008 International Conference on Software Engineering* (Vol. 30, pp. 9-14). Leipzig, Germany: ACM.

Jiang, B. (2002). Key Elements of a Successful Project Manager. *Project Management*, *8*(1), 14–19.

Jiang, J. J., Klein, G., & Chen, H. G. (2006). The effects of user partnering and user non-support on project performance. *Journal of the Association for Information Systems*, *7*(1), 68–88.

Jiang, J. J., Klein, G., & Chen, H.-G. (2001). The relative influence of IS project implementation policies and project leadership on eventual outcomes. *Project Management Journal*, *32*(3), 49–55.

Jiang, J. J., Klein, G., & Margulis, S. (1998). Important behavioral skills for IS project managers: The judgments of experienced IS professionals. *Project Management Journal*, *29*(1), 39–43.

Johnson, J. (1995). Chaos: the dollar drain IT project failures. *Application Development Trends*, *2*(1), 41–47.

Johnson, S. D., Suriya, C., Seung Won, Y., Berrett, J. V., & La Fleur, J. (2002). Team development and group processes of virtual learning teams. *Computers & Education*, *39*(4), 379–393. doi:10.1016/S0360-1315(02)00074-X

Johnston, H. R., & Carrico, S. R. (1988). Developing capabilities to use information strategically. *Management Information Systems Quarterly*, *12*(1), 37–48. doi:10.2307/248801

Jones, M., & Karsten, H. (2008). Gidden's structuration theory and information systems research. *Management Information Systems Quarterly*, *32*(1), 127–157.

Jones, M., Orlikowski, W. J., & Munir, K. (2004). Structuration theory and information systems: A critical reappraisal. In Mingers, J., & Willcocks, L. (Eds.), *Social theory and philosophy for information systems* (pp. 297–328). Chichester, UK: John Wiley & Sons.

Joshi, A., Pandey, N., & Han, G. (2009). Bracketing team boundary spanning: An examination of task-based, team-level, and contextual antecedents. *Journal of Organizational Behavior*, *30*(6), 731–759. doi:10.1002/job.567

Jost, G., Dawson, M., & Shaw, D. (2005). Private sector consortia working for a public sector client - factors that build successful relationship: Lessons from the uk. *European Management Journal*, *23*(3), 336–350. doi:10.1016/j.emj.2005.04.012

Jurison, J. (1999). Software project management: The manager's view. *Communications of the Association for Information Systems*, *2*(17), 1–57.

Kahn, W. A. (1990). Psychological conditions of personal engagement and disengagement at Work. *Academy of Management Journal*, *33*(4), 692–724. doi:10.2307/256287

Kakabadse, N. K., Kouzmin, A., & Kakabadse, A. (2001). From tacit knowledge to knowledge management: Leveraging invisible assets. *Knowledge and Process Management*, *8*(3), 137–154. doi:10.1002/kpm.120

Kamara, J., Augenbroe, G., Anumba, C., & Carrillo, P. (2002). Knowledge management in the architecture, engineering and construction industry. *Construction Innovation*, *2*(1), 53–67.

Kaplan, R. S., & Norton, D. P. (1992). The balanced scorecard: measures that drive performance. *Harvard Business Review*, (Jan.-Feb.), 71-79.

Kappelman, L. A., McKeeman, R., & Zhang, L. (2006). Early warning signs of it project failure: The dominant dozen. *Information Systems Management*, *23*(4), 31–36. doi:10.1201/1078.10580530/46352.23.4.20060901/95110.4

Karim, M. R. A. (2003). Technology and improved service delivery: Learning points from the Malaysian experience. *International Review of Administrative Sciences: Creating Self-Confident Government* (p. 69, 191). London: Sage.

Karim, M. R. A. (1999). *Reengineering the public service: leadership and change in an electronic age*. Kuala Lumpur, Malaysia: Pelanduk Publications.

Karim, M. R. A., & Khalid, N. (2003). *E-government in Malaysia*. Kuala Lumpur, Malaysia: Pelanduk.

Karlsen, J. T., Graee, K., & Massaoud, M. J. (2008). The role of trust in project-stakeholder relationships: a study of a construction project. *International Journal of Project Organisation and Management*, *1*(1), 105–118. doi:10.1504/IJPOM.2008.020031

Kaulio, M. A. (2008). Project leadership in multi-project settings: Findings from a critical incident study. *International Journal of Project Management*, *26*(4), 338–347. doi:10.1016/j.ijproman.2007.06.005

Keil, M. (1995). Pulling the plug: Software project management and the problem of project escalation. *Management Information Systems Quarterly*, *19*(4), 421–447. doi:10.2307/249627

Keil, M., Mann, J., & Rai, A. (2000). Why software projects escalate: an empirical analysis and test of four theoretical models. *Management Information Systems Quarterly*, *24*(4), 631–664. doi:10.2307/3250950

Keil, M., Rai, A., Mann, J., & Zhang, G. P. (2003). Why software projects escalate: the importance of project management constructs. *IEEE Transactions on Engineering Management*, *50*, 251–261. doi:10.1109/TEM.2003.817312

Keil, M., & Robey, D. (1999). Turning around troubled software projects: an exploratory study of the de-escalation of commitment to failing courses of action. *Journal of Management Information Systems*, *15*(4), 63–87.

Kelleher, D., & Levene, S. (2001). *Knowledge management: A guide to good practice.* London: British Standards Institution.

Kelley, J. E. (1961). Critical-path planning and scheduling: mathematical basis. *Operations Research, 9*(3), 296–320. doi:10.1287/opre.9.3.296

Kempster, S. (2006). Leadership learning through lived experience: A process of apprenticeship. *Journal of Management & Organization, 12*(1), 4–23.

Kendric, T. (2003). *Identifying and managing project risk.* New York: AMACOM Div American Mgmt Assn.

Kerzner, H. (2006). *Project management: a systems approach to planning, scheduling, and controlling* (9th ed.). Haboken, NJ: John Wiley and Sons.

Kerzner, H. (2009). *Project management* (10th ed.). Hoboden, NJ: John Wiley & Sons.

Keyzerman, Y. (2003). Trust in virtual teams. In *Proceedings of Professional Communication Conference (IPCC 2003)* (pp. 391-399). Orlando, FL, USA.

Khalifa, M., & Verner, J. M. (2000). Drivers for software development method usage. *IEEE Transactions on Engineering Management, 47*(3), 360–369. doi:10.1109/17.865904

Kheng, C. B., & Al-Hawamdeh, S. (2002). The adoption of electronic procurement in Singapore. *Electronic Commerce Research, 2*, 61–73. doi:10.1023/A:1013388018056

Kim, H.-W., & Pan, S. L. (2006). Towards a process model of information systems implementation: the case of customer relationship management (CRM). *The Data Base for Advances in Information Systems, 37*(1), 59–76.

Kim, K. H., & Moon, K. C. (2003). Berth scheduling by simulated annealing. *Transportation Research Part B: Methodological, 37*, 541–560. doi:10.1016/S0191-2615(02)00027-9

Kim, P. H., Dirks, K. T., & Cooper, C. D. (2009). The repair of trust: A dynamic bilateral perspective and multilevel conceptualization. *Academy of Management Review, 34*(3), 401–422.

Kirby, C., & Wagner, A. (1999). The ideal procurement process: The vendor's perspective. *Gaylord Information Systems.* Retrieved from http://www.ilsr.com/vendor.htm

Kirsch, L. J. (1997). Portfolios of control modes and IS project management. *Information Systems Research, 15*, 374–395. doi:10.1287/isre.1040.0036

Kirsch, L. J. (2004). Deploying common systems globally: the dynamics of control. *Information Systems Research, 15*(4), 374–395. doi:10.1287/isre.1040.0036

Kirsch, L. J., & Haney, M. H. (2006). Requirements determination for common systems: turning a global vision into a local reality. *The Journal of Strategic Information Systems, 15*(2), 79–104. doi:10.1016/j.jsis.2005.08.002

Kirsch, L. J., Sambamurthy, V., Ko, D. G., & Purvis, R. L. (2002). Controlling information systems development projects: the view from the client. *Management Science, 48*(4), 484–498. doi:10.1287/mnsc.48.4.484.204

Kirytopoulos, A. K., Leopoulos, N. V., & Diamantas, V. K. (2008). PERT vs. Monte Carlo simulation along with the suitable distribution effect. *International Journal of Project Organisation and Management, 1*(1), 24–46. doi:10.1504/IJPOM.2008.020027

Kleindorfer, G. B. (1971). Bounding distributions for a stochastic acyclic network. *Operations Research, 19*(7), 1586–1601. doi:10.1287/opre.19.7.1586

Kleiner, Y., Rajani, B., & Sadiq, R. (2006). Failure risk management of buried infrastructure using fuzzy-based techniques. *Journal of Water Supply: Research & Technology - Aqua, 55*(2), 81–94.

Klein, G. (2003). *Intuition at Work: Why Developing Your Gut Instincts Will Make You Better at What You Do.* New York, NY: Doubleday.

Klein, G. A., Calderwood, R., & MacGregor, D. (1989). Critical decision method for eliciting knowledge. *IEEE Transactions on Systems, Man, and Cybernetics, 19*(3), 462–472. doi:10.1109/21.31053

KLICON. (1999). *The role of information technology in knowledge management within the construction industry (Project report of knowledge learning in construction group).* Manchester, UK: University of Manchester, Institute of Science and Technology.

Klingel, A. R. (1966). Bias in PERT completion times calculations for a real network. *Management Science, 13*(4), 476–489. doi:10.1287/mnsc.13.4.B194

Knecht, G. R. (1974). Costing, technological growth, and generalized learning curves. *Operational Research Quarterly, 25*(3), 487–491.

Knorr, E. (2005). Anatomy of an IT disaster: How the FBI blew it. *Infoworld.com.*

Kock, N. (2001). The ape that used email: understanding e-communication behavior through evolution theory. *Communication of the AIS, 5*(3), 1–29.

Kock, N., & Nosek, J. (2005). Expanding the boundaries of e-collaboration. *IEEE Transactions on Professional Communication, 48*(1), 1–9. doi:10.1109/TPC.2004.843272

Kodama, M. (2007). *Project-based organisation in the knowledge-based society.* London: Imperial College Press.

Kogut, B., & Zander, U. (1992). Knowledge of the firm, combinative capabilities and the replication of technology. *Organization Science, 3*(3), 383–397. doi:10.1287/orsc.3.3.383

Korhonen, P., & Halme, M. (1990). Supporting the decision maker to find the most preferred solutions for a MOLP-problem. In proceedings of the *9th International Conference on Multiple Criteria Decision Making (pp. 173-183)*, Fairfax, Virginia.

Koskela, L., & Howell, G. (2002a). The theory of project management: explanation to novel methods. *Proceedings of IGLC-10.*

Koskela, L., & Howell, G. (2002b). The underlying theory of project management is obsolete. *Proceedings of the PMI Research Conference.*

Kraemer, K. L., & King, J. L. (1977). *Computers and local government: Volume 1, a manager's guide.* New York: Praeger.

Kruchten, P. (2000). *The rational unified process an introduction.* (2nd ed.) Reading, MA: Addison-Wesley.

Kumar, A. (1989). Component inventory costs in an assembly problem with uncertain supplier lead-times. *IIE Transactions, 21*(2), 112–121. doi:10.1080/07408178908966214

Kushchu, I., & Borucki, C. (2004). Impact of mobile technologies on government. *mGovLab.* Retrieved October 22, 2008, from http://www.mgovernment.org/resurces/mgovlab_ikcb.pdf

Kwak, Y. H. (2005). A Brief History of Project Management. In E. G. Carayannis, Y. H. Kwak & F. T. Anbari (Eds.), *The Story of Managing Projects. An Interdisciplinary Approach.* Westport, Connecticut: Praeger Publishers.

Kwon, T. H., & Zmud, R. W. (1987). Unifying the fragmented models of information systems implementation. In Boland, R. J., & Hirschheim, R. A. (Eds.), *Critical Issues in Information Systems Research* (pp. 252–257). New York: John-Wiley.

Laffont, J. J., & Tirole, J. (1990). The Politics of Government Decision-Making - Regulatory Institutions. *Journal of Law Economics and Organization, 6*, 1–31.

Langer, N., Slaughter, S. A., & Mukhopadhyay, T. (2008). Project managers' skills and project success in IT outsourcing. In *Proceedings of the 29th International Conference on Information Systems*, Paris.

Laplante, P. A., & Neill, C. J. (2004). The demise of the waterfall model is imminent and other urban myths. *ACM Queue; Tomorrow's Computing Today, 1*(10), 10–15. doi:10.1145/971564.971573

Larman, C. (2004). *Agile and iterative development: A Manager's Guide.* Reading, MA: Addison-Wesley.

Larman, C., & Basili, V. R. (2003). Iterative and Incremental Development: A Brief History. *IEEE Computer, 36*, 47–56.

Lazarsfeld, P. F., & Rosenberg, M. (1957). *The language of social research: a reader in the methodology of social research.* Glencoe, IL: Free Press.

Leach, L. P. (2000). *Critical Chain project management.* Artech House.

Leach, L. P. (2003). Schedule and cost buffer sizing: How to account for the bias between project performance and your model. *Project Management Journal, 2003*(2), 34-47.

Lee, A. S., & Baskerville, R. L. (2003). Generalizing generalizability in information systems research. *Information Systems Research, 14*(3), 221–243. doi:10.1287/isre.14.3.221.16560

Lee, D. M. S., Trauth, E. M., & Farwell, D. (1995). Critical skills and knowledge requirements of IS professionals: A joint academic/industry investigation. *Management Information Systems Quarterly, 19*(3), 313–340. doi:10.2307/249598

Lee, D., Trauth, E., & Farwell, D. (1995). Critical Skills and Knowledge Requirements of IT Professionals: A Joint Academic/Industry Investigation. *MIS Quarterly, 19*(3), 313–340. doi:10.2307/249598

Lee-Kelley, L. (2002). Situational leadership: managing the virtual project team. *Journal of Management Development, 21*(5/6), 461–476. doi:10.1108/02621710210430623

Lee, S., Tan, X., & Trimi, S. (2005). Current practices of leading e-government countries. *Communications of the ACM, 48*(10), 99–104. doi:10.1145/1089107.1089112

Leifer, R., & Delbecq, A. (1978). Organizational/environmental interchange: A model of boundary spanning activity. *Academy of Management Review, 3*(1), 40–50. doi:10.2307/257575

Leon, F. (2008). *Courses of artificial intelligence*. Retrieved July 5, 2009 from http://eureka.cs.tuiasi.ro/~fleon/curs_ia.htm

Levin, G., & Rad, P. F. (2005). Requirements for effective project communications: differences and similarities in virtual and traditional project environments. Retrieved from www.AllPM.com.

Levina, N. (2006). Collaborating across boundaries in a global economy: Do organizational boundaries and country contexts matter? In *Proceedings of the 27th International Conference on Information Systems*, Milwaukee, WI.

Levina, N., & Vaast, E. (2005). The emergence of boundary spanning competence in practice: Implications for implementation and use of information systems. *Management Information Systems Quarterly, 29*(2), 335–363.

Levina, N., & Vaast, E. (2006). Turning a community into a market: A practice perspective on information technology use in boundary spanning. *Journal of Management Information Systems, 22*(4), 13–37. doi:10.2753/MIS0742-1222220402

Levina, N., & Vaast, E. (2008). Innovating or doing as told? Status differences and overlapping boundaries in offshore collaboration. *Management Information Systems Quarterly, 32*(2), 307–332.

Levy, F. K. (1965). Adaptation in the production process. *Management Science, 11*(6), B136–B154. doi:10.1287/mnsc.11.6.B136

Leydesdorff, L., & Etzkovitz, H. (1996). Emergence of a Triple Helix of University-Industry-Government Relations. *Science & Public Policy, 23*, 279–286.

Liao, S. H., Cheng, C. H., Liao, W. B., & Chen, I. L. (2003). A Web-based architecture for implementing electronic procurement in military organizations. *Technovation, 23*(6), 521–533. doi:10.1016/S0166-4972(02)00006-8

Liao, W. M. (1979). Effects of learning on resource allocation decisions. *Decision Sciences, 10*(1), 116–125. doi:10.1111/j.1540-5915.1979.tb00011.x

Li, C.-L., Cai, X., & Lee, C.-Y. (1998). Scheduling with multiple-job-on-one-processor pattern. *IIE Transactions, 30*, 433–445.

Li, M., & Gao, F. (2003). Why Nonaka highlights tacit knowledge: A critical review. *Journal of Knowledge Management, 7*(4), 6–14. doi:10.1108/13673270310492903

Lindgren, R., Andersson, M., & Henfridsson, O. (2008). Multi-contextuality in boundary-spanning practices. *Information Systems Journal, 18*(6), 641–661. doi:10.1111/j.1365-2575.2007.00245.x

Lin, W. T., & Shao, B. B. M. (2000). The relationship between user participation and system success: a simultaneous contingency approach. *Information & Management, 37*, 283–295. doi:10.1016/S0378-7206(99)00055-5

Lin, Y., Wang, L., & Tserng, P. (2006). Enhancing knowledge exchange through web map-based knowledge management system in construction: Lessons learned in Taiwan. *Automation in Construction, 15*(6), 693–705. doi:10.1016/j.autcon.2005.09.006

Lipnack, J., & Stamps, J. (2000). *Virtual teams: people working across boundaries with technology*. New York: John Wiley & Sons, Inc.

Liu, H., & Lu, Y. (2002). From strategic risk measurement to strategic risk management. Retrieved 31 May, 2009 from http://findarticles.com/p/articles/mi_hb6419/is_7_79/ www.chinareview.org/News/manage/image/78105926.doc

Lock, D. (2007). *Project Management* (9th ed.). Hampshire, UK: Gower.

Love, P., Edum-Fotwe, F., & Irani, Z. (2003). Management of knowledge in project environments. *International Journal of Project Management, 21*, 155–156. doi:10.1016/S0263-7863(02)00089-3

Lowry, P. B., Roberts, T. L., Romano, N. C., Cheney, P. D., & Hightower, R. T. (2006). The impact of group size and social presence on small-group communication - does computer-mediated communication make a difference? *Small Group Research, 37*(6), 631–661. doi:10.1177/1046496406294322

Ludwig, A., Mohring, R. H., & Stork, F. (2001). A computational study on bounding the makespan distribution in stochastic project nets. *Annals of Operations Research, 102*(1), 49–64. doi:10.1023/A:1010945830113

Lynch, T., & Gregor, S. (2004). User participation in decision support systems development: influencing system outcomes. *European Journal of Information Systems, 13*(2), 286–301. doi:10.1057/palgrave.ejis.3000512

Lynch, T., & Gregor, S. (2004). User participation in decision support systems development: influencing system outcomes. *European Journal of Information Systems, 13*, 286–301. doi:10.1057/palgrave.ejis.3000512

Lyne, C. (1996). Strategic procurement in the new local government. *European Journal of Purchasing & Supply Management, 2*(1), 1–6. doi:10.1016/0969-7012(95)00022-4

Lyytinen, K. (1999). Empirical research in information systems: On the relevance of practice in thinking of IS research. *Management Information Systems Quarterly, 23*(1), 5–28. doi:10.2307/249406

Lyytinen, K., Mathiassen, L., & Ropponen, J. (1998). Attention shaping and software risk - A categorical analysis of four classical risk management approaches. *Information Systems Research, 9*(3), 233–255. doi:10.1287/isre.9.3.233

MacKenzie, C. M., Laskey, K., McCabe, F., Brown, P. F., & Metz, R. (2006). *Reference Model for Service Oriented Architecture 1.0 (Committee Specification soa-rm-cs)*. OASIS.

Mahring, M. (2002). *IT project governance*. Stockholm, Sweden: Economic Research Institute (EFI).

Mahring, M., & Keil, M. (2008). Information technology project escalation: a process model. *Decision Sciences, 39*(2), 239–272. doi:10.1111/j.1540-5915.2008.00191.x

Malcolm, D. G., Roseboom, J. H., Clark, C. E., & Fazar, W. (1959). Application of a technique for research and development evaluation program. *Operations Research, 7*(5), 646–669. doi:10.1287/opre.7.5.646

Malhotra, A., Majchrzak, A., & Rosen, B. (2007). Leading virtual teams. *The Academy of Management Perspectives, 21*(1), 60.

Mann, J. (2003, August 4-5). Preventing runaway IT projects: protecting auditors from entrapment. In *Proceedings of Americas Conference on Information Systems*, Tampa, FL.

Marchewka, J. T. (2006). *Information Technology Project Management*. New Jersey: Wiley.

Marcolin, B., Compeau, D., Munro, M., & Huff, S. (2000). Assessing User Competence: Conceptualization and Measurement. *Information Systems Research, 11*(1), 37–60. doi:10.1287/isre.11.1.37.11782

Marcus, G. E., & Fischer, M. M. J. (1986). *Anthropology as cultural critique: an experimental moment in the human sciences*. Chicago: University of Chicago Press.

Markus, M. L. (1983). Power, politics, and MIS implementation. *Communications of the ACM, 26*(6), 430–444. doi:10.1145/358141.358148

Markus, M. L., & Mao, J. Y. (2004). Participation in development and implementation - updating an old, tired concept for today's IS contexts. *Journal of the Association for Information Systems, 5*(11-12), 514–544.

Markus, M. L., & Saunders, C. (2007). Looking for a few good concepts… and theories… for the information systems field. *Management Information Systems Quarterly, 31*(1), iii–vi.

Marr, B., & Schiuma, G. (2001). Measuring and managing intellectual capital and knowledge assets in new economy organisations. In Bourne, M. (Ed.), *Performance Measurement Handbook*. London: GEE Publishing Ltd.

Marrone, J. A., Tesluk, P. E., & Carson, J. B. (2007). A multilevel investigation of antecedents and consequences of team member boundary-spanning behavior. *Academy of Management Journal*, *50*(6), 1423–1439.

Martin, J. (1991). *Rapid Application Development*. New York: Macmillan Publishing.

Martin, P. Y., & Turner, B. A. (1986). Grounded theory and organizational research. *The Journal of Applied Behavioral Science*, *22*(2), 141–157. doi:10.1177/002188638602200207

Matsuo, M., Wong, C. W. Y., & Lai, K.-H. (2008). Experience-based learning of Japanese IT professionals: A qualitative research. *The Journal of Strategic Information Systems*, *17*(3), 202–213. doi:10.1016/j.jsis.2008.03.001

Maurer, F., & Melnik, G. (2006). Agile methods: moving towards the mainstream of the software industry. In []. Shanghai, China.]. *Proceedings of the International Conference on Software Engineering*, *28*, 1057–1058.

Mayer-Schonberger, V., & Lazer, D. (Eds.). (2007). *Governance and information technology: From electronic government to information government*. Cambridge, MA: MIT Press.

Mazur, J. E., & Hastie, R. (1978). Learning as accumulation: A reexamination of the learning curve. *Psychological Bulletin*, *85*(2), 1256–1274. doi:10.1037/0033-2909.85.6.1256

McCall, M. W. Jr. (2004). Leadership development through experience. *The Academy of Management Executive*, *18*(3), 127–130.

McCauley, C. D., & Hezlett, S. A. (2001). Individual development in the workplace. In Anderson, N., Ones, D. S., Sinangil, H. K., & Viswesvaran, C. (Eds.), *Handbook of Industrial, Work & Organizational Psychology* (pp. 313–335). London: Sage.

McConnell, S. (1996). *Rapid Development: Taming Wild Software Schedules*. Redmond, WA: Microsoft Press.

McConnell, S. (2003). *Professional Software Development*. Reading, MA: Addison-Wesley.

McGee Woodward, M. (2005). *Measuring the payoffs of strategic risk management*. Retrieved July 5, 2009 from http://findarticles.com/p/articles/mi_hb6419/is_7_79/ai_n29236259/

McInerney, C. (2002). Knowledge management and the dynamic nature of knowledge. *Journal of the American Society for Information Science and Technology*, *53*(12), 1009–1018. doi:10.1002/asi.10109

McIntyre, E. V. (1977). Cost-volume-profit analysis adjusted for Learning. *Management Science*, *24*(2), 149–160. doi:10.1287/mnsc.24.2.149

McKeen, J. D., Guimaraes, T., & Wetherbe, J. (1994). The Relationship Between User Participation and User Satisfaction: An Investigation of Four Contingency Factors. *MIS Quarterly*, *18*, 427–451. doi:10.2307/249523

McMurtrey, M. E., Downey, J. P., Zeltmann, S. M., & Friedman, W. H. (2008). Critical Skill Sets of Entry-Level IT Professionals: An Empirical Examination of Perceptions from Field Personnel. *Journal of Information Technology Education*, *7*, 101–120.

McVeigh, C. B. J. (1995). The Right Stuff—Revisited: A Competency Perspective of Army Program Managers. *Program Manager*, *24*(1), 30–34.

Mendel, B. (1999). Overcoming ERP project hurdles: experts offer tips on avoiding 10 problems that plague many ERP implementation projects. *InfoWorld*, *21*(29), 87.

Merna, T., & Al-Thani, F. (2008). *Corporater Risk Management*. Hoboken, NJ: John Wiley & Sons.

Middleton, P. (2000). Barriers to the efficient and effective use of information technology. *International Journal of Public Sector Management*, *13*(1), 85–99. doi:10.1108/09513550010334506

Miler, J., & Gorski, J. (2004). Risk identification patterns for software projects. *Foundations of Computing and Decision Sciences*, *29*(1-2), 115–131.

Miles, B. M., & Huberman, A. M. (1994). *Qualitative Data Analysis: An Expanded Sourcebook* (2nd ed.). London: Sage.

Miles, M. (1979). Qualitative data as attractive science: the problem of analysis. *Administrative Science Quarterly*, *24*, 590–601. doi:10.2307/2392365

Miles, M. B., & Huberman, A. M. (1994). *Qualitative data analysis: An expanded source book* (2nd ed.). Thousand Oaks, CA: Sage.

Millennium Challenge Corporation. (2009). *Threshold quarterly report August 2008*. Retrieved June 18, 2009, from http://www.mcc.gov/documents/qsr-albania.pdf

Mingers, J. (2004). Real-izing information systems: Critical realism as an underpinning philosophy for information systems. *Information and Organization, 14*, 87–103. doi:10.1016/j.infoandorg.2003.06.001

Mintzberg, H. (1973). *The Nature of Managerial Work*. New York: Harper & Row Publishers.

Misic, M. M., & Graf, D. K. (2004). Systems analyst activities and skills in the new millennium. *Journal of Systems and Software, 71*(1-2), 31–36. doi:10.1016/S0164-1212(02)00124-3

Mokyr, J. (1990). *The lever of riches*. Oxford, UK: Oxford University Press.

Monaco, F. M., & Sammarra, M. (2007). The berth allocation problem: A strong formulation solved by a Lagrangean approach. *Transportation Science, 41*(2), 265–280. doi:10.1287/trsc.1060.0171

Montealegre, R., & Keil, M. (2000). De-Escalating information technology projects: lessons learned from the Denver international airport. *Management Information Systems Quarterly, 24*(3), 417–447. doi:10.2307/3250968

Moorthy, R., & Teo, C.-P. (2006). Berth management in container terminal: the template design problem. *OR-Spektrum, 28*(4), 495–518. doi:10.1007/s00291-006-0036-5

Morris, P. W. G. (2001). Updating the project management bodies of knowledge. *Project Management Journal, 32*(3), 21–30.

Morris, P. W. G., Crawford, L., Hodgson, D., Shepherd, M. M., & Thomas, J. (2006). Exploring the role of formal bodies of knowledge in defining a profession – The case of project management. *International Journal of Project Management, 24*(8), 710–721. doi:10.1016/j.ijproman.2006.09.012

Mothe, C., & Quélin, B. (2000). Creating competencies through collaboration: The case of EUREKA R&D consortia. *European Management Journal, 18*(6), 590–604. doi:10.1016/S0263-2373(00)00052-9

Muhr, T. (2008). *Atlas.Ti - the knowledge workbench, scientific software development*, Berlin.

Müller, R., & Turner, J. R. (2005). The impact of principal-agent relationship and contract type on communication between project owner and manager. *International Journal of Project Management, 23*, 398–403. doi:10.1016/j.ijproman.2005.03.001

Mumford, E. (1983). *Designing Participatively: Participative Approach To Computer Systems Design*. Manchester: Manchester Business School.

Munns, A. K., & Bjeirmi, B. F. (1996). The role of project management in achieving project success. *International Journal of Project Management, 14*(2), 81–87. doi:10.1016/0263-7863(95)00057-7

Mutch, A. (2002). Actors and networks or agents and structures: Towards a realist view of information systems. *Organization, 9*(3), 477–496. doi:10.1177/135050840293013

Mutch, A. (2007). Concerns with "Mutual constitution": A critical realist commentary. In Stahl, B. C. (Ed.), *Issues and trends in technology and human interaction* (pp. 230–244). Hershey, PA: IGI Global.

Nah, F. F., Lau, J. L., & Kuang, J. (2001). Critical Factors for Successful Implementation of Enterprise Systems. *Business Process Management Journal, 7*(3), 285–296. doi:10.1108/14637150110392782

Nakagawa, T., Tani, S., Yasunobu, C., & Komoda, N. (2005). Business risk management based on a service portofolio approach for an equipment–providing service. In Nardelli, E., & Talamo, M. (Eds.), *Certification and security in inter-organizational e-service* (pp. 85–90). Boston: Springer Boston Press. doi:10.1007/11397427_6

Nanda, R. (1979). Using learning curves in integration of production resources. In *Proceedings of 1979 IIE Fall Conference* (pp. 376-380).

Nandhakumar, J., Rossi, M., & Talvinen, J. (2005). The dynamics of contextual forces of ERP implementation. *The Journal of Strategic Information Systems, 14*, 221–242. doi:10.1016/j.jsis.2005.04.002

Napier, N. P., Keil, M., & Tan, F. B. (2009). IT project managers' construction of successful project management practice: A repertory grid investigation. *Information Systems Journal, 19*(3), 255–282. doi:10.1111/j.1365-2575.2007.00264.x

NDR. (2003, March). Data, information, and knowledge. *No Doubt Research*. Retrieved from www.nodoubt.co.nz

Nedelko, Z. (2007). Videoconferencing in virtual teams. *Business Review (Federal Reserve Bank of Philadelphia)*, *7*(1), 164.

Neef, D. (2001). *e-Procurement: From strategy to implementation*. Upper Saddle River, NJ: Prentice Hall.

Neely, A., Adams, C., & Kennerley, M. (2002). *The performance prism: the scorecard for measuring and managing business success*. Financial Times.

Nellore, R., & Balachandra, R. (2001). Factors influencing success in integrated product development (IPD) projects. *IEEE Transactions on Engineering Management*, *48*(2), 164–174. doi:10.1109/17.922476

Nelson, R. R. (2007). It project management: Infamous failures, classic mistakes, and best practices. *MIS Quarterly Executive*, *6*(2), 67–78.

Nembhard, D. A., & Osothsilp, N. (2001). An empirical comparison of forgetting models. *IEEE Transactions on Engineering Management*, *48*(1), 283–291. doi:10.1109/17.946527

Nembhard, D. A., & Uzumeri, M. V. (2000). Experiential learning and forgetting for manual and cognitive tasks. *International Journal of Industrial Ergonomics*, *25*(3), 315–326. doi:10.1016/S0169-8141(99)00021-9

Nerur, S., & Balijepally, V. G. (2007). Theoretical reflections on agile development methodologies. *Communications of the ACM*, *50*(3), 79–83. doi:10.1145/1226736.1226739

Neuman, W. L. (2003). *Social research methods: Qualitative and quantitative approaches* (5th ed.). Boston, MA: Allyn and Bacon.

Newman, B., & Conrad, K. (1999). A framework for characterizing knowledge management methods, practices, and technologies. In *proceedings of The Knowledge Management Forum in support of The Introduction to Knowledge Management*. West Richland, WA: Spring.

Newman, M., & Sabherwal, R. (1996). Commitment determinants to information systems development: a longitudinal investigation. *Management Information Systems Quarterly*, *20*, 23–54. doi:10.2307/249541

Nickols, F. (2003). *The knowledge in knowledge management*. Retrieved from http://home.att.net/~OPSINC/knowledge_in_KM.pdf

Nidumolu, S. (1995). The effect of coordination and uncertainty on software project performance: residual performance risk as an intervening variable. *Information Systems Research*, *6*(3), 191–219. doi:10.1287/isre.6.3.191

Noble, G., & Jones, R. (2006). The role of boundary-spanning managers in the establishment of public-private partnerships. *Public Administration*, *84*(4), 891–917. doi:10.1111/j.1467-9299.2006.00617.x

Nonaka, I. (1991). The knowledge-creating company. *Harvard Business Review*, *69*, 96–104.

Nonaka, I. (2007). The knowledge-creating company. *Harvard Business Review*, *85*, 162–171.

Nonaka, I., & Takeuchi, H. (1995). *The knowledge-creating company: How Japanese companies create the dynamics of innovation*. Oxford, UK: Oxford University Press.

Nørbjerg, J. (2002). Managing incremental development: combining flexibility and control. *Proceedings of the Tenth European Conference on Information Systems*, 229-239.

O'Sullivan, E., Rassel, G. R., & Berner, M. (2008). *Research methods for public administrators* (5th ed.). New York: Pearson-Longman.

Ocker, R. J. (2005). Influences on creativity in asynchronous virtual teams: a qualitative analysis of experimental teams. *IEEE Transactions on Professional Communication*, *48*(1), 22–39. doi:10.1109/TPC.2004.843294

Olsson, N. O. E. (2008). External and internal flexibility–aligning projects with the business strategy and executing projects efficiently. *International Journal of Project Organisation and Management*, *1*(1), 47–64. doi:10.1504/IJPOM.2008.020028

Orlikowski, W. J. (1992). The duality of technology: Rethinking the concept of technology in organizations. *Organization Science*, *3*(3), 398–427. doi:10.1287/orsc.3.3.398

Orlikowski, W. J. (1993). CASE tools as organizational change: investigating incremental and radical changes in systems development. *Management Information Systems Quarterly, 17*(3), 309–340. doi:10.2307/249774

Orlikowski, W. J. (2000). Using technology and constituting structures: A practice lens for studying technology in organizations. *Organization Science, 11*(4), 404–428. doi:10.1287/orsc.11.4.404.14600

Orlikowski, W. J. (2005). Material works: Exploring the situated entanglement of technological performativity and human agency. *Scandinavian Journal of Information Systems, 17*(1), 183–186.

Osborn, C. (1995). SDLC, JAD, and RAD: Finding the Right Hammer. Retrieved April 28, 2008, from faculty.babson.edu/osborn/cims/rad.htm#SDLCvsJADvsRAD.

Panayiotou, N. A., Gayialis, S. P., & Tatsiopoulos, I. P. (2003). An e-procurement system for governmental purchasing. *International Journal of Production Economics, 90*, 79–102. doi:10.1016/S0925-5273(03)00103-8

Pan, S. L., Pan, S. C., Newman, M., & Flynn, D. (2006a). Escalation and de-escalation for commitment to information systems projects: insights from a project evaluation model. *European Journal of Operational Research, 17*(3), 1139–1160. doi:10.1016/j.ejor.2005.07.009

Panteli, N., & Davison, R. M. (2005). The role of subgroups in the communication patterns of global virtual teams. *IEEE Transactions on Professional Communication, 48*(2), 191–200. doi:10.1109/TPC.2005.849651

Papadimitriou, H. C., & Steiglitz, K. (1982). *Combinatorial optimization: Algorithms and complexity.* Mineola, N.Y: Dover Publications, Inc.

Papazoglou, M. P. (2008). *Web Services: Principles and Technology.* Harlow, England: Pearson.

Park, M. Y., & Kim, H. K. A. (2003). A scheduling method for berth and quay cranes. *OR-Spektrum, 25*, 1–23. doi:10.1007/s00291-002-0109-z

Parnas, D. L., & Clements, P. C. (1986). A rational design process: how and why to fake it. *IEEE Transactions on Software Engineering*, 1–12.

Parr, A., & Shanks, G. (2000). A model of ERP project implementation. *Journal of Information Technology, 15*, 289–303. doi:10.1080/02683960010009051

Pauleen, D. J., & Yoong, P. (2001). Relationship building and the use of ict in boundary-crossing virtual teams: A facilitator's perspective. *Journal of Information Technology, 16*(4), 205–220. doi:10.1080/02683960110100391

Pawlowski, S. D., & Robey, D. (2004). Bridging user organizations: Knowledge brokering and the work of information technology professionals. *Management Information Systems Quarterly, 28*(4), 645–672.

Pegels, C. C. (1976). Start-up of learning curves - some new approaches. *Decision Sciences, 7*(4), 705–713. doi:10.1111/j.1540-5915.1976.tb00714.x

Pescuric, A., & Byham, W. C. (1996). The new look of behavior modeling. *Training & Development, 50*(7), 24–31.

Pettigrew, A. M. (1990). Longitudinal field research on change: theory and practice. *Organization Science, 1*(3), 267–292. doi:10.1287/orsc.1.3.267

Pich, M., Loch, C., & De Meyer, A. (2002). On Uncertainty, Ambiguity and Complexity in Project Management. *Management Science, 48*, 1008–1023. doi:10.1287/mnsc.48.8.1008.163

Pinedo, M. (2008). *Scheduling: theory, algorithms, and systems-3rd edition.* New York: Springer.

Pinto, J., & Kharbanda, O. (1995). *Successful Project Managers: Leading Your Team to Success.* New York: Van Nostrand Reinhold

PMI Standards Committee. (2004). *A Guide to the Project Management Body of Knowledge (PMBoK Guides)*: Project Management Institute.

PMI. (2004). *A Guide to the Project Management Body of Knowledge.* (3rd ed.) Project Management Institute.

Polanyi, M. (1996). *The tacit dimension.* New York: Anchor Day Books.

Polanyi, M. (1997). Tacit knowledge. In Prusak, L. (Ed.), *Knowledge in Organizations.* Boston: Butterworth-Heinemann.

Poppendieck, M., & Poppendieck, T. D. (2003). *Lean Software Development: An Agile Toolkit* (1st ed.). Boston: Addison-Wesley Professional.

Powell, A., Gabriele, P., & Blake, I. (2004). Virtual teams: a review of current literature and directions for future research. *The Data Base for Advances in Information Systems*, *35*(1), 6.

Premkumar, G., Ramamurthy, K., & Crum, M. R. (1997). Determinants of EDI adoption in the transportation industry. *European Journal of Information Systems*, *6*(2), 107–121. doi:10.1057/palgrave.ejis.3000260

Probst, G., Raub, S., & Romhardt, K. (2000). *Managing knowledge: Building blocks for success*. West Sussex, England: John Wiley and Sons Ltd.

Project Management Institute. (2002). *Project manager competency development (PMCD) framework*. Newton Square, PA: Project Management Institute.

Project Management Institute. (2004). *A guide to the project management body of knowledge (PMBOK Guide)* (3rd ed.). Newton Square, PA: Project Management Institute.

Provan, K. G., Fish, A., & Sydow, J. (2007). Interorganizational networks at the network level: A review of the empirical literature on whole networks. *Journal of Management*, *33*(3), 479–516. doi:10.1177/0149206307302554

Puschmann, T., & Alt, R. (2005). Successful use of e-procurement in supply chains. *International Journal of Supply Chain Management*, *10*(2), 122–133. doi:10.1108/13598540510589197

Ragu-Nathan, B. S., Apigian, C. H., Ragu-Nathan, T. S., & Tu, Q. (2004). A path analytic study of the effect of top management support for information systems performance. *Omega*, *32*(6), 459–471. doi:10.1016/j.omega.2004.03.001

Rakitin, S. (2001). Manifesto Elicits Cynicism. *IEEE Computer*, *34*(12), 4.

Ranasinghe, M. (1994). Quantification and management of uncertainty in activity durations network. *Construction Management and Economics*, *12*, 15–29. doi:10.1080/01446199400000003

Ravichandran, T., & Rai, A. (2000). Quality management in systems development: an organizational system perspective. *MIS Quarterly*, *24*(3), 381–415. doi:10.2307/3250967

Raz, T., Barnes, R., & Dvir, D. (2003). A critical look at Critical Chain project management. *Project Management Journal*, *34*(4), 24–32.

Rehring, E. (2006). Germany's tolling success. *Traffic World*, *270*(6), 14.

Reijniers, J. J. A. M. (1994). Organization of public-private partnership projects, the timely prevention of pitfalls. *International Journal of Project Management*, *12*(3), 137–142. doi:10.1016/0263-7863(94)90028-0

Richards, L. (2002). *Using NVivo in Qualitative Research*. London: Sage Publications.

Richardson, W. J. (1978). Use of learning curves to set goals and monitor progress in cost reduction programs. In *Proceedings of 1978 IIE Spring Conference* (pp. 235-239).

Ritchie, J., & Spencer, L. (1994). Qualitative data analysis for applied policy research. In Bryman, A., & Burgess, R. G. (Eds.), *Analyzing qualitative data* (pp. 173–194). London: Routledge. doi:10.4324/9780203413081_chapter_9

Robb, D. J., & Silver, E. A. (1993). Scheduling in a management context: Uncertain processing times and non-regular performance measures. *Decision Sciences*, *24*(6), 1085–1108. doi:10.1111/j.1540-5915.1993.tb00505.x

Robertson, P. J. (1995). Involvement in boundary-spanning activity: Mitigating the relationship between work setting and behavior. *Journal of Public Administration: Research and Theory*, *5*(1), 73–98.

Robey, D., Farrow, D. L., & Franz, C. R. (1989). Group process and conflict in system development. *Management Science*, *35*(10), 1172–1191. doi:10.1287/mnsc.35.10.1172

Robinson, H., Carrillo, P., Anumba, C., & Al-Ghassani, A. (2004). Developing a business case for knowledge management: The IMPaKT approach. *Construction Management and Economics*, *22*(1), 733–743. doi:10.1080/0144619042000226306

Robinson, H., Carrillo, P., Anumba, C., & Al-Ghassani, A. (2005). Knowledge management practices in large construction organizations. *Engineering, Construction, and Architectural Management, 12*(5), 431–445. doi:10.1108/09699980510627135

Roebuck, D. B. (2002). *Colonel mustard in the library with the knife... experiencing virtual teaming.* Paper presented at the 67th Annual Meeting of the Association for Business Communication, Cincinnati, OH.

Roebuck, D. B., & Britt, A. C. (2002). Virtual teaming has come to stay--guidelines and strategies for success. *Southern Business Review, 28*(1), 29–39.

Roijakkers, N., & Hagedoorn, J. (2006). Inter-firm R&D partnering in pharmaceutical biotechnology since 1975: Trends, patterns, and networks. *Research Policy, 35*(3), 431–446. doi:10.1016/j.respol.2006.01.006

Ronen, B., & Trietsch, D. (1988). A Decision support system for purchasing management of large projects. *Operations Research, 36*(6), 882–890. doi:10.1287/opre.36.6.882

Rose, J., Jones, M., & Truex, D. (2005). Socio-theoretic accounts of is: The problem of agency. *Scandinavian Journal of Information Systems, 17*(1), 133–152.

Rose, J., Pedersen, K., Hosbond, J. H., & Kræmmergaard, P. (2007). Management competences, not tools and techniques: A grounded examination of software project management at WM-data. *Information and Software Technology, 49*(6), 605–624. doi:10.1016/j.infsof.2007.02.005

Rosenau, P. V. (1999). Introduction: The strengths and weaknesses of public-private policy partnerships. *The American Behavioral Scientist, 43*(1), 10–34.

Rosencrance, L. (2007). *Survey: poor communication causes most IT project failures.* Retrieved July 5, 2009 from http://www.computerworld.com/action/article.do?command=viewArticleBasic&articleId=9012758

Ross, J. W., & Beath, C. M. (2002, winter). Beyond the business case: New approaches to IT investments. *MIT Sloan Management Review*, 51-59.

Ross, J., & Staw, B. M. (1986). Expo86: An escalation prototype. *Administrative Science Quarterly, 3*(1), 274–297. doi:10.2307/2392791

Ross, R. J., & Staw, B. M. (1993). Organizational Escalation and Exit: Lessons from the Shoreham Nuclear Power Plant. *Academy of Management Journal, 36*(4), 701–732. doi:10.2307/256756

Rousseau, D. M., Sitkin, S. B., Burt, R. S., & Camerer, C. (1998). Not so different after all: A cross-discipline view of trust. *Academy of Management Review, 23*(3), 393–404.

Royce, W. (1970). Managing the Development of Large Software Systems. *Proceedings of IEEE WESCON*; 1-9.

Royer, I. (2002). *Escalation in organizations: The role of collective belief.* Denver, CO: Academy of Management Conference.

Royer, I. (2003). Why bad projects are so hard to kill. *Harvard Business Review*, 49–56.

Rubenstein, D. (2007). Standish group report: There's less development chaos today. *Software Development Times on the Web.* Retrieved from http://www2.sdtimes.com/content/article.aspx?ArticleID=30247

Rubin, J. Z., & Brockner, J. (1975). Factors affecting entrapment in waiting situations: The Rosencrantz and Guildenstern Effect. *Journal of Personality and Social Psychology, 31*, 1054–1063. doi:10.1037/h0076937

Rubin, J., Brockner, J., Small-Weill, S., & Nathanson, S. (1980). Factors affecting entry into psychological traps. *The Journal of Conflict Resolution, 25*, 405–426. doi:10.1177/002200278002400302

Sabherwal, R., & King, W. R. (1992). Decision Processes for developing strategic Apps of IS: A contingency approach. *Decision Sciences, 23*(4), 917–943. doi:10.1111/j.1540-5915.1992.tb00426.x

Salaka, V., & Prabhu, V. (2008). Project management and scheduling for enterprise integration. *International Journal of Project Organisation and Management, 1*(2), 167–184. doi:10.1504/IJPOM.2008.022190

Saleem, N. (1996). An empirical test of the contingency approach to user participation in information systems development. *Journal of Management Information Systems, 13*(1), 145–166.

Santos, F. M., & Eisenhardt, K. M. (2005). Organizational boundaries and theories of organization. *Organization Science, 16*(5), 491–508. doi:10.1287/orsc.1050.0152

Sarker, S., & Lee, A. S. (2003). Using a case study to test the role of three key social enablers in erp implementation. *Information & Management*, *40*, 813–829. doi:10.1016/S0378-7206(02)00103-9

Sauer, C., Gemino, A., & Reich, B. H. (2007). The impact of size and volatility on IT project performance. *Communications of the ACM*, *50*(11), 79–84. doi:10.1145/1297797.1297801

Saunders, M., Lewis, P., & Thornhill, A. (2007). *Research Methods for Business Students* (4th ed.). Harlow, UK: Pearson Education Limited.

Schambach, T. (1994). *Maintaining professional competence: an evaluation of factors affecting professional obsolescence of information technology professionals.* Ph.D. dissertation, University of South Florida.

Schmidt, C. W., & Grossman, I. E. (2000). The exact overall time distribution of a project with uncertain task durations. *European Journal of Operational Research*, *126*(3), 614–636. doi:10.1016/S0377-2217(99)00316-1

Schmidt, J. B., & Calantone, R. J. (2002). Escalation of commitment during new product development. *Journal of the Academy of Marketing Science*, *30*(2), 103–118. doi:10.1177/03079459994362

Schonberger, J. R. (1981). Why projects are ""always" late: a rationale based on manual simulation of a PERT/CPM network. *Interfaces*, *11*(5), 66–70. doi:10.1287/inte.11.5.66

Schultze, U. (2000). A confessional Account of an Ethnography about Knowledge Work. *Management Information Systems Quarterly*, *24*(1), 3–41. doi:10.2307/3250978

Schwaber, K. (1995). The Scrum Development Process. Retrieved April 28, 2008, from www.controlchaos.com/old-site/scrumwp.htm.

Schwalbe, K. (2007). *Information technology project management* (5th ed.). Boston: Course Technology.

Scott, R. W. (2001). *Institutions and Organizations* (2nd ed.). Thousand Oaks, CA: Sage.

Seneviratne, S. J., & Garson, G. D. (Eds.). (1999). *Information technology and organizational change in the public sector*. Hershey, PA: IGI Global.

Shanks, G., Parr, A., Hu, B., Corbitt, B., Thanasankit, T., & Seddon, P. B. (2000). Differences in critical success factors in ERP systems implementation in Australia and China: A cultural analysis. In H. R. Hansen, M. Bichler, & H. Mahrer (Eds.), *The European Conference on Information Systems* (Vol. 8, pp. 537-544). Wienna: Wirtschaftsunivsitat Wien.

Shenhar, A. J. (1998). From theory to practice: Toward a typology of project management styles. *IEEE Transactions on Engineering Management*, *45*, 33–48. doi:10.1109/17.658659

Shogan, A. W. (1977). Bounding distributions for a stochastic PERT network. *Networks*, *7*(4), 359–381. doi:10.1002/net.3230070407

Sholler, D. (2008). *2008 SOA User Survey: Adoption Trends and Characteristics* (Gartner No. G00161125).

Siggelkow, N. (2007). Persuasion with case studies. *Academy of Management Journal*, *50*(1), 20–24.

Skulmoski, G., Hartman, F., & DeMaere, R. (2000). Superior and Threshold Project Competencies. *Project Management*, *6*(1), 10–15.

Smith, H., & Keil, M. (2003). The reluctance to report bad news on troubled software projects: a theoretical model. *Information Systems Journal*, *13*(1), 69–95. doi:10.1046/j.1365-2575.2003.00139.x

Smith, J. (1989). *Learning curve for cost control*. Norcross, GA: Industrial Engineering and Management Press.

Smunt, T. L. (1986). A comparison of learning curve analysis and moving average ratio analysis for detailed operational planning. *Decision Sciences*, *17*(1), 23–35.

Snow, A. P., & Keil, M. (2002). The challenge of accurate software project status reporting: A two-stage model incorporating status errors and reporting bias. *IEEE Transactions on Engineering Management*, *49*, 491–504. doi:10.1109/TEM.2002.807290

Snow, A. P., Keil, M., & Wallace, L. (2007). The effects of optimistic and pessimistic biasing on software project status reporting. *Information & Management*, *44*(2), 130–141. doi:10.1016/j.im.2006.10.009

Somers, T., & Nelson, K. (2001). The impacts of critical success factors across the stages of enterprise resource planning implementations. In []. Washington, DC: IEEE Computer Society.]. *Proceedings of the Hawaii International Conference of System Sciences, 8*, 1–10.

Sommerville, I. (2006). *Software engineering* (8th ed.). Harlow, UK: Pearson Education.

Spencer, S. M., & Spencer, L. M. (1993). *Competence at work: Models for superior performance.* New York: John Wiley.

Stability pact – eSEEurope initiative. (2002). Stability pact – eSEEurope initiative. *eSEEurope agenda for the development of the information society, a cooperative effort to implement the information society in South Eastern Europe.* Retrieved October 30, 2008, from http://www.eseeuropeconference.org/agenda.pdf

Standish Group. (2001). *Extreme CHAOS.* The Standish Group International Inc.

Stangor, C. (2004). *Research methods for the behavioral sciences* (2nd ed.). New York: Houghton Mifflin.

Stapleton, J. (1997). *Dynamic Systems Development Method: The Method In Practice.* London: Addison-Wesley.

Staw, B. M. (1997). The escalation of commitment: an update and appraisal. In Shapira, Z. (Ed.), *Organizational Decision Making* (pp. 191–215). Cambridge, UK: Cambridge University Press.

Staw, B. M., & Ross, J. (1987). Behavior in escalation situations: antecedents, prototypes and solutions. In Staw, B. M., & Cummings, L. L. (Eds.), *Research in Organizational Behavior* (pp. 39–78). Greenwich, CT: JAI Press.

Steenken, D., Voss, S., & Stahlbock, R. (2004). Container terminal operation and operations research – A classification and literature review. *OR-Spektrum, 26*, 3–49. doi:10.1007/s00291-003-0157-z

Stephens, M., & Rosenberg, D. (2003). *Extreme Programming Refactored: The Case Against XP.* USA: APress.

Stoddard, D., & Jarvenpaa, S. (1995). Business process redesign: Tactics for managing radical change. *Journal of Management Information Systems, 12*(1), 81–107.

Stones, R. (2001). Refusing the realism-structuration divide. *European Journal of Social Theory, 4*(2), 177–197. doi:10.1177/13684310122225064

Strauss, A., & Corbin, J. (1998). *Basics of Qualitative Research: Techniques and Procedures for Developing Grounded Theory* (2nd ed.). Thousand Oaks, CA: Sage Pulications.

Stubbart, C., & Smalley, R. (1999). The deceptive allure of stage models of strategic processes. *Journal of Management Inquiry, 8*(3), 273–287. doi:10.1177/105649269983005

Sukhoo, A., Barnard, A., Eloff, M. M., Van der Poll, J. A., & Motah, M. (2005). Accommodating Soft Skills in Software Project Management. *Issues in Informing Science and Information Technology, 2*, 691–704.

Sule, D. R. (1978). The effect of alternate periods of learning and forgetting on economic manufacturing quantity. *AIIE Transactions, 10*(3), 338–343.

Sullivan, R. S., Hayya, J. C., & Schaul, R. (1982). Efficiency of the antithetic variate method for simulating stochastic networks. *Management Science, 28*(5), 563–572. doi:10.1287/mnsc.28.5.563

Sumner, M., Bock, D., & Giamartino, G. (2006). Exploring the linkage between the characteristics of it project leaders and project success. *Information Systems Management, 23*(4), 43–49. doi:10.1201/1078.10580530/46352.23.4.20060901/95112.6

Sutton, R. I. (1987). The process of organizational death: disbanding and reconnecting. *Administrative Science Quarterly, 32*(4), 542–569. doi:10.2307/2392883

Swan, J., & Scarbrough, H. (2005). The politics of networked innovation. *Human Relations, 58*(7), 913–943. doi:10.1177/0018726705057811

Swanson, E. B. (1974). Management information systems: appreciation and involvement. *Management Science, 21*(2), 178–188. doi:10.1287/mnsc.21.2.178

Swanson, E. B., & Ramiller, N. C. (2004). Innovating mindfully with information technology. *Management Information Systems Quarterly, 28*(4), 553–583.

Taboada, H. (2007) *Multi-objective optimization algorithms considering objective preferences and solution clusters.* Unpublished doctoral disseratation. Rutgers University, New Jersey.

Taboada, H., & Coit, D. W. (2007). Data clustering of solutions for multiple objective system reliability optimization problems. *Quality Technology & Quantitative Management Journal, 4*(2), 35–54.

Taboada, H., & Coit, D. W. (2008). Multiple objective scheduling problems: determination of pruned Pareto sets. *IIE Transactions, 40*(5), 552–564. doi:10.1080/07408170701781951

Tang, Q. C., & Cheng, H. K. (2006). 2007). Optimal strategies for a monopoly intermediary in the supply chain of complementary web services. *Journal of Management Information Systems, 23*(3), 275–307. doi:10.2753/MIS0742-1222230310

Tapio, S. (2004). *Key competences for lifelong learning: A European reference framework*: European Commission. Directorate-General for Education and Culture, Brussels.

Taylor, F. W. (1911). *The Principles of Scientific Management.* New York: Harper & Brothers.

Taylor, H. (2005). A critical decision interview approach to capturing tacit knowledge: Principles and application. *International Journal of Knowledge Management, 1*(3), 25–39.

Taylor, P. J., Russ-Eft, D. F., & Chan, D. W. L. (2005). A meta-analytic review of behavior modeling training. *The Journal of Applied Psychology, 90*(4), 692–709. doi:10.1037/0021-9010.90.4.692

Teodorescu, H. N., Zbancioc, M., & Voroneanu, O. (2004). *Knowledge based systems. Applications.* Iaşi, Romania: Performantica Press.

The Economist. (2008, February 14). A special report on technology and government. 3-18.

Theofanis, S., Boile, M., & Golias, M. M. (2009). (in press). Container terminal berth planning: Critical review of research approaches and practical challenges. *Journal of the Transportation Research Record.*

Thompson, R. L., Smith, H. J., & Iacovou, C. L. (2007). The linkage between reporting quality and performance in IS projects. *Information and Management, 44*, 196-205.

Thompson, R. L., Smith, H. J., & Iacovou, C. L. (2007). The linkage between reporting quality and performance in IS projects. *Information & Management, 44*, 196–205. doi:10.1016/j.im.2006.12.004

Tijssen, R. J. W., & Korevaar, J. C. (1997). Unravelling the Cognitive and Interorganisational Structure of public/private R&D Networks: A Case of Catalysis Research in the Netherlands. *Research Policy, 25*, 1277–1293. doi:10.1016/S0048-7333(96)00908-0

Tiwana, A. (1999). *The knowledge management toolkit: Practical techniques for building a knowledge management system.* Upper Saddle River, NJ: Prentice Hall.

Tiwana, A., & Bush, A. A. (2007). A comparison of transaction cost, agency, and knowledge-based predictors of IT outsourcing decisions: A U.S.-Japan cross cultural field study. *Journal of Management Information Systems, 24*(1), 259–300. doi:10.2753/MIS0742-1222240108

Todd, P., McKeen, J., & Gallupe, R. B. (1995). The Evolution of IT Job Skills: A Content Analysis of IT Job Advertisements From 1970 to 1990. *MIT Quarterly, 19*(1), 1–27. doi:10.2307/249709

Towill, D. R., & Cherrington, J. E. (1994). Learning curve models for predicting the performance of advanced manufacturing technology. *International Journal of Advanced Manufacturing Technology, 9*(3), 195–203. doi:10.1007/BF01754598

Trafford, S., & Proctor, T. (2006). Successful joint venture partnerships: Public-private partnerships. *International Journal of Public Sector Management, 19*(2), 117–129. doi:10.1108/09513550610650392

Trietsch, D. (2005). The effect of systemic errors on optimal project buffers. *International Journal of Project Management, 23*, 267–274. doi:10.1016/j.ijproman.2004.12.004

Trietsch, D. (2005a). Why a critical path by any other name would smell less sweet? Towards a holistic approach to PERT/CPM. *Project Management Journal, 36*(1), 27–36.

Trietsch, D. (2006). Optimal feeding buffers for projects or batch supply chains by an exact generalization of the newsvendor result. *International Journal of Production Research, 44*, 627–637. doi:10.1080/00207540500371881

Trimi, S., & Sheng, H. (2008). Emerging trends of m-government. *Communications of the ACM, 51*(5), 53–58. doi:10.1145/1342327.1342338

Tserng, H., & Lin, Y. (2004). Developing an activity-based knowledge management system for contractors. *Automation in Construction, 13*(6), 781–802. doi:10.1016/j.autcon.2004.05.003

Tuckman, B. W. (1965). Developmental sequence in small groups. *Psychological Bulletin, 63*, 384–399. doi:10.1037/h0022100

Turley, R. T., & Bieman, J. M. (1995). Competencies of Exceptional an Non-Exceptional Software Engineers. *Journal of Systems and Software, 28*(1), 19–38. doi:10.1016/0164-1212(94)00078-2

Turner, J. R., & Müller, R. (2005). The Project Manager's Leadership Style as a Success Factor on Projects: A Literature Review. *Project Management Journal, 36*(2), 49–61.

Turner, J. R., & Müller, R. (2006). *Choosing appropriate project managers: Matching their leadership style to the type of project*. Newton Square, PA: Project Management Institute.

Turner, J. R., & Simister, S. J. (2004). *Gower manual for project management*. Bucharest, Romania: Codecs Press.

Tushman, A. A. (1986). Technological discontinuities and organizational environments. *Administrative Science Quarterly, 31*, 439–465. doi:10.2307/2392832

Tushman, M. L. (1977). Special boundary roles in the innovation process. *Administrative Science Quarterly, 22*(4), 587–605. doi:10.2307/2392402

Tushman, M. L., Newman, W. H., & Romanelli, E. (1986). Convergence and upheaval: Managing the unsteady pace of organizational evolution. *California Management Review, 29*(1), 29–44.

Tushman, M. L., & Scanlan, T. J. (1981). Boundary spanning individuals: Their role in information transfer and their antecedents. *Academy of Management Journal, 24*(2), 289–305. doi:10.2307/255842

Tushman, M., & Romanelli, E. (1985). Organizational evolution: A metamorphosis model of convergence and reorientation. In Cummings, L. L., & Staw, B. M. (Eds.), *Research in organizational behavior* (pp. 171–222).

Tversky, A., & Kahneman, D. (1981). The Framing of Decisions and the Psychology of Choice. *Science, 211*, 453–458. doi:10.1126/science.7455683

Umble, E. J., Haft, R. R., & Umble, M. M. (2003). Enterprise resource planning: Implementation procedures and critical success factors. *European Journal of Operational Research, 146*, 241–257. doi:10.1016/S0377-2217(02)00547-7

Umble, E. J., & Umble, M. M. (2002). Avoiding ERP implementation failure. *Industrial Management (Des Plaines), 44*(1), 1–25.

UN E-government survey. (2008). *From e-government to connected governance*. Retrieved November 3, 2008, from http://unpan1.un.org/intradoc/groups/public/documents/UN/UNPAN028607.pdf

US GAO. (2006). *Weak controls over trilogy project led to payment of questionable contractor costs and missing assets, GAO Report to Congressional Requesters*. Washington, DC: Government Accountability Office.

Utterback, J. M. (1994). Radical innovation and corporate regeneration. *Research Technology Management, 37*(4), 10–18.

Van Maanen, J. (1995). An end of innocence: The ethnography of ethnography. In *Representation in Ethnography* (pp. 1–35). Thousand Oaks, CA: Sage.

van Marrewijk, A. (2007). Managing project culture: The case of the environ megaproject. *International Journal of Project Management, 25*(3), 290–299. doi:10.1016/j.ijproman.2006.11.004

van Marrewijk, A., Clegg, S. R., Pitsis, T. S., & Veenswijk, M. (2008). Managing public-private megaprojects: Paradoxes, complexity, and project design. *International Journal of Project Management, 26*(6), 591–600. doi:10.1016/j.ijproman.2007.09.007

Van Slyke, R. M. (1963). Monte Carlo methods and PERT problem. *Operations Research, 11*(5), 839–860. doi:10.1287/opre.11.5.839

Veenswijk, M., & Berensde, M. (2008). Constructing new working practices through project narratives. *International Journal of Project Organisation and Management, 1*(1), 65–85. doi:10.1504/IJPOM.2008.020029

Venkat, V., Jacobson, S., & Stori, J. (2004). A post-optimality analysis algorithm for multi-objective optimization. *Computational Optimization and Applications, 28*, 357–372. doi:10.1023/B:COAP.0000033968.55439.8b

Venugopal, C. (2005). Single goal set: A new paradigm for it megaproject success. *IEEE Software, 22*(5), 48–53. doi:10.1109/MS.2005.135

Vitale, I. B., & Beath, C. M. (1986). Linking information technology and corporate strategy: an organizational view. In *Proceedings of the Seventh International Conference on Information Systems,* San Diego, CA (pp. 265-276).

Vlaar, P. W. L., Van den Bosch, F. A. J., & Volberda, H. W. (2006). Coping with problems of understanding in interorganizational relationships: Using formalisation as a means to make sense. *Organization Studies, 27*(11), 1617–1638. doi:10.1177/0170840606068338

Vlaar, P. W. L., Van den Bosch, F. A. J., & Volberda, H. W. (2007). On the evolution of trust, distrust, and formal coordination and control in interorganizational relationships: Toward an integrative framework. *Group & Organization Management, 32*(4), 407–429. doi:10.1177/1059601106294215

Vlach, J. (2007). *Public-private partnership as a basis of the development of public procurement.* Bratislava, Slovakia: Transparency International Slovensko. Retrieved July 20, 2009, from http://www.icoste.org/Roundup1105/Vlach1105.pdf

Volkoff, O., Strong, D. M., & Elmes, M. B. (2007). Technological embeddedness and organizational change. *Organization Science, 18*(5), 832–848. doi:10.1287/orsc.1070.0288

Walker, D., Wilson, A., & Srikanthan, G. (2001). *The knowledge advantage (K-Adv) for unleashing creativity and innovation in construction industry* (Tech. Rep. No. 2001-004-A). Institute of Construction.

Walsham, G. (1995a). The emergence of interpretivism in is research. *Information Systems Research, 6*(4), 376–394. doi:10.1287/isre.6.4.376

Walsham, G. (1995b). Interpretive case studies in is research: Nature and method. *European Journal of Information Systems, 4*(2), 74–81. doi:10.1057/ejis.1995.9

Walther, J. B., & Ulla, B. (2005). The rules of virtual groups: trust, liking, and performance in computer-mediated communication. *The Journal of Communication, 55*(4), 828. doi:10.1111/j.1460-2466.2005.tb03025.x

Ward, J. (1995). *Principles of information systems management.* New York: Routledge.

Ward, J., Hemingway, C., & Daniel, E. (2005). A framework for addressing the organisational issues of enterprise systems implementation. *The Journal of Strategic Information Systems, 14*, 97–119. doi:10.1016/j.jsis.2005.04.005

Webber, S. S., & Torti, M. T. (2004). Project managers doubling as client executives. *The Academy of Management Executive, 18*(1), 60–71.

Weick, K. E. (1995). *Sensemaking in organizations.* Thousand Oaks, CA: Sage.

Weiser, M., & Morrison, J. (1998). Project memory: information management for project teams. *Journal of Management Information Systems, 14*(4), 149–166.

Weiss, G. (1986). Stochastic bounds on distributions of optimal value functions with applications to PERT, network flow and reliability. *Operations Research, 34*(4), 595–605. doi:10.1287/opre.34.4.595

Wenger, E. (1998). *Communities of practice: Learning, meaning, and identity.* New York: Cambridge University Press.

White, D., & Fortune, J. (2002). Current Practice in Project Management - an empirical study. *International Journal of Project Management, 20*, 1–11. doi:10.1016/S0263-7863(00)00029-6

Whyte, G., & Fassina, N. E. (2007). Escalating commitment in group decision making. In *Proceedings of the Academy of Management*, Philadelphia.

Whyte, G. (1986). Escalating commitment to a course of action: a reinterpretation. *Academy of Management Review, 11*(2), 311–321. doi:10.2307/258462

Wiegers, K. E. (1999). Customer Rights and Responsibilities. Retrieved April 28, 2008, from www.processimpact.com/articles/customer.html.

Wikipedia. (2009). Social theory. *Wikipedia.* Retrieved October 31, 2009, from http://en.wikipedia.org/wiki/Social_theory

Williams, P. (2002). The competent boundary spanner. *Public Administration, 80*(1), 103–124. doi:10.1111/1467-9299.00296

Williams, T. A. (1992). Practical use of distributions in network analysis. *The Journal of the Operational Research Society, 43*(3), 265–270.

Wilson, J. M., Straus, S. G., & McEvily, B. (2006). All in due time: the development of trust in computer-mediated and face-to-face teams. *Organizational Behavior and Human Decision Processes, 99*(1), 16–33. doi:10.1016/j.obhdp.2005.08.001

Wollmer, R. D. (1985). Critical path planning under uncertainty. *Mathematical Programming Study, 25,* 164–171.

Womer, N. K. (1979). Learning curves, production rate, and program costs. *Management Science, 25*(4), 312–219. doi:10.1287/mnsc.25.4.312

Womer, N. K. (1981). Some propositions on cost functions. *Southern Economic Journal, 47*(2), 1111–1119. doi:10.2307/1058169

Womer, N. K. (1984). Estimating learning curves from aggregate monthly data. *Management Science, 30*(8), 982–992. doi:10.1287/mnsc.30.8.982

Womer, N. K., & Gulledge, T. R. Jr. (1983). A dynamic cost function for an airframe production program. *Engineering Costs and Production Economics, 7*(1), 213–227. doi:10.1016/0167-188X(83)90015-0

Woo, J., Clayton, M. J., Johnson, R. E., Flores, B. E., & Ellis, C. (2004). Dynamic knowledge map: Reusing experts' tacit knowledge in the AEC industry. *Automation in Construction, 13,* 203–207. doi:10.1016/j.autcon.2003.09.003

Wright, M. K., & Capps, C. J. (2008). Information technology customer service: 'Best Practices' processes for operations. *Journal of Applied Business Research, 24*(3), 63–76.

Wright, T. P. (1936). Factors affecting the cost of airplanes. *Journal of the Aeronautical Sciences, 3*(2), 122–128.

Wu, J. H., Chen, Y. C., & Chang, C. (2007). Critical IS professional activities and skills/knowledge: A perspective of IS managers. *Computers in Human Behavior, 23*(6), 2945–2965. doi:10.1016/j.chb.2006.08.008

Yano, C. A. (1987). Planned leadtimes for serial production systems. *IIE Transactions, 19*(3), 300–307. doi:10.1080/07408178708975400

Yano, C. A. (1987a). Setting planned leadtimes in serial production systems with tardiness costs. *Management Science, 33*(1), 95–106. doi:10.1287/mnsc.33.1.95

Yelle, L. E. (1976). Estimating learning curves for potential products. *Industrial Marketing Management, 5*(2), 147–154. doi:10.1016/0019-8501(76)90037-7

Yelle, L. E. (1979). The learning curve: Historical review and comprehensive survey. *Decision Sciences, 10*(2), 302–328. doi:10.1111/j.1540-5915.1979.tb00026.x

Yelle, L. E. (1983). Adding life cycles to learning curves. *Long Range Planning, 16*(6), 82–87. doi:10.1016/0024-6301(83)90011-0

Yin, R. K. (1994). *Case study research: Design and methods.* London: Sage.

Yin, R. (1994). *Case study research: Design and methods* (2nd ed.). Beverly Hills, CA: Sage.

Yin, R. (2003). *Case study research - design and methods.* Thousand Oaks, CA: Sage Publications.

Yin, R. (2003). *Case study research: Design and methods* (3rd ed.). Thousand Oaks, CA: Sage.

Yin, R. K. (2003). *Case study research Design and Methods* (3rd ed.). London: Sage Publications Inc.

Yong, J. S. L. (2003). *E-Government in Asia: Enabling public service innovation in the 21st century.* Singapore: Times Edition.

Yu, A. G., Flett, P. D., & Bowers, J. A. (2005). Developing a value-centred proposal for assessing project success. *International Journal of Project Management, 23,* 428–436. doi:10.1016/j.ijproman.2005.01.008

Zack, M. (1999). Managing codified knowledge. *Sloan Management Review*, *40*(4), 45–58.

Zahniser, R. (1995). Timeboxing For Top Team Performance. Retrieved April 28, 2008, from www.belizenorth.com/articles/TIMEBOX.htm

Zeleny, M. (1982). *Multiple criteria decision making*. New York: McGraw Hill Higher Education.

Zhu, K., Kraemer, K. L., Xu, S., & Dedrick, J. (2004). Information technology payoff in e-business environments: An international perspective on value creation of e-business in the financial services industry. *Journal of Management Information Systems*, *21*(1), 17–54.

Zmud, R. W. (1980). Management of large software efforts. *Management Information Systems Quarterly*, *4*, 45–55. doi:10.2307/249336

Zwikael, O., Cohen, Y., & Sadeh, A. (2006). Non-delay scheduling as a managerial approach for managing projects. *International Journal of Project Management*, *24*(4), 330–336. doi:10.1016/j.ijproman.2005.11.002

About the Contributors

John Wang is a Professor in the Department of Management and Information Systems at Montclair State University (USA). Having received a scholarship award, he came to the USA and completed his PhD in operations research from Temple University. Due to his extraordinary contributions beyond a tenured full Professor, Dr. Wang has been honored with a special range adjustment in 2006. He has published over 100 refereed papers and six books. He has also developed several computer software programs based on his research findings. He is the Editor-in-Chief of *International Journal of Applied Management Science, International Journal of Information Systems and Supply Chain Management*, and the *International Journal of Information and Decision Sciences*. He is also the EIC for the *Advances in Information Systems and Supply Chain Management Book Series*. He has served as a guest editor and referee for many other highly prestigious journals. He has served as track chair and/or session chairman numerous times on the most prestigious international and national conferences. Also, he is an editorial advisory board member of the following publications: Intelligent Information Technologies: Concepts, Methodologies, Tools, and Applications, End-User Computing: Concepts, Methodologies, Tools, and Applications, Global Information Technologies: Concepts, Methodologies, Tools, and Applications, Information Communication Technologies: Concepts, Methodologies, Tools, and Applications, Multimedia Technologies: Concepts, Methodologies, Tools, and Applications, Information Security and Ethics: Concepts, Methodologies, Tools, and Applications, Electronic Commerce: Concepts, Methodologies, Tools, and Applications, Electronic Government: Concepts, Methodologies, Tools, and Applications, and other IGI Global titles. Furthermore, he is the editor of *Data Warehousing and Mining: Concepts, Methodologies, Tools, and Applications* and the *Encyclopedia of Data Warehousing and Mining* 1st and 2nd editions. His long-term research goal is on the synergy of operations research, data mining, and cybernetics.

* * *

Hesham S. Ahmad received his BSc in civil engineering from the Jordan University of Science and Technology and his MSc in Management Information Systems from Amman Arab University. He was a Project Manager in a variety of construction and road projects before joining the University of Birmingham (UK) in October 2006. He is currently a PhD research student within the Safety, Risk and Reliability Management Research Group of the School of Civil Engineering and working on a project entitled 'Development of KM models to simplify knowledge management implementation in construction projects'.

Min An (BEng (Hons), MSc, PhD, CEng, MIMechE, MCICE, MIEngD) is a Reader in Project and Transport Risk Management in the School of Civil Engineering of the University of Birmingham (UK). He is the leader of Safety, Risk and Reliability Management Research Group and also is the Director of MSc/PgD Construction Management programme. He received his BEng and MSc in Civil Engineering from Xian Jiaotong University (China) and PhD in Civil & Offshore Engineering from Heriot-watt University (UK). His research interests are in project management, safety risk and reliability management, project risk management and project decision-making.

Roman Beck is the E-Finance and Services Science Chair at Goethe University, Frankfurt, Germany. His research focuses on the creation, sourcing, and management of knowledge intensive IT services and has been published in journals such as Communications of the ACM, Communications of AIS, Electronic Markets, Information Systems Frontiers, Information Technology & People, and others. Oliver Marschollek is a doctoral student at the Chair of E-Finance and Services Science at Goethe University, Frankfurt, Germany. His research focuses on public private partnerships and the management of IT megaprojects as well as the use of the grounded theory method in IS. His research has been presented at the European Conference on Information Systems (ECIS) and the International Research Workshop on IT Project Management (IRWITPM) where he received a best paper award.

Juan Miguel Gomez-Berbís is an assistant professor at the Computer Science Department of the Universidad Carlos III de Madrid. He holds a PhD in computer science from the Digital Enterprise Research Institute (DERI) at the National University of Ireland, Galway and received his MSc in telecommunications engineering from the Universidad Politécnica de Madrid (UPM). He was involved in several EU FP V and VI research projects and was a member of the Semantic Web Services Initiative (SWSI). His research interests include semantic web, semantic web services, business process modeling, b2b integration and, recently, bioinformatics.

Constanța-Nicoleta Bodea is a professor of project management and artificial intelligence at the Academy of Economic Studies (AES), Bucharest, Romania. She directs a Masters Program in Project Management, and is the head of the Economic Research Department at AES. She is the chair of the "334 Technical Committee - Continuing Education Standards" at the Romanian Association for Standardization - ASRO, president of the Project Management Romania Association (since 2000), chair of the Education & Training Board of the International Project Management Association - IPMA (since 2007), project manager of more than 20 R&D and IT projects in the last ten years, contributor and author of 11 books and more than 50 papers on Project Management, Information Systems, and Artificial Intelligence, being Honored by IPMA with the *Outstanding Research Contributions* (2007).

Maria Boilé is an associate professor of transportation in the Department of Civil and Environmental Engineering at Rutgers University, co-Director of the Freight and Maritime Program (FMP) at the Center for Advanced Infrastructure and Transportation (CAIT), and academic fellow in the Center for Supply Chain Management of the Rutgers School of Business. Dr. Boilé's areas of research and interest include freight logistics, intermodal network modeling, freight and maritime systems analysis, port and marine terminal operations. Her recent research work includes empty intermodal container management; modeling of container terminal operations; modeling of shipper and carrier behavior and interactions within an intermodal network environment; IT assisted intermodal freight network modeling for transportation contingency planning; logistics facility location/allocation modeling; and statistical analysis of freight data. Her research has been sponsored by the US Department of Transportation (US DOT), National Science Foundation, Federal Highway and Federal Transit Administration, State DOTs, the Port Authority of New York and New Jersey, and the New York Metropolitan Transportation Council. Professor Boilé has authored and co-authored over one hundred journal and conference articles and book chapters. She is a member of several professional societies and serves on various committees and editorial advisory boards. She is a member of the Eno Transportation Foundation's Board of Regents.

Tanya Bondarouk is an assistant professor of Human Resource Management at the University of Twente, the Netherlands. She holds two PhDs: in Didactics (1997) and Business Administration/HRM (2004). Since 2002 she has been busy with the emerging research area of Electronic HRM. Her main publications concern an integration of Human Resource Management and social aspects of Information Technology Implementations. Her research covers both private and public sectors and deals with a variety of areas such as the implementation of e-HRM, management of HR-IT change, HRM contribution to IT projects, roles of line managers in e-HRM, implementation of HR Shared Service Centers. She has conducted research projects with the Dutch Ministry of Interior and Kingdom Relations, Dow Chemical, Ford, IBM, ABN AMRO bank, Shell, Unit4Agresso. Among her current research projects are Implementation of HR Shared Service Centers at the Dutch Ministry of Defense, Large Non-academic Hospital, and the Belgian Federal Public Health Service. Since 2006 she is involved in organizing European Academic Workshops on e-HRM, and International Workshops on HRIS.

Charles Capps teaches strategy and human resource management. He is a lifetime certified Senior Professional in Human Resources. Dr. Capps' industry experience as a human resource development (HRD) practitioner includes establishing and managing a large petrochemical training program where the world's record in safety was set. As a consultant, Dr. Capps trained hundreds of law enforcement professionals in strategic management for the Law Enforcement Management Institute of Texas (LE-MIT). In addition, Dr. Capps has provided management and human relations training to national and international corporations.

Houn-Gee Chen earned his PhD from the University of Wisconsin-Madison, 1988. Prior to joining National Taiwan University, he was a faculty member at University of Notre Dame and National Tsing Hua University. His research interests include e-commerce, management information systems, information technology, project management, and software quality. Professor Chen has published near 70 articles in refereed journals like *Decision Sciences, Communications of ACM, IEEE Transactions, Journal of MIS, Journal of AIS, Information & Management, Database, JCIS, IJPR, J. of Manufacturing Systems, Int. J. of Man-Machine Studies,* Computers and OR, and others. He is currently the editor-in-chief of *Journal of Information Management* and serves at the editorial board for *Comparative Technology Transfer and Society, Journal of Knowledge and Learning Objects, International Journal of Management and Decision Making,* and *International Journal of Internet and Enterprise Management.*

Andrew P. Ciganek is an assistant professor in the Information Technology/Business Education Department in the College of Business and Economics at UW-Whitewater. Prior to UW-Whitewater, Dr. Ciganek was an assistant professor of computer information systems at Jacksonville State University. His research interests include examining the managerial and strategic issues associated with the decision-making process of innovative technologies. Dr. Ciganek earned his PhD in management information systems from the Sheldon B. Lubar School of Business at the University of Wisconsin – Milwaukee in 2006.

Yuval Cohen is the head of the Industrial Engineering program at the Open University of Israel. His areas of specialty are production planning, industrial learning, design of manufacturing control systems, and logistics management. He has published many papers in these areas. Dr. Cohen served several years as a senior operations planner at FedEx Ground (USA) and received several awards for his contributions to the hub and terminal network planning. He received his Ph.D. from the University of Pittsburgh (USA), his M.Sc. from the Technion — Israel Institute of Technology, and B.Sc. from Ben-Gurion University. Dr. Cohen is a Fellow of the Institute of Industrial Engineers (IIE), and a full member of the Institute for Operations Research and Management Sciences (INFORMS).

Ángel García-Crespo is the head of the SofLab Group at the Computer Science Department in the Universidad Carlos III de Madrid and the Head of the Institute for promotion of Innovation Pedro Juan de Lastanosa. He holds a PhD in industrial engineering from the Universidad Politécnica de Madrid (Award from the Instituto J.A. Artigas to the best thesis) and received an executive MBA from the Instituto de Empresa. Professor García-Crespo has led and actively contributed to large European Projects of the FP V and VI, and also in many business cooperations. He is the author of more than a hundred publications in conferences, journals and books, both Spanish and international.

Michael J. Cuellar is an Assistant Professor of Computer Information Systems at North Carolina Central University. His research focuses on the areas of project management, outsourcing and social theory for Information Systems. He has substantial experience in industry having held management positions for EDS and American Software managing software product development and infrastructure services, as well as systems management sales. He has published papers at conferences and journals such as JAIS, the e-Services Journal and the European Journal of Operational Research, ICIS, AMCIS, and the International Research Workshop on Project Management,. He is a member of the Association for Information Systems, Project Management International and the Academy of Management.

Maria-Iuliana Dascălu has a Master Degree in Project Management from the Academy of Economic Studies (AES), Bucharest, Romania (2008), and a Bachelors Degree in Computer Science from the Alexandru-Ioan Cuza University, Iasi, Romania (2006). She is a PhD candidate in Economic Informatics at the Academy of Economic Studies, combining her work experience as a programmer with numerous research activities. Her research relates to computer-assisted testing with applications in e-learning environments for project management. Her interests are algorithm design, artificial intelligence, IT project management, project management methodologies, risk management, e-learning systems, and knowledge management. Maria-Iuliana Dascălu is a Certified Project Management Associate (2008).

Mihalis Golias is an assistant professor in the Department of Civil Engineering at the University of Memphis, an affiliated faculty an affiliated faculty at the Center for Intermodal Freight Transportation Studies, at the University of Memphis, and an affiliated faculty at the Center for Advanced Infrastructure and Transportation, at Rutgers University. His core expertise is in the field of freight and maritime operations with a focus on freight intermodal terminal operations modeling and management and applications of optimization based evolutionary and memetic algorithms. He possesses experience with data mining, optimization, transportation planning, and traffic operations and management. His recent research work includes container terminal operations; drayage operations; intermodal freight network modeling; traffic congestion and travel time reliability; ITS assisted operational strategies to relief truck traffic related externalities; scheduling and routing of commercial vehicles to reduce related vehicle mileage; and capital and operational network improvements to increase transportation efficiency.

Robert Wayne Gregory is a Ph.D. candidate at the Institute of Information Systems at Johann Wolfgang Goethe University, Frankfurt, Germany. His research interests focus on global sourcing, information technology project management, and the financial services industry. He presented his research at several international conferences and workshops, including International Conference on Information Systems (ICIS), Americas Conference on Information Systems (AMCIS), European Conference on Information Systems (ECIS), IFIP Working Group 8.2, and Hawaii International Conference on System Sciences (HICSS) where he received a best paper award. He has also published in the journal Information Technology and People.

Marc N. Haines is a Senior Architect at Ictect, Inc. and adjunct faculty in the Sheldon B. Lubar School of Business Administration at the University of Wisconsin-Milwaukee. His research has been published in the *International Journal of Human Computer Interaction, Communications of the ACM, Information Systems Management, Information Resources Management Journal*, and other publications. He has chaired the HICSS mini-track on strategies and technologies for service-oriented architectures. As a member of the *Organization for the Advancement of Structured Information Standards* (OASIS), he is contributing to open standards development. His research interests include strategies and technologies for enterprise integration and IT architecture, as well as organizational issues concerning the implementation of enterprise systems.

William (Dave) Haseman is Wisconsin Distinguished Professor and Director of the Center for Technology Innovation in the Sheldon B. Lubar School of Business at the University of Wisconsin-Milwaukee. Dr. Haseman also serves as the Director of the UWM SAP University Competence Center. He received his PhD from the Krannert Graduate School of Management at Purdue University and served previously on the faculty at Carnegie-Mellon University. His research interests include groupware, Web services, decision support systems, services oriented architecture, emerging Internet technologies and enterprise resource planning. Dr. Haseman has published a book and a number of research articles in journals such as *Accounting Review, Operations Research, MIS Quarterly, Decision Support Systems, Information Management, Information Systems*, and *Database Management*. He served as Conference Chair for Americas Conference on Information Systems (AMCIS) in 1999 and as Conference Chair for International Conference on Information Systems (ICIS) for 2006.

Rugayah Hashim is an Associate Professor of Management Information Systems at the Faculty of Administrative Science and Policy Studies, Universiti Teknologi MARA (UiTM), Shah Alam, Selangor, Malaysia. She obtained her Ph.D degree in Information Management from Universiti Teknologi MARA and her Master of Business Administration majoring in Management Information Systems from Oklahoma City University, USA. Her research interests include information systems, electronic government, business value of information technology, strategic use of information technology to improve organizational performance, social capital and sustainable development. She has presented her research papers at several international conferences such as the International Conference on Information Systems and Its Applications, International Conference on Electronic Government, conferences organized by the International Business Information Management Association (IBIMA), International Conference on Educational Research and Practices (ICERP), European Conference on e-Government (ECEG), International Conference on Local Governments, and IT Governance International Conference (ITGIC). Her articles have appeared in the Turkish Online Journal of Educational Technology (TOJET) and the Journal of Administrative Science. She has also published a book chapter. Subsequently, she is also on the board of several international conference committees and refereed journals. She has won several awards including an International Award for Best Research Paper, and several local ones on innovations.

Jack Shih-Chieh Hsu is assistant professor of information management in the College of Management at National Sun Yat-Sen University, Taiwan. He received his PhD from the MIS Department at the University of Central Florida and his Master's of information management from National Chung Cheng University, Taiwan. His research interests include information technology project management, mental models, and team coordination. He has published in *Information & Management*, *Communications of the AIS*, and other journals. He is an active participant in the AIS special interest group on information technology project management.

James Jiang is professor of management information systems at the University of Central Florida. He obtained his PhD in information systems at the University of Cincinnati. He is also the honorary Sun Yat-Sen Management Chair Professor of Information Management at National Sun Yat-Sen University, Taiwan. His research interests include IS project management and IS service quality management. He has published over 100 academic articles in these areas in the journals such as *Decision Sciences, Decision Support Systems, Journal of Management Information Systems, Communications of ACM, IEEE Transactions on Systems Men & Cybernetics, IEEE Transactions on Engineering Management, Journal of AIS, European Journal of Information Systems, Information & Management, Data Base, Journal of Systems & Software, Information Resources Management Journal*, and *MIS Quarterly*. Currently, he is an AE of MIS Quarterly and the *Information Resources Management Journal*.

Gary Klein is the Couger Professor of Information Systems at the University of Colorado in Colorado Springs. He obtained his PhD in management science from Purdue University. Before that time, he served with the company now known as Accenture in Kansas City and was director of the Information Systems Department for a regional financial institution. His research interests include project management, technology transfer, and mathematical modeling with over 140 academic publications in these areas. He teaches programming, project management, and knowledge management courses. He is a Fellow of the Decision Sciences Institute, Vice Chair of Membership and Community Relations for the AIS SIG on

IT Project Management, and an active member of the Institute of Electrical and Electronic Engineers, the Association for Computing Machinery, INFORMS, the Association of Information Systems, and the Project Management Institute.

Sadan Kulturel-Konak, PhD is currently an associate professor of management information systems at Pennsylvania State University, Berks Campus which she joined in 2003. She received her degrees in Industrial Engineering; BS from Gazi University, Turkey in 1993, MS from Middle East Technical University, Turkey in 1996 and from the University of Pittsburgh in 1999, and PhD from Auburn University in 2002. Her research interests are in modeling and optimization of complex systems and robustness under uncertainty. In addition, she has research interests in participation of women in information systems and engineering, and teaching and learning with virtual teams. She has published her research in *IIE Transactions, OR Letters, INFORMS Journal on Computing, INFORMS Transactions on Education, International Journal of Production Research, European Journal of Operational Research*, and *Journal of Intelligent Manufacturing*. She is a member of *INFORMS, IIE, Alpha Phi Mu*, and *Phi Kappa Phi*.

Daniel L. Lohin is currently an Information Security Analyst for Booz Allen Hamilton in Northern VA. He received his BS in information sciences and technology from the Pennsylvania State University and is currently pursuing a master degree in information security from George Mason University. His primary interest is in network security monitoring and incident analysis.

Clifford R. Maurer is currently an instructor of information sciences and technology at Pennsylvania State University, Berks Campus, which he joined in 2001. He received a BS degree in Ed, mathematics from Bloomsburg University and MS in engineering science from the Pennsylvania State University. He has participated in projects; especially IT projects, at all levels of involvement. He also has extensive experience and training in developing and managing teams.

Ricardo Colomo-Palacios is an assistant professor at the Computer Science Department of the Universidad Carlos III de Madrid. He has been a faculty member of the Computer Science Department at Universidad Carlos III de Madrid since 2002. His research interests include software process improvement, software project management and information systems. He received his PhD in computer science from the Universidad Politécnica of Madrid (2005). He also holds a MBA from the Instituto de Empresa (2002). He has been working as software engineer, project manager and software engineering consultant in several companies including Spanish IT leader INDRA.

Richard Peterson has achieved excellence through passion, dedication, and commitment to his profession and to his students and faculty colleagues. He is "outstanding" in the true sense of the word. Rich grew up in Conneaut Lake, in northwestern Pennsylvania and went to nearby Edinboro State University for his Bachelor's degree in Speech Communication and elementary education in 1966. He continued on to Pennsylvania State University to earn a Master's in Speech Pathology in 1971 and a PhD in 1974 in Speech Communication. After leaving Penn State, Rich held several posts at INPUT, an information services subscription research company, and with McGraw-Hill Companies, the global publishing, media, and financial information corporation. At McGraw-Hill, he served as Vice President and Director of New Product Development and also as Head of Mergers & Acquisitions. He later created his own firm,

IMPACT Research, Inc., an Information Technology management consulting practice that focused on the needs of organizations for efficient and effective administrative and management process. In 1992, Rich joined Montclair State University in New Jersey first as an adjunct faculty member, and in 1996, as a full-time faculty member. He has taught courses ranging from Management Information Systems to Decision Support Systems. Rich has published many academic journal articles and chapters on information ethics and security. His honors include the 2009 Outstanding Empirical Research Paper from Decision Sciences Institute, the 2009 Service Award from the International Academy of Business and Public Administration, and the Outstanding Service Award for Service Learning in 2000 from Montclair State University. Today, Rich is Chair of Montclair State's Department of Management and Information Systems, which serves 500 undergraduate and graduate students in Hospitality Management, Operations Management, Management, and Management and Information Systems. His wife, Susan, is Director of Marketing at McGraw-Hill Construction Division.

Marcos Ruano is a consultant at Amvos Consulting, Spain. Formerly he was a research assistant of the Computer Science Department at Universidad Carlos III de Madrid. He holds a BSc in Computer Systems from Universidad de Valladolid and a MSc in Computer Science from Universidad Carlos III de Madrid. He has been involved in several research projects as information management engineer and software consultant.

Huub J.M. Ruël is an assistant professor of International Human Resource Management at the University of Twente (The Netherlands), before that – at the American University of Beirut (Lebanon), Kuwait-Maastricht Business School (Kuwait), and the University of Utrecht (The Netherlands). He holds a PhD in Business Administration/Human Resource Management. His thesis focused on implementation of IT's in office-environments. His main research focus is Human Resource Information Systems/e-HRM in global companies, combining the IT, HRM and International Management field. In 2004 he published a book *e-HRM: innovation or irration?* together with dr. Tanya Bondarouk, in which the results of e-HRM implementation in five large international companies were presented. Huub J.M. Ruël has authored several follow-up publications on this topic since then.

Kozeta Sevrani is an Associate Professor of Management Information Systems and head of the Department of Mathematics, Statistics and Applied Informatics, at the Faculty of Economy, University of Tirana, Albania. She is in the Editorial Board of several international journals and does an extended work in consulting private companies and government agencies in Albania. Her research interests include: digital divide; issues and solutions in building information infrastructure, e-business, e-learning, and e-government in developing countries, particularly in Albania. She has presented her work in numerous national and international conferences. Her work has been published in several journals and she has co-authored two books.

Stefan Smink is a project management trainee at Sodexo Altys, Amsterdam Airport, the Netherlands. He holds a professional bachelor degree (BEng) from the University of Applied Sciences Windesheim, Zwolle, the Netherlands and a Master of Science degree in Business Administration (MScBA) from the University of Twente, the Netherlands.

Heidi A. Taboada is an assistant professor in the Department of Industrial Engineering at The University of Texas at El Paso. Her research focuses on developing new tools for solving and analyzing optimization problems with multiple objective functions. Other of her research interests lie in the areas of applied operations research, biologically inspired methods, and algorithms, including evolutionary computation, system reliability modeling and optimization, risk analysis, data mining and pattern recognition. Her work has been published in *IEEE Transactions on Reliability, Reliability Engineering and System Safety, IIE Transactions and Quality Technology and Quantitative Management, among others.*

Hazel Taylor is an Assistant Professor at the Information School, University of Washington, Seattle. She holds a Ph.D. from Queensland University of Technology, Brisbane, Australia. Prior to joining the Information School, Dr. Taylor taught at the University of Waikato in New Zealand, and at the Hong Kong University of Science and Technology, and conducted research in Hong Kong on risk management and tacit knowledge in IT projects. Her teaching and research focuses on IT project management and risk management with an emphasis on tacit knowledge and decision making in these areas. Dr. Taylor has published a number of articles and book chapters on aspects of project management, risk management, outsourced projects, tacit knowledge and decision making. Prior to her academic career, Hazel worked in industry with manufacturing, construction and government organizations, both as a systems manager and an IT project manager.

Sotirios Theofanis is the Director of Strategic Planning at Rutgers University's Center for Advanced Infrastructure and Transportation (CAIT) and Co-Director of the Freight and Maritime Program (FMP) at CAIT. His recent research work includes empty intermodal container management; modeling of container terminal operations; modeling of shipper and carrier behavior and interactions within an intermodal network environment; IT assisted intermodal freight network modeling for transportation contingency planning; logistics facility location/allocation modeling; and statistical analysis of freight data. He has a plethora of experience with real world applications as he has served as the executive vice president of supply chain management and logistics of the LOULIS Group, as the president and CEO of Piraeus Port Authority, Greece, the CEO of the Thessaloniki Port Authority, S.A., Greece, and as the Director for Port Planning of the Hellenic Ministry of Merchant Marine.

Dan Trietsch is a professor of industrial engineering at the College of Engineering, American University of Armenia, Yerevan, Armenia. He holds a PhD degree in Operations Research (summa cum laude), a Master's of business administration (cum laude), both awarded by Tel Aviv University, and a Bachelor's of science in mechanical engineering (Technion). In the past he had worked as an engineer and consulted with large project organizations. His research interests include the design of highway networks, Euclidean Steiner trees, statistical quality control, system theory, project scheduling and control, and stochastic economical balance principles. His first paper on optimal safety time in a project context (with Boaz Ronen) has been written in 1986. His 2005 PMJ paper, *Why a critical path by any other name would smell less sweet: Towards a holistic approach to PERT/CPM*, listed several challenges in project scheduling and control (and exposed serious shortcomings of Critical Chain). This paper tackles one of those challenges. He is also the author of *Statistical Quality Control: A Loss Minimization Approach* (World Scientific, 1999) and a co-author of the recently published *Principles of Sequencing and Scheduling* (with Kenneth R. Baker, Wiley, 2009).

Silvana Trimi is an Associate Professor of Management Information Systems at the University of Nebraska – Lincoln. Her research interests include: E-government, M-government, Web 2.0, Social Networking, Internet-based Organizational Innovation, Digital Convergence, Security and Privacy, ERP, Organizational Justice, and Knowledge Management. Her studies have been published in a number of journals including Communications of the ACM, International Journal of Production Research, Communications of the AIS, Information and Management, Industrial Management and Data Systems, International Journal of Public Administration, International Journal of Knowledge Management, and others.

Jill Palzkill Woelfer is a PhD student in Information Science at the Information School. Jill has extensive professional experience working in IT-related functions in the medical products manufacturing sector. Since 2008, she has worked as a research assistant for the Institute for Innovation in Information Management on projects focused on the learning and behavioral competencies of IT project managers, and on a project regarding critical success factors for geographically dispersed technology teams. Jill is an alumna of the Executive Master of Science in Information Management program, and also pursues research in the role of information technologies in life skills development of homeless young people.

M. Keith Wright has a Ph.D. in Management Science and Information Systems from the University of Texas at Austin, and has published in leading journals in the areas of project management, information services management, expert systems, and program comprehension. Dr. Wright now teaches project management and systems analysis but has extensive previous information systems development experience in several large organizations including United Airlines, Levi Strauss, National Semiconductor, and Advanced Micro Devices.

Angus G Yu is a Lecturer of Management Science in the Division of Management, Stirling University in the UK. He earned his BSc (First Class Hons) from Zhejiang University, his MBA from Heriot-Watt University and his PhD from Stirling University. He has had extensive operational and project experiences in manufacturing and IT service sectors. His current research focuses on the management of application software suppliers in large-scale information systems development projects. He is particularly interested in applying agency theory in analysing complex relations within the project environment. He is also interested in developing and applying organizational theory to studying projects as temporary organizations. He is a member of the Chartered Institute of Purchasing and Supply (MCIPS).

Ofer Zwikael is an Associate Professor and Deputy Head of School at the School of Management, Marketing and International Business of The Australian National University (ANU) College of Business and Economics at Canberra Australia. Previously he was a senior lecturer at the Victoria Management School, at the Victoria University of Wellington. Dr Zwikael is also active with the Project Management Institute (PMI), as the Research Director at the New Zealand PMI Chapter Executive Board and as an accredited Project Management Professional (PMP®). He has lead, trained, mentored and consulted projects and programme groups in dozens of organisations in NZ, Asia and Europe, including Motorola, Nestle, Teva, and Nationwide Bank (UK). He has also lead workshops, keynote presentations and seminar all around the world.

Index